A History of Christianity
in the World

A History of Christianity in the World

SECOND EDITION

Clyde L. Manschreck

Chavanne Professor of Religious Studies
Rice University

Prentice-Hall, Inc., Englewood Cliffs, New Jersey 07632

Library of Congress Cataloging in Publication Data

Manschreck, Clyde Leonard, 1917–
  A history of Christianity in the world.

  Bibliography: p.
  Includes index.
  1. Church history. I. Title.
BR145.2.M3 1985   270   84–11660
ISBN 0–13–389354–5

Cover design: Lundgren Graphics, Ltd.
Manufacturing buyer: Harry P. Baisley

Printed in the United States of America

10 9 8 7 6 5 4

ISBN 0-13-389354-5   01

Prentice-Hall International, Inc., *London*
Prentice-Hall of Australia Pty. Limited, *Sydney*
Editora Prentice-Hall do Brasil, Ltda., *Rio de Janiero*
Prentice-Hall Canada, Inc., *Toronto*
Prentice-Hall of India Private Limited, *New Delhi*
Prentice-Hall of Japan, Inc., *Tokyo*
Prentice-Hall of Southeast Asia Pte. Ltd., *Singapore*
Whitehall Books Limited, *Wellington, New Zealand*

Contents

Preface   vii

1   Presuppositions and the Beginnings
    of Christianity   1

2   In Conflict with Rome   16

3   In Quest of Authority   28

4   The System Makers, in Search of a Theology   38

5   Counterculture and Controversy   53

6   Augustine, Paradigm of Western Theology   67

7   Imperial Disintegration, Papal Ascendancy   79

8   Eastern Orthodoxy   93

9   Struggle for Independence and Sovereignty   104

10   Reform, Crusade, Dissent, and Triumph   115

11   Ecclesiastical Domination   128

12   Disruption   140

13   Reformation   158

14   Explosive Expansion   178

15   The Catholic Renewal
and Counter Reformation   194

16   The Reformation in England   210

17   State Sovereignty: Puritan Revolt,
Thirty Years' War, and Absolutism   228

18   The Age of Reason and Piety   243

19   Reaction to the French Revolution   263

20   The American Experiment   280

21   Retrenchment, Outreach, Reappraisal,
and Uncertainty   307

General Bibliography   336

Index   345

Preface to the Second Edition

The opportunity to revise this volume is one the author welcomed. It permitted reassessment, corrections, shortening of some passages and lengthening of others, and the addition of new data, including a map. Throughout the book passages have been rewritten, and some entirely new material has been added, particularly with regard to the women's movement, the increasing importance of blacks in Western society, the religious ferment swirling around Fundamentalism and Liberalism, and post–Vatican II developments in Roman Catholicism. The basic theme of the dangers of claiming sovereignty for the church, state, or individual remains central, as does the importance of this theme for Christian living. When church or state dominates society, as has often been the case, then the injustice, immorality, and oppression that so frequently accompany inordinate power occur. Modern times have witnessed the individual asserting sovereignty with equally dire results. Human usurpation of divine sovereignty has failed repeatedly, leaving much of the past strewn with negative consequences. These assertions of sovereignty pervade church history, from the persecutions of the early Christians to the uncertainty of the twentieth century, with church, state, and individual vying for finality, but they have not overshadowed the glorious achievements inspired by Christianity in the world. This history seeks to portray both.

To the many students who have offered criticisms and suggestions for the chapters in this book the author is indebted. Two students in particular should be mentioned. Murray Wagner, a doctoral student at the Chicago Theological Seminary, contributed the major research and writing of Chapter 8, and Peter Kaufman, a doctoral student at the University of Chicago, assisted in the production of Chapter 12. Their help is gratefully acknowledged.

Clyde L. Manschreck

1

Presuppositions and the Beginnings of Christianity

PRESUPPOSITIONS

Christianity began with Christ. Such a truism would seem to be obvious, but such a statement put in the past tense presupposes a linear view of history that does not do justice to the immediacy of faith. Existentialists have taught us that without "immediacy of faith" Christianity is a fraud, an institutionalized stumbling block. Yet Christianity without historical moorings loses its identity, for "immediacy of faith" finally makes public distinctions impossible and private distinctions folly. It would be more acceptable perhaps to say that Christianity begins with Christ; this would not exclude either side of the equation, but neither would it solve the dilemma of faith in relation to history.

Christianity begins with Christ, but who is Christ? The one depicted in the Gospels? Protestantism generally asserts this and uses the Bible as its authority, but examination discloses different views of Christ among the Gospel writers, and the apparently older letters of Paul show little interest in the supposed facts about Jesus. Individual Protestants have assumed varied stances for interpreting Scriptures, with the result that widely divergent portraits of Jesus emerge, with no way to determine which is "true."

Many Christians assume the inerrancy of the inspired Scriptures, and then resort to elaborate schemes of dispensations and ages to explain away biblical incongruities. Presupposing that God wrote the Scriptures and that God could not possibly be inconsistent, they end not with the literal word of God but with a rationalistic scheme which they have imposed on the Bible. On the other hand, Unitarians insist truth is where you find it, whether in the Bible or in the morning paper. They also end with a rationalistic scheme of truth consistent with their desires and ideals.

Catholicism asserts tradition and Scripture as equal authorities, both being products of the Holy Spirit, who dwells supremely in the Pope, the infallible interpreter of the Christ of Scripture and tradition. Yet the Pope is human and his finite judgments cannot be elevated above doubt by appeal to magisterium. Still other people insist on the primacy of the Spirit directly imparting the secret truths promised in John, but which usually vary from individual to individual.

Presuppositions basically determine our understanding of Christianity and its relevance in our lives. Cognizance of this from the beginning may help us to assess new facets of truth and save us from the idolatrous intolerance that has written such bloody chapters in church history. Being too open to it may leave us in such profound doubt (which also has its presuppositions) that we have no place to stand, and so we succumb to circumstances; or we may perceive in doubt itself a divine smashing of idols, in preparation for more fulfilling human relationships. In any event, presuppositions shape the way we regard Christianity. They set limits to our selection and interpretation of data. They almost always reflect our milieu and produce a pale replica of what is or is hoped for.

Numerous examples can be drawn from church history. In 1863 Joseph Ernest Renan published his *Life of Jesus*. Influenced by rationalism, he assumed that the miracles and all supernatural elements were froth to be discarded in any true picture. Consequently he depicted Jesus as an ordinary man, a peasant preacher, with common human emotions. He treated the resurrection as a legend, born of the credulous enthusiasm of Jesus' early followers, especially Mary Magdalene's strong imagination and fantasy fired by the power of her love. "The passion of one possessed," he wrote, "gave to the world a resuscitated God."

In 1925 Bruce Barton, a successful advertising man, published *The Man Nobody Knows*. He pictured Jesus as a business go-getter. "Wist ye not that I be about my Father's *business*" (Luke 2:49) provided the basic orientation. Jesus was not a weakling, a man of sorrows, a shrinking violet, a willing victim of the cross. On the contrary, he was dynamic and inspiring, a thinker, doer, leader, outdoorsman, mixer, a man. He founded modern business by taking twelve ordinary men and building a corporation. Jesus was like David Lloyd George, Henry Ford, and J. Pierpont Morgan! Wrote Barton: Jesus' motto might well have been, "Never explain; never retract; never apologize; get it done and let them howl!"

Hitler's theologian, Alfred Rosenberg, at a time when Hitler was trying to vilify Jews without alienating Christians, used selected data from philology, religion, anthropology, and history to prove that Jesus was not a Jew but an Aryan. In 1970, John Marco Allegro, a British philologist and theologian, published a sensational book, *The Sacred Mushroom and the Cross*, in which he maintained the New Testament was written as a sort of cryptic handbook for a mushroom-eating fertility cult. Influenced by Freud, he sought to show that all religions root in sex.

No stance is without presuppositions. They are our foundations and guidelines to truth; they undergird our values, standards, and ideals; they form the framework within which we move. Yet presuppositions by their very nature cannot be proved; they can only be affirmed. This makes all knowledge tenuous and vulnerable. Even science does not escape this vulnerability. The two great tests of scientific truth are utility and conformity to nature, yet science remains uncertain about what nature is, and "it works" rests on a subjective basis. Christianity has received much criticism in the twentieth century precisely because people have questioned the adequacy not of Christianity necessarily but of the presuppositions through which we have interpreted it.

In writing this brief history of Christianity, the author is aware that much will have to be omitted and condensed. In doing this, the judgments of past and present historians, critics, philosophers, artists, theologians, and laity will be used to advance a consensus, which the critical student can deal with as a kind of base line from which to operate. Still, more than this will be attempted, for the author sees Christianity moving through history from persecution to privilege, to dominance, to reform, to decline, to uncertainty.

The achievements of Christianity have all proved imperfect. They may have served well in their time, and still have a relevance that should not be arrogantly dismissed, but they have almost always become so ossified and institutionalized that they work more like idols than fruits of the living Spirit. Other Christians, moved by the Spirit or their own desires, have repeatedly moved Christianity forward, toward some beaconing ideal, some standard that seems to embrace truth. In turn such standards have been questioned and shattered by others. This is known as the Protestant principle: no stance, dogma, institution, or value is final. To regard any as final or absolute is to court idolatry. Yet each achievement or failure uncovers something significant for the meaning of Christianity, without which we would today be vastly poorer. This is the Christian community's living legacy, transmitted in history and faith. The trust that this is so, and that our destiny is to press on to "perfection" even though vaguely intuited, as through a dark glass, dissipates the despair of hopeless nihilism. The prevalent uncertainty in the twentieth century may be seen by future interpreters as the shattering of the intellectualizing of Christianity. Reason, great as it is, may also prove to be a false idol that cannot bear final trust. However, intellectualizing, like other edifices built in Christianity, is not to be denigrated per se. Without it something vital in the history of Christianity would be missing, just as without the ancient martyrs, whom modern Christians often dismiss, something vital would be lacking.

The author presupposes that divine love, *agape*—self-giving, unmerited, freely bestowed love, given to the just and the unjust—was revealed in Christ; that Christ endured the cross and was resurrected to reveal that nothing, not even death, can separate us from God's love; that this love operates in God's providence; that we are invited to respond with the same kind of love to others; that as the rain and sunshine fall on the clean and unclean, so is this love offered to all; that we often fail to respond to agape and introduce radical disharmony in the universe by inordinate self-seeking, as if we were the center of everything. The effects reverberate through all of life. What agape actually means for us goes to the core of Christianity, and in one way or another church history articulates our struggle to come to terms with it. Sometimes we have accepted it in joy and gratitude and translated it into our life styles, sometimes we have smothered it in institutionalism, sometimes we have horribly distorted it. How we experience agape, whether through preaching, sacraments, Scripture, intuition, or persons, is a mystery. The history of Christianity is *one* record of how agape has been received, what it has meant, and what it may mean for the present.

The above is, of course, a confessional stance that has many ramifications. While such presuppositions are acknowledged, the author does not seek to make them obtrusive nor to propagandize, but various interpretations will reveal their presence. Good scholarship and all that it connotes about objectivity, evidence, and substantiation will be attempted, but no one escapes his own time. This kind of a beginning, cursory though it be, indicates the skeptical milieu of the twentieth century. Except on the basis of a confessional stance, who can say what is finally right or wrong? Dialogue with the past may help us to understand not only Christianity but also who we are as its heirs. To study history is to study ourselves.

BASIC WRITINGS

Christianity may have been a gigantic hoax or a mushroom-eating cult, but the New Testament writings, despite their inadequacies, still remain the most reliable accounts of the beginnings of Christianity. If they are rejected as legitimate documents, then the basis on which they are rejected should in fairness be applied to all other documents. Critical appraisal is not necessarily rejection, but even here one should be aware of the limitations of one's presuppositions. The author accepts the New Testament writings as legitimate, and feels that they must be critically examined with all available internal and external evidence, and that finally the reader must make a personal decision as to what they mean.

By the time Paul's letters were written, Christianity was already well under way. Various sources indicate it had spread, albeit sparsely, far beyond Jerusalem. A group of Christians was already in Rome. Others were in Antioch, where according to Acts they were first called Christians. And it is probable that some had made their way into other urban centers of the Roman Empire and into Ethiopia, which today boasts of its Christian antiquity. Legend, which is not to be discounted just because it is not precise, holds that some refugees from the early persecutions in Jerusalem carried Christianity into Arabia, India, and outer China.

The dates of Paul's letters, our first written documents about Christianity, cannot be exactly determined. There are too many variables. Judging, however, from Paul's own letters (particularly Galatians) and from other sources (particularly Acts), scholarly consensus places the writing of Paul's letters between 45 and 63 A.D. The other New Testament writings followed, one or two possibly as late as 150. None came directly from Jesus. Information about him circulated orally. Paul's letters gave little data about Jesus—no miracles, no parables, and only a few isolated sayings. Some thirty years after Christ's death the first Gospel appeared, the word "gospel" coming from the Anglo-Saxon *god-spell,* meaning "good tidings" of Jesus' life, death, and resurrection. Of the three synoptic Gospels, from the Greek word *synopsis* because they are so much alike, Mark appears to have been written first, probably around 60 A.D. Mark has little not also in Matthew and Luke, and where variations occur Mark is invariably in agreement with Matthew or Luke. Matthew and Luke seldom agree on data in opposition to Mark. Such collation points to the earlier authorship of Mark, with Matthew and Luke drawing on him for their accounts, although Roman Catholicism officially puts Matthew first. Many scholars posit a common earlier source, called *Q* from the German *Quelle.*

The Gospel of John, noticeably different from the other three, contains no parables of Jesus; it features long discourses of Jesus with his disciples. John mixes in his own interpretations, especially with regard to the relation of Christ to the Father and of the union of Christ with his followers. Acts is an account of the first thirty years of the Christian movement, and the Revelation to John is an apocalypse concerned with the future.

Twenty-one of the twenty-seven books of the New Testament are letters, most of them purporting to be from Paul. All the New Testament books were written in *koine* or common Greek, and the original manuscripts no longer exist. However, the texts have been preserved in old Greek manuscripts, in quotations in other works, and in translations into other languages, particularly Syriac, Latin, and Coptic. More than 300 manuscripts of all or parts of the New Testament date from the second to the eighth century, in contrast to other ancient writings which often have been preserved in only one or two manuscripts from the Middle Ages. The selections for the New Testament canon came from a much larger body of literature. Whereas most of the books were accepted by 200 A.D., the number of twenty-seven was not finally settled until the latter part of the fourth century.

A brief "factual" sketch of early Christianity, drawn from multiple New Testament sources, might read as follows:

"Jesus, the founder of Christianity, was born about 4 B.C. in Bethlehem shortly before the death of Herod the Great. His parents, Mary and Joseph, were pious Jews; whether they had other children is disputed. Jesus learned the trade of a carpenter, but other data about his life before he began his ministry are unknown. Between 26 and 29 A.D. Jesus was drawn to the preaching of John the Baptist, a prophetic figure proclaiming the advent of the long-expected messianic kingdom and calling for repentance. Baptized by John in the Jordan River, Jesus soon became convinced that he was the Messiah of a spiritual rather than political kingdom. Active chiefly in Galilee and North Palestine, he soon attracted a large following, drawn by his strangely authoritative words and unusual deeds of healing. Rome suspected another uprising. Jesus proclaimed the end of the present order and the beginning of the kingdom of God, already signaled by his miraculous deeds. His own disciples seemed to doubt, but his following increased. Despite indications of powerful opposition, he witnessed in Jerusalem. Acclaimed by the people on his entry, within five days he was arrested, accused of blasphemy and sedition, tried, and crucified as a criminal. Pontius Pilate, Rome's procurator of Judea, 26–36 A.D., presided. Jesus' ministry had lasted a year, three at most; he died young, under thirty-five. Despondency and fear settled over his disciples. Then, on the third day (counting the crucifixion as the first) reports circulated that Jesus had risen from the dead and that he had appeared to his disciples and others. Ecstasy seized his followers. They were convinced that God had raised him from the grave. They began proclaiming that the Jews' Messiah had come, had been rejected and killed, but had risen from the dead. Their numbers increased. By believing in him, they said, they received the power and comfort of his Spirit manifest in their changed lives.

"Disturbed religious and political leaders mounted a persecution. One Christian, Stephen, was stoned to death by a mob; others were imprisoned; some fled; some were not molested. Peter and James became leaders of the Jerusalem congregation. The most fanatical persecutor of the new sect was Saul, a man educated for the rabbinate, but he was himself converted. Under the name of Paul he became the new movement's highly successful missionary to the Gentiles. His journeys took him through Asia Minor, Greece, and eventually to Rome. He established numerous congregations, many of which (Ephesus, Corinth, Antioch, Philippi) became influential Christian centers. He was eventually arrested, taken to Rome for trial as a Roman citizen, and put to death, probably during the reign of Nero. About 44 A.D. a severe persecution broke out in Jerusalem, instigated by Herod Agrippa I, a vassal-king over Judea. The Apostle James was beheaded. Peter was arrested, escaped, and went to Rome where he was crucified during Nero's persecution. To quell Jewish rebellion, Rome destroyed Jerusalem in 70 and 135 A.D., greatly diminishing that city as a center for Christianity. Christians believed the two destructions signified divine reprisal against the Jews for rejecting Jesus."

But such a brief "factual" sketch of Christianity is a summary selected from many documents and conveys little of the inner power that enabled Christianity to become the moving force that shaped so much of Western culture. A fuller picture is possible only when one reads the early accounts themselves, and possibly only if one believes.

When one reads the four Gospels, what features stand out? What would a careful reader in the early church identify as the central theme in each Gospel? The different Gospel emphases significantly stand out.

The Gospel according to Mark, written about 60–65 A.D., presents Jesus as the Son of God (1:1, 11; 5:7), but the presentation is against a backdrop of tragic misunderstanding. Everyone seems to desert Jesus— the common people, his disciples, the women, even God. The narrative begins abruptly, without any birth stories, and by the end of chapter three the Scribes, Pharisees, John's disciples, and the Sadducees are arrayed against Jesus, and the fanatic Herodians are plotting his death. Jesus' own relatives believe he is mentally ill (3:20–35). His disciples do not understand him and do not want to be implicated in his difficulties with the authorities. After he stills the storm, they wonder who he can be (4:35–41). After Jesus feeds the five thousand, they do not understand who he is. In chapter eight Peter confesses Jesus is the Christ, but immediately demonstrates he does not understand; he reproves Christ for talk about dying and rising again, and in turn is rebuked by Christ for siding with the devil. Repeatedly the disciples are afraid to ask Jesus what he means by resurrection (9:10ff., 20–32). Peter denies Jesus three times, as predicted, and one young man tears off his clothes in escaping arrest with Jesus (14:52). Even the women desert Jesus at the cross. No disciples are at the crucifixion, and the women are watching from a distance (15:40). The death of Jesus seems to end everything: "My God, my God, why hast thou forsaken me?" (15:34). A brief Resurrection account sharpens its dramatic effect. The women who behold the tomb empty flee, trembling and bewildered, afraid to tell anyone (16:8).

Mark's Messianic Secret may have been a device to answer criticism of the Christian movement. As Mark is the first of the Gospels, and as the letters of Paul had not yet been published, outsiders might well have been asking why they had not heard more about Jesus. Mark's theme seems to be one reply. Jesus himself kept it secret to prevent false hopes and misunderstanding about his messiahship. He was not the king expected by James and John (10:35–37). He had to prepare his followers to understand him as "the suffering Messiah" who must die on the cross, who would show the nature of his kingdom through the conquest of death. The fruitless fig tree that was cursed even though it was not the season for figs (11:12–14, 20–21) might symbolize the fruitlessness of Jewish ritualism and the final barrenness of all of life. The fig tree is connected with the cleansing of the temple (11:15–19), which causes the chief priests to seek to destroy Jesus "because they feared him." The story of the woman who anoints Jesus is significant because she is really the first (other than the demons and the readers) to recognize that Jesus is the suffering Christ. Jesus' miracles in Mark signify his conquest of death; however, Mark does not want people to rest with the signs but with the signal victory of Christ over death, which left the women amazed.

The Gospel according to Matthew reflects most of Mark, but the additions and emphases give Matthew a distinctive tone, making it a manual of Jesus' teachings. It stresses fulfilled Old Testament promises, the New Law in contrast to the Old, and the Resurrection.

For almost everything connected with Jesus, Matthew finds a parallel in the Old Testament; Jesus fulfilled the old promises. Birth stories (1:1–2:25) found only in Matthew make this clear. Jesus is born of a virgin because Isaiah prophesied it. He is born at Bethlehem, as Micah prophesied. Herod tries to kill the babies, a fulfillment of what Jeremiah said. Jesus' parents take him to Egypt to fulfill "I called my son from Egypt." Jesus returns not to Bethlehem but to Nazareth because a prophet said, "He shall be called a Nazarene." Matthew pictures Jesus as fulfilling the

Old Testament. Other Gospels also do this, but in Matthew it receives unusual emphasis. For example, Matthew has Jesus ride into Jerusalem on two animals instead of one (21:1–9). This contradicts the other Gospels but fulfills what was said by the prophet Zechariah (Zech. 9:9).

Matthew also stresses the New Law over the Old by placing Jesus, the giver of the New, in relation to Moses, the giver of the Old. When Moses was born, a tyrannical king was trying to kill off the babies, so also with Jesus. Moses supposedly wrote five books, and so Matthew organizes his Gospel around five books or groups of sayings. Moses issued his basic teachings from a mountain, and so did Jesus. The Sermon on the Mount (5–7) makes the New Law much more strenuous than the Old—makes it impossible for us to keep, as Martin Luther said later, so that we are forced to rely on divine love if we are to be saved. Far from relaxing demand, the New Law elevates inner obedience. The Old Law forbade murder; the New forbids even anger. The Old forbade adultery; the New, even looking at a woman with lust. The Old forbade false swearing; the New, all swearing. The Old demanded an eye for an eye; the New says not to resist injury. The Old enjoined love of neighbor and hatred of enemy; the New, love for enemy and prayer for persecutors. Christians are further enjoined not to be anxious about what they shall eat, drink, and wear. They are first to seek the kingdom of heaven, and all other needs will be taken care of.

A, if not *the*, basic message seems to be that God has bestowed abundant love upon us and that we are to respond by showing such love to all. The law is something the Christian willingly fulfills, not to gain a reward but to express joyful gratitude for divine benefits already given. Jesus dispatches the twelve disciples saying, "Heal the sick, raise the dead, cleanse lepers, cast out demons. You received without pay, give without pay" (10:5ff.), and Jesus' parable of the Sheep and Goats (25:31–46) equates love of neighbor with love of Christ. Matthew's parable of the vineyard workers (20:1–16) places spontaneous, undeserved love on a higher level than distributive human justice; God's dealing with us is not a matter of equal exchange. Matthew's parable of the unforgiving servant (18:23–25) warns us that God expects us to treat others as he has treated us, or dire consequences will follow.

The Gospel according to Matthew is not a biography of Jesus in the usual sense, although the first four chapters do depict the genealogy and birth stories, the baptism and temptation, followed by the Galilean ministry (4:18–15:20), his work further afield (15:21–20:34), and the last week in Jerusalem, with emphasis on the Passion and Resurrection (21:1–28:20). Matthew incorporates almost all of Mark but leaves out connotations of the Messianic Secret and corrects certain passages that might have been awkward for Christians to explain. For example, he omits any reference to "not the season for figs" in the story of the cursing of the fruitless fig tree (21:18ff.).

The two-volume Luke-Acts was the first conscious history of Christianity. Its precise date is uncertain but probably 80–85. Mark, Matthew, and other works preceded, for Luke (presumably Luke the physician and friend of Paul—Colossians 4:14; II Timothy 4:11; Philemon 24) refers to "many" narratives as having been undertaken (1:1). Luke's theme—at least a central theme—pictures Jesus as the Savior who brings mercy and forgiveness of sins to all who will accept. This theme of forgiveness receives special emphasis and points beyond itself. Biblically, sin, illness, and death are joined, so that forgiveness of sin, like the acts of healing, points directly to the Resurrection, an emphasis in this Gospel as well as in the sermons reported in Acts. Because the Resurrection was a doctrine emphatically embraced by the early church, Luke's theme is singularly important.

Christ's mission of forgiveness is universal; Luke traces the genealogy of Jesus back to Adam, the father of the race (3:38), rather than simply to Abraham, father of the Jews, indicating that forgiveness is for all mankind. He includes the rejected poor (6:20–25), the despised Samaritans (10:30–37; 17:11–19), women (7:36–50; 8:3; 10:38–42), Gentiles (2:32; 3:6; 24:47), and lepers (5:12–13). Luke does not exclude even the worst of our sinners, and it is only in the Gospel of Luke that Jesus speaks from the cross saying, "Father, forgive them, for they know not what they do" (23:24), and only in Luke that he says to the penitent thief who asks to be remembered, "This day you shall be with me in paradise" (23:43).

The birth and childhood stories found only in Luke also stress the theme of forgiveness (1:1–4:19). Mary hails God's mercy in sending a Savior. Zechariah sings of a redeemer bringing salvation, forgiveness, and light. The angels herald a "Savior, who is Christ the Lord." Simeon praises "the salvation of God, a light of revelation for the heathen and a glory to the people of Israel." John's proclamation of Christ's coming includes a line from Isaiah not in the other Gospels, "and all flesh shall see the salvation of God." In his first sermon, recorded only in Luke, Jesus says he is sent to "proclaim the acceptable year of the Lord."

The theme continues to be emphasized throughout the Gospel of Luke in the famous parables of the Good Samaritan (10:25–37), the Prodigal Son (15:12–32), and the Pharisee and the Publican (18:1–14). The poor receive special attention and blessing, because poverty was considered a consequence of sin (Deuteronomy 28). The poor recognize their need and accept the Savior. "Blessed are the poor . . . the hungry" (6:20–26), and blessed is the poor man Lazarus (16:19–31).

But death, the wages of sin, appears finally to claim Jesus, and gloom settles over his followers. They scatter. Luke pictures two despondent disciples on the road to Emmaus (24:13–36) following the crucifixion. "We had hoped that he was the one to redeem Israel." But, of course, he died. When a stranger reveals himself as the risen Christ, they are overjoyed, and return to Jerusalem, where they learn about and experience other appearances.

The conviction that God supremely revealed himself in the Resurrection of Jesus and that forgiveness of sin is a foretaste of divine mercy and the possibility of a changed life becomes the theme that motivates the early Christians, according to Luke's second volume—Acts. Jesus "was not abandoned to Hades, nor did his flesh see corruption" (Acts 2:31). This was the theme of the early preaching and was what disturbed the high priest, the commander of the temple, and the Sadducees; the disciples "were teaching the people and proclaiming in Jesus the resurrection from the dead" (Acts 4:2).

Luke's Gospel is not scientific history; it is a witness to what the early Christians believed and experienced in Christ. The historicity of what the Gospel records is one thing, the witness to an existential reality, another; but the two can be separated only at the peril of rendering the Gospel lifeless. Luke's Gospel is an interpretation of what Christ meant. The overcoming of the universal realities of sin and death carried a universal appeal that undergirded the rapid spread of the new movement.

In the second volume, Acts, Luke shows the ever-expanding outreach of Christianity. After Pentecost the disciples are persecuted, some driven out of Palestine. The experience of Peter with Cornelius (Acts 10) opens the way for a mission to the Gentiles. And then Paul makes increasingly distant journeys until he reaches Rome, the capital of the empire. Thus Luke, drawing on a variety of sources, pictures the universal good news becoming geographically triumphant in the world.

The Gospel according to John differs markedly from the synoptics. Written about 95–100, John's Gospel concentrates on the divine Christ, the sublimity of his teachings, the effects of his miracles. Its stated purpose is to convince us "that Jesus is the Christ, the Son of God" so that we may "have life in his name" (20:31). Its seven miracles are performed in the presence of many beholders as if to allay doubt about authenticity. They are stupendous, astonishing, to compel belief in Christ as the Son of God, the last miracle being the raising of Lazarus.

John's Gospel is ninety percent different from the synoptics, in organization, style, and content. Here one finds a three-year instead of a one-year ministry. The locale of Jesus' activity is not Galilee but Jerusalem. The cleansing of the temple comes at the beginning rather than at the end of Jesus' ministry. Here is no Messianic Secret; Jesus is proclaimed as divine from the very beginning; he is the pre-existent Logos; he was with God in the beginning; he is the principle of life and light in the world; he became incarnate that believers in knowing him might know the Father. Here are no parables. Instead of short sayings, Jesus gives long speeches or discourses about himself and his relationship to the Father. The Gospel has a Greek tone, a "spiritual" thrust: Jesus is more than human; he is the Christ—majestic, aloof, mystifying, moved by a transcendent power to which we have access only through him, which he has come to represent and present to those who will believe. He is the door, the way, the vine, the truth, the light, and the life. There is no baptism, no temptation, no transfiguration, and no agony in Gethsemane. Everything that Jesus does seems to have been divinely prescheduled, and he acts according to plan. He does not deviate. The schedule calls for him to go to the cross, so he does not ask to be relieved, saying "Let this cup pass from me" (Matthew 26:39, cf. Luke 24:42; Mark 14:36). Instead, Jesus exclaims, "And what shall I say? 'Father, save me from this hour'? No, for this purpose I have come to this hour. Father, glorify thy name"

(12:27–28). Jesus is the Logos, the light and life of men, and apart from him is darkness and death. But those who believe have eternal life now. The belief of doubting Thomas (20:24–29) is an appropriate climax, if not to the whole Gospel, at least to this aspect. Jesus is also the principle of life; he is more powerful than death. The last of the seven great miracles in John is the raising of Lazarus (11:1–53), not recorded in any other Gospel. Many believe, but others are alarmed, lest Jesus attract so many followers that the Romans take action to destroy the nation. The miracle prefigures the Resurrection of Jesus (19–21). Death has no dominion over him nor over those who believe in him. John highlights the Resurrection of Jesus as the distinction between the Christians and Jews.

Because Paul's letters are the earliest written records that we have of Christianity, they are especially valuable for reflecting the ethos of the Christian community, and deserve to be considered alongside the Gospels for what they tell us about Christ. Yet Paul's letters were not collected and circulated until after 90 A.D., until after at least three of the Gospels were circulating. Paul's letters were apparently preserved by the individual churches to which he wrote. This delayed general access to the Pauline epistles may well account for their having less influence in the early church than did Matthew, which was easily the most popular Christian writing and was placed first in the New Testament canon. Because Matthew stresses the continuity between Judaism and Christianity and makes the new law even more strenuous than the old, this may also account for some of the legalistic tendencies in second-century Christianity that seem so contrary to Paul's emphasis on the Christian's freedom from the law. Some early Christians—like the Ebionites (from the Hebrew word for poor, "Ebion")—exalted ascetic poverty as the way to salvation, used only the Gospel of Matthew, strictly observed the Mosaic Law, and rejected Paul as a heathen. The Nazarenes of Syria manifested similar notions, although they did not completely reject Paul. The great theological acceptance of Paul came much later with the interpretations of Augustine and Luther. Yet any picture of Jesus would be incomplete without dealing with the reflection of Jesus in Paul's letters.

Paul's experience of the risen Christ (Acts 8:1–3, 9:1–6; Galatians 1:11–17) ended his fanatical persecution of Christians and began a remarkable effort to extend Christianity among the Gentiles. Wherever he went, Paul started congregations, and to those congregations he later wrote letters. All the letters attributed to Paul could not have come from him, but little doubt exists about the genuineness of I Thessalonians, Galatians, I–II Corinthians, Romans, Philippians, Philemon, Colossians, and Ephesians. The earliest letter dates about 45 A.D., the latest about 63. Paul's letters make up one-fifth of the New Testament and are nearer in time to Jesus than any of the Gospels, yet Paul does not depict a single miracle of Jesus, nor relate a single parable, nor give any direct teachings of Jesus. Possibly Paul assumed that the people to whom he was writing knew about the parables, miracles, and teachings of Jesus, but it is more likely that these were displaced by the things that Paul considered more significant. He emphasized resurrection, justification, love, and hope, not as stilted doctrines but as dynamic relationships in divine revelation and human response.

The Resurrection was primary for Paul, as he himself said. In that event he saw the decisive act of God revealing two things: that Jesus was indeed the Messiah and that his victory over death supremely revealed the love of God for us. "For I delivered to you as of first importance what I also received, that Christ died for our sins in accordance with the Scriptures, that he was buried, that he was raised on the third day . . ." and appeared to the apostles, to many others, and finally to Paul (I Corinthians 15:1–11). Chapter fifteen caps the entire I Corinthians letter, rising even above the magnificent heights of chapter thirteen, for the love of the earlier chapter rests on the agape disclosed in the Resurrection. Paul's experience of the resurrected Christ convinced him that God acted supremely in Jesus to overcome the final enemy—death. Triumphantly he wrote, "Death is swallowed up in victory. O Death, where is thy victory? O Death, where is thy sting?" (I Corinthians 15:54–55). Without the Resurrection, declared Paul, all preaching is in vain, all faith is futile (15:12–17). If Christ has not been raised, we are still in our sins, and everything ends in the grave (15:17–18). "But in fact Christ has been raised from the dead." For Paul, the Resurrection meant that God had begun the destruction of the "last enemy" (15:20–28). People needed no longer succumb to sin saying, "Let us eat and drink, for tomorrow we die" (15:33). There was hope; God's power had been supremely revealed. "Thanks be to God, who gives us the victory through our Lord Jesus Christ" (15:57).

The Resurrection was for Paul the divine vindication that God had acted in Christ to do what we could not do—fulfill the law. Death was for him the sure sign that sin was being punished by God, but in Christ that universal punishment was abrogated (Romans 6:23). Christ was raised from the dead. "God shows his love for us in that while we were yet sinners Christ died for us," saving us from the "wrath of God" (Romans 5:8–9), and bringing those who believe into a new relationship of reconciliation and joy in God (Romans 5:10–11).

By faith, not by reason, we believe and are united with this Christ (I Corinthians 1:17–2:16; Romans 1:16–32). Out of joy rather than duty believers strive to show love to others (Romans 3:1–6:20). Paul's letter to the Romans shows this integral connection. Chapters 1–11 discuss faith, and chapters 12–16 discuss the expression of faith in love toward others. Throughout I Corinthians Paul is concerned with what this love means in various practical situations. In Galatians he vehemently defends God's action in Christ as abrogating the *necessity* of keeping the law and then declares that the believer acts in love toward others and *keeps* the law as an expression of love rather than duty.

Paul believed that nothing can separate us from "the love of God in Christ Jesus our Lord"—"neither death, nor life, nor angels, nor principalities, nor things present, nor things to come, nor powers, nor height, nor depth, nor anything else in all creation" (Romans 8:38–39). His conviction enabled him to brave beating, stoning, shipwreck, ridicule, insult, and hate, and his fervor was apparently shared by those early Christians who suffered martyrdom. A later writer summarized Paul when he wrote, "We love, because he first loved us" (I John 4:19).

Paul's missionary journeys, three or more in number, took him into remote areas in Asia Minor, to cities on the European and Asian sides of the Aegean Sea, to Rome, and possibly to Spain. He was the Apostle to the Gentiles. His experience of the risen Christ convinced him that we stand justified before God because Christ perfectly fulfilled the law and overcame sin and death, something humanity in all its striving had not been able to do. We receive this gift of justification in faith (Romans 3:21–26). Although we keep the law as an expression of "faith acting in love," we are not bound by law. Paul insisted on this liberty of believers. The Gentile does not have to be circumcised, does not have to become a Jew, in order to be justified in Christ. Such would negate the cross of Christ (Galatians 2:21). Paul expressed this forcefully in Galatians, a letter sometimes called the Christian declaration of independence from the law of the Old Testament. Whether Gentiles should first become Jews to be Christians occasioned conflict with leaders in Jerusalem (Acts 15:1–35), and brought Peter and Paul into temporary disagreement (Galatians 1:1–2:21). But Paul did not do away with the law; he simply insisted that the motive for keeping the law (God's will) be love engendered by the indwelling Spirit rather than slavish duty. In doing so, he freed the expanding Christian movement from sectarian ties to Judaism (Romans 3:21–31). One may be circumcised as an act of love, or not; one may eat meat sacrificed to idols, or not. The controlling factor for Paul is love rather than fear of punishment, for the supreme punishment (death) has been overcome in Christ's resurrection. Sin is conquered not by our keeping the law, for it is impossible even to know all the law, but by the gift of the indwelling Christ, who gives victory now over sin (Romans 8:1–2) and hereafter over death (Romans 8:11).

Paul's letter to the Colossians echoes this theme. In response to some disturbers who were preaching a theosophy of heavenly beings and the necessity of ascetic and ritualistic practices (2:16–23), Paul emphasizes the supremacy and universal all-sufficiency of Christ for the church and the individual (1:1–3:4) and stresses a consequent ethic of Christian love (3:5–4:1).

In Ephesians Paul sublimely pictures the unity of Jews and Gentiles, brought together by the love and grace of God in Christ. He depicts those who are the body of Christ, the Church, as already blessed and destined to reveal the "mystery" and "power" and "unsearchable riches of Christ," which will ultimately unite all things in God.

CONCLUSIONS

This brief survey of some of the basic literature in the early church leaves many exegetical questions untouched. The student can go to biblical commentaries for important pro and con discussions of discrepancies, textual problems, dates, and authorship. The concern here is to note the overall thrust and presuppositions. The "facts" of the Gospels and of Paul's letters have difficulty withstanding the buffeting of rationalistic scrutiny. We do not even know who Mark, Matthew, Luke, and John were. They could well have been immediate disciples of Jesus as traditional scholarship has asserted, or they might have come into the Christian community without having known Jesus in person and written their accounts from various records and remembrances of Jesus. We know a little more about Paul, but he was not one of the original disciples. Whatever their immediate relationship to Jesus, these writings, along with the other New Testament works, are the earliest reflections of Jesus that are known, and for this reason they hold a special place of authority in Christendom. Why they were not written earlier may have been due to eschatological expectations about the end of the world or the practice of oral transmission that was much in vogue.

Although these writings differ in emphases, key beliefs or presuppositions that were basic to the life of the early community emerge:

1. At the center stands the Resurrection, a vindication of everything that Jesus taught and did. Even the lordship of Christ rested on the Resurrection, for without the conquest of death, the lordship was not complete. That the early church believed this was a historical event is abundantly evident, but "proof" of the Resurrection rests on one's presuppositions, or faith stance.

2. The Resurrection convinced Jesus' followers that he was more than human, that he was divine, that in him God had acted. The Resurrection validated the authority of his teachings and miraculous deeds. He taught as one having authority, and his claims superseded even those of Moses. His authority was not simply that of another wise man; he himself seemed to be the authority. His miraculous deeds were not those of a magician or ordinary healer; they were signs pointing to his lordship over life and death.

3. The Resurrection validated Jesus as Savior—his forgiveness of sins. The common biblical tradition (Genesis 3:1–19) made death the result of sin, so that Jesus' victory over death rendered credible his forgiveness of sin, made his promises (as to the dying thief) more than mere words.

4. The Resurrection revealed a new dimension to the power and love of God. Jesus showed that death is not the final power, thus accrediting his insistence on love as the basis of human life; not even death can separate one from the love of God in Christ, cried Paul. God cares, even the hairs of one's head are numbered, and this God will not finally be defeated. At the heart of the universe is love: return good for evil, love God and love your neighbor as yourself. The letter known as I John, written toward the end of the first century, makes love the core of Christian life: "He who does not love does not know God; for God is love" (1 John 4:8).

5. The Resurrection vindicated Jesus' claims—some oblique, some direct—to be the Messiah, the king long looked for in Jewish tradition, but his kingdom was not of this world. Yet he had promised to come

again. Eschatological expectations developed, as varied as the many implications of Jesus' words about his kingdom and his kingship. Paul (especially in I Thessalonians and I Corinthians) looked for an imminent return of Christ. The Gospel of John tended to spiritualize this expectation, but Mark 13, Matthew 24–25, Luke 21, and the Revelation to John gave it an apocalyptic, destruction-of-the-evil-of-this-world turn. In any case, eschatology implied the establishment of the sovereign rule of God, an ideal that has beckoned Christians with varying degrees of intensity throughout the centuries.

These are the assumptions, presuppositions, or faith stances that marked the early Christian community. They rest on and also reaffirm God as Creator, Sustainer, and Sovereign as in the Old Testament. They are not "historical facts," but neither can they be separated from history, for to do so is to make Christianity an abstraction. The conviction that beyond death is a sovereign God who loves us and who in Christ revealed his lordship over death released the early Christians to a new way of life "in Christ." How succeeding generations experienced, interpreted, abused, institutionalized, abandoned, rationalized, and lived this universal message is the story of Christianity in the world.

2

In Conflict with Rome

Christianity entered the world as a subversive element. It acknowledged but one sovereignty—the sovereignty of God—and soon collided with the sovereign claims of the Roman Empire and the cult of imperial divinity. Acceptance of Jesus as Lord made all human institutions and human beings less than absolute, less than final, less than sovereign. The collision took the form of persecutions that lasted 250 years. The Christian belief in the sovereignty of God has repeatedly functioned as a subversive element in culture, for it has provided impetus for criticism, rejection, and reform of the status quo. Earthly loyalties, however lofty, cannot be absolute. Belief in the sovereignty of God has often been vague and often has been translated into mundane human action, but this belief has kept Christianity from becoming completely acculturated. "Render therefore to Caesar the things that are Caesar's and to God the things that are God's" (Matthew 22:21; Mark 12:17; Luke 20:25), "We must obey God rather than men" (Acts 5:29), and "If God be for us, who can stand against us?" (Romans 8:31) are expressions of divine sovereignty that have echoed through church history in the lives of martyrs, conscientious objectors, pacifists, and revolutionaries. This was the belief that caused early Christians to resist Rome's absolute claims; that caused "heretics" to defy particular forms of Christianity in Roman Catholicism, Lutheranism, Calvinism, and Anglicanism; that caused Christians to protest the absolute claims of national sovereignties in Russia, the United States, France, and

Germany. It is the rootage, although generally unacknowledged, that feeds campus unrest, conscientious objection, and upheaval in the second half of the twentieth century.

Whereas the Incarnation and Resurrection differentiate Christianity from Judaism, the sovereignty of God joins them, and the same subversive element has been evident in the history of the Jews—for strong belief in the sovereignty of God tends to erode the sovereign claims of nations.

Prior to the time of Jesus, in the Maccabean period (167–63 B.C.), the Jews had known a period of independence. It had come to the Jews after centuries of domination by Assyria, Babylonia, Persia, and Greece. But the independence had been far from ideal, and the rival factions vying for power finally invited the intervention of Rome in 63 B.C. However, the peace that Rome brought was intermittently broken by insurrectionists who wanted to return the land to Jewish control, thus manifesting the sovereignty of God as in ancient times. Among these were the Zealots, one of whom, Simon, was associated closely with Jesus. This tie and the crowds that Jesus attracted apparently caused Rome to think that Jesus might be the center of an incipient revolt, a factor that contributed to his crucifixion, for Rome desired peace almost at any price in her territories. Rome, normally tolerant of new religious beliefs, could not grant the key belief in the sovereignty of God, for it undercut the sovereignty of Rome. Neither could the Jews grant the sovereignty of Rome when it impeded their religious affirmations. In 41 A.D., after Caligula announced his intention to erect a statue of himself in the temple at Jerusalem so that he might be more readily worshiped by the Jews, he was assassinated. To avoid further revolt, the Jews were granted exemption from emperor worship, but were carefully watched for possible new outbreaks. Jesus, "King of the Jews," appeared to be the center of just such a possibility, and he was crucified.

But the Jews in Palestine subsequently enjoyed no real peace, as Josephus in his *Wars of the Jews* so graphically tells us. In 66 A.D. the Zealots in Jerusalem instituted an uprising in which the Roman garrison was butchered. When the Roman army from Syria was repulsed, Nero dispatched Vespasian and his son Titus to quell the rebellion. A general religious war in Palestine ensued. For four years the land was devastated by war, Titus finally taking and demolishing the city of Jerusalem in 70 A.D. after a siege of five months. Other cities like Masada resisted siege for two years. When the walls of Masada were finally breached, the Roman legions found only one old woman and another with five children. During the night the husbands had killed their wives and children, and then ten selected men killed the husbands. Nine hundred sixty died. During the war the Romans seized booty, much of which was used to adorn Vespasian's Palace of Peace in Rome, and deported 97,000 captives as spoils of battle. Sixty-five years later, during the revolt of Bar Kochba, Jerusalem was again demolished. Afterward, Jerusalem rapidly faded as a strategic center. Many Christians believed the destruction of Jerusalem in 70 and again in 135 were signs of God's displeasure toward the Jews for having rejected Jesus as Messiah.

Just when Rome distinguished Christians from Jews is not known, but even if clearly distinguished from the beginning, it would have made little difference, for the Christian insistence on God's sovereignty also collided with the cult of emperor worship, the symbol of Roman unity and loyalty. The earliest Christians were, of course, Jews. Jesus was a Jew. The disciples and Paul were Jews, and Jesus did practically all his work among Jews. Their expectations and beliefs were Jewish. They shared the same Bible, prayers, rituals, and liturgy. They believed in the sovereignty of God the Creator, the lord of history. They looked for establishment of divine rule through a promised Messiah. Some Jews, the Pharisees, believed in a resurrection (Acts 23:6–10).

Their chief differences centered on the Christian belief that Jesus was God Incarnate, the long-expected Messiah—a belief vindicated for Christians by the Resurrection. He was a Messiah whose kingdom was not political but spiritual, whose power was not simply over life but also over death. The earliest Christian confession was "Jesus is Lord." The Incarnation, Resurrection, and felt power of the Spirit gradually produced differences. The shift of the Sabbath to Sunday for worship to symbolize the Resurrection, and from the Passover to the Lord's Supper to symbolize unity with one another and Christ were significant changes. The exaltation of Jesus and the Holy Spirit, culminating in the controversial doctrine of the Trinity, which appeared to many to depart from monotheism, was another. The two great commandments to love God and neighbor telescoped Old Testament morality, which Christians accepted, for Jesus had come not to destroy but to fulfill the law. Yet belief in Jesus' atonement dictated the cessation of various sacred rites that affected ethical expressions and further differentiated the Christians. Paul's ministry to Gentiles, his claim that faith in Christ rather than human works justifies, his abrogation of the necessity of circumcision and exclusiveness shocked the early Christians in Jerusalem (Acts 15, Galatians 1–5). While the Jerusalem Christians blamed high Jewish officials for the crucifixion of Jesus, their own orientation was toward Jewish customs. A miraculous vision was necessary to open Peter's mind to non-exclusiveness (Acts 10). Even so, the relative exclusiveness of the Christian community in Jerusalem continued to contrast sharply with the non-Jewish ways of converted Gentiles. Jerusalem Christians were dubbed Christians of the "Circumcision" (Eusebius, *History,* 4:5). Although many ties and beliefs were alike, differentiations did develop, and the two destructions of the Holy City seemed to show divine disapproval of the Jews' rejection of Christ.

With nationalistic Judaism squelched in the East, Rome did not proceed vigorously against Jews in other areas, and probably did not clearly distinguish Christians from Jews until about the end of the first century. Complicating the confusion during this period was the tacit exemption of Jews from emperor worship and the Christians' claim that they were the true Jews, the true continuation and heirs of the ancient prophecies and promises. Differences among the Jews were not uncommon and probably meant little to the Roman rulers except when disruptions occurred. Not only did the priestly leaders, the Sadducees and Pharisees, differ with one another in significant beliefs and in attitudes toward outsiders, but there were differences between the Essenes and the related Qumran community (whose existence was recently brought to light by discovery of the Dead Sea Scrolls in 1947).

Pliny the elder, Philo, and Josephus have all left descriptions of the Essenes, "the pious ones," who came into existence in the second century B.C. They were separatists, living in isolated, highly organized communes in Judea but principally near the western shore of the Dead Sea. They shared their frugal belongings. Marriage seems to have been allowed, but full-fledged Essenes were expected to be celibate. They did not actively proselytize. Recruits came largely from orphaned children cared for by the community. Strict rules for entrance, including a three-year novitiate, solemn vows of obedience and secrecy, stringent discipline, and expulsion for infractions kept the community relatively small. They rejected slavery, oaths, and war, although some of them were Zealots against the Roman domination. Esoteric knowledge about the names of angels and the special qualities of roots and stones, exegesis of the Scriptures to uncover inner meanings, piety in the keeping of ceremonies and the Sabbath, and predictions about the future marked their activities. Although different in some respects, the Qumran community was a related group, greatly concerned with prophecy and God's expected intervention in history. Their founder-hero was "the Teacher of Righteousness" who was dispelled from Israel by a "wicked priest." They rejected the official priestcraft at Jerusalem and lived communally in a house on the northwest shore of the Dead Sea. Their connection with the Maccabean revolt and the bloody fighting in the Jewish war of 66–70 that took place at Qumran is not certain.

With the rapid growth and pervasiveness of Christianity in the empire, Rome increasingly distinguished it from Judaism and eventually regarded it as a new internal threat that for the sake of unity in the empire would have to be exterminated. The ethos of the time made a secular state in the modern sense a virtual impossibility.

Not until the second century were Christians persecuted on the basis of the name itself (*nomen ipsum*). Not until then were they seen as a new internal threat distinguishable from the Jews in Palestine. The Book of Revelation, if written at the close of the first century as most scholars conclude, clearly indicates a severe persecution of Christians in Asia Minor on the basis of *majestas* (Rome's sovereignty), but does not clearly distinguish between Christians and Jews. However, the correspondence between Pliny and Emperor Trajan about 112 indicates a definite policy against Christianity as illicit and unlawful (*religio illicita, non licet esse Christianos*).

In the first century Rome persecuted Christians on the basis of police power, *coercitio*. Christians were disturbers of the peace. This, Tertullian reports, was the nature of the move against Jesus, who was crucified under Emperor Tiberius (14–37). It underlay the stoning of Stephen (Acts 6:8–7:60) and the beheading of James (Acts 12:2). The emperor's right to use police power without recourse to the courts, even though Rome prided itself on due process of law, provided the basis for Nero's persecution in 64. To divert suspicion of arson from himself, Nero (54–68) accused the Christians of burning Rome. Tacitus (ca. 60–120), in his *Annales* (XV, 44), after denigrating Christians for "moral enormities" and "pernicious superstition," reports:

Those who confessed were first seized, then on their information a great multitude were convicted, not so much of the crime of incendiarism, as of hatred of the human race. The victims who perished also suffered insults, for some were covered with the skins of wild beasts and torn to pieces by dogs, while others were fixed to crosses and burned to light the night when daylight had failed. Nero had offered his gardens for the spectacle and was giving a circus show, mingling with people in the dress of a driver, or speeding about in a chariot. Although they were criminals who deserved the most severe punishment, yet a feeling of pity arose since they were put to death not for the public good but to satisfy the rage of an individual.

Suetonius in *Vita Neronis*, XVI, mentions suppressing Christianity as "a new and vicious superstition." Clement of Rome (30–97) refers to tortures suffered by women. However, Nero's persecution did not extend beyond Rome.

Under Galba, Vespasian, Titus, Otho, and Vitellius persecutions of Christians were sporadic, scattered, and slight. They were blamed for bad business, storms, diseases, riots, and crimes. Serious persecution did not come until Domitian (81–96). Avowedly hostile to Christians and Jews, Domitian persecuted both fiercely. Occasioned by hesitancy of Jews to pay the Capitoline Jupiter tax, levied after the fall of Jerusalem as a substitute for the temple tax, oppression was especially heavy in the East and in Rome. Domitian accused Christians of crimes, confiscated their property, exiled some, and decreed death for others. I Peter 4:14–16 and Revelation 2:13 and 6:9 may refer to Domitian's persecution, but the evidence does not indicate treatment of Christians as traitors. Nerva (96–98) reversed Domitian's policy and recalled many of the banished. Nerva did not treat Christianity as legal, nor did he regard it as a crime. However, by the time Pliny ruled as governor of Bithynia (111–13), Rome did regard Christians as subversive. To be a Christian was a crime against the state. Refusal to sacrifice to the emperor was treason.

Emperor Trajan (98–117) revived laws against secret associations, and about 111–13 Pliny found himself confronted with the problem of what to do with large numbers of Christians in his area. He wrote to Trajan for instructions. From every rank, age, and sex Christians had been apprehended. Should they be equally punished, the old and young, the weak and strong, simply for being Christian? If they repented, cursed Christ, and sacrificed to the emperor, should they be acquitted? Should anonymous accusations be received? Should they be sought out? Pliny had already put some to death for their obstinacy and tortured others to get confessions. His procedures had already restored the sacred imperial rites and caused the temple to be frequented again, but the large numbers of Christians involved in all this made him hesitate to proceed further.

Pliny believed that many could be reclaimed if repentance were permitted (Pliny, *Epistles*, X, 96). He did not receive answers to all of his questions, but Trajan's reply set the standard treatment of Christians for a century. He approved Pliny's procedure and added, "They ought not to be sought out; if they are brought before you and convicted they ought to be punished, provided that if anyone denies that he is a Christian, and proves this by worshiping our gods, he shall be pardoned as a result of his recantation, however much he may have been under suspicion in the past. No attention should be paid to anonymous charges. They constitute a bad precedent and are not worthy of our age" (Pliny, *Epistles*, X, 97).

The most notable martyr in this period was St. Ignatius (ca. 35–115) who died sometime during the reign of Trajan. He was one of those whom Pliny said were "sent to the City" because they were Roman citizens. He was taken to Rome under military guard, "chained to ten leopards," as he said. On the way, he sent letters to several churches in which he manifested a passionate desire for martyrdom, lauded the Resurrection, exalted the office of bishop, insisted on the humanity and divinity of "our God Jesus Christ," warned against Judaizers, and called the Eucharistic bread the "flesh of Jesus Christ." (Cf. Chapter 3, p. 36.)

Emperor Hadrian (117–38) continued the policies of Trajan, with insistence apparently on due process and penalties for those who brought false accusations. Second-century Christian writers like Quadratus and Aristides indicate that many suffered, and tradition holds that Roman bishops Alexander and Telesphorus, St. Symphorosa and her seven sons, and Eustachius died under Hadrian. In Palestine the Jews revolted when Hadrian founded a colony, Aelia Capitolina, on the site of Jerusalem, and more than half a million Jews perished during the rebellion (132–35). Hadrian's legions dispersed thousands of the survivors and banned Jews from the city.

Although Antonius Pius (138–61) protected Christians from mob violence when they were blamed for natural calamities, he did put Christians to death and is remembered for one famous martyrdom, that of Polycarp, the bishop of Smyrna (ca. 69–155). Polycarp, a disciple of the apostle John and a friend of Ignatius, went to Rome about 154 to help adjust a dispute about Easter and died at the stake in the persecution by Pius. Polycarp's staunch piety, anti-Gnosticism, and apostolic traditionalism endeared him to many contemporaries. When asked to renounce Christ and swear by Caesar, he refused saying he could not blaspheme the one whom he had served eighty-six years. The *Martyrdom of Saint Polycarp*, written to observe the first anniversary of Polycarp's death, tells how he was seized by mounted police, how he withstood threats, how the flames enveloped his body without touching him, how the executioner's spear brought blood which put out the fire, how his body eventually burned and gave off a fragrance of spices, and how a dove flew up from his ashes. The dove in addition to symbolizing purity and the Holy Spirit may also account for the increasing worship of saints. An eagle flying up from the burning pyre of the emperors signified apotheosis.

Numerous evidences of persecution come from the reign of Marcus Aurelius (161–80), a Stoic philosopher who disdained Christianity as a fanatical superstition, dangerous to the state because of its doctrine of Resurrection. The defenses of Christianity from Melito, Miltiades, Athenagoras, and Justin Martyr did not prevent a stormy time for the church. Justin Martyr, who wrote the first formal defense of Christianity about 150, died in Rome around 166. Celsus and Lucian wrote bitter tirades against the Christians, not only blaming them for natural disasters and insurrections, but also attacking the reliability of the Scriptures. Christians suffered in Asia and in Europe at the hands of authorities and "Marauding hooligans." About 170 Melito wrote: "The race of worshipers of God in Asia is now persecuted by new edicts as it never has been heretofore; shameless, greedy sycophants, finding occasion in the edicts, now plunder the innocent day and night." In addition to existing laws, Marcus Aurelius decreed exile for anyone who tried to influence others by talking about divine wrath. Eusebius, the historian, in Book V of his *Ecclesiastical History,* has left an eye-witness account of the persecutions at Lyons and Vienne in France in 177. "Not only were we excluded from public houses, baths, and markets, but also forbidden, every one of us, to appear in any place whatsoever." Mobs subjected them to insults, blows, the stocks, imprisonment, plunderings, the arena, fire in the iron chair, and stonings. Brought before the forum by the authorities, the accused Christians were publicly examined and subjected to torture. Some heathen servants, fearing torture, told of Thyestean feasts and Oedipean incests among the Christians, thus arousing the populace to new heights of rage. Sanctus, after being burned over the tender parts of his body with red-hot brass plates, was thrown into prison and retortured in the same manner a few days later. Bishop Pothinus, though ninety and ill, was kicked and beaten before the governor and hurled into a dungeon where he died two days later. The virgin Blandina, a slave, mangled and broken in torture, was finally gored by a bull. Corpses of martyrs choked the streets. Dogs feasted. After six days' exposure, the multilated bodies were burned and the ashes dumped into the Rhone river to make resurrection more difficult.

During the reign of Commodus (180–92), who tended to favor Christians, the first phase of the persecutions came to an end. They had been of varying intensity, sporadic, and limited, despite the fact that hundreds of Christians suffered death. They developed a feeling of rejection and hatred of the state and the world. Even though the world had been created good, the Fall had so corrupted the world that Christians looked upon it as evil. The change occasioned by the persecutions may be seen by contrasting Paul's letter to the Romans and the Book of Revelation. In Romans 13 Paul accepted the state as good, as an institution ordained by God from whom all power comes. He urged Christians to obey the authorities, for the power of the state is to curb evildoers. A similar stance is seen in I Peter 2:12, 15 and 3:16, even though these passages reflect persecutions already under way. The Book of Revelation, however, pictures the state as the enemy of God's people. The author wants vengeance; he rejoices in anticipation of the state's coming destruction (Revelation 18:20); and the martyred saints cry out from beneath the throne of God in heaven, "O Sovereign Lord, holy and true, how long before thou wilt judge and avenge our blood on those who dwell upon the earth?" (6:10; cf. 11:18; 16:6). The writer considers the state satanic; only Christ's return can end the struggle of the church with this world's evil forces. The Book of Revelation, written during the reign of Domitian or later, displays toward the state a vastly different attitude from that manifested in Romans 13.

Beginning with Septimus Severus (193–211) the persecutions became more severe supposedly with the purpose of forcing the assimilation of Christianity into the plurality of religions under the imperial cult. In 202 Christians and Jews both suffered; their claims of One Lord and One God were too subversive to be tolerated. During this persecution Leonides, the father of Origen, was beheaded. Tertullian tells the story of Perpetua, a noble woman, whose heathen father, holding her baby, pleaded with her to renounce Christianity and save herself, and of Felicitas, a slave woman, who was delivered of her baby just in time to be cast with Perpetua to the wild beasts. Clement of Alexandria writes that "many martyrs are daily burned, confined or beheaded before our eyes." But this persecution was relatively brief. With the exception of a short outburst under Maximinus Thrax (235–38), Christians lived generally in peace until the time of Decius. Philippus Arabs (244–49) may even have been a Christian. Origen wrote letters to him and his wife Severa.

Decius (249–51) mounted the first systematic, general persecution of Christians, vigorously proceeding against them as atheistic and seditious. Following the celebration of the thousandth anniversary of the founding of Rome, a belief prevailed that Rome's misfortunes were due to the displeasure of the gods who, because of Christianity, were being neglected. Decius' edict in 250 demanded that everyone sacrifice to the gods and the genius of the emperor on a fixed day or suffer confiscation, exile, torture, or death. Many nominal Christians complied or connived with officials to secure certificates of sacrifice saying they had; they were later excommunicated by Christians as *lapsi*. Others suffered the penalties. Origen was tortured. Bishops Fabianus of Rome, Babylas of Antioch, and Alexander of Jerusalem were put to death. Bishop Cyprian of Carthage fled, saying the Lord had not yet granted him the grace of martyrdom.

Gallus (251–53) continued the persecution started by Decius, in addition blaming the Christians for outbreaks of pestilence and famine. In 257, after a few years of reprieve, Valerian (253–60) issued a rescript forbidding Christians to assemble or to use their cemeteries on pain of death. He ordered bishops, presbyters and deacons to be seized and punished immediately; senators, nobles, and Roman knights to lose their rank and property, and their heads if they persisted in being Christians; matrons to be deprived of their goods and exiled; and members of Caesar's household who confessed, to sacrifice their property and be sent to Caesar's estates in chains (Cyprian, *Epistles*, LXXX:1). Sixtus II of Rome was martyred. Cyprian of Carthage felt he had now received the grace for martyrdom and went to the scaffold. A multitude accompanied him to his execution, a presbyter bound his hands, and the faithful caught his blood in their handkerchiefs.

During the next forty-six years, until the reign of Diocletian (284–305), Christians enjoyed peace, prospered, increased in numbers, and built places of worship. But their allegiance to One Lord still posed a threat to imperial sovereignty, and Diocletian decided on extermination, the final solution, even though he had respected Christianity for some twenty years and even though his wife Prisca and daughter Valeria were catechumens. Diocletian extolled his own divinity, called himself Lord and Master of the world, and made supplicants approach him on their knees. His persecution exceeded all others in brutality, intensity, and terror. In

303 he issued three edicts, followed by a fourth by Maximian in 304, and a fifth by Galerius in 308. Eusebius and Lactantius have supplied us with details. Churches were to be destroyed, Scriptures burned, Christians deprived of their offices and civil rights and imprisoned, and all were to sacrifice to the gods or die. Regardless of rank or age, suspects were racked, scraped, flogged, dragged, and maimed. Lawsuits were received against Christians, but they could not be plaintiffs in questions of wrong, adultery, or theft, and when found to be Christians they were summarily killed. Whole families were led to execution. Servants with millstones tied about their necks were cast into the sea, others strangled. Crowds were herded together, ringed with wood, and burned. One man who tore down an edict was seized, tortured, and slowly roasted. The prisons bulged. Executioners became weary, their swords dull. Beasts overly gorged on human flesh turned away. Beginning with the burning of the church in Nicodemia, the persecution raged through the empire except in Britain, Gaul, and Spain, where Constantius, the father of Constantine, held sway—though he did allow some property to be destroyed to avoid the charge of insubordination. Retiring to private life in 305, Diocletian left affairs of the empire in the hands of his subordinates, among whom a struggle for power ensued. By 307 no less than six generals claimed to be Augusti. In 311 when Galerius lay dying of a horrifying disease that rotted the lower part of his torso, after a year of unsuccessful medicines and surgery, he issued an edict of limited toleration and besought the prayers of Christians. But events were already in motion that would totally alter church-state relations. In 306 Constantine had become ruler of the West—Gaul, Spain, and Britain—and in 312 he led a victorious army over the Alps and into Rome. For either political or religious reasons, or both, he chose to protect Christians, and in 313 joined with Licinius in issuing the famous Edict of Milan. The co-emperors proclaimed that "Christians and all others should have liberty to follow that mode of religion which to each of them appeared best." This toleration was "absolute" and "unconditional" for Christians, who were specifically mentioned throughout the edict. The edict ordered that all appropriated property of Christians formerly bought or received by gift be restored immediately, and that restitution for loss sustained by such action be sought from the public treasury. The church had suddenly become an accepted, favored institution.

In other decrees Constantine enhanced the status of the church. In 313 he ordered the subsidizing of expenses of certain ministers in Africa and exempted all clergy from public duties that would draw them away from ministerial services. In 319 he decreed burning for soothsayers and in 321 legalized bequests to the church and made Sunday a day of rest for all except farmers.

Constantine and Licinius eliminated their rivals, divided the empire for awhile, and then fought each other, until in 323 Constantine emerged the sole ruler. In an effort to secure religious unity he sent armed forces against the dissident Donatists of North Africa and in 325 convened the Council of Nicaea. About 325 Eusebius finished his *Ecclesiastical History*, in which he lauded Constantine as "God's dearly beloved," "the all-gracious emperor," and "the most exalted person living." He pictured opposition to Constantine as opposition to God's own. In 330 Constantine selected Byzantium for his capital and renamed it Constantinople, thus leaving a large share in the shaping of the West to the rapidly developing church in Rome. On his deathbed in 337 he received baptism. Although a revival of paganism occurred under Julian (361–63), by 380 in the reign of Theodosius I (379–95) Christianity was enforced as the *only* official religion of the empire.

The consequences of the persecutions are difficult to assess. Rather than stopping the growth of Christianity, they advertised and enhanced its appeal. People dared to be heroic; many wanted to be martyred. Both Ignatius and Polycarp asked that nothing be done to hinder their triumphant witness with their blood. The belief was strong that Christ would crown those who suffered in this life. Concomitant with this attitude was the belief that, although God created this world good, human sin had rendered it so corrupt that it was hardly a fit place in which to live. Mixed with biblical notions about seeking the kingdom of heaven first (Matthew 6:25–34) and letting nothing in this world come before one's allegiance to Christ (Matthew 19:16–30, Luke 14:25–33), and with Greek notions about the unreality of material things, this attitude produced an ethos of asceticism—a rejection of this world and its evils in favor of spiritual reality and an otherworldly hope. Persecution undoubtedly contributed to the feeling that the world was grossly evil, but with the abatement of the persecutions asceticism did not cease. Instead, it increased. In the Middle Ages, "ascetic" was a synonym for "religious." The persecutions provided favorable conditions for asceticism, but asceticism involved far more than a reaction to the persecutions, as we shall see in Chapters 3–5.

To approximately the same degree did the persecutions affect eschatology, which pertains to last things—the final destiny of the individual and of the human race. Persecution served to heighten expectations of divine judgment on this world; its cessation contributed to a transference of the Kingdom of God to the church in the world. In general, eschatology in the Christian community was at first strong and then tended to wane, except during periods of stress. The persecutions provided such periods. But again, eschatology is much more complex than its recurrence during periods of stress might suggest. It was a hope, an ideal; it was tied to God's sovereignty and the expectation of that sovereignty's becoming actual. As such, eschatology fostered (and continues to foster) a basis from which to criticize the present.

Usually associated with times of suffering, eschatology embodies the hope of a divine righting of things—vindication of the just, judgment on the unjust. Old Testament eschatology is linked with the expectation of a messianic king and finds expression in Daniel, the latter parts of Job, Ezekiel, Zechariah, Psalms 49 and 73, Isaiah, and in the apocryphal Book of Jubilees and Enoch. In the New Testament eschatology assumes a prominent place, especially in Mark 13, Matthew 24–25, in Jesus' parables of the wheat and the tares, the drag net, the man who stored his grain, and in Jesus' urgent injunctions to "repent for the kingdom is at hand." Albert Schweitzer's startling studies, *The Mystery of the Kingdom of God*

(1901, 1925), and *The Quest of the Historical Jesus* (1906, 1910), upheld eschatological expectations of a speedy end of the world as the key to Jesus' ministry. However, an imminent judgment on the world in the Gospels is attenuated. The kingdom is both present and future. "Repent for the kingdom is at hand" provides an eschatological context for ascetic rejection of the world, but the command to preach the gospel in all the world provides for social acceptance and responsibility. "Thy kingdom come" points to an imminent end, whereas "give us this day our daily bread" points to stability. Celibacy might have been a better state for those expecting an immediate end, but marriage was both honored and blessed by Jesus. Mark 13 and Matthew 25 depict a cataclysmic end, although saying that no one knows the time and place and stressing preparation. But the Gospel of John, presumably a later writing, spiritualizes the judgment and the return of Christ.

Expectation of the end of the world is quite direct in Paul's letters. The dead will soon be resurrected, and Jesus will come triumphant to judge and reward (I Thessalonians 4:9–5:11). Christians are to wait patiently, maintain their callings, get married if they must but not beget children because the time is short and continence and virginity are preferred (I Corinthians 7:17–31; Romans 13:11–14). But Ephesians does not stress the imminent end of the world; rather, it stresses Christ as the living power that binds all into one, holy, catholic, and apostolic church that is to be coterminous with humanity; purity in marriage is enjoined; and Christians are to put on the armor of God as if for a long battle.

Eschatological apocalypses dominate the Book of Revelation, which was written under severe and growing persecution. The martyred dead in heaven cry out for vengeance on the wicked of this world, and catastrophe follows catastrophe when God unleashes minions of judgment, until finally there is a new heaven and new earth without death and tears. The Book of Revelation notes the idolatry, tyranny, and injustice of the Roman Empire—not the benefits of authority as in Romans 13. And by speaking of the 144,000 undefiled, it fostered asceticism, virginity, fasting, and poverty.

Noncanonical writings indicate that the imminent end of the world was strongly expected among Christians at the turn of the first century, even though many unfulfilled years had passed and some discontent and impatience had developed. Clement of Rome inveighs against this discontent. Christ was expected to return triumphant over all enemies. There was to be a resurrection of the dead and a day of judgment. Christians were enjoined to watch and be ready. Such allusions are found not only in Clement of Rome, but also in the *Didache*, Barnabas, and Papias. These expectations and the persecutions engendered aloofness from the world and otherworldly hopes, but the commands to love, to evangelize, and to create a good reputation drove Christians to associations in the world. Clement of Rome includes submission to and intercession for rulers in his liturgical prayer.

In the second century eschatological fervor waned. Gnostic writers abandoned or rationalized the old views, and Christians during the relative periods of peace in the second century associated more freely with the world. But the old views and aloofness are still found in the *Shepherd of Hermas*, Diognetus, Justin Martyr, and Tatian, along with the hope of triumph over the empire.

In the period of the great thinkers (180–250) eschatology continued but there was great disappointment. Origen, the greatest writer of the period, stressed the spiritual coming of Christ and criticized the preachers of judgment and chiliasm—the violently inaugurated thousand-year reign of Christ. But Tertullian and Montanus expressed extreme eschatology and called for strict fasting, martyrdom, moral earnestness, and refusal of carnal pleasures. They discouraged marriage and denounced second marriages as adultery. Tertullian prayed for a postponement of the final judgment because of the horrible things that were to precede it, and Hippolytus postponed the end by 200 years. By the third century eschatology had lost its edge, although it had by no means disappeared. Lactantius, Arnobius, and Victorinus still talked about the reign of Antichrist in the world but a growing worldliness tended to prevail along with the general belief that Christ would not return so long as the empire lasted. Christian writers heaped lavish praise on those emperors who tolerated the new religion, especially Constantine. Harmonization tended to check eschatology; persecution and developing asceticism tended to keep it alive. Throughout the first three centuries the eschatological scene was mixed, paralleling to a considerable extent the off-and-on persecutions. With Constantine's acceptance and promotion of the church, eschatological expectations shifted toward a realization of hope in the individual and in the church now. Concern for the individual's place in heaven, hell, and purgatory and the ecclesiastical domination of worldly affairs increasingly displaced expectations of the overthrow of this world. The Constantinian church had little reason to promote either eschatology or aloofness. Christianity was soon the only legal religion in the empire, and by 416 only Christians could serve in the army. The church had passed from persecution to privilege, and with the passing had gone eschatology.

3

In Quest of Authority

Very soon after the death and resurrection of Christ, problems developed within the Christian community that gave impetus to what Ernst Troeltsch has called the greatest sociological achievement of the time—the formation of the Christian church. The struggle was bitter, complicated by the persecutions, eschatological expectations, burgeoning missions, and invading ideas. But, by the end of the second century the Christian community had an organized clergy, a creed, and a canon. Excrescences and deviations had been answered. A set authority (creed and canon) and a fluid authority (the clergy) had been established. Although these authorities, later designated Scripture and Tradition, often have been buffeted and blemished, they have basically shaped Christianity for 2,000 years.

Loyalty and a sense of the mystical presence of Christ held the early Christians together. Inexplicably Christ was in them, and they were his body in the world (I Corinthians 12, Romans 12, John 14, 15, 17). They met together for prayer, the singing of hymns, and worship. They called one another "brother" and "sister." They shared their goods. To be admitted to the community one had to believe, either through direct contact with Christ or through the power of the Spirit (Acts 2). The sign of repentance and forgiveness was baptism, symbolizing death to sin and resurrection to new life in Christ through the indwelling of the Spirit (Acts 2:1–4, 38; 9:3–19; 10:47; 11:15–17). Baptism also commemorated Christ's baptism (Matthew 3:16; Mark 1:9–11; Luke 3:21–22), when the

Holy Spirit descended upon him; pledged the receiver to a renunciation of evil ways; and marked the beginning of a new life. Each Sunday Christians ate a common meal of bread and wine in remembrance of Christ's last supper with the disciples; the bread was "his body" and the wine "his blood" of the new covenant between them and God. Only full-fledged members could share in this sacred meal. Unworthy members were to abstain lest damnation fall upon them (I Corinthians 11:27–30); and some with serious faults had to be excluded (I Corinthians 11:17–30; 5:1–13). The Old Testament and Jewish customs furnished the Christians with ethical guidelines, but the acceptance of Jesus as the Messiah implied changes that came forth dramatically in the activities of Paul. Who was unworthy? Those who lied, lusted, sued in court, robbed, defrauded? What constituted grounds for exclusion? Adultery, murder, apostasy, incest, uncircumcision, eating meat sacrificed to idols, false ideas? What discipline should Gentile converts without a background in Jewish life be expected to observe? These questions surfaced very quickly in the early church, in situations involving Paul's converts. They centered around the problems of the Judaizers and the antinomians, and the Gnostics. Their resolution left a legacy of legalism and asceticism.

If the Judaizers had triumphed, Christianity might have remained a Jewish sect, for the Judaizers were Jewish Christians who regarded Jewish Levitical laws as binding. They insisted on circumcision, abstinence from forbidden meats, etc., in such a way as to make righteousness dependent upon observing rules. Paul's experience of Christ and his prior failure to find peace in keeping the law would not allow him to accept such a view. In Christ he experienced a love that did not rest on human merit but on the mercy of God. The key was not faith in legalistic deeds but in God (Galatians 3:11; Romans 1:17; Hebrews 2:4). Faith preceded law, said Paul, for Abraham's covenant with God was received in faith long before Levitical law. The law was given as a guideline, a custodian, until the promise to Abraham could be fulfilled (Galatians 3:23–29). In Christ the promise was fulfilled. By dying on the cross Christ redeemed us from the curse of the law and revealed the primacy of faith (Galatians 3:10–14). Now that Christ has come, said Paul, to insist on the custodian is to reject the fulfillment and to live by something that has always been secondary. "I do not nullify the grace of God; for if justification were through the law, then Christ died to no purpose" (Galatians 2:21).

When emissaries from Jerusalem visited the churches that Paul founded at Galatia and insisted on circumcision, Paul angrily argued that the Galatians were to live by faith in Christ and not be enslaved to a set of rules. The source of your righteousness, he exclaimed, is not the law but Christ! He pleaded that they allow no one, not even Peter, James, or John, to make them Jews by submitting to circumcision. To receive circumcision is to separate from Christ, to fall from grace. Christians through the Spirit, by faith acting in love, live righteously. "For in Christ Jesus neither circumcision nor uncircumcision is of any avail, but faith working through love" (Galatians 5). Love is greater than law, not necessarily contrary to it. Paul wrote, "Christ has set us free . . . only do not use your freedom as an opportunity for the flesh, but through love be servants of one another. For the whole law is fulfilled in one word, 'You shall love your neighbor as yourself!' " (Galatians 5:1, 13–14). To the Romans Paul wrote, "For we hold that a man is justified by faith apart from works of law. . . . Do we then overthrow the law by this faith? By no means! On the contrary, we uphold the law" (3:28, 31).

As Acts reveals, Paul won the argument, but it took a miraculous vision to convince Peter (Acts 10, 11) and a conference in Jerusalem to resolve the matter (Acts 15). Even so, the Ebionites, who lasted into the fourth century, upheld the entire law as necessary to salvation. They hated Paul, rejected his letters, considered him a heathen. Opposition continued in Jerusalem long enough for leaders there to be called "bishops of the circumcision."

Paul's arguments may well have been too convincing, for some Christians embraced antinomianism; if righteousness is by faith, not law, if we are free, then let us sin that grace abound (Romans 3:8, 6:1–23; Galatians 5:13–14). The antinomians rejected all law, but Paul knew that law was needed to curb evil tendencies (Romans 7:13–25). Antinomianism became more acute when linked with Gnosticism. Nicolaitans (Revelation 2:6, 14f.) practiced licentiousness saying only the spirit mattered, and Ophites glorified the serpent of the Garden of Eden. Antinomianism continues to plague Christianity.

Gnosticism disrupted Paul's churches at Corinth and Colossae. Traces of it are found in I John and the Pastoral Epistles (I–II Timothy, Titus). Early Christian writers like Ignatius, Irenaeus, Tertullian, and Hippolytus wrote refutations of its ideas. Gnosticism, from the Greek *gnosis*, was secret knowledge. It took many forms, depending on who was its principal spokesman. In the Christian community, three of its most influential advocates were Basilides, Valentinus, and Marcion. It drew upon the Greek philosophical dualism of body-spirit, the body being inferior, unreal, and evil. Only the spirit was deemed real. Salvation meant freeing the spirit from material bondage. Everything turned on that key presupposition of the spirit's superiority. Extended and applied, the dichotomy of body-spirit yielded strange fruits, which the mainline Christians fought to reject.

Gnosticism's secret knowledge came to a favored few through direct revelations and secret traditions from the apostles. It usually had a mythology saying God was too spiritual to have been involved in creating this world. That mundane task was the work of a Demiurge, a fallen creature removed from God by a series of emanations. Demiurge created and rules the world. He created people with varying bits of spirit, so that the Gnostics spoke of different grades of human beings. Some were very spiritual, whereas others had such small amounts of spirit that they could hardly be distinguished from animals. Various rites were designed to free those bits of spirit, the real persons, from their fleshy embodiments. Christ came to show the way, but he was not incarnate, he merely used the body of Jesus. Since spirit is immortal, Christ did not die, and there was no resurrection; the man Jesus died on the cross. Docetism, from the Greek word for "seeming," derives from this notion that Christ merely seemed to be human.

Basilides, a second-century teacher at Alexandria, posed a system purportedly from Peter, of 365 eons emanating from God. The god of the Jews was a low eon, very far removed from the pure reality of God. He created the world and subjugated humanity. The supreme God then sent Nous (mind) into the world on a rescue mission. This spiritual Nous dwelt without contamination in Jesus to show us how to rid ourselves of matter and reascend to God. Data on Basilides' system is unfortunately sparse.

Valentinus (d. ca. 160), a teacher in Rome, received his gnosis in a vision. He posed a Platonic parallelism between the realms of ideas and phenomena. Its myth had an eternal primal Being whose silent contemplation became his spouse, for God is love and love must have an object. Then a process of emanations produced twenty-eight eons, in sexual pairs, symbolizing various attributes of divinity. Together they constituted the fullness of reality (*pleroma*). A dividing line (*horos*) separated reality from unreality (*kenoma*). All was well until Sophia, the twenty-eighth eon, feeling lonely attempted to leap into the heart of the All-Father, primal Being. In doing so, Sophia kicked a hole in the horos, and reality began to drain away. In the process, Demiurge was born outside pleroma. He created the visible world, imprisoning bits of reality in human beings. The All-Father then projected the last pair of eons—Christ and the Holy Spirit—to rescue reality. When reclaimed, a great wedding will be held in heaven, and matter will sink into nothing. The Soter, Christ, united with the man Jesus at the time of his baptism to reveal true gnosis to pneumatics (the Valentinians), who alone will enter into pleroma. Psychics (Christians who live by faith and good works) will make it only to a middle realm. Hylics (those submerged in matter) will suffer eternal perdition.

Gnosticism was a serious attempt to answer the problem of evil. What is evil? How can one be freed from it? Gnostics answered, we are essentially spiritual; the world is evil, unreal; salvation is escape from this world. Gnosticism posited a docetic Christ, no human incarnation. It denied history and God's activity in the world. It posited predestination: only those who have a portion of the spirit can be saved. Generally it fostered an ascetic ethic, rejection of sex and physical matters, a debasement of the body, and a cultivation of the spirit. However, by making the spirit everything and the body nothing it also fostered physical license; some Gnostics justified licentiousness by saying their bodies, not they themselves, were indulging. Stress on privileged gnosis led some to assumptions of arrogant superiority, a form of Gnosticism that troubled the Corinthian church.

Marcion (d. ca. 160), who perhaps left a more lasting mark than any of the others, was not a Gnostic in the sense of having an elaborate cosmic theosophy. He was a Christian, possibly the son of a bishop, well versed in Scriptures, and may have been excommunicated from the church in Rome for immorality. Over a large part of the Roman empire he established communities committed to the thesis that love is the central element of Christianity. The Old Testament and its laws he regarded as the antithesis of love and rejected them. Leading Christians of the day, Irenaeus of Lyons, Tertullian of Carthage, and Hippolytus of Rome, entered the lists against him. His followers flourished in the second and third centuries, only to be engulfed in Manicheism, although a few remnants endured for centuries.

Marcion's careful study of the Old Testament convinced him that the God Jesus revealed was just the opposite of the Jewish god revealed in the Scriptures. In his *Antitheses* he contrasted the two. The god of the Old Testament demanded justice, an eye for an eye; he called down fire from heaven, and he would associate only with the righteous. The Old Testament god contradicted himself, at one time forbidding images and at another commanding Moses to set up a brazen serpent. He was less than omniscient, for he had to ask Adam where he was and he had to descend to earth to find out what the builders of the Tower of Babel were up to. As the creator of Adam he introduced evil into the world and made physical sex the means of reproduction. He was wholly a god of law, capricious and cruel, who chose such bloodthirsty, lustful men as David to enforce his will. By contrast the God of Jesus was a God of love, insisting that his followers love their enemies, return good for evil. Christ forbade his disciples to call fire down from heaven, and he associated with sinners and harlots. Marcion's Bible consisted of his own *Antitheses*, the Gospel of Luke, and ten of Paul's letters (not the Pastorals), all carefully edited so as to leave nothing contrary to the basic thesis of love. Contrary elements were simply false excrescences. He rejected the Old Testament altogether. Marcion believed that the Apostles were too much under the influence of the Jews to understand the profound contrast between law and love. Paul alone understood that.

Marcion has no syzygies, no birth stories, no resurrection. Christ simply appeared about 29 A.D. He was docetic, and his salvation is not of the body but only of the spirit. Because Christ is love, Marcion posited no judgment. Believing that only the spirit is real, he advocated strict ascetic self-discipline. He rejected marriage, pagan festivities, flesh, and wine, and allowed only celibates to be baptized. Salvation is the escape of the spirit from matter.

The Judaizers, antinomians, and Gnostics left permanent marks on Christianity, particularly a tendency to legalism and asceticism. The persecutions and eschatology enhanced this tendency, which steadily increased in the early church. But more than that a resolution of these problems meant that the church had to declare its own canon, confess its beliefs, and establish an authentic leadership. This resulted in setting up the New Testament, the Apostles' Creed, and ecclesiastical offices.

Because of their own life experiences, those who personally knew Jesus understood his ministry in different ways, despite a strong common core. The oral tradition was still prominent, so that people remembered and quoted the words and deeds of Jesus. The return of Jesus loomed large in the minds of believers; the expectation prevailed that he would return during the lifetime of those who had been associated with him. When this did not happen and as original associates with Jesus began to dwindle, the need for literature for use in worship and to preserve the memory of events and words was felt. Thus, scholars believe, the Gospels and related writings came into existence. It is not surprising that the

Christians did not immediately canonize their writings. This did not happen for the Old Testament until the Jewish rabbis got together at Jamnia in 90 A.D. to weed out spurious literature that had become associated with Judaism. It happened for the Christians during the second to fourth centuries under the pressure of Gnosticism and the need to specify authoritative records.

Individual writings and letters were treasured and preserved by local congregations and read repeatedly in worship services. Copies were circulated to other churches in exchange for other writings. A common feeling of validity prevailed for the most part about the letters of Paul and the four Gospels. Paul's letters were collected sometime after 90. Acts shows no knowledge of the collected letters, but other writings at the turn of the century do. The four Gospels appear together shortly after 100 A.D. In about 150 Tatian published his *Diatessaron,* the four Gospels in a continuous narrative, which became a standard text of the Gospels in Syriac churches until the fifth century. In other areas John's obvious differences from the synoptic Gospels caused some concern. However, references in the literature of the time indicate that the four Gospels, thirteen letters of Paul, Acts, I Peter, and I John received general acceptance quite early, but that Hebrews, James, II Peter, II and III John, Jude, and Revelation were questioned in many circles. In addition, some writings like the letters of Barnabas, Ignatius, and Polycarp, the *Shepherd of Hermas, Acts of Peter,* the *Didache, Gospel of Thomas,* and the letter of Clement of Rome were received in some churches, though by no means in a majority. Apostolic authorship gradually became the test for acceptance, and the number of accepted writings began to sift down to the twenty-seven that now comprise the New Testament.

In response to Gnosticism and Marcionism, the church at Rome sponsored, alongside the Old Testament (the Septuagint version that included the apocrypha), a New Testament of twenty-two books that were to be read in worship services and appealed to as authorities in doctrinal controversies. Irenaeus of Lyons, Tertullian of Carthage, and the Muratorian fragment reflect this situation. The Muratorian fragment, discovered by Muratori in 1740, dates from the late second century and recognizes the four Gospels, Acts, the Pauline letters (except Hebrews), the Apocalypse of John, two Epistles of John, Jude, and the Apocalypse of Peter (not now included in the New Testament). It rejects two letters, one to the Laodiceans and the other to the Alexandrians, as heretical forgeries under the name of Paul, and counsels against reading the *Shepherd of Hermas* in public worship.

Around 200 A.D. Clement of Alexandria added Hebrews to the Pauline list and included the letters of Barnabas, Clement of Rome, and the Preaching of Peter (now lost) to the remaining writings. His quotations of Scripture indicate that he may have had a canon of some thirty books. In the third century Origen recognized our twenty-seven books plus Barnabas and the *Shepherd of Hermas.* The Eastern churches generally shied away from Revelation, and the Western churches from Hebrews. In the fourth century bishops and then synods began specifying some books as canonical and others as apocryphal until the writings finally sifted down to twenty-seven, not so much because of fiat from an overreaching authority as from a self-authenticating quality in the writings themselves and the practical needs they met. The Easter letter of St. Athanasius in 367 designated our present twenty-seven canonical books of the New Testament and seemed to settle the matter. Practically speaking, however, and apparently without a synod such as the Jews held at Jamnia, the Christians had a canon (a list of authoritative books) by the end of the second century. Gnostic writings were not included.

Christianity's oldest confession of faith, the Apostles' Creed, originally known as the Old Roman Symbol, was also developed about 150 in reaction to Gnosticism and the need for an identifying statement. A medieval legend held that the Apostles' Creed was composed under the inspiration of the Holy Spirit on the tenth day after the ascension of Jesus, each one of the apostles in turn contributing one of the phrases of the creed as known today. We now know that its original form was much briefer and that phrases were added to meet various needs. It originated in Rome where both Valentinus and Marcion had been teachers. Each phrase seems to be directed against a Gnostic notion. If it had been a simple summary of Christian belief, it seems strange that nothing is said about miracles, the teachings of Christ, the fulfillment of prophecy, missions, and so forth. The Gnostics denied the creation of this world; the creed asserts, "I believe in God, the Father all-mighty, maker of heaven and earth." The Gnostics presented a docetic Christ; the creed emphasizes that Christ was born, suffered and was crucified under Pontius Pilate, died, and was buried. The Gnostics considered the body evil and rejected the Resurrection; the creed boldly asserts the resurrection of the body. The Gnostics spoke loosely about a final judgment, Marcion having none at all; the creed speaks of Christ sitting at the right hand of the Father from whence he will come to judge the quick and the dead. The Gnostics held that only they could be saved; the creed upholds forgiveness of sins.

References to the creed appear frequently in early Christian literature. Although the exact present wording of the creed can be traced back only to the eighth century, the present form can be approximated in the fourth century, and the short form can be traced back to about 150. Churches and individuals apparently felt free to make changes.

In addition to the need for a canon and a creed, the early church also felt the need for the authority of authentic leadership. With so many voices being raised, some of them claiming direct and superior revelation, it was only natural to turn to the apostles for a way out of the confusion. Although Christ had promised to send a Spirit (John 14:15, 25; 15:26; 16:7–11) who would reveal still more truth to believers, the early Christians felt that additional truth would not contradict truth already revealed by Jesus. The Christian community turned to the apostles for guidance to determine an authoritative canon. If the reliable source for what Jesus really taught was to be found anywhere, it would be found in the apostles and their immediate successors. In this way the Apostolic Succession, the unbroken line of authority back to the original disciples, came into use.

Those churches that could claim apostolic foundations seemed to have telling voices of authority and to enjoy superior status, especially the church at Rome, which claimed both Peter and Paul as founders, thus according her tradition double reliability.

Paul's letters indicate that he wanted a sense of order in his churches, with various workers doing their tasks under the inspiration of the Spirit for the good of the whole body. He named apostles, prophets, teachers, workers of miracles, healers, helpers, administrators, and speakers in tongues, and admonished all of them to work together in love for the good of all (I Corinthians 12:13). In Philippians he spoke of bishops and deacons (Philippians 1:1). Other accepted writings spoke of elders and presbyters. Over these, of course, was Paul's own superintendency, a position which Timothy and Titus as Paul's delegates to Ephesus and Crete similarly enjoyed. From the data now available, distinct lines of authority are obscure, and the course of development is not clear, but by 100 A.D., the churches were generally headed by bishops or presbyter-bishops with deacons as helpers, all of them chosen by the people. A felt need for unity seemed to be the determining factor. As the church was one, its faith and practices should be uniform. Paul had excoriated divisive leaders at Corinth for breaking Christ up into factions (I Corinthians 1). Faced with a hostile world, a world that the church hoped to evangelize, a united front was obviously a desirable source of strength.

The appeal to unity, a hierarchical view of the ministry, and the necessity of submission to elected clergy—with an undertone of apostolic succession—were central themes in one of the most influential letters in the early church. That letter was written by Clement of Rome to the Corinthians about 96 A.D., toward the end of Domitian's reign. Deeply concerned with unity in the whole church, Clement, probably a bishop or leading presbyter in the church at Rome, wrote to protest the takeover of the Corinthian church by a group of young ascetic Gnostics claiming to have special spiritual gifts. Clement did not specifically assert superior authority for the church at Rome, but the church of Peter and Paul felt it had a duty to intervene and also to send envoys to rectify matters. The letter pointed to the church at Rome as a model of unity and to Abraham as a pattern of obedience and righteousness, and appealed to the order in nature as an example of what ought to prevail everywhere. While apostolic succession per se was not quite clear, it was implied. Fixed offices of bishop, presbyters, and deacons were clearly depicted as better than the unsettling free activity of the spirit.

A giant step forward in internal organization was taken by Ignatius when he exalted the office of bishop as the church's center of unity and fortress against heresy. While on his way to martyrdom in Rome, Ignatius wrote letters to various churches. In his letters to the Ephesians, Smyrneans, Magnesians, Trallians, and Philadelphians, he glorified the bishop saying that avoidance of schisms required obedience to church authorities. Presbyters, deacons, and laymen must all follow the bishop. The bishop represents God. Deference to the bishop is deference to God. The bishop is administrator, liturgist, and prophet. To the Smyrneans Ignatius wrote:

> Shun divisions, as the beginning of evils. Follow your bishop, as Jesus Christ followed the Father, and the presbytery as the Apostles; and to the deacons pay respect as to God's commandment. Let no man do anything pertaining to the church apart from the bishop. Let that be held a valid eucharist which is under the bishop or one to whom he shall have committed it. Wheresoever the bishop shall appear, there let the people be; even as where Jesus may be, there is the universal church. It is not lawful, apart from the bishop, either to baptize or to hold a love feast; but whatsoever he shall approve, this is well pleasing also to God; that everything that is done may be sure and valid.

He used the term "Catholic Church" in his letter to the Smyrneans, but used it in a spiritual rather than territorial sense to refer to the infinite Spirit of Christ rather than a domain. He was troubled by the Judaizers, who threatened schism; and he was troubled especially at Smyrna by the docetists, who denied the reality of Christ saying that matter is evil and that there was no real incarnation, no real person, no death, and no resurrection. Against the Judaizers he posited the divinity of Christ; against the docetists, the genuine humanity of Christ. Intensely devoted to Christ, he mystically identified the bishop with Christ, thus making the bishop the center of unity. Ignatius succeeded Peter as the bishop of Antioch, strongly recommended the primacy of Rome, but made no mention of the apostolic succession, although the implication of orthodoxy through the bishop was unmistakable.

Appeal to the apostolic tradition to counteract spurious assertions about Christianity was strong in Polycarp (ca. 69–155), bishop at Smyrna, who was a disciple of the Apostle John and a friend of Ignatius and, according to Irenaeus, an acquaintance of some of the other apostles. He hated Gnostic departures from the apostolic tradition, from "the word which has been given us from the beginning." And he exhorted the Philippians to love and harmony. The Syrian Christians glorified Polycarp's martyrdom at the venerable age of eighty-six.

These writings of Clement, Ignatius, and Polycarp held the germ of papal primacy—exaltation of the bishop, apostolic foundation, apostolic succession, and the need for unity. On apostolic foundation and succession, Rome held a distinct advantage, especially after Eastern leadership was crushed in the fall of Jerusalem in 70 and 135. Roman primacy became more manifest when Irenaeus of Lyons in 185 declared that every church should agree with the Roman church as "a matter of necessity." Although Irenaeus had leadership in faith rather than judicial supremacy in mind, he expressed a general feeling at the time that opened the door to further assertions of authority. The destruction of Jerusalem left a vacuum of leadership in the East, further dissipated by jurisdictional quarrels and confusion over Gnostic claims. Rome, with its apparent strength, gradually filled the emptiness. In 190, after a synod voted to adopt the Roman practice of celebrating Easter on Sunday, Victor, bishop of Rome, boldly excommunicated those churches that hesitated to go along. Victor also excommunicated Theodotus, the moneychanger, for proclaiming that Jesus was just an anointed man. Victor's boldness enhanced the position of Rome.

When the conflict over authority through the inspiration of the spirit or through the tradition of succession erupted in Montanism around 155–170, the orthodox reply emphasizing unity came from Hippolytus, the bishop of Rome. He stood in apostolic succession with Peter and Paul; the tradition handed down from the apostles seemed more reliable than the unsubstantiated ecstasies of the Gnostic spiritualists.

Montanism originated in Phrygia in Asia Minor, near the villages of Colossae, Laodicea, and Hierapolis. Montanus, a mutilated former priest of Cybele, was seized by the Spirit and began prophesying. Two women, Prisca and Maximilla, who had left their husbands, joined him in his ecstasies. Maintaining that the Holy Spirit was speaking through them, they urged people to prepare for the eschaton and to journey to Pepuza, where the new heavenly Jerusalem was to be established. Preparation meant being ascetic, disdaining the world, practicing celibacy, fasting, abstaining from eating meat, enjoying no pleasures, having no art, and wearing no ornaments. The age of the Spirit had come. During his half-conscious ecstasies, Montanus often spoke as if he were the Holy Spirit, or even the Father, not just a divine instrument, thus giving his pronouncements divine sanction. Not even Marcion had posed so great a threat to the authority and jurisdiction of the established clergy, whom the Montanists said had grown lax. Montanus admitted women to the universal priesthood, saying endowment by the Holy Spirit was superior to ecclesiasticism. Montanism was a lay movement. It splintered the churches in Asia Minor and won a notable convert in Tertullian of Carthage, one of the most dynamic intellectuals of the third century. But the main body of Christians rejected Montanism, not because it promoted the miraculous gifts of ecstasy but because it engendered divisiveness.

Persecutions from the outside as well as attacks from assailants and critics like Celus and Lucian undoubtedly contributed to the felt need for unity, causing the Christians to close ranks, molding the church into a sociological reality. Developments within, that potentially could shatter unity, could hardly be favored—especially when those developments appeared to contradict the experience of the apostles closest to Jesus.

The complexity of the establishment of authority in canon, creed, and clergy is not to be obscured. Other factors played roles, not the least of which was the hammering out of theological positions (Chapter 4), which reflected the various pressures and events impinging on Christianity. In the process, the church did in fact become a sociological reality, soon to vie with other institutions for status and power. Whether that development was inherent in Christianity or whether some inherent essence in Christianity was lost in the process cannot be easily determined. For better or for worse, Christianity was launched in the world. By the end of the second century it had a set and fluid authority—canon, creed, and clergy—flexible enough to change, stable enough to maintain continuity.

4

The System Makers, in Search of a Theology

Westerners seem to have a compulsion to put everything in order, into a comprehensive whole, only to find that it cannot be done with any finality. Subsequent events and other minds make new assessments necessary. Yet, Christianity would be poorer if Irenaeus, Tertullian, Clement of Alexandria, and Origen had not struggled with perennial human problems. Contexts change, but the problems remain basically the same.

Prior to the "systematizers," surviving Christian literature, in addition to the New Testament canon, connotes limited responses to immediate situations. The chief form of early literature was the letter—those of Clement of Rome, Ignatius, and Polycarp being good examples—but there were also manuals, apologies, sermons, apocalypses, and poetry. Of these the *Didache, Letter of Barnabas, Shepherd of Hermas, First Apology of Justin,* and Athenagoras' *Plea Regarding Christians* ought at least to be mentioned. They all reflect immediate concern for preserving the apostolic message.

Judaizers, antinomians, Gnostics, persecutions, and critics like Celsus and Lucian produced the context. Celsus, about 177, mounted a literary attack on Christianity. His stance was that of a pagan rationalist, alarmed by the rapid expansion of Christianity. Origen wrote an eight-book reply in which he extensively quoted from Celsus, thus preserving the views of Christianity's earliest recognized literary assailant. A sophisticated skeptic, Celsus ridiculed Christianity as a mammoth hoax nourished by superstitious slaves, women, children, and mechanics. Far from being divine, he wrote, Jesus was born of an adulterous affair between a poor seamstress and a soldier named Panthera. The flight to Egypt was to escape disgrace. Celsus regarded Peter's denial, Judas' treachery, and Jesus' death as proofs that Jesus was not divine. Credulous disciples fabricated the Resurrection. Besides, worms hope in resurrection, rational souls do not. How could the pure, omniscient God become flesh? How incredible that God should die on a cross as a common criminal! How incredible that God should have created this evil world in six days, that he should be directing history, and that he should care enough about people that he should reveal a scheme of redemption! God is no more concerned about human beings than he is about monkeys and flies. Celsus concluded that Jesus was an impostor, that the disciples were either deceived or deceivers, that Christians were intellectually incompetent and potentially dangerous. With the refusal of Christians to serve in the army, if Christians gained control of political life, the empire would collapse. While he did not attack Christians for immoralities, Celsus thought it ridiculous that robbers who turned Christian ceased to be robbers. He proposed that Christians give up social life and live as celibates in the desert.

Lucian of Samosata (ca. 120–200) used wit and ridicule to satirize Christians. He wove his satire about Peregrinus Proteus, an historical person. Proteus, a thoroughly contemptible man who was guilty of adultery, sodomy, and parricide, joined the Christians of Palestine and won a reputation as a prophet, leader, author, and interpreter of Christian books. Imprisoned for his faith, he was visited by Christians and exalted as a confessor. Gifts poured in. Later he was excommunicated for eating forbidden food! He became a cynic, lived filthily, and in 166 at Olympia martyred himself before a large crowd in the name of philosophy by jumping into a funeral pyre—in mockery of the exemplary deaths of Christians. To Lucian, Jesus was a "crucified sophist" and his followers simpletons.

Nevertheless, despite multiple difficulties, Christianity won converts. The trickle of first-century literature swelled to a steady stream during the second, confronting opponents, changing and being changed.

The *Didache*, or *Teaching of the Twelve Apostles*, discovered in 1873, shows concern lest Christians drift away from apostolic morals and customs. Some passages indicate it came from the second century, whereas the main portion points to the late first century, 70–90. A writer of the second century probably put two earlier manuscripts together to make a church manual. The first part of the *Didache* gives ethical injunctions on the way of life and the way of death. The way of life enjoins Christians to love God and neighbor: Pray for your enemies, abstain from carnal passions, turn the other cheek, give to any who beg, do not commit adultery, do not murder a child by abortion or kill a newborn infant, do not lie or grumble, do not put on airs, do not turn back on the needy. . . . "For the Father wants his own gifts to be universally shared . . . If you have what is eternal in common, how much more should you have what is transient!" The way of death involves murders, adulteries, fornications, thefts, idolatries, hypocrisies, malice, jealousy, haughtiness, and boastfulness. People following the way of death "corrupt God's image, turn their backs on the needy, oppress the afflicted, defend the rich, unjustly condemn the poor." This section concludes with a practical note: "If you can bear the Lord's full yoke, you will be perfect. But if you cannot, then do what you can." The author obviously knew Matthew and Luke.

The second part of the *Didache* is a church order, possibly reflecting a rural setting. It speaks of baptism, after public instruction, in running or non-running water, warm or cold, by immersion or by pouring (affusion) on the head three times "in the name of the Father, Son, and Holy Spirit," with both the baptizer and the one baptized fasting for one or two days in advance. It speaks of prayer without hypocrisy, quotes the Lord's Prayer, advises praying it three times daily, and cites one other prayer for use after the Lord's Supper. It speaks favorably of apostles and prophets, warns against prophets who seek money or stay in one place longer than two days, yet insists that genuine prophets and teachers should be paid "for they are your high priests." A description of the Lord's Day mentions coming together, breaking bread, giving thanks, confessing, offering a sacrifice, and if at variance with a neighbor, refraining from participation until reconciliation. It speaks of electing bishops and deacons and honoring them, as if there might be some conflict between them and the traveling prophets and teachers. The essay concludes with warnings about being ready for the return of the Lord "on the clouds of the sky." Gnosticism is notable by its absence.

The *Shepherd of Hermas*, about 160, is concerned with penance and forgiveness of post-baptismal sin. The author, Hermas, was a Christian slave, sold in Rome to a woman named Rhoda, who set him free. By questionable means he became a successful merchant, and lost everything in a persecution. He then did penance. His book, an allegory calling the church to repentance, resulted from visions of an angelic shepherd. Its three parts consist of five Visions, twelve Mandates, and ten Similitudes. It was immensely popular. Although considered by Irenaeus and others as "divine scripture," it was gradually consigned to an apocryphal status. The Visions give symbols of the church saying post-baptismal sins can be forgiven once. The Mandates urge repentant Christians to live in faith in one God, with sincerity, humility, truth, love, chastity, patience, trust, and joy. The Similitudes present parables of Christian principles.

Two allegories had far-reaching influences—the church as a tower built on a rock rising out of water, and the parable of the vineyard worker. In the tower allegory, the stones represent individual believers. As they emerge cleansed from the baptismal water, they fit into the tower. If they become marred, they can be reclaimed, but only once. Hermas thus symbolizes the necessity of water baptism and upholds limited forgiveness of post-baptismal sins, but murder, adultery, and idolatry are not included. The rock symbolizes pre-existent Logos; the door to the tower, Christ. In the vineyard parable, a slave labors far more than is required, and for the extra work the owner makes him a co-heir with his son. Thus Hermas set the stage for works of merit and supererogation, a development that led eventually to a penitential system with a treasury of merits. Hermas considered fasting, celibacy, and martyrdom as supererogatory means for meriting the kingdom of heaven. He viewed Christianity as a new law, stressed ascetic and legalistic duties, and implied that outside the church there is no salvation. Tertullian later severely criticized his leniency.

The *Letter of Barnabas,* 70–135, struggles with the problem of the Old Testament. The author argues that the Old Testament is an elaborate allegory prophesying the Christian church. The Judaic scapegoat is a prefiguration of Christ; water in the Old Testament, a prefiguration of baptism; trees and poles, a prefiguration of the cross. The Jews in their literalism simply misunderstood the real meaning of the Old Testament. The prohibition of pork really forbids association with men who are like swine. The prohibition of hyena flesh warns against seduction and adultery. Seeing only the exterior, the Jews colossally misconceived true law and hardened their views in external customs. True circumcision is of the heart, which the Jews would see if they understood, for example, that Abraham's circumcision of his "18 and 300" servants symbolizes Christ and the cross of grace: I is 10, H is 8, signifying Jesus, and T is 300, signifying the cross. The separation of the figures signifies that grace is yet to come. Moses' breaking of the first tablets of laws signifies that the new law of Christ is to displace the old. As if to discount the destruction of the temple in Jerusalem, Barnabas says the real temple is spiritual. Although Barnabas asserts that Christians keep the new law not out of necessity but because of forgiveness of sins and the indwelling Holy Spirit, his emphasis on keeping various rules is so strong that he speaks of doing works for the "ransom of your sins." But a literal keeping of the Jewish law is not necessary. Christ in his Resurrection abolished death. In forgiving us our sins and in renewing our hearts, Christ makes us new creatures, thus demonstrating the resurrection in us. Christians relate, therefore, not to an external law but to the living law of Christ, and are the true inheritors of the old covenant. As God created the world in six days, and as one day is like 1,000 years with the Lord, Barnabas envisioned an eschaton at the end of 6,000 years. Instead of rejecting the Old Testament as evil, Barnabas simply allegorized everything to fit his Christian convictions. In doing so he set a non-historical pattern for Old Testament exegesis for the next 1500 years!

As Barnabas preserved the Old Testament for Christianity in a kind of dying-rising baptism in allegory, so Justin Martyr (ca. 100–166) and Athenagoras (later in the same century) helped preserve philosophy. Just as the Old Testament promises and prophecies find their fulfillment in Christ, so the insights and ideals of philosophy find their completion in Christ, contended Justin. The Logos inspired the Jewish prophets and finally became fully manifest in Christ. The Logos, the immanence of the transcendent God in the world, also inspired the philosophers, but their speculations, said Justin, are incomplete apart from the manifestation of the full Logos in the Son of God. Justin was thus the first of the Christian thinkers to conceive of secular and sacred history as converging in Christ. The God of Plato and the God of the Old Testament are the same. To Plato, God revealed his will through nature and an implanted moral consciousness, an inner light, given to all but without the revealed clarity of the Old Testament. Justin did not develop the inner light in a Gnostic sense, nor did he regard the soul as having immortality. Neither did the incarnation of the Logos mean for Justin that Christ only seemed to be an historic human being. Christ was fully man. He suffered, died, and was resurrected. He was the full Logos. The Logos given to the prophets and the Greeks was partial.

Justin embraced Christianity after years of searching and finding only incomplete truth in pagan philosophies. In Christianity he believed that he had found the only truly rational creed, which he vigorously defended in his *Dialogue with Trypho the Jew* and his *First Apology*. His descriptions of early church life, including the central place of baptism, the eucharist, and the moral earnestness of the community, are among our most valuable. Wearing his philosopher's robe, he propagated his views in Rome and Ephesus, especially against Marcion. For refusing to sacrifice to the emperor, he was scourged and then beheaded in 166, during the reign of Marcus Aurelius.

Athenagoras in his *Plea Regarding Christians* continued many of the thoughts of Justin but is chiefly remembered for his spirited defense of Christians against charges of atheism, cannibalism, and incest. He was the first to elaborate a philosophical explanation of the Trinity and to do an entire essay on the validity of the Resurrection.

While this literature generally preserves earlier conceptions of Christianity, the influences of other patterns of thought begin to surface, a process that inevitably changed, compromised, and contributed to Christianity—the price (or reward) of being relevant to the world. As Christianity expanded into the Greco-Roman world and endeavored to communicate its message, it employed Hellenistic thought forms that subtly affected many of its beliefs. God was more and more abstractly conceived in static Platonic terms of the Immutable Infinite, and Christ, in the universal Stoic terms of Logos. Sin came more and more to signify ignorance, and redemption to signify knowledge. Immortality of the soul tended to displace resurrection of the body.

The concerns of these early writers with the preservation of apostolic tradition and teaching culminated in the writings of Irenaeus (ca. 130–202). That he could designate "heresies" as such and that his writings could receive such wide acclaim indicate the extent to which orthodoxy had been established in canon, creed, and clergy.

Irenaeus was born in Asia Minor, received a Greek education, traveled widely in the Roman world, furthered Christianity in Gaul, and became the Bishop of Lyons following the great persecution there in 177. The end of his life is shrouded in mystery. He simply disappeared, and although tradition grants him a martyr's death, no one seems to know quite when or how it occurred. In his boyhood Irenaeus knew Polycarp and thus had a direct link with the apostolic fathers. In his time the New Testament was already accepted as sacred alongside the Old Testament, even though some questions remained about a few books. Because Peter and Paul had both worked in Rome, Irenaeus looked to that church and its tradition through the apostolic succession as a principal source for the basic truths of Christianity. He regarded the Gnostics in general, and Valentinus and Marcion in particular, as heretics who had strayed from the truth and broken the unity of the one faith received in Christ, passed on by the apostles, and embodied in Scripture and creed. Although he shows considerable skill in dealing with Greek influences on Christianity, Irenaeus was basically a missionary and pastor, caring little for philosophical speculations. "The true way to God is love. It is better to be willing to know nothing but Jesus Christ the crucified, than to fall into ungodliness through over-curious questions and paltry subtleties."

Because he saw Gnosticism as a threat to a unity of believers clearly linked by canon, creed, and clergy to Christ, Irenaeus wrote *Adversus Haereses*, at the request of a friend who wanted to know and refute Valentinus. *Against Heresies* is divided into five books. Book I explains somewhat sarcastically the various heresies of the Marcosians, Ebionites, Nicolaitans, Marcionites, Encratites, Cainites, and Valentinus. Book II expounds on the absurdities of "their evil teachings" and shows them "nakedly for what they are." Book III sets Scripture and tradition against heresies, with an emphasis on God as Creator and Christ as Redeemer. Book IV defends the Old and New Covenants against Marcion, and Book V concludes with discussions of redemption, Resurrection, and the millennium, in which Irenaeus posits the eventual return of all of nature to God. He combats Gnosticism with reason, Scripture, and church teachings, showing especially how Gnostics pervert Scriptural passages.

Irenaeus believed that God created matter and form, and that all creation is dependent on God. He has no Demiurge; God is involved in the world. The Son and Father are not separate. Christ did not begin to exist; he was with the Father from the beginning. Created in the image of the immortal God, we are capable of attaining immortality because God intended us to be perfect. God allowed us to fall to teach us to curb our pride, but the Fall did not introduce original sin. Yet because we are bogged down and blinded by sin, the Incarnation became necessary. The Son came to help us, thus revealing that God is merciful and loving. Christ recapitulated the perfect life, step by step, so that we might again see our possibilities. The Incarnation was not docetic; Christ was truly and fully human, and exhibited what perfect Man was intended to be at every level of life. Irenaeus even infers from John 8:57 that Christ lived to be an old man and that his ministry lasted at least ten years. Christ was what God intended every person to be. Thus God is revealed to us, and us to God, and we are reconciled to God. We were so created that if we grow to our full stature, God will bestow immortality on us. Perfect Man, Christ, attained that full stature. He fulfilled the conditions for entering the divine life; he showed our human possibilities; he abrogated the law by fulfilling it. In principle Christ broke Satan's grip for everyone. The Incarnation was no pretense; the divine entered this life to show us how to recover the image of God. Irenaeus goes all the way with his anti-Gnosticism, positing the recapitulation or return to God of all of nature. The world is not evil per se; our bodies are not evil. God created both. Believers are likened to two-toed animals, one toe pointing to things of this world and the other to heaven. Against the Gnostics, Irenaeus sets the church's teachings, unbroken in apostolic succession, substantiated in canon, confirmed in reason, and witnessed in the Apostles' Creed. His authority is the validated faith of a community of believers.

Irenaeus furnished much of the theological thought of the man whom many scholars consider the greatest Western theologian of the patristic period, next to Augustine—Quintus Septimus Florens Tertullian (ca. 145–220). The exact dates of his birth and death are not known; however, he was a native of Carthage, received a good education, and became a practicing lawyer in Rome. When about fifty, he accepted Christianity, returned to Carthage, and rose to the office of a presbyter. Rigorist in his general attitude, he was drawn from Catholicism toward the Montanists, whom he officially joined around 207. He is especially remembered for his legalistic explanation of the Trinity, being the first to apply that term to the three Divine Persons—Father, Son, and Holy Spirit. He is also remembered for his stern moralistic asceticism; for his asserting an authority of the Spirit over against the authority of ecclesiastical institutionalism; and for his sharp defense of Christianity against Jews, Gnostics, heathens, and heretics.

Vituperative, witty, eccentric, sometimes shallow and one-sided, Tertullian nevertheless had penetrating insights into Christian doctrine and life. Thirty-one of his many writings still exist and divide readily into three categories. First are those defenses of Christianity that he wrote shortly after his conversion, e.g., the *Apology* and *The Testimony of the Soul.* Second are those vigorous attacks against the Gnostics and other deviators, his *Prescriptions against Heretics, On the Flesh of Christ, On the Resurrection of the Flesh, Scorpiace,* and *Against Praxeas.* Third are those works enjoining ascetic practices, written both before and after he became a Montanist. Before he joined the Montanists, Tertullian wrote *On the (Lord's) Prayer, On Baptism, On Patience, On Penance, On the Virgin's Veil, To his Wife,* and *On Women's Dress;* after joining the Montanists, *The Soldier's Crown, On Idolatry, Exhortation to Chastity, On Flight in Persecution, On Monogamy, On Fasting,* and *On Chastity.* They differ in that Montanism made Tertullian even more severe. Although many scholars find fault with Tertullian, his influence on the Western church can hardly be doubted.

In about 197 Tertullian wrote the first plea for religious liberty, his famous *Apology,* in which he defends Christianity against outside attacks. He claims equality and toleration for Christians as inalienable rights, given by God, and exonerates Christians from the odium of absurd accusations. Christians are honorable people, live exemplary moral lives, pay taxes, serve in the army, engage in business. They are loyal, even though their monotheism prohibits granting divine honors to the emperor. They pray God for the safety of the emperor. Christians pray even for their enemies and persecutors, as anyone who reads their Scriptures can see. They desire peace; they are not disturbers nor perpetrators of calamities. They pray that God's judgment on the world will be delayed. Yet Christians, says Tertullian, are not granted the rights in court that are accorded even to the worst murderers. Criminals can defend themselves, hire lawyers, plead their innocence, reply, and cross-examine, but Christians are not allowed to defend themselves. "That alone is looked for, which the public hate requires—the confession of the name, not the investigation of the charge."

That all persons in their innermost being bear witness to God is the burden of Tertullian's *Testimony of the Soul.* Although Tertullian believed in traducianism, i.e., that the soul is transmitted by parents to the off-spring, he also believed that the soul springs from God and continually longs for God. If not prevented by selfish desires and passions, the soul will by nature tend upward until it comes to God.

Tertullian's writings against the Gnostics are extremely interesting, because he rests his arguments on the faithful transmission of Christ in canon, creed, and clergy, whereas in writings after he became a Montanist he rejects this idea of authentic Christianity in favor of the authority that lies in the immediate activity of the Spirit in spiritual men and women. *Prescriptions against Heretics,* ca. 200, develops Tertullian's earlier view of authority. Christ's Incarnation was prophesied and promised in the Old Testament; it happened. The revelation in Christ was an historical event. It was communicated to others through the writings of the apostles, the canon. It was also communicated to others through apostolic preaching, the common core of which is expressed in the baptismal profession of faith, the creed. The creed leaves room for variant interpretations, but not for anything completely contrary to Scripture. The revelation was also transmitted by a regular, responsible clergy, especially in the churches founded by the apostles themselves. Authentic Christianity rests with a believing community reaching back to the original revelation in Christ—validated in canon, creed, and clergy! It does not rest on philosophical speculations, "What has Christ to do with Plato, Jerusalem with Athens?" In the eyes of reason, it may be absurd, says Tertullian, but "I believe because it is absurd." He denies that heretics have any right to interpret the Scriptures; the Bible belongs to the church. Christians need not even listen to Gnostic appeals to Scripture; Gnostic mutilations of Scripture show they are outside the traditional, universal, historic communion. Their sophistical argumentation contradicts canon, creed, and clergy.

But when Tertullian became a Montanist, he gave up on the estab-lished clergy; to him they had become morally lax; they had sacrificed the strenuous demands of Christ to institutional expediency. They were no longer credible. He turned to the Montanists, who looked to the Spirit, rather than apostolic succession, for guidance. Their lives, he said, vali-dated their claims.

The strict discipline of the Montanists matched Tertullian's own moral austerity. He denounced as blasphemous the growing leniency of the church at Rome and Carthage toward adultery and fornication as forgiv-able sins. Bishop Callistus of Rome, 218–22, took decisive steps in this direction. The Montanists shunned worldliness, rejected pleasure, prohib-ited ornaments on clothing, condemned second marriages, and said mortal sins after baptism were unpardonable. Believing in the impending final catastrophe and judgment of the world, Tertullian could hardly remain content in a communion that had grown lax and comfortable.

On Idolatry, whether written just before or after the shift to Montan-ism, typifies Tertullian's austerity. In this essay he is concerned with how Christians can live in the world without compromising their deepest be-liefs, and his statements often are incongruous with what he says in ar-guing that Christians are loyal citizens of Rome. *On Idolatry* calls for as full a break with the world as possible, because Christians are forbidden to worship idols, and any normal participation in the affairs of the world involves one in idolatrous customs and ceremonies. Idolatry is murder, for idolatry condemns one to perdition; idolatry is fraud, for idolatry defrauds God of his honors. In fact, for Tertullian, almost any sin can be reduced to idolatry. The Christian cannot be a soldier without idolatry because the military observes ceremonies for the emperor. A Christian cannot be a merchant because merchants cater to idolaters. He cannot help build or decorate a shrine for pagan purposes. He cannot be an astrologer or magician, or a teacher, or a public official without contributing to idolatry. To decorate one's house or shop on a festival day is idolatry, and so forth. In other writings he argues that Christians are to avoid circuses, theatres, amusements, vanity, and luxury partly on account of immorality but mostly on account of their idolatrous connections. Although some might consider Tertullian too extreme, he is one of the first to see that culture religion compromises loyalty to God.

In his tract *Against Praxeas,* Tertullian develops his concept of the Trinity. Praxeas was a Monarchian who subordinated Christ to God by saying that Christ the Son was one of the three modes of God. Other Monarchians could not accept Christ as divine and explained him as the energy or power of God. Tertullian acknowledged that God is one in substance and then asserted, as if dealing with a legal matter, that the three persons (Father, Son, and Holy Spirit) are simply three roles or functions of the one God. In each function or role the full God acts, just as the full person acts in his different roles as father, husband, and magistrate. Christ was not less than God. Tertullian also asserted that Christ was one person with two natures, not obliterated, fused or obscured; Christ was fully human and fully divine, an assertion that later rocked the church for over a century but nevertheless stood, not on reason but on faith.

Despite the difficulties of some of his conceptions, Tertullian left a heritage of asceticism, gave the West its basic understanding of the Trinity and the two natures of Christ, and placed an emphasis on the Spirit that continues to haunt ecclesiastical institutionalism.

Clement of Alexandria (ca. 150–215) clearly illustrates how presuppositions shape one's religious outlook. Schooled in philosophy, Clement made the assumption that the river of truth is one, that all truth comes from the universal Logos, that philosophy as well as religious revelation is a gift from God. Faith is requisite to both because, says Clement, one cannot demonstrate First Principles. First Principles are accepted in faith, and faith rests on grace. Thus Clement made the sufficient reason of philosophy and the faith of prophets compatible. And since the source of truth for both is the same Logos, to investigate one is to investigate the other, and to come to the same conclusions. Having a philosophical background, Clement proceeded to apply philosophical notions to various aspects of Christian life. In answer to those who objected that secular philosophers were of the devil and had borrowed from Moses, he said we ought to recognize the gold in the wallets of thieves as gold. Clement

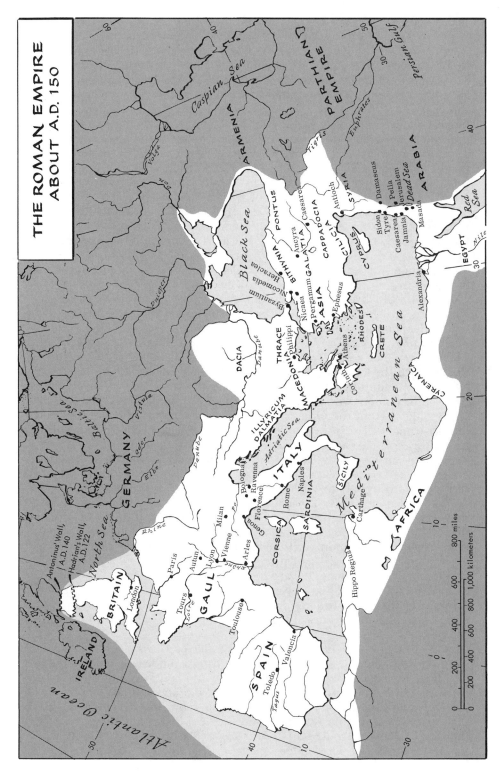

THE ROMAN EMPIRE
ABOUT A.D. 150

Atlantic Ocean

IRELAND

BRITAIN
London

Antoninus' Wall,
A.D. 140
Hadrian's Wall,
A.D. 122

North Sea

Baltic Sea

GERMANY

Vistula

Oder

Elbe

Rhine

Don

Volga

Dnieper

Caspian Sea

Dniester

Danube

Black Sea

ARMENIA

PARTHIAN
EMPIRE

Persian Gulf

Euphrates

Tigris

Paris

Tours

GAUL

Autun

Lyon
Vienne

Arles

Toulouse

SPAIN

Toledo

Valencia

Tagus

Loire

Rhône

Genoa

Milan

Po

Bologna
Ravenna

Florence

Rome

Naples

ITALY

CORSICA

SARDINIA

SICILY

Carthage

Hippo Regius

AFRICA

Mediterranean Sea

DACIA

Danube

THRACE

ILLYRICUM
DALMATIA

Adriatic Sea

MACEDONIA

Philippi

Byzantium

Nicomedia
Heraclea

BITHYNIA

PONTUS

Nicaea

Pergamum

ASIA

Ephesus

Corinth
Athens

RHODES

CRETE

GALATIA

Ancyra

CAPPADOCIA

Caesarea

CILICIA

Antioch

CYPRUS

SYRIA

Damascus

Sidon
Tyre

Caesarea

Pella
Jerusalem
Jamnia

Dead Sea

Masada

Alexandria

EGYPT

Nile

Red Sea

ARABIA

CYRENAICA

Antioch

800 miles

1,000 kilometers

47

shied away from invoking biblical texts but averred that examination
would show his thoughts conformed to the New Testament.

An Athenian by birth, Clement studied both Christianity and philosophy in several cities, and finally cast his lot with Pantaenus, whom he
succeeded in 190 as head of the catechetical school at Alexandria. Valentinian Gnosticism, the latest thing in theological speculation, was vogue in
the educated circles of Alexandrian society, and ordinary Christianity
appeared a bit drab in comparison. Both Basilides and Valentinus had
taught in Alexandria. Pantaenus rationalized the apostolic tradition, but it
remained for Clement to make Christianity intellectually and ethically
acceptable to the cultural people of the city on the Nile. He did so by
treating philosophy as a superior elaboration of Christianity, and in the
process he introduced elements that seem alien to believers like Polycarp,
Irenaeus, and Tertullian. Clement fled in 202 to escape the persecution
of Severus, and possibly suffered a martyr's death in 215.

Clement's chief works are *The Exhorter* (*Protreptikos*), a polemical exhortation urging pagans to convert to Christianity; *The Tutor* (*Paidagogos*),
a discussion of Christian manners and morals; and the unfinished *Miscel-
lanies* (*Stromateis*), which may have been an oblique way of suggesting some
of the deeper things he intended to put into a projected volume called
The Teachings (*Didaskalos*) but feared to do so on account of persecution.
Clement was not content with the Gnostic notion that this is a debased
world which the Christian should avoid by practicing asceticism or ignore
by disdainful indulgence of the body. He discussed advocates of both.
Nor was he content with the determinism implied in the body-soul drama.
Everything is from the One, the Being beyond nature, the absolute, the
indescribable. Christ is the Logos of God, present and active in the world,
giving the world existence, imparting truth to prophets and philosophers,
dependent on God only existentially. But Clement's interest is basically
ethical. This Logos became human to instruct us in right living and to
conduct us to eternal life. Although Clement attempted to avoid docetism,
he does not quite succeed, for the soul of Christ is impassible and Christ
does not really have physical and emotional needs as others do. Christ
dies as a ransom for us and overcomes the devil, but Clement puts far less
emphasis on this than on Christ as the supreme teacher-revealer pointing
the way to immortality. In relating ourselves to Christ, we are to believe
and to obey his teachings. We are fettered in sin, but we have free will; we
choose the way we will go; we can at any time grasp the salvation that God
offers. The first step is taken in faith, and advancement comes through
knowledge and love, until inward fellowship with God and immortality
are reached.

At this point Clement introduces grades of Christians. Those who
simply accept the illumination that Christ brings and live by faith, without
knowing, are *pistics;* they follow Christ without really knowing why. To be
baptized is to enter into this grade. Those who know in addition to this
are superior Christians, *pneumatics.* They live on a level with men like
Plato. Despite occasional qualifications, Clement makes ignorance, not sin,
the key to human troubles. If one chooses the worse way, it is due to
ignorance. Virtue is knowledge, and vice is ignorance. To know what is

right is to do what is right. The Christian life for Clement becomes a matter of being reasonable, of being moderate with regard to sex, clothing, dancing, drinking, and eating. Prudence is better than cowardice or rashness, a reasonable partaking of food better than gluttony or starvation, and, in the use of things of this world, temperance is better than excessiveness or denial. Clement regards marriage and the procreation of children as good, lust as bad. Second marriage he thinks should be avoided if one hopes to attain perfection, but even second marriage is not inherently inferior. Celibacy, virginity, vegetarianism, and teetotalism are not superior per se. A tendency toward asceticism creeps in because Clement values knowledge so highly. But in the main Clement avoids the extreme asceticism that considers physical things evil and disdains them, or that feels the body cannot affect the soul and allows physical licentiousness. Because we are rational and can choose, Clement also avoids the inherent determinism of the Gnostics. But Clement's praise of knowledge (*gnosis*) knew no limits; beyond faith one is to follow knowledge to immortality; ignorance is sin. Only the Gnostic *pneumatics* cultivate perfection; the *pistics* just trust and obey.

By making Christianity philosophical, Clement made it palatable to Alexandria's cultured society, which could identify with the *pneumatics*. Unfortunately, he left the impression that Christianity should cater to the intellectually superior and merely tolerate the *pistics*.

When the persecution of 202 forced Clement to flee, a precocious young man, whose father, Leonides, had just been martyred, assumed the direction of the catechetical school of Alexandria. This was Origen (ca. 184–254), only eighteen at the time, a theologian who became one of the most controversial figures in all of church history. He left his stamp on Christian thought, but after 300 years of stormy debate was officially condemned as a heretic by the Fifth General Council that met at Constantinople in 553. Extremely ascetic, given to fastings, vigils, and poverty, he is said to have emasculated himself in an excess of zeal after reading about the voluntary eunuchs in Matthew 19:12. Whether this act is hearsay or fact, Origen's capacity for self-discipline and his spiritual bent render it credible. Much to the anger of the Bishop Demetrius of Alexandria, who was trying to assert episcopal control in Egypt, Origen while still a layman preached on one of his speaking tours to Palestine, and fifteen years later, in 230, accepted ordination at the hands of the bishop there. For the first offense Demetrius recalled Origen from Palestine; for the second he deprived him of his teaching chair, and with the compliance of the bishop of Rome and an Egyptian synod deposed him from the priesthood and sent him into exile. Origen's declaration just after his ordination that even the devil could be saved did not help his case. Origen then established a school at Caesarea in Palestine. In 250, during the persecution of Decius, he suffered imprisonment and prolonged torture, which contributed to his death a few years later.

Because he felt that an accurate biblical text was essential to his own interpretations and to his frequent arguments with Jewish and Gnostic scholars, Origen published his famous *Hexapla,* a synopsis, side by side, of six texts of the Old Testament: first the Hebrew itself, then a transliteration of the Hebrew into Greek, followed by the four Greek translations then in use of the Septuagint, Theodotion, Aquila, and Symmachus. Origen then proceeded to write extensive and numerous commentaries in which he explained the biblical passages in three senses—literal, moral, and allegorical. Origen was ambiguous about the importance of the literal text; historically it had little significance. However, it did have significance as a kind of vehicle for the mysticism in which Origen believed. The inner meaning or soul of a passage concerned him most. Allegory, a common device made popular by Barnabas, Hermas, and especially the Old Testament scholar Philo, allowed Origen to extract from Scripture meanings that meshed perfectly with his prior assumptions and convictions. He took to the Bible a set of ideas that he substantiated by use of allegory. He found his doctrines everywhere. Keen insights and what many have regarded as perversions resulted.

Origen started with the presupposition that nothing should be said about God that is unworthy, and his allegorical method allowed him enough leeway to do just that. God is Perfect Being, not Infinite Being, which is inconceivable and incomprehensible because of the nature of infinity. But even Perfect Being is beyond man's limited capacity to conceive and comprehend, although man can say that God is at least this and more. Origen thought of Perfect Being as the perfect balance of all virtues. This Perfect Being expresses himself in three hypostases, as Father, Son, and Holy Spirit. The Father and Son are hypostases of the same God and are coequal because there could not be a Father without a Son. God is recognized as the Father through the Son, who is his image. As God is eternal, the begetting of the Son is an eternal act. The Son has no temporal beginning; He eternally proceeds from the Father in a spiritual way. Son and Father have the same will and thought, and presumably express the same full sovereignty, but when all of Origen's statements are tabulated the Son turns out to be subordinate. The Son is second; the Son cannot precede the Father; the Son is relative Truth; petitions are to be addressed to God, presented by Christ; the Son mirrors the Father, is dependent on the Father. The Holy Spirit also is subordinate, less than the Son, brought into being through the Son, and active only in the souls of saints whose superior gnosis enables them to make contact with the Holy Spirit. To the Father, Son, and Holy Spirit Origen assigns, respectively, existence, rationality, and sanctity.

According to Origen, this world did not begin as the result of an accident (Sophia's leap into the heart of the All-Father), but as an attempt on the part of God to retrieve fallen souls through education and training. Suffering and pain are not purposeless; they are part of God's redemptive scheme, his justice but also his goodness, for by them God would point fallen souls back to the higher realms from which they came. Order and beauty serve the same purpose. The first act of creation was not this world, but a realm of intelligences in ethereal bodies, who were endowed with reason and free will. Tiring of always adoring God, these spiritual beings allowed their love to lapse. An hierarchical order of celestial bodies resulted. Some fell into sin, becoming demons or souls imprisoned in bodies. God then created this world as a temporary place of trial and judgment to redirect fallen souls. Depending on the quality of life on earth, the soul at death ascends upward, or descends downward still further. The ascent and descent will go on for a long time, but God will not finally be defeated. In the end all moral creatures will be saved. Evil is distance from God, privation of good, brought about by misuse of free will. The ascent back to God may be painful, with periods of backsliding descent, for souls always have free will. The pain that comes from wrong choice is God's way of noting error. Thus Origen avoided determinism.

In theory, we are free to extricate ourselves, our souls, but in actuality this is very difficult, for we have lapsed so far from God that we see God dimly, as through a dark glass. This situation made the Incarnation and Atonement necessary. The Logos became human for our sake, to teach, to exemplify, to guide. Jesus linked Logos and flesh in one person, uniting divinity and humanity, but Origen failed to maintain the integrity of one nature, for the divinity in Jesus did not suffer; the humanity in Jesus suffered and died, not the divinity. After the ascension the humanity was absorbed entirely in the divinity. Christ is to Christians what Moses was to the Jews. He is a physician to sinners, a teacher to those made pure. We partake of this mystically, through baptism, the Eucharist, and spiritual gnosis, which cooperates with the Holy Spirit to achieve sanctity. Christ is a propitiation, a ransom, to break the hold of Satan who would drag us even father from God, but how Christ is a propitiation is not quite clear. Faith is explained as an act of free will as well as divine grace; it is the first ascending step toward knowledge and understanding. The soul is rational, and knowledge unto perfection is the goal. Since to know is to do, faith unfolds in works, making works essential to salvation as we ascend to God. The body is, of course, left behind. When God is all in all and even Satan is redeemed, the process may begin all over, for souls will still possess free will.

Allegory enabled Origen to preserve the unity of the Bible, to show the fulfillment of the Old Testament in Christ. It also enabled him decisively to answer the Marcionites who tended to take the Old Testament literally. His assumption of free will allowed him to answer the determinism implied in the writings of Celsus. *Contra Celsus* has a double value, for Origen preserved his opponent's thoughts by quoting large passages in order to answer them.

But Origen's philosophical assumptions also left many controversial questions. What about the eternality of worlds, spiritual resurrection, universalism, recurrence of the Fall, pre-existence of souls? Did Christ really teach these? Origen was such a prolific author that few people took the time to read all his writings, fewer still made the effort to translate him into Latin, and those who did felt free to omit and change. When Rufinus translated Origen's *Commentary on Romans* into Latin, he not only paraphrased and abbreviated but changed and added passages. Origen's principal work, *De Principiis,* a systematic explanation of Christian thought about God, mankind, the world, and Scripture is recoverable only from less than first-rate translations. *Exhortation to Martyrdom,* written during the persecution of Maximinus in 235, is an excellent example of Origen's ascetic austerity. *On Prayer,* a treatise on the communion of the soul with

God, was widely read in his day. But controversy soon clouded the memory of Origen, aroused suspicion, and prompted official action against him, one result of which was the non-preservation of his books.

Although St. Pamphilus, Athanasius, Basil, Didymus, Jerome, and Gregory of Nazianzus supported Origen, opposition mounted. Epiphanius (ca. 375), described Origen's doctrines as heretical and was seconded by Jerome, who had previously defended Origen. Theophilus of Alexandria, after supporting Origen, convoked a Council at Alexandria in 400, which condemned him. Bishops in Italy, Syria, and Palestine supported the council's action, and Theophilus went on to say Origen was the "hydra of heresies." A revival of Origenism in the next century prompted the Emperor Justinian in a letter to Mennas, the patriarch of Constantinople, to brand Origen as a heretic, an action that led a Council at Constantinople in 543 to specify, refute, and condemn a long list of Origenistic errors. Pope Vigilius concurred. The Origenistic monks at Jerusalem split over whether all men would finally become like Christ or whether Christ was really a different creature. The Fifth General Council at Constantinople, 553, again condemned Origen, and the one bishop who dissented was deposed. Much of the prolonged controversy was due to Origen's ideas, but just as much resulted from a complexity of conflicting personalities and politics in the Arian disputes of the following century.

5

Counterculture
and Controversy

Accommodation versus non-accommodation with the world reached a climax in the fourth century in two seminal happenings: (1) the withdrawal of thousands of laymen from the church, whose status had shifted from that of persecution to luxury and honor, and (2) the Nicene controversy over the nature of Christ. Constantine's Edict of Milan had ended the persecutions, but the unity for which he hoped did not follow. Many Christians believed the new partnership of church and state compromised true Christianity. Rather than be a part of the compromise, thousands withdrew to the solitude of the deserts and wilds. In the beginning, monasticism was a massive lay movement, a counterculture, in protest against institutional worldliness. The Council of Nicaea in 325 was called by Constantine in an attempt to resolve theological differences over the nature of Christ and thus establish a basis of unity in the empire. Resolution was not achieved. Instead, raging controversy erupted and continued for 150 years. The partnership of church and state did not have an auspicious beginning.

Although the massive monastic movement in the fourth century was primarily a reaction to a secularized, worldly Christianity, other factors were also present. Some early hermits wanted to elude taxes; others, the economic necessity of raising a family. Some believed isolation was necessary to avoid temptation; others wanted opportunity to think and pray. And some, e.g., criminals hiding, had no religious motivation. Asceticism pervaded the movement, partly out of a desire to return to strenuous early Christianity, but mostly out of a mistaken identification of Christianity with dichotomous Greek thought, which exalted the soul and debased the body.

Christianity had its birth in Judaism. For a hundred years those within and without Christianity considered it a sect of Judaism, so close were their ties. But only obliquely, if at all, can asceticism be claimed for the Jewish tradition, making asceticism prima facie an influence of Hellenistic ideas. The Jews believed in the goodness of God's created world and in God's control of history. Jewish holidays celebrated the mighty acts of God—the rescue from Egypt (Passover), preservation in the wilderness (Feast of Booths), rededication of the Temple in 165 B.C. (Hanukkah), etc. For the Jews this world was not a place from which God was absent in ineffable transcendence. The human body was not evil. Sex was the divinely ordered means of reproduction. Rejection of the Baal fertility gods and temple prostitution resulted from the belief that God's sovereignty extends over all of nature. The Rechabites' refusal to drink wine and live in houses signified not asceticism but a longing for primitive days when people thought more of God than of physical comforts. Resurrection and immortality of the soul were ambiguous in Judaism because the Jews emphasized life now and posited no dualism of temporal body and immortal soul until Persian-Greek dualism arrived bringing ascetism. Then the Essenes, Therapeutae, and Dead Sea Scroll communities appeared. The Essenes believed in immortality of the soul only. They generally practiced celibacy and apparently excluded women, but they allowed some members to marry and to procreate so that the group could survive. The Therapeutae near Alexandria allowed women, but they dwelt in separate huts. Both groups lived rigorously and frugally and spent much time in purification rites and contemplation. The Dead Sea Scroll communities, apparently related to the Essenes, expected and prepared for an eschaton. But these ascetic elements were not an ancient tradition.

However, bodily discipline, as in fasting, did form part of the ancient tradition. Such discipline was not intended to denigrate things as evil, but to assert precedence of the Creator over creation. Nevertheless, self-discipline, when combined with the notion that spirit is more important than body, spawned asceticism. Many New Testament passages lent themselves to this interpretation, so that what Troeltsch calls the "heroic ethic" of Christianity soon took on characteristics of asceticism. Given the legitimate desire of Christians to be holy, to seek God above all else, and given the pervasive Greek notion that spirit is more significant than body, it was easy to slip from a strenuous ethic into asceticism. Many New Testament passages seemed to point to a "higher" reality for which Christians must strive: "Be not anxious about your life, what you shall eat or what you shall drink" (Matthew 6:25); "You must be perfect, as your heavenly Father is perfect" (Matthew 5:48); "If any man would come after me, let him deny himself and take up his cross and follow me" (Mark 8:34); "Sell what you have, and give to the poor, and you will have treasure in heaven" (Mark 10:21); "If any one comes to me and does not hate his own father and mother . . . and even his own life, he cannot be my disciple" (Luke 14:26); "God is spirit, and those who worship him must worship in spirit and truth" (John 4:24); and Paul's injunctions to contend against the "old" man (Romans 8:13; I Corinthians 9:26ff.). Eschatological expectations and the persecutions seemed to indicate the same thing. And the sacraments, controlled by the clergy, seemed to be a mystical link between this world of sense and the transcendent world of suprasense. Consequently, for many Christians ascetic exercises soon became synonymous with keeping the demands of the Gospel; things difficult and contrary to nature rated as doubly religious. In the process sin was confused with matter, and creation itself declared bad. Groups developed within the church devoted to fasting, prayer, contemplation, poverty, virginity, celibacy, and martyrdom as superior ways of gaining heaven. Ignatius, who longed for martyrdom, called such groups the brides and jewels of Christ. The Ebionites believed that poverty was essential to salvation. Many people gave away their property at the time of conversion, thereby expecting to be more holy. The Marcionites regarded procreation as diabolical and would not allow married people to join their churches. Justin Martyr, Tertullian, Jerome, and Cyprian all accepted marriage, but they regarded it as inferior to celibacy, and Hieracas of Egypt made virginity a condition of salvation. This side of Christianity asserted itself in the monastic withdrawal, as if the church's partnership with the state was a sell out.

But another side of the Christian tradition rejected asceticism as incongruous with beliefs in God the Creator and the Incarnation. This side found expression in the Apostles' Creed, rejection of docetism, and acceptance of this world as good. It impelled Christians to become more and more responsibly involved in society.

Tension between these two sides brought about the sanction of a double ethic, symbolized in marriage and celibacy. A lower ethic for most, a higher ethic for clergy! Celibacy, largely because of Paul's injunctions (I Corinthians 7:32–40), was an early general ideal; but Paul's expectation of an immediate eschaton did not abrogate marriage. Peter, Philip, and probably Paul were married, and bishops were enjoined to have only *one* wife. Prohibitions against remarriage for clergy quickly developed, as well as against a first marriage after ordination. Married priests and bishops were expected to observe sexual abstinence. The synods (councils) of Elvira, 306; Arles, 314; Ancyra, 314; and Nicaea, 325, concerned themselves with these problems. Jerome, Augustine, and Chrysostom excessively praised virginity; Popes Siricius, Innocent I, Leo I, and Gregory I made celibacy mandatory for clergy, even though not everywhere enforced. Chastity for laity was extolled, but did not generally displace marriage.

In the tension between marriage and celibacy, asceticism tended to prevail. In the Middle Ages "ascetic" and "religious" became synonymous. Monasticism was largely responsible for asceticism's triumph. Celibate monastics embraced the rigoristic tendencies in Christianity and practiced them in isolation. Then, obversely, in the succeeding centuries, celibate monastics became the most potent socializing force in Western culture.

Before the fourth century, monasticism already had two basic models. The eremitical model, from which the term "hermit" comes, was for the individual seeking salvation. Paul of Thebes (d. ca. 340) and St. Anthony (d. ca. 356) were its founders. Pachomius (ca. 292–346) founded the cenobitic or communal model, in which monks lived in small communities.

The little known about Paul of Thebes comes from Jerome's *Life of Paul*. He fled to the desert during the Decian persecution and is said to have lived alone in a cave for over a hundred years. St. Anthony is supposed to have visited him twice, once when Paul was 113 years old and again to bury him. A palm tree and two lions represent Paul in art.

The reputed father of monasticism was St. Anthony, born in Coma, Egypt, during the Decian persecution. His biographer was Athanasius, himself an ascetic admirer of monks even though he was an active, controversial metropolitan bishop. Strongly drawn to religious reflection, Anthony was early impressed by Christ's words to the rich young man to sell his goods. On the death of his parents, Anthony disposed of his inheritance, keeping only enough to care for his sister. Later, in obedience to "take no thought for the morrow," he disposed of everything, left his sister with a society of virgins, and began living as an ascetic in his native village. He then moved to a mountain cave, where he strove to subdue his passions and attain purity of thought. Becoming known and sought after for advice, he retreated to deeper mountainous solitude, but appeared in Alexandria in 311 to encourage Christians facing persecution and again about 350 to preach against Arianism. He fasted for long periods, neglected his body, prayed constantly, and tried to think about spiritual things, only to be buffeted by tormenting demons. Even emperors sought his advice. Tradition has enshrined him as the patron saint of gravediggers, basketmakers, butchers, and domestic animals. Although much about Anthony is legend, his impact was substantial.

About 320, Pachomius, a soldier who converted to Christianity, founded a communal monastery on the Nile in Southern Egypt. While his monks lived in different cells and did the usual fasting and praying, they worshiped regularly together, wore similar clothing, and worked set schedules. Profits from basketmaking and farming were given to the poor. Pachomius served as abbot. This "common life" proved so popular that Pachomius established eleven communities, nine for men, two for women.

In the fourth and fifth centuries, literally thousands of Christians expressed their religion in monasticism, often in bizarre ways, without benefit of sacraments, Bible, or clergy. They lived in caves, trees, tombs, holes, and mud huts. They killed the bath, encouraged vermin, fasted inordinately, seldom slept, wore coarse clothing, went barefooted, and attempted to outdo one another in physical discomfort. The more they tried not to think of sex, the more they failed, so that sex was a constant problem. Some would not look at women, others would not allow a female cat about. Perhaps the most unusual eremitical or anchoritic monk lived near Antioch—Simeon Stylites (d. ca. 459). He sat atop a pillar sixty feet high on a yardwide disc for thirty-six years!

Although monasticism developed radical types especially in Syria, it slowly changed, becoming more organized and related to the church. Though a lay movement, ordination for monks in the East became customary, and monasticism served as a model for the Greek church. In the West, monasticism increasingly furnished leaders for the church, candidates for priesthood frequently being required to have monastic training. Monasticism never completely lost the isolation that marked its beginnings, but isolation proved impractical, and as changes developed monasticism became one of the most involved institutions in European culture. In the East contemplation predominated; in the West, social work and missions.

One of the major agents of change in the East was Basil of Caesarea in Cappadocia (ca. 330–79). After receiving a good education and dissatisfied with worldly affairs, he turned to a life of monasticism, secluding himself as a hermit on the Iris river near Neo-caesarea about 358. He preached and traveled in Syria and Egypt to extend his knowledge of the monks, but ill health and the repeated urging of friends prompted him to accept the post of bishop of the see of Caesarea in 370, an office he held until his death. For nine years he was engaged in the bitter post-Nicene theological controversies. Theologically devoted to Origen, Basil came into contact with Athanasius, and eventually helped persuade opposing Nicene factions that they held virtually the same views on the nature of Christ. Although a theologian of stature, his greatest influence came through his monastic Rule which provided Eastern monasticism with structure and brought the church and monastery into a working relationship. His Rule, in the form of questions and answers, avoided the extremes of asceticism and set forth an ideal of perfect service to God through communal obedience. It emphasized poverty, chastity, prayer, hymns, labor, Bible reading, and social work, especially the care of the poor and orphans. However, contemplative monasticism prevailed over social activity in the East. As bishop, Basil was able to appoint priests to serve the monks, a step toward incorporating monasticism into the life of the church. No one did more than Basil to set the direction of monasticism in the Greek and Russian churches, where his Rule became standard. Basil's Rule was adopted at Chalcedon, 451, and received its present form from revisions made by St. Theodore of Studion early in the ninth century. The extent to which Basil's sister Macrina helped write the Rule is controversially disputed.

A major agent of change in Western monasticism was Jerome (ca. 347–420), who successfully united the movement with scholarship and service. Although not a great theologian, his passion for asceticism, relics, and pilgrimages, his credulity and superstition, and his concern for religious books projected the spirit of medievalism. An angelic vision turned Jerome away from youthful wildness and classical studies to life as a desert hermit near Antioch, where he spent several years studying "God's books." When he returned to Antioch, at the urging of many friends he accepted ordination as presbyter and studied briefly in Constantinople under Gregory of Nazianzus. After the Council of Constantinople in 381 he journeyed to Rome where he served as secretary to Pope Damasus. Damasus commissioned him to make a Latin translation of the Bible, which he did, completing the New Testament between 386 and 391, and the Old in 405. This Vulgate translation encountered opposition but was gradually accepted, and in 1546 the Council of Trent made it the official Roman Catholic Bible.

Jerome promoted monastic ideals, especially among the rich women of Rome, many of whom practiced monasticism privately or turned their homes into monasteries. Among these were Paula, Eustochium, and Melania the Elder. Paula later became head of Jerome's convent at Bethlehem, succeeded by her daughter Eustochium, and Melania founded a convent on the Mount of Olives. When Pope Damasus died, rumors circulated that Jerome might become Pope, but Siricius was elected, and Jerome expediently left Rome for the East. His outspoken biblical criticism had gained him many enemies, and a mob angry over his monastic houses for women put speed behind his departure. Paula, aged thirty-six, a widow, accompanied him, leaving her four children on the dock weeping. After establishing themselves in Antioch, Jerome and Paula journeyed in Palestine and Egypt, and in 386 at Bethlehem started separate monasteries for men and women and a hospice for pilgrims. Jerome extravagantly praised Paula. She completely accepted asceticism, forsaking "her palace glittering with gold to dwell in a mud cabin." On their travels she prostrated herself before the rediscovered cross, wept and prayed at the stable, liked the tomb of Jesus, fasted excessively. She ate no flesh, drank no wine, bathed only when ill, slept on bare ground with a goat hair cover, performed menial tasks, sprinkled her food with ashes and learned Hebrew so she could sing psalms with Jerome each morning.

Jerome's ascetic ideals matched those of Paula. Although he accepted papal authority, he described the church as a den of serpents, and repeatedly urged people to withdraw from worldly corruption and temptations. He accepted marriage as an institution for the procreation of virgins, but promoted virginity as superior, noting that the second day of creation, prefiguring marriage, was the only day the Lord did not bless. He pictured housecleaning, husband-pleasing, and child-rearing as things that "distract a person from thoughts of God." He attacked opponents of relics and any who said that Mary had other children. Jerome exerted a wide influence on monasticism through his immediate followers and through his biblical translations, commentaries, and the social services his monasteries rendered. When "barbarian" armies beset and sacked Rome in 410, refugees streamed into Palestine, using the monasteries as hostels and hospitals.

Although Basil and Jerome were key figures in monasticism, there were many others. It was a massive lay movement that attracted thousands of Christians, a counterculture of withdrawal that metamorphosed into a potent social force in the course of a century. (See Benedictines, Chapter 7).

The sharp controversies that beset both church and state in the prolonged Nicene struggle heightened the appeal of monasticism, but did not help with the unity that Constantine desired. When Constantine legalized Christianity, he expected it to unify an empire sorely needing unity. Before Diocletian, during a seventy-year period, twenty-three emperors ruled. Of that number twenty were assassinated, one fell battling the Goths, one died a prisoner of the Persians, and one perished from the plague. Constantine had hoped for peace and unity, but both eluded him. An ominous note for the future occurred when Constantine ordered military force against the dissident Donatists in North Africa. Henceforth church and state would work together to destroy opposition.

The Donatists were North African Christian rigorists who believed that they had the right to exclude from their communion those who proved unfaithful in time of persecution. Their controversy, nourished by nationalistic feelings, reached back to the time of Cyprian in the third century, but the Donatist problem as such erupted shortly after the Diocletian persecution. The Numidian Donatists refused to accept Caecilian, the Bishop of Carthage, on the grounds that the one who consecrated him in 311 had been a traitor (*traditor*) during Diocletian's persecution. In his place they elected Majorinus, who was soon succeeded by Donatus, whose name became attached to the Numidian schismatics. When a Roman commission investigated and ruled against the Donatists in 313, they appealed to the synod of Arles in 314, and then to the emperor in 316. Rebuffed on each occasion, the Donatists still refused to yield, and Constantine resorted to coercion. However, military force did not bring the hoped-for resolution, and after five years, in 321, Constantine recalled the imperial army. During the succeeding years the Donatists greatly increased their numbers. When violence erupted in 347, during the rule of Constans, the state again exerted repression, this time for a period of fourteen years, but the schism persisted. In 405 the state again interfered, and in 411 a large conference at Carthage ruled against the Donatists. Although visibly weakened by these efforts and by the theological treatises against them from Augustine, they continued as a schismatic group until destroyed by the Muslim expansion in the seventh and eight centuries.

What was at stake? The distribution of imperial church funds at first, but more than that, a concept of the church and the sacraments. The Donatists insisted that the church was a congregation of saints, that its leaders had to be holy. They maintained that sacraments administered by unworthy ministers were invalid. The Donatists rebaptized those who came to them from the orthodox Catholic Church and insisted that they alone were the true church, undefiled, one, and holy. The orthodox church maintained the validity of sacraments even when administered by one living in sin; once baptized, always baptized; the sacrament was efficacious regardless of the character of the minister. The Donatists' practice of reordaining ministers directly threatened the authority of the orthodox church to represent Christ. A century later, Augustine answered that the sacraments are valid for those who receive them in faith, even if the priest is not blameless, because the church is merely the custodian of the means of grace for the benefit of all. But the Donatists were not persuaded either by force or by argument. The first attempt of Constantine to achieve religious unity failed.

His second attempt, at the Council of Nicaea in 325, was only minimally more successful. Taken together, the two failures might be viewed as early indicators of the uneasy partnership of two social institutions, each claiming sovereignty. The Nicene controversy began as a local dispute between a priest and his bishop about the nature of Christ, but it harbored momentous political and theological implications. If the church said Christ was not fully divine, then there was no revelation, no incarnation. If the church said Christ was not fully human, then there was no escape from the death that ends all nature. Nihilism, a feeling of meaninglessness, lurked in the controversy. Emphasis on the divine nature of Christ opened the way to Gnosticism and its devaluation of this world, whereas emphasis on the human nature eliminated a transcendent reference and, as Athanasius recognized, left the church with no essentially higher authority than that of the state and rendered all of life meaningless.

The initial dispute was between Arius (ca. 250–336), a priest in Alexandria, and Alexander (d. 328), the city's bishop. Previous theologians, particularly Origen, were ambiguous about the human nature of Christ. Bishop Alexander, a stern leader, had welded the Egyptian church together, and at a gathering of his presbyters and clergymen in 319 essayed to give a theological disquisition on the Trinity. He asserted that God was always, and the Son was always; "at the same time the Father, at the same time the Son; the Son coexists with God, unbegotten; he is ever-begotten, he is not born-by-begetting; neither by thought nor by any moment of time does God precede the Son; God always, Son always, the Son exists from God himself."

Arius took issue and began preaching just the opposite from his pulpit, saying that before Christ "was begotten or created or appointed or established, he did not exist; for he was not unbegotten. . . . If the Father begat the Son, he that was begotten had a beginning of existence; hence it is clear that there was (a time) when the Son was not. It follows then of necessity that he had his existence from the nonexistent."

Alexander believed that the Son was eternal, uncreated, in essence the same as the Father. Arius believed that the Son was a created being, created out of nothing, first-born of all creatures and the agent in creating the world. He believed that "The Son has a beginning" and that "God is without a beginning." For Arius, Christ was God but a lower God, not one with the Father in either essence or eternity. The Logos, he contended, became incarnate by taking the place of the reason in the man Jesus, so that Christ was neither fully God nor fully human, but a third something.

Bishop Alexander called a synod in Alexandria in 320 which excommunicated Arius and excoriated his sympathizers. Arius then appealed to his personal friend, Bishop Eusebius of Nicomedia, and the controversy greatly enlarged until the East was in turmoil with charges, countercharges, and recriminations. Constantine, who feared another schism, sent his trouble-shooter, Bishop Hosius of Cordova, Spain, to reconcile the parties. Instead the dispute grew more heated, and Constantine convened the Council of Nicaea in 325. Of the 318 bishops who attended, at government expense, only six came from the West. The Emperor Constantine, though not baptized, was present, signifying the importance attached to the proceedings. Many lower clergy also attended, at government expense.

Three parties emerged at Nicaea: the large majority, who were uncommitted on the issues at hand, led by the historian Eusebius of Caesarea; the followers of Arius, led by Eusebius of Nicomedia; and the supporters of Alexander. The Arian statement of Eusebius of Nicomedia was rejected, and then Eusebius of Caesarea offered a baptismal creed used in his home church as a compromise. Although Eusebius wrote home otherwise, the creed was significantly amended, probably at the suggestion of the emperor, who surmised that more political unity lay in a union of the middle party and the anti-Arians. Added were the key phrases, "begotten, not made," "of one essence (*homoousion*) with the Father," and "came down and became man." Rejected were "there was when he was not" and "he was made of things that were not." *Homoousion* proved to be the principal symbol. Arius and the two bishops who did not sign the creed were banished. After considering the date for Easter, readmission of Melitian schismatics, treatment of those who weakened under persecution, discipline, and prayer while standing, the council adjourned. Before the delegates reached home, opposition boiled. Many in the middle party thought the creed suggested Sabellianism—one God manifested in three modes. Eusebius of Nicomedia and Theognis of Nicaea spoke out and were promptly exiled by Constantine.

A new phase developed in 328. Eusebius and Theognis, through the influence of court friends, were allowed to return home. That same year Alexander died, and the gifted Athanasius (296–373) became bishop. Although banished five times, he remained the Bishop of Alexandria the rest of his life. At Nicaea he had championed both the full divinity and full humanity of Christ. Already he had written *On the Incarnation of the Word* expounding how the union of the Logos with humanity restored the image lost in the Fall and how the Resurrection wiped out death, the consequence of sin. He saw in Arius' view of Christ as a being created less than God the same fatalism that he saw in the failure of Roman culture. He believed Romanism rested on the myth of an eternal world of nature endlessly proceeding in cycles, and as nature is limited, this meant for Athanasius that all human affairs were basically determined. He felt that this underlying defective myth had cut the nerve of endeavor in Roman culture, that an *arché*, a cause of causes, which would give meaning to life, simply could not be found in nature. What is in space and time cannot ultimately be the cause of what is in space and time, said Athanasius, and so he looked for a new starting point that could be directly apprehended by its working and power. This he found in the Trinity, and believed that the consciousness of it was part of the original spiritual legacy of mankind. When the consciousness of the *arché* became obscured in the Fall, it was revealed in Christ and continues to be renewed in consciousness by the Spirit. Athanasius was contending that apart from the Incarnation and the Resurrection, apart from the divinity and humanity of Christ, we are still trapped in the meaningless cycle of nature. Without the transcendent incarnate and the barrier of death broken, we are trapped in the inertia of determinism. Athanasius wanted to get at the purely spiritual character of reality: we are not related ultimately to nature, but to God. Consequently, to say that Christ was less than God meant for Athanasius no ultimate revelation, and to say he was not fully human meant no escape from death. Athanasius believed that through Christ, fully divine and fully human, the revelation and resurrection became ours, that only in the trinitarian *arché* could frustration and meaninglessness be dissipated. Systems based on cyclical nature could lead only to blind groping for moral and intellectual reality. To his culture he offered renewal of both. Christ became human that we might become divine. In Arianism he saw no escape from the cultural malady of his time, and none opposed Arianism more vigorously.

Having friends at court, possibly the emperor's sister, Eusebius of Nicomedia on his return resorted to political machinations and personal attacks to secure vengeance. By 330 he had obtained the condemnation of Eustathius of Antioch, who had spoken against Arius, and had persuaded Arius to present a cleverly worded retraction to Constantine, who not only then released him from banishment but also ordered Athanasius to restore Arius to his pulpit in Alexandria. Eusebius meanwhile maneuvered two assemblies in Tyre and Jerusalem in 335 to vote to restore Arius, and when Athanasius refused, Constantine banished him to Gaul, the first of five banishments. Eusebius also pushed his temporary advantage against others and succeeded in having Marcellus of Ancyra, who had spoken against Arius, deposed for heresy. Even though Arius died in 336 on the evening before his restoration, the Nicene faith had officially been overthrown. Eusebius baptized Constantine in 337 when the emperor lay on his deathbed.

A circus of theological-political confusion ensued. Constantine's three sons partitioned the empire. Constantine II took control of Britain, Gaul, Spain, and part of Italy; Constantius took Asia Minor, Syria, Egypt; and Constans received North Africa, Italy, and the Danube. When Constantine II died in an attack on Constans in 340, Constans became ruler of the West, Constantius ruler in the East.

All the bishops were allowed to return from exile during the transition, and Athanasius was back in Alexandria in 337. When Eusebius became Bishop of Constantinople in 339, however, he influenced Constantius to banish Athanasius a second time. Athanasius joined a number of other refugees in Rome, where they were welcomed by Bishop Julius. A Roman synod in 340 declared that Athanasius and Marcellus had been unjustly deposed. Ecclesiastical rivalry between the East and West deepened when the Eastern bishops then called two synods in Antioch in 341 and not only protested the action at Rome but adopted new creeds without reference to Nicaea. With the death of Eusebius in 341, Constans and Constantius sought to settle the entire matter in a general council that was called to meet at Sardica in 343, but when it appeared that Western bishops would outnumber Eastern bishops, the latter refused to attend. Athanasius and Marcellus were approved by the council at Sardica, which, under the leadership of Hosius of Cordova, boosted Roman primacy by enacting rules saying that any deposed bishop had the right to appeal to the Bishop of Rome for a new trial, and that until a decision was made the bishopric was to remain vacant.

When the Arian bishop of Alexandria died in 347, Constans let Athanasius return. He received an enthusiastic welcome, and his stay lasted nine years. But the political tides again turned; in 350 Constans was murdered, and in 353 after Constantius had stablized his control, he decided that Athanasius was too troublesome to tolerate. In two synods, at Arles in 353 and at Milan in 355, Constantius virtually forced the Western bishops to abandon Athanasius. The few who did not go along with the emperor, like Hosius, were banished, and military might was used to force Athanasius from Alexandria in 356, his third banishment. He joined the monks of Egypt. In the following year the Eastern bishops at the synod of Sirmium forbade the use of the term *ousia*, signifying the oneness of Father and Son, on the grounds that it was unscriptural, and at Nice in 359 the bishops agreed on "we call the Son *like* the Father, as the holy Scriptures call Him and teach." *Homoios* and *homoiousios* prevailed as symbols. The Son was like the Father. Constantius forced other synods to come to the same agreement. This was the creedal statement about Christ that Ulfilas took to the Goths on his missionary travels, so that some of the Germanic tribes that came into the Roman Empire in later centuries were nominally Arian Christians.

In 361 Constantius died, and Julian, who hated Christianity, became emperor. He let all the exiles return home, hoping they would fight and knock each other out. So Athanasius was back in Alexandria in 362; and, because he was so popular and successful against heathenism, in the same year Julian exiled him again, the fourth time. By now the controversy had widened to include the nature of the Holy Spirit, the semi-Arians joining the conservatives at Antioch in a statement that the Holy Spirit was not a creature. So many people had crossed from one side of the argument to the other that some of the theological distinctions seemed blurred. Yet Athanasius was exiled once more. Julian died in 363, and Jovian, who ruled only one year, allowed Athanasius to return in 364. Valentinian I (364–75) then ruled the West with his brother Valens (364–78) as co-regent in the East. Valens came under the influence of Arians at Constantinople and condemned Athanasius to his fifth and final exile, 365. He returned in 366 and died in Alexandria in 373. To the end he worked to build up the Nicene party and to maintain the full divinity and full humanity of Christ. In the process his deep concern for asceticism helped promote monasticism in the West.

With the death of Athanasius, the early antagonists had passed, and new theologians—Basil of Caesarea in Cappadocia and his brother Gregory of Nyssa, and Gregory of Nazianzus—attempted to resolve the theological dilemma. These three bishops brought about the Nicene-Constantinopolitan statement at the Council of Constantinople in 381. Omitting anathemas but retaining *homoousios*, this "Athanasian" creed defined Christ as "the only-begotten Son of God, begotten of the Father before all the ages, Light of Light, true God of true God, begotten not made, of one substance with the Father, through whom all things were made. . . ." The statement was not without political impact for when Theodosius became sole emperor in 380 he decreed that all people under his rule "should live by that religion which divine Peter the apostle is said to have given to the Romans, and which it is evident that Pope Damasus and Peter, bishop of Alexandria, a man of apostolic sanctity, followed; that is that we should believe in the one deity of Father,

Son, and Holy Spirit with equal majesty and in the Holy Trinity according to the apostolic teaching and the authority of the gospel" (Codex Theodosianus XVI).

The creed and the edict legalized in the empire that Christianity teaching one divine essence in three hypostases—one substance, three persons. Heretics, schismatics, and pagans were subjected to fines. The emperor ordered all pagan temples closed, decreed death by sword for those who continued in pagan sacrifices, forbade lawsuits and business on Sunday, and invalidated wills made by Christians turned pagan.

The first sixty-eight years of the partnership of church and state were hardly an unmixed blessing. In addition to the withdrawal by a massive segment of the laity from a church they felt had become too worldly, a bitter theological dispute made mockery of any religious unity. And just as the monastic movement continued into the next century and beyond, so the Nicene controversy continued beyond the Council of Constantinople.

After Constantinople the dispute centered not so much on the relationship of the Son to the Father as on the relationship of the human to the divine in Christ. What part of Christ was human? What part divine? Was he two-thirds human, one-third divine? And so forth. After seventy more years of dispute over the intricacies of Apollinarianism, Nestorianism, and Eutychianism, the Council of Chalcedon in 451 finally issued a definition that has become historic rather than conclusive: Christ was "as regards his manhood begotten, for us men and for our salvation, of Mary the Virgin, the God-bearer; one and the same Christ, Son, Lord, Only-begotten, recognized in two natures, without confusion, without change, without division, without separation; the distinction of natures being in no way annulled by the union, but rather the characteristics of each nature being preserved and coming together to form one person and subsistence. . . ."

The long Nicene struggle exemplified the significance that the early church attached to the divine-human Christ; it marked the effort to keep the revelation of the historical Christ in the Christian purview; it also highlighted human infirmities and the inability to capture in human definitions what Christ meant. Yet the effort was not without reward; it witnessed to the significance of the "transcendent" for finding meaning in life.

After the death of Theodosius in 395, the imperial Eastern and Western administrations, which had existed for a century, became a permanent division of the empire. The West had its capital at Rome and Ravenna; the East, at Constantinople (Byzantium). While the empires rivaled and interacted with one another, their political and ecclesiastical developments took different turns. In the East the state maintained itself more or less intact until the fifteenth century and largely predominated over the church. In the West, the state succumbed to the incursions of the "barbarians," and in the disruptions the church predominated.

These state-church tendencies were already predictable in the lives of two of the fourth century's most influential ecclesiastics: Chrysostom of Constantinople and Ambrose of Milan. Both of them were eminent preachers, both were strongly influenced by monasticism, both came from noble families and received training in law, and both were active in the relations of state and church. In Chrysostom a concern for contemplation, holiness, and liturgy predominated, and in Ambrose a concern for large social issues. They symbolize the future of the church in the East and the West. In the East, where the Nicene controversy raged and the emperors were generally Arian, the state tended to dominate; in the West, the church tended to prevail, in part at least because its Christ was not confined to the created order and so provided a basis from which to judge all earthly sovereignties. Some scholars credit Ambrose with authorship of the so-called Athanasian Creed at Constantinople in 381.

St. John Chrysostom (ca. 347–407) studied both law and theology in Antioch but felt the call to monasticism so strongly that he resided as a monk in his home while his widowed mother was still living. When she died ca. 373, he retreated to the caves about Antioch and for eight years lived so austerely as a hermit that his health was undermined, making continuance impossible. In 381 he became a deacon and in 386 a priest, serving at Antioch with the special duty to preach, at which he excelled. Drawing most of his texts from the Bible, eschewing allegory, and emphasizing the strenuous life, he became known as the foremost biblical expositor of the century. In 398 he was made Bishop (Patriarch) of Constantinople, where his practical, ascetic reforms and uncompromising honesty met stiff resistance from the Empress Eudoxia, who felt that his fulminations against fine lace and the shady actions of Jezebel were directed against her, and from Theophilus, the Bishop of Alexandria, who felt that he instead of Chrysostom should have been elevated to the bishopric of Constantinople. In his zeal against worldliness and laxity, Chrysostom made tactless mistakes, unceremoniously sacked a number of lax priests, and was soon arraigned before the Synod of Oak in 403 on twenty-nine fabricated counts ranging all the way from liking Origenism to derogatory remarks about the empress and chewing lozenges in church. Theophilus had packed the synod with cronies from Egypt, and the emperor executed the synod's condemnation by exiling Chrysostom to Bithynia. Chrysostom preached a rousing farewell sermon in which he likened Eudoxia to Jezebel and Herodias. One day later an earthquake shook the city, the people became enraged, and the superstitious empress recalled Chrysostom. In the following year he was again banished, for resuming the duties of an episcopal office from which he had been deposed and for denouncing ceremonies at the dedication of a silver statue to the empress. This time, despite widespread protest from as far away as Rome, he was whisked away to Syria, and died in 407 on a deliberately forced march in severe weather to remote Pityus. Although he fought evil in high places, he did not successfully resist the state. It was Rome that finally forced Patriarch Atticus to place Chrysostom's name on the diptych list of departed saints read at the eucharist.

Quite the opposite occurred with St. Ambrose (ca. 339–97), son of a civil officer in Gaul. Trained in law and appointed in 370 to be governor of the area about Milan, Ambrose's promising civil career was suddenly interrupted by a popular call to become bishop. When the Arian bishop of Milan died in 374, a struggle ensued over the theology of his successor.

Ambrose unexpectedly appeared in the doorway to quiet the proceedings, and was hailed as an emissary sent by God. Within one week he was baptized and made bishop. He saw the events as a divine hand laid upon him, gave away all his possessions, studied theology, and was soon recognized as an unusually able administrator and preacher. The boldness of his preaching and strong moral convictions directly affected the conversion of Augustine. Like Chrysostom he was ascetic, excessively extolled virginity, and promoted monasticism. Unlike Chrysostom he successfully brought fundamental belief to bear on leaders in high places, as if the whole church were speaking through him. In his struggle in 385 with Justina (mother of Valentinian II), he maintained the independence of the church against civil encroachment. Ambrose, strongly Nicene in his view of Christ, did not want the Arians to have a church in Milan. When Justina tried to take over a basilica, Ambrose organized the congregation to sit and sing hymns (since some of these were his, he is often called the father of Christian hymnody), and forced the youthful emperor and his mother to withdraw. In 390 Ambrose demonstrated the power of the sacraments and his own moral boldness by excluding the Emperor Theodosius from communion. The emperor had vengefully executed 7,000 Thessalonicans for a mild insurrection in Thessalonica. Theodosius invited the citizens to the amphitheater, and at a given signal they were slain by soldiers strategically stationed among them. Ambrose protested and forbade Christian communion to the emperor until he did penance. Ambrose also fought remaining vestiges of paganism and successfully opposed repeated efforts to restore the Altar of Victory, a pagan shrine, in the Roman Senate House. His letter to Valentinian II on this subject (Epistle 18) illustrates his ability to make practical application of deep theological convictions. His best writing is *On the Office of the Ministry,* an ethical treatise drawn from Scripture and the insights of Cicero. When noting the significant figures of the fourth century, one cannot ignore Ambrose. He lived what Athanasius had fought for. Insistence on the divinity of Christ was oblique protest against sovereignty of state. It meant that ultimately the church's Lord is above all created entities. Christ, as part of the created order, would have had a status not different essentially from that of the emperor. In Ambrose met the divinity of Christ and the sovereignty of the church.

6

Augustine, Paradigm of Western Theology

The paradigm of Western theology, Aurelius Augustine (354–430), bishop of Hippo, stands at the close of the early history of Christianity. In his own life experiences he encountered all the major problems of the early church and in his writings bequeathed to the future seminal answers that have influenced Christianity and secular thought ever since. The medieval church, Aquinas, Luther, Calvin, and Pascal drew heavily on him. So did Kant, Hegel, Marx, and Whitehead, and so do hundreds of other thinkers in widely diversified fields, even though they may not acknowledge their indebtedness.

Four controversial subjects shaped his thought: (1) Manicheism, which led him to reject basic Gnostic tenets about reality and evil; (2) the Donatists, who made him think through the sacraments and the political order, (3) Pelagianism, which elicited his views on sin and free will, and (4) paganism, which evoked his philosophy of history. Although the *The Confessions*, *The City of God*, and *The Enchiridion* are his best known works, he wrote some fourteen treatises against the Manicheans, six against the Donatists, and fourteen against the Pelagians, in addition to a number of philosophical works just after his conversion, and numerous sermons, letters, and commentaries during his lifetime.

MANICHEISM

The driving force in Augustine's life was his intense desire to find happiness. Emotionally, intellectually, and spiritually he could not find it until his heart rested in God, as he says at the beginning of *The Confessions*, and ultimately not in this life of destruction and death, as he asserts in *The City of God*. He affirms life in the present but does not consider it final.

The Confessions, a first in such spiritual autobiography, not only reveals the inner life of Augustine but is a rich source of information about events that occurred before its completion in 400. Augustine was born in Tagaste in North Africa of a pagan father and Christian mother. After a good education at Carthage, he abandoned himself to physical pleasure. At seventeen he had a mistress and at eighteen a son, Adeodatus. In 373 he became associated with Manicheism. To him it was a double boon. As the latest vogue of the smart, intellectual set, it suited his rational vanity, and its assertion of the spirit as the real part of man allowed him to indulge in physical lust without feeling guilt. After all, the real Augustine was not indulging. This was the period when he prayed, "Make me chaste and continent, O Lord, but not yet" (*Confessions* 8).

Manicheism was a syncretism of elements of Gnosticism, Zoroastrianism, Buddhism, and Hinduism—imported from Persia. Its founder was the little known Mani (ca. 216–76), reputedly a writer and artist who believed that he was divinely called. He wandered through the East preaching and making disciples, and was finally martyred by Zoroastrian priests. In an elaborate nature myth he pictured the world as a dualism of light and darkness. Mani equated the light with spirit and goodness, the darkness with matter and evil. In the beginning they existed as upper and lower realms, until the beings of darkness launched an attack to secure light from the upper realm. A cosmic war followed in which the demons initially won and trapped portions of the realm of light. To rescue the light, the high God created the visible world and heavens. The twelve constellations of the zodiac served as a giant bucket lift for the rescued light, which was dumped into the moon and, when it became full, was emptied into the sun. To imprison bits of light, the demons created man, a discordant being in the image of Satan, but compounded with light, the soul. Salvation was to know the true relation of body-spirit and to liberate the spirit by living ascetically. To help us, the God of light sent messengers—Adam, Noah, Abraham, Zoroaster, Buddha, Jesus, Paul and Mani. Receivers were of two classes, the hearers and the perfect. Their ascetic strictness differentiated them. The perfect, standing on the threshold of liberation, took vows of total asceticism. The hearers lived less strenuously in the hope of being reincarnated and achieving liberation next time. Since the body is evil, the true Christ was docetic, not really human, and Mani pictured himself as the Holy Spirit, the ambassador of light. Augustine remained a member of the Manichean sect for nine years. It catered to his intellectual pride; he scorned the Scriptures, calling attention to interpolations and self-contradictions, and he easily bested simple Christians in argument. The Manicheans insisted on truth through reason; the church seemed to impose truth and terrify people into accepting. During this period Augustine was a hearer and evil was for him a substance. The real Augustine was not sinning.

But Augustine's reason was not satisfied. In the Manichean myth, he could find no reason for the cosmic fighting. He could not understand how an incorruptible God could be subject to violence from the realm of darkness. And the "superior" morality of the Manicheans when compared to that of Christian monks seemed somewhat tawdry. He was disappointed in the elect. He could not see that philandering cohabitation was superior to marriage just because in marriage one was more likely to beget offspring and thus imprison light in matter. This argument merely deepened Augustine's growing sense of moral inadequacy; simple monks could control their passions better than he.

After nine years as a Manichean, Augustine became a skeptic; he had already learned enough from reading Neoplatonism to doubt that evil was a substance. Rather, in the system of Neoplatonism, in which everything emanated from the Nous, evil was more nearly privation, negation, alienation, or absence of the good. When Augustine left Carthage to teach rhetoric in Rome, he was also reaching for a new philosophy of life. Neoplatonism, which he continued to study in Victorinus's translations of Plotinus (205–70) and Porphyry (233–304), increasingly shaped his thought and moved him further from Manicheism. But Neoplatonism, like Gnosticism, devalued the body and this world, and did not comprehend the depth of sin in the spiritual being of man. Disappointed in his teaching in Rome, in 384 Augustine accepted a government appointment to teach rhetoric in Milan. There he met Ambrose. He wanted to believe—he thought of the Christian God as the highest good, and felt even more ashamed of his own profligacy in comparison with ascetic monks—but not until his garden experience could he convert to Christianity. In a state of self-condemnation he rushed into a garden where he heard a voice telling him to "take up and read." He opened his Bible at random to Romans 13:13ff. and read, "Let us conduct ourselves becomingly as in the day, not in reveling and drunkenness, not in debauchery and licentiousness, not in quarreling and jealously. Put on the Lord Jesus Christ, and make no provision for the flesh, to gratify its desires." His character was transformed. A feeling of miraculous relief came over him. While awaiting baptism, he retreated with some of his friends to Cassiciacum, where they discussed Christianity and he wrote his early philosophical essays. In the following year, 387, on Easter eve, he was baptized by Ambrose at Milan.

On the death of his mother (*Confessions* 9) and son, Augustine in 388 returned with some friends to North Africa to set up a monastery at Tagaste. In his writings he began combating the Manicheans. In 391 the people demanded that Bishop Valerius of Hippo ordain him to the priesthood. Augustine consented and four years later became the ruling bishop of Hippo. By 400 he had finished his profoundly moving *Confessions*, addressed as a prayer to God, the spiritual odyssey of his struggle to find fulfillment.

Keenly conscious of his long battle to understand and overcome sin, Augustine in the *Confessions* profusely thanked God for his grace and mercy, for having melted away his sin as if it were ice. He conceived of religion as an intensely personal relationship with God. Recalling past events, he saw the hand of God guiding and preparing him, allowing him to suffer agonies that his bliss might be the sweeter. In all his wanderings, he wrote, he found no real happiness because he sought that which was less than God. He was seeking and exalting himself, pretending to be God, making himself and his desires the false center of everything. He had willfully turned away from the source of light and life to darkness and death. As a baby he disrupted family order by demanding that his parents satisfy his wants. Later, his sexual immorality disrupted social order to satisfy his own physical lusts. On seeing cruel games he laughed demonically and felt no responsibility to change anything. But it was the famous incident of pear-stealing that worried him most (*Confessions* 2). Why had he stolen? He did not like the company of the boys with him, the pears were green, he was not hungry, he tossed the pears to some pigs, and he was not moved by the excitement. Then why? Augustine finally realized that he "was imitating the liberty and omnipotency of God," trying to usurp the place of God. Sin lodges in will, not in nature or the body. God is the center of everything, yet as in the Fall we try to be the center, and this disrupts everything. When we sin, be it theft or murder, we proclaim ourselves God and the fulfillment of our wants as ultimate. False joy and despondency follow because our efforts originate in a corrupt source and seek a false goal. "I sinned in that I sought pleasures, sublimities, truths, not in God but in his creatures, myself and others. And thus I rushed into griefs, confusions, errors" (*Confessions* 1). We inherit a status of original sin from Adam, wrote Augustine. Originally we were able to sin and not to sin. Now, however, we are able only to sin. Why God rescued and forgave him Augustine could not fathom; he could only return thanks, marvel, and rejoice. He felt blessed, directed by God.

DONATISM

As the sole bishop of Hippo after 395, Augustine was concerned about the implications of Donatism for the nature of the church. In 400 he finished his anti-Manichean works and wrote *On Baptism* against the Donatists. The Donatist schism was almost a century old (see Chapter 5). Various emperors were unable to suppress it. Opposing factions had developed among the Donatists and Augustine at first tried to bring about reconciliation. However, when a three-day conference at Carthage in 411 failed to resolve differences between Donatists and Catholics and among the Donatists themselves, imperial edicts then forbade Donatist assemblies on penalty of death.

The Donatists did not reject episcopacy. They simply demanded that bishops be holy, saying sacraments administered by unholy clergy were invalid. Cyprian (d. 258) had denied the validity of baptism by heretics, and had warned against contamination by association with unworthy priests. Since theirs was the only church that had maintained its purity despite persecutions and that demanded purity of its bishops and members, the Donatists asserted that they were the one true church. Only their sacraments were valid. Their strength lay in the maxim that the people of God should be holy.

The Catholic position rested on the validity of the sacrament as such. The administrant may change, but baptism is baptism, and ordination is ordination, because not we but the Holy Trinity bestows the gift. Faith is required in the recipient, but holiness or unholiness in the administrant makes no essential difference. Unholy persons are in the church, as the parable of the wheat and tares indicates, and the Donatists err in trying to lay claim to final blessedness. The Catholic Church derives holiness from its custody of the sacraments, not from the worthiness of its priests, although in the eschaton the tares will be separated out.

Augustine built on the Catholic position. Only saints compose the true church, but in the empirical institution are both good and evil persons, a condition that is to be tolerated according to Jesus' parables. The church is universal, in all the world, not confined to a corner in Africa that claims to have only holy people. The church is the keeper of the sacraments, which are gifts of God; the validity of the sacraments is not destroyed or enhanced by the moral state of the administrant. If it were, salvation would depend on us rather than on God. In baptism and ordination God bestows an indelible character that the church dare not repeat. This, of course, forced Augustine to accept Donatist baptism and ordination, but he argued that the individual living outside the unity of the church does not realize the full benefit of the sacrament. He is cut off from universal communion, fellowship, and hearing of the true word. That the individual and the church might be built up, Augustine pleaded with the Donatists to return to the fold of the universal church. Consequently, Augustine defined a sacrament as a sign, a symbol, an occasion for the invisible grace of God. In baptism God forgives sin, but only life in the universal church permits the full realization of what this means. The Donatist sacrament itself is valid, but unfortunate. The true church unites its members in the Spirit and in love; the Donatists fragment, separate, and foment hate. Acceptable as Augustine's view is, it is not without a double edge. Augustine stretched, if he did not betray, both the Spirit and love that he advocated.

For the sake of unity and an environment in which the sacraments might fully function, Augustine urged the state to use force against Donatists and heretics. He quoted Luke 14:23, "Compel them to come in." He argued that coercion and persecution were good or evil depending on the goal sought. Elijah persecuted and slew false prophets (1 Kings 18:40), Christ compelled Paul to embrace truth (Acts 9:1–18), Moses afflicted the Hebrew people (Exodus 5:9). He also argued that since the Donatists had originally appealed to the state, they should not complain when the state's judgment went against them. Formerly Augustine had asserted that force should not be used to compel heretics to come into the church, lest the church be contaminated, but in view of the good resulting from such compulsion, he had changed his mind (*Letters,* 93). Without coercion, many people would simply languish away in Donatism, never know the joy of truth. It is better to lead people to God with love, "but those are certainly more numerous who are corrected by fear" (*Letters*, 185). Lost sheep who resist coming back to the fold should for their own good be brought back with the pain of the whip; but Augustine wanted reclamation, not revenge. Augustine's arguments regarding compulsion passed into the medieval church, which readily sanctioned death now to save the soul from the future eternal fires of hell, thus choking heretical dissent and preserving unity.

Augustine's view of the Donatists was linked to his view of the state. On the death of Theodosius, the emperor who made Christianity the only legal religion in the empire, Ambrose gave an oration expressing the hope that the church and empire might rule as partners, each with special power and authority from God, each serving to guarantee and bolster the work of the other. Augustine regarded the church as the superior in that arrangement, but nevertheless felt that governments were permitted and empowered by God to maintain peace and order, to be dikes against sin. He sanctioned coercion and violence as a means of restraining evildoers and declared that Christians should tolerate even atrocious forms of government. Not that Christians need such restraints, but others do. This was the basis for his asserting the just war theory. A war is just if it is fought under recognized leadership, has the restoration of peace and vindication of justice as its end, is motivated by love, has some possibility of success, and is undertaken for the good of society. Inasmuch as Christians are involved in the secular world, they can serve in government and the military, for both were ordained by God, but priests should abstain from war to serve altars. Since the church is superior to the state (though neither is fully good or fully bad), Augustine felt that the state should follow the guidance of the church.

PELAGIANISM

The third conflict that shaped Augustine's thought was with Pelagius. Pelagius, a learned lay monk from Britain, came to Rome about 385. The low morality of Roman life shocked him. He believed strongly in free will and our ability not to sin. God would not have given commands he did not expect to be obeyed: we are always able to make moral and immoral choices. Pelagius reacted sharply to the notion that original sin keeps us from doing good. When a bishop quoted Augustine's plea, "Grant what Thou commandest and command what Thou wilt" (*Confessions* 10:40), Pelagius felt that morality was imperiled. To say we are not responsible for good and evil deeds was, for Pelagius, to invite indulgence in sin. Consequently, he attacked Augustine's statement. Pelagius believed we are created with free will and never lose it. Free will, law, and Jesus' example constitute God's grace. Without these we cannot save ourselves; with them we can. At any moment we can turn to God and obey. Free will makes ethical behavior the responsibility of every person. Pelagius denied original sin. Adam's sin was a bad example that we have chosen to follow; original sin is nothing more than habit and social influence, and we should not surrender supinely to them. Sin is really self-generated, and we, becoming accustomed to it, sin even when we do not want to, and then retreat behind "original sin." Pelagius advocated a morally vigorous Christianity. Pelagius' fame spread; he published a popular commentary on St. Paul's epistles; his disciples multiplied; Celestius, a fellow countryman practicing law in Rome, joined him. A clash with Augustine (and Jerome, the other major opponent of Pelagianism) was not long in coming.

When Rome was sacked in 410, Pelagius and Celestius fled to North Africa, hoping to contact Augustine. Unable to do so, Pelagius made his way to Palestine and deepened the controversy about his ideas by publishing *On Free Will.* Between 418 and 420, he disappeared. Celestius remained in Carthage to be ordained, only to be blocked by a letter from deacon Paulinus of Milan to Augustine accusing Celestius of six errors: (1) Adam was made mortal and would have died even if he had not sinned; (2) the sin of Adam injured only Adam and not the whole human race; (3) infants are in the same state in which Adam was before his fall; (4) the whole human race does not die because of Adam's death or sin, nor will it rise because of Christ's resurrection; (5) the law as well as the Gospel leads to the kingdom of heaven; (6) people without sin lived even before Christ. Although these views were inimically stated, they were not falsified. In 411 an advisory synod in Carthage decided against ordaining Celestius. He left for Ephesus, and Augustine began writing tracts and letters against this new threat.

Pelagius' views rested on the assumption that there are no sinful people, only sinful acts, that sins are separate acts of the will, that righteousness is the reverse of such acts, that one is always able to choose between the two. Conduct does not affect the essence of our free will. In Augustine (and in Ambrose before him) a certain synergism of cooperation with God in conversion can be seen, but the implications of Pelagianism drove Augustine to a belief in predestination, irresistible grace, and divine control of all that happens. Augustine was unwilling to admit that Pelagius even understood the problem. Whereas Pelagius held that acts only incidentally affect our nature, Augustine believed that will is inseparable from acts and that each act affects the will.

Augustine's experience showed him that one cannot overcome sin merely by willing to do so; evil is too powerful. Something deep within our nature has to be changed. The law and the example of Jesus simply made Augustine's own inability more poignant. Augustine's experience led him to attribute salvation solely to grace. Adam did not just sin, he became a sinner. In pride, in self-love, he turned from God; the result was ignorance, concupiscence, and death. Turning from God disoriented Adam's will, blinding him to truth. Once disoriented, the will was powerless to re-orient itself. Adam the sinner begat sinners, passing his character on to posterity. Original sin was real for Augustine, not merely guilt. Its penalty was death. For him it was not just imitation, but generation, for concupiscence always occurs in generation and is passed on to children, though not imputed to the regenerate as sin. Marriage for Augustine was good, celibacy better.

In God's bestowal of grace, faith conquers ignorance, love displaces self-centeredness, and hope triumphs over death. Grace is the cause of salvation; it initiates good in us and actively continues. Grace reorients and endows us with a good will and the capability of doing good. Grace is irresistible. Some people are elected, predestined to be saved. Others are called, but not saved. Others are damned, said Augustine. None can complain because all deserve damnation for their sinfulness. The various ordinances of the church are means whereby the set number of the elect is realized. All happens according to the mysterious, inexplicable, omnipotent will of God. This connotes determinism, a factor in Augustine's thought still being debated.

Synods at Jerusalem and Diospolis in 415 accused Pelagius of heresy, but he adroitly cleared himself. However, the North African councils of Carthage and Mileve in 416 condemned his teachings, and Pope Innocent I (402–17) not only approved their actions but also excommunicated Pelagius and Celestius. When Zosimus became Pope (417–19), Celestius appealed to him in person. On the basis of a statement of faith and a Roman synod's finding of orthodoxy, Zosimus declared Celestius innocent and criticized the African synods for acting too hastily. In defiance of the Pope, in 418 a large council at Carthage issued a set of canons holding that Adam became mortal by sin, that children should be baptized to remit original sin, that grace is more than law, that sacramental grace is necessary for right living, and that sinlessness is impossible. In the same year Emperor Honorius issued a rescript condemning Pelagius, Celestius, and their followers to exile, and Pope Zosimus followed suit, changing his previous view.

The Pope's letter required all bishops to subscribe, but in southern Italy, Bishop Julian of Eclanum and eighteen others refused to comply. Julian conducted a vigorous anti-Augustinian campaign from exile in Constantinople, accusing Augustine of demeaning marriage and reasserting Manicheism. Neither reason nor Scripture, he asserted, recognizes original sin; we are not totally depraved. Sin is in the will, not in a substance or character passed on in generation. Julian was repeatedly exiled by local civil powers and by Theodosius II in 430. The Council of Ephesus, 431, again condemned Pelagianism as a heresy.

However, opposition to Augustine continued for another century. Prosper and Hilary from the Gallic church thought predestination crippled preaching, ethical endeavor, and reproof. They insisted that God assists the human will to do what is good. As Christ died for all, the will of each person is to blame for non-salvation. Similar modifications may be found in John Cassian, who asserted that while salvation is attributable to celestial grace, we do cooperate, and our freedom is preserved in the process.

Practical churchmen feared that Augustine's doctrines pushed to an extreme would have God compelling us to sin, baptism robbed of its value, fatalism drowning freedom, God capriciously saving a few, some indulging in libertinism, etc. Vincent of Lerins attacked Augustine's views as innovations, contrary to what the church has everywhere and always taught. The synod of Orange, 529, settled for semi-Pelagianism. The synod rejected irresistible grace in favor of sacramental grace and human freedom to assert free will, abandoned predestination. But the question of sin and grace persists and repeatedly recurs in church history. To what extent are we free? To what extent is life determined?

PAGANISM

Alaric, leader of the West Goths, after two previous marches on Rome, captured and sacked the city in 410. The event sent psychic shock waves throughout the empire. Eternal Rome had fallen! Since Christianity had been in ascendancy less than a century, it was blamed for the fall. The pagan gods were venting their wrath. In 412 Augustine began writing *The City of God* (considered by many to be his greatest work) in order to show that destruction was the logical outcome of a civilization like that of Rome. The twenty-two books of this monumental opus were not finished until 426, just four years before the death of Augustine, when the Vandals were besieging Hippo.

Augustine himself explains the outline. The first five books refute the argument that the destruction of Rome resulted from the ban that Christianity placed on pagan cults. The next five books expose the worship of pagan deities as a poor investment for life after death. These ten books are highly polemical, journalistic in style, primarily negative. The next twelve books, Augustine noted, are "devoted expressly to meeting the criticism that we have refuted other positions but have not declared our own." Books 11–14 trace the rise of the divine and earthly cities; 15–18, their growth; and 19–22, their proper ends.

For Augustine history has a beginning and an end; it is not an eternal repetition of cycles. It begins in creation, climaxes in Christ, and concludes on the day of judgment. Conflict between the cities of God and man provides history's drama. The real causes of worldly catastrophe stem from assertions of arrogant pride and self-sufficiency, seen first in the revolt of the angels and then in human rebellion. God is the source of all good, but in the Fall Adam wilfully turned to himself, to the world of creatures. Disoriented, humanity now can achieve only relative goods—of which the earthly city is one. But God grants grace to a selected few who, in directing their love toward God, form the heavenly city. The two cities, commingled in this world, vie with each other throughout history, but in the church the city of God has begun its fulfillment.

The earthly city and the heavenly city, relatively identified with the state and the church respectively, are formed by love (*amor*), which motivates all our actions. Love directed toward the creature is *cupiditas;* it can never bring complete happiness. Love directed toward God is *caritas;* it alone holds the possibility of complete happiness. Love of self (the creature) to the exclusion of God creates the earthly city; love of God to the exclusion of self creates the heavenly city. The state is not completely bad, nor the church completely good. They are approximations of the two cities.

Profound pessimism pervades Augustine's conception of all earthly institutions. Human sinfulness renders all our achievements less than good. Sin roots in the Fall, which contaminated the whole human race. Yet, even before the Fall, God predestined some to be saved by grace; these constitute the true city of God. Through God's grace they seek happiness not in creaturely ends but in God who alone is the source of eternal happiness. All others seek happiness in inferior objects, and continually meet with pathetic failure. People are filled with self-centered drives for power, glory, wealth, pleasure. They lust, hate, pretend, and cheat. In seeking for themselves, they set up their own selfish standards. Anarchy would result except that enlightened self-interest establishes some order for self-preservation. Thus the state came into existence, to keep people from exterminating each other. The state is one utilitarian means of curbing greed. God permitted, but did not create, the earthly city or state. It guarantees relative peace and order, relatively curbs violence; its basis is self-seeking; it exists because of immorality; it is a dyke against sin. In our self-centeredness we vie for advantages. The strong conquer; the weak submit to find some peace rather than annihilation. Kingdoms rise and fall; their foundations make it impossible for them to endure. God's providence allows some to last longer than others, depending on whether they promote the relatively higher goods, such as justice and liberty. A kingdom without justice is but piracy on a large scale, but in the end all kingdoms in this world are ephemeral.

Augustine conceives of God saving individuals, not political regimes, for the Christian's home is not in this world where coercive power prevails. Yet Christians are not to abandon worldly affairs; they are to submit to political authority. They are to help mitigate violence, sin, and injustice, not for themselves, for Christians really need no government, but because God commands them to love. Also, it is better to have secular society ruled by good people. Christians should tolerate imperfect governments, cooperate, and obey, so long as they command nothing contrary to the word of God. Thereby God exercises the righteous. Christians are pilgrims in the world, living now by faith, using the state's peace, acknowledging the state's relative goodness, but looking to the hereafter.

Against culture Augustine places Christian eschatology. History moves by the providence of God toward the elimination of the state and the enthronement of the heavenly city as the one and only final society. Only in God can be found the happiness, peace, and order that all seek. This is profoundly presented in Book 19. Augustine believed in resurrection. At death, the soul and body separate; but on the final day of resurrection all decayed bodies will in an instant rejoin souls. Thus Augustine rejects a final dichotomizing of soul and body. The misery and eternal death of the damned will be their estrangement from the life of God. The happiness and eternal life of the saved will be just the opposite.

The final and eternal union of soul and body as seen in the *Enchiridion* and *The City of God* indicates the extent to which Augustine basically rejected Manichean and Neoplatonic thought. For Augustine the body is not extraneous to the real person, even though Augustine believed that in this world, because of sin, ascetic practices are necessary to reorganize human priorities—the ultimate goal being God. He maintained a dualism of Creator-creature, not soul-body. Instead of eternal emanation or eternal realms, Augustine depicts a personal God whose creative act brought the universe into being. God created matter; it is not evil. Members of the Trinity are not emanations of the One; they are consubstantial, equal. To speak of one is to speak of all. Nevertheless, Augustine makes numerous allusions to and eulogizes Neoplatonism. This is especially strong from the time of Augustine's conversion to the writing of the *Confessions*, and then it fades, leaving behind a tint, if not a discoloration, on the doctrinal fabric woven by Augustine the theologian-churchman. Neoplatonism influenced Augustine to love God for the sake of self-fulfillment, whereas the New Testament emphasizes self-giving as a consequence of what God has done for man.

The question about the abiding influence of Neoplatonism raises one final question concerning the authority, or presuppositions, of Augustine. On what does the mature Augustine finally rest his case? The answer has multiple facets, as if to match the rich variety of his life and thought. True to the earlier affirmation of the church in its struggle for authority, Augustine appeals first to Scripture. Scripture is for him "the supreme and heavenly pinnacle of authority" (*Letters*, 82). To the canonical Scriptures alone the Christian owes unhesitating assent (*On Nature and Grace*, 61). He insists on the absolute authority of every word of Scripture; none of it can be treated as unauthoritative without endangering the whole. Christians are to be subject to the Scriptures; they are not to subject the Scriptures to themselves (*Against the Manichean Faustus*, 32; *Letters*, 40).

But the supreme authority of the Scriptures depends on their apostolicity, and behind the apostles stands Christ. The Scriptures via the apostles link us to the revelation in Christ. Human beings wrote the Scriptures, but they were inspired by the Spirit, and in one place at the end of the *Harmony of the Gospels*, Augustine argues that Christ wrote the Scriptures because we are members of the body of Christ, who is the head. The apostles were the agents for the establishing of the church, the transmitting of God's will, and the embodying of the will in Scripture. To the authority of the revelation of Christ in the apostolic Scriptures Augustine repeatedly appeals.

However, since everything is not contained in Scripture, Augustine also appeals to the generally accepted custom of the church, to tradition, because the church gives continual expression to the revelation. The church also safeguards the transmission and authenticity of the Scriptures: "I would not believe the Gospel except I were moved thereto by the authority of the Catholic Church." By this Augustine means the testimony of the whole universal church, from the beginning to the present, which bears witness to the canonical Scriptures. He does not limit the living authority of the church to the contemporary church. He also appeals to universal over local councils, and acknowledges that later councils may have more insight than earlier ones, because of experience.

Behind Augustine's appeals to Scripture and the church stands his doctrine of sin and the necessity of grace to restore us to a right relationship with God. Sin abrogates general revelation for us and necessitates special revelation and grace. The church is the keeper of the Scriptures, which bear the revelation, and it is in the church that gradual growth toward full restoration in the city of God occurs. The church mediates between sinners and that which can again lead them to truth. Although Augustine also brings reason to bear on various beliefs and customs and appeals to individual leaders, he returns to the revelation in Scripture as his basic authority—safeguarded against misappropriation by the continuity of apostolic succession and tradition.

Still another aspect of authority finds expression in Augustine—existential faith. This was Augustine's own experience. Apart from a redirection of the will through the grace of God (predestination, election), the Scriptures and the church hold no special authority. In the historical order, Scriptures and the church constitute Augustine's authority. In the order of living experience, faith is primary, even though Augustine's own experience of conversion was not apart from biblical and church influences.

Augustine died while the Vandals were besieging Hippo, but he left the church with a philosophy of history that transcends destruction and tragedy. Neither happiness nor salvation depends on what transpires in this world. During the Middle Ages the church became increasingly identified with the city of God, lessening the effect of Augustine's eschatology in its bearing on culture, and progress became the secularized form of Augustine's view of history.

7

Imperial Disintegration, Papal Ascendancy

In the fifth century the vaunted Roman Empire in the West crumbled rapidly, so that Emperors Honorius (395–423) and Valentinian III (425–55) presided over a dying regime. Between them came the usurper Joannes, and after them ten more rulers in the span of twenty-one years. Alaric, the Visigoth, in 401 made his first but unsuccessful incursion into Italy. In 406 the Vandals crossed the frozen Rhine River and overran Gaul. In 408 Alaric again invaded Italy, besieged Rome, but left on receipt of ransom. However, when Honorius refused to grant Alaric's request for the Visigoths to settle permanently in northern Italy, he put Attalus on the throne in Rome, and consigned Honorius to virtual exile. In 409 Rome withdrew its legions from Britain. In the following year Alaric captured and sacked Rome, sending psychic reverberations through the empire. However, no massacre occurred; Alaric issued orders that life should be spared. He wanted recognition for himself and his people, and regarded Rome as necessary to his plans. In the East his military prowess had gained permission for the Visigoths to settle in Bulgaria and he had been recognized as master of Illyricum, but in Italy violent anti-German feeling blocked any share in government. Shortly after the capture of Rome Alaric died, and leadership passed to his brother Ataulf, who regarded himself as more or less a servant of the Roman Empire. Ataulf married the sister of Emperor Honorius and withdrew into southern Gaul, where he checked the Vandals and eventually settled in Aquitaine. Honorius regained his throne in 416, and the Vandals retreated into Spain, where they laid waste the country. With the aid of the East, Valentinian III was enthroned in 425 at the age of six, but he and his mother coped poorly with the rapid events. When Gaiseric became king of the Vandals in 428, they crossed over into Africa, pillaging and plundering, forcing Rome to acknowledge them first as *foederati* (Roman subjects bound by treaty to Rome) and then after the fall of Carthage in 439 as sovereign rulers of North Africa. The Vandals' naval fleets freely raided the coasts of Italy and Sicily, and little-known other barbarians breached remote parts of the empire. Valentinian did temporarily halt Attila the Hun, in 451, but he murdered his best general Aetius, and was in turn murdered by Maximus, who married his widow Eudoxia. To keep the Huns from taking over Italy, Eudoxia called in the Vandals, who sacked and plundered Rome for fourteen days. Following Valentinian, ten weak rulers held sway, until Odovakar, leader of the Herulian and other German bands in the pay of Rome, deposed Romulus Augustulus, the last of the imperial line in the West. By 476 the ancient Roman Empire had come to an end.

This was the fluid, unstable political situation in which the papacy was forced to forge its way. It was the one enduring institution in a cultural vacuum, and had three advantages: the strong leadership of Pope Leo I (440–61), who insisted on the primacy of the Roman bishop over all other ecclesiastics and secular rulers; a band of devoted men in the monks, who were further organized and mobilized for the Middle Ages through the work of Benedict of Nursia; and a philosophy in Augustine's *City of God* that allowed the church to withstand the fluctuations of the earthly city. In the long struggle that ensued between church and state during the next thousand years, the papacy proved to be the overall architect that shaped Western Europe.

While the West struggled with the barbarians, the Eastern church struggled with theological niceties, and in the process became more and more subservient to the state. Following the Council of Constantinople in 381, disputes over the relation of the divinity and humanity in the Incarnation disrupted the East. How could one conceive of the human-divine in the historical Christ? As the bishop of Constantinople (428–31), Nestorius attacked the propriety of calling the Virgin Mary the Mother of God, a practice gaining in popularity with the growing devotion to Mary. For political as well as theological reasons, Cyril of Alexandria and the Egyptian monks opposed Nestorius. Both sides appealed to Rome, which in 430 voted against Nestorius, and in 431 the Council of Epheseus summoned by the emperor pronounced a sentence of deposition on Nestorius, sending him back to his old monastery at Antioch. In 435 the emperor condemned Nestorius' books and in 436 banished him to exile in Upper Egypt. Nestorius apparently believed in two different natures and two different persons in Christ. Only the human nature was born and developed through the stages of human growth, for one could hardly speak of God being two years old! Nestorius postulated a conjunction rather than a union of the natures. He championed the humanity of Jesus in opposition to the monophysitism that developed later in the thought of

Eutyches, an elderly monk of Constantinople. Eutyches and his supporters emphasized the godhead of Christ so strongly that they came to deny the humanity of Jesus. The controversy raged on, embroiling almost all of the East.

At the Council of Chalcedon in 451, some 500–600 bishops, all but two from the East, voted to accept the doctrine in Pope Leo's tome that Christ was truly human and divine, and that in the historical Christ "each nature preserves its own characteristics without diminution." The Council specifically repudiated the views of Nestorius and Eutyches and asserted the doctrine of One Person in Two Natures in Christ. But the controversy continued to disrupt the empire. The Nestorians, who withdrew to Persia, and the Monophysites, who became strong in Syria and Egypt, actually posed the threat of dismemberment of the empire. These opponents clashed frequently in bloody violence and riots.

When Zeno became emperor (474–91), he resolved to bring the factions together and in 482 issued his *Henotikon* or Edict of Reunion. The *Henotikon* reaffirmed the faith published by the "318 holy Fathers assembled at Nicaea" and confirmed by "the 150 holy Fathers in council at Constantinople" as the "irreproachable faith" of the empire. It anathematized Nestorius and Eutyches and their followers, and asserted that Christ "is one, not two," in no wise divided or phantomized. But by suggesting that there may have been error at Chalcedon and by presuming that the state could settle a question of faith, the *Henotikon* aroused the ire of the papacy. Pope Felix III (483–92) anathematized the emperor and the bishops who subscribed to it and was in turn excommunicated by Patriarch Acacius in 484, creating a schism that lasted until the ascension of Justin (518–27).

Justin, known for his cruelty and ignorance, reaffirmed the definition of Chalcedon, literally forcing the two-nature-one-person doctrine on the Eastern churches, and his nephew Justinian (527–65) succeeded temporarily in restoring the religious unity of the East and West. Justinian reconquered North Africa from the Vandals in 534; wrested control of Italy from the Ostrogoths, after their king Theodoric the Great (493–526) had taken it from Odovakar; and extended his rule over Sicily, Illyricum, and Dalmatia. While he reasserted orthodoxy, he also personified Caesaropapism, taking it upon himself to close the last of the pagan academies in Athens, persecute the Marcionites and Samaritans, destroy Egyptian temples, condemn Origen, and segregate the Jews. Justinian insisted that the monarch's will was supreme over all political and ecclesiastical affairs and thus legitimized Caesaropapism in subsequent Byzantine history. The Justinian Code of 529, revised in 534, harmonized Roman law with Christian ideas. It began with a statement of faith and anathemas against heretics, and exerted great influence on the further development of Western Europe. Although Justinian built churches, palaces, public baths, and monasteries throughout the empire, his greatest architectural achievement was the magnificent Hagia Sophia in Constantinople in 538, whose enormous dome evokes a feeling of ethereality.

But theological debate continued to rack the East. In the seventh century monotheletism occupied the central forum. Was Christ's will divine, human, or both? Did he have one, two, or three wills? Emperor Heraclius (610–41) and Pope Honorius (625–38) agreed on the "one will of our Lord Jesus Christ," only to have the Sixth Ecumenical Council of Constantinople in 681 issue a statement that each of the two natures in Christ operates with a will proper to it. But by that time the East had its hands full trying to ward off the Persians at the beginning of the century and after them the Muslims. (For further developments, see Chapter 8.)

MOHAMMED

The Persian expansion under Chosroës II (589–628) ravaged the Near East and Egypt, and Chosroës' armies camped within a mile of Constantinople, briefly restoring Persia's boundaries to those attained by Darius I. But by the time of Chosroës' death, Heraclius had successfully turned the tide back, and a new challenger from the Arabian deserts had arisen.

Little is known about the life of Mohammed (570–632), founder of one of the world's major religions. Orphaned at the age of six, he grew up under the guardianship of an uncle in the Quraysh tribe, which had control of the Ka'bah and the food concessions for the thousands of visiting pilgrims. The Ka'bah—with its sacred Black Stone, idols associated with biblical and Arabian history, and the Zemzem well kicked up by the infant Ishmael when Hagar left him to search for water (Genesis 21:8–21)— served as a national religious shrine for the Arabs. Mohammed's early acquaintance with religion left him with a resolve to do something about the idolatrous worship connected with the Ka'bah's goddesses, phallic symbols, angels, fairies, jinn, and the ghouls who robbed graves to obtain flesh for their midnight orgies. He disliked the drunkenness and gambling which often led to quarrels and warfare among tribesmen, and he hated the burying of unwanted infants. His feelings about religion enlarged when he made caravan trips to Syria and Palestine, first as a camel driver with his uncle Abu Talib, and later as the business manager of the rich widow Khadijah, whom he married. He conducted business with Jews and Christians and later liberated and adopted the Christian slave boy Zaid. His two sons by Khadijah died in childhood; only one of four daughters, Fatima, survived. Wider religious contacts and increased time for leisure caused him to reflect for long periods on religion. He often went to the hills about Mecca just to brood. One night while in a cave on Mt. Hira, he had a vision of the angel Gabriel telling him to recite. He went home and produced the entire ninety-sixth sura of the Koran. Thinking that he might be insane, he said he waited for a second appearance, at which time Gabriel commissioned him a Prophet of the Lord. After that, the revelations that constitute the Koran came frequently.

In the marketplace Mohammed began proclaiming the Day of the Lord, a day of doom for those who had cheated, lied, and not cared for the poor and orphaned. He believed strongly in a day of resurrection, final judgment, and everlasting fire. People were struck by the unusual flow of poetic inspiration from his lips, but they were also unconvinced. After four years he had made only forty converts, most of them from his immediate family, some slaves, and some women. The Quraysh, disturbed by his constant attacks on the Ka'bah and its idols, sought to break up his meetings by hurling filth on him and his hearers. When both his protectors, Khadijah and Abu Talib, died, more violent measures followed, until Mohammed feared for his life. This was the time when six men from Medina, a city 300 miles to the north, sought him as the leader who might bring their city's two tribes together. In 622 he and his followers made their great Hegira to Medina, just in time to escape being assassinated.

There he became the undisputed leader of a religious theocracy, getting much of his sustenance from robbing caravans from Mecca—which instigated the Meccan war in 630. By digging a ditch around Medina, Mohammed warded off the Meccans, and in a bold counterattack captured their city. Within eight years Mohammed had become the strongest chieftain in Arabia! Although he stripped the Ka'bah of its idols and images, he paid tribute to the Black Stone and magnanimously granted amnesty to his opponents.

By 632 Mohammed was dead, but he had already set in motion beliefs that would unify the Arabian peoples in one brotherhood. He stopped child exposure and outlawed tribal fighting. He established laws against adultery, drinking, gambling, defrauding; he elevated the status of women and provided for the protection of orphans. By violent as well as non-violent means he consolidated the Arabs' religious energies in the worship of one God, Allah, whose will was made known in the prophet Mohammed and in the Koran. He inspired them with the conviction that to them the final revelation had been made; that Adam, Noah, Abraham, Moses, and Jesus were but forerunners of the greatest prophet; that they were divinely appointed to bring all peoples into submission to the will of God. This sense of divine guidance produced in the Muslims (the submitters) a fanatical determination that manifested itself in sweeping conquests. They were not afraid to die, believing that death in combat on behalf of Allah would ensure entrance into paradise. If they lived and won, they reaped the rewards of booty. By 635 their armies had conquered Damascus. Jerusalem fell in 638, and by 640 all of Palestine and Syria. By 641 all of Egypt had succumbed, and the Muslims had begun their advance across North Africa. To the East they conquered Iraq in 637, and by 649 had subdued all of Persia. After a twelve-year campaign ending in 652, the Muslims controlled most of Asia Minor. In subsequent years they pushed into Chinese Turkestan and Mongolia and southward into India. After traversing the plains and deserts of North Africa, their armies swept through Spain into France and were defeated at Tours in 732 by Charles Martel's Franks.

Although Christianity survived in North Africa and the Near East, it was decidedly modified. Thousands of Christians became Muslims; the remainder were effectively cut off from the rest of Christendom for centuries to come. Constantinople maintained itself against the Muslims until 1453, and by that time had expanded northeastward into the vast areas of Russia. Rome was absorbed in creating a civilization among the "barbarians" of the West.

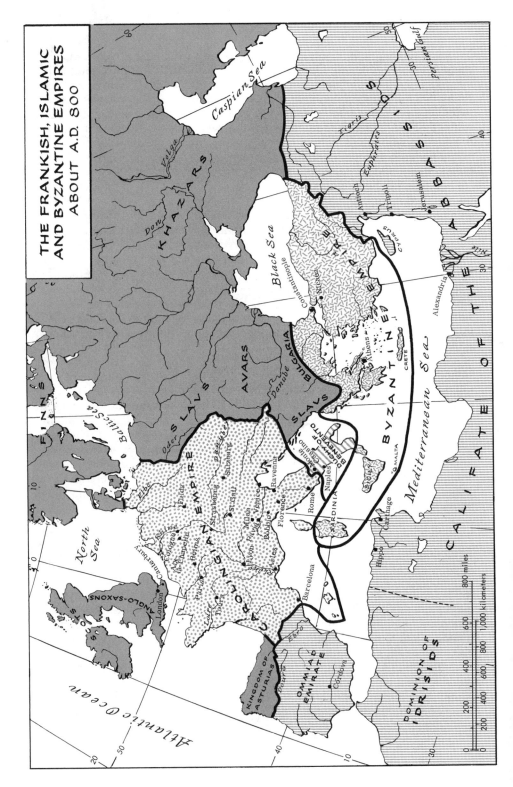

THE FRANKISH, ISLAMIC
AND BYZANTINE EMPIRES
ABOUT A.D. 800

CaspianSea

Volga

KHAZARS

Don

Black Sea

BULGARIA

Danube

AVARS

SLAVS

SLAVS

Constantinople

Nicaea

Athens

CRETE

BYZANTINE

EMPIRE

Mediterranean Sea

FINNS

Baltic Sea

Oder

Elbe

CAROLINGIAN EMPIRE

Danube

Regensburg

Salzburg

Fulda

Rhine

St. Gall

Milan

Ravenna

Bobbio

Venice

Florence

Rome

Naples

MONTE CASSINO

BENEVENTO

SPOLETO

Cologne

Aix-la-Chapelle

Reims

Paris

Lyon

Rhône

Arles

SARDINIA

SICILY

MALTA

CALIFATE OF THE ABBASIDS

Tigris

Euphrates

Antioch

Tripoli

Jerusalem

Damascus

CYPRUS

NILE

Alexandria

Persian Gulf

North
Sea

ANGLO-SAXONS

Canterbury

London

Tours

Strasbourg

Barcelona

Ebro

KINGDOM OF
ASTURIAS

Douro

OMMIAD
EMIRATE

Cordova

Tagus

Hippo

Carthage

DOMINION OF
IDRISIDS

Atlantic Ocean

0   200 400 600 800 miles
0 200 400 600 800 1,000 kilometers

PAPAL PRIMACY

Rome's most stabilizing force during the fifth century was the papacy's unflinching assertion of primacy, a dogma that helped to insure its independence from Eastern Caesaropapism and to secure dominion over the developing barbarian empires. Geography and politics were factors in this development, but hardly as important as the people's faith that Rome's authority through its double apostolic succession from Peter and Paul was more to be trusted than that of other traditions. Jerusalem had suffered destruction twice, and the East seemed continuously embroiled in theological-political rivalries. Rome alone seemed stable. Ignatius pointed to the primacy of Rome; Clement of Rome upheld Roman unity as a model for Christendom; Victor excommunicated churches that did not subscribe to Rome's date for Easter and excommunicated Theodotus for denying the divinity of Christ; Irenaeus urged churches to agree with Rome as a matter of necessity; Tertullian spoke of the bishop of Rome as the "bishop of bishops"; Cyprian mentioned the bishop of Rome as succeeding to the place of Peter; the Council of Sardica in 343 gave deposed bishops the right to appeal to Rome, said Rome should be consulted about vacant bishoprics, and granted Roman bishops the right to adjudicate quarrels, etc. The tradition was impressive.

Although Stephen of Rome invoked Matthew 16:18 in his quarrel with Cyprian over baptism, the Petrine text was not seriously used as a foundation for primacy until the time of Pope Damasus (366–84). He commissioned Jerome's Vulgate translation, promulgated a biblical canon, acted as the judge of all religious matters, and claimed that the Council of Nicaea was authoritative only because his predecessor, Pope Sylvester, had approved its decisions. Pope Innocent I (402–17) also asserted that no religious question should be decided without Rome's cognizance. However, not until Pope Leo I (440–61) was papal primacy asserted in the full sense. Leo was convinced that the Lord had committed to him, the successor of St. Peter, the care of the whole church. He insisted people should honor Peter through him, and declared resistance to his authority was a sure way to hell. He exegeted "Petra" in Matthew 16:18ff. as referring to Peter and his confession, and Christ as the "rock" on which the church is built, but he held that by transfer of authority the Lord made Peter the rock in virtue of his confession, and on him built the indestructible church. The keys, he declared, were committed to Peter specifically and to the other disciples generally, and that Rome therefore has a primacy reaching back to Christ. Divine providence brought both Peter and Paul to Rome. Anyone who does not acknowledge the Roman bishop as head of the church is not of the body of the church.

Relentlessly Leo fought Pelagianism and Manicheism. Africa submitted to his authority by 443. He confirmed Anastasius of Thessalonica in his office but reserved the right of bishops under Anastasius to appeal to Rome. He fought heresies in Spain. He sent his Tome to Chalcedon in 451, not to be discussed, which he forbade, but as a statement to be received as from Peter himself. Leo boldly confronted Attila the Hun in 452 and turned him away. In 455 he deterred the Vandals from senseless slaughter, but could not prevent their looting and pillaging Rome.

Pope Gelasius I (492–96) furthered papal primacy by claims that priestly power is above kingly power and that there can be no legitimate appeal from the chair of Peter. In civil affairs, clergy are to submit to the emperor, but in ecclesiastical affairs, the emperor is to submit to the Pope. The fight from 498 to 506 between Symmachus and Laurentius for the papal throne did not enhance papal prestige. Bloody battles erupted, cloisters were burned, nuns insulted, priests murdered. Yet the decision of the Synod of Rome in 501, to accept Symmachus without further investigation on the ground that a council should not presume to judge a successor of Peter, did further papal primacy. Although Justin and Justinian rendered the papacy subservient de facto to the Eastern emperor for a time, Leo and Gelasius had already laid foundations for the expansion of papal power in the Middle Ages.

THE BENEDICTINES

A second stabilizing factor in the West during the breakup of the empire was the "Patriarch of Western monasticism," Benedict of Nursia (ca. 480–542). Formed to be self-sustaining, self-contained units, his monasteries were centers of stability, learning, art, and worship throughout Western Europe during the violent early centuries of the Middle Ages. His rule was first adopted in Italy, was carried to England by Augustine of Canterbury, where it clashed with Irish and Scottish monasticism, and was brought back to the Continent by missionaries in the seventh and eighth centuries. It was the universal rule for monasticism. Isolated as most of the monasteries were, for many of them it was their only link with Rome. Besides providing an example of religious living, Benedictine monasticism also inculcated a sense of Roman legal order.

Benedict spent his early life in a territory controlled by "barbarian" kings—Odovakar, the Visigoth who in 476 displaced the last of the old imperial line, and Theodoric (493–526), the Ostrogoth who murdered Odovakar at a banquet. Theodoric practiced religious tolerance for twenty-five years, saying that rulers who pretended to dictate in religious affairs were usurping the prerogative of God. But when the Eastern Emperor Justin, who accepted Nicene orthodoxy, tried to conquer the West and stirred many of the Catholics of Italy to rebellion against Theodoric's Arianism, the latter became ruthlessly intolerant and made Catholicism a crime. He put his friend Boethius to death. While in prison under sentence to die, Boethius wrote his classic, *The Consolation of Philosophy.*

Born at Nursia, educated in Rome, Benedict was so shocked by the immorality of his time that he retreated to the Abruzzi mountains and lived for years in a rocky cave near Subiaco. Many sought his advice, and a few nobles sent their children to him for instruction. In the environs of Rome he established twelve monasteries, each with twelve monks. In 525 Benedict established the famous monastery at Monte Cassino, near Naples.

The rule of St. Benedict centered in the Divine Office, around which was organized the monks' life of worship, work, and study. Although drawing freely on previous rules, especially St. Basil's, the rule of St. Benedict did not stress ascetic poverty, nor did it discourage possessions, thus enabling the Benedictines to do works of mercy. As the prologue indicated, the Benedictine's basic goal was to attain heaven by good deeds. The rule revolved about the abbot. He was chosen on the basis of merit by the whole group. If conniving brothers elected one who would abet their conniving, the area bishop could intervene. The abbot was not to rule autocratically but was to be considerate of needs and weaknesses, and was to seek counsel of the entire group in important matters. After receiving counsel, the abbot decided, and all brothers were expected to obey. The abbot was to be learned in the law, and able to deal gently but firmly with vice. If the monastery was large, he was to be assisted by deans. The abbot could at times impose special restrictions for discipline in "food, drink, sleep, chatter, and mirth," to insure special purifying, praying, and abstaining.

Joining the monastery was not easy. One had to knock and suffer insults for four or five days before being allowed inside. An older brother was then assigned to observe and judge the seeker for his fitness to join. After months of testing, the seeker took vows and promises before the entire congregation and was admitted.

The Benedictine monks owned everything in common except the few necessary possessions that were given to each—cowl, tunic, shoes, socks, girdle, knife, pen, needle, handkerchief, and tablet—but even these were gifts and had to be returned when new ones were issued. They were not to *own* anything. Their beds were frequently searched to prevent the hiding of personal items. Their clothing was to be only what the climate dictated, the cheapest sort, and they had an extra cowl and tunic solely to permit washing. Gifts and letters could be received only on permission of the abbot. All shared according to need.

The day was carefully divided to allow for work, worship, study, and sleep, but the schedule could be varied. Praises were to be given to God seven times daily. During the two daily meals (three in case of demanding labor), a brother read from the Bible or a suitable book. The daily allowance of food included a pound loaf of bread, a pint of wine, two cooked vegetables, and fruit in season; there was no meat except in cases of illness. Monks assigned to kitchen duty received an extra slice of bread and cup of wine. Fasts occurred frequently. Silence was enjoined at all times, with severe penalties for breaking it. During periods for study, supervisors checked to see that all were so engaged. The monks slept on separate beds in one large room, if possible, with a candle burning. They slept clothed. At a given signal they arose and began the day. Contumacious and disobedient brothers were excommunicated if they did not change after three warnings. The sick and guests received special treatment. The sick could eat meat and take a bath. Guests could arrive at all hours; rich or poor they were to be received with elaborate bowing and the kiss of peace. A special guest kitchen was maintained. The sick and guests were to be welcomed as one would welcome Christ. These self-contained Benedictine monasteries with their own water, garden, mill, bakery, and different trades, became centers of hospitality, learning, worship, and liturgical art—beacons of light in the Dark Ages.

Between 580 and 590 the Lombards destroyed Monte Cassino, scattering the monks, causing most of them to go to Rome. There the rule was adopted and carried to England by Augustine of Canterbury and back to the Continent by missionaries headed by Boniface, who in 751 crowned Pepin king of the Franks, the dominant people of the time.

Through its monasteries, especially Benedictine monasticism, the church became the transmitter of culture to the barbarians, who in the sixth through eighth centuries laid the foundations of nationalism in Western Europe. The barbarians were not simply wild savages. Some of them, like Alaric, had been in the service of Rome. Others like Ataulf married into highly situated Roman families. In general the barbarians had a lower civilization than that of Rome, but they were not without their own virtues. Their massive movements in the fifth and sixth centuries were prompted by pressures from peoples who had pushed across the Ural mountains into Europe from Asia. The Huns were among these. The extended frontier lines of the empire could not hold them back. They spilled across the Danube into the Balkan areas and across the Rhine into the plains of Gaul. When they could, they settled into agrarian patterns, sometimes beside the old Roman inhabitants, sometimes after subduing them. They were not marauding nomads, and they did not exterminate the old populace, but they did appropriate land and property. In their settlements, the old populace frequently outnumbered the newcomers. The religion and the language of Rome tended to prevail, so that Catholicism and Latin eventually became two of the Middle Ages' most visible universals. The invaders were superstitious and were mystified by the claims and deeds of the church. When Pope Leo I boldly confronted Attila and Gaiseric, it was said Peter and Paul walked beside him. Some of them were already nominally Arian Christians, having been touched, even though remotely, by the missionary activities of men like Ulfilas (ca. 311–83). His maternal grandparents had been carried off in a Gothic raid, and when he became a Christian bishop he resolved to take the gospel to the Visigoths. He invented the Gothic alphabet and translated the Bible into the Gothic tongue, so that through Ulfilas many of the barbarians knew something about Arian Christianity. Yet sermons like those of the bishop of Braga indicate a vulgar culture of divinations, auguries, incantations, and even the worship of mice and moths along with Christianity as late as 550. In the fusion that eventually came between the invaders and the older settlers, a violent rural society emerged. Lines of communication were disrupted, currencies of exchange folded, and London and Paris became relatively small villages. The church itself became rural, landholding. Missionaries had to be self-supporting. The Benedictines had a structure for just such a situation.

The barbarians were also tribal and eventually moved into tribalism's larger form—nationalism. Because leadership and authority came from the tribal head, the prince prevailed over the priest, and a continuing struggle between the Roman church and the state church marked the Middle Ages. Later this rivalry is called Gallicanism vs. Ultramontanism.

Pacifism as the Christian way faded into the background when church and state joined under Constantine and faded even more with the influence of the barbarians. They were warlike, tyrannical; took their priests into battle with them; made Peter who cut off the soldier's ear their patron saint; sewed the cross instead of the horsetail on their banners. To Augustine's idea of the just war they added a dimension of honor and glory in conquest and inaugurated the Crusades. What greater honor and glory than to fight infidels and heretics for God! The church conceiving itself as the representative of God on earth readily employed them. The earlier church-state partnership by 416 said only Christians could serve in the army. But the militant crusading church went farther. It chose violence as a major means of extending and defending the gospel. The shift came gradually but ineluctably. Generally the barbarians were heavy drinkers, but they were more chaste than the Latins and were shocked by the immorality in the empire. Sylvanian, an historian, said the barbarians were allowed to overrun the empire because they were better men. Attila the Hun was known as "the Scourge of God," a minister of God's vengeance. Augustine pictured Rome's inner corruption as the cause of its collapse.

In the three centuries following the fall of Rome, the barbarians carved out places for themselves in the old Roman empire and became the new political leaders of Europe. In the fusion they and the church were changed. The church became a feudal institution, but a strong papacy and monasticism infused society with Christian culture.

The conversion of the Franks through Clovis (466–511) proved to be a signal victory of the church, for the Frankish kingdom dominated Western Europe in the succeeding centuries. Clovis passed directly from paganism to the Nicene faith, perhaps because he saw that it would widen his support among the older populations and aid him in his conquests. This may also have motivated his marriage to Clothilda, a Catholic, in 493. Their first son was baptized a Christian but died shortly afterward, and when their second son became ill, Clovis blamed Christianity. However, Clothilda prayed successfully for her son's recovery, and Clovis went into a battle with the Alemanni promising that he would become a Christian if Christ would grant him victory against what seemed to be overwhelming odds. Clovis won, and kept his promise. On Christmas day, 496, he and 3,000 of his soldiers were baptized in the cathedral at Rheims. He extended his kingdom from the Rhine to the Pyrenees by driving the Visigoths into Spain. In 508 he chose Paris as his capital, and united two of the major factions among Franks by prompting a son to patricide and then taking vengeance on the murderer. At best Clovis' Christianity was crude; he ruled with violence, once splitting the head of a soldier for breaking a vase he wanted. Clothilda spent her last days after Clovis' death in the abbey of St. Martin of Tours, saddened by the internecine war of her sons. Chilperic (561–84), one of the worst of the Merovingian line, displayed exceptional cruelty by inflicting blindness on any who dared to disobey his commands. From the *History of the Franks* of Gregory of Tours we learn much about the times. One queen ordered her physicians to be executed if they failed to cure her. They were. A duke buried one of his servants and a maid alive because they were married without his consent. Sexual immoralities were rife, even among bishops, contrary to the chastity of the Germanic tribes pictured by Tacitus about four hundred years earlier. A set of Salic laws from about 500 shows that rape was punishable but the fines were not heavy, nor was the fine for killing a Roman. Laws against drawing blood with one's fists, and inflicting wounds that left the brain exposed or gashes extending from the ribs to the entrails, indicate a heavy degree of personal injury. Women could not inherit land. Laws against stealing pigs, sheep, cattle, and fences show not only an agricultural life base but also the fact of such theft.

In the seventh century the royal Merovingian line from Clovis became increasingly degenerate, and practical rule passed into the hands of the powerful mayors of the palace. One of these was Charles Martel, who won fame in 732 by defeating the Muslim Moors at Tours, a small town only one hundred miles from Paris. Whereas Charles did not claim kingship, his son Pepin the Short was elected and crowned king of the Franks. He was crowned first by Boniface the missionary in 751 and then by the Pope in 754, doubly signifying that royal kingship is bestowed by the church. This was the beginning of the Carolingian line of Frankish kings, so called because of its greatest member, Carolus Magnus, Charlemagne (742–814). Throughout this period the church had its difficulties; often there seemed to be little difference between the barbarians and the nominal representatives of Christianity; but Christian culture, though compromised, gradually prevailed.

A second signal victory for the church was the acceptance of Roman Christianity at the Synod of Whitby in England in 664, made possible by the foresight of one of the greatest of the medieval Popes, Gregory I (590–604). Gregory was born in Rome in 540, just fifteen years before the demise of the Ostrogothic kingdom in Italy. He grew up midst the victories of the Lombards, who under their king Alboin carved out a kingdom in Italy that lasted from 568 to 774. Gregory was the principal reason why the Lombards did not conquer all of Italy in his lifetime. He was the actual ruler of the Italian peninsula. Through him papal primacy in spiritual matters and Roman order in secular affairs made their impact on the new kingdoms of Western Europe.

As the son of a Roman nobleman, Gregory at first sought a career in civil administration. At the age of thirty-three he was prefect of Rome, in charge of the city's grain supplies, aqueducts and sewers, finances, and other civil affairs. But Gregory's mystical longings drew him toward monasticism, and in 574 he sold his family estates in Sicily. He used part of the money to found six monasteries in Sicily, one in Rome, and distributed the rest to the poor. He entered the monastery in Rome, hoping to lead a life of contemplation, but was called back by the Pope to be an envoy seeking aid from the court of Constantinople. He got no help and in 585 returned to Rome to become abbot of his monastery. His contemplations resulted in the writing of his famous commentary on Job, the *Magna Moralia,* a work used as a model of exegesis throughout the Middle Ages. Drawing on Augustine and Origen, he probed the literal, allegorical, and moral meanings of passages of Job, not mechanically, but with a certain flair. He warns against obscuring the plain clarity of some passages and delves into the mysteries of others. Of the passage in Job 31, which enjoins acts of love toward the poor, widows, and orphans, he says: "It [love] is like a river, both shallow and deep; in it a lamb may walk and an elephant swim."

Gregory accepted his election to the papacy by the people and clergy of Rome only after an inward struggle, for he longed to escape the prison house of this world of flesh. However, his skill and integrity were obviously needed. Floods, famine, bubonic plague, and a Lombard invasion were threatening to wipe out the city. The East was unable and unwilling to help. Believing firmly in angels, demons, and the power of relics, Gregory led a penitential procession to rid the city of the illness, and legend says that the likeness of a plague angel sheathing his sword appeared in the sky over the mausoleum of Hadrian. He set the civil affairs of Rome in order, collected taxes, provided for welfare, repaired buildings and streets, and raised and trained an army to repel the incursions of the Lombards. Technically he was under the emperor, but in fact he acted independently, and in 592–93 he concluded a significant treaty of peace with the Lombards. On his own authority he appointed governors over certain areas and increased his own papal patrimony until the papacy was the largest, wealthiest, and most powerful institution in all of Italy. Like Pope Leo, he believed that he was a servant of the servants of God, that the papacy was established by God to oversee all ecclesiastical and political affairs, and that he should not hesitate to assert what was God's will. When the patriarch in Constantinople claimed the title of "universal bishop," he objected on the grounds that it wantonly affronted the authority of the Roman see established by God. He deliberately heard appeals from Eastern clergy against their patriarch and blocked the Empress Constantia's attempt to move the head of St. Paul to a church she was constructing.

The state's duty, he said, is to provide conditions for the church's work. The marks of the true church, i.e. Roman, are holiness, for it includes and can develop saints; unity, for it stands against heretics and schismatics; universalism, for it embraces all; sacerdotalism, for it is the proper channel of salvation; and apostolicity, for it has an authoritative succession from Christ. This concept conflicted with the barbarians' tribal concept of using priests as mere spokesmen for the community. In the following centuries, Gregory's view prevailed.

Although Gregory is one of the four Latin doctors of the church, along with Jerome, Ambrose, and Augustine, he was far from an original theologian. For the most part he restated Augustine's views and missed their profundity. But what he advocated suited and helped shape the medieval mind. He regarded the number of the elect as fixed, but seemed to dismiss the implied determinism, insisting that one can be rescued from the fetters of original sin by Christ through baptism, and that after baptism, sins can be expiated by meritorious works, provided they are accompanied by penance. He considered the mass a repetition of the sacrifice of Christ that would benefit either the living or the dead. He helped fix the previously fluid belief in purgatory as a place for purification beyond this life by decreeing that such a belief was essential to faith.

The order with which Gregory conducted his affairs carried over into later times. He efficiently managed the papal estates. From his lands in Africa and Italy, manned by serfs and slaves, he imported materials for churches and monasteries and food for the populace. He collected money to ransom war captives, and ruled that a church should sell its sacred vessels for such purposes. People trusted him; funds rolled in. His annual income exceeded a million dollars. Yet he did not use it for himself. He believed strongly in eschatology, disdained human schemes, and lived as if he was facing death. He argued that order in society was essential if everyone was to fulfill his proper vocation and reflect the order of heaven. Only if order prevailed could diverse occupations contribute to the whole. Gregory conceived of this as a chain of command linking the priest to the bishop to the Pope. It proved to be a structure admirably fitted to medieval life.

In his book *Pastoral Care* written shortly after being elected Pope, Gregory described the true bishop—one who is thoroughly trained for his task, who has genuine spirituality, who despises pleasures of the flesh, understands people, and teaches by example; one who is devoted to preaching, to admonition against sin, and to being a minister instead of a master. Gregory gives practical instructions to thirty-six paired opposites: men-women, sick-well, rich-poor, joyful-sad, etc.

In his *Dialogues,* a collection of tales about holy men, Gregory displayed the deep credulity that marked his age. The second book is devoted to Benedict of Nursia, whom he greatly admired. The bygone saints had miraculous extrasensory perception revealing inward human thoughts; they raised the dead, cured the ill, predicted catastrophes, and altered the course of streams. Such pious credulity abetted similar attitudes in the Middle Ages. To Gregory is credited the Gregorian Sacramentary, one of the earliest forms of the Roman liturgy, which became standard in the Frankish kingdom. He also fostered the Roman school of cantors and probably authored the Gregorian chant, so important to medieval music.

One of Gregory's boldest acts was to extend papal sway beyond the Alps not only by interfering in local church affairs but also by sending Augustine with forty monks in 596 to reestablish the church in the British Isles, a move that proved to be extremely consequential for papal domination in the future (see Chapter 9, p. 106).

Gregory the Great is not unduly named; he permanently affected the spiritual and secular life of the Middle Ages.

8

Eastern Orthodoxy

Ecumenism has been a dominant motif in twentieth-century church history. Christians have come to recognize the painful limits of their divisions, leading a major portion of Christendom to draw back together in witness to the universalism of the Gospel. But at mid-century most expressions of Christian unity had yet to include in their conversations one-third of the Christian world, the Eastern Orthodox Church.

Americans have usually been heedless of the Orthodox, with their few numbers representing a mere peculiar minority. In the popular Protestant mind the identity of Orthodoxy is somehow confused with Roman Catholicism, allowing the enemies of ecumenism from the political and theological right to seize upon the misconception in their agitation against Christian unity. Carl McIntire, self-styled fundamentalist preacher, once assailed the prospect of including the Orthodox in the World Council of Churches by raising the ominous spectre of ritual cross-bearing, pompous banners, and candle processions to blur the rites of the Eastern Church with the "papal pageantry in the Vatican at St. Peter's." To be sure, the greatest fear he was able to arouse came from the fact that the greater part of Orthodox membership is Russian. Therefore, he would argue, their clerics must clearly be disguised Soviet agents in liturgical garb. Few have been convinced by McIntire's noisy polemic. After 1950 the ecumenical movement officially included the Orthodox Church. Yet most Christians of the Western world still regard Orthodoxy as somehow alien. Eastern Christianity remains mysteriously veiled to Western eyes. In so many respects the history of its life, its civilization and its language is not our story. Yet that seemingly remote half of Christendom has had the longest continuous Christian tradition. It has never been breached by a Protestant Reformation. The sixteenth-century upheaval that denied Rome's claim to catholicity continues to divide Christians of the West into Catholics and Protestants. But the break was not the first major schism to dismember the church as the body of Christ. The first rupture to sever Christendom came in 1054, after a series of tensions; East and West parted ways, cutting through the church's history with two separate traditions.

To understand Eastern Orthodoxy and the marks of its faith that distinguish it from the Western Christianity, we must return to examine the fundamental causes of the first great schism. At the same time, we can soberly note that the lingering division that politically alienates East and West had its beginnings in ecclesiastical history over a thousand years ago.

THE BYZANTINE EMPIRE

In 330, the Roman Emperor Constantine (311–37) moved the capital of the empire from Rome to the mouth of the Bosporus at the site of the ancient fortress town of Byzantium. The new city was consecrated to Christ and named Constantinople. There were good reasons for the change in location. The new capital was closer than Rome to the intersection of imperial trade routes. The site was also chosen as a proper spot for establishing a bulwark to withstand the onslaught of Eastern tribes. A barbarian people were migrating into the empire from the steppes of a vast uncharted region that would come to be known as Russia.

In the East, Christianity was able to mount enough strength to secure the faith from the competing ideologies and religions of the ancient world. In the West, the shift to Constantinople sharply diminished the political importance of Rome to the empire. However, new powers were unintentionally transferred to Rome's bishop, the Pope, and the papal office became the heir to Caesar's mantle. The result was of momentous consequence for the Western world. Rising in the power vacuum, the Pope achieved an enormous political authority. Henceforth, the papal office came into continued rivalry with secular rulers throughout the medieval period.

No such church-state rivalry existed in the Byzantine culture. In the East the term Caesaropapist best describes the relationship between secular and religious authorities. Briefly, it means the subordination of ecclesiastical affairs to monarchical control with frequent state interference into priestly functions. The consequence was a church made into a virtual department of the state apparatus. Though there were strong Byzantine critics of the arrangement, the primacy of the state over the church was never substantially altered. The eventual heir of Byzantine Christianity, the Russian Orthodox Church, easily adjusted to the concept, even under the post-revolutionary rule of the communist Soviet government. The problems of a church whose life is subjected to the intrigues of emperors and the whims of empresses will heavily mark every consideration of Eastern Orthodoxy.

The use of the term Caesaropapist to describe church-state relations of Orthodox Christendom brings protest from historians of the Byzantine. They point out that the emperor was never a priest and that he might be excommunicated by the patriarch. Time and again emperors were excommunicated and even driven into submission. The term preferred by Byzantinists to characterize the Eastern church-state pattern is _symphonia,_ or harmony, in which the spiritual and civil authorities each supported the other. Yet it must not be forgotten that the emperor controlled the election of the patriarch (the head of the Eastern church), and even conciliar decisions of the church were not valid without his consent.

The concept of _symphonia,_ however, needs a more thorough understanding if we are to grasp the cultural and religious significance of Eastern Orthodoxy. The notion allowed division of function in which the church left civil administration entirely in the hands of Christian rulers of state, while it attended to the enrichment of the liturgy and the rigors of contemplative life. But the whole of Byzantine society believed itself to be under the patronage of God and the Mother of God. The Virgin Mary would intervene at crucial moments in battle to deliver the enemy unto the faithful. The emperor was the Lord's anointed, after the manner of King David. The empire's successes were not attributed to sound policies but to the favor of heaven.

Nowhere is the concept of _symphonia_ more manifest than in Byzantine art and architecture. In the grandeur of the Hagia Sophia, a temple erected by Emperor Justinian (527–65), the harmony of Orthodoxy appears with dazzling brilliance. Against the towering heights of the dome, the Virgin Mother stands lifting her child unto the presence of God, the Pantocrator, emperor of the universe. This magnificent cathedral, still the most important structure in Eastern Christendom, captures in its stone and mosaic the Orthodox vision of the unity and harmony of the cosmos.

The reign of Justinian, architect of Byzantine civilization, was disrupted by internal antagonisms that obscured the Orthodox vision of harmony. Two lagging Christological controversies grew out of dissatisfactions with the Council of Chalcedon's (451) dogmatic solution. Monophysitism and Monotheletism both gave the characteristic Eastern interpretation to the person of Christ by stressing his divinity at the expense of his humanity. These dissenting views challenged the orthodoxy defined by the ecumenical councils and accepted by the West. The Eastern dissidents refused to adhere entirely to the formula that held the Father and the Son to be fully equal and of the same substance or being.

We need not give detailed consideration to the subsequent distortions brought to traditional Christology by the "mono" heresies. But it is necessary to stress the theological tendency of the East, which put it at odds with the West. Byzantine Christianity continued to elevate Christ's divinity above his humanity, but even the "divinity" was considered less than the Father. The result is of no mean consequence. "Mono" Christology not only continues to hold a prominent place in Eastern theology but lives on wherever the humanity of Christ is neglected. If Christians believe that Christ was not fully divine, they are left with no ultimate revelation; and if Christians refuse to believe that Christ fully assumed human flesh, they are left with a savior who belongs more to the world of spirits than to the world of history where flesh-and-blood humans live and die. A Christology that is not quite human restricts the activity of the church. In Eastern Orthodoxy the church's mission was defined by "a department of state." Among Protestant fundamentalists in the United States a spiritualized doctrine of Christ limits church affairs to "a sanctuary of personal religion." In both cases the social contract would deny the church the right to "meddle" in the affairs of Caesar unless it is either to support public policy or to minister to the spiritual and private needs of individuals. "Mono" Christianity tends to be of the world but not in it.

Divisions among Christians of the East made impossible a united front against the advance of Mohammed's armies. Confident that Allah would deliver the unbelievers (Christians included) into the hands of his chosen people, the sons of the prophet swept around the southern shore of the Mediterranean and up to the Pyrenees. The Western church never fully shared the agony of the East in their struggle to survive the Islamic expansion. Muslim power in the West was broken with Charles Martel's victory at Tours in 732. But the East lived on under continual threat of destruction. Because East and West were not equally affected by the Muslim conquests, another wedge of suspicion and distrust drove Christendom to sharper division.

While external threats to the East increased, yet another internal struggle further weakened the empire from within. The issue was iconoclasm: the shattering of images, traditionally so vital to religious expression in the Byzantine. Emperor Leo III, "the Isaurian" (717–41), motivated by both theological and political reasons, decided that images were idolatrous and must be destroyed. There were those who resisted and were punished, often with death. Iconoclasm released a furor of protest and racked the East with painful division. The Roman Bishop, Pope Gregory III (731–41) aligned himself with the pro-image side. Christian unity at that time hung together by a thread.

One last dogmatic clash destroyed all semblance of Christian catholicism. Rome had introduced the *filioque* clause into the creed (the Holy Spirit proceeded from the Father *and* the Son). The Byzantine church, for reasons originating with the Eastern subordination of the Son to the Father, rejected the notion that the Spirit could proceed from them both. Finally two uncompromising personalities, the Orthodox Patriarch Michael Cerularius (1043–58) and Pope Leo IX (1049–54) excommunicated each other, adding anathemas for good measure. After July 1054, there were no more illusions about the unity of Christendom. Symbolically, the empire was broken over a conjunction.

THE BIRTH OF RUSSIAN CHRISTIANITY

The divided East and West went their separate ways with few hopes for reconciliation. The Byzantine church sought to increase its influence over northern tribes. Missionaries were sent to convert the Slavic peoples to Christianity. Eventually the Slavs entered into Christendom with the efforts of both Rome and Constantinople. Thus they have never been ecclesiastically united. The Czechs, Slovaks, and Poles were converted by German Catholics and therefore look to Rome for authority. The Serbs, Bulgarians, and Russians, though ecclesiastically independent, are Christians of the Byzantine rite. The modern states of Poland and Czechoslovakia are largely Roman Catholic. At the same time, the two nations speak Slavic tongues. The cultural contradictions between Eastern and Western traditions have engendered an ambivalence of national spirit among Czechs, Slovaks, and Poles that continues into the present East/West conflict.

From 989 until the Bolshevik Revolution of 1917, Russia was the daughter of Byzantium in religion, alphabet, and art. According to legend, 1000 years after Christ, Prince Vladimir of Kiev (980–1015) discovered which of the religions was best. Spokesmen for the great religions came to Kiev—Jews, Muslims, Western (Roman) Christians, and Eastern (Byzantine) Christians—to persuade Vladimir to embrace their faith. Unable to make a decision on the basis of their pleadings, the prince dispatched a commission to observe the rites of these religions in their respective countries. The Muslim practice they found to be too dour and severe (they forbade the use of alcohol and perhaps Vladimir knew he could not survive Russian winters without vodka). The Jews living in exile from their homeland were passed over. The Latin rites of Rome were thought dull and without beauty. But in Constantinople the emissaries were convinced by the overwhelming artistry of the Byzantine liturgy and the churches. They clinched the decision for Vladimir. Russians became Christians of the Eastern Church in 989. Thousands were lined up on the River Kiev, the ceremony was read, and they immersed themselves.

Aesthetics, however, did not figure most prominently in Vladimir's decision for Byzantine Christianity. Between 860 and 1043 the Russians had made six attempts to take Constantinople—so old is the drive to the Bosporus for secure access to the Mediterranean. Vladimir took as his wife the sister of the Eastern Emperor Basil II (963–1025) and gained entry to the Bosporus through marriage and the faith of his bride.

Politically, Orthodoxy served the Russian prince extremely well. The doctrine of divine right of kings buttressed his authority in establishing a social order. Under Vladimir's son Yaroslav (1036–54) a civilizing process began to work its way across the steppes. Four hundred Byzantine churches and a great cathedral were erected. Valdimir had previously made education compulsory, and slowly Russia began to lift itself out of its barbarism to establish the beginnings of a great civilization, one that stood for a millennium.

Ivan the Great (1462–1505), who may be regarded as the first national sovereign of Russia, annexed rival principalities, deported many of the troublesome aristocracy to central Russia, and consolidated a diversity of people from the Baltic to the Urals. Most important to the future of the Russian Church and of great political consequence was the marriage of Ivan to Zoë, niece of the last Emperor of Constantinople (1472). The union established the claim of the Russian rulers to be the successors of the Byzantine emperors and the protectors of Orthodox Christianity. It also introduced into Moscow the Eastern conception of the autocrat as ruler. Ivan took the title Tsar (Caesar) and adapted the quasi-religious practices of court ceremony.

The fifteenth century witnessed the further conquest of the Byzantine by Muslim armies. They pressed on up the Balkan Peninsula to capture Budapest and lay siege to Vienna itself. The desperate Patriarch of Constantinople was willing to bargain with the Pope of Rome at the Council of Florence (1439), hoping for troops from the Christian West to help stay the Turkish onslaught. Negotiations failed and Constantinople fell to the conquering Muslims.

The fall of Constantinople in 1453 left only the Russian diocese of the Patriarch of Constantinople free of alien control. By the second half of the fifteenth century, Moscow was the only major city in all the East ruled by a Christian prince. The Russian Church, under the influence of the monk Philotheos, formulated a theory of Moscow's divine election. It was believed that God had ordained four successive empires: Babylon, Persia, Macedonia, and Rome; and that Rome would preserve the faith until the Second Coming. The first Rome had fallen through heresy; the second because it compromised with the papacy; but the third Rome would discipline the life of faith until the end of history. Thus the holy mission that Byzantium once carried had passed to Moscow, giving Russia an infallible authority to defend the faith and to illuminate the whole universe with its wisdom. It has been observed that the Marxist vision of post-Revolutionary Russia can be understood as a desacralized Soviet model of the Third Rome, ordained by the forces of history to free and unite the proletariat of the world.

The theory of the Third Rome was further elaborated by monks and clerics who declared the Tsar to be God's vicar on earth, the supreme head of the state and the church. The doctrine served to elevate the place of the Dukes of Moscow over other Russian princes, bringing consolidation through centralization. The integration of Russia continued apace as Ivan IV "The Terrible" (1533–84) ascended the throne. In the early years of his reign he was successful in breaking the power of provincial governors. During the war years at mid-century, Ivan conquered the Tartars and extended the rule of Imperial Russia along the entire course of the Volga, opening the way for east and southeast expansion. But his reign was drenched with the blood of those he massacred in near orgies of passion and cruelty. He left the peasants more subjected than ever. He divided the land into hostile camps and brought the people to the edge of anarchy.

Ivan's reach was limited. It was limited by the other ruler of Russia, the church. The fear of God was everywhere. Strict rules of ritual bound even the Tsar. The priests saw to it that he washed his hands after giving audience to ambassadors from outside the pale of Orthodoxy. The Third Rome, as sovereign over every Christian kingdom, had to prevent any possible defilement of the sacred contents of the faith, which Russia, the holy crucible, held in its protection. Anathema was to be laid down against all heresy and the impious heterodoxy of Rome.

The Third Rome doctrine was given authority by various legends similar to those that ratified the papacy in the West (e.g., Donation of Constantine). Most important in the history of Russian Orthodoxy was the arrival of fugitive Patriarch Jeremiah of Constantinople in Moscow. Protected by the Tsar, he agreed to preside over the consecration of an independent Patriarch of Moscow and Russia (1589).

Of all the Patriarchs of Moscow, Nikon (1605–81) is best known to history. Nikon, elected to the office in 1652, set out to actualize the Tsar's leadership over all Orthodox Christians by giving the liturgy a universal language, namely Greek. Russian liturgy translated into Greek! "Never!" cried the opposition under Archpriest Avvakum. How could the Third Rome, citadel of unwavering orthodoxy, compromise the faith by making the least concession to the Greeks? The Greeks were filled with intrigue and suspected of collaboration with Muslims and Romanists. The Russian Church had already condemned the Greek usage of three instead of two fingers in making the sign of the cross. "Come, Orthodox People," cried Avvakum, "suffer tortures for the two finger sign of the cross," and the "Old Believers" did just that. Perhaps 20,000 died of self-immolation to win the martyr's crown.

The liturgical reform undertaken by Nikon resulted in the schism of "Old Believers." The last half of the seventeenth century was marked by hysterical apocalyptic fervor, group suicide, and wild prophecies of the approaching end of time. How can such excess be understood? Why such violent response to measures that today seem like trivia? Imagine the mass suicide of modern Roman Catholics in protest over the Vatican II decision to say the mass in the vernacular rather than in Latin. Impossible! But modern Roman Catholics do not understand the church liturgy in the same way as seventeenth-century Russian Christians regarded their liturgy. Ritual and worship were the sum of religion. Piety focused on religious art, liturgy, icons, and music, much as it did in Byzantium. It was only natural that religious Russians reacted with horror when the Patriarch, with the Tsar's support—both of them the appointed guardians of pure Orthodoxy—introduced innovations and additions to the infallible truth.

At the apocalyptic fringe of the "Old Believers" a number of sects proliferated, which ranged from the more biblically based Baptists, Stundists, and Molokans to the highly ecstatic Khlypty, Sukhobors, and Dukhobors. All suffered varying degrees of legal penalties. Some were exiled, and others remaining in the Soviet Union to this day, are still regarded with disfavor by both church and state. As alien as the behavior of the schismatics and sectarians seems to present observers, they must be recognized as the only religious groups to offer any resistance to the church-state establishment. They were therefore considered both seditious and heretical.

Peter the Great (1682–1725) undertook to alter the course of Russian-Byzantine culture by forcing upon it a process of Westernization. He adopted Western dress, cut his beard, and sought to import from Germany and France the Enlightenment learning of rationalism and deism. Peter's effort at changing the culture took a secular course, which had far-reaching consequences for the church. He sharply reduced ecclesiastical authority by eliminating the independent office of patriarch. A new synodal form of church government gave the Tsar greater control over religious affairs. With the reorganization, the crown took over the management of the church's revenues, which came from one-third of the land of Russia, worked by serfs. The clergy were turned into a virtual auxiliary police force. They were made to use the confessional as an instrument of political espionage. The priestly vocation was degraded by its burden of governmental work. Clerics were used and humiliated by the state and resented as agents and extortioners by the peasants. The hostility of the working class toward the church was building. It would be violently released by the Bolsheviks.

Peter may have been one of the less lovable figures of modern history, yet his achievement was immense. He gave Russia an army and navy, opened the ports to Western trade, and founded schools and academies. His efforts were to wrest Imperial Russia out of its Eastern isolation and make her a permanent factor in the affairs of the Western world. Russian Orthodoxy came to exert a new and powerful influence on the intellectual tradition of the West. Long considered the least articulate portion of Christendom, the Church of Russia had always excelled in the magnificence of its art and music and in its liturgical splendor. But the nineteenth century witnessed a flowering of literary activity. When intellectual expression began to be heard, however, it was not from the clergy but rather from the laity.

Modern literary eloquence was first given to the spirituality of Russian Orthodoxy under the rigid and reactionary reign of Nicholas I (1825–55). Under severe censorship Russia produced a generation of brilliant writers, thinkers, and musicians: drama by Ostromsky (1823–86) and later Chekhov (1860–1904); and music by Glinka (1803–57), Borodin (1838–87), Moussorgsky (1839–81), Tchaikovsky (1840–93) and Rimsky-Korsakov (1844–1908). The novel reached its height by mid-century in the works of Dostoyevsky (1821–81), Tolstoy (1828–1910), and Gorki (1868–1936). They gave life's meaning and its non-meaning a most profound interpretation.

Russia reacted against Enlightenment opinions imported from the West. The antipathy toward Napoleon transformed all things French into contemptible vices. Many intellectuals associated with the Slavophil movement, which rejected all imitation of European society and lauded the primitive virtues of the Russian soul and the Russian peasant. Dostoyevsky became a prominent member of this group. He more than any other single writer brought to Western Christendom the depth and power of Orthodox Russia. Leo Tolstoy was another of the extraordinary writers of the period. His radical rejection of war, the state, and the judicial system led him to the attack in heaping harsh criticism upon the Orthodox

Church. He denounced its affairs and intrigues with the standing order. Tolstoy's eccentric sectarian interpretation of the Gospel got him excommunicated, but his search for ethical integrity stands as one of the few attempts in the entire history of Eastern Orthodoxy that fully rejects all attempts to accommodate the Christian faith to prevailing cultural values.

ORTHODOXY AND THE U.S.S.R.

Peter the Great, under the influence of Enlightenment forces for secularization, initiated the process in Russia that eventually extricated the church from civil life in the legal and formal sense. This process had been retarded under the rule of several emperors. During World War I the real power remained in the hands of an ecclesiastic, Gregory Rasputin (1872–1916), "the mad monk," who dominated the neurotic Empress Alexandria. The government was completely discredited in public eyes. Rasputin was murdered and Russia was in general revolt. On November 7, 1917, the Russian Bolshevik revolution broke out under the leadership of Nikolai Lenin (1870–1924). He was convinced that the war was the imperialist venture of capitalist nations. The movement destined to rule or influence at least half of the globe for the yet foreseeable future was under way. The Empire Christianized by Vladimir's acceptance of the faith in 989 was at an end.

The mission transferred in 1453 from the fallen citadel of the faith in Constantinople to the Russian Third Rome was now given over to a modern secular agency that was no less intent on taking its "good news" unto all the nations. The church fell on bitter times for reasons that have been repeated across the history of Christianity. Wherever the church had closely allied itself with the standing order's reaction to revolutionary ferments, it quickly fell victim to the reprisals of the revolutionaries once they gained power.

In 1917 the Governing Synod (Sobar) of the Russian Orthodox Church realized their long awaited desire to restore the office of Patriarchate, which Peter had abolished. The decision was reached under the thunder of guns in Red October. The restored office was not to have the autocratic functions of the past. It was to be subject to the governing synod of the church. However, the Bolshevik government soon made clear their intention to extirpate Christian influence everywhere. All church lands and buildings were confiscated without compensation. Civil marriage was made compulsory. Religious instruction was everywhere forbidden and all church literature was strictly censored.

The Soviet crackdown on institutional religion led to the first overt conflict between the church and the new state. Patriarch Tikhon (1917–25), the first of the holders of the restored patriarchal office, declared war. He refused to recognize the Soviet government. The Sobar ratified his policy. Orthodox resistance led to riots and casualties on both sides. But within a year Tikhon had retreated from his stand in overt opposition to the state and sought to establish the widest possible autonomy for the church within the limits prescribed by the civil authorities. His efforts were defeated with his arrest and imprisonment. In May, 1922, a schismatic group of collaborationists called the "Living Church" seized ecclesiastical control and recognized the Soviet government.

The new *modus vivendi* left the church with little legal authority. Upon his release from prison, Tikhon signed a document that yielded much of the freedom he had so fervently tried to save. His successor, Metropolitan Sergei (1926–43) continued to work for conciliation between church and state. Under extreme pressure he paid the price of accepting the full terms of the government. The church became so subordinated to Soviet interests that even Joseph Stalin acknowledged the services of Orthodoxy in the national interest.

Sergei's successor, Alexis (1943–70), willingly continued the policy of cooperating with the state, supporting Soviet policy in every decision. He also denounced the "Cold War" opposition of the West, the United States in particular. There remain very few official sources of discontent within the Orthodox Church over its relationship to the Soviet government. The arrangement seems to be the Caesaropapist notion of division of responsibilities in an unequal partnership. The main difference between the church's position under the rule of Byzantine emperors and their Tsarist successors and the church under Soviet rule is that now the government is officially anti-religious. No longer are Russian rulers protectors of the faith. It has been observed that the present state of the Russian Orthodox Church is in most respects the same as it has been throughout most of its history. Orthodoxy continues its historic affair with the prevailing culture, blessing its public virtues and restricting its religious pronouncements to matters of the private conscience.

Tolstoy, as we have noted, provides the history of Russian Christendom with the sectarian protest against acculturated religion. He rejected cultural claims to authority and understood the commands of Christ to contradict those of the world. The position was in sharp contrast to the Eastern theological interpretation of culture, which did not find Christ and the world to be in sharp tension. Creation was believed to be the medium of God's wisdom and grace. The highest values of its culture were recommended by the guardians of the faith as expression of God's will.

The phenomenon of acculturated religion is sharply criticized by most Christian theologians. The primary objection is against the reduction of God as Lord and judge over history to a place in the process where God can conveniently serve as a divine agency to ordain the political and cultural consensus. The tendency to domesticate the faith to a particular ideology, national system, or cultural form inevitably occurs in every society. It is in no way peculiar to Russian Orthodoxy. It even occurs in states and nations with legally separate covenants of church and state but nonetheless fosters a de facto civil religion. Nations everywhere practice cultural religion in celebrations of public piety. They ratify their claims to righteousness at football half-time shows and political prayer breakfasts. Such quasi-religious public functions in the West make evident the facts of *symphonia* in our own society. The separate traditions that still divide Christendom into East and West merge to share a dubious phenomenon that corrupts the "holiness" of the faith with accommodation. Yet the two traditions have also met in the cause of Christian unity, giving witness to the "oneness" of the faith. That the Ecumenical Movement in 1961 brought together Christians of the East and West after a thousand years of mutual misunderstanding and distrust is indeed a major chapter in the story of the twentieth-century Christian church.

9

Struggle for Independence and Sovereignty

The great struggle of the Middle Ages was for independence and sovereignty. It was a contest between titans—church and state—and in the end the church won. But it was a Pyrrhic victory, for papal primacy and implied infallibility on which the church built its case suffered from what Augustine called the essence of sin: the human attempt to imitate the liberty and omnipotency of God. Replete with heroic deeds and dedicated believers, the Middle Ages witnessed ecclesiastical drives to put the institutional church at the center of all life, and in the process the church subtly traded service for domination, prophecy for order, and agape self-giving for the self-fulfillment of eros. This is not to say that the church did not contribute much to Western thought and religious life. It did. Nor is it to say that the church acted wrongly in so directing affairs, for the Middle Ages stand as a monument to the triumph of the church in society. It is to say that absolute sovereignty is more than human institutions can bear. Mistakes accumulated, oppression grew, and authority eroded, until the church could not hold back the eruptions that came in the Middle Ages and in the Reformation of the sixteenth century. In the twentieth century state sovereignty may well be suffering from the same liberty and omnipotency identified by Augustine, resulting inevitably in disharmonies and disruptions. But this overall interpretation forges ahead, for in the fifth to seventh centuries, the church was by no means in control even though the theoretical basis for its eventual triumph had already been laid. On the contrary it struggled to survive.

Early in the fifth century, Rome withdrew its far-flung legions from Britain to defend more vital boundaries. This isolated the islands for two centuries, the time when Irish monasticism led by St. Patrick grew. Most of Patrick's life is shrouded in legend, but the general outline is known. He was born about 389 in Britain and was reared in the church. His father may have been a deacon. Around 405, he was seized by Irish raiders and carried as a slave to Ireland. After six years of slavery, he escaped, passed himself off as a caretaker of dogs, and sailed for France. Having landed on the shores of France, Patrick was credited with a small miracle. A drove of pigs appeared when he prayed for food. After wandering for some years, Patrick received his call to save the unborn babies of Ireland. He then turned up in the strict Pachomian monastery at Lerins on a Mediterranean island, where he trained for some fourteen years. Apparently he was ordained bishop and in 432, according to legend, he sailed with twenty-four helpers for Ireland. Some earlier Christianizing in Ireland had been done by Palladius, but Patrick found the island thoroughly pagan, given to a nature worship of Druids who predicted the future.

With astounding energy and tact, for there were no martyrs in Ireland, Patrick overcame the island's paganism and established so many monasteries that the land came to be called the Island of Saints. With Britain falling to the pagan Anglo-Saxons in the fifth century, Ireland evolved its own brand of Christianity. It was the only country where ascetic monasticism completely dominated the developing church, probably because monasticism adapted well to rural situations. The dioceses were not organized around towns, which were few, but around monasteries, ruled over by abbots rather than bishops. Minor as well as important differences emerged in the course of years. Curiously the clergy did not have to be celibate, Easter was celebrated on a date different from that at Rome—which posed the question of who had authority to set the date, Roman primacy was not accepted, monks wore a tuft of hair on the head with the remainder shaven rather than vice versa, and one immersion rather than three at baptism was practiced. These differences later occasioned tension with missionaries from Rome. Among the contributions of the Irish monasticism were (1) the introduction of classical Latin, which scholars later carried to the Continent, (2) private lay confessions and penance, and penitential books that described in detail what had to be done to make satisfaction for specific sins, (3) a strong emphasis on this life as a pilgrimage, one's true home being in heaven, and (4) a missionary effort that extended from Ireland and Scotland all the way to Italy.

About 563 Columba founded the monastery at Iona off Scotland, and Aidan, a monk from Iona, established a mission in Northern England on the island of Lindisfarne, which became a center for scholarship and missions. Columbanus of Bangor, who spent many years at Iona, went to the Continent with twelve companions around 589. During the following twenty-five years he preached, started schools, and founded monasteries in Burgundy, Switzerland, and Northern Italy, where as late as 614 he established a monastery at Bobbio.

This Irish (Celtic) missionizing conflicted with Roman Christianity, especially the Benedictine monasticism introduced into England by Augustine, who after a perilous journey from Rome reached England in 597. Venerable Bede (673–735) tells this story in his *Ecclesiastical History of the English Nation*. Augustine had with him forty monks, but made few gains until he approached King Ethelbert through his Queen Bertha, a Frankish princess who influenced her husband to accept Christianity. Even so, Augustine had to meet Ethelbert in an open field where the clear air would diminish the saint's supposed power to make tails grow from the backs of his enemies. Ethelbert gave him a residence at Canterbury, and on Pentecost, just one year after Augustine arrived, Ethelbert and 10,000 of his subjects were baptized. Relics, books, and instructions came from Rome. Although Augustine died about 605, the work continued, but not without setbacks. After Ethelbert, Eadbold actively persecuted the missionaries. When Aethilburga, daughter of Bertha, became the queen of Edwin of Northumbria, Paulinus accompanied her and in 627 he baptized hundreds in the River Glen and established his see at York, the second historic archbishopric of England.

Political as well as religious differences heightened the tensions between Roman and Celtic Christianity. However, at the Synod of Whitby, 664, Oswy of Northumbria, when assured the keys had been given to Peter, declared for Rome saying he did not want to be shut out of heaven. Northern Ireland accepted Rome's jurisdiction in 696, Iona in 720. Other territories followed, and unity with Rome once more prevailed. From the Celts came zeal and learning, from Rome, order and authority.

In a short time intrepid Benedictine monks from Great Britain began missionizing Europe. Wilfred, who was at Whitby and who became bishop of York, began the work. He called for missionaries to go to Frisia, and monks began swarming over northwestern Europe. Willibrord worked in Frisia and along the Rhine; he organized a diocese and became bishop at Utrecht. The most successful of these missionaries was Boniface (680–754), whose overall work unified monasticism and the papacy, giving the latter a firm hold on the developing transalpine church. Trained in a monastery from the age of five, a scholar, preacher, and administrator, Boniface began his mission with little success in Frisia about 716. On gaining the support of both the Pope and the increasingly powerful Frankish leader, Charles Martel, his conversions of pagans multiplied rapidly. In 719 Pope Gregory II commissioned Boniface "in the name of the unshaken authority of Peter" to spread "salvation-bringing fire" among "whatsoever tribes are still lingering in the error of unbelief," and in 722 consecrated him bishop. Boniface swore to uphold the purity and unity of the one universal church. He boldly converted heathen, as when he chopped down the Oak of Thor, and he brought a sense of moral and intellectual inspiration wherever he went, especially in Gaul. By order of the Pope he excoriated remaining Irish practices that differed from those of Rome. He founded numerous dioceses and became the archbishop of Mainz.

Boniface's greatest achievement was the crowning of the son of

Charles Martel, Pepin the Short, as king of the Franks, in 751. The coronation was a deliberate copy of Solomon's crowning in I Kings 1. Childerich, the nominal king, was shorn of his locks and sent into a monastery. Pepin, who was educated by the Benedictine monks of St. Denis near Paris, received the Pope himself (Stephen II) in 754, with a great show of obeisance, and was reanointed by the Pope. He promised to protect the Pope against his enemies and in 756, after defeating the Lombards, made to the Pope his famous donation of the papal states, consisting of twenty-two cities and their environs stretching across Italy from Rome to Ravenna. This unusual act rested heavily on a fabled document. According to an old legend Pope Sylvester had cured Constantine the Great of leprosy and in return had received grants of land in the West. The story was fictional, but around 754 a document purporting to be "The Donation of Constantine" appeared. Centuries later Nicholas of Cusa, 1433, and Lorenzo Valla, 1440, definitely established it as a forgery, but it had wide acceptance in the eighth and succeeding centuries. In the Donation, Constantine bestowed on Sylvester all his imperial powers and dignities, which the Pope humbly returned, and in addition bestowed on the universal Pope all the cities of Italy and the Western regions. Pepin's own kingship was confirmed by the Pope, and in donating the papal states Pepin was but returning lands to their "rightful" overlord. The Eastern emperor's request that the lands be returned to him was rejected. The dependence of the papacy on the Eastern empire had ended. Henceforth the papacy issued its own coins and dated documents by its own regnal year or that of the Frankish kings, the new emperors in the West. The focus in the struggle for domination had shifted. By energetically supporting Boniface's work, Pepin greatly enhanced the standing of the church and set the stage for the Caesaropapism of Charlemagne. Boniface spent his last years evangelizing in Frisia, where he was murdered.

On the death of Pepin, Carloman and Charlemagne divided the kingdom, with the latter becoming sole ruler on the voluntary retirement of Carloman to a monastery in 771. King Charlemagne (768–814) swore to revitalize the spiritual and intellectual life of his realm. It was not an abstract need. Despite the efforts of the Benedictines, learning had sunk to dismal lows. Vast amounts of ancient literature and philosophy had been forgotten, and the monasteries preserved for the most part only those writings that they thought had ecclesiastical value. Benedictine monasteries were still the centers for clerical and lay education, but this education was nothing to boast about. In the two centuries since Benedict, decadence had taken its toll. The light of the monasteries was bright only because of the nearly total darkness of the Dark Ages.

Charlemagne inaugurated a period of revitalization by inviting to his court at Aix-la-Chapelle the most renowned scholars of the time to form the nucleus of a palace school where administrators for the state and the church could be trained. Chief among these was Alcuin (735–804), head of the cathedral school at York, trained in the tradition of Bede. Others included the Lombard, Paul the Deacon; the Frank, Einhard; Rabanus Maurus; and the Visigoth, Theodulf. Their writings and the cathedral and palace schools they established kept the intellectual life of the time flickering. Because of the Muslim conquests, supplies of papyrus became scarce, forcing the monks to use animal skins for the copying of books, which in turn caused them to write smaller and in time to develop the *minuscule* system of small letters with capitals to begin sentences. Compared to the old Roman *majuscule* of capital letters, it proved highly utilitarian and later served as a model for the first printing. Inferior and limited as the cathedral and palace schools were, they nevertheless taught generations of men to read and write and appreciate books.

Lauded by Alcuin, Charlemagne considered himself a second David destined to restore classical and biblical learning, a ruler who would make Augustine's *City of God* a reality in his realm, one in whom the theocracy of the Old Testament would again manifest itself. He was God's anointed, second to none, not even the Pope. He extended his kingdom from the Pyrenees to the Danube, including France, Holland, Belgium, Germany, Austria, Hungary, Italy, and a fourth of Spain. When the Lombards tried to revolt, Charlemagne ruthlessly put them down, and as a reward the Pope conferred on him the title of King of the Franks, King of the Lombards, and Patrician of the Romans. For thirty-three years, 772–804, Charlemagne sent his armies against the Saxons. Though finally subdued, some 3,000 chose death rather than adopt Christianity. Charlemagne quelled further revolts by resettling thousands of men, women, and children, and sending in Franks to replace them. Without consulting the Pope, he conducted his own religious synods, often dictating their decisions. He condemned Nicaea for approving the reverence of pictures, and censured adoptionist Christology.

Through capitularies (laws) that he freely promulgated, Charlemagne sought to establish both clerical and lay justice and order. He decreed the death penalty for eating meat during Lent; killing a priest, bishop, or deacon; burning an alleged witch or eating an alleged witch's flesh; burning the dead on pyres; robbing a church; practicing heathen rites; and refusing to be baptized. These were laws especially for the Saxons. He charged the clergy to improve the condition of the churches, promote zeal in learning, set a holy example, and employ the lectionary prepared by Paul the Deacon. His rules for the monasteries forbade drunkenness; feasting; fornication; sodomy; hunting with dogs, hawks, or falcons; secular moonlighting; lot casting for church property; and favoritism in promotions. Priests could not be ordained without an examination, and everyone in the kingdom, lay and clerical, twelve or older, had to swear an oath of fidelity to Charlemagne. He reserved the right to approve all clerical appointments and to depose refractory clerics. Throughout the empire he sent clerical and lay messengers to investigate and report to him injustices and misconduct.

During Charlemagne's reign, the Popes were relatively weak, constantly embroiled in petty Italian politics. In 799 Pope Leo III was ambushed and brutally beaten by some of his enemies, who also publicly accused him of immorality and heresy. Charlemagne journeyed to Rome and adjudicated the case in the Pope's favor. To offset the implied superiority of the state in this adjudication, Leo unexpectedly placed a crown on Charlemagne's head while he was praying at St. Peter's on Christmas Day in the year 800, and then fell down before him in a posture of submission. In history the coronation implied papal supremacy.

Charlemagne left his kingdom to his son Louis the Pious (814–40), and on the death of Louis after a three-year period of confusion and struggle, the kingdom was divided by his three sons. Charles the Bald (843–77) got France, Louis the Bald (843–75), Germany, and Lothair (843–55) the section in between, Lorraine. Thus divided and weakened, Western Europe fell prey to almost constant raids and invasions from the Vikings, Muslims, and Magyars. Civil order virtually disappeared.

Temporarily the papacy, because of the strong character of Pope Nicholas I (858–67), enjoyed a period of independence and supremacy. About 850 the famous Pseudo-Isidorian or False Decretals appeared. They consisted of letters from ante-Nicene popes, a collection of canons of councils, and letters of Popes from Sylvester I to Gregory II, plus the Donation of Constantine. Most of these documents were spurious, but they were widely accepted for many centuries. They purported to show the superior authority of the church over that of secular rulers and asserted that priests were not subject to secular rulers or their courts, that they were immune from taxes, and that the Pope could be removed from his office only by God. The channel of authority is from God to Peter to priests to others. Nicholas accepted these documents and came close to asserting papal infallibility. His power was immense, and greatly enhanced by three events: (1) When Lothair accused and forced his wife to admit incest so that he could secure a divorce and marry a concubine, Nicholas declared that the church would never sanction his remarriage and compelled him finally to reinstate his wife. The Pope appeared to be the guardian of morality and marriage. (2) When the Patriarch Ignatius of Constantinople refused to allow the unsavory uncle of the Eastern emperor to take communion, the emperor deposed Ignatius and appointed Photius, a very learned man, in his place. Ignatius, however, appealed to Nicholas, who officially deposed Photius. Photius then accused the Pope of heresy in such things as celibacy, filioque, shaving of beards, eggs during Lent, and so forth. In this controversy the Pope appeared to be the upholder of morality against Eastern corruption. (3) When Hincmar, the controversial Archbishop of Rheims, deposed a priest and the latter appealed to the Pope, Nicholas took his side, leaving the impression that the Pope was the champion of the little man. Priests were often regarded as no better than the bishop's serfs.

But the papacy's independence and supremacy soon waned. With the collapse of Carolingian power, Pope John VIII (872–82) fell prey to the power designs of a group of Italian nobles who bribed a servant to poison him. Impatient with the slow poison, the conspirators broke into the Pope's bedchamber and beat his brains out with a hammer. Having prospered in the rise of the Franks, the papacy declined with their fall.

The papacy of the tenth century is known largely for its corruption and in-fighting in petty Italian politics. Monstrous depravity became commonplace. A series of popes were mixed up with or descendants of two exalted prostitutes, Theodora and Marozia, particularly the degenerate Popes John X, XI, and XII. One Pope is said to have used the papal palace as a brothel and to have seized visiting pilgrims for his purposes. The papacy was but another position in a game of political chess.

When Otto I, ruler of Saxony (936–73), became dominant in Germany, Pope John XII (955–64), famed for his pleasure, vice, and perfidy, sought Otto's aid to enhance his own political power in Italy, particularly against King Berengar II in the North, an old enemy of Otto. Otto, in imitation of Charlemagne, invaded and subdued Italy in 962. Pope John XII, only twenty-five at the time, rewarded him with the crown of Holy Roman Emperor, which as Voltaire said, was neither holy, nor Roman, nor imperial. As soon as Otto withdrew from the city, Pope John regretted the implied vassalage of the papacy and initiated political intrigues with Otto's foes. Angered and desirous of controlling the wealth of the church, Otto returned to Rome in 963, captured the city, put the Pope to flight, and convoked a synod, which deposed John for immorality and then elected a layman, Leo VIII, to the papal throne. Leo received all his ecclesiastical orders in two days. In the following year, after the departure of Otto, John seized the papacy again, cancelled the synod's actions, and died. The people of Rome then chose Benedict V, only to have Otto return, reinstate Leo VIII, and after him to put John XIII on the papal throne. The papacy had never been so completely dominated by the state; even the Roman people were forced to swear that they would never elect a Pope without the emperor's consent.

Otto II and Otto III continued the policies of their predecessor but were never able to subdue for long the various rebellious factions within their vast holdings. Tedious wars and internecine strife also blocked the universal ambitions of the Bavarian and Franconian kings Henry II, Conrad II, Henry III, and Henry IV. All of them manipulated the papacy for their own political advantage. In the eleventh century papal prestige sank to a historic low. Benedict IX (1033–48) became Pope at the age of twelve. When a little older, he wanted to marry but the father of the girl refused unless he relinquished the papacy. So Benedict sold the papacy to Gregory VI for 2,000 pounds of silver. This infuriated the Roman people, who then elected Sylvester III as Pope. King Henry III, disgusted, intervened. He called the Synod of Sutri, which in 1046 caused all three Popes, accused of simony, to be deposed. Henry then appointed Clement II of Germany, who on Christmas Day obligingly crowned the king emperor. In less than three years he appointed two others—Popes Damasus II and Leo IX.

Recovery from such a long moral slump and political manipulation seemed virtually impossible, but two developments were well under way—a new doctrine of the sacrament of communion that would give the celebrant of the Mass added power, and clerical reform in the monasteries that would give spiritual life a new image. Both of these found expression in the pontificate of the powerful Gregory VII (1073–85).

At about the time of the Pseudo-Isidorian Decretals, a significant doctrine of the Lord's Supper was emerging—transubstantiation. It did not become generally accepted, however, until 200 years later, when it became one of the principal weapons of the church in its struggle with the state for sovereignty. Superstition, religious longing, and a feeling that life on earth was brief combined to make the church's claim that the sacraments were necessary to attain heaven very important in the Middle Ages. The fact that excommunication could actually deprive a king of his subjects' support indicates the pervasiveness of the awe in which the sacraments were held. Transubstantiation greatly enhanced this belief.

In 831 Paschasius Radbertus, abbot of the French monastery at Corbie, published *The Body and Blood of the Lord.* He maintained that in the mass, when the priest speaks the consecration, the bread and wine are changed into the body and blood of Christ—not for those who have doubts, but for believers. This, he said, was the creative act of God *through the priest.* The change was substantial and metaphysical, not visible; outwardly the elements remained the same. It was a symbol because of the visible elements and a truth because of Christ's presence. While he did not use the term transubstantiation, he spoke once of the bread changing into a lamb, and the idea was definitely there. Rabanus Maurus, abbot and theologian of Fulda, supported this new view but denied any absolute identity between the sacramental and historical Christ.

Ratramnus, a monk at Corbie, in opposition to Radbertus, wrote an essay maintaining an Augustinian view. No real change occurs in the elements. The sacrament is a symbol and occasion for the working of God. The bread and wine are memorial signs of what we spiritually receive. They are in no way changed into the body of Christ. Transubstantiation was also opposed by Gottschalk (ca. 808–68), who in his day represented a revival of radical Augustinianism. He clearly demonstrated that Augustine believed strictly in human dependence on God. This implied that the entire church structure was dispensable, because salvation depends wholly on God and not on any human effort. Although some scholars argued that Augustine taught foreknowledge rather than predestination, they were no match for Gottschalk's firsthand knowledge of Augustine. Gottschalk's theory was too threatening, and a synod at Mainz in 848 condemned him as a heretic. He was scourged almost to death and was imprisoned in a monastic cell until his death.

Berengar of Tours voiced similar Augustinian views, saying Christ was in the elements only through thought. He was condemned by synods at Rome and Tours, and in 1059 Cardinal Humbert forced him to sign a statement that communicants actually bite the body of Christ during communion.

Although transubstantiation did not become official dogma until the Fourth Lateran Council, 1215, and was not officially defined until the Council of Trent, 1545–63, it increased the awe of the communicants who believed they were partaking of the actual body of Christ, and heightened the power of the priest through whom the miraculous change occurred.

Elevation and adoration of the host became common in the twelfth century. Pope Honorius III in 1217 decreed bells be rung at the moment of change so that people everywhere might bow in worship. Care was taken that crumbs not be eaten by mice or trampled underfoot and that spilled wine be extracted from altar cloths and drunk or the area of spillage burned over. In an age devoted to veneration of the Virgin Mary and all the saints and to belief in the miraculous powers of relics, the ability to change bread and wine into the flesh and blood of Christ greatly enhanced the power of the papacy. Only a priest could do this, and every priest by ordination was linked to the papacy and its claim of primacy in apostolic succession.

Concomitant with this development was a growing desire for clerical reform. The Benedictine monasteries, for all their virtue, gradually declined. As the Benedictine monasteries depended heavily on the disciplinary guidance of the abbot, the general slump of the church affected the quality of available leaders. Worldly intrusions engulfed the monasteries in the weaknesses of the age. Yet there were those who longed for something better.

A significant step toward reform started with the monastic Congregation of Cluny in southern Burgundy. In 910 Duke William of Aquitaine founded Cluny in a deliberate attempt to revive the ancient Benedictine order. It was to be independent of all secular rulers, free to elect its own abbot, free to follow the old Benedictine rule. To avoid control by local bishops, it was made responsible only to the papacy. The Cluniac reform strictly adhered to the old rules and soon gained wide renown for piety. Older monasteries affiliated, and Cluny appointed priors to supervise their activities. Eventually over 300 houses joined Cluny in an effort to renovate spiritual life. Through Oda, the archbishop of Canterbury, and Aethelwald, the abbot of Abingdon, the reform movement spread to England. In the form of a third order, it reached laity, as at Hirschaw in Germany, where whole families adopted monastic ideals. Although emperor Henry III (1039–56) regarded the church as a department of state and interfered directly in the election of popes, he did support the Cluniac efforts to rejuvenate spiritual life. He forbade children of clergy to hold state and church offices and outlawed simony—the custom of buying ecclesiastical positions. Cluny profoundly affected religious life. It lessened lay investiture and slowly began freeing the church from secular domination. Many Cluniacs became bishops and applied the ideals of Cluny to their dioceses. They influenced synods to promote reform by enforcing celibacy and even mitigated the horrors of private warfare by promoting the Peace of God, 989, which limited the combatants in war by excluding priests, abbots, deacons, clerks, women, children, laborers, pilgrims, tools of work, donkeys, monasteries, and cemeteries; and the Truce of God, 1017, which limited the acceptable times for fighting by excluding Saturday to Monday and the holy seasons. Unfortunately the church raised armies to enforce the peace and eventually increased the fighting.

The Cluniac reform reached the zenith of its influence in the pontificate of Gregory VII, who sought to apply its principles to the papacy itself. Gregory's goal was direct and clear. If the church is to be independent of civil rulers, it must be pure; it must control itself. Immorality must be stamped out of the priesthood and simony must be eliminated completely.

Even before he became Pope, Gregory, also known as Hildebrand, exerted a reforming influence on the papacy. Henry IV (1056–1106), who became king of the Germans at the age of six, was unable to direct papal affairs, and Hildebrand became the guiding force. He had been a Benedictine monk at Rome, had visited Cluny, had received a good education, and was given to the practice of severe asceticism and veneration of the Virgin Mary. Having traveled widely and associated with Henry III, he was well aware of the high stakes in the struggle of church and state. When his friend, Bishop Bruno of Toul, was elected to the papacy, Hildebrand accompanied him to Rome, the two of them entering the eternal city as barefooted pilgrims. On the advice of Hildebrand, Bruno did not receive the crown from the emperor. This symbolic assertion of church over state continued during the pontificate of Bruno as Leo IX (1049–54). Assisted by Hildebrand, Humbert, and Peter Damian, Leo undertook a semi-successful crusade against clerical concubinage and simony (also known as lay investiture). Synods agreed to excommunication for offenders, but to have enforced this would have left Rome without priests, for most of them had bought their positions. A penance of forty days was substituted. Many of the clerical concubines became servants in the papal palace—not a very satisfactory compromise for celibacy.

Hildebrand displayed his real power in 1058, when after the brief reigns of Victor II and Stephen IX, the Roman nobility elected Benedict X to the papacy. Hildebrand was temporarily in Germany. He raised a small army, expelled the usurper, and seated Nicholas II (1059–61) on the throne. Nicholas' reign was distinguished by the establishment of the College of Cardinals in 1059 to elect future Popes. The College provided a buffer between the emperor and the papal throne. Further moves against priestly concubinage and simony provoked violent battles in the streets of Milan.

Pope Alexander II (1061–73), the first to be elected by the College of Cardinals, was chosen outside of Rome by the cardinals, and conducted to and consecrated in Rome with the aid of Norman soldiers, with whom Hildebrand had negotiated for protection. An anti-Hildebrand party elected antipope Cadalus, backed by young Henry IV, who was consecrated as Honorius II in 1061 and maintained a schism for ten years. The great struggle between Henry IV and Hildebrand was about to be joined, for Alexander just before his death had refused to give Henry a divorce and had summoned him to Rome to answer charges.

On the death of Alexander II, Hildebrand ordered a fast for three days, and was then acclaimed by the people and elected by the cardinals as Pope Gregory VII (1073–85). Dedicated to the austere ideals of Cluny, Gregory sought to enforce clerical celibacy not only as a purer state but as a means of freeing the church from the world. In 1074 he prohibited future marriages and ordered married priests to dismiss their wives or give up reading mass. Clerical marriage from his viewpoint was no better than fornication. Laymen were urged not to take the sacraments from such guilty priests. Havoc resulted. Priests were insulted, tortured; some were driven to suicide, some even murdered. Legal wives became harlots, and legitimate children, bastards. But Gregory moved relentlessly forward, unseating those bishops who opposed him, especially in the north. He enforced clerical celibacy, but at a great price and without permanence, for at the time of the Reformation in the sixteenth century the church was licensing clerical concubines and taxing the children of bishops.

Gregory precipitated the struggle with Henry IV by prohibiting lay investiture of bishops, a practice very dear to the civil ruler, for the church had acquired much of the taxable land and the civil ruler needed to have control of bishoprics. The Pope suspended some bishops in Germany. Henry, fresh from a victory over the Saxons, resented this interference with an ancient imperial custom and boldly appointed some bishops to sees in Italy itself. Gregory threatened excommunication, and Henry replied by calling some disgruntled bishops to the Synod of Worms in 1076, which declared Hildebrand unfit to be Pope because of treason, witchcraft, and immorality. Henry wrote him an insulting letter insisting that he vacate the papal throne.

In the following month of February, 1076, Gregory, in the name of St. Peter and the divine Trinity, deposed Henry for his "unheard of arrogance and iniquities," placed him under anathema, and relieved his subjects of keeping oaths sworn to him. When German political factions decided to support the Pope's action, Henry IV found himself without followers. In desperation he decided to swallow his pride and plead with the Pope for restoration. The two of them met at Canossa, 1077, when the Pope was journeying north to a diet at Augsburg. Henry stood penitently in the snow for three days, barefooted and thinly clad, seeking an audience. Gregory finally relented, and after exacting promises absolved Henry. But neither Gregory nor Henry acted subsequently in good faith. Gregory began supporting Henry's rival Rudolph, and when Henry regained control in Germany, the Pope excommunicated and anathematized him a second time saying he had not kept his promises. The year was 1080.

Whereas before the people had supported the Pope, in the second anathema they supported Henry, believing that the Pope had overstepped himself in demanding detailed control of the state. Henry invaded Rome and put rival Pope Wibert on the throne; in 1084 Wibert crowned him holy Roman emperor. The Normans, engaged in the East, were temporarily unable to help Gregory, but they soon returned to Italy, drove out the Germans, and in their fury sacked, raped, and pillaged Rome, selling many of its inhabitants into slavery. Although reinstated in 1085, Gregory died in the same year, a sadly disillusioned man, a bitter refugee in Salerno. Spiritual power without military assistance appeared weak, and spiritual power with state backing seemed to boomerang. Gregory's mistake was not in trying to make the church independent and pure but in trying to make the church dominant. He wanted not separation but control. But Gregory's struggle was not all in vain, for early in the following century Henry I of England in 1107 and Emperor Henry V of Germany in 1122 concluded concordats that left the investiture of the spiritual office of bishop in the hands of the Pope, although the bishop was to be answerable to the civil ruler in temporal matters.

10

Reform, Crusade, Dissent, and Triumph

The Cluny attempt to make the church independent of and sovereign over the state had come to a dramatic confrontation at Canossa, but the conflict was by no means resolved. It may well be that the monastic reform movement aimed solely at spiritual independence, even though what spiritual independence for the church in the world might mean is not clear. In any case the events that left Pope Gregory VII stunned and thinking that the end of the world was at hand did not deter the reform efforts already going forward on a broad front.

The Cluny reform did indeed reach its zenith under Gregory and afterward decline, especially in the twelfth century when Cluny became wealthy and self-indulgent, causing Peter the Venerable (1122–57) to heap scorn upon it. Under the leadership of Abbot Odilo, ca. 994, the monks at Cluny adorned their cloisters with marble, art, carvings, and other ornamentations. Individually the monks practiced austerity; collectively they ate from gold plates. Such luxurious accouterments appeared incongruous with monastic poverty, and protest movements developed.

In 1084, Bruno of Cologne quit teaching at Rheims cathedral to establish an extremely strict, contemplative order of monks near Cartusia at the Grande Chartreuse. At first it had no rule; its demands were simply renunciation of the world and mortification of the flesh. The monks lived in separate cells, daily devoting many hours to silent contemplation. Each monk had his own garden and prepared his own food. They met only for the night office, mass, and meals on feast days. Loneliness, austerity, and silence marked their religious vigils. Though some of the Carthusians became scholars, mystics, and writers, their impact on the Middle Ages was limited. For the most part they achieved spiritual separation and the anonymity of cultivated silence.

The Cistercians were quite different. In 1098, Robert of Molesme, sick of the laxity and degeneracy of the Cluniacs, founded a stringent Benedictine monastery at Citeaux, France. In obvious protest of the worldly Cluniacs, the Cistercians fostered plainness. They shunned images, crosses of gold, marble, carvings, expensive mouldings, stained glass, and decorated vestments. They wore straight, narrow, undyed habits, lived strictly within their meagre income, practiced vegetarianism, and devoted themselves to manual labor and contemplation. They later admitted lay brothers to assist them in their farming and the reclaiming of forests.

The most famous of the Cistercians was Bernard (1090–1153), who joined them in 1113. A noble, at the age of twenty-two he was disgusted with life. But after an experience of conversion, he led thirty companions to the monastery with him. During his year of probation, he exceeded even the strict Cistercians in austerity, often prolonging his prayers, fasting to excess, and finally having a nervous breakdown. When a sister house was established at Clairvaux in 1115, he was chosen as its abbot. So severe were his practices, so emaciated his body, so bitter his criticisms of the worldly tendencies of the church, so sharp his tongue against overindulgence, so censorious his remarks about pride, injustice, and greed that he was soon recognized as the embodied conscience of Europe. Bernard accepted the church's faith, taking such delight in its mystery and the inability of reason to explain it that he was led into a kind of mysticism. He longed for a love so intense that its expression would be an imitation of Christ. Even though his condemnation of Abelard at the Council of Sens in 1140, the preaching of the Second Crusade, and his manner of denouncing evil might belie it, love dominated his perspective. Love and Christianity were for him synonymous. In writing on the stages of love, Bernard discussed love for ourselves, love of God for derived benefits, love of God for himself alone, and love of ourselves for God's sake so that we may fittingly do the work of God in the world, that is, love our enemies and neighbors. Bernard added that if enemies continually thwart the will of God, they are God's enemies and we are to hate them for his sake. Blinded by his own rationalization, Bernard found in love the very basis for his hate.

Nevertheless, Bernard's moral integrity, passionate devotion to love, knowledge of the Bible, and fearless attacks on evil made him one of the most respected men in Europe. Princes, kings, and Popes sought his advice. Common people sang his hymns—"Jesus the very thought of Thee," "Jesus, Thou joy of loving hearts," "Of Him who did salvation bring." Disputants came to him to settle ecclesiastical and civil quarrels. Crowds heard him preach. The Cistercians begged him to rewrite their constitution to offset trends toward relaxation. Legends told of even the devils and dumb creatures obeying his commands. In the contested papal election of 1130, when a split College of Cardinals elected two Popes, Bernard's moral status swung the victory from Anacletus to Innocent II. The new Pope then showered favors on the Cistercians. Under Bernard's leadership they grew phenomenally. For the guidance of Eugenius III, elected Pope in 1145 on the strength of his friendship with Bernard, he wrote *Some Considerations,* a set of ascetic counsels.

Perhaps Bernard's greatest legacy was the piety he inspired through his mystical contemplation of Jesus' wounds, which he linked with atonement and the divine Christ. For him such contemplation led not to quietism but to an imitation of Christ—an active, practical expression of love with which people of any standing could identify. Such imitative love was for him the whole of Christianity.

Concomitant with the monastic reforms were the Crusades. Gregory VII attempted a crusade in 1074 and raised an army of 50,000 for Henry IV to lead against Constantinople, but their quarrel made this impossible. Gregory's immediate successor was an aged friend who died within a year. After him came the much younger Urban II (1088–99), a disciple of Gregory with a similar commitment to make the church pure and independent. Urban, however, could not enter Rome until antipope Guibert of Ravenna (Clement III) was unseated. In 1089, with the help of a Bavarian army Urban assumed the papal throne, only to have Henry IV bring Guibert back in 1090 and send Urban into exile for three more years. When Henry's son Conrad defected in favor of the Pope, Urban crowned him king of Italy and in 1094 once more regained the papal palace. In 1095 Urban convoked the Council of Clermont, to bring general reform to the church and enforce the Truce of God. But in the meantime a situation had developed that offered the opportunity of uniting the warring nobles of Christendom in a religious venture under papal direction that would turn attention from the papacy's internal difficulties.

The new situation was the expansion of the Seljuk Turks, who had burst out of their Asiatic plateau between China and Persia and overrun the Near East. They had swept to the shores of the Mediterranean, and in 1071 had annihilated a Byzantine army in Asia Minor at Manzikert and had proceeded to the outskirts of Constantinople itself. With the death in 1092 of the Turkish leader, Malik Shah, the Byzantine Emperor, Alexius Comnenus, believed the time was ripe to strike a blow to regain his territories. In 1095 he sent an appeal to Urban for military assistance. Urban saw an opportunity to unite the West, to heal the East-West schism, to elevate the papacy, and to wrest the entire holy land from the control of the Muslims.

Another—and possibly the more important—factor leading to the Crusades was the general religious fervor of the common people. With the advance of the Seljuk Turks, access of Christian pilgrims to the Holy Land became more difficult. The Seljuk Turks who adopted the Muslim religion did not like the pilgrimages that Christians made to expiate their sins. The Cluny reform had made trips to Palestine highly desirable. In 1065, the Bishop of Bamberg led a tour group of 7,000 to the holy places of Jerusalem. Such pilgrimages had become part of the penitential system. Confession and absolution were not considered sufficient; the penitent had also to make satisfaction for transgressions, both to impress the memory and to rectify by a good act what sin had undone. These satisfactions commonly consisted of fasting, biblical recitations, religious journeys, alms, prayers, scourgings, and so forth. Depending on the seriousness of the sin, acts of satisfaction might extend over weeks or even years. Many could not afford the time, so substitutions became common. One could give an equivalent in money or hire another person to perform the necessary works. Outfitting a crusader was regarded as a prime means of satisfaction.

Holy warfare was not new. As early as John VIII (872–82) the papacy had promised soldiers fighting the Saracens in Italy as much absolution from sins as the Pope himself could give. Since the Crusade in the eleventh century was to rescue the holy places associated with Christ from the hands of desecrating infidels, the pious could hardly have imagined anything more suitable. A contemporary chronicler, Leo Cassinensis, attributed the first Crusade in 1095 directly to the fervor of penitents.

In 1095 concern for the Holy Land reached a feverish pitch. Trade on the Mediterranean had been disrupted and visitors to Palestine brought back wild tales of profanation of relics, ill treatment of pilgrims, and capture of Christians for sale into slavery. Peter the Hermit, who carried a huge wooden cross and rode an ass around Europe, had been to Jerusalem and in the Church of the Holy Sepulchre had dreamed that Christ was begging Christians to purge the city of infidels.

At the Council of Clermont in 1095 Pope Urban II delivered one of the most outwardly successful sermons of all time. Preaching in French, he pictured the desecration of Jerusalem and Antioch, said Christ would lead any army that went to the rescue, and promised cancellation of debts, exemption from taxes, and a crown of eternal life to all participants. To the nobles he promised fruitful new lands. As the law of primogeniture left many younger sons without inheritances, the promise of new lands was especially appealing. In a frenzy the crowd chanted, "God wills it," and moved forward to take the crusader's oath by sewing crosses on their garments. Some burned crosses into their flesh.

Emotions ran high. Before an official Crusade could be organized, huge groups of pilgrims began the long march to the East. Most of these unofficial bands pillaged as they went and met with disaster in Hungary. Only one group, under Peter the Hermit, reached Constantinople. To prevent looting, Comnenus rushed them to Asia Minor, where the Turks ruthlessly butchered some 7,000 and piled the bodies in a heap to rot. Peter escaped.

The first official Crusade in 1096 came largely from France under the leadership of Godfrey of Lorraine, Hugh of Vermandois, Bohemund of Tarentum, Robert of Normandy, and Raymond of Toulouse. By different routes they proceeded to Constantinople, argued with Comnenus about the disposition of conquered lands, and then invaded the Holy Land. The leaders seemed most interested in carving out principalities for themselves. A nephew of Bohemund, Tancred, took over Edessa. Bohemund stopped at Antioch. Raymond settled the area of Tripolis. Only a small band reached Jerusalem in 1099. They marched around the walls as

Joshua did at Jericho but the walls remained intact. Then on Good Friday, after siege and assault, and after a vision of St. George appeared in the sky, at exactly three o'clock, the hour of Christ's death, the invaders breached the walls. Great slaughter followed. The streets ran with blood. Godfrey in a white linen suit conducted a thanksgiving service in the Church of the Holy Sepulchre, and then he and his men resumed the massacre. Tears of women and children did not save them. Some accounts say that all the inhabitants were slain. Godfrey refused to wear a crown of gold where Christ had worn a crown of thorns. On Christmas Day in 1100, following the death of Godfrey, his brother Baldwin was crowned the king of Jerusalem.

But these gains proved to be temporary. In less than fifty years, the Turks had retaken Edessa, and Bernard of Clairvaux, fearing that the infidels might reconquer everything, trumpeted the Second Crusade, 1147–49. Led by Louis VII of France, who was doing penance for having burned a church with 1200 people in it, and Conrad III, who was emperor, the Second Crusade failed miserably, largely because of quarrels between Louis and Conrad. By 1187 Jerusalem was again in the hands of the Turks, and the Third Crusade, 1189–92, was mounted to retake the holy city from Saladin. However, Emperor Frederick Barbarossa died before reaching Palestine, and internal feuds brought failure except for the capture of Acre by Richard I of England. The Third Crusade showed that the crusading ardor had cooled. The Fourth Crusade, 1201–04, was inspired by Pope Innocent III. He envisioned the papacy at the head of a great religious conquest. But the crusaders got completely out of his control. The Venetians incited them to seize Zara from Hungary, and the deposed emperor of Constantinople persuaded them to attack Constantinople and put him back on the throne. The whole Crusade was a boondoggle. The Crusaders did little more than fight other Christians. They did capture and loot Constantinople and sent back to Europe thousands of relics. The Venetians, the real winners, secured valuable trading concessions in the Aegean Sea.

Although there were other Crusades (like the Children's Crusade in 1212 led by the shepherd boy Stephen, which netted the sea captains of the Mediterranean thousands of slaves), the grandiose scheme of the church militant had run its course. The tangible results are debatable. The West was temporarily united. Papal indulgences to offset punishment for sin grew, knowledge and commerce increased, the spirit of nationalism budded, and the church's ability to wield power was demonstrated. Some free communities emerged by buying their freedom from overlords who needed money for pilgrimages, and three new orders of knighthood to protect the Holy Land were founded—the Hospitalers, the Templars, and the Order of Teutonic Knights. However, Islam was not permanently checked, the East-West schism not healed, the Holy Land not won, the church not purified. Reactions came in the rise of heresies and the rejection of the militant culture of the age by men like St. Francis.

The medieval period in Western culture was by no means simplistic and monolithic. The church did tend to dominate, but both within and without tensions existed that called orthodoxy into question. The development of national, sovereign states based largely on affinities of language and geography rather than religion steadily eroded the universal claims of the church.

The rise of universities in the twelfth and thirteenth centuries contributed to this development. Universities depended heavily on papal and princely patronage and enhanced orthodoxy in many respects, but they also encouraged new thought. The University of Paris originated with the cathedral school of Notre Dame and the canons of St. Victor and St. Genevieve at the beginning of the twelfth century. It received a charter in 1200 from Philip Augustus of France and a grant of papal statutes in 1215. Oxford University in England, modeled after Paris, began about the same time and achieved eminence by the mid-thirteenth century. In 1209 a migration of scholars from Oxford joined the canons of Cambridge and by 1233 Cambridge University was recognized. Peter Abelard (1079–1142), one of the most brilliant teachers of the period, attracted large crowds of scholars to Paris by questioning and in debate demolishing views held by some of the most cherished mentors of the day. Logic intoxicated him with delight and seemed to promise a solution to all mysteries. Something should be believed, he said, not because it came from God but because reason convinces us that it is so. In an irritating treatise called *Sic et Non* (*Yes and No*) he compiled conflicting passages from the Fathers without resolving the issues thus raised. He taught that we inherited punishment but not guilt from Adam, that intention makes an act either good or bad, that ancient philosophers received divine revelations, and that Christ's life and death were intended to awaken love in us. He questioned the reality of universals (such as Justice, Truth, and the Trinity, as if a perfect ideal of each existed) and argued that the whole essence of divinity was not in each of the three divine persons, but instead that each was an attribute of the godhead. Bernard of Clairvaux, who could condone neither Abelard's theology nor his tragic love affair with Heloise, procured the condemnation of Abelard's assertions at the Council of Sens in 1141 and successfully thwarted an appeal to Pope Innocent II. Abelard was regarded as a critical doubter, and theologians realized that dependence on his kind of dialectical logic could lead to institutional and theological chaos. (See also Chapter 11.)

One of Abelard's disciples, Arnold of Brescia (1100–55) persistently raised his voice against the worldliness of the church. After studying with Abelard in Paris, he returned to Brescia and mounted a virulent attack on ecclesiastical immorality. Clerical vice, he said, was the result of the church's attempt to control the world. He urged the church to give all property and secular dominion to the state and return to the poverty and simplicity of the early church. Priests, he said, should be poor, should own no land. They should have nothing to do with secular authority. The true church and its ministers should shun wealth, for wealth and power nullify salvation and destroy the value of the sacraments. Better than the priestly absolutions and satisfactions were the direct confessions of one Christian to another. These ideas were not necessarily heretical, but they were radical. Alarmed nobles and prelates forced him to flee from Brescia in 1139. Bernard considered Arnold's ideas dangerous enough to secure his condemnation at the same council that condemned Abelard in 1141. In 1145 Arnold showed up in Rome, joined in the civic revolt against temporal papal dominion, and established a rival government that lasted ten years. Pope Eugenius III (1145–53), a Cistercian monk and Bernard's own protégé, spent nearly all of his pontificate outside of Rome. Not until seven months before he died, when he made a treaty with Frederick Barbarossa, was Eugenius able to re-enter Rome. His successor, Pope Adrian IV (1154–59), engaged Frederick to destroy Arnold in return for coronation. Frederick then captured, hanged, and burned Arnold, and scattered his ashes on the Tiber.

Protest continued against papal worldliness and dominion. In the eleventh and twelfth centuries a much more heretical form of objection developed. It came from the Cathari, who spread rapidly from Hungary into France, Spain, Italy, and Germany. Cathari stood for "pure" in some circles, and "heretics" in others. They revived orthodox as well as heretical practices. Although similar to the ancient Manichees, they were not just a rebirth of that sect. They were an organized protest against Roman Catholicism. The true church endures and does not persecute, they said. Against them the papacy inaugurated the Inquisition and mounted a crusade, both of which were monumental for their cruelty.

The Cathari (commonly called Albigenses because of their large settlement near Albi, France) believed in a dualism of body and soul, material and spiritual worlds, evil and good. Essentially, each person is a spirit, temporarily trapped by evil powers in a prison house of flesh. One's goal is not to gain more and more worldly goods but to rid oneself of them, including the body, and to re-enter the world of pure spirit. They practiced a severe asceticism, believing that the greatest sin was human reproduction because it extended the prison bondage. The higher class of Cathari, the *perfecti* or perfect, subjected themselves to *endura*, a rite of slow starvation that brought the final consolation of forgiveness of sins and restoration to the kingdom of God. They rejected marriage, war, property, oaths, and all products related to animal reproduction such as eggs, milk, butter, and cheese. They ate fish, but otherwise were strict vegetarians. The lower class of Cathari, the *credenti* or believers, accepted these ideals but were not expected to fulfill them perfectly until given the grace to do so. In this life they could marry, own property, and even conform to Roman Catholicism, hoping however to receive consolation before death, and short of that, reincarnation.

They avidly read the New Testament, stressed its moral earnestness and injunctions to love, and made vernacular translations. They believed that the Roman Catholics had mistaken biblical allegories for literal truths and as a consequence were actually serving the devil. Christ was not truly human; he did not die nor did he rise from the grave. He was an angel created in heaven that appropriated a body only to meet us on our own level and show us the true way to redemption—the way of the Cathari. They rejected the cross and the sacraments as being no more than symbols of materialism.

Although the records of the suppression of the Cathari may be exaggerated, there is little doubt that they were subjected to cruelties. At

Cologne in 1145, three women and eight men believed to be Cathari were burned to death. At Oxford in 1161 thirty of them were branded on the forehead and flogged. In England, Henry II (d. 1189), blinded and castrated those believed guilty of Catharism—blinding so they could not see this evil world, castration so they could not imprison more spirits. The councils of Rheims, 1148, Third Lateran, 1179, and Verona, 1184, condemned them, the Lateran council enjoining princes to take action. In 1184 Pope Lucius III established an early form of the Inquisition by requiring bishops to examine under oath all their subjects for heresy. Heresy and harboring a heretic brought excommunication. Church leaders felt that the Cathari had to be stopped, if not by persuasion, then by force, lest the entire body of Christ be poisoned. Since the Old Testament said that an apostate should be stoned, the New Testament that a body might be destroyed for the sake of the soul, Augustine that a rotten limb should be amputated, and the Justinian Code that deniers of the Trinity should be executed, the church felt it had ample justification for harsh measures. In 1199 Pope Innocent III declared heresy a capital crime and called on Philip II of France to conquer the heretics by force of arms, promising him plenary indulgence and their lands if he did so. Innocent thus inaugurated a crusade against the Cathari that lasted from 1207 until 1244. In 1209 the "Slay all, God will know his own" massacre occurred at Beziers, the papal legate reporting that 20,000 men, women, and children were slain. Pope Innocent III congratulated the Crusaders for having won remission of sins and new wealth. At Minerve 140 *prefecti* were burned, and hundreds of prisoners had their ears and noses cut off. Violence continued throughout the century.

Decrees of the Fourth Lateran Council, 1215, provided for the secular punishment of heretics, the confiscation of their property, excommunication for those unwilling to proceed against heretics, and complete forgiveness of sins for those cooperating. In 1220 the Inquisition was turned over to the newly formed order of Dominicans, and in 1229 the Synod of Toulouse systematized inquisitorial rules, leaving the alleged heretic with virtually no rights. Bernard Gui in his *Inquisitor's Manual,* 1300, disclosed that the inquisitor was not subject to the law, only to the papacy. He was the prosecutor and judge. The "trial" was secret, and the accused had to prove his innocence. The victim could have no counsel, nor were his accusers identified. Favorable witnesses were charged with abetting heresy. The accused as well as the witnesses were tortured. Testimony of children and criminals could be received against a person but not for him. If he confessed, the death penalty might be reduced to life imprisonment, although Emperor Frederick II directed that in such a case he should lose his tongue for having assailed the church. One was never completely acquitted. Cases could always be reopened. Because the Cathari were using the Bible, the Synod of Toulouse denounced all vernacular translations, and forbade the laity to possess Scriptures.

In 1233 Pope Gregory IX ordered the Dominicans to exterminate the Cathari, especially the Albigenses in France, and in 1252 Pope Innocent IV authorized torture as a means of getting information and confessions. By the end of the fourteenth century the Cathari had disappeared.

However, from 1306 to 23 they were still strong in Toulouse. During that period 143 alleged Cathari were condemned to wear crosses, 307 imprisoned, 69 corpses exhumed and burned, and 42 put to death. Condemnation and exhumation of the dead, sometimes after thirty years, made confiscation of property possible. Of the 930 suspects brought before Bernard Gui, the property of not one went unconfiscated. Inquisitor Eymeric reported a languishing of the Inquisition in 1369 because no more wealthy heretics remained!

The Cathari disappeared in the fourteenth century but not the Inquisition. It continued against heresy and dissent. It reached its zenith under Torquemada at the end of the fifteenth century, was reinstituted in 1542 to curb Protestantism, and was not officially ended until 1834. The suppression of dissent was thorough and cruel and extended over 700 years. As Lord Acton said, it left a stench that has not yet been eradicated.

Lumped with the Cathari and persecuted along with them were the Waldenses, even though the two groups were quite different in their beliefs. In the eyes of the papacy, the Waldenses like the Cathari were disturbers of the unity of the universal church. Their commitment to simple, Sermon-on-the-Mount religion constituted a criticism of ecclesiastical worldliness. Peter Waldo (d. 1218), a wealthy merchant of Lyons and founder of the Waldenses, received his inspiration not only from the New Testament but also from the story of St. Alexis, who renounced his possessions, went on a pilgrimage, and returned to live for many years as a beggar under his parents' porch—unrecognized until he died. Troubled in conscience by his own wealth, Waldo provided for his wife and family, gave away all that remained, and began a career of itinerant preaching. He wanted to be perfect, according to Matthew 19:21. He preached, using memorized portions of the Bible translated by a friendly priest, and soon attracted such crowds from all classes that local authorities became concerned. Waldo journeyed to Rome during the Third Lateran Council in 1179 to seek official permission to preach, only to have Alexander III praise him for his poverty and tell him that doctrinal preaching required much training and had to be done under local clerical supervision. The commission that heard Waldo regarded him and his followers as ignorant laymen and suspected Waldo of Arianism for saying Mary was the Mother of Christ instead of the Mother of God. On not receiving permission to preach, Waldo and his followers resolved to obey God rather than men. In 1184 the Council of Verona excommunicated the Waldenses for disobedience, but they spread quickly into Northern Italy, the Alps, the Rhine Valley, Germany and along the Danube River—strengthened especially by many Lombard Humiliati, also forbidden to preach in 1184. Waldo's arbitrary exercise of authority sparked a schism in Lombardy in 1210, and Innocent III's organization of Poor Catholics, who used Waldensian practices to win Waldenses to Catholicism, slowed the movement. In France and Spain repeated persecutions resulted in their annihilation. Yet the Waldenses have continued to maintain themselves in the Piedmont and the Alps until the present.

The Waldenses believed in the Bible, took the Sermon on the Mount seriously, went out preaching in pairs. They rejected oaths, war, property;

they begged for food. Persecution forced them to share their goods communally. They quit begging, commissioned some to evangelize while others worked, and eventually took up arms in self-defense. Any who helped them could have their property confiscated. Pressed by violent opposition, the Waldenses bitterly assailed the clergy, denounced the papacy, used the Bible rather than the cross as their symbol of Christianity, refused to say the Apostles' Creed, and proclaimed sacraments given by unworthy priests invalid. They rejected veneration of saints, masses for the dead, images, relics, tithes, indulgences, capital punishment, purgatory, and all but two of the church's sacraments. They heard confessions and ordained their members for ministry. Though tainted somewhat by Catharism, the Waldenses wanted to purify the church by a return to simplicity. The papacy, however, saw the Cathari and Waldenses not only as heretical, disruptive groups but also as serious threats to medieval unity. Other groups were also seen as threats. Even the Poor Catholics who were organized to match the poverty of the Waldenses were eventually forbidden to preach and forced to join established orders. The papacy could not annul its sacraments and void its priesthood, nor admit that faith in God might be something other than the mandates of Rome.

Although the Cathari and Waldenses constituted the main thrusts of protest in the Middle Ages, there were many others—the free-thinking Beghards, Bogomiles, Humiliati, mystics, Runcarii, and Amalricians. Reminiscent of the early church whose eschatology provided a transcendent basis for criticism of the world, in the Middle Ages eschatology had a rebirth. Apocalyptic speculations came preeminently from Joachim (ca. 1132–1202). A Cistercian monk devoted to the church and founder of his own monastery at Fiore, Joachim directed that his writings be submitted posthumously to the papacy. They were and were condemned by the Lateran Council in 1215 and again by Alexander IV in 1256. Joachim saw a Trinitarian division in history. The first age was that of the Father, the period of law for humanity; the second that of the Son, the period of grace; and the third that of the Spirit, the period of spiritual freedom, to start about 1260. It would be accompanied by the rise of new religious orders and the establishment of the spiritual church. Gerard of Borgo San Donnino, a Spiritual Franciscan, believed the third age would be lived under the Eternal Evangel that he excerpted in 1254 from Joachim's writings. By implication Joachim's treatises superseded the Old and New Testaments. Whether intended or not, Joachim's works became the basis for apocalyptic speculations critical of a church mired in worldliness. His ideas were especially promulgated later by the Spiritual Franciscans, who were subjected to the Inquisition.

In the pontificate of Innocent III (1198–1216) the medieval church reached a climax of power. Neither before nor since has the papacy basked in such heights of domination. In Innocent the theories of papal supremacy over all spiritual and secular affairs came to fruition. He firmly believed that God is the source of all power, that the Pope is Christ's vicar, and that no king can rightly rule unless he serves the vicar of Christ. Innocent's one consuming desire was to extend the *plenitudo potestatis* of the Roman see over all of Christendom. That desire did not go unsatisfied. He controlled Europe from Canterbury to Constantinople, from Coimbra to Upsala. He made kings his vassals, created the Inquisition, promoted the Fourth Crusade, engineered the Fourth Lateran Council, and realized within himself the awful power to bind and to loose. Yet his triumph was not without much shedding of blood.

Two things contributed greatly to Innocent's success: his own ascetic convictions, and the awe with which the sacraments had come to be held. Born Lothario Conti, Innocent came from a family of Popes, studied theology and law at Paris and Bologna, and became a cardinal-deacon at the age of twenty-nine. When forced out of papal service by a rival family, Innocent withdrew from the world and immersed himself in asceticism. This was the time when he wrote *Contempt of the World, Misery of the Mortal Estate, Four Kinds of Marriage,* and *The Mystery of the Sacrament of the Altar.* This ascetic rejection of the world enabled him as Pope to act out of concern for principles rather than self. He knew that the sacrament of the altar and ordination linked all priests to Rome and its claim of primacy; he realized the necessity of keeping that link free from simony, investiture, and immorality. Innocent conceived himself as standing between God and man, in control of the priests who controlled those sacraments that enabled a person to avoid hell and acquire heaven. He understood the power of transubstantiation, which only the priest could bring about, and he made it the official doctrine of the church. Thus he capitalized on a potent religious feeling that pervaded the Middle Ages. In the mass, through the power of the priest, the individual came into direct contact with Christ and his grace. Ever imminent death made such grace desirable. Neither serf nor king could stand without it.

Innocent felt that final authority could not be divided between church and state. One had to dominate. As the keys had been given to Peter and his successors, Innocent staunchly believed that he must not neglect the high stewardship that he held as God's supreme representative on earth. "Feed my sheep" meant that he was to interpret the word of God to the church in sermons, commentaries, and pronouncements. In this he was Melchizedek, the priest, ministering to the priests of the Vicar of Christ, insisting that the church be pure, objecting to absenteeism, pluralism, simony, inefficiency, and immorality. "I will build my church" meant that he was to bring the church to its proper place of eminence in the world, as he did in his numerous conflicts with secular powers. In this he was Melchizedek, the king, employing the keys to bring about proper submission, endeavoring to make the church strong, centralizing Christian society under the office established by God. Innocent believed he was to direct the church and rule the world not because of his own inherent power, but because he had been chosen by God to do so.

Innocent was no great theologian, but his ascetic bent, study of the Bible, and desire for ecclesiastical efficiency fostered in him an ideal of purity. He ordered the abbot of Cluny to correct abuses in the Cluniac order. He prohibited clerical marriages and punished offenders. He sent many absentee bishops back to their bishoprics. He stripped some clergy of their multiple benefices. To keep the church pure within, he authorized the Inquisition and sent crusading armies against the Cathari and

Waldenses. He wisely, albeit cautiously, gave tentative approval to the Dominicans and Franciscans (see Chapter 11), thus keeping the thirteenth century's two vigorous monastic orders within the church's orbit of control. A series of events enabled Innocent to assert his claims:

1. When Henry VI of Germany died in 1197 at the age of thirty-two, Henry's widow warded their very young son, Frederick II, to Innocent and also gave him Sicily that Frederick might later receive it back as a fief. Taking advantage of the temporary imperial chaos, Innocent declared that while the electors should elect their emperor, he as Pope had the "right and authority to examine the person elected" and that only he could invest the crown. Innocent was guardian of the future emperor.

2. In the German struggle for the crown, Innocent supported Otto, then switched to Philip when it appeared that Otto would be defeated. The assassination of Philip, however, caused the Pope to switch his support back to Otto, who won in Germany and was crowned at Rome by Innocent in 1209. But tension between Otto and Innocent soon resulted in Otto's seizure of papal lands in central Italy, causing Innocent to put forth the young Frederick II as anti-emperor in 1212. Frederick defeated Otto at Bouvines in 1214 and was crowned German king at Aachen in 1215. Although he had no love for papal supremacy, he accepted the Pope's feudal control of his domains. Innocent appeared to have achieved a base of invincible power.

3. When Philip II of France divorced his wife Ingeborg of Denmark in order to marry an attractive young girl, Innocent placed the kingdom under interdict, forbade public celebration of church rites, and eventually brought Philip to submission. Innocent appeared as a champion of marriage.

Similar actions not only gained territorial rights for Innocent but also won him a reputation as defender of morality. As the price for an adulterous affair with the wife of a count, King Peter of Aragon turned his kingdom over to the Pope in 1204 and then received it back as a fief. King Alfonso IX of Leon gave up his wife to whom he was blood-related. Innocent resisted the aspirations of a bastard to the throne of Denmark. He deposed the king of Navarre for making a treaty with the Moors. He helped establish a legitimate line of kings in Sweden. He incited the bishops of Poland and Norway to reform. And the kings of Serbia and Bulgaria granted Innocent the right to wear their crowns. Innocent's victories were not always lasting, but they demonstrate the far-reaching power of his pontificate and the implementation of his concept of the papacy as above all human institutions.

4. Innocent had to fight long and hard against King John of England (1199–1216) but finally wrested England from John's control and gave it back as a fief. John's character left much to be desired. He ruthlessly killed those people that he regarded as threats to his throne, plundered churches and convents, divorced his wife to take another, and longed to control Canterbury and the appointment of bishops. When the Pope, against the wishes of John, appointed Stephen Langton archbishop of Canterbury, John seized the property of Canterbury, and Innocent

retaliated by putting England under interdict—despite the threat of John to mutilate every Italian on the island. The Pope's interdict of England in 1208 directed that church burials cease, religious services be drastically curtailed, monasteries be closed to usual visits, churches remain shut, the cross be put outside without ceremony. In 1209 Innocent excommunicated the king himself, and in 1212 declared that John was unworthy to be king and that Englishmen need no longer obey him. John fearfully punished those who sided with Innocent, but in 1213, with the prospect of an invasion from France, he submitted, surrendered the "whole realm of England and Ireland" to "God and the Roman Church" for "remission of our sins," swore fealty to the Pope and his successors, and promised to remit a thousand marks sterling each year. The interdict was lifted, but Innocent's victory was somewhat hollow, for in 1215 the barons of England pressed their Magna Carta, which demanded certain basic rights for Englishmen and freedom for the Church of England. Although Innocent III declared that this was interference with his vassalage rights and that the Magna Carta was henceforth null and void, and although John raged and ate straw saying he had signed the document under duress, the Magna Carta became the cornerstone of English law.

Ecclesiastically the Fourth Lateran Council, 1215, crowned Innocent's attempt to manifest the full power of the church. The council anathematized the Cathari and invited a Crusade against them; made transubstantiation the official dogma of the church on the Lord's Supper; legalized and promoted the Inquisition; warned clergymen against worldly theaters, executions, drinking contests and inns of ill repute; ordered that Jews wear a special garb "to protect them"; excoriated those who said Father, Son, and Holy Spirit were one only semantically speaking; sought to control trade in sham relics; licensed collectors of charity; required confession and communion at Easter on pain of excommunication.

Neither before nor since has the domination of the papacy been so complete over human affairs.

11

Ecclesiastical Domination

The thirteenth century marked the predominance of the church in Western culture. The 1200s, inaugurated by Pope Innocent III, saw the rise of
two new dynamic monastic orders, brought scholasticism to a climax in
Thomas Aquinas, and witnessed the popular reality of the church as the
agent of God in the directing of all earthly affairs. Never before had the
church enjoyed such preeminence. Compared to the persecuted church
in the Roman empire, the tables had turned completely and the church
was now the sovereign mistress of society. However, the Kingdom of God
had not come, and the near collapse of papal institutionalism in the next
century demonstrated that all was not well. In the succeeding centuries,
sovereignty over society passed from the church to a multitude of national
states, each claiming and fighting for sovereignty, a situation that in an
interrelated culture has moved inexorably from one war to another. The
thirteenth century, although followed by disruption, witnessed the pinnacle of the church in control of secular and spiritual affairs.

Innocent III, discussed in the previous chapter, had the foresight to
sanction the thirteenth century's two most influential orders, the Dominicans and the Franciscans, the former tending to support the worldly
dominance of the church and the latter tending to posit an alternative
example of service. In the course of the century the two orders became
rivals, especially in the intellectual realm of university teaching. At first
the Franciscans shunned scholarly pursuits, but soon provided that cer-

tain members of the order be given university training that others might in turn be trained in theology. Both orders provided relative security and freedom for dedicated and proven teachers who could not find or were tired of the competition for ecclesiastical and secular preferments and benefices. Only the rare and highly popular teachers could live from the fees paid by their students. The friars infused the thirteenth century with intellectual fervor and dominated education in Europe until 1350. Dominican theologians included Robert Bacon, Albertus Magnus, Thomas Aquinas, and Meister Eckhart; the Franciscans had Alexander of Hales, Bonaventura, Duns Scotus, and William Occam. The list includes the greatest constructor and the greatest destroyer of medieval thought, respectively—Aquinas, a Dominican, and Occam, a Franciscan.

More by accident than design the begging friars lived in towns wealthy enough to support organized communities of poverty. But poverty, a means for the Dominicans and an ideal for the Franciscans, proved impossible. They found that they had to have some property, that they could not be utterly poor, although they strove to possess as little as possible. Their houses, donated by the rich and near rich, soon formed a familiar sight in the larger cities. In contrast to the older orders, which were rural and stable, the new friars were urban and mobile.

The Dominican order, founded by the Spaniard Domingo de Guzman (1170–1221), began almost fortuitously. In 1206 Dominic heard a conversation in Montpellier between a bishop and three Cistercian abbots whom Innocent III had assigned to combat heresy in Languedoc. He realized that the abbots had failed and others would fail if they depended on ecclesiastical pomp and dignity, which the Albigenses considered an affront to true religion. He believed the Albigenses would listen only if apostolic poverty accompanied the preaching. To reach the Albigenses, he traveled as a poor man, wore no shoes, begged for food, preached along the roads and in the marketplaces. Threatened and ridiculed, Dominic had only meager success, and his peaceful mission was foreclosed in 1208 when Innocent III's policy of force began to take effect.

Dominic's mission was preaching and poverty, which he deemed necessary for communication. In 1214, with the aid of a rich man of Toulouse, Dominic gathered a group of men to win heretics and heathen by preaching to them the Word and living simply. Dominic supplemented preaching with instruction, and his dream of a learned, preaching order of mendicant friars took shape. The Fourth Lateran Council denied him and his friars papal recognition, but in 1216 Honorius III sanctioned their mission. In 1220 their rule, adapted from that of the Augustinians with added emphasis on preaching and simple living, was confirmed.

In 1217 at Toulouse Dominic and fifteen of his followers laid plans for an expanding world mission. They deployed to strategic points in Spain, Paris, Bologna, and Rome to preach, teach, win, and train others, and within another four years had organized in eight countries—France, England, Germany, Lombardy, Hungary, Spain, Provence, and the Papal States. From the beginning they stressed learn ng, making it a rule that no one could preach without having had three years of theological training. A cosmopolitan movement and the first order to be based on learning, they established themselves in the fast-growing universities and soon gained renown for their scholarship. Dedicated to combat heresy and heathenism, the Dominicans became the watchdogs of the church's Inquisition, and Aquinas clarified the doctrines and practices of the church in a monumental system of theology that is still basic in Roman Catholic circles. With their added interest in far-flung missions to the heathen, the Dominicans contributed heavily to ecclesiastical orthodoxy.

The same could not be said for the Franciscans. Although the Dominicans and Franciscans became intense rivals and had many goals in common, the Franciscan movement symbolized reform, redirection, and rededication. Francis repaired churches and insisted that his followers obey priests and bishops, yet his espousal of poverty as an ideal for all Christians constituted a constant criticism not only of the comfortable clergy but of the laity and the burgeoning materialism of the times. Unlike the Dominicans, who bolstered orthodoxy, the Franciscans frequently suffered persecution and excommunication as heretics. Francis' own life was one of dedication to apostolic poverty and imitation of Christ. He lived within the church, but not without tension. The Spiritual Franciscans who tried to continue his way of life met with official condemnation. Francis' life of poverty, spontaneity, and self-denying service contrasted sharply with the church's sovereign preeminence in spiritual and secular affairs.

Giovanni Bernardone, St. Francis (1182–1226), was the son of a rich cloth merchant of Assisi. Capitalism in the modern sense was just beginning to take hold of Europe's commercial enterprises, and trading in Assisi was profitable. Although Francis as a young man indulged himself in carefree irresponsible gaiety, throwing big parties and giving away large portions of his father's goods, he revolted against the economic greed of those times and questioned why men should strive to get money. In a war between the rich and the poor in 1201, Francis found himself siding with the poor—much to the distaste of his father; he was captured, and spent a year in prison in Perugia. There he had time to think, and after being freed found resumption of his former ways impossible.

Affected by tales of romantic chivalry and stories of early Christians renouncing all worldly goods to follow Christ, Francis resolved to devote his life to the ideal of lady poverty. He would beg for his livelihood but would not accept any more than was necessary for each day; he would work but only to serve, not to accumulate wealth. He would store nothing and own nothing. He would live from day to day rejoicing in the abundance of God's gifts, in creation, in creatures, in pain. He would live in the forest, if necessary, trusting God to supply his needs. He would have no rule in which to take pride, only the Holy Spirit to give spontaneous guidance.

Francis' conversion was not sudden. His restless spirit found no immediate way to proceed. He journeyed to Rome, saw how little pilgrims contributed at St. Peter's shrine, and noisily dumped all his money through the grating for offerings. He then went outside, exchanged clothes with a beggar, and begged. Returning to Assisi, he compelled himself to kiss the rotting hand of a leper, and then to serve the needs of the leper outcasts in the lazar houses. They were the first to call him St. Francis. One day while in the chapel of San Damiano praying and meditating on the wounds of Christ, Francis believed he heard a voice commanding him to repair God's house. Interpreting the voice literally, Francis began doing just that. Liberality with his father's money, however, caused his father to have him thrown in jail, where he underwent repeated floggings for obduracy. By now Francis was in full revolt. In court he dramatically stripped himself naked, gave his clothes to his father, thus legally and symbolically severing all ties with his family. A priest gave him a cloak. His renunciation was complete.

For three years he repaired chapels and churches in and around Assisi and attended the lepers. From friendly priests he learned to read. On hearing Christ's instructions to his disciples in Matthew 10, Francis resolved to preach that the kingdom of heaven is at hand. He discarded his sandals, walked barefoot, carried no wallet or purse, wore only a single tunic girded with a piece of rope. People began to listen with respect. His first followers were Bernard of Quintavalle and Peter Catani, the former a wealthy Assisian and the latter a doctor of law who had studied at Bologna. Both distributed their goods to the poor and joined Francis in the freedom of renunciation. Soon others came. The fact that so many joined the Franciscan movement in the thirteenth century indicates widespread dissatisfaction with social conditions and a hungering for religious fulfillment. Many, already begging because of their poverty, switched to Francis' religious venture.

Because of previous trouble with the Waldenses, papal authorities hesitated to approve the Franciscans, but in 1210 Innocent III's dream of a beggar upholding the church prompted him to grant informal papal approbation. If there was a rule as early as 1209–10, it was simply an acceptance of biblical injunctions to leave all, give to the poor, and live a life of poverty and self-denying service in Christ. By a kind of intuition Francis decided who should join. But the growing numbers of brothers necessitated organization and rules, and the order gradually lost much of its original spontaneity. When Francis returned from an unsuccessful trip to Egypt to convert the Muslims, around 1220, he found internal discord among his followers about whether they should own property. With his hands he attempted to demolish a house that some brothers had built. He seemed to be a mother hen unable to cover and control her hatching chicks. Reluctantly Francis consented to rules, rules he feared would lead to pride in keeping them; and he accepted the use of property rather than ownership, which he feared would lead to material attachments.

However, Francis was not happy with these compromises; he perceived a different spirit in the Second Rule, 1221, which insisted on vows of poverty, obedience, chastity, standards of prayer, habits for novitiates, and other regulations. The Third Rule was confirmed in 1223 by Pope Honorius III, who thus officially sanctioned the order, but each rule seemed to depart further from the spirit of Francis. The Third Rule in particular reflected the interests of the papacy. The first item required the brothers minors to obey and observe the gospel in poverty and chastity. Francis was bound to obey and revere Pope Honorius and his successors, and the brothers were bound to obey Francis and his successors. They were expected but not required to sell their goods and give the money to the poor. Newcomers, after a year's probation assumed irrevocable bonds. Clerical brothers were to perform divine service according to the rules of Rome, and lay brothers were to say seventy-six Paternosters daily and pray for the dead. The brothers were not to ride, quarrel, argue, become angry, receive money, or be idle. They were to trust the Lord to provide through alms. None was to preach without examination and approval. A cardinal was to serve as corrector and protector of the order. The rule did not encourage learning. Francis objected to a brother having even a psalter, saying it would lead to pride and more possessions; he cursed brother Peter Stacis for trying to start a house of study in Bologna. However, after the death of Francis, the pressure for education could not be resisted. Seventy new universities started in Europe between 1200 and 1250. By 1234 the Franciscans had a flourishing seminary with 214 students at St. German des Pres. In 1212 the Poor Clares order for women was organized.

Francis helped preserve religion for the masses; he believed a religious person need not be learned and intelligent. But he also lived by paradoxes. Self-denial led easily to asceticism, yet he was not an ascetic. He gloried in God's creation, felt related to nature, preached to birds, and tamed wolves. His *Canticle to the Sun,* written after forty days of fasting on Monte Alverno, was an Italian hymn of joy and praise for the sun, earth, moon, and even death. He concentrated on the wounds of Christ until he received the stigmata, bringing together in his body a mystical joy in creation and crucifixion—the unsearchable mercies of God.

He recognized that rules were necessary and also that they led almost inevitably to difficulties and divisions. The first large split among the Franciscans occurred between those who wanted to adhere strictly to the rules and those who wanted to preserve, though they unwittingly institutionalized, the spirit of Francis, who before he died was widely believed to be a saint. The church so declared in 1228. The Spirituals tried to adhere to the spirit of Francis and were widely persecuted, especially when through the writings of Joachim of Fiore they seemed to herald an age of the spirit which would supersede the church. Other dissensions plagued the Franciscans, for the infectious spontaneity of Francis resisted institutionalization and repeatedly challenged established patterns.

Innocent III, the Dominicans, and the Franciscans loomed large in the thirteenth century, but one intellectual giant dominated that century. His name was Thomas Aquinas (1225/27–74), a Dominican scholar who applied a synthesis of Plato and Aristotle to medieval ecclesiastical thought and created a systematized theology that has continued to dominate Roman Catholicism into the twentieth century. Although the Franciscan Order for a time forbade the friars minor to study Aquinas and a few bishops with whom he had argued condemned some of his works, the Dominicans in 1278 officially adopted his teachings and in 1323 he was canonized by Pope John XXII. In 1567 Pope Pius V pronounced him a Doctor of the Church, and in 1879 Pope Leo XIII made his writings required reading for all Catholic students of theology and philosophy. He is the patron of all Catholic universities, and in 1923 Pope Pius XI reiterated his authority as a teacher. No theologian has equaled the influence of Aquinas in Roman Catholicism.

Scholasticism, of which Aquinas is the acknowledged master, was concerned with the essence of reality. What is real? What is truth? How are faith and reason related? It reached its climax in Aquinas, but it did not begin with him.

The scholastics sought answers to these questions largely through the avenues of reason, preferring to defend the faith, to which they were almost totally committed, by intellectual reasoning rather than biblical authorities. They drew heavily upon the ancient Greeks, particularly Plato and his eternal forms of Goodness, Truth, Justice, etc., the things on earth being mere imitations. This fitted well with the ascetic bent of religious life in the Middle Ages and represents an enduring aspect of early Gnosticism. With the reintroduction of Aristotle into Western culture via Arabic scholarship, Aristotle became increasingly important. Averroes (1126–98), a Muslim of Cordova, became known as "the commentator" on Aristotle. He stressed the eternity of the world and the human race; denied personal immortality, freedom of the will, and moral responsibility; separated God from providential action in the world by a series of emanations; and posited one intellect for the human race in which individuals participate. His works gained acceptance in the University of Paris until they were combatted by Aquinas and condemned in 1270 and again in 1277. Moses Maimonides (1135–1204), a Jewish scholar of Cordova, who wrote much of his work in Arabic, sought to harmonize Jewish revelation and Aristotelian reason, and heavily influenced Albertus Magnus and Aquinas. This new Aristotelian thrust in learning became widely available through the Latin translations of William of Moerbeke (1215–86), a close friend of Aquinas.

The incongruities between Platonic and Aristotelian thought pushed the scholastics of the Middle Ages into long and intricate arguments about whether reality resides in the concept or the individual things. The realists maintained that only the ideal, the concept, the universal, is real. The nominalists maintained that the ideals or universals are merely names, and that reality resides in the individuals. A great deal was at stake, for if the nominalists were correct, then by implication such things as the Trinity, the Universal Church, absolute Justice, God, Purity, and so forth would be abstractions, mere names. Aquinas' greatness rests on his successful synthesis of the two in support of church doctrine and practice. In the fourteenth century the erosion of Aquinas' synthesis rested heavily on the ascendancy of nominalism.

Among the scholastic predecessors of Aquinas were Anselm of Canterbury (1033–1109), William of Champeaux (1070–1121), Roscellinus of Compiegne (d. 1125), and Peter Abelard (1079–1142).

Anselm is remembered for his high papalism over against the king of England, but even more so for his arguments on the existence of God and the atonement. He accepted revealed truth but maintained that we must exercise our reason in apprehending it. In this he was a realist. The *Proslogion* is an attempt to prove the existence of God without reference to empirical things. It stands on the notion that God is that than which nothing greater can be conceived. Since conceiving of God as existing would be greater than not existing, it follows that God exists. "If that thing than which no greater thing is conceivable can be conceived as non-existent, then that very thing than which a greater is inconceivable is not that than which a greater is inconceivable!" This is the classic ontological proof for the existence of God. *Cur deus homo?* was equally a classic masterpiece, seeking to prove the necessity of the incarnation and redemption on rational grounds. Anselm rejected the ransom theories of atonement, prevalent since the days of Gregory I, on the grounds that humanity owes nothing to the devil. Anselm's satisfaction theory is grounded on the idea that the creature owes all honor to God the creator and that sin consists of withholding the honor that is due to God. In withholding honor one violates his obligation as a rational creature. Sin having been committed, it cannot simply be forgiven, for such non-punishment of unatoned-for sin would introduce disorder into the divine kingdom. To preserve order (justice), the withheld honor must be rendered or punished. Otherwise, either God is not just to himself, or he is powerless to do what he ought to do, which Anselm pronounced blasphemous. The honor of God demands that satisfaction or punishment follow every sin. Since the satisfaction must be commensurate with the dishonor, satisfaction can be rendered for human sin only by God. And since only we ought to render the satisfaction, it can be done only by one who is both God and human—Christ. Christ's mere obedience was not enough; that is demanded of every creature. But since he did not sin, death was not required. Christ's death was an offering of his free will, not of debt, and God could not leave so great a gift unrewarded. Since Christ needed neither gift nor pardon, he willed his claim on God to us. God's great mercy toward the sinner is thus revealed in the Father, saying, "Receive my only Son, and offer him for thyself," while the Son says, "Take me, and redeem thyself."

William of Champeaux, who studied under Anselm of Laon and Anselm of Canterbury, founded the Order of St. Victor and became a teacher of renown at the cathedral school of Paris. In the Platonic tradition, he was a realist who believed that universals come before individuals, that the reality of the individuals comes from the general class or universal in which it participates. Humanity precedes individual persons. God comes first; Father, Son, and Holy Spirit share together in God. Individual particulars are aspects of the substance of the class or universal.

Roscellinus, a popular priest and teacher in Brittany, is sometimes called the father of nominalism. In the tradition of Aristotle, he maintained that universals are derived from our observation of individuals. Species and class are no more than words, abstractions; nothing in reality corresponds to them. Because he held that God is a concept and that the divine reality is the three persons, he was accused of tritheism and condemned for heresy at the Synod of Soissons, 1092.

Peter Abelard, who studied under William of Champeaux, Roscellinus, and Anselm of Laon, took a mediating position, saying that only individuals exist, but that individuals are expressed in universals. The universal's function is logical, enabling us to think; nominalism alone would lead to a breakdown of thought; realism (universalism) alone would lead to pantheism. There are real universals, but we cannot experience them. We go from particulars to general concepts, which do not absolutely represent the real universals. As mentioned earlier (Chapter 10), many of his ideas became suspect. He trusted basically in our rational ability to arrive at truth, saying it is good to doubt because doubt leads to inquiry, inquiry to understanding, and understanding to conviction. True faith must be won through knowledge and understanding. Since to doubt and to be mistaken are not sins, he believed that heretics should not be coerced. He argued that intention renders an act sinful or not, thus leaving the possibility that even the crucifiers of Christ, if they intended good, did not sin. He discarded both the ransom and satisfaction theories of atonement, saying the devil has no claim upon us and that forgiveness cannot demand satisfaction. He posits the moral theory, saying that Christ's death is a revelation of God's full love and that it arouses a love toward God in us when we realize that God does not allow the suffering to be final. The Resurrection is final. Atonement is in the responsive love awakened in one's life by a kind of sympathetic moral influence when one learns about Christ's life and death. As in Luke 7:47, awakened love is the ground of forgiveness.

Although Abelard may not have intended it, others saw that his views tended to detract from the machinery and moral practices of the church. His views on the Trinity were condemned at the Council of Soissons in 1121, and other views at the Council of Sens in 1141 under pressure from St. Bernard. Nevertheless all of these dialectical struggles with the realities of faith and reason contributed to the system of Aquinas.

Thomas Aquinas, related through Count Landulf of Aquino to the Emperor and the King of France, received a good education in the Benedictine school at Monte Cassino and Naples, and in 1244, despite the objections of his family, who held him prisoner for fifteen months at Roccasecca, he joined the Dominicans. At Paris he came under the influence of Albertus Magnus (1200–80), who introduced him to Aristotle. He accompanied Albertus to Cologne and returned to Paris in 1252 to lecture in the Dominican Convent of St. Jacques, where he wrote a defense of the mendicant orders. Subsequently he taught at Anagni, Orvieto, Rome, Viterbo, Paris, and Naples. During his lifetime he wrote sixty books including commentaries on Aristotle, Lombard, Dionysius, Boethius, and various books of the Bible. His work culminated in two *Summae. Summary of the True Catholic Faith Against the Gentiles*, 1259–64, was designed as a handbook for missionaries. The *Full Summary of Theology*, unfinished at his death, crowned his theological thought and formed the basis of subsequent Catholicism. Reginald of Piperno completed the *Summa theologiae* by drawing on Thomas's commentary on Lombard. Written over a period of nine years, the summary concerns itself with God, creation, human destiny, Christ as the way to go to God, the Sacraments, and Last Things. From God—to God—through Christ and the sacraments of the church.

Aquinas held that philosophy examines the natural order in the light of reason, and that theology examines the supernatural order in the light of revelation in God's word. Although reason is used in theology, revelation does not fall within the province of philosophy. But philosophy cannot contradict theology because truth cannot contradict truth. Human reason can demonstrate some truths of revelation, and it can show that other truths are supra- rather than anti-rational, but there is a realm in which reason cannot hold sway. For Aquinas, faith and knowledge are not mutually exclusive. One believes at that point at which one does not know, but faith and knowledge are not antithetical. The goal of both is Being, and although reason cannot finally grasp Being, it can make faith plausible. Faith and reason, revelation and reason, are not inherently antithetical.

In reaction to the Averroists, who from their study of Aristotle posited a truth of reason and a truth of revelation (double truth), Aquinas believed that there is one truth apprehended in different ways and to a different extent by reason and faith. Both are directed toward the truth of Being. Faith, he maintained, deals with revealed knowledge apprehended through feeling and will. Reason deals with natural knowledge apprehended through sense perception and intellection. For Aquinas they are distinct but overlapping cognitive faculties. Whereas such Christian truths as the Trinity, purgatory, Resurrection, original sin, and the Incarnation are beyond the province of reason, reason can indicate their probability and develop a rationale for them. Accepting or rejecting them is a matter of the will, a moral decision. But from the effects of God's activity in the world, reason can point to the existence of God and his providence. The arguments of reason must rest on the facts of the natural world, and so Aquinas bases his famous five arguments for God's existence on observable data. His proofs of God are known as inferential knowledge: (1) Since things in this world move, and since change necessitates an unmoved Mover, God must exist. (2) Since every effect has a cause, and we behold in this world a series of causes and effects, there must be a first Cause—God. (3) Since contingency is that of which the non-existence can be thought, and since we can imagine the non-existence of everything in this natural world, there must be something that is non-contingent or no thing would now exist. That which is non-contingent is God. (4) Since we make judgments of good, better, and best, we imply that the supreme is God. (5) Since means are subordinate to ends in nature, we say that there is a purpose in nature, which implies a Purposer, God.

The argument from the contingency of everything in the world was Aquinas' key proof of God. Drawing on Aristotle he asserted that existence and essence are one in God, that God is pure actuality, thinking thought, pure spirit. To conceive of God as such is to conceive of him as thought and will, he being the object of both thought and will because in God they are inseparable. God's thought and will are set on perfection, which means they are set upon good, which means they are set upon love. God's love is defined as the will that seeks the good of all. Reason can thus show, argues Aquinas, that the primary nature of God expresses itself in love for all being.

Although the arguments of reason can be very powerful, they do arise out of concrete experiences that cannot properly be applied to God at all. Since God is spirit, corporeal terms cannot be ascribed to God, who is infinite by definition. Even the observations that arise from mind and human spirit cannot be applied to God literally, for God is much greater than mere human concepts such as justice and love. We cannot go directly from human concepts arising out of our natural experience to descriptions of God, except by analogy. Only analogical predication is permissible in speaking of God. Things exist in this world; their status is not that of non-being or nothing. Analogically, it is more true of God to say that he exists than to say that he does not. But God does not exist as a thing, for human concepts cannot be literally applied to God.

God's justice and mercy are shown in giving good things for the benefit of all. His activity is aimed at perfection, at good, which means love. The Trinity cannot be rationally demonstrated, but belief in the Trinity is necessary for salvation because it specifies that God's love is directed toward human salvation. The Trinity is accepted by faith in God's revelation, and reason can help make it plausible. "To believe is to think with assent."

God is self-subsistent; his creation is dependent. For Aquinas creation is *ex nihilo* (out of nothing). It occurred at a moment of time—the first moment. We know this on the basis of revelation, but to dispute it is to argue that the world always was. However, for Aquinas time is a form of change and begins when changeable things begin. Creation reflects God; it is not God. Nevertheless, God is present everywhere as first cause, efficient cause, and ground of being. This is known as concurrence. Each creature has the power of secondary cause, but all power in creation comes ultimately from God. All things move by the will of God, although God moves the will of each creature in accordance with the nature of that creature's will. In developing this thesis, Aquinas was attempting to safeguard the invulnerability of personal existence and the final power of God. We make choices, but we are responsible to God. Unfortunately, Aquinas failed to avoid determinism, which arises inevitably from the contention that the will is ultimately moved by God.

Yet Aquinas would not say that God is responsible for sin. The mystery of this is beyond the grasp of reason. God has provided both internal and external aids. (1) He has provided two internal insights to give guidance for moral living: *Synteresis,* which is an infallible faculty whereby one knows there is a difference between good and bad, and *conscientia,* a fallible faculty that seeks to specify what is good and bad. On the basis of these insights, one seeks the seven virtues of truth, justice, courage, temperance, faith, hope, and love, or the seven vices of pride, sloth, greed, envy, wrath, gluttony, and lechery. Even though the human concepts will always be less than perfect, by using will and reason one can develop *conscientia* into either habitual virtues or habitual vices. Reason can carry one a long way, but only after being redeemed can one do good works of merit. (2) In addition to the internal aids, God has provided us with external aids for guidance in the moral life, namely intrinsic and external law. Intrinsic law has two aspects: the eternal law or plan for the world, which is in God's mind, and natural law, which is an expression of eternal law in creation. Human reason can appropriate natural law and by inferential analogy the eternal law, since the natural law is an effect of God's activity. External law is also open to us in the form of divine pronouncements and human laws.

The divine pronouncements are in the form of moral law, the Ten Commandments, and are valid everywhere. Moral law is an expression of natural law. The divine pronouncements also take the form of judicial laws of social and political organizations as in Exodus, Leviticus, and Deuteronomy, and of ceremonial laws relative to particular communities. Human laws are our positive understanding of the above.

Human reason can use these internal and external aids, which God mercifully has provided for all, but one needs the sacraments of grace to achieve actual righteousness. Before the Fall we possessed the natural powers of reason and an additional gift (*donum superadditum*) that made actual righteousness a reality, but in the Fall, although we retained our rational powers, we lost the power of actual righteousness. Thus one needs infused grace to achieve the good life. The church is the vehicle of grace through the sacraments, and the means of grace are the seven sacraments: Baptism, Lord's Supper, Penance, Confirmation, Marriage, Ordination, and Extreme Unction—one for each of the major happenings in a person's life.

Grace is a vital key in the thought of Aquinas. Without grace, writes Aquinas, an individual is like a sick man who can move but not wholly or perfectly unless he is made well with the aid of medicine. Grace is a force from God, a supernatural thing, an inflowing, an infusion, which actually makes one like and pleasing to God. In effect grace creates a new nature in us that makes us capable of doing good. Before grace (even though all motion is grounded in God) one can act fittingly but not worthily so as to merit eternal life. After receiving grace one cooperates with God and merits eternal life. Aquinas tended to emphasize cooperation in order to avoid determinism. Aquinas thus contributed meritorious good works to righteousness, and this became one of the main aspects of medieval religious life.

The infusion of grace works forgiveness, but Aquinas stresses that grace makes one capable of doing good works. Grace is the source of meritorious works, and the goal of meritorious works is the righteous life on earth and eternal life in heaven. One may even earn more merit than necessary to gain eternal life, and the extra merit may be transferred to others. The ideal way to earn merit is to live an ascetic monastic life—forsaking possessions, sensual pleasures, and worldly success.

The seven sacraments, paralleling the five physical and two social needs of humanity, are God's ordered means of conveying grace to us. The seven are of course defined, controlled, and administered by the church, which necessitates an ordered hierarchy. The priest is the key person for giving the sacraments, but some are reserved for the bishop—that is, the bishop has plenary authority to grant or refuse sacraments within his territory. Above the bishops stands the final, universal authority of the Pope. He is the supreme primate. He is above all rulers, lord of the church and lord of the world, a view adopted by the Second Council of Lyons in 1274.

Aquinas gave little tolerance to heretics. He justified their excommunication and execution, for since their sin affects not just some material thing but the soul, they should be more quickly and severely punished than forgers and robbers. Yet the church showed them mercy by admonishing them twice, hoping for their return, before excommunicating them and turning them over to secular powers for extermination. Yet mercy on the part of the church did not mean that they would not lose their property. If they kept their property, other people might not be deterred from heresy. Death would follow any relapse.

Thus, the church with its sacraments stands at the pinnacle of the human quest for knowledge and Being. Scholasticism generally assumed that the teachings of the church, its customs and practices, are true if ecclesiastically sanctioned. Anything contrary to orthodoxy is condemned, while orthodoxy itself is proved to be reasonable. Aquinas did not believe in the Immaculate Conception of Mary, which was still being debated. All knowledge must finally serve the church. The church stood at the top of a social pyramid and acted as the intermediary between God and mankind.

Aquinas believed that God is the author of the revelation contained in the Scriptures. God inspired the various writers by transient impression and then confirmed their views in history by miracles and signs. As God is the author of the Scriptures, they are binding in their authority. But with the introduction of heresy, supplementation of the Scriptures with systematic statements in creeds, councils, and the Fathers became necessary, as did a supreme authority—the Pope—for deciding final definitions of faith. Thus, the Pope is supposed to speak in harmony with Scripture, but the Pope stands as the higher authority. Papal infallibility did not become dogma until 1870, but already in the Middle Ages and before it was present in Roman Catholicism.

Ironically, as if absolute sovereignty was too much for anyone to bear, at the very moment of triumph of scholasticism and its exaltation of the church, forces of disruption were already in process. By 1300 they would become manifest, and other social and relgious centers would undercut and weaken the sovereignty of the papacy.

12

Disruption

In 1274, the year of the death of Aquinas, scholasticism reached its height. It provided theological support for the sovereign claims of the church in both ecclesiastical and political affairs. It seemed to bring together into one magnificent system all the divergent elements of the Middle Ages. But appearances were deceiving. Within twenty-five years after Aquinas, state sovereignty began once more to defy the extreme claims of the papacy, Neoplatonic nominalism found a new base for spiritual and secular truth, conciliarism asserted itself as the supreme authority in Christianity, mystics arose who bypassed the machinery of the church, Renaissance humanism blossomed, and many of the laity sought a more personal relationship with God than that offered by the sacerdotally controlled, infused grace of a worldly church. Reactions became manifest as early as 1277 when Stephen Tempier, Bishop of Paris, and Robert Kilwardby, Archbishop of Canterbury, condemned some of Aquinas' teachings, and again in 1284 when John Peckham, Archbishop of Canterbury, did the same.

But the most spectacular reaction came when the grandiose claims of Pope Boniface VIII (1294–1303) confronted the rising national sovereignties of France and England. Boniface took seriously the primacy of his office and the theology that justified papal supremacy. He gave the papal crown its present tiara, the three crowns symbolizing the trinitarian power embodied in the occupant of the papal throne; publicly declared,

"I am the emperor, I am the Pope"; and claimed to be "the sole source and depositary of canon law." In fact, however, Boniface possessed neither real power, theological acumen, nor diplomatic tact. His arrogance led to radical, fundamental criticism of the church.

In the second year of his pontificate Boniface issued his famous *Clericis laicos*. It brought him into direct conflict with the powerful monarchies of France and England. The *Clericis laicos* forbade the clergy to pay taxes to secular powers, except by papal permission, and threatened with deposition and excommunication any who participated in such "a terrible abuse of secular power." However, taxation of the clergy and church property was not new. It had been allowed for the Crusades and to combat the heresies of the Cathari. Besides, the church's vast accumulations of property, if left exempt, made the tax burden of others heavier. King Edward I of England and Philip IV of France, pressed by the demands of war, had resorted to taxing the property holdings of the clergy. But Boniface saw this as a threat to the immunities and liberties of the church, and issued his *Clericis laicos*. This assertion of sovereignty by one who in reality had little power angered both Edward and Philip. Edward reacted by outlawing the clergy in England, and Philip by prohibiting the export of money from France.

Faced with a serious loss of revenue, Boniface hesitated, as seen in his bull *Etsi de statu,* and then proceeded. Acting in a manner reminiscent of Innocent III, Boniface claimed Scotland as a fief and forbade Edward to invade it. However, Edward summoned parliament to Lincoln and secured a declaration forbidding him to answer to the Pope for his temporal rights. When Boniface sought to settle with France through a council in Rome, Philip refused to let the French clergy participate. In this defiance, Edward had his parliament, Philip his Estates-General behind him.

Undismayed, and unable to assess the nationalistic situation realistically, Boniface in 1302 issued his bull, *Unam sanctam,* the most extravagant claim to universal temporal sovereignty to come out of the Middle Ages. Boniface asserted control of both swords, said all temporal power should be directed by a priest, and claimed that resisting the Pope was the same as resisting an ordinance of God. "We therefore declare, say, and affirm that submission on the part of every person to the bishop of Rome is altogether necessary for salvation." In this he was the true successor of Gregory VII and Innocent III, but his claims also made reform councils, which the powerful universities and others were increasingly calling for, completely unnecessary.

Philip promptly summoned an assembly that charged Boniface with heresy and immorality and called for a general council to try him. Noting the travel plans of the Pope, Philip sent William Nogaret, a jurist, and Sciarra Colonna, a personal enemy of Boniface, with a mercenary force to intercept the Pope at Anagni and compel him to submit. They captured Boniface on September 7, 1303. Although Philip's men plundered the palace where the Pope was staying and threatened and imprisoned Boniface for three days, he refused to yield. Freed by friendly forces, a month later Boniface died, never quite recovering from the shock and ill treatment he had received.

Boniface's successor, Pope Benedict XI (1303–4), tried to conciliate Philip but felt morally bound to issue a bull against the outrage at Anagni. One month later, under mysterious circumstances, Benedict died. Eleven months passed before Pope Clement VI (1305–13) was chosen. Although the cardinals at Rome elected Clement, he was crowned at Lyon and never ventured to return to Italy. Completely dominated by France, Clement moved the papacy to Avignon in 1309, thus beginning what is known as the Babylonian Captivity. He condemned Boniface, and at the Council of Vienne (1311–12), with Philip's army standing nearby, he suppressed the Knights Templars, gave their lands to the French king to finance a Crusade that he never made, and later tried the leading Templars for heresy. The Templars' grand master and sixty-nine knights suffered death at the stake. The Council of Vienne also proclaimed that the papacy was supreme in the church, but supremacy under such circumstances meant little. The papacy had become a French institution. Its prestige withered.

A feeling that the church should be ruled by a representative council, conciliarism, began to grow. The Babylonian Captivity (1309–77) with the papacy at Avignon, and the Great Schism (1378–1417) with two and then three popes reigning at the same time, caused scholars from many walks of life to question the authority of the papacy.

English opposition to the papacy mounted and combined with increasing nationalism to diminish papal power in England. The Statute of Provisors in 1351 denied the papacy the right to fill English benefices, and the Law of Praemunire in 1353 forbade appeals to Rome. (Henry VIII later used this law to accuse the English Catholic clergy of treason.) In 1366 parliament declared that the king could not give his kingdom to the Pope as a fief.

This was the atmosphere in which John Wycliffe (1328–84) launched his attack on the papacy. The papacy was still at Avignon, and the Great Schism, with one Pope at Avignon and another at Rome, was imminent. When Wycliffe received his doctorate from Oxford, he expected a plush appointment from the Pope, and when he did not get it, he entered the service of King Edward III, who in 1374 appointed him to Lutterworth, his only pastorate. In the same year he represented the king in a dispute with the Pope, who still regarded England as a fief and was demanding tribute. Wycliffe appealed to English law and had ideas about righteous stewardship that were not fully explicated until he published *On Divine Lordship* in 1375 and *On Civil Lordship* in 1376. Basing his theology on the superior authority of Scripture over the papacy, Wycliffe developed his view of righteous stewardship. Everything belongs to God, he said; God is the Creator and Lord of all. Every creature is a servant. Human lordship is neither permanent nor unlimited. Human lordship is by the grace of God. It is really stewardship, and if a person, particularly a priest, is immoral or unfit, he can and should be replaced. Wycliffe thought the church should do this, but if it could not or would not act because of its own weakness or corruption, then secular powers might do so. His second essay *On Civil Lordship* placed all possessions on this level. If a steward, be he king or priest, fails to render good service, then whatever he has may be taken from him. Priests and kings are not masters, but stewards. Wycliffe's idea was radical and disturbing. If he had not specifically forbidden the use of force against even tyrannical civil order, his ideas might have exploded into revolution. As it was, he was accused of fomenting the peasants' uprising in 1381. But most of his barbs he directed at the church, which he believed should have no authority over the temporal realm. He traced the fall of the church back to when Constantine endowed it with property and favors. With corruption rife in the church, Wycliffe's ideas seemed like an invitation to civil rulers to confiscate church holdings. John of Gaunt, the son of King Edward III, did just that, thus righteously satisfying his own greed. In *On the King's Office* Wycliffe depicted a territorial church ruled by the king, a situation realized under Henry VIII. In 1377 Pope Gregory XI issued five bulls against Wycliffe demanding his arrest.

However, the Great Schism that followed the death of Gregory seemed to substantiate Wycliffe's call for reform. In 1377 at Rome Urban VI became Pope. France expected him to return to Avignon, and when he did not, the French cardinals claimed treachery and elected a Pope of their own, Clement VII. These two Popes then anathematized each other and virtually divided Europe. During the thirty-nine years of schism, many voices demanded reform.

Wycliffe continued to publish his writings, based on Scripture and ever more radical. In 1378 *On the Pastoral Office* called for clerical poverty, declaring that not much is required for frugal, moral living and everything extra must be distributed to the poor. Immoral or negligent priests, Wycliffe said, should not be supported with money or attendance at services. *On the Eucharist,* 1380, rejected transubstantiation, the cornerstone of papal power, in favor of a theory of "remanence," according to which the bread and the wine of the mass remain just that even after consecration. He refuted the notion that "a hog, a dog, or a mouse can eat our Lord." They eat only the material elements. Christ is sacramentally, not physically, present in the elements. Wycliffe called on Ambrose, Augustine, Anselm and Pope Nicholas II's decretal in 1059 to show the early church did not have transubstantiation. But this rejection of transubstantiation caused many of his friends to shun him. In 1382 the synod at the Blackfriars Convent condemned ten of his statements as heretical, and some of his disciples departed or recanted. After Wycliffe's death, his followers, the Lollards, whom he had sent out two by two to preach the Gospel, suffered persecution under Kings Henry IV and V, who wanted papal support for their questionable dynastic claims. The Lollards continued their preaching and circulation of the Bible in vernacular translations, and in the *Lollard Conclusions* of 1394 severely denounced transubstantiation, exorcisms, material greed, priestly pretensions, immorality, holding religious and secular offices simultaneously, prayers for the departed, pilgrimages, image and relic worship, auricular confession, war, indulgences, and immature vows of continence. The Lollards were ruthlessly suppressed at Oxford University, and in 1401 parliament's *De Haeretico Comburendo* authorized burning them as heretics. Lollardy went underground where it thrived among the poor and later emerged in the sixteenth century as a social factor in the Reformation.

Onslaughts against the papacy and Aquinas' system continued. Although Duns Scotus (1265–1308) was also a scholastic, his views contributed to the dissolution of scholastic theology. He believed that universals are before, in, and after objects, and that the goal of nature is the individual, of which an eternal image exists in God's mind. Scotus' theory of knowledge thus emphasized experience of individual objects, from which conceptions of universals rise in the perceiver's mind, the individual thus superseding the universal in existence. He agreed with Aquinas that revelation and reason (which he tended to distrust) do not contradict each other; he disagreed with Aquinas on the primacy of the will. Aquinas had combined reason and determinism; Scotus combined free will and indeterminism. He asserted primacy of will in God and human beings. God can do as he pleases, unbound by laws of rationality; God is free. However, God acts in an orderly fashion, said Scotus, because he wills to do so. In humanity, the primacy of will means that we act as we will; we are not constrained or moved by anything more powerful. God is omnipotent, but does not infringe on human freedom. This freedom of will makes us responsible for our acts, and only on this premise is meritorious activity intelligible.

For Scotus, original sin is lack of actual righteousness. Sin is an act of will preferring something less than God, and grace is necessary simply because God has so willed it. God could restore a person at any time, but he has chosen to do this by grace—by restoring us to a relationship of favor with God. According to Scotus, we can do meritorious works, but without a relationship of favor they would not be acceptable to God. For Scotus, justifying grace is God's willing to accept our meritorious works. Even Christ's work is not efficacious without God's willing to accept it. The church's practice of meritorious satisfaction is acceptable because God so wills, said Scotus. Augustine thought that in the Fall humanity lost its proper status in creation, that reason was impaired, requiring a creative act by God for restoration. Aquinas thought human reason was not impaired, but that we lost the gift that made actual righteousness possible and need grace to restore it. Scotus thought we lost our moral-ethical relationship to God in the Fall and that grace restores the right relationship, grace being God's willing to accept human good works.

Although Scotus' theology resembled Aquinas' scholasticism and in some respects advanced it, Scotus' emphasis on experiencing the individual object and his emphasis on the indeterminate nature of things because the will is free helped disintegrate the medieval synthesis. His theology was adopted by his Franciscan order, the rivalry between Franciscans and Dominicans thus heightening the differences between Scotus and Aquinas. Scotus was the first major theologian to defend the Immaculate Conception of Mary, against Aquinas arguing that the eternal Christ made it possible. He also insisted the Incarnation would have taken place even without a Fall.

However, Scotus did not radically depart from the medieval ethos. Although he stressed that nothing can be the substance of faith that is not derived from Scripture or a declaration of the church, the latter was primary. Since the church determines the canon of Scripture, to accept Scripture is to accept the authority of the church.

William Occam (1280–1349), a Franciscan nominalist and student of Scotus, was the chief voice among many whose further criticism of the medieval synthesis approached disintegration. Yet it remained for others to draw the implied revolutionary, logical conclusions; Occam submitted fully to the dogmas of the church. That others saw his teachings as dangerous is borne out by the fact that he was never advanced to the status of teacher at Oxford; the chancellor of the university charged that his teachings were dangerous. Summoned to Avignon to give an account of his views, he incurred the wrath of Pope John XXII by siding with the Spiritual Franciscans, was excommunicated, and had to flee from Avignon to Bavaria, where he remained in the employ of Emperor Louis, himself excommunicated, from 1328 to 1349. In 1330 his attack on the Pope regarding the question of poverty brought him expulsion from his order and a sentence of perpetual imprisonment. Subsequent writings developed political ideas sharply critical of the papacy's pretensions.

Occam maintained that universals do not objectively exist; they are tools of thought and exist only subjectively in the mind. We experience individual objects. From them we form pictures in our minds, representative mental copies. From what is common in these pictures we form concepts, or universals. They have no objective existence. Even though they correspond in a sense to existing reality, universals are abstractions— names, not realities at all.

Having established his position on universals, Occam in his *Centilogium* assaulted the traditional dogmas of the church. Dogmas cannot be scientifically proved; they can be believed on faith, but not demonstrated in reality. The arguments for demonstrating the existence of God must go because the validity of the causal argument on which all of them depend cannot be shown. So also for the Trinity, the soul, transubstantiation, creation, moral values, etc. We believe these things on the basis of infused faith, not on the basis of knowledge. Such things cannot be proved from what we experience in this world. Theology is based only on faith; it has no basis in knowledge; theology should not be made systematic, because its truths are revealed, nor should one attempt to derive truths from the accepted theological truths. We accept them on faith because they are revealed, given. Because of infused grace, Christians can easily believe things to which their natural powers cannot assent. So Occam accepted the dogmas of the Roman Catholic Church.

But Occam also exalted the authority of the Holy Scriptures. Nothing is to be believed that is not contained in the Bible or cannot be inferred from it. Scripture has greater authority than an assertion of the church. The ancient creeds merely summarize biblical data or answer heresies. The Pope does not declare new truths of religion; he enunciates what is already there. Although Occam accepted the teachings of the church, and bowed to the authority of the Pope, he paved the way for others to appeal to Scripture as final.

In the employ of Louis of Bavaria, Occam applied his ideas to politics. As universals are descriptive, abstract words, and only particulars are real, the church is merely an aggregate of individuals. It is not some form in which people participate and become Christians. Not being a unity it has no common spirit. The will of the church is a summary of the wills of individuals. But neither the community constituting the church, nor the Pope, nor priests, nor councils are infallible. Occam preferred placing final authority in a council representative of the entire church, including women, but even that he did not think would be infallible.

Many of these ideas culminated in the devastating political theory of Marsiglio (Marsilius) of Padua (1275–1342). He propounded the theory that the emperor has absolute supremacy over the Pope—can elect, censure or depose him—but that both emperor and Pope are finally subject to the will of the people whom they represent. Marsilius finished his *Defensor Pacis* (*In Defense of Peace*) about 1324, and when he was discovered as its author took refuge in 1326 with Louis of Bavaria. Pope John XXII anathematized the *Defensor Pacis* in 1327, and in 1342 Pope Clement VI repeated the excoriation. Marsilius declared that the basis of all power is the people. To them all rulers, whether in the state or the church, are responsible. Rulers are simply executors to implement the will of the people. Their authority pertains not to them as persons but to the office to which the people call them to perform tasks of maintaining peace, justice, equity, and order. They rule by virtue of office and can be replaced if they do not satisfactorily fulfill the duties of that office. They are to be removed not by tyrannicide or violence but by an orderly expression of the people's will.

To the church he applied the same principles. All ecclesiastical power is based on the will of the people who constitute the church. Priests and popes represent the people; they have their offices to perform particular tasks, and when they perform unfittingly, they can be judged and removed. This should be done, thought Marsilius, through a council of priests and laity. As the state is the unifying power in society, the church should be completely subordinate to the emperor. The church has no inherent jurisdiction, only what historically has been granted by the state, which the state can also withdraw. At the pleasure of the state, it can use but not own property. In the order of medieval society, Marsilius reversed the channels of power, placing the emperor above the Pope, and the people above both.

Although Louis of Bavaria established himself in the Vatican in 1328 and installed an antipope, Nicholas V, for two years, the ideas of these radical thinkers were actualized only gradually. Yet they fomented state independence of the church, scriptural authority, and the laity as compeers of the clergy.

With two Popes reigning during the Great Schism, each anathematizing the other, many voices cried for reform, among them Conrad of Gelnhausen, Heinrich of Langenstein, Peter of Ailli, John Gerson, and Nicholas of Clémanges. The agitation for a reforming council became so great that the cardinals of both Popes finally issued a call for a council in Pisa in 1409. Neither the Pope at Avignon nor the one at Rome attended. Pisa declared both of them deposed, and elected Alexander V to be Pope. But the Popes at Avignon and Rome refused to be deposed, so that

Christendom was faced with the spectacle of three Popes. The situation was intolerable, yet it lasted for six long years.

Finally, the newly elected Emperor Sigismund and the Pope of Pisa called the Council of Constance (1414–18). It represents the height of conciliar power. An array of ecclesiastical and secular figures from cardinals and princes to writers of bulls and buglers attended. In 1415 the council disposed of all three Popes; it jailed and then deposed John XXIII, successor to Alexander V; Roman Pope Gregory XII resigned; but Avignon Pope Benedict XIII proved intractable and did not actually vacate until July 26, 1417. He claimed he was the only cardinal since before the schism, and, if the schism Popes were invalid, he alone had the right to elect a Pope. On April 6, 1415, the council issued its *Sacrosancta* decree: "The ecumenical council assembled at Constance represents the whole church. It derives its authority immediately from Christ. Everyone, even the Pope, owes obedience to it in all that concerns the faith, the unity of the Church and the reform of both head and members." Unless set aside by a council, it declared its canons and decrees were immutable.

Actually the Council of Constance was not very successful as a reforming body, even though it ended the schism. That the council's views were not really different from traditional dogma was demonstrated by the council's order to exhume and scatter the bones of Wycliffe and to put John Hus to death. After the election of Cardinal Oddo Colonna of Rome as Pope Martin V, November 11, 1417, the council's interest in reforms virtually ceased.

Yet by constituting itself the supreme governing body in Christendom, it changed the papacy from an absolute to a constitutional monarchy. Although the transformation did not last, it set a historic precedent that emerged again in Vatican II in the drive for collegiality. With the decree *Frequens,* October 9, 1417, the Council of Constance provided for the next two councils to be convoked within five and seven years respectively, and then every ten years. If such action had been carried out, the Pope would have remained the executive of the church but under the control of a representative council meeting frequently. However, papal ultramontanism was not so easily laid aside. Martin V dragged his feet on implementing the *Frequens* decree. Within five years he called a council, but it died for lack of attendance. Then seven years later he reluctantly called the Council of Basel.

Martin V died before the Council of Basel opened in 1431, and Pope Eugenius IV (1431–47) and the Council of Basel were soon embroiled in a struggle over papal versus conciliar authority. Attendance at Basel was poor, and Eugenius after a series of misunderstandings ordered its adjournment. The council refused; they would not listen to the bull of dissolvement. They renewed the decree of *Sacrosancta* and reprimanded the Pope. Eugenius declared his superiority, but after two years of infighting, during which the council moved to cut off his revenues, he reversed himself and proclaimed the council legitimate. The Council of Basel proceeded to act as the supreme authority in the church, deciding lawsuits, issuing indulgences, decreeing reforms, appropriating taxes, and so forth.

When the question of union with the Greeks came up, the Greeks responded to the Pope's suggestion of Ferrara as the place for a council. Eugenius ordered the Council of Basel translated, but in defiance the majority remained at Basel. Now the council lost all restraint, and made conciliar authority a matter of faith. When Eugenius refused to accept the claim, the council deposed him as a heretic, June 25, 1439, and a little over four months later elected Felix V in his place. But Eugenius refused to step down and continued with the council at Ferrara. Because of the pressue of expenses, he transferred the council to Florence and still later to Rome, working out an agreement with the Greeks that acknowledged the Pope as the head of the whole church and the guide of all Christians. Even though the agreement did not last, it was a signal victory for Pope Eugenius and further weakened the claims of the Council of Basel.

Meanwhile, the support of the Council of Basel dwindled. Many countries, for political as well as religious reasons, remained neutral. When the Council of Basel in 1443 transferred itself to Lausanne where Felix V resided, countries gradually drifted to the side of Eugenius. After several major nations declared for Eugenius, Felix resigned in 1449. By 1460 Pope Pius II was able to issue his *Execrabilis,* which excommunicated anyone who appealed to a council. Reform continued to be in the minds of people, but the conciliar period was over. The papacy had won. The Lateran Council, 1512–17, again condemned conciliarism and proclaimed papal supremacy.

That the Council of Constance represented a shift of power rather than of doctrine is clear from the treatment given Wycliffe and John Hus (1373–1415). Although Wycliffe's writings were condemned by Gregory XI in 1377 and by the Blackfriars Council of London in 1382, and his followers subjected to burning as heretics in 1401, the Council of Constance in 1415 nevertheless condemned 267 of his statements as errors, ordered his books to be burned, and his bones to be exhumed. Wycliffe's appeal to Scripture, stress on stewardship, advocacy of apostolic poverty, rejection of transubstantiation, and attacks on the worship of saints, on pilgrimages, on pluralities of offices, and on other abuses were too radical for a worldly church that had already condemned the Spiritual Franciscans, Waldenses, and Cathari. The Council of Constance further expressed its basic conservatism in the condemnation of Hus, who disseminated many of Wycliffe's ideas in Bohemia. In condemning Hus the council revolutionized the Bohemians and set in motion theological and political forces that directly influenced the Reformation in the next century.

Hus was educated at the University of Prague, ordained a priest in 1401, and chosen rector of the university in 1402. Although his ideas are similar to those of Wycliffe (whose works filtered into Bohemia following the marriage of Anne, the sister of King Wenceslaus IV, to Richard II of England), many of his thoughts were developed in studies and controversies before he became acquainted with Wycliffe. As the popular preacher in the Czech language at Bethlehem Chapel at Prague, Hus advocated the New Testament as the law of the church, Christ-like poverty as the Christian ideal, reform of abuses such as pilgrimages, Christ as the head of the church rather than the Pope, abolition of clerical immoralities, and a predestinated church of the elect. Even though the university condemned forty-five of Wycliffe's ideas in 1403, Hus continued to preach reform, and soon became the recognized leader of a religious movement deeply rooted in a pietistic mysticism among the people and in a growing nationalism. The papacy in Rome ordered Hus to cease preaching in 1407, but in 1409 the Council of Pisa elected a third Pope to offset the schism Popes. This new Pope, Alexander V, received backing from Wenceslaus and Hus, and Hus continued to lead the nationalistic Czechs at the university. Yet one year later Alexander V ordered the retraction of all Wycliffite doctrines and the cessation of preaching in private chapels, including Bethlehem Chapel; in 1411 Pope John XXIII, Alexander's successor, excommunicated Hus and in 1412 interdicted his followers. For political reasons Wenceslaus then exiled Hus from Prague, but in the meantime Hus had become a national hero. After two conferences failed to achieve accord, Hus appealed from the papacy to a general council. During his exile Hus wrote *On Simony* and *On the Church* (much of it from Wycliffe) and denounced the Pope as Antichrist. In this context, under safe-conduct from Emperor Sigismund, Hus ventured to go to Constance. There he fell victim to political intrigue, was imprisoned, tried, and burned as a heretic. His ashes were shoveled into a cart and dumped into the Rhine. Not quite a year later, Jerome of Prague, Hus' compatriot, was condemned and burned at the stake, May 30, 1416, on the same spot as Hus.

When news of Hus' execution reached Prague, the country seethed with revolt. On September 2, 452 of the most prominent Czech and Moravian nobles met in Prague and pledged themselves to defend the reforms for which Hus died. Although Hus had not strongly advocated the cup for the laity, communion in both kinds soon became the rallying cry of the Hussites. They used a red cup against a field of black on their army banners. The council placed Prague under interdict, but virtually the entire population reacted violently. Armed bands of common people attacked monasteries and churches, expelled those who refused to offer communion *sub utrague specie* (under both kinds). By February 1416 all the Prague churches were in the hands of reform clerics, and the revolt spread throughout the country. The reform party, known as Utraquists (from *sub utraque specie*), took over most of the churches, and the university solemnly declared for the chalice early in 1417. In February 1418, Pope Martin V pronounced a crusade against Bohemia that with King Wenceslaus' support brought a general restoration of Roman Catholicism in 1419. Popular protest led the king to allow three Utraquist churches in Prague.

The restoration produced resentment, especially in southern Bohemia, where a powerful party developed known as the Taborites, named for Mount Tabor, where often as many as 42,000 assembled to hear Utraquist preachers and take communion in both kinds. When Wenceslaus suddenly died in 1419 and Sigismund became heir apparent, popular resentment boiled. A Prague diet demanded that Sigismund grant freedom of preaching, communion *sub utraque,* and honor to Hus and Jerome, in response to which Sigismund hurled 1,600 Utraquist priests and laymen into the abandoned silver mines at Kutna Hora and joined the

Pope in a declared crusade against the Czech heretics in 1420. Prague, John Zizka (1360?–1424), and other Hussite leaders successfully resisted the royal armies and adopted the famous Four Prague Articles: freedom of preaching, the sacrament in both kinds, exemplary living and no secular power for priests and monks, and punishment of all mortal sins. However, the Hussites were not united. Conservative Praguers wanted to retain the old worship; radical Praguers wanted a new social order; Taborites wanted their own community; the Adamites practiced nudity; and the followers of Peter Chelčický (1381–1460), repudiated all killing and accepted the state only as a necessary evil. Zizka eventually emerged as a gifted military leader, united the Hussites, and successfully resisted the restoration efforts of Sigismund. After Zizka's death, the Hussite armies continued their successes until 1434, when political-religious intrigue factioned the Hussites and pitted Czechs against Czechs. The Taborite defeat at Lipany brought Sigismund to the throne in January 1436. Failing to keep promises made to the Utraquists, Sigismund was forced to flee in 1437 and died while retreating. After Albrecht II of Austria had ruled only one year, George of Poděbrady, head of the Utraquist party, took control as regent for Albrecht's son. When the latter died in the plague of 1457, George was elected king, brilliantly reigning until his death in 1471, despite the Pope's declaring him a heretic in 1466 and sending a Hungarian army against him.

Hus' influence reverberated across Europe, affecting the Reformation in Germany, the Moravians, and the rising nationalism that increasingly challenged the sovereignty of the papacy and the medieval synthesis. When the Turks took Constantinople in 1453 and advanced into Europe, many believed the invasion was punishment for the sins of the church.

Mysticism, which spread widely in medieval Europe in the fourteenth and fifteenth centuries, further eroded ecclesiastical power. The mystics in varying degrees represented a criticism and bypassing of the formal sacerdotalism of the church. Their advocacy of direct contact with God made ecclesiastical machinery, sacraments, satisfactions, and even prayer unnecessary. The most outstanding of the mystics was Meister Eckhart (1260–1327), and the most outstanding representatives of practical mysticism, sometimes referred to as mystical pietism, were John Tauler (1300–61) and Thomas a Kempis (1380–1471). They influenced thousands of common people and spread a negative ethos regarding the church as an institution, even though they did not want to attack the church directly. They stood for an Augustinianism of direct contact with God that did not require sacerdotal mediation. They passed beyond asceticism and righteousness to an ecstatic vision of perfection or even a unification and identification with God.

Eckhart, a Dominican who became one of Germany's most famous preachers, could conceive of God only negatively. He believed in a Neoplatonic pure mysticism in which God is beyond being and non-being but is also present in the soul and in the world. The only reality in humanity and in nature is the divine spark of God, wholly uncreated. This divinity is in everything; whatever makes us appear as individuals is unreal. Eckhart strove for a complete loss of individuality, for complete union of the divine spark in him with God, for the loss of any consciousness of "I," and in this sense for immersion and identification with God. He lectured in Paris but did most of his teaching and preaching in Strassburg and Cologne. In 1326 he was accused of heretical teachings and tried in Cologne, but died while his case was being appealed to Rome. He was willing to submit to the church's judgment, but in 1329, two years after Eckhart's death, Pope John XXII condemned twenty-eight of his statements as either dangerous or heretical. The attempt to express the inexpressible made many of Eckhart's words sound pantheistic.

Eckhart insisted that a person prepare himself intellectually and morally with good works but that such externals will not sanctify; at best they can only prepare the way for the ecstatic realization of oneness with God. He stressed spontaneous love as an expression of God in the human soul. In this, Christ was his pattern and example. But it is God who by grace must finally enter into the divine human soul. This lifts one beyond consciousness of identity, beyond time and space, to divine unity. Following in the train of Eckhart came men like John Ruysbroeck (1293–1381), John Tauler, Henry Suso (1295–1366), and Thomas a Kempis.

Eckhart's best known disciple, Tauler, also a Dominican, worked in Strassburg, Cologne, and Basel during a time of great social stress in Germany. The Black Death of 1348 through 1349, long wars, distrust of the papacy in Avignon, and economic hardship made the quiet mysticism of Tauler attractive to the common people. He condemned dependence on outward works and ceremonies and spoke of vital religion being born of God within, yet without stressing loss of identity and pantheism. He laid more stress on love and ethical piety than on intellectual discipline, asserting that the vision of God finally comes as God wills. If we would be truly religious, we must surrender all that is accidental and transitory, destroy self-will, and humbly follow the guidance of the Holy Spirit. He preached union with God not so much for the sake of unification as for the resulting enlargement of love and strength for self-sacrifice. Henry Suso, also a disciple of Eckhart, extolled suffering as the way to the exquisite love of God.

Although these men differ in particulars, they followed the mystical steps of purification, illumination, and unification. We are to imitate Christ, renounce ourselves, and thus prepare our souls for the gift of ecstasy and the loss of the self in the totality of God. The accouterments of religion are secondary; they are externals; they help only obliquely.

Eckhart, Tauler, and Suso inspired thousands of laymen and clergy in the Rhine valley to practice a form of mysticism emphasizing intense personal transformation and union of their souls with God. They called themselves the Friends of God and for the most part remained within the church, loosely organized, though some did form themselves into separate societies. From this circle came the anonymous *German Theology,* probably written by several authors, which so greatly affected Luther that he republished it in 1516 and 1518. It insisted on self-denunciation and renunciation of "I" and "Mine." This movement emphasized not so much ecstatic unification or pantheism as it did holy living brought about by inward transformation. John Ruysbroeck, a Flemish priest also influenced by Eckhart, came from this circle. Writing in Flemish, he popularized mystic contemplation and directly influenced Gerhard Groot (1340–84), a Carthusian monk, who traveled through the Netherlands preaching against ecclesiastical abuses and calling for internalized, sincere religious living. With his disciple Radewyn he founded the Brethren of the Common Life, popularizers of the *Devotio Moderna*, the new devotion, which stressed simple, undogmatic Christianity. To encourage one another, the Brethren lived in houses and had rules like monks but did not take permanent vows or practice mendicancy. Laymen and clerics could continue their chosen vocations. They established schools, gave free instruction, and copied books. Two of their famous houses, at Windesheim and at Deventer, where Erasmus received his early education, profoundly affected cultural life in the Lowlands. Thomas a Kempis, schooled by the Brethren at Deventer, produced Christianity's most widely used devotional book, *The Imitation of Christ*. It enjoined the simple piety of moral imitation of Christ.

This widespread mystical movement in the fourteenth and fifteenth centuries represented not only a bypassing of the externalized sacramentalism of the church, which had begun to sell indulgences for the living and the dead, but also a deep longing for a more satisfying answer to human nature and destiny. Popular preaching, study of the Scriptures in the vernacular, the Babylonian Captivity, the Great Schism, and conciliarism helped widen the breach between the mystics and organized Christendom.

The disruption of the medieval synthesis was but part of a larger movement known as the Renaissance (1300–1517), a complicated period of social change that had many foci. Individualism, secularism, and rationalism were important motifs in the period, but so were other developments such as emerging nationalism, urbanization, and industrialization. Most of what we term modern had its roots or significant growth in the Renaissance. Industry advanced especially in the Low Countries and northern Italy, where cloth, arms, leather materials, and hardware were produced. Capitalist forms of ownership developed; trading companies and corporations grew. Latin was still the international language, but national tongues were becoming stronger. Professional soldiers who served where they could get the highest wages were displacing the military obligations of vassalage. When they were not paid, as often happened in the Hundred Years' War, when the treasuries of France and England were exhausted, they ravaged the countryside. The Hundred Years' War (1337–1453) saw England ousted from the continent but strengthened the monarchies in both countries, despite the fierce War of the Roses (1453–85) over succession to the English crown. The Holy Roman Empire declined until it included little more than Germany, and the Golden Bull of 1356 made the emperor an elected official by limiting the electorate to four secular rulers and three archbishops. In Italy, where the Renaissance flourished, Milan, Florence, Venice, the Papal States, and Naples dominated, rivaling each other for trade, lands, and prestige. Spain, long the scene of civil wars, was united through the marriage of Ferdinand of Aragon to Isabella of Castile. His accession came in 1474 and hers in 1479. They virtually took control of the church, seeking through the Inquisition to root out heretics. In 1492 they completed the defeat of the Moors in Granada and sponsored Columbus' voyage to the New World. Following victory in Granada they sought to terminate Jewish influence in the country by demanding that the Jews be baptized as Christians or emigrate. Many left, causing a brain-drain, but others converted and were severely persecuted as Marranos who had become Christian in name only. The capture of Constantinople in 1453 enabled the Ottoman Turks to consolidate their power and prepare for expansion across Africa and through the Balkans. The fall of Constantinople also prompted the fast-developing Russian Orthodox Church to proclaim Moscow the "third Rome," divinely destined to rule the political and religious affairs of the world, a claim that Western powers lightly dismissed.

In general, more concern for humanity per se prevailed. Interest in ancient Greece and Rome tended to offset interest in biblical lands, and study of secular literature often prevailed over scriptural endeavors. In art, architecture, and sculpture, themes no longer exclusively religious displaced the central medieval emphasis on God. Early leaders in this new turn were Giotto (1276–1337), Dante (1265–1321), Francesco Petrarch (1304–74), and Boccaccio (1313–75), all from Florence. Florence dominated in the early Renaissance as she did in the later period with Fra Angelico, Michelangelo, Donatello, Filippo Lippi, Botticelli, and Leonardo da Vinci.

Giotto succeeded in using the newly discovered third dimension of perspective in art to give his paintings a realistic, dramatic, human quality that is noticeably absent from the classic stereotypes of earlier medieval works. His style is intensely personal and original and although he is still concerned with religious themes, Giotto represents a break with the past. His interest lies in solid human beings rather than ethereal visions of heaven.

Dante, Italy's greatest poet, had his property confiscated and was exiled from Florence after his involvement in anti-papalist politics there in 1301; he spent the last part of his life wandering from one Italian city to another. Between 1311 and 1318 he wrote *On Monarchy,* in which he maintained that peace is the best condition for mankind and that it can best be secured through a universal emperor in whom all temporal power should be vested. Although Dante was regarded as an orthodox man, he argued strongly against all the biblical passages and historical instances that seemed to point to papal supremacy in the world. In his greatest work, *The Divine Comedy,* Dante makes an imaginary, allegorical trip through hell, purgatory, and paradise. He is guided first by Virgil, symbolizing reason, and in paradise by Beatrice, symbolizing faith. With amazing vividness and sharp detail Dante pictures various people, some contemporary, in each stage of his journey. He discovers several Popes in hell and only one in heaven. His criticisms of the church are not superficial; a recurring theme reiterates that good works without faith, and morality without religion, will not merit salvation. At the end he stands in the presence of God in the ecstasy of mystic love. For religious ideas he draws heavily on Aquinas and medieval tradition, but his artistic portrayals, interest in classical antiquity, and anti-clericalism point to the future.

Petrarch embodies two sides of the Renaissance. On the one hand he wrote 300 Italian sonnets to Laura, a married woman whom he loved, and on the other he furthered research by collecting old manuscripts and starting libraries. Exiled from Florence for his family's political activities, Petrarch wandered through Europe searching for and copying classical manuscripts, thus preserving some of our only copies of ancient literature. In his religious poetry he stressed the transitoriness of human life and in his vernacular poetry the passion of worldly living. Yet despite his new style of poetry and his love for pagan culture, Petrarch, like most of the artists of his time, was deeply grounded in medieval thought while pointing to future changes.

Petrarch's friend Boccaccio, author of Europe's first novels, is a forerunner of the modern writers who virtually ignore Christianity and frankly celebrate the joys of this world, nature, love, and the flesh. Boccaccio's *Decameron* is a collection of tales told by three men and seven women as they wait out the ravages of the Black Death on an estate near Florence. Drawn from many walks of life, the tales concern thieves, whores, and hypocrites as well as idealists, aristocrats, and honest commoners. They are racy, ironic, amusing, tragic, earthy. The church figures only in satire. Like Chaucer's (d. 1400) *Canterbury Tales* they furnish us with vivid pictures of medieval people. Boccaccio's *Fiammetta*, the first psychological novel in Europe, immortalizes the author's love for Maria, a married woman who succumbed to the Black Death. Boccaccio wrote largely in the vernacular, apparently simply for the amusement and diversion of his readers. His interests are religious only obliquely.

Leonardo Bruni (1370–1444), still another critical spirit of Florence and protégé of the Greek emigré Manuel Chrysoloras (d. 1415), promoted a skeptical and secular attitude by translating several of Plato's dialogues into Latin and attempting to place the study of the humanities in the service of an increasingly new historical and political consciousness. Believing ethics to be more important than speculative knowledge, he furthered a "civic humanism" by explicating the political implications of his favorite classical treatises. Due to the efforts of men like Bruni, Marsilio Ficino (1433–99), and Pico della Mirandola (1463–94), by 1469 the Platonic academy of Florence could boast of the first complete translation of Plato.

Lorenzo Valla (ca. 1406–57) and Nicholas of Cusa (ca. 1400–64) embody the critical, scholarly spirit of the time beyond Florence. Although Valla served as apostolic secretary during the last period of his life, he declared himself an Epicurean and in 1440 he proved that the *Donation of Constantine* was spurious and bitterly attacked the temporal power of the papacy. In proving the falsity of the *Donation* he employed historical and form criticism, thus promoting if not originating these two scholarly methods. In subsequent writings he showed the inadequacies of the Vulgate when compared to the Greek New Testament, and toward the end of his life sharply assailed the pretensions of scholasticism's attempt to harmonize an understanding of God's omnipotence with human free will. Although his sustained critique of the religious life was not printed until 1869, he condemned asceticism as utter folly.

Nicholas of Cusa, considered by many to be the best mind of his time, used his critical acumen to declare the falsity of the *False Decretals* and the *Donation of Constantine.* As a cardinal and a philosopher, he sought to reform the church—first as a conciliarist but then as a papal supporter when he felt the conciliarists had gone too far with their demands. In 1433 he wrote his *Catholic Harmony,* outlining a reform program for the church and empire. In 1459 Pope Pius II named him vicar-general of Rome, to reform and govern Rome and the patrimony of St. Peter. Intellectually he advocated learned ignorance, *docta ignorantia,* as the highest stage of human comprehension. Man cannot attain absolute, simple, infinite Truth via reason and the rules of logic; God or Truth lies beyond such intellectual endeavor. Only by intuition can one discover God, who is the center and the circumference of the world. Reason is relational. It works by comparing that which is unknown to that which is known. But since the infinite is incomparable, it must remain beyond the grasp of reason. Our intellect is related to truth as a polygon is to a circle; no matter how often the polygon's angles are multiplied, its angles will never equal the circle. Influenced by Eckhart, Nicholas depicted God as embracing all opposites—"where speech, sight, hearing, taste, touch, reason, knowledge, and understanding are the same, and where seeing is one with being seen and hearing is one with being heard . . . and speaking with hearing, and creating with speaking." For Nicholas, Alpha and Omega become the same in God. His interest in reconciling opposites led Nicholas to show the affinities between the Koran and the Bible and to seek the reunion of the Greek and Roman branches of Christianity.

The papacy from 1300 to 1517 was less than admirable as a Christian institution. The Babylonian Captivity (1309–77)—so called because Petrarch compared the period of the papacy in Avignon to the period of the Jews in Babylon—the Great Schism (1378–1415), the election of a third Pope by the Council of Pisa in 1409, and the conciliarist struggle that followed the Council of Constance left many Christians with the feeling that the papacy was not a true representative of the spirit of Christ. When the Council of Basel in 1439 elected a second Pope, Felix V, Europe—to avoid another disastrous schism—rallied round the Roman papacy. The Council of Basel lost its authority and appeal. Pope Nicholas V (1447–55) consolidated papal power against conciliarism by persuading antipope Felix and the Council of Basel before it dissolved in 1449 to submit to Rome. He also suppressed the attempt of Stefano Porcaro to make Rome a republic. The best of the Renaissance Popes, Nicholas eschewed nepotism, promoted reform, and founded the Vatican Library. His Jubilee in 1450 celebrated the end of the Council of Basel schism.

But the same could hardly be said for those Renaissance Popes after Nicholas. Pope Calixtus III (1455–58) was known for his nepotism, his illegitimate son, an unsuccessful attempt to launch a crusade against the Turks, and his exonerating of Joan of Arc. Pope Pius II (1458–64), after being a convinced conciliarist most of his dissolute life, was absolved of excommunication and reconciled to the papacy. As Pope he proclaimed a crusade against the Turks and issued his famous bull in 1460 excommunicating anyone who appealed to a general council over the papacy. Pope

Paul II (1464–71) further strengthened the power of the papacy, especially in its rivalry with other Italian states. With Pope Sixtus IV (1471–84) the political ambitions of the papacy became uppermost. He wanted the papacy to be supreme everywhere and freely used nepotism and intrigue to achieve his ends. He warred against Florence and undertook a building program, including the Sistine Chapel, which required extensive taxation and led to subsequent financial abuses. His bull of 1476 made belief in the availability of indulgences for souls in purgatory an article of faith. Pope Innocent VIII (1484–92) openly sought to advance the welfare of his children and scandalously sold offices. His successor was Rodrigo Borgia as Pope Alexander VI (1492–1503). Notoriously immoral, although politically sagacious, Alexander secured the papacy through bribery and was concerned principally with promoting the welfare of his daughter Lucrezia Borgia and his ruthless son Caesar Borgia. His tactics brought invasions of Italy from France and Spain. Pope Julius II (1503–13), the most warlike of the Popes, brought a measure of respect to the papacy, patronized Renaissance art, but failed in his attempt to accomplish reform. And Pope Leo X (1513–21) never comprehended the depth of the revolt that began with Martin Luther. He accepted his office saying, "Now we have the papacy, let's enjoy it." Like some of his predecessors he promoted the affairs of his family, spent lavishly, patronized the arts, and enlarged the Papal States. The Lateran Council of 1512–17 again condemned conciliarism and asserted papal superiority.

The Renaissance Popes seemed unable to understand the nature of the widespread discontent with the papacy and its ecclesiastical control. Nor did they grasp the significance of the contemporary forces of change. The disruption of the medieval synthesis eroded the authority of the papacy, and the Popes themselves forfeited the respect of western Christendom long before Luther launched his revolt in 1517.

The dissolution of the medieval synthesis generally shook confidence in human ability to grasp divine truth and turned attention to things of this world. The nominalists had called into question all ideals, thereby undercutting the supramundane claims of the church. Lorenzo Valla and Nicholas of Cusa had shown that the *Donation of Constantine,* used to advance the welfare of the church in its contest with territorial rulers, was a forgery. Perhaps other claims of the church were equally spurious, and dogmas once accepted as sacrosanct no more than barriers to prevent close examination of mundane motives and goals. The church's deep involvement in secular affairs and its vying for wealth and status like other political powers seemed to belie its claims that spiritual things are more important than material goods. Mistakes and immoralities among the clergy undermined the assertion that a clerical vocation was either special or superior to others. People increasingly doubted not only that the papacy had any monopoly on revelation but also that the spiritual foundations on which the church rested its hierarchical control were valid. This prevalent uncertainty generated more interest in immediate affairs, about which they had definite knowledge and experience. Action prevailed over contemplation, and the body, through which action takes place, became increasingly important. Asceticism proved less and less popular. Renaissance man gave his attention to life now. This relativity of knowledge, particularly with regard to anything beyond this world, was one of the most significant legacies of the dissolution of the medieval synthesis. Albrecht Dürer (1471–1528) in his enormously provocative engraving *Melancholia*, 1514, caught the spirit of the time. Mankind in the form of a winged woman sits brooding, hesitant to move into the future, despite the tools of knowledge and craftsmanship with which she is surrounded. In the background a flying demon with the word "melancholia" on its wings offsets a bright sun and rainbow. Perhaps the woman senses the conflict that will come with the changing times, for there was still enough resistance left in the older institutions and enough vitality in the newer ones to inflame the sixteenth century with tumultuous wars and persecutions. The human need to believe with some certainty in things that transcend this life may well be a significant factor in accounting for the rapid spread of the Reformation in the sixteenth century. Evangelical Protestantism rested its claims not on reason but on faith and asserted the Bible as God's divine word, thus bypassing a thousand years of questionable ecclesiasticism and temporarily giving hope once more in something beyond death.

13

Reformation

On the eve of Martin Luther's *Ninety-five Theses* in 1517, Europe was hovering on the brink of momentous change. The authority of the church had been eroded but was by no means eliminated. Priorities had subtly and complexly altered. Three powerful nations that followed their own self-interest rather than the dictates of the papacy had emerged, indicating that a shift in sovereignty from church to state had taken place. They were France, England, and Spain, each with recognizable geographical boundaries, vernacular speech, and a vague consciousness of being unified, and each with despotic monarchs who crushed local nobles and guilds and assumed their prerogatives.

In France the struggle of the French to expel the English from the continent, a struggle known as the Hundred Years' War, 1337–1453, brought prestige to the monarchy and a sense of unity to a feudally divided people. Unscrupulous though he was, King Louis XI (1461–83) extended his royal control over almost all of France and enabled the Bourbons to assert their absolute rule.

In England the War of the Roses, which began about 1453 between rival barons, plunged that nation into such bloody disorder that Henry VII in 1485 was able to capitalize on the disgust of the people, crush the remnants of feudal power, and establish the Tudor dynasty. The Tudors gave English merchants a sense of security and order, adding to the British nationalism that reached spectacular heights under Elizabeth I.

Spain, the most Catholic of these three emerging nations, gained a sense of unity in its long fight to rid the country of Moors and in the marriage of Ferdinand of Aragon and Isabella of Castile in 1469. Under Charles I (1516–56), who was also Holy Roman Emperor Charles V, and Philip II (1556–98), Spain rose to national glory and power.

This shift in sovereignty from church to state is manifested in the fact that during the turbulent sixteenth century the temporal sword usually determined whether Roman Catholicism or Protestantism prevailed.

The Renaissance, as the term implies, heralded new developments (see Chapter 12). It especially prompted an interest in worldly affairs as seen in the works of those artists who brought the Renaissance to magnificent flower—Fra Angelico (1387–1455), Donatello (1383–1466), Filippo Lippi (ca. 1406–69), Sandro Botticelli (1444–1510), Donato Bramante (1444?–1514), Giorgione (1477–1510), Raphael Sanzio (1483–1520), Leonardo da Vinci (1452–1519), Michelangelo Buonarroti (1475–1564), and Titian (1477–1576). They treated religious subjects, but they also experimented with color, light, forms, and substances. Like Filippo Lippi, who was released from his vows by Pope Pius II for immoral living, they were not known generally for their ascesticism or piety, but for pushing forward the frontiers of their art. Leonardo da Vinci, a many-sided genius—inventor and engineer as well as painter—used his mastery of technique to imbue his art with a new sense of realism and psychological insight, as in his *Mona Lisa* and *Last Supper*. Michelangelo portrayed human emotions on a monumental scale in his ceiling frescoes, *Creation of Man* (1508–12), and *The Last Judgment* (1533–41), as well as in his sculptured works of *David* and *Moses*. Bramante and later Palladio capitalized on the insights of classical antiquity to push architecture into new ventures that emphasized human achievement. These individualistic Renaissance artists clung to the old forms while projecting the new. They were orthodox and rebellious at the same time, undeterred in celebrating the sensuous and the nude along with older religious aspirations, with worldly themes gradually gaining ascendancy.

Secular ideals received embodiment in two influential books, radically different in their tone. One was Machiavelli's *The Prince* and the other Castiglione's *The Courtier*. Emperor Charles V kept copies of both along with the Bible beside his bed.

Niccolo Machiavelli (1469–1527), primarily a Florentine diplomat, is remembered chiefly for his writings. His *Discourses on Livy* lauded the ancient Roman republic and upheld rule by law, equality, and subordination of religion to the state, but Machiavelli's *Prince* was different. He wrote it about 1513 from exile after losing his position as chancellor and serving a brief prison term. It was not published until 1532. He dedicated *The Prince* to Lorenzo de' Medici, Duke of Urbino, hoping the Medici would undertake to unite Italy against foreigners. Having observed the political shrewdness and ruthlessness of Caesar Borgia, son of Pope Alexander VI, in *The Prince* he assumed human depravity, saying that if a prince is to preserve and extend his rule, as he should, he must be especially adept at war and let nothing interfere with his goal. In this world of selfishness, duplicity, and violence, such things as justice, mercy, promises, treaties, and honor are luxuries that the realistic ruler cannot afford—unless they promote his goals. The prince is to do anything, use any means, foul or fair, to secure his ends; this might mean assassination, tyranny, magnificence, or kindness—anything. He is to be as wise as a lion and wily as a fox, taking nothing for granted from his subjects, inasmuch as human selfish motives outweigh loyalty and affection. The prince is to give the appearance of rectitude, which men imagine they value, although they care little for actual virtue. He is to be cruel or merciful to secure the fearful or respectful following of his subjects, whose support he must have. He is justified in executing rivals and must never appear weak or wavering. His rule must prevail, if necessary at the expense of ideals, principles, and truth. Machiavelli's cynical approach to politics has earned him the reputation, whether fully justified or not, of being the great glorifier of selfishness and immorality in politics.

Baldassare Castiglione (1478–1529), poet, ambassador, and courtier at Urbino, published *The Courtier* in 1528, some twelve years after writing it. In sharp contrast to Machiavelli, Castiglione based his views not on the assumption of human depravity but on the goodness of man and the possibility of improvement. Instead of any means to achieve his ends, Castiglione laid down standards for his ideal courtier—skill in military affairs, honest counsel to one's prince, justice, graceful bearing, good manners, learning, writing ability, appreciation of art, and prowess in sports. Without succumbing to religious piety, Castiglione combined many spiritual aspects of medievalism with secular idealism, and for over a century set the tone—including a double sexual standard—for courtly behavior. The book went through 100 editions.

These two books, with their minor emphasis on religion, point to a growing disenchantment with the ecclesiasticism that had once dominated European culture. Before the end the sixteenth century, three giants who mark a transition to modern culture—Michel de Montaigne (1533–92), who invented the essay; William Shakespeare (1564–1616), who poured his genius into drama; and Miguel de Cervantes (1547–1616), who achieved satirical greatness through the novel—would write their masterpieces with almost no treatment of religion.

Discovery of new lands would soon turn the face of Europe toward the West, new trade routes would be mapped, gold from the New World would alter economics, cities on the Atlantic would grow to prominence, and the Mediterranean cities of Venice, Milan, and Genoa would gradually decline as commercial centers. Columbus led the way in 1492 in his search for a passage to India's riches. Vasco da Gama reached India in 1498 via South Africa, and Magellan's crew after his death in the Philippines in 1521 completed the circumnavigation of the globe. Even though Europe during the sixteenth century was more concerned with immediate contingencies on the continent, these voyages opened new perspectives, opportunities, and hopes. Many believed that God in his providence was giving mankind another chance to establish the Kingdom in new, unspoiled lands.

With the invention of the printing press about 1455 by Johann Gensfleisch of Gutenberg, the dissolution of the medieval synthesis, and new geographical discoveries, people seemed to be freed of many of the old restrictions. In almost every respect, Europe bustled with new economic, political, and social vigor, but change did not come quickly, and the old institutions did not easily yield. Not until 1648, the end of the Thirty Years' War, would it be evident that religion, whether Protestant or Catholic, had ceased to be the organizing motif of European culture and that sovereignty over culture had passed from the church to nations vying with one another for supremacy. In particular the papacy clung to its Gregory VII-Innocent III-Boniface VIII image of itself and asserted its sovereignty whenever and wherever temporal forces permitted it to do so. The century began with the horrors of the Inquisition in Spain and ended with the death in 1598 of Philip II of Spain whose great ambition was to use his power to make Europe completely Catholic, thereby bringing glory to Spain.

After the Pope's *Execrabilis* of 1460 the papacy resisted calls for a reforming council, fearing that a council would democratize the church's power structure. With the Pope's armies fighting like other armies for advantages in Italian politics, Andrew Zamometič, bishop of Granea, near Saloniki, in 1482 issued a call from Basel to depose Pope Sixtus IV and reform the curia and the church. His voice did not go unheard. Emperor Frederick III wavered and then imprisoned the bishop, and the Pope laid an interdict on the city. Ulrich Surgant of Basel, a professor at the university, actively supported the idea of a reform council, and maintained that one could legally be convoked by the emperor, the cardinals, or even a single bishop. In 1498 the king of Portugal threatened to call a council if Pope Alexander VI did not mend his personal conduct and nepotism, and King Louis XI of France intrigued for a council to further his own political aspirations. The University of Paris officially recognized conciliar theory, and Padua and Pavia became known as centers for conciliar agitation. In 1511, two jurists, one a member of the court of Pope Julius II, expounded conciliar superiority. Although the call for a council during the Renaissance was often no more than a maneuver in a game of political chess, it indicated that the discontent with hierarchical absolutism that provoked the rise of conciliarism was by no means dead, and also that a declining and much-buffeted papacy still harbored great strength.

In Florence, fiery Dominican friar Girolamo Savonarola (1452–98) strongly reacted to worldliness and sought to purify the city of vanities, while at the same time being heavily involved in Florentine politics. The sixty-year rule of the Medici ended in 1494 when the Florentines kicked them out. Florence then tried to establish a "pure" republic. Heavily influenced by the dramatic preaching of Savonarola, the Florentines in 1496 gathered up their vanities—nude pictures, masks, frivolous books, secular song sheets, ornaments, mirrors, and paintings by Boticelli—and burned them in a huge street bonfire to commemorate the austerities of Lent. Disgusted with the notorious immoralities of Pope Alexander VI, Savonarola called for a council to reform the church. But Savonarola was in no position to challenge the papacy. In the year of the Lenten burning, he was forbidden to preach; in the following year the Pope excommunicated him for not obeying; and on May 23 of the next year he was convicted of heresy and after a month of torture was publicly hanged and burned with two companions on a specially constructed platform in the city's square. His activities and temporary success reflected the prevalent discontent. Many admirers even beyond Italy acclaimed him as a hero. Medals were struck in his honor, and relics of drops of his blood, bits of clothing, and locks of his hair circulated widely in Europe. Luther later hailed Savonarola as an early evangelical and published some of the comments on Psalms that Savonarola had written while in prison. But Savonarola's reforms were as much politically as religiously inspired, and his powerful opponents reacted in kind.

The Spanish Inquisition, a complex of religious, political, and economic factors, symbolized the power still remaining in Catholic ecclesiasticism. The Inquisition had operated intermittently over long periods of time during the Middle Ages. Its basic purpose was to control expressions and activities unwanted by the church. In the thirteenth and fourteenth centuries it was directed largely against the errant Cathari, Waldenses, and the Spiritual Franciscans, who preached poverty as an absolute for Christians. In 1478 the infamous Spanish Inquisition began, and in 1542 the Holy Office of the Inquisition was revived to combat Protestantism. Although some inquisitors said only spiritual weapons should be used against heterodoxy and some hesitated to use extreme physical measures, before the Inquisition ran its course historians estimate that between 5,000,000 and 15,000,000 people lost their lives.

Having received its form under Pope Innocent III, the Inquisition by the end of the thirteenth century had spread to all of Latin Christendom with the exception of England. The Dominicans excelled as inquisitors, diligently searching for heretical suspects and subjecting them to examination including the *infama* (torture), which Pope Innocent IV legalized in 1252 and Pope Alexander IV blessed in 1261. In 1484 Pope Innocent VIII instructed inquisitors to use torture, not only to procure convictions but also to dramatize the horrors of hell. As confession could end torture, many victims confessed to heinous crimes and words. Suspected heretics could be imprisoned for many years, cases could be reopened any time, and trial after death was not uncommon. The *Inquisitors' Manual* of Nicolaus Eymericus (d. 1399) graphically revealed the rules of procedure (see Chapter 10). If found guilty a person could be sentenced to wear yellow crosses as penance, languish in prison for a few years or life, or die by burning, hanging, drowning, or quartering. In a single day in 1245 at Montsegur, 200 Cathari were burned. Those individuals and towns that objected to these acts of the church suffered harsh repressive measures.

To control the nation even more tightly than usual, the new rulers of Spain, Ferdinand and Isabella, in 1478 inaugurated the worst period of Inquisition. The long struggle to expel the Moors tended to make the Spaniards identify patriotism with Catholic orthodoxy. Under Domingo de Torquemada, chief inquisitor in Spain, 1483–98, the church's repression of dissidents reached horrifying heights. In 1492 the Jews who refused to convert to Christianity were exiled and those who converted became subject to the Inquisition. Torquemada surrounded himself with an organization of volunteer spies, many of whom joined his staff to protect themselves. Although immediate confession of heresy usually saved a victim's life, it did not save him from loss of property and imprisonment. Inquisitorial records indicate that under Torquemada over 10,000 were burned, and over 100,000 imprisoned. About every tenth person was a woman who would not conform to the church's expectations.

Under Ximenes, inquisitor general in Spain, 1507–17, an excess of 2,500 suffered death, more than 40,000 received severe punishments, and over 1,300 who could not be apprehended were burned in effigy. Ximenes had reform and renewal in mind (see Chapter 15), but such crushing repression resulted that Spain never had a Reformation and did not experience the full flowering of Renaissance humanism.

The intellectual ferment, commonly termed humanism, that stirred Italy, and especially Florence, during the Renaissance laid heavy emphasis on the study of the humanities, the recovery of sources in Roman, Greek, and Hebraic thought. Neither the ecclesiasticism of the medieval church, nor the finely wrought arguments of scholasticism, nor the otherworldly ideals of the monks greatly interested the humanists. Knowledge of this world and its cultural affairs claimed their attention. Somewhere the civilization of the West had gone astray and the attempt of the humanists to draw directly from the best thought of the ancients represented a broad reform effort. They desired to drink directly from the fountains of early Christianity, believing that to know the good would also lead to doing the good, and to correcting the abuses of a corrupt church. The simplicity of Christ's religion seemed to have little in common with indulgence buying and ecclesiastical pomp, and Christ's direct parables and spirit of love seemed far removed from scholastic hair-splitting and heretic hunting. Leaders among the humanists were Pico della Mirandola (1463–94), Leonardo Bruni (1370–1444), and Marsilio Ficino (1433–99) in Italy; Jacques LeFevre d'Etaples (1455–1536) and Olivetan (ca. 1506–38) in France; John Colet (1467–1519), Thomas Linacre (1460–1524), and Thomas More (1478–1535) in England; Juan Luis Vives (1492–1540) and Ximenes (1436–1517) in Spain; Rudolf Agricola (1443–85), Johann Reuchlin (1455–1522), and Conrad Celtes (1459–1508) in Germany; and Desiderius Erasmus (1466/69–1536) in Holland.

For the most part the humanists were irenic, armchair reformers, change agents but not revolutionists, although sharply critical. They relied on intellectual dialogue, learning, and the pen to achieve their goals. They accused Luther of barbarism, and reacted in horror at the bloodshed and devastation that accompanied so much of the Reformation. They valued law, order, and equity, praised intellectual pursuits, prized learning, believed in people as basically good who, if they would but use their rational powers, could achieve wonders. Despite their bitter assaults on ecclesiasticisim, the humanists for the most part remained Roman Catholic.

Johann Reuchlin exemplifies the humanists in Germany. At twenty he published a Latin dictionary and in 1506 an epoch-making Hebrew grammar, the first in Germany. Deeply interested in Hebraic cabalistic literature, Reuchlin soon clashed with the Dominicans and their Jewish convert, Pfefferkorn, who in 1509 through some friends at court received a mandate from Emperor Maximilian to destroy any Jewish literature that opposed Christianity. Pfefferkorn could not read Hebrew, but he issued hate pamphlets and went through Germany demanding that Jews surrender their books for burning. Many Jews paid bribes to keep the most precious works. Asked for an opinion, Reuchlin advised establishing chairs of Hebrew in universities so that the literature could be properly assessed and purged if necessary. Pfefferkorn, inquisitor Jakob van Hoogstraten, and the Dominicans of Cologne then began a savage vilification of Reuchlin. Reuchlin replied with *Augenspiegel,* and soon humanists from Germany and other countries got involved realizing that freedom of scholarship was at stake. Universities took sides. Pfefferkorn sued, but Reuchlin won acquittal of heresy, and the Dominicans then appealed to Rome. To defend his name, Reuchlin in 1514 published *Letters of Renowned Men,* supportive testimonies from famous people. Then in 1515 *Letters of Obscure Men* appeared. Many Dominicans believed it was a reply from their side; actually it was scathing satire, in a series of humorous letters that obscure monks addressed to their spiritual guide. One famous letter asked how much guilt one would incur if on Friday he ate a boiled egg that turned out to have a chicken in it, and whether wormy cheese was really meat. Others bared the Dominicans' pettiness, greed, laziness, and ignorance. Although authorship of the letters remains unknown, scholarly evidence points to Crotius Rubianus and Ulrich von Hutten, humanist friends of Reuchlin, as the probable authors. Pope Leo X ordered all copies of the book burned, excommunicated its authors, whoever they might be, condemned Reuchlin's *Augenspiegel,* and saddled him with court costs. Drained of funds and energy, Reuchlin made his peace with the church, and died a broken man, estranged from his beloved grand-nephew, Philip Melanchthon, who had become a colleague and ally of Luther in Wittenberg. Although Philip Melanchthon (1497–1560) was a renowned scholar, colleague, and ally of Luther, Reuchlin chose to be estranged from him and despite his difficulties not to depart from the Roman Church.

Erasmus stands above all the others as the acknowledged prince of humanists. He wanted to synthesize faith, reason, and practice, so that society would be reformed and culture would flourish. All about him he saw social excesses and religious hypocrisy. He hated pilgrimages, image veneration, indulgences, illiteracy, and the sanctity of filth. The philosophy of Christ, he said, was better than the intricacies of scholasticism, true piety better than false pretense, and learned wisdom superior to the corrupt and violent ways of the world. The son of a wayward priest, Erasmus of Rotterdam received his early education from the Brethren of the Common Life in Deventer, developed a love for the classics, and to avoid poverty became an Augustinian monk. He had no love for either the monastic or priestly life, and eventually in 1517 won a waiver of his vows. As a student in Paris, where he received his theological training, Erasmus found a mixture of the old and the new learning. For the old he had little enthusiasm. He often cut classes to escape the intricacies of scholastic disputation. Occam's formal logic had become an end in itself, and disagreements on the most trivial meanings of terms frequently erupted in violence. Erasmus wanted no part of the arid lectures or petty quarrels. Instead he found himself drawn to the inner circles of the Parisian society of letters. In 1496 he began his incredibly long list of publications with a slender volume of poetry. When Erasmus went to England in 1499 for the first of several visits, the frivolity and hospitality of the intelligentsia fascinated him, but the Greek scholarship of Linacre, the theological acumen of Colet, and the gentle social genius of More impressed him more. The social, academic, and religious elements of humanism, all present in the Oxford community where Erasmus made so many lasting friendships, furthered Erasmus' hopes to forge religion and culture into a new synthesis.

The *Adages*, first published in 1500, a kind of classical anthology of sayings from ancient authors to which Erasmus added comments, soon grew into a celebrated volume of wit and learning quoted all over Europe. Every passing year brought faith and reason, religion and culture, closer in Erasmus' mind. In 1503 he wrote *The Handbook of a Christian Knight,* which pictured the Christian as a soldier fighting the lures of evil with the weapons of knowledge and prayer. If one would be a moral, Christian person, he must be vigilant, cultivate piety, and acquire knowledge of salutary ideas. For Erasmus, religion and learning contributed to culture and were in turn benefited. This neatly packaged idea engaged Erasmus throughout his life.

In 1506 Erasmus visited Italy. He saw the worldliness of warrior Pope Julius II in full military state riding behind the Holy Sacrament through the breached walls of conquered Bologna. Later he spotlighted papal crimes in a dialogue between St. Peter and the ghost of Julius. After his return from Italy and while visiting Thomas More, Erasmus wrote *In Praise of Folly,* published in 1511, one of his most comprehensive satires. He pillories hypocrisy, greed, ineptness, and ignorance in almost every corner of society, religious and civil. He pictures Folly as a female professor who, with her attendants Self-love, Pleasure, Wantonness, Flattery, and Laziness, is the true spirit promoting all human activities. Without Folly the world would cease to function, trade would stop, no children would be begotten, and superstition would be abandoned. This unsanctimonious spoof delighted the humanist world. But Erasmus also had a more serious purpose, to synthesize culture with piety. At the end he eulogized childhood innocence and saintly meditation.

In 1516 Erasmus published his famous Greek New Testament, followed by a Latin translation in 1519. He sought to correct over 600 errors in the long cherished Vulgate of St. Jerome. But truth did not automatically prevail. For Erasmus and his allies these editions and annotations marked the supreme interpretive service that scholarship could perform for culture. For his enemies the editions presumed to tamper with revelation, as if the uncleansed and prurient tools of secular disciplines had invaded the inner sanctums of ecclesiastical authority. Erasmus' Greek New Testament proved to be epoch-making as a stimulator of biblical research and as a basis for further definitive scholarship. In the same vein he edited the writings of many of the early Church Fathers including Origen, Basil, Cyprian, Jerome, Ambrose, and Augustine, as well as many of the ancient works of Cicero, Seneca, Aristotle, Ptolemy, Euripides and Galen.

In *On the Education of a Christian Prince,* 1516, written for the future Emperor Charles V, Erasmus lauded biblical and classical education as a guiding panacea for princes and pleaded in the name of wisdom for an end to the madness of war among Christians. Erasmus issued his *Colloquies* in 1522 as dialogues to promote good grammar and conduct, but in subsequent revisions the *Colloquies* became a massive satire on the ills of society.

Erasmus endeavored to infuse culture with piety to produce a synthesis of both, and in his person he embodied a confluence of the two, but his "philosophy of Christ" never really penetrated to the essentials of the theological problems of his day. By 1517 another Augustinian monk had intruded upon the scene in distant Saxony. With ninety-five articles on religion, Martin Luther launched a new epoch in ecclesiastical history.

Erasmus and the humanists in general found testimony of God's presence and will in human power and wisdom; Luther found that same power and wisdom to be an abyss of pride, impotence, and ignorance. Although Luther drew upon humanistic studies, he prized faith above erudition, providence above free will. No religion in or of culture could calm the young Luther. Human righteousness was not God's righteousness. For Luther the supreme disposer was not man but God. No one knew better than Erasmus that a profound change was taking place. Erasmus believed he had rescued humanism from paganism and turned it toward Christ, but, he wrote, "While I was fighting a fairly equal battle, lo! suddenly Luther arose and threw the apple of discord into the world."

Although Erasmus at times seemed to condone the activites and ideas of Luther, the two of them clashed sharply in 1524 and 1525 over the question of free will, Erasmus basing his argument for free will on reason and human goodness, Luther basing his contrary arguments on faith and the depths of sin (see p. 173). When Erasmus died in 1536, he was still a loyal Roman Catholic, critical but not revolutionary.

With the publication of Luther's *Ninety-five Theses* in 1517 the ethos of the late Renaissance suddenly burst into new dimensions that profoundly affected all of Christendom. The *Ninety-five Theses* struck a telling blow against the waning authority of the church, but Luther's stand at Worms in 1521 was even more decisive, for there Luther defied not only the church but also the empire with his own subjective judgment of truth. In that paradigmatic act at Worms, Luther not only bequeathed to Protestantism its two pillars of authority—the Bible and conscience—but he also introduced into the very base of Protestantism and modern culture the volatile element of individual subjectivism that threatens all social authority. Although such subjectivism was by no means new in Western thought, the drama at Worms rendered it paradigmatic. In the historical events that followed, Luther himself retreated from its consequences, but like the nominalists before him, Luther had delivered a shattering blow to authority.

Assessments of Martin Luther (1483–1546) vary widely, depending on the stance of the assessor. To Pope Leo X he was a stiff-necked, notorious, damned heretic; to Philip Melanchthon and many of his contemporaries, a second Elijah, a new Paul. For 400 years, from Thomas Murner in 1520 and Johann Dobneck in 1549 to Hartmann Grisar and Heinrich Denifle in the twentieth century, Roman Catholic writers pictured Luther as a seven-headed monstrosity, a sick monk driven by sex, a desperate criminal, a destroyer of culture, a misguided radical. Since 1950, however, many Catholic scholars have hailed him as a profound reformer. To Goethe he was a genius; to Nietzsche, a vulgar peasant. Luther regarded himself as a tool in the hand of God.

Many far-reaching forces converged in the sixteenth century to make the Reformation possible, but its immediate origins lay in the complex struggle of Martin Luther to find religious fulfillment. Born at Eisleben to parents on the rise from peasants to burghers, Luther received a bachelor's degree in 1502 and a master's degree in 1505 from the University of Erfurt. He had just begun to study for a career in law when he was overwhelmed by fear of death and eternal punishment in hell if he should die before earning salvation. In 1505, terrified by a sudden thunderstorm, Luther vowed to become a monk. Against the wishes of his father, a short time thereafter Luther entered the Augustinian monastery at Erfurt. After a two-year probation and with only partial reconciliation to his father, Luther received the sacrament of ordination. But being an Augustinian did not quell his fear of death and the haunting doubt that he, a sinful man, could never satisfy the righteous demands of God. Outwardly Luther was a model of piety and diligence, inwardly he was racked by guilt, doubt, and anxiety. Despite endless *Ave Marias* and *Pater Nosters,* vigils, scourgings, fastings, confessions, and weeping, Luther found no comfort, no feeling of sacramental absolution, no arousal of love for God. Men were expected, with the grace of God, to do sufficient good works—acts of charity, ceremonies, penance, pilgrimages, etc.—to merit salvation, but Luther felt that everything he did was hypocrisy and that his works were paltry in comparison to the righteousness demanded by God. He did not love God; he feared and hated him. The great commandment to love God was like a curse, and God was like a hound of heaven waiting to destroy him. Far from loving God and neighbor, Luther knew that his first love was himself. His religious works were farces.

To break the tension of Luther's struggle to find salvation and to have a spokesman in Rome in a merger dispute that had arisen among the Augustinians, in the winter of 1510–11 Luther's monastery sent him with a fellow monk to the Eternal City. Profoundly shocked and disappointed by the religious superficiality and worldliness of Rome, Luther returned to Germany and immersed himself in study of the Bible in preparation for an appointment as professor of theology at the new University of Wittenberg. He later commented that he had carried onions to Rome and brought back garlic. When Luther received his doctorate October 19, 1512, his spiritual conflict was still unresolved. Just when he had his famous tower experience is questionable. Many say that it came late in 1512 or early 1513 and that his notes, particularly on Psalms, imply this. Others that it did not come until after the *Ninety-five Theses,* because salvation by faith is not clearly manifested in them, and because Luther says that for fifteen years he wore himself out trying to attain righteousness by his own works. The traditional date is 1512–13, based also on Luther's comments, its advocates maintaining that Luther only gradually recognized and expressed the external consequences of his experience. In the tower room of the Augustinian friary at Wittenberg, while studying the Bible, Luther felt that he had suddenly found a gracious God. We by our works do not compel God to accept us; God already accepts and loves us, as demonstrated in the Incarnation in Christ, who died while we were yet sinners. We live by faith, trust a God who cares. Good works are not a prior condition; to trust in one's own works is to blaspheme the gift of God in Christ. In 1545 Luther described his attempt to unlock the meaning of Romans 1:17:

> After I had pondered the problem for days and nights, God took pity on me and I saw the inner connection between the two phrases, "The justice of God is revealed in the Gospel" and "The just shall live by faith." I began to understand that this "justice of God" is the righteousness by which the just man lives through the free gift of God, that is to say "by faith." . . . Thereupon I felt as if I had been born again and had entered Paradise through wide-open gates. Immediately the whole of Scripture took on a new meaning for me. I raced through the Scriptures, so far as my memory went, and found analogies in other expressions. [Translated by E. Harris Harbison, in Kenneth M. Setton and Henry R. Winkler, eds., *Great Problems in European Civilization*. N.Y.: Prentice-Hall, Inc., 1954, pp. 252–53.]

In the place of an angry God Luther had discovered a merciful God. The justice of God meant that because of Christ sinners are acquitted of guilt. Luther had been concerned with the active justice of God, which condemns sinners; he had experienced the passive justice of God, which imputes to those chosen a status of righteousness through Christ. This forgiveness or acceptance occurs *sola fide* (by faith alone). It is not the product of reason, or of good works, or of anything originating with us (see Romans 3:28, 5:8; Ephesians 2:8–9; Galations 3:19–21). God mysteriously, gratuitously chooses some to be saved. These are the elect. We can claim no merit in the process. Natural man is inclined toward evil, and everything he does is tainted. We are justified before God by faith alone, by accepting God's forgiveness in faith, not by forcing God to forgive sins on account of good works. Luther felt released from his torment and illumined, and the ramifications of justification by faith alone marked the remainder of his life. Soon he was to see that one does good works not to earn entry into heaven but to express joy and gratitude for what God has already done.

By emphasizing Scripture as the authoritative channel through which the revealed Word of God reaches those granted faith, Luther undercut the dominant claims and practices of the church for a thousand years. Although Luther heavily stressed the two sacraments he believed to be biblically sanctioned, justification by faith and the preached Word became central in Protestantism. Luther's rejection of transubstantiation and any superior vocational status for the priest, along with his massive blow at the prior necessity of good works for salvation, effectively loosened the religious hold of an already heavily criticized ecclesiasticism and yet left the people with something that rang true to believe in. The individual with a Bible—like Luther in his tower—would symbolize the Protestant Christian. Authority would lodge in each person's conscience, rather than in the Pope. The Bible, rather than the sacerdotalized structures of a hierarchical priesthood, would bear the revelation of God. Luther did not immediately recognize these consequences; they became manifest only gradually in the historical events that followed.

The event that initially propelled Luther into the limelight was the Mainz Indulgence of 1515, to which he responded with his *Ninety-five Theses*. An indulgence was an officially sanctioned means whereby the church could transfer the extra merits earned by Christ and the saints to the credit of another person so that the guilt of his sin could be remitted or punishment in purgatory alleviated. Although the granting of indulgences to those who were in purgatory was in vogue, this practice was not dogmatized until Pope Leo's *Cum Postquam,* November 9, 1518. Popes Urban II in 1095 and Innocent III in 1187 had promised soldiers indulgences for fighting against the Muslims, and Hugo of St. Cher in the thirteenth and Alexander of Hales in the fourteenth century had theologized about the treasury of the merits of Christ and the saints, saying that they could be used by the Pope, who had the key to the fabulous chest. By the time of Clement VI's indulgence in 1350 (to stimulate trade), the indulgence had become a business enterprise to raise money for the papacy. Pope Sixtus IV in 1476 offered an indulgence for the dead, in addition to indulgences for the living, to anyone who could pay the price.

Luther viewed indulgences as a mockery of true religion, a denial of the gift of God in Christ. When Johann Tetzel, a Dominican, came to the borders of Saxony hawking indulgences and making extravagant claims about their full efficacy, even for the dead in purgatory, even if one had violated the Virgin Mary, Luther felt bound to protest the entire business. His response was the *Ninety-five Theses,* nailed, as Philip Melanchthon said, on the Wittenberg Castle Church door October 31, 1517. The Castle Church housed almost 18,000 relics, collected by Elector Frederick of Saxony and his predecessors. Offerings from the pious who came to view the relics provided an endowment and revenue for Wittenberg's new university. Included in the collection were bones from a host of saints, a complete skeleton of a baby slain by Herod, a twig from Moses' burning bush, pieces of Mary's girdle, feathers dropped by angels, and a tear shed by Jesus when he wept over Jerusalem. With the proper prayers and payments, one could cancel almost 2,000,000 years in purgatory. Elector Frederick would not allow Tetzel to come into Saxony for fear that Tetzel's wares would detract from his own.

Like the ordinary person, Luther did not know that an elaborate deal had been arranged between Albert of Brandenburg, Pope Leo X, and the Fugger bankers. Albert, a Hohenzollern prince-bishop, already had the bishoprics of Magdeburg and Halberstadt, even though he was too young to have any and the canon law prohibited holding more than one. And he wanted a third, the Archbishopric of Mainz. Such privileges required large bribes and fees. Albert borrowed the money from the Fuggers, using as security the promise of an indulgence in his territory, and paid off the Pope's agents. By secret agreement half of the indulgence money was to go to the Fuggers and half to the Pope. The people were told the indulgence fund would rebuild St. Peters' Church in Rome. Luther was unaware of this big business arrangement; he reacted because some of his students and townspeople were crassly exhibiting indulgence certificates to verify forgiveness of their sins. Luther dramatically questioned the indulgence traffic by challenging anyone to dispute his ninety-five articles. Indulgences, said Luther, pose a false picture of what Christ meant when he commanded us to repent, for repentance means inward and outward contrition. To those who truly repent, God for Christ's sake freely grants plenary remittance of both punishment and guilt. The Pope has no power to forgive any sin; he can only declare and confirm God's forgiveness. He can remit only those penalties imposed by himself. Absolution without personal repentance is worthless. The people have been deceived. Indulgences are a fraud, detrimental to the Word and worship of God. Poor people would be better off buying food. No saints have earned extra merits, and the merits of Christ are free. If the Pope cared for people, he should, if he had the power to do so, empty purgatory not for the sake of money but for love. Indulgences fish for money; the Gospel fishes for men. "To deem the papal pardon so great that it can absolve a man even if he had violated the mother of God is sheer madness. . . . It is blasphemy to say that an indulgence cross which is adorned with the papal arms and erected in a church has the same value as the cross of Christ." In short, Luther said, the traffic in indulgences harms not only religion but the papacy itself. Instead of true religion, indulgences foster deceit, immorality, skepticism, and irreverence.

Luther had struck a telling blow. He had dared to call the church's best means of funding a fraud and to declare that the Gospel and its promises supersede even the claims of the Pope. The theses were printed and widely circulated, and pent-up resentment of ecclesiastical abuses spilled forth. Within weeks Luther became a German hero. The serious implications of the theses were clearly evident in the two sets of counter-theses published by Tetzel and his Dominican friends. The second set of fifty theses was written in 1517 and publicly debated January 21, 1518. Tetzel upheld papal supremacy and infallibility, saying that the Pope cannot err in matters of faith, that defined Catholic truth contains no falsehood, that Christians must obey papal statutes, and that dissenters are manifest heretics. Nevertheless, Germany was like a hornet's nest, and the sale of indulgences fell sharply.

Attempts to silence Luther forced him step by step to realize the revolutionary character of his challenge. The first two attempts came in 1518. One was a blast from Sylvester Prierias, Master of the Sacred Palace and Papal Inquisitor, and the other was a visit from Cardinal Cajetan. The Dominicans were very active in Rome and persuaded the Pope to summon Luther to Rome for examination on suspicion of heresy and subversion of papal power. In the citation Prierias claimed that the Pope is virtually the universal church, that he is infallible, that whoever does not rely on the

Pope or questions indulgences is a heretic. He branded Luther as a leper, libeler, calumniator, and dog. Luther could not believe that the document came from the Pope. He regarded it as a forgery. Christ, not the Pope, is the embodiment of the church, Luther declared; if the Pope is, what odium must be borne by the church because of Popes like Julius II and Boniface VIII "who entered the church as a wolf, governed it as a lion, and died like a dog." Since Popes and councils may err, said Luther, he would trust Christ. In August Luther went to Augsburg for Cardinal Cajetan's fatherly talk, but Cajetan wanted no discussion of the situation, only submission on the part of Luther, and Luther would not submit without being shown his error either by the weight of Scripture or by reason. Luther stood his ground, despite the *Cum Postquam,* which against "certain religious in Germany" declared that papal indulgences did apply to both the living and the dead. From his own university and the University of Paris Luther received supportive declarations.

On January 4 and 5, Karl von Miltitz, papal nuncio, suavely talked with the Elector Frederick, presenting him with a Golden Rose and promising him legitimization for his two bastard sons, and with Luther, promising him the whole case would be fairly decided in Germany if Luther would but keep silent. He exceeded his instructions and reported to the Pope that Luther was ready to recant. Luther saw through Miltitz's dissimulation and lack of authority.

The most significant attempt to silence Luther was the Leipsic Disputation with Johann Eck, June 27–July 16, 1519, an elaborate affair lasting almost three weeks and attracting wide attention outside Germany. Eck maneuvered Luther into agreeing with Hus that belief in the supremacy of the Roman Church was not necessary for salvation. Luther openly defied the church's authority, and Eck jubilantly called him a heretic. In the pamphlet warfare that followed, many humanists supported Luther.

Elector Frederick shrewdly protected his prize professor, and Charles V, who already had enough votes to be chosen emperor, was reluctant to court further trouble in Germany. But on June 15, 1520, Pope Leo X issued his famous bull, *Exsurge Domine,* branding Luther a wild boar in the Lord's vineyard and giving him sixty days to recant. Months later, on December 10, urged on by cheering students, Luther publicly burned the bull and other papal documents outside the walls of Wittenberg. The bull *Decet,* January 3, 1521, finalized Luther's excommunication.

In the meantime, Luther's three 1520 essays appeared. *The Appeal to the German Nobility* played on the patriotic feelings of Germans, and smashed the three "walls" erected by the papacy. The papacy is not superior to the state, said Luther, nor is the Pope the only one who can interpret Scripture and call a council. All Christians enjoy the same spiritual status. By baptism, every Christian is part of the body of Christ, and although each part has its particular vocation, no vocation is better than another; a baker's vocation is just as sacred as a monk's. All parts contribute to the common good of the body. When one part of the body gets out of line, other parts must correct it. Luther urged the nobility to correct the abuses of the church. All Christians are priests and parts of the body of Christ; all are equal.

The Babylonian Captivity scored withdrawing the cup from the laity and dogmatizing transubstantiation as acts imprisoning the sacrament of the Lord's Supper in order to heighten the power of the priest. Luther rejected transubstantiation as a human innovation. Only Baptism and the Lord's Supper were instituted by Christ; the other so-called sacraments were invented by men to enhance the rule of men. Thus he undercut the medieval claims of the church.

The essay on *The Freedom of the Christian Man* set freedom in the context of ethics. The Christian man is both free and bound. He is free in that he does not have to keep multitudinous rules in order to be saved; he is justified by faith alone. However, he is bound in that his experience of justification by faith impels him out of sheer joy and gratitude to show to others the same kind of love revealed to him in Christ. Luther urges every Christian to be a Christ to his neighbor.

Luther's early career climaxed at the Diet of Worms on April 18, 1521. Summoned before the august gathering of imperial and ecclesiastical dignitaries at Worms, when asked to revoke his heresies, Luther replied that unless he was convinced by Scripture or by clear reason (for he did not trust either Popes or councils, knowing that both had erred and contradicted themselves many times), he could not and would not act contrary to his conscience, which was captive to the Word of God. "I cannot do otherwise, here I stand, so help me God." Luther's dramatic stance uplifted Scripture interpreted by right reason (conscience) as the twin authorities of Protestantism. Roman Catholics at the time perceived this as the gateway to chaos and schism, for the real issue at Worms was not Holy Scripture but who should interpret Scripture—the Pope or an individual Christian. If the latter, then the possibility of as many forms of Christianity as there are individuals loomed. The issue at stake was papal infallibility versus subjective conscience. Both sides accepted Scripture, but each interpreted it quite differently.

Luther used Scripture and conscience to break through the sovereignty of Roman Catholicism. He bequeathed to Protestantism in particular and Western culture in general the volatile problems of subjective individualism, which has been a prime factor in the multiple divisions within Protestantism and which opens the door to the breakdown of all social authority and to anarchy. Luther's Roman Catholic opponents at Worms quickly recognized that his stance would make each person sovereign and lead to anarchy, and Luther soon recognized the same thing and fell back on the state to prevent chaos. Luther successfully challenged the sovereign authority of Rome but not that of the state. He needed the aid of the state to combat the power of Rome, and subsequent events put the state in complete control. This trading of sovereignties was manifested and symbolized in the primary creed of Lutheranism—the Augsburg Confession, drawn up by the theologians, but publicly confessed and signed by the ruling princes.

Luther left Worms on April 26, in the midst of the general excitement and political maneuvering that followed his bold statement. On May 4, his supporters staged a kidnapping and secreted him in the Wartburg Castle for eleven months to safeguard his life. After the Elector of Saxony and others who inclined toward Luther had left Worms, young Charles V drafted an imperial edict, dated May 8 but actually signed May 26, in which he condemned Luther's views as a cesspool of heresies. Charles ordered all his subjects, on pain of treason and loss of property and privileges, to hunt Luther down as a "notorious and stiff-necked heretic," destroy his books, and seize for themselves the property of "his friends, adherents, patrons, maintainers, abettors, sympathizers, emulators, and followers."

But the political realities favored Luther, who worked during the remainder of the 1520s to structure and consolidate the new religion. Some of Luther's adherents still considered Luther's actions a reform movement within Catholicism; Luther realized the break was irreparable. At the Wartburg Castle he finished translating the New Testament into German, and in 1523 and 1526 wrote his *Order of Worship* and the *German Mass* to bring liturgy into conformity with justification by faith. An evangelical hymnal, edited by Johann Walter and containing four hymns by Luther, appeared in 1524 to promote congregational participation in worship. While Luther was still at the Wartburg Castle, in 1521 Philip Melanchthon, a humanist who had come to Wittenberg University in 1518 to teach Greek, published his *Loci Communes,* the first systematic theology of the new movement. Luther agreed so fully with its contents that he said it deserved a place in the scriptural canon. Lutheranism was well launched.

However, although a shaky peace prevailed among the secular princes, Lutheranism was not without significant disturbances. In 1524 and 1525 Erasmus, the critic, and Luther, the reformer, clashed over the question of free will. After much urging on the part of his Catholic friends, Erasmus published his *Diatribe De Libero Arbitrio (On Free Will)* in 1524. He sent presentation copies to Duke George, an avowed foe of Luther, and to Pope Clement VII and Henry VIII. He proposed an academic discussion of the place of free will in salvation, for he could not accept Luther's view of the impotence of the human will and the worthlessness of human works. Reason was not completely extinguished in the Fall, Erasmus argued, and God's commandments imply that we can keep the divine law. If we have no free will to choose and to act responsibly, then the Bible's promises and threats mean nothing. This semi-Pelagian stance barely touched Luther's central problem—the inward pervasiveness of sin causing all human deeds to be tainted, making righteousness impossible. In 1525 Luther replied with *De Servo Arbitrio (On the Bound Will)* in which he developed justification by faith alone against Erasmus' moralism, and declared that if God is not ruling, then his promises are empty and we are left with despair. He would not admit that Erasmus even understood the problem. Erasmus retorted vituperatively with *Hyperaspistes,* but Melanchthon persuaded Luther not to reply, and the controversy ended. Because Luther had denigrated human rational powers, many humanists withdrew from the new movement thinking it was headed for social barbarism. The humanists placed their trust in education and reason. Luther, seeing that reason had been used to bolster scholasticism, regarded reason apart from faith as a tool of Satan.

In 1525 the Peasants' Revolt erupted in all its fury, with tragic consequences for the peasants and the evangelical movement. More than any other event it shows that Luther was committed to the sovereignty of the state. The peasants' complaints were not new; the 1525 uprisings climaxed a series of revolts reaching back to the Middle Ages. The peasants wanted relief from burdensome taxes, tithes, rents, labor services, and flagrant encroachment on their privileges. In Luther they saw a champion. They took Luther's words on freedom and faith out of context and applied them to their social difficulties. Freedom, as they said in their *Twelve Articles* in 1525, meant release from serfdom, inasmuch as all are free as Christians. Luther's views on vocations and the priesthood of all believers suggested a more egalitarian society. And Luther's denunciations of the corruptions and abuses of monasticism invited seizure and confiscation of church properties. In their *Twelve Articles* the peasants demanded the right to choose and depose their own pastors, withdrawal of the cattle tithe imposed by men, release from serfdom, hunting and fishing rights, communal ownership of forests and meadows, payment for extra services, abolition of the hated death tax, and the right in the future to present or withdraw demands in accordance with the Scriptures. The peasants swore to obey Scripture, and believed their demands to be in full accord with God's Word.

In his *Admonition to Peace: A Reply to the Twelve Articles of the Peasants,* April, 1525, Luther scorched the princes for their tyranny, intolerance, cruelty, and unjust exactions. He said peasants should have the right to choose pastors who would preach the Gospel, that their social demands were just. At the same time, he deplored insurrection and appeal to the sword, and advised arbitration. He rebuked the peasants for seriously misinterpreting the Gospel, for using the Gospel as a lever to better their own physical conditions. He pointed out that the patriarchs had slaves and that slaves and prisoners can have Christian freedom, for Christian freedom is not a physical status. He objected to making all men equal and turning the spiritual kingdom of Christ into a physical kingdom in this world. Luther refused to draw the social inferences that the peasants saw in his theological concepts. He would not identify the Gospel with their demands. Instead he implied that Christianity is properly concerned with eternal life in heaven, and that Christians should bear patiently the wrongs and sufferings of this life and calmly await their awards in the next world.

Luther's theological admonition soon gave way to a call for the princes to use armed force. Within weeks the unrest and occasional violence among Germany's 300,000 peasants erupted into ravaging and pillaging. On April 16, peasants stormed Weinsberg and massacred its inhabitants. Scores of castles and cloisters were plundered and burned. Thomas Müntzer (ca. 1490–1525) at Mühlhausen and other fiery preachers among the peasants openly called for slaughter in the name of God. Luther believed that the sword of government had been given by God to the princes, and that the peasants, even though treated unjustly, were not justified in taking the sword into their own hands. In his eyes they had become robbers and murderers, faithless and perjured. In his infamous essay, in May, 1525, *Against the Robbing and Murdering Hordes of Peasants,*

Luther called on the nobles to use any means available to suppress the rebels. "Smite, slay, and stab, secretly or openly . . . as if among mad dogs," he urged, "lest the whole land be ruined." The peasants deserved death, Luther argued, because they had broken their oath of fealty, resorted to rioting and plundering, and masked their terrible sins with the name of the Gospel.

Germany's nobility, Lutheran and Catholic, combined to crush the uprising. On May 15, at Frankenhausen, 50,000 peasants armed mainly with clubs and pitchforks were overwhelmed and wretchedly butchered. Subsequent reprisals left the peasants utterly defeated and demoralized. According to one eye-witness account, at Wernitz a priest and four peasants were beheaded and seven others had their fingers cut off. At Kitzingen fifty-eight had their eyes gouged out. At Königshofen the Swabian forces slew 4,000 on Friday and 8,000 more on Monday with a loss of 150 men. At Rothenburg more than 17 were beheaded and their bodies left all day in the market place. An estimated 100,000 perished. Obviously, Luther had opted for the ruling powers, causing the lower classes, when they had the choice, to shun religion or to join sects that rejected both the established church and the state. Albrecht Dürer designed a monument for any who might wish to celebrate the victory: a base with dozing cattle and sheep, a shaft with symbols of peaceful labor, and at the top a peasant sitting on a chicken coop with a sword thrust between his shoulder blades.

Luther's marriage, June 13, 1525, so soon after the uprising, to Catherine von Bora, a former nun, seemed ill-timed and started malicious tongues wagging. Yet it established a pattern of marriage for pastors throughout Protestantism.

In 1526 the German evangelicals won a significant concession from the Diet of Speier (Spires). Ostensibly because Emperor Charles V wanted peace in Germany while he dealt with the Turks, who were threatening Austria; the French, who were constant rivals; and the papacy, whose machinations he could not always trust, the German evangelicals secured a suspension of the Edict of Worms. Each prince was to be responsible for religion in his territories until a general settlement of the religious question. Until 1529, this left the evangelicals free to organize and consolidate along scriptural lines. The Diet of Speier in 1529 revoked this concession, causing the evangelicals to protest that religion should be a matter of free conscience. From that protest, Protestantism derives its name.

1528 was a signal year for Lutheranism. Luther had challenged the sovereignty of the papacy, but the ally that he courted in doing so was the state. The development of that alliance put the state in final control of both religion and education. This significant shift in sovereignty was legalized in 1528 when the *Visitation Articles,* guidelines for churches and schools, were enacted into law. It was further cemented for Lutheranism in the historic Confession of 1530 made by the princes at Augsburg. Acceptance of state sovereignty by the early Protestants—Lutherans, Zwinglians, Calvinists, Anglicans, Reformed, Presbyterians—contributed greatly to the rise of the claim to absolute sovereignty on the part of the world's nations, a concept undergoing radical questioning in the late 1900s. The church-state partnership in 313 resulted in the dominance of the church; the church-state partnership in the sixteenth century resulted in the dominance of the state.

By 1530 divisions had already occurred among the evangelicals, as evidenced in their inability to agree on the sacrament of the Lord's Supper. The most dramatic disagreement was that between Luther and Zwingli (see Chapter 14) at Marburg in 1529. By 1530, with the Turks repulsed in their drive toward Vienna, Emperor Charles V felt free to deal with the religious question. In an effort to achieve concord, all parties were invited to present their beliefs. The Elector of Saxony commissioned Melanchthon to draw up the final statement. It rested heavily on prior evangelical documents, but, in the hope of achieving peace, softened belligerency toward Roman Catholicism. Luther, still under the imperial ban, stayed at Coburg. As the day of reckoning approached, the evangelical princes and representatives of cities drew closer together. On June 25, 1530, they all boldly stood for two hours while the Augsburg Confession was read before the imperial diet. It is the Protestants' major creed, on which almost every other evangelical creed is based. At its center stands justification by faith. It elevates faith over meritorious works. It places authority in the biblical Word of God interpreted by conscience. It rejects transubstantiation, withdrawal of the cup, propitiatory mass, invocation of saints, enumeration of sins. It accepts civil government and the duty of Christians to hold office. Yet in other respects it is thoroughly Catholic, for it claims not to have strayed from Scripture and the early Fathers.

Zwingli's confession was presented on July 3, and the Tetrapolitan Confession of Strassburg, Constance, Memingen, and Lindau on July 11. The Roman Catholic *Confutation* composed by Eck and other Catholic theologians was presented first on July 13, but the emperor considered its 351 pages too long and too vituperative, so that it was rewritten and submitted again on August 3. Negotiations and committee discussions yielded little fruit and the Protestants dispersed in September.

Although the Lutherans were refused a copy of the *Confutation*, on the way home, working from notes, Melanchthon drafted the *Apology to the Augsburg Confession*, published in 1531, a superior theological work judged by many to be one of the best explanations of the Augsburg Confession.

The diet settled nothing. The Protestants were given until April 15, 1531, to reconsider their stance and rejoin the Catholics. But renewed threats from the Turks and shrewd political maneuvering on the part of the Lutheran Smalcald League gave them peace for sixteen years. The Catholics took measures to counter Protestantism, but not until after Luther's death, February 18, 1546, did open warfare come.

On April 25, 1547, the Lutherans, betrayed by one of their own leaders, suffered defeat by imperial forces at Mühlberg. But Catholic rulers of Lutheran subjects proved unviable. After the failure of the imposed religious compromises of the Augsburg and Leipsic Interims, the former betrayer of the evangelicals betrayed the Catholics. The ensuing Peace of Passau, 1552, brought general quiet until the more permanent settlement of the Peace of Augsburg in 1555, which established the principle of *cuius regio, eius religio* (whose region, his religion) and allowed any who could not conform to emigrate. Within Lutheranism state sovereignty was well entrenched. Those who really carried out Luther's stance at Worms regarding individual conscience were the Anabaptists. They rejected both papal and state sovereignty and asserted the ultimacy of the consecrated individual's conscientious interpretation of God's Word.

14

Explosive Expansion

The explosive reform detonated by Luther reverberated throughout Europe, causing a rift in Christendom greater than that between Roman Catholicism and Greek Orthodoxy. Switzerland especially felt the reverberations. Ulrich Zwingli (1484–1531), about the same time as Luther, began agitations that resulted in widespread evangelical reform in the Swiss cantons. Dissatisfaction with Zwingli's policies prompted the main beginning of the Anabaptists, a group of New Testament Christians who rejected the established church and its ties with sovereignty of state in favor of voluntaryism and individual autonomy in religion. After the death of Zwingli on the battlefield at Kappel, evangelical leadership in Switzerland shifted to John Calvin (1509–64), whose *Institutes of the Christian Religion* in 1536 and subsequent work in Geneva made him the acknowledged leader of Protestantism. Calvin's impact was primary, Luther's secondary, in the expansion of Protestantism in France, along the Rhine River into Holland, in England, Scotland, and the United States. Calvin's stamp is clearly noticeable in the Reformed Church of the Rhine Valley, Puritanism in England, and Presbyterianism in Scotland. Martin Bucer (1491–1551) and John Knox (1505–72) played important roles in these developments. Long before the end of the sixteenth century, diversity clearly marked Protestantism. The inherent subjectivity in the Protestants' twin authorities of Scripture and conscience led quickly to fragmentation.

Ulrich Zwingli, a native of Wildhaus, came under the influence of religion and humanism early in his life. Being gifted in music, at the age of twelve he almost became a monk in order to train other monks in music. However, he finally chose an alternative route to the priesthood—a humanist education at Vienna and Basel, where he came under the influence of Thomas Wyttenbach and Erasmus—and secured an appointment in 1506 as parish priest at Glarus, a large, wealthy church. In 1510 he published a fable in which he pictured a shepherd (the Pope) protecting his sheep against a marauding leopard (the French) and a stealthy fox (the Venetians). He became a reformer only gradually. His experience as a field chaplain led him to protest Swiss mercenary service for any except the Pope, which endeared him to the papacy, but Zwingli's study of the Bible and the Church Fathers led him also to question some of the church's practices. He wholeheartedly received Erasmus' Greek New Testament in 1516, and his study of it and reading of the sources inclined him toward an Erasmian philosophy of Christ. He grew increasingly critical, so that his departure from Glarus was not entirely voluntary. As the pastor at Einsiedeln for two years, 1516–18, Zwingli concentrated on the Bible and found more fault with Roman Catholicism. He openly attacked pilgrimages and Bernard Samson's selling of indulgences. Current papal authority and practices, he said, could not be justified in Scripture.

Nevertheless, in 1518 Zwingli received appointment as Acolyte Chaplain to the Pope, which led subsequently to his new pastorate in Zurich, finally enabling him to realize his political and ecclesiastical ambitions. Despite this honor from the papacy, by the time Zwingli became chief pastor of Grossmünster, the principal church of Zurich, January 1, 1519, he had already made the Bible his authority. Discarding selected Gospel and epistle texts, he began expounding Scripture verse by verse, book by book. By 1525 he had preached through the entire New Testament. Throngs attended his regular services, and to accommodate even wider audiences, he preached special market-day sermons.

Zwingli's moral integrity has often been questioned. At the time of his appointment to the Zurich pulpit, he was investigated for alleged heresy and seduction of a young girl. He denied both charges, but freely admitted incontinence and insisted that his vow to celibacy did not necessarily include chastity. When the city council found him not guilty of moral abuse or heresy, he called on the council to support his ministry, a tactic he later adroitly used to get his own theological views enacted into laws. The petition of Zwingli and ten other priests in 1522 to the Bishop of Constance for permission to marry indicated that he was moving rapidly away from Catholicism. The petition rested mainly on biblical texts, but noted that if the appeal were granted, it would but legalize the widespread priestly cohabitation already being practiced. Although the petition went unanswered, Zwingli began living with a wealthy widow, whom he publicly married two years later on April 2, 1524.

Outward reform in Zurich began in 1522 with Zwingli's vigorous preaching against Lenten fasts and rules. When the Bishop of Constance objected, Zwingli cited scholars and the New Testament, and pressed his point with the city council, which eventually agreed that the New Testament did not impose Lenten fasts but that they should be observed for the sake of good order. That did not satisfy Zwingli and his followers, who in August received a ruling from the council that henceforth all religious customs should be based on the pure Word of God. This undercut the authority of the Bishop of Constance and established civil rule in accordance with the Word as the reform principle of Zurich.

This set the stage for the crucial debates in 1523 for which Zwingli prepared his *Sixty-seven Articles.* He ably argued the authority of the Bible over the church, salvation by faith, the mass as a remembrance not a sacrifice, the right of priests and nuns to marry. He denied that good works merit salvation, that saints should be invoked, that priests mediate between God and man, that monastic vows are binding, that there is a purgatory, that anything is required of a Christian except what the Bible commands. The council implemented these new ideas with new regulations, and the turn away from Catholicism was virtually complete. Before the year ended the council forbade images and performance of the mass. In place of the latter, Zwingli instituted the love feast, a memorial in remembrance of Christ. Instead of the golden chalice that he used as a Catholic priest at Glarus, he now celebrated the supper using a simple wooden bowl. Instead of transubstantiation, he held that the elements were purely symbolic and commemorative. He wished to eliminate anything, any creature, that might detract from the worship of the Creator. Consequently he removed from the churches all kinds of ornaments— clerical robes, tapestries, frescoes, relics, crucifixes, candles, and images. Bell-ringing, chanting, and organ-playing ceased. In 1527 Zwingli had the great organ in Zurich dismantled.

Zwingli's best theological work appeared in 1525, a *Commentary on True and False Religion.* He believed the Bible was authoritative for faith and practice, that the Bible revealed God's will for all humanity, that the Christian should reject everything not expressly enjoined in Scripture. He believed in an omnipotent God who wills and directs us and has foreordained the elect, and that election is made known through a faith experience. But he did not believe in original sin, regarding it only as a moral disease that did not involve personal guilt, and his humanism compelled him to hold that the Spirit operates outside the sacraments and has inspired such men as Socrates, Cato, and Hercules.

Soon other Swiss cantons succumbed to the influence of Zwingli. Zwingli's friend, Johann Oecolampadius (1482–1531) won Basel; a debate in 1528 of the *Ten Theses* by Zwingli and others turned Berne to Protestantism; and St. Gallen, Schaffhausen, and Mülhausen followed. Martin Bucer (1491–1551) won Strassburg for the evangelical cause, but his efforts to unite Zwinglianism and Lutheranism proved futile. He brought together Luther and Zwingli, with their two assistants, Melanchthon and Oecolampadius, in the Marburg Colloquy in 1529, and although the two Protestant leaders could agree on most points they could not agree on the Lord's Supper. Luther believed in the real presence of Christ in the elements of the Lord's Supper, even going so far as to say the recipient chews the body of Christ with his teeth. On the conference table he wrote *"Hoc est corpus meum"* (This is my body—Matthew 26:26) and insisted that

Christ meant that the bread was his body. Zwingli referred to John 6:48–63 to show that Christ was speaking figuratively, not literally of the body. And there they angrily parted company. The theological and political union of the two was not to be; each said the other was inspired by the devil. Zwingli presented a separate confession at Augsburg in 1530. He was killed in battle while leading troops against the Roman Catholic cantons.

Earlier in his career Zwingli clashed with some of his co-workers and instituted one of the most tragic chapters in church history. Some question remains about the origins of Anabaptists (so-called for rebaptizing adults). Some say they began with Carlstadt when he left Wittenberg to cast his lot with the peasants; others that they began with the peasants for whom Thomas Müntzer was a spokesman; others that they went back to the Waldenses and Cathari. The main part of Anabaptism originated in Switzerland in reaction to Zwingli's stand on infant baptism and failure to promote a genuinely New Testament church.

Conrad Grebel (1498–1526) and Felix Manz (1498–1527), both educated members of prominent Swiss families, worked closely with Zwingli. His preaching convinced them on scriptural authority. Grebel became a convert in 1522, and hoped for a believers' church without the mass and papal trappings. Zwingli proceeded cautiously, after every step waiting for the city council to pass laws implementing the changes. Grebel, Manz, and a few others began meeting in the home of Manz' mother to study their Hebrew and Greek Bibles. Soon convinced that infant baptism was not scripturally justifiable, that baptism was merely a symbol as Zwingli had preached, that baptismal regeneration of infants was therefore a contradiction, and that Zwingli was not following his own biblical dictum, they declared that baptism could be properly administered only to adults who freely believed the Gospel. This threatened the delicate union of church and state that Zwingli had learned to manipulate. He feared tampering with infant baptism would arouse antagonism that could undo the entire reform.

Balthasar Hubmaier (1480–1528), a former priest who worked among the peasants at Waldshut, joined Zwingli in Zurich. In May 1523 he had doubts about infant baptism and declared that Zwingli shared his views. At Waldshut in 1524 Hubmaier defended eighteen reform propositions, one of which stated that every Christian should believe and be baptized for himself.

Irritated by the direct and implied criticisms of Grebel, Manz, and Hubmaier, Zwingli met his critics in preliminary talks, and early in 1525 faced them in public debate before the city council. Grebel, Manz, and Wilhelm Reublin, a pastor near Zurich, opposed Zwingli unsuccessfully, and on the following day, January 18, the council ordered parents to have their infants baptized within eight days or leave the city "with wife and child, goods and chattels." Zwingli's arguments were not scripturally conclusive, but he had accurately assessed the mind of the council. On January 21 the council ordered Grebel and Manz to cease their Bible meetings. Reublin and several other pastors who continued to object were banished.

According to *The Oldest Chronicle of the Hutterian Brethren,* Grebel, Manz, George Blaurock (Cajacob) who was a Catholic priest and a recent

EUROPE, 1550
THE HOLY ROMAN EMPIRE

Atlantic Ocean

SCOTLAND
St. Andrews
Edinburgh

IRELAND

ENGLAND
Cambridge
Oxford
London
Canterbury

Paris
Loire
Tours
FRANCE

Bay of Biscay

Toulouse
Carcassonne

PORTUGAL

Madrid
Toledo
SPAIN

OTTOMAN

0		200		400		600 miles

0		400		800 kilometers

BOUNDARY OF THE HOLY ROMAN EMPIRE: ▪▪▪▪▪▪▪▪▪▪▪▪▪▪▪▪▪▪▪▪▪▪▪

visitor to Zurich, and several others met secretly on the night of January 21, 1525, to ponder their plight. Blaurock spoke convincingly about one having a true faith learned from the Word, and manifesting it in love and true godliness, despite tribulation. The group prayed, until Blaurock, overcome by the Spirit, knelt and implored Grebel to baptize him. Grebel did, and Blaurock in turn baptized the others. "Soon thereafter several others made their way to them, . . . Balthasar Hubmaier of Friedberg, Louis Haetzer, and still others, . . . some preachers and other persons, who were soon to testify with their blood." Although immersion came to be the accepted form of baptism, in the beginning sprinkling was widely used. With one bucketful of water Reublin is said to have baptized three hundred believers. Persecution fell heavily on the early leaders, nearly all of whom became martyrs. But the movement spread rapidly, arousing old fears of heresy and treason among Zwinglians, Catholics, and Lutherans. By 1535, an estimated 50,000 Anabaptists had been put to death for their faith.

State-church authority fell quickly on Grebel, Manz, and Blaurock. All three were jailed for their preaching in and out of Zurich. Sentenced to life imprisonment in March, 1526, Grebel escaped from prison and resumed preaching, only to die of the plague in the same year. He was twenty-eight.

Felix Manz was the first Anabaptist martyred by the Protestants. In March, 1525, he was arrested and confined with thirteen men and seven women in the Tower in Zurich, with nothing to eat but bread and water, until "they either give up the ghost or surrender." Zwingli likened his treatment of the Anabaptists to Peter's treatment of Ananias (Acts 5). When Manz denied opposing all civil government and favoring a communism of goods, he was set free, only to be arrested several more times for preaching. But in 1526 the council decreed death for anyone who rebaptized, and on January 5, 1527, Manz was sentenced to die by drowning. He was bound in a doubled-up position and pushed from a boat into the water of the Limmat River in Zurich. He was twenty-nine.

On the day of Manz' execution, George Blaurock was whipped out of town. But Blaurock would not give up preaching repentance and baptism. He took the place of a Tirolese preacher whom the Catholic authorities had burned at the stake. On August 14, 1529, he was himself arrested by the Catholic authorities, and after severe torture, was burned at the stake on September 6. He was found guilty of leaving the priesthood, refusing to invoke Mary, repudiating the mass and confessional, and discrediting infant baptism.

Among those banished from Zurich in 1525 was Michael Sattler. Undaunted, he began evangelizing in Württemberg but within a year and a half was burned at the stake. On February 24, 1527, he presided over the meeting at Schleitheim that produced the first Anabaptist confession of faith, written largely by him and aimed at erring brothers. The Schleitheim Confession stated that the Swiss Brethren were agreed on seven articles: (1) Baptism for adults who have "learned repentance and amendment of life, and believe truly that their sins are taken away by Christ." (2) The use of the ban after secret admonition twice so that all who partake of the Lord's Supper may be one in mind and love. (3) Exclusion from the breaking of the bread of any who are not united by baptism in the "one body of Christ which is the church of God and whose Head is Christ." (4) Separation from the evil and wickedness of the world, from all popish and antipopish works, meetings and church attendance, drinking houses, civic affairs, and abominations, from all use of the sword and weapons of force. (5) Pastors who have good standing in and out of the communion, to read, admonish, teach, warn, discipline, ban, pray, and lead the faithful, who shall be supported by the church, and disciplined by the church if they fall into sin, and who in case of martyrdom shall be succeeded by others chosen and ordained by the church "in the same hour." (6) Nonuse of the sword in connection with the ban, refusal to serve as a judge in worldly disputes, or to serve as a magistrate or a prince since they employ the sword. (7) Rejection of all swearing and oath-taking.

Zwingli in 1527 and Calvin in 1544 both wrote treatises against these articles. Michael Sattler could not reply. Three months after the confession he was burned as a heretic. The Roman Catholic authorities of Austria arrested him near Rothenburg on the Neckar, where he was brought to trial on May 17 and executed on May 21. He and his thirteen fellow prisoners were charged with multiple heretical practices. After severe torture, he was burned. His fellow male prisoners were beheaded, the women drowned. His wife was drowned a few days later.

Still another early martyred leader was Balthasar Hubmaier. Imprisoned in Zurich in 1525, he "recanted" under torture, was released, fled to Moravia and resumed evangelizing. Hubmaier enjoyed success in Moravia, but only for a brief time. Early in 1528 Archduke Ferdinand had him arrested, taken to Vienna, and tried for treason and heresy. After being paraded through Vienna and having his flesh torn with hot pincers, he was burned at the stake. Three days later his wife, who had encouraged him at his execution, was drowned in the Danube River. Four years earlier, in 1524, he had written *Concerning Heretics and Those Who Burn Them,* the earliest plea in the sixteenth century for complete religious toleration. In thirty-six brief articles he had argued that the burning of heretics is contrary to what religion is all about, contrary to the Bible, and of the devil.

The Anabaptists plagued the mainline Protestants and the Catholics for one basic reason: they endangered the union of church and state. They were subversives. Church and state were so closely linked that any fundamental criticism, any forming of a new communion, even pacifism, appeared to be seditious. Anarchy might result. If the country were invaded, a large body of citizens could not be counted on to resist. Anabaptists frequently said the threatening Turks were not as bad as bloodthirsty, graceless Christians. In any event, the Bible enjoined them not to resist evil, but to return good for evil, to pray for their enemies. The established church and state rationalized that for the good of society Anabaptists had to be eradicated. The Anabaptists would not accept the absolute sovereignty of either the church or the state: they sought to establish a counterculture based on the Bible. Using a rationale of law and order, Luther, Melanchthon, Zwingli, Bucer, Calvin, Henry VIII, and

Queen Elizabeth I subscribed to, justified, and sanctioned violent treatment of the Anabaptists. When the state clearly became the sovereign entity in Western culture, persecution of the descendants of the Anabaptists did not cease, even in the twentieth century. Their choosing to "obey God rather than men" still threatens human sovereignty. They are tolerated, but only so long as the body politic is not considered to be in grave danger. In the twentieth century, sovereignty of state reigns, and the arguments against dissenters and disturbers who threaten it are not essentially different from those used against Anabaptists.

Unfortunately, violent apocalypticism tended to discredit even the peaceful Anabaptists. Whether this fringe violence was inherent in Anabaptists' biblical hermeneutics, or whether it was a religious mania stemming from the stress of persecution, or both, cannot be determined. Biblical literalism led some to preach from housetops, go without clothing, forsake their families, become as little children. Hans Hut, who was opposed at Nikolsburg by Hubmaier, advocated a doctrine of free love, mysticism, and sharing of goods. He preached that Christ would come in 1528 to inaugurate his kingdom and would give the elect swords to slay priests and nobles. In 1527 Hut was killed while in prison, and his corpse was sentenced to burn at the stake.

The apocalypticism that eventually led to the debacle of Münster found a firm believer in Melchior Hofmann (1495–1543), an ex-Lutheran pastor and free-lance Anabaptist along the Rhine River. Although a furrier by profession, he acquired an extensive knowledge of the Bible, wrote voluminously, and ably preached from Stockholm to Strassburg. His numerous followers in Holland were called Melchiorites. The Swiss Brethren, however, would not accept him as a brother. The Swiss particularly objected to his writings on the Parousia (Second Coming), which he announced would occur in 1534; to his notion regarding the human nature of Christ—although born of Mary, he did not partake of her nature; and to his deferral of baptism for converts on the grounds that the time was not propitious. Many of the Melchiorites remained a secret party within Roman Catholicism. When a Frisian seer prophesied that Hofmann would return to Strassburg, be arrested, and greet the Lord's return within a year, Hofmann hurried back there and solicited arrest. The council promptly complied, imprisoning him in May, 1533. After languishing in solitary confinement for ten years, he died in 1543.

One of his converts was Jan Matthis of Haarlem, a baker, who in 1533 broke with Hofmann and started his own violent attempt to prepare a city for the coming of the Lord. He and his apostles seized control of Münster in 1534 and established a military communistic regime that lasted approximately a year. Matthis decreed death or banishment for all who refused rebaptism. For the common good, he confiscated the property of all heretics. Many refugees poured into Münster, believing that the Parousia was at hand. Matthis' daily revelations instructed him to drive out the sick and aged and to execute any critics. When Matthis was killed in a sortie against the besieging army of the bishop, Jan Bockelson, a bankrupt businessman of Leiden who had been one of Matthis' twelve disciples, took charge. He, too, ruled despotically by means of expedient revelations. He legalized polygamy, taking for himself fifteen wives, including the widow of Matthis, and had himself crowned King David. But the besieging army, made up of Catholics and Lutherans, eventually reduced the inhabitants of Münster to starvation. On June 24, 1535, the city was betrayed and fell. The besiegers allowed the women and children to leave the city but massacred all the men capable of bearing arms. A year and a half later, Brockelson and two other leaders, after being tortured to death, were exhibited in cages suspended from St. Lambert Church. The cages are still hanging. The repression was more brutal than the revolt, but the Münster experiment branded the Anabaptists in the common mind as revolutionaries.

Obbe and Dirk Philips, Menno Simons, and Jacob Huter began picking up the pieces and redirecting the Anabaptists toward their originally more peaceful ways. Obbe and Dirk Philips, illegitimate sons of a Dutch priest, were converted to Anabaptism in 1533 by two of Jan Matthis' apostles. When these apostles attempted to take over Amsterdam, they were quickly arrested along with fifteen Melchiorites, tortured on the wheel, and burned to death at the stake. The disaster discredited apocalypticism for Obbe and Dirk, who turned to a peaceful ministry more like that of the Swiss Brethren. In 1537 Obbe ordained a converted Roman Catholic priest, Menno Simons of Friesland, to the office of elder. Menno had openly joined the Anabaptists in the previous year. Menno more than anyone else saved the remnants of Anabaptists in the Lowlands. Painstakingly he purged the radicals and gathered communities of dedicated, earnest, peaceful believers who today bear his name—the Mennonites.

In 1529 a Swiss minister by the name of Jacob Huter joined a group of Swiss Brethren who in 1526 had fled to Moravia for refuge. Hubmaier was their early mentor. Inspired by Acts 4:34ff. and a sense of necessity, the refugees pooled their resources and established Bruderhofs for communal living. Huter, who became their leader in 1533, stressed pacifism. But in 1536 Huter was burned at the stake for heresy. Hundreds of others suffered the same fate, for King Ferdinand was determined not to have a dissident "Münsterite" group in his lands while the Turks were threatening. Huter's apology of 1536 masterfully depicts the Anabaptists as earnest, sincere, peaceful followers of Christ. Although persecution caused emigration and scattering, the Huterites have endured to the present, though in some countries they still suffer for their rejection of state sovereignty.

The Schleitheim Confession marks the central core of early Anabaptists. They were trying to follow the commands of Christ completely, not to win salvation as Luther charged, but simply to obey God's will and to show forth the fruits of their faith. They refused the oath, which was an annual way of showing citizen loyalty, broke the locks on their houses and barns in order to share goods, practiced pacifism, expected suffering, and separated from society in order not to be contaminated. Their doctrine of believers' baptism caused them to reject original sin, and their belief that all could keep Christ's commands caused them to reject the predestination and bondage of the will at the heart of classical Protestantism. They believed free will was essential for moral choices, in this being more like the humanists. Eventually they developed a strong legalism that marked their subsequent development. Voluntaryism and believers' baptism rather than infant baptism provided a mature religious commitment and basis for church membership. Rejection of the sovereignty of church or state made them forebearers of religious toleration. In the enshrinement of individual conscience as a final interpretative authority, they, like Luther at Worms, opened the way to diversity and the kind of social anarchy that Luther sensed in the Peasants' Revolt. They used consensus and the ban to check such tendencies, but shunned physical violence.

During these turmoils the foremost leader of the second generation of Protestants emerged—John Calvin (1509–64). He stands midway between Luther and Zwingli in theology, and produced for Protestantism its most comprehensive theological system and model holy community. He and his followers dominated the second phase of Protestantism and clashed violently with Roman Catholicism for control of Western Europe.

Calvin, the son of a secretary to the Bishop of Noyon, France, prepared for a legal career with studies at Orleans, Bourges, and Paris, only to become interested in humanistic studies and eventually to switch to religion. In Paris he came into contact with Jacques Lefevre d'Etaples (1455–1536), a humanist whose commentary on Paul's letters had already raised doubts about transubstantiation as well as the merit of human works. Like many other humanist scholars, Lefevre believed increased knowledge would bring reform to the church. He was not the innovator of a new institution. Around him gathered other scholars who by 1530 had produced the entire Bible in French. Among his admirers was William Farel (1489–1565), who later persuaded Calvin to help in the reform of Geneva. How interested Calvin was in religion in this early period is not known. His first book, a commentary on Seneca's *Mercy*, in 1532, did not touch on religion. But between 1532 and 1534 Calvin underwent a conversion in which he, like Isaiah, experienced the glory of God and the sinfulness of man. In 1533 when Nicolas Cop assumed the rectorship of the University of Paris, Calvin assisted in the writing of the inaugural speech, which called for a return to the pure Gospel. Both he and Cop fled Paris. Calvin, disguised as a vinedresser, escaped in a basket. In the following year, 1534–35, the zeal of the Paris reformers brought on a persecution in which two hundred were arrested and twenty martyred. This was the persecution that prompted Calvin to write his *Institutes of the Christian Religion*, a small volume in 1536 when first published, but which Calvin greatly enlarged until the final edition in 1559. Since his basic ideas did not change, the book mirrors a lifetime of theological thought. Calvin prefaced it with a plea to Francis I of France (1515–47) to end the persecution of his loyal subjects.

Almost overnight Calvin was hailed as the new champion of the French Protestants. When Calvin's travels brought him to Geneva in 1536, Farel induced him to stay to help make Geneva, which had recently pulled away from Roman Catholicism, a model Christian community. The next two years were rough. Although Calvin produced the *Genevan Confession of Faith*, 1536, and his first *Catechism*, 1537, Roman Catholics, liberals, and libertines mustered sufficient opposition in 1538 to force him and

Farel to leave Geneva precipitously. Calvin worked among the refugees in Strassburg for three years, had contact with other religious leaders, wrote his *Reply to Sadoleto*, who was trying to woo Geneva back to Catholicism, and in 1541 was invited to return to Geneva to restore order and stave off the drift to Rome. From 1541 until his death, Calvin molded Geneva, seeking to make it a model Christian community to the glory of God. For twenty-three years he preached, organized, disciplined, and wrote, more in the spirit of the Old Testament than the New. Geneva was a theocracy, directed in the will of God by Calvin.

Calvin took the absolute sovereignty of God as his basic principle. God is omnipotent, free, holy, glorious, just, and good. Human beings are weak, sinful, depraved, corrupt. They are unable to do any works of merit. All deserve to perish. However, through the Incarnation God reestablished contact with humanity, gratuitously granting justification by faith and belief in Christ as the divine Word, Creator, Redeemer, Prophet, Priest, and King. Not all are justified. Only the elect truly hear and believe the Gospel. Election is the work and will of God, from all eternity, and one's realization of election in justification by faith is an act of God and the Holy Spirit. Election is the reason why people respond differently to the preached Word. All are sinners and justly condemned by God, who in his inscrutable wisdom and mercy nevertheless eternally elected to save some through the merits and grace of his Son—salvation for some, reprobation for all others. Why did God elect as he did? Because it pleased him to do so. Election precedes faith; it does not depend on faith; faith, the disciplined life, and one's calling are but manifestations of it. We are saved by God's gratuitous mercy; we are damned by our own depravity. Yet everything is as God ordains. "He governs heaven and earth by his providence, and regulates all things in such a manner that nothing happens but according to his counsel. . . . Predestination we call the eternal decree of God, by which he has determined in himself, what he would have to become of every individual of mankind. . . . Nevertheless God cannot be called the cause of sin, nor the author of evil, nor subject of any guilt. . . . Man falls as God's providence ordains, but he falls by his own fault."

If this doctrine does not meet rational human standards, Calvin replies that God, not puny human reason, is sovereign. God has revealed his will in his inspired Word, which only a few people, like Calvin, with the aid of the Holy Spirit, truly understand.

Although God's grace is irresistible and irreversible, it may remain unknown. As those who are elected manifest the presence of the Spirit in disciplined morality and calling, this prompted some Calvinists to do good works to convince themselves of election. Because Calvin wanted to glorify God, he rigorously disciplined Geneva's vocations, manners, and morals. In this he was like the Anabaptists and their separated communities. But he joined with this the medieval notion that the secular power should cooperate with and protect the church. The result was an extensive and intensive system of social control. He extended his discipline to the entire community, maintaining that there is no adequate means for determining which are true Christians (i.e., elected and grafted into Christ by faith) and which are false. Everyone must have the opportunity to hear the true Word truly preached, and for the glory of God all must conform to his Word. Calvin instituted compulsory enforcement of pure doctrine and discipline; God's sovereign will was not to be mocked.

The instrument of control was a Consistory of twelve elders—laymen of good repute and members of the city council—and six ministers that heard reports once a week of moral infractions. Penalties included fines, imprisonment, excommunication, banishment, and death. Between 1542 and 1546, fifty-eight people were executed and seventy-six banished. Adulterers, witches, blasphemers, and traitors were sentenced to death, a child was beheaded for striking his parents, and a critic executed for putting a sign on Calvin's pulpit. Other infractions included profanity, fighting, dancing, playing cards, carousing, laughter or loud noises in church, promiscuous bathing, gambling, theatrical performances, not attending or coming late to services, obstinacy, baptism by midwives, apostasy, and interest in excess of five percent. Pilgrimages, paternosters, idols, papal feasts, and fastings were all forbidden. Saloons were made into restaurants equipped with French Bibles for reading. Houses could be checked without notice at any time. No one, regardless of status, escaped the "fraternal correction" of the Consistory. Even the pastors examined themselves and their fitness for the ministry four times a year. The Consistory operated under the city council, but in 1553 Calvin won the right of the church to excommunicate without any further sanction. Although he had bitter opponents, Calvin dominated Geneva, like a tyrant according to his enemies, like an emissary from God according to his friends and the thousands of refugees who poured into Geneva.

After the massacre of the Waldenses, the burning of twenty-two of their villages in 1545, and the institution of the policy of Henry II of France (1547–59) to exterminate heretics and their books, as many as 5,000 Christians (about thirty percent of the population of Geneva) sought refuge under Calvin. For them Calvin provided jobs, brought in new industries, retrained adults, and established schools so that they might in their vocations properly glorify God and not be a parasitic burden on the community. They formed the bulwark of much of Calvin's power.

Calvin never sought honors for himself. His salary was a mere $600 a year, supplemented with a house, garden, two tubs of wine, twelve bushels of wheat, and enough broadcloth for a new coat each year. He was not ordained. In 1540 he married a widow with two children; his only son died in infancy. Severity marked his domination of Geneva, but in his private life he exhibited love and warmth.

The most noted instance of his control was the execution of Michael Servetus on October 27, 1553. Servetus was a native of Spain, a renowned physician, and a critic of orthodoxy. As early as 1531, while only twenty years of age, Servetus (1511–53) published the results of his early biblical studies in *On Errors of the Trinity*. It was an acrid attack on varying trinitarian theories and contentions prevalent among Catholics and Protestants. He did not find the Trinity in the Bible, did not think three beings in one Godhead could be justified, and felt only disgust for self-serving orthodoxy and ecclesiastical pomposity. If the Christian is to believe only what is in the Bible, then, said Servetus, orthodoxy's "three-headed Cerberus," the Trinity, must go. It has no biblical basis, the Son is not coeternal with the Father, and it is ridiculous to speak of the Trinity as the divine three in one, the same, yet different. The book created a storm of protest, and inasmuch as anti-trinitarianism was, like rebaptism, punishable by death in imperial Roman law, Servetus was compelled to go underground and to live for twenty-two years in France under an assumed name.

In later years Servetus chose Calvin as his special target, corresponding with and writing bitter criticisms of him. Servetus not only rejected the Trinity, but openly rejected original sin and infant baptism, and lauded the Anabaptist concept of the church as a voluntary community of regenerated believers. When Calvin sent him a copy of the *Institutes* for his instruction, Servetus returned it with copious, contemptuous, marginal notes. Servetus' masterpiece, the *Restitution of Christianity*, appeared anonymously in 1553, but to Calvin he impudently sent a copy under his own name. The *Restitution* was aimed chiefly at Calvin's *Institutes*. It was more than Calvin could stand. Years before he had guessed the identity of his correspondent, but now, through a friend, Calvin exposed Servetus to the Inquisition in France and supplied evidence for his heresy. Servetus was arrested and tried, but escaped from jail just before his sentencing. In effigy he was strangled and burned along with copies of his new book. In his flight toward Naples, he stopped at Geneva, went to church, was recognized, denounced by Calvin, and arrested on charges of heresy. How much Calvin's struggle for political power in 1553 affected his actions is not known, but the outcome is certain. The Genevan Council found Servetus guilty of obstinately spreading heresy and sentenced him to death by burning. Seven years earlier Calvin had vowed that if Servetus ever came to Geneva he would not leave it alive. On the day after sentencing, Servetus was chained to a stake, his book fastened to his arm, sulphur and straw rubbed into his hair. But the straw and fagots were damp and Servetus died only after half an hour of agony and screaming. At the end he cried, "O Jesus, Son of the Eternal God, have pity on me!"

Theologians and governments approved, including Melanchthon, Bullinger, Wittenberg, Basel, Berne, and Zurich. Heresy threatened the body politic; it was like a rotten limb that had to be amputated; the heretic could mislead and poison others. Harsh immediate action was necessary.

However, not all approved, and when the clamors reached Calvin, he wrote his *Defense of the Orthodox Trinity Against the Errors of Michael Servetus*, 1554, upholding the necessity of severely dealing with heretics in order to glorify God. The best criticism of Calvin was Sebastian Castellio's anonymous *Concerning Heretics* (1554). In it Castellio pleaded for the right of conscience in religion. The burning of heretics is far removed from Christ's spirit and words, and there are always the dangers that someone will be mistaken for a heretic or that a heretic will be punished more than Christian discipline requires. "To kill a heretic," he said, "is not to defend a doctrine, but to kill a man."

Servetus was not the first nor the last to be put to death in Calvin's Geneva, only the most famous. In 1903 some loyal "sons of Calvin" erected an "expiatory monument" on the site of Servetus' execution.

Despite the obvious criticisms that can be leveled against Calvin's excesses and harsh discipline, his religion of the majestic sovereignty of God attracted thousands of followers. Calvinists increased phenomenally in Holland, France, Scotland, and England, and also in parts of Germany, Poland, Hungary, and America. They suffered martyrdom by the thousands in their push against Roman Catholicism, particularly in Holland and France. Part of the appeal lay in the doctrine of election and God's providence, in the consummate skill with which Calvin expounded it, in the inherent democratic tendencies in the city-state of Geneva and the synod, in the paradoxical dynamic of Calvinism, in its biblically based insights into human nature and destiny. Calvin would have attributed its success to providence, to God's inscrutable will for the world.

Henry II's campaign against heretics in France did not keep the Huguenots (Calvinists) from winning adherents. By 1559 French Huguenots numbered 400,000. They had 49 regular churches and about 2,000 preaching places. Unconnected with the state, they developed a synodal system with democratic, self-governing principles. A consistory of laity and pastors governed local congregations. In 1559 the French Calvinists met secretly in Paris and produced the Gallican Confession. Written under Calvin's supervision, the Gallican Confession summarizes his thought. Its principal statements include belief in the triune God revealed in creation and in the Word; the Old and New Testament as containing all that is necessary for salvation and for regulating this life; God's governing by his sovereign will all that happens in the world; the Fall rendering mankind totally corrupt; predestination to election or damnation before the creation of the world; election showing God's mercy, condemnation his justice; salvation through the Incarnation of Jesus Christ, God and man in one person, through whom we are reconciled to God by faith; regeneration of the elect to newness of life; renunciation of purgatory, pilgrimages, indulgences, and monastic vows; the Church as those who follow God's Word and use his sacraments; equality of ministers; infant baptism; and ordained authority. Persecution and religious wars in France, Scotland, England, and Holland drove the Calvinists to develop theories of resistance and rebellion against authorities that defy the will of God. At best, such resistance could only be inferred from Calvin.

Scottish Presbyterianism and English Puritanism embodied and also modified Calvinism (see Chapters 16 and 17), but the most general modification resulted from the Arminian controversy in Holland, where Calvinism had grown strong. Jacobus Arminius (1560–1609) studied Calvinism at Geneva and Basel, but developed doubts about divine election before Creation. Appointed professor at the University of Leiden in 1603, he disputed bitterly with Franciscus Gomarus, a strict Calvinist, about unconditional election and irresistable grace. After Arminius' death, his disciples expanded his views in the Remonstrances of 1610, in which they asserted that all who believe in Christ and persevere shall be saved, that Christ's atonement is universal and all can be saved, that without divine grace one cannot be saved, that God's grace can be resisted, and that the possibility of losing grace needs further study. This repudiation of strict Calvinism divided numerous Dutch churches. Many

Remonstrant preachers were banished and over 200 lost their pulpits. The Synod of Dort, 1618–19, reasserted strict Calvinism. Arminianism now connotes liberal religious views. Nevertheless, Calvinism rode the wave of the future and greatly influenced Christian life and culture during the next 400 years.

15

The Catholic Renewal and Counter Reformation

Roman Catholics have with some justification rejected "counter reformation" as an adequate description of their church during the sixteenth century. Movements toward reform, independent of the Lutheran situation, had already started within many Catholic circles. Yet it is also true that the Lutheran upheaval with its wide ramifications stirred the Roman Catholic Church to take countermeasures that determined the direction of Catholicism through the next 400 years. A strong grassroots drive toward renewal came in the early decades of the century. Even Luther could be counted as one of those seeking renewal. However, the Protestant schism became so significant that the papacy mounted major thrusts to counter it, thrusts that shaped Catholicism well into the twentieth century.

Four developments dominated the Catholic sixteenth-century scene: (1) renewal, (2) the Society of Jesus, (3) the Council of Trent, and (4) the appeal to force, all of which were inextricably intertwined and helped produce a vigorous Catholicism in the last half of the century.

RENEWAL

The desire for Catholic renewal was widespread and manifested itself in many quarters. The earlier mystics' search for a more personal relation to God and the humanists' return to the sources and their scathing ridicule of clerical ineptitude, ignorance, and impiety provided a broad background for this movement (see Chapters 12 and 13). It surfaced in clerical circles in men like Savonarola and Ximenes and in the formation of the Oratory of Divine Love and other new orders.

Luther praised Girolamo Savonarola (1452–98) as an evangelical reformer and published some of his prison comments on the Psalms (see Chapter 13). Savonarola was a Dominican friar in Florence, Italy, during the grossly immoral pontificate of Alexander VI (1492–1503), the former Roderigo Borgia whose chief concern seemed to be the promotion of his two children, Caesare and Lucrezia Borgia. Under Alexander VI the papacy was so worldly that touring monks openly preached against it. With more zeal than political sagacity, Savonarola attempted to reform religion in Florence. By 1494 his eloquent preaching and warnings of dire judgment so profoundly affected the people that he virtually controlled the city, subjecting it to ascetic austerity, even discouraging marriage. During the Lenten season of 1496 citizens collected and burned great piles of "vanities." Frustrated Florentine politicians and the papacy did not approve. Two years later Savonarola was hanged and burned as a heretic in the public square at Florence. The bell at St. Mark's church, which summoned people to hear Savonarola, was removed, publicly flogged, and sentenced to banishment! Although Savonarola was more a politician than a saint, he symbolized a desire for reform. Engravings and medals were struck in his honor; drops of his blood, pieces of his hair, and bits of his ashes were preserved as relics. He marks a surge toward renewal some twenty years before Luther.

Cardinal Ximenes (1436–1517), although remembered for his continuance of the Inquisition begun under Torquemada, inaugurated a religious revival that profoundly affected all of Spain (see Chapter 13). He combined force, education, and moral severity in an attempt to purify and promote ecclesiastical order. He was both a zealous medieval churchman and an ardent humanist scholar. Being the queen's confessor, he enjoyed royal approval and affected the political and social tone of Spain as well as its religious and intellectual life. The key to his activity was his love of orthodoxy and anything that promoted it and his hatred of heresy and anything that denigrated the church. Consequently he fought heretics, preached a crusade against the Moors, eliminated many monastic abuses, tried to stop clerical irregularities, established schools, and fostered humanistic research. As a Franciscan who had taken the traditional vows of poverty, obedience, and chastity, he renounced honors, practiced asceticism, lived like a hermit, wore a hair shirt, curtailed clerical concubinage, and enforced stringent morality in the monasteries. As a humanist scholar, he promoted biblical and medical studies and founded the University of Alcalá. In 1522 his famous Complutensian Polyglot, the Bible in original languages, appeared posthumously, intended for clerical study rather than general lay reading of the Scriptures, to which he was opposed. As a churchman with high office and power he launched campaigns of preaching and violence against deviators from the faith and infidels. In 1507 he became head of the Spanish Inquisition, putting to death more than 2,500 people and imprisoning and torturing more than

40,000 more. After ten years as Grand Inquisitor, he incurred the disfavor of Charles V and was about to be deposed when he died. Despite his faults, Ximenes prepared the way for Ignatius Loyola and typified the agitation within Catholicism toward renewal.

The Oratory of Divine Love, established in Rome in 1517 by Gregorio Cortesi, typified another move toward renewal that profoundly affected Catholicism primarily because so many future leaders in Catholicism were connected with it even though later they did not implement reform in the same ways. Among these were Caraffa (1476–1559), Sadoleto (1477–1547), Cajetan (1480–1547), Contarini (1483–1542), and Ghiberti (1495–1543). The Oratory included about sixty lay and clerical members who dedicated themselves to reforming their own lives and the lives of those about them, hoping thereby to rejuvenate devotion to Christ and his church. They diligently participated in the mass and the sacraments, established orphanages and hospitals, cared for the sick, fasted, gave alms, went on pilgrimages, and met frequently for prayer, preaching, and discussion. Although they were dispersed by Charles V's plunder of Rome in 1527, their earnest dedication inspired later reforms. Largely from this group came the committee that Pope Paul III appointed to investigate clerical immorality. In March 1537, the committee made its sensational report, *Consilium de Emendenda Ecclesia*, noting in its twenty-six sections a host of glaring abuses—prostitution, concubinage, graft, bribes to pervert justice, non-residence, multiple benefices, worldly bishops, poor schools, indulgence excesses, simony, superstition, monastic scandals and the like. The report was so drastic that it was finally put on the list of unfavorable and undesired works. When word of the report leaked to Protestants, they claimed substantiation for their wildest accusations. Pope Paul III virtually shelved the report, although in 1540 he did insist that some eighty bishops return to their sees.

Some members of the Oratory, like Contarini, tried reform through humanism. He was conciliatory toward Protestants and felt that Catholic-Protestant doctrinal differences could be reconciled through earnest dialogue. To this end he worked, especially in his conversations with Melanchthon at Ratisbon in 1541. The two of them agreed to a statement on justification by faith but could not agree on celibacy, the priesthood of all believers, sacerdotalism, and papal authority. They felt a sense of triumph in their agreement on justification by faith, only to be rebuffed on the one hand by the Pope and on the other by Luther. Contarini died a disappointed man, his dream shattered.

Another member of the Oratory, Caraffa, who later at the age of 79 became Pope Paul IV (1555–59), pushed for reform through force. Caraffa, fiercely loyal to the church, declared he would burn his own father if he was a heretic. He forced Jews to wear yellow hats and live in ghettos. He recommended establishment of the Holy Office of the Inquisition, 1542, in order to curtail defections to Protestantism. Bernardino Ochino, head of the Capuchins, and Peter Martyr Vermigli of the Augustinians had already been converted. The Office of the Inquisition, which was part of the appeal to force, was composed of six cardinals headed by Caraffa. All Catholics were subject to its authority; it could imprison on mere suspicion, confiscate property, torture and condemn to execution. Toleration of heretical views was not one of Caraffa's virtues. As Pope he left many sees vacant rather than appoint worldly clerics, and set up an index of forbidden writings that included the works of Luther, Erasmus, Henry VIII, Machiavelli, Peter Abelard, and Allah (the Koran). Under his direction literally thousands of books were collected and burned. He advocated extreme asceticism, even going so far as to clothe some of the naked figures in the Sistine Chapel. Although he and Contarini shared a desire for reform, their methods differed radically.

Philip Neri, founder of the Oratorians, 1574, continued and revived much of the old order's ascetic ideals and commitment to renewal.

An immediate offshoot of the Oratory of Divine Love was the formation of the Theatines by St. Cajetan, Caraffa, and others in 1524. Their aim was reform of the secular clergy and nobility; they were priests but accepted no benefices. Under vows of chastity, obedience, and absolute poverty, the Theatines practiced strict asceticism, cared for the indigent and sick, and concerned themselves with preaching and liturgy. From the bishopric of Theate where the group started, its monastic houses spread throughout Italy, Spain, France, Germany, Poland, Austria, and Portugal.

Directly influenced by the Oratory were the Barnabites or Clerks Regular of St. Paul, organized by St. Anthony Zaccaria of Cremona in 1533 to combat rife immorality by prophetic preaching and example; and the Sommaschi, started by Jerome Emilian about 1527 but not approved until 1540, who concerned themselves with relieving misery wherever manifested, working in hospitals, orphanages, and homes for prostitutes, caring for the sick and burying the unwanted.

Out of the turmoil of tension and renewal in the Franciscan Order came the establishment of the Capuchins by Matteo da Bascio. In 1525 he received verbal permission from Pope Clement VII to wear a habit that he maintained was authentically in keeping with that worn by St. Francis, and to exhort people everywhere by his example to turn to God. In 1528 this order of ascetic Franciscan hermits was formally recognized and the Capuchins rapidly increased. Their small houses with narrow windows without glass and doors so low that one had to stoop to enter symbolized humility, and their restricted diet of bread and water and a few fruits and herbs showed their asceticism, but they endeared themselves to the populace by their unusual charity and service, only to suffer attacks from jealous Minor Observant Friars and to receive a serious setback when the head of their order, Bernardino Ochino, an outstanding orator, defected to the Lutherans in 1542 and later married. Yet they survived and grew.

Other renewal groups included the Ursulines, organized by St. Angela Merici in 1535, to teach and care for children; the Brothers of Mercy, begun by St. John of God in 1540, also to care for the sick in hospitals and asylums; the Brothers of the Good Death, founded by Camillus de Lellis, a former soldier and gambler who founded hospitals and devoted themselves to caring for incurables; the Angelicals of St. Paul, devoted to work with orphans and penitent girls, and later the Daughters of Mary, devoted to education—both begun by Ludovica Torelli.

Scores of oratories, associations, and orders seeking religious re-
newal and reform burst forth in the early part of the sixteenth century.
The masses reverenced relics and frequented shrines. Itinerant monks
raised their voices in towns and villages. Laity and priests eagerly read
books concerned with prayer and devotions, such as Kempis' *Imitation of
Christ*, Ludolph's *Life of Christ*, Cisneros' *Exercises of the Spiritual Life*, Vivès'
Manual of a Soldier of Christ, and others. Individual men like Ghiberti in
Italy, John Fisher in England, Stanislaus Hosius in Poland, and Johann
von Eich in Germany sought to establish religious seriousness in their
dioceses. An abundance of evidence points to grassroots ferment and
religious quickening in Roman Catholicism, but it was essentially ascetic in
orientation and did not threaten the foundations of medieval Christianity.
Renewal of piety and seriousness characterized its expressions.

THE SOCIETY OF JESUS

A part of this movement toward renewed piety but also important enough
to be in a category by itself was the Society of Jesus. Ignatius Loyola
(1491–1556), founder of the Jesuits, forcefully stated the principle and
foundation of his religious endeavors in the first part of his *Spiritual
Exercises:* "Man was created to praise, reverence, and serve God our Lord,
and by this means to save his soul." Man's free will enables him to serve or
not to serve, as he chooses. Hardly any statement could be more antithetical to Luther's justification by faith alone and Calvin's doctrine of election.
Loyola interpreted his principle and foundation to mean radical obedience to the Church Militant, in this case to the Pope. At the end of his
famous exercises, he attached rules for upholding the ideas of the church,
which included the following: "Laying aside all private judgment, we
ought to hold our minds prepared and prompt to obey in all things the
true Spouse of Christ our Lord, which is our holy Mother, the hierarchical Church," and "To arrive at the truth in all things, we ought always to
be ready to believe that what seems to us white is black, if the hierarchical
Church so defines it." [Quoted from *The Spiritual Exercises of St. Ignatius of
Loyola*, tr. by W. H. Longridge (London: A. R. Mowbray & Co., Ltd.,
1955), pp. 197f.] The rules also urged the exercitant to praise everything
pertaining to the hierarchical church—confession, the sacrament, canonical hours, vows of religion, veneration of relics, invocation of saints, fasts,
images, jubilees—and to save criticism for official ears rather than public
hearing. The secret of the Jesuits lay not in rigid discipline alone but in
the dedication and genius of the founder of the Society.

A Spanish cavalier of noble lineage, Loyola served as a page under
Ferdinand and Isabella and had dreams of an army career, but in 1521
during a French attack on Pampeluna, a cannon shot tore away his left
calf and broke his right shin. He was sent home to Loyola where his right
leg was rebroken, reset, and a protruding bone sawed off, all without
anesthesia or stimulants. Such was his stamina. During the long days of
recovery he read Kempis' *Imitation of Christ*, Ludolph's *Life of Christ*, and
Vayad's *Golden Legend*, books that caused him to reassess his entire life.

He vowed he would be a soldier for Christ and excel the deeds of saints of the past. The resolution gave him peace and joy unequaled in his dream fantasies of chivalry, fair ladies, and temptations of the flesh. Never again did lusts of the flesh control him; henceforth he would be concerned with the salvation of his soul—thus he reminisced in later life.

By 1522 Loyola had regained enough strength to journey to the Benedictine abbey at Montserrat near Manresa, where he scrupulously confessed his sins, made a vow of perpetual chastity, exchanged his cavalier's clothes for the pilgrim's sackcloth, gave the monastery his mule, hung up his dagger and sword, espoused poverty, and began his wanderings as a new soldier of Christ. Cisneros' *Exercises of the Spiritual Life* inspired his own spiritual exercises.

Thwarted in his attempt to imitate Christ by caring for the sick in Jerusalem, Loyola returned from Palestine to Spain in 1524 intent on acquiring an education in order to combat Protestant heretics. Within the space of four years he advanced from a school for boys in Barcelona to the University of Paris. So many men and women followers were attracted to him that he was investigated three times by the Inquisition, subjected to forty days in jail, and ordered not to preach for three years. At the University of Paris a small group gathered about him to practice his spiritual exercises: Francis Xavier, later an apostle to the Orient, Diego Lainez, who succeeded Loyola as head of the Jesuits, Pierre Lefèvre, Alfonso Salmeron, Nicholas Bobadilla, and Simon Rodriguez. In 1534 this group, in the Parisian church of St. Mary on Montmartre, at the crypt of St. Denis, knelt to take communion, vowed lives of poverty and celibacy, and resolved to go to Jerusalem to help the poor, or if that proved impossible, to place themselves at the disposal of the Pope. By 1537, after doing hospital work in Venice and taking priestly orders, they abandoned plans to go to Jerusalem and turned to Rome for guidance, hoping they might be used as a spiritual army to combat heretics. After some hesitation and opposition, Pope Paul III approved the Society of Jesus on September 27, 1540, with the provision that its members be limited to sixty and that each remember daily his vow to fight "for God under faithful obedience to one most holy lord, the Pope, and to the other Roman pontiffs who succeed him, . . . to obey without evasion or excuse, instantly," as well as the usual vows of poverty and chastity.

The Spiritual Exercises received final form about 1548. Few other books rival it in influence. Every prospective Jesuit as well as thousands of laity have used it to deepen their own sense of spiritual dedication. The exercises, designed for four weeks, could cover a longer or shorter period. Their aim was to lead one to complete service to God and humanity. The phenomenal success of the Jesuits attests their effectiveness. By spiritual exercises Loyola meant every method of examination of conscience, meditation, contemplation, and prayer to rid the soul of all inordinate attachments and to find the will of God in the ordering of life to win salvation for one's soul. He wanted recruits to make themselves indifferent to all created things, even health and honor, so as to be free to serve God. The first week concentrated on sin to purify the retreatant's soul. The second week focused on the life of Christ, to inspire the retreatant to greater knowledge and love of Christ. The third week revolved around Christ's passion to help the retreatant to decide to follow Christ. The fourth week centered on the triumph of the Resurrection to free the retreatant from false attachment to creatures, worldly ambitions, and honor. Each week was a prolonged meditation in which the conscience was probed to prompt thanksgiving, prayer, accountability for one's sins, pardon, and resolve to amend. Human frailty, death, judgment, and hell received detailed attention. By imagination, the retreatant was to feel, taste, hear, see, and smell the horrors of hell, and in the same way to visualize the events in Christ's life, his sufferings and Resurrection. In the end the exercises led to placing the mind and body under the direct guidance of the Holy Spirit.

The Society was unrealistically limited to sixty members at the time of its approval. It grew phenomenally. By 1626, the Jesuits had 15,000 members and 803 houses; by 1750, 22,000 members. They were entrusted with significant ecclesiastical tasks, especially at the Council of Trent, but their chief fields of endeavor were education and missions. They had no distinctive dress and felt that a cultivation of asceticism would debilitate their energy; their one aim was to restore the Catholic Church to its previous dominance.

Believing that human reason was to be cultivated so that one would choose the right, the Jesuits concentrated heavily on education. Before or shortly after Loyola's death in 1556, Roman, German, Greek, Hungarian, and English colleges were established at Rome, in addition to colleges at Vienna, Bavaria, and Munich. By 1626 the Jesuits had 476 colleges and 36 seminaries; by 1750, 669 colleges, 176 seminaries, and 700 lower schools in France alone. During the Generalate of Claudio Aquaviva (1581–1615) the educational practices received permanent form and remained in force until the dissolution of the Society in 1773. In an attempt to make every student a faithful son of the church, to restore the old religion to its glory, and to resist innovations, the Jesuits employed a tight lower school curriculum of grammar, philology, poetry and rhetoric, with almost no attention given to history, geography, and mathematics. Latin, the official language of the church, was used in instruction; no modern languages were officially taught until 1832. To eliminate heretical ideas, censors carefully expurgated every text, and books read in private had to be approved in advance. Students could not attend executions, except of heretics. Classes opened and closed with kneeling prayer, and the mass, pilgrimages, catechism, and Gospels received special attention. Teachers demanded instantaneous, blind obedience, and encouraged a system of spying. Memory and emulation were the means of learning. Yet, despite obvious shortcomings, the schools of the Jesuits were better than what prevailed previously. They were rationally grounded and thoroughly disciplined. No single instrument served the Catholic Counter Reformation quite so effectively as the schools of the Jesuits. Linked with the personal efforts of men like Robert Bellarmine (1542–1621), a spirited apologist for Catholicism, and Peter Canisius (1521–97), a powerful leader in Germany, the schools helped reclaim many territories that had fallen to the Protestants.

The Jesuits scored spectacular achievements in missions. Before the end of the sixteenth century Jesuit missionaries had pushed boldly into India, Japan, China, the Philippines, Indochina, the Congo, Morocco, Brazil, Peru, Paraguay, the United States, and Canada. Francis Xavier (1506–52), a member of the original group in Paris, led the vanguard. In 1541 he set sail for Goa, a Portuguese colony on the west coast of India. After laboring there and in southern India, he proceeded to the Malay Peninsula and then to Japan, where he landed in 1549. Three years later, while attempting to break into China, he died on the little island of Sancion. He relied heavily on perfunctory baptism, the mass, ceremonies, songs, the aid of children, memorized prayers, and the catechism. He preached in 52 different kingdoms and baptized over 1,000,000 persons. He sowed seeds and they grew. Matteo Ricci (1552–1610), the apostle to China, and hundreds of others continued the world missions begun by Xavier. Many suffered martyrdom. In the expansion of Christianity they wrote a stirring chapter, yet not without its seamy side, which in Mexico included the enslavement of the Indians and in South America their exploitation.

The very success of the Jesuits militated against them. Through their educational institutions they influenced the minds of thousands of youth. Through their confessionals they influenced the affairs of state, especially by being confessors to rulers in France, Germany, Bavaria, Poland, Portugal, and Spain. In their zeal to promote the church, they acquired property—houses, lands, factories, banks, jewelry, silver, gold—and developed two infamous ethical doctrines known as probabilism and mental reservation. Probabilism permitted them, especially in the confessional, to declare any act to be perfectly acceptable to Christ if there was any probability that it might be all right. Mental reservation allowed them to withhold part of the truth or leave a wrong impression if the end for such action seemed good. Blaise Pascal (1623–62) scathingly ridiculed them for ruthlessness, unscrupulousness, and untrustworthiness in his *Provincial Letters,* and Feodor Dostoyevski (1821–81) mounted a similar attack in his tale of the Grand Inquisitor in *The Brothers Karamazov.* In the dispute that occasioned the ridicule by Pascal, the Jesuits were defending the doctrines of freedom of the will and the saving grace of good works, both of which were integral to the foundations of their Society. Their opponents argued that free will denied the omnipotence of God and that good works denied the efficacy of grace, both of which derived from Augustine. The immediate occasion for the dispute centered in Cornelius Jansen (1585–1638), who as director of the new University of Louvain vigorously opposed the aspersions of the Jesuits. After years of detailed research, Jansen wrote *Augustinus,* published posthumously in 1640, in which he defended St. Augustine's doctrine of grace. This affronted the Jesuits and a bitter fight ensued. The Cistercian convent at Port-Royal came under Jesuit fire during this period, not only because Jansenist views were espoused there under the leadership of Jansen's friend, Saint-Cyran, but also because his successor, Antoine Arnauld, published two books in 1643—*On Frequent Communion* and *The Moral Theology of the Jesuits*—in which he attacked the Jesuit stance. In 1653 the Jesuits succeeded in persuading Pope Innocent X to condemn as heretical five propositions culled from *Augustinus.*

Pascal, whose sister was a nun at Port-Royal, entered the lists against the Jesuits with his *Provincial Letters* in 1656. The conflict disturbed all of Catholicism. A shaky truce was established in the Church Peace of 1668, only to break out again when Pasquier Quesnel (1634–1719), who though educated by the Jesuits published his *Moral Reflections,* which reaffirmed Jansenist principles. Persecuted and imprisoned, he finally fled to Holland. In 1713, Pope Clement XI, in the bull *Unigenitus* formally condemned 101 propositions from Quesnel's book. Meanwhile, Port-Royal suffered persecution; its buildings were finally destroyed and even its graves dug up. Many Jansenists fled to the Netherlands, where they established the Jansenist communion (Old Catholics).

Similar controversies and political involvement caused the successes of the Jesuits to boomerang. Protestant hatred of them knew almost no bounds, but the severest blows came from within Catholicism. Roman Catholic rulers regarded the Pope as an Italian prince and the Jesuits as his militia. The Jesuits had turned the tide of the Reformation and distinguished themselves in theology, education, and missions; they had grown wealthy and powerful; but they had also employed intrigue and subversion to promote papal interests at the expense of other civil rulers. In 1759 Portugal banned the Jesuits, accusing them of plotting regicide. In 1761 and 1764 France blamed the whole Society for the financial delinquency of one. Their schools were closed, foundations dissolved, and property confiscated. In 1767 King Charles III suppressed the order in Spain, allegedly for disloyalty and intrigue against the crown. The Bourbon kings wanted the order suppressed everywhere and brought such heavy pressure against the papacy, including threats of invasion, that in 1773 Pope Clement XIV issued his *Dominus ac Redemptor,* which dissolved the Society of Jesus. Papal prestige suffered sharply! The Jesuits were not restored until 1814, after the French Revolution and the defeat of Napoleon. Throughout the nineteenth century the Jesuits continued their support of a conservative papacy (see Chapter 19).

THE COUNCIL OF TRENT

If representative conciliarism had its triumph at Constance, ultramontane papalism had its come back at Trent. The papacy did not want a general council and delayed convoking one, but the Council of Trent (1545–63) enhanced papal power and set Roman Catholic guidelines for four centuries. The dicta of Trent were not significantly questioned until Vatican Council II (1962–65), which created a new liberal atmosphere in Catholicism, although the extent of the actual changes is debatable.

The Council of Constance issued its *Sacrosancta* on the superiority of councils over Popes and decreed its *Frequens* on the periodicity of councils, but both were effectively shelved in succeeding events. Pope Martin V did not implement the actions of Constance until just before his death, and his successor Eugenius IV scuttled the Council of Basel. These actions made the decrees of Constance little more than dead words. In 1460 Pope Pius II's *Execrabilis* set aside the supremacy of councils and made any call for a council an affront subject to excommunication. Yet calls for reforming councils continued.

In the sixteenth century, the specters of Constance and Basel still lingered in Rome, and the papacy did virtually nothing to convoke a council before the pontificate of Paul III (1534–49). He was the first of a series of Popes bent on setting the affairs of the church in order. After him, Paul IV (1555–59), Pius V (1566–72), and Sixtus V (1585–90) showed an ascetical zeal for reform similar to that of Gregory VII. They brought the Catholic reform movement to its height. Paul III reluctantly convened the Council of Trent, yielding finally to pressure from Emperor Charles V, lower clergy, and the universities. Significantly, representatives from the universities and lower clergy were not invited to Trent. They had spearheaded troubles at Basel. A hundred theologians and canonists served as consultants at Trent but had no vote. Only archbishops, bishops, important abbots, and heads of religious orders could vote. Protestants were invited to join the discussions without vote, and a few attended briefly. Philip Melanchthon and Johann Brenz canceled their plans to attend in 1552. Luther said that he would participate only if the council was not dominated by the papacy and took Scripture as its final authority. Both conditions were summarily dismissed. Attendance at the council fluctuated. Some 255 prelates signed the decrees but only between 60 and 70 were present for the most important transactions.

Although heated debates and even fisticuffs marked the twenty-five sessions of the Council of Trent, the council was dominated by the papacy and its emissaries. Preaching was confined to two Jesuits, Salmeron and Lainez, both fiercely loyal to the Pope and strongly anti-Protestant. They spoke first and last on all major motions. Through committees and personal messengers the papacy exerted its influence. Not a single concession was made to the Protestant perspective. Every challenged dogma was reaffirmed. Cardinals Reginald Pole and Girolamo Seripando, both humanists, argued vainly for doctrinal statements that the Protestants could accept. The definition of dogma on all disputed points constituted the main purpose of the council; in that it succeeded very well. Its secondary purpose, reform, which Charles V especially wanted, was only partially achieved.

Contrary to Luther's demand, the council after vigorous debate moved quickly to place tradition on a par with Scripture as an authoritative source in faith and morals, leaving tradition in the person of the Pope to prevail in conflicting interpretations. It also sanctioned the Apocrypha as having canonical standing, thus retaliating against Luther's remark in his 1534 translation of the entire Bible that the Apocrypha was not considered canonical by the Jews. And it adopted the Latin Vulgate of Jerome as the church's official translation of the Bible despite the various errors noted by humanist scholars. "If anyone receive not, as sacred and canonical, the said books entire with all their parts, as they have been used to be read in the Catholic Church, and as they are contained in the old Latin Vulgate edition; and knowingly and deliberately contemn the traditions aforesaid; let him be anathema."

The council defined justification by faith with a slightly Protestant tone, but it stated that faith is progressive and that good works are integral to the process, preservation, and increase of faith, and that we cooperate with the grace of God and merit justification. Because the Protestants accepted only two sacraments, baptism and the Lord's Supper, as biblically grounded, the council reaffirmed the conferring of grace through the church's traditional seven sacraments—baptism, eucharist, confirmation, penance, extreme unction, order, and matrimony. In elaboration of the eucharist, the council reasserted complete transubstantiation and declared the mass to be a propitiary sacrifice to obtain merits for both the living and the dead. The cup was to be withheld from the laity, and only Latin was to be used in the ceremony, two actions that tended to elevate the status of the priest.

Other actions included giving an indelible character to ordination, extolling celibacy and virginity as better than marriage, making marriage valid only when performed by a priest before two witnesses, condemning divorce and prohibiting remarriage as long as the other partner is alive, asserting that purgatory exists and that souls detained there can be helped by the good works of the living, enjoining veneration and invocation of the saints, calling for the honoring of relics and proper use of images, and reasserting the efficacy of indulgences, which should be guarded against abuse.

Every major reform proposal failed, despite the efforts of Emperors Charles V and Ferdinand and the liberal French and Bavarian prelates. Episcopal residence by divine right was successfully combatted, leaving the papacy in final control of all bishoprics and eliminating any hint of collegiality. Communion in both kinds was left a possibility at the discretion of the Pope, depending on circumstances. Attempts to reform the Roman curia, limit the use of excommunication, allow the mass in the vernacular, and encourage reading of Scripture in the ethnic tongues made no headway. Abuse of indulgences received scant attention, and the central issue of buying and selling indulgences was bypassed.

Because of political exigencies, war, and plague, the council met irregularly over a period of eighteen years, sessions 9 through 11 being held at Bologna in 1547, the others at Trent. In 1564 Pope Pius IV ratified the actions of the council and issued his creedal summary known as the Tridentine Faith. Drawn as a personal statement, it began, "I, ———, with a firm faith believe and profess . . ." Each succeeding paragraph repeated the "I." The actions of Trent were confessed as personal belief, including all traditions: the Pope as the only valid interpreter of Scripture, propitiatory sacrifice of the mass, transubstantiation, communion in one kind, purgatory, veneration of saints, honoring of relics, affirmation of indulgences, obedience to the Pope, anathema on all heretics, no salvation outside the Catholic faith, and a pledge to transmit Catholicism to all dependents and subjects.

At Trent doctrinal victory belonged to the papacy; it received a mandate of absolutism that was made explicit in the statement of papal infallibility at Vatican Council I in 1870. No other council was needed, so complete was the package handed the papacy. After 400 years, Vatican

Council II was sensational precisely because it challenged the adequacy of Tridentinism.

To complete papal control, Pope Pius IV formally established the Index of Prohibited Books, 1564, and later the Congregation of the Index was formed to revise the list from time to time. This was intended to safeguard the faithful against the corruption of heretical ideas, but intolerance is a frequent assessment of the act.

THE APPEAL TO FORCE

On the theory that "untruth" should not have the same privileges as "truth," Roman Catholicism throughout the Reformation period appealed to force to promote, establish, and keep its domination. The revival of the Holy Office of the Inquisition, 1542, marked the use of force on a personal level. Suggested by Caraffa (later Pope Paul IV), the revived Inquisition was promoted by new orders, especially the Jesuits, and became the international arm of Catholicism to curb defection to Protestantism. In territories where the ruling powers backed Roman Catholicism, the Inquisition was virtually absolute. An accused person had practically no rights and little support for fear of guilt by sympathetic association. Even though a person accused might be freed, he was never acquitted; his case could always be reopened, even without notice. Every Catholic or former Catholic was subject to the Inquisition. Even those in high places did not escape, particularly because the defection of men like Bernardino Ochino, head of the Capuchin order, attracted wide attention. Papal secretary Carnesecchi, Cardinal Morone, Archbishop Carranza of Toledo, and scores of other high officials felt the brutality of the Inquisition. Teachers were especially vulnerable. One of the Inquisition's most famous victims was Giordano Bruno, a philosopher-scientist, who, for his teachings on the eternity of the universe and atomic theory of matter, his pantheism, and rejection of miracles, was tried before the Inquisition and burned at the stake in 1600. The property of the victim went to the state or the church. Quarrels over its disposition eventually helped weaken the procedure.

The appeal to force undergirded a series of religious wars remembered especially for their atrocities. The first was the attempt by Charles V to restore by force the Catholic unity of the Holy Roman Empire. The Schmalkaldic War (1546–47) was brief, with Duke Maurice of Saxony joining the emperor for political reasons and forcing the other Protestants to succumb. But Maurice's Lutheran subjects would not change. After several years of unsatisfactory maneuvering, Maurice turned on the emperor in 1552. The turmoil ended in the Peace of Augsburg, 1555, with its renowned principle of *cuius regio, eius religio* (whose region, his religion), a tenuous compromise making the religion of the ruler the religion of the land, which lasted until the outbreak of the Thirty Years' War in 1618.

The second appeal to war occurred in France. The Huguenots (Calvinists) had increased phenomenally. In 1559 they managed to hold a secret synod in Paris where they adopted the forty articles of the thoroughly Calvinistic *Gallican Confession*. By 1561 the Huguenots had over 2,150 local congregations with about 400,000 adherents. Although a distinct minority in France, so many nobles joined the Huguenots that they became a political threat. After a series of incidents and intrigues, the Catholic House of Guise achieved governmental power and launched a persecution of the Protestant House of Bourbon (King Henry of Navarre), which precipitated a series of intermittent religious wars lasting until 1593. The climax of atrocities in these civil wars came in the infamous massacre on St. Bartholomew's Day, August 24, 1572, in Paris. The planned marriage of the heir of Navarre, eventually Henry IV of France, to Margaret of Valois, the sister of King Charles IX, posed the possibility of a Protestant inheriting the throne of France. Queen Mother Catherine de Medici resolved that it would not take place. She plotted with various Catholic leaders to strike on the day of the wedding. When the nobles were assembled, at a given signal of church bells, the Catholic conspirators put on white armbands, drew swords and guns, and began killing all the Protestants they could find. Paris mobs entered the action and before the carnage ended it spread to the provinces, some 8,000 Protestants being murdered in Paris and 20,000 in the environs. Contemporaries described the atrocities: "The streets were covered with dead bodies, the rivers stained, the doors and gates of the palace bespattered with blood. Wagon loads of corpses, men, women, girls, even infants, were thrown into the Seine, while streams of blood ran in many quarters of the city. . . ." Bodies were hacked, mutilated, beheaded and dragged through the streets; even packs of children joined in the horrors. Henry saved his life by professing Catholicism, only to return later to Protestantism. A reaction of shock swept over Europe, except in Italy, Spain, and France. The severed head of Admiral Coligny, a staunch Huguenot, was sent as a trophy to the Cardinal of Lorraine. Pope Gregory XIII thanked God for the event, ordered a *Te Deum*, proclaimed a jubilee, and struck a medal bearing on one side the inscription "Ugonotorum stranges, 1572" (slaughter of the Huguenots) with an angel upholding the cross as prostrate Protestants are being slain, and on the other a bust of the Pope himself. French medals showed Charles IX fighting the hydra of heresy with fire and a club. Many Huguenots became refugees, hundreds fleeing to foreign lands, others banding together in fortified cities. Though the Protestants were weakened, the civil war dragged on in France until 1593, when Henry IV again professed Catholicism in order to secure the throne. Not forgetting his Huguenot compatriots, in 1598 he issued the Edict of Nantes asking that the past be forgotten and guaranteeing freedom of conscience to the Huguenots. In the following century Cardinal Richelieu under King Louis XIII (1610–43), successor to Henry IV, used the Jesuits to harass the Huguenots. Many suffered martyrdom. Louis XIV (1643–1715) in 1685 revoked the Edict of Nantes. Churches were closed, pastors banished, and troops quartered in Huguenot homes. Some 30,000 "converted" to Catholicism, but an estimated 50,000–250,000 emigrated to England, America, and Prussia.

The third appeal to war came in the Netherlands and ran an equally disastrous course. When Philip II became ruler of Spain (1556–98), he was determined to check the growth of Protestantism in his subject provinces of the Netherlands. Anabaptism and Lutheranism had taken root there in the 1520s and thirties, but Calvinism in the twenty years after the publication of the *Institutes* had increased phenomenally. Almost half the population had become Calvinists. The fact that Calvinism provided a basis for resisting tyranny by force, whereas Anabaptism and Lutheranism did not, undoubtedly made it attractive to the nationalistic Netherlanders. Philip II had almost boundless contempt for the Protestants, regarding them as little better than traitors. When the Protestants rebelled in 1565 because of high taxes and Spanish governmental interference with their freedom of religion. Philip proceeded against them with force. In 1567 he sent the Duke of Alva with 10,000 soldiers to quell the rebels. The Protestant leaders Egmont and Hoorn were taken by treachery, tried, and then executed in the public square at Brussels. For six years Alva terrorized the territory, executing hundreds, imprisoning thousands. His rule was so oppressive, the exaction of taxes so ruthless, that Catholics and Protestants temporarily joined forces to expel him. But, the religious conflict continued with little abatement until 1609, the Catholic southern provinces (Belgium) remaining under Spanish rule and the Protestant northern provinces (Holland) finally emerging from the struggle. In England the Counter Reformation's appeal to force climaxed in the disaster of the Spanish Armada of 1588 (see Chapter 16). Unfortunately, these events made an almost indelible imprint on the conscience of Protestants, creating an animosity toward Catholicism that has lasted well into the twentieth century.

The second half of the sixteenth century saw a reinvigorated Roman Catholicism standing firm against Protestantism. However neither Catholics nor Protestants clearly discerned that sovereignty had shifted to national states. The treaty ending the Thirty Years' War in 1648 paid scant attention to religion, even though religious differences instigated the conflict. Protestantism succumbed in large part to cultural religion, as seen in territorial churches, and Catholicism had to retreat further from control of temporal affairs, despite its many concordats and treaties. Sovereign national states increasingly controlled external human affairs.

Yet the Counter Reformation obviously bore fruit in the second half of the sixteenth century. Vigorous leaders on numerous fronts enabled the Roman Catholics not only to stop the advances of Protestantism but also to win back many territories lost to the evangelicals. Pope Pius IV (1559–65) was the first of five Popes who energetically reformed and promoted the church. Pius IV successfully brought the Council of Trent to its final sessions and promulgated and executed its decrees during his pontificate. He imposed the profession of Tridentine faith on all ecclesiastical office holders, published a new Index in 1564, prepared a Roman Catechism for priests, and instituted reforms in the college of cardinals. To check the further spread of Protestantism, he even agreed with the emperor in 1564 to concede the chalice to the laity in Germany, Hungary, Austria, and several other countries. The concession was later abolished.

Pope Pius V (1566–72) corrected his predecessor's inclination toward nepotism and worked zealously to reform the church. He applied ascetic practices and regularity to the church, compelled bishops to abide by the Council of Trent, and used the Inquisition to curb Protestant inroads into Spain and Italy. Although his excommunication of Elizabeth I in 1570 backfired, he imbued Catholicism with a sense of renewed dedication. He had the Roman Catechism translated into several languages, revised the Breviary and Missal, declared Thomas Aquinas a Doctor of the Church in 1567, brought out a new complete edition of Aquinas' works, and in 1571 joined the Spanish and Venetian fleets in stopping the Turks at Lepanto.

Pope Gregory XIII (1572–85), known especially for his Gregorian Calendar devised in 1582, concentrated chiefly on reform and restoration of the faith. Working closely with the Jesuits, Gregory established numerous seminaries and colleges and took a special interest in Far East missions.

Pope Sixtus V (1585–90) patronized the arts and scholarship and concentrated on administrative reform in the church and papal states, often with ruthless methods.

Pope Paul V (1605–21), although he suffered several political setbacks, lived an exemplary life, enforced the decrees of the Council of Trent, promoted social work and missions, and completed building St. Peter's.

These five Popes helped immeasurably to revamp the image of the papacy. But they were not alone. In St. Teresa (1515–82) and Francis de Sales (1567–1622) mystical piety reached spectacular heights. St. Teresa of Avila led a routine life as a Carmelite nun until the age of forty, when she was converted to a life of perfection while praying before a statue that portrayed Christ being scourged. Despite frequent illness, she spent the rest of her life in intense devotions, ascetic exercises, self-mortification, and reformation of the Carmelite Order. She often entered into mystical ecstasies of union with God, spoke of "spiritual marriage," and once reported that Christ was physically present. In the face of almost constant opposition, the "seraphic virgin," as she was later canonized, established sixteen reformed branches of the Carmelite order for women, and fourteen for men, wrote a number of books on the "science" of prayer, and left an autobiography with psychological insights into her character. Few mystics have ever joined their quietism with such practical ability and ceaseless activity. Among those Teresa influenced directly was St. John of the Cross (1542–91) whose devotional classics, *Ascent of Mount Carmel* and *Dark Night of the Soul*, probe the soul seeking through faith and suffering to be fitted for union with the divine.

Even more successful in the promotion of mystical piety was Francis de Sales (1567–1622), whose *Introduction to the Devout Life*, 1618, became one of the most popular devotional books of all time, translated into almost every European language. As the Bishop of Geneva (1602–22), although unable to live there, he vigorously combatted Calvinism. He was an ideal son of the Counter Reformation, educated by the Jesuits, given to a life of self-denial, noted for his preaching, and completely devoted to the church. His kindness and devotion prompted him to establish the Order of the Visitation in 1610, an order of women who vowed to do works of charity among the poor, but he also resorted to coercive measures when the occasion demanded. His preaching reached many; the bull in 1665 that canonized Francis claimed he had converted 72,000 heretics.

Giovanni da Palestrina (1524?–94), "the Father and Prince of Church Music," saved music for Roman Catholic divine worship at a time when the Council of Trent was seriously considering banning it. Palestrina demonstrated that it need not be cheap and inferior. He rejected all embellishments and secular strains that might detract from the arousal of true devotional feeling, and set the official pattern for the pure polyphonic form of ecclesiastical music with his *Missa Papae Marcelli* in 1565. Serving as choirmaster of St. John's Lateran, St. Peter's, Santa Maria Maggiore, and as Composer to the Papal Chapel, he dominated liturgical music in Europe, producing more than 90 masses and 500 motets for the church year in addition to numerous offertories, litanies, hymns, spiritual madrigals, magnificats, and lamentations. His *Improperia* is still traditionally sung in the Sistine Chapel on Good Friday. The austere beauty and vigor of his music matched the reform efforts of the Counter Reformation.

Three of the most active controversialists, theologians, and churchmen, who worked closely with the Jesuits to combat Protestantism, were Peter Canisius (1521–97), who won back much of southern Germany, Charles Borromeo (1538–84), whose reforms in morals and education had great effect in Milan and Switzerland; and Robert Bellarmine (1542–1621), who forcefully defended Catholicism in clear, systematic apologies.

At the beginning of the seventeenth century the Roman Catholic Church seemed strong once again in central and southern Europe. But in England it had lost almost completely to state sovereignty, and the inroads of Protestantism and the development of nationalistic trends made efforts to reassert papal supremacy increasingly anachronistic. Yet the Tridentine stance of ultramontanism (papal supremacy) has continued to dominate Roman Catholicism through Vatican Council I (1869–70) to Vatican Council II (1962–65). Whether or not Vatican II instituted fundamental changes remains to be seen.

16

The Reformation in England

The struggle for royal supremacy dominated the story of the Reformation in England—a struggle that gave the English Reformation a distinctly political emphasis and that had no religious giant such as Luther, Zwingli, or Calvin at its center.

Because they threatened royal supremacy, Roman Catholicism, Puritanism, and then the free church movements were considered subversive. Yet in a sense none of the major contenders for power over England won. The Act of Toleration in 1689 undercut royal supremacy in religion, disfranchised Roman Catholicism, and acknowledged the legal rights of free church dissenters. The power of the monarch lessened, that of Parliament enlarged. The factor that prevailed in the end was nationalism; religion with its universal claims ceased to be the organizing center of English culture. The old partnership of church and state gave way to national sovereignty, displacing the universal authority of Rome in Western culture. In Wittenberg the drama centered about a monk concerned with the salvation of his soul; in Geneva the drama revolved about one of God's elect glorifying God in this world; in England the drama took the form of royal power breaking the hold of the papacy. Nationalism rapidly filled the vacuum of broken church authority.

Rising nationalism was the underlying force that enabled Henry VIII (1509–47) to make his dramatic break with Rome. For 300 years papal supremacy had been eroding in England, and Henry VIII's takeover was the culmination of a long trend. The trend was complex but it is discernable in several key events. One of these was the *Magna Carta*, which punctured papal control. In 1213 Pope Innocent III wielded enough power to force King John of England (1199–1216) to declare his kingdom a papal fief and to pay a feudal tax to the Pope as his overlord (see Chapter 10). To back his demands Innocent III commissioned a crusading French army under King Philip Augustus to invade the British Isles if necessary. Two years later, in 1215, the barons of England wrung from King John the famous *Magna Carta,* a constitution guaranteeing them various rights, which became fundamental in English law. Pope Innocent protested on the grounds that the barons were interfering with a papal vassal, for Innocent correctly recognized that his own power as well as that of the king was being curtailed. Nevertheless, the *Magna Carta* stood, one of the first in a series of laws that eventually saw the proscription of Roman Catholicism in England.

The law of *Praemunire,* 1353, further eroded papal supremacy in England. During the Babylonian Captivity when the Popes were residing at Avignon in France, the English Parliament passed the famous law of *Praemunire,* which made appeals to Rome acts of treason. And in 1366 Parliament officially invalidated King John's acceptance of papal lordship in the previous century, thus wiping out the national humiliation of John's having made England a papal fief. The Great Schism (1378–1415) (with a Pope at Avignon, another at Rome, and after 1409 a third at Pisa, each claiming to be the supreme arbiter of human spiritual affairs) added to the erosion of papal claims. Henry VIII revived the old 1353 law of *Praemunire* and used it to browbeat the clergy into submission. That the clergy, Parliament, nobility, and people offered little resistance is an indicator of the nationalistic feeling that gave Henry his base of strength. Not for some foreign power, not for the Pope, but England for Englishmen! It was no empty cry, and the feeling that England was destined by Providence for some special mission in the world would continue to grow until the British Empire reached its height in the nineteenth century.

A third factor was mounting anti-Romanism. Wycliffe had given it a boost by promoting an ideal of the church based on good stewardship of God's gifts, an ideal quite contrary to the image of Rome as self-serving ecclesiasticism (see Chapter 12). He believed that poverty would make the church more Christlike and that the true church is composed of the elect who live by the Scriptures. English clerics were known neither for their poverty nor their Scriptural living. Wycliffe's contention that unworthy and idle clerics should be deprived of their soft livings was responsible in part for the Peasants' Uprising in 1381 and for the communistic trend that developed among his followers, the Lollards. Wycliffe took Scripture as his authority and began a translation of the Bible to give common people access to the Word. In 1380 he denied transubstantiation, on which he believed much of Rome's power rested. Wycliffe and the Lollards fed an underground anticlericalism among the populace that lasted into the sixteenth century.

John Oldcastle was the last visible, general leader of the Lollards, and was accused of both heresy and subversion. Arrested and tried in

1413, he escaped from prison in 1414 and led a march on London. King Henry V, who was currying Roman approbation of his dynastic claims, defeated the marchers at St. Giles' Fields. Fifty-two of the marchers were publicly executed. Later, in 1417, Oldcastle was captured, hanged, and burned. But Lollardy was not squelched, as civil and clerical records throughout the century abundantly verify. Incomplete records of court actions in a few scattered localities in the 1400s show 395 abjurations, 15 purgations, 27 burnings, and 6 executions in addition to numerous indictments, arrests, and accusations for Lollard activity. The following century saw a resurgence of Lollardy, especially as seen in John Foxe's *Acts and Monuments*. In London, Bishop Fitzjames persecuted 40 Lollards in 1510 and 37 in 1517, four of whom were burned. In Kent, Archbishop Warham between 1511 and 1512 burned 5 and forced nearly 50 abjurations. In Berkshire, 120 were forced to abjure, 3 burned. In Coventry, 7 were burned in 1519. In Buckinghamshire in 1507, 60 were induced to recant, 2 burned. Such scattered records indicate that Lollard anticlericalism ran deep in English life.

In Henry VIII's time, pluralities of benefices, non-residence, non-preaching, and the sumptuous living of many English prelates continued to engender popular indignation. For a clergyman to hold eight benefices was not uncommon. Cardinal Thomas Wolsey was papal legate, minister of state, Archbishop of York, and held four bishoprics. Enormously wealthy, he had over 500 persons in his household, and two of his residences eventually became royal palaces—Hampton Court and York Place (Whitehall). From 1515 to 1529 he virtually ran England, having control of clerical appointments, correction, absolution, and degrees. He bestowed preferments on his natural son, Thomas Wynter, making him an archdeacon in two places, prebendary in five, and rector in two, and giving him offices of chancellor, dean, and provost, while he was still a schoolboy. Such flagrant abuses inflamed anticlericalism in England, and provided a seedbed for humanistic criticism and Lutheran reform.

A fourth development centered in the humanists who, like their counterparts on the Continent, aimed their barbs at clerical ignorance and immorality. So important was the humanistic renaissance in England that some scholars make the English Reformation an outcome of this New Learning. Early in the sixteenth century both Oxford and Cambridge were strongholds of the humanism that was sweeping Europe. Erasmus often visited both universities; he taught at Cambridge from 1510 to 1513. The English renaissance is frequently said to have begun in 1485 with the reign of the first Tudor king. King Henry VII as well as Lady Margaret, the grandmother of Henry VIII, encouraged humanistic studies. Many English scholars went to Italy to study and returned to become intellectual and religious leaders in England. Among these were William Grocyn (1446–1519), Thomas Linacre (1460–1524), and John Colet (1467–1519). Grocyn and Linacre became celebrated lecturers at Oxford. Colet, who absorbed the biblical views of Marsilio Ficino and Pico della Mirandola of Florence, made his great contribution in London at St. Paul's Cathedral, where he expounded Paul's epistles in lectures and sermons and founded St. Paul's school for boys. He sought to reform the clergy and to eliminate corruption, superstition, image worship, relic veneration, and indulgence abuses, saying such housecleaning should come before drives to rid the land of alleged heresy.

Sir Thomas More (1478–1535), an intimate friend of Colet and Erasmus, expressed his humanistic attitudes in *Utopia*, 1516, a biting satire of social and religious matters. In Utopia religion was based on the dictates of reason and the laws of nature. People of varying shades of belief participated in a common service. They could have religious differences so long as these did not lead to persecution. By following a few rational rules the people lived in peace with one another. People enjoyed equality, worked only six hours a day, and had time for intellectual pursuits. They elected their king and others to represent them in the governing process. Despite the implied criticism of the established order, More wanted to combat ignorance, strife and injustice rather than to overthrow the papacy. Like many humanists he remained a faithful Catholic.

Even though the papacy patronized humanism, the New Learning with its motto of "back to the sources" constituted a subtle bypassing of the ecclesiastical establishment of the time. More's *Utopia* held out an ideal of what society might be, an alternative to the prevailing tired forms, and Erasmus' ridiculing of greedy priests, ludicrous monks, and irrelevant bishops left scars on the *corpus Christianum*. These humanists helped prepare the way for the Reformation in England, if not by making a highway, then at least by leveling a few rough places.

Fifth, Lutheran ideas were also invading the British Isles, providing among those who accepted them yet another milieu for Henry's takeover. Although England did not have a Luther or a Calvin, many travelers, scholars, merchants, and traders brought revolutionary ideas and books across the channel, despite efforts by the government to prevent them. Luther's writings poured into England, particularly through the London shipping terminal in the Stilyard. Pope Leo X considered the spread of Luther's ideas so dangerous that he wrote Cardinal Wolsey urging him not only to prohibit the import of Lutheran books but also to promote their burning. In 1521 the first spectacular burning took place at St. Paul's Cathedral, London, after a two-hour sermon on Luther's errors by Bishop John Fisher. With 30,000 people watching, Cardinal Wolsey excommunicated Luther and all his followers and gave the signal for the bonfire. Another big book burning occurred in 1525. Cardinal Wolsey in 1526 forced a group of Stilyard men to march around a bonfire with fagots hanging from their necks to signify that they also deserved to be burned.

Henry VIII published his *Assertion of the Seven Sacraments* in July of 1521, and John Clerk elaborately presented the essay to Pope Leo. Henry called Luther a calumniator, schismatic, and menace to society. Even though his essay did not pulverize Luther's arguments in the *Babylonian Captivity,* it did win a title, "Defender of the Faith," from the Pope. Almost exactly a year later, Luther replied, calling Henry an ass, a fool, and a liar. Although Luther later apologized for being so rash, the brief flare-up brought more attention to Luther's views. John Fisher wrote three tracts against Luther in 1523 and 1525; Sir Thomas More, using the pseudonym William Ross, responded to Luther in 1523, lambasting him with insults.

At Cambridge a group of humanist "heretics," ten of whom later became Protestant martyrs, met during the 1520s at the White Horse Inn. Thomas Bilney, the first Englishman burned for Lutheran opinions, Robert Barnes, an ambassador to Germany later executed as a heretic, and Hugh Latimer, martyr under Queen Mary, were among its leaders. Opposition seemed to make the new ideologies all the more exciting.

As important as any of these was the sixth factor—Henry's own personal desires and ambitions. Henry VII was the first in a new line of English Tudor kings. To strengthen the line politically, Henry VII arranged for Arthur, his oldest son, to marry Catherine of Aragon, daughter of Ferdinand and Isabella of Spain. When Arthur died five months later leaving no heir, Henry VII preserved the alliance with Spain by betrothing his younger son, Henry, to Catherine. A special dispensation from the Pope set aside the proscriptions in Leviticus 21:14 against a king marrying his brother's widow. For twenty-five years Henry VIII staunchly defended papal supremacy; the validity of his marriage and his children's claims to be the throne depended on it. However, of the six children born to him and Catherine only one daughter, Mary, survived. Henry grew increasingly anxious. A woman had never ruled England. He began to doubt the legitimacy of his marriage and to feel that his having no male heir might be God's judgment for marrying his brother's widow. These circumstances and the shapely figure of Anne Boleyn, who refused to share his bed without sharing his crown, prompted Henry to petition the Pope for a divorce—for reasons of state. Pope Clement VII, unwilling to alienate Emperor Charles V, who was Catherine's nephew and whose armies were dominating Rome, refused to invalidate the former dispensation. Stung by this refusal, Henry searched for alternatives and soon acted on the suggestion of Thomas Cranmer (1489–1556), an aspiring young scholar, that he seek an opinion "out of the word of God" from the universities and canonists of Europe, thereby bypassing the papacy. If they found the first marriage contrary to divine law, then there never had been a valid union, and the king would be free to marry without reference to Rome. The Pope could set aside church law, but a dispensation could not set aside a law of God.

Numerous negotiations and intrigues transpired. In 1530 Oxford and Cambridge decided in favor of Henry. French universities and even Bologna in Italy followed. Cranmer became an immediate favorite of the court, and Cardinal Wolsey was stripped of his posts of honor and accused of treason for having broken the statute of *Praemunire* of 1353 by accepting his office from the Pope. He died in 1530 on his way to the Tower before he could be tried for treason. Henry played with the same legal tactics to intimidate all of the clergy of England, who not only submitted but presented him with a gift of £118,000 and an ambiguous statement that he was the supreme lord of the church, as far as permitted by the law of Christ. In 1532 the Convocation of Clergy agreed not to enact any new canons without royal assent, to submit all previous canons to a committee appointed by the king, and to withhold from the Pope the annates (first year's income) of each English benefice. The clergy of England had submitted!

In January of 1533 Henry threatened to take the annates outright (which he later did) to force the Pope to name Thomas Cranmer Archbishop of Canterbury. In that same year the Convocation and the court of the new Archbishop decreed "that the said pretended marriage was and still is null and invalid . . ." and that henceforth "Henry VIII and Lady Catherine . . . are absolutely free from all marriage bond." Earlier in the year Henry secretly married Anne Boleyn.

Henry now needed only the sanction of Parliament to make his triumph complete, and that, too, came easily. Reacting to Pope Clement's threat to excommunicate Henry, Parliament legalized the supremacy of the king. In 1533 in the Restraint of Appeals, known as the legal principle of the English Reformation, Parliament declared that all cases having to do with religion "shall be from henceforth heard, examined, discussed, clearly, finally, and definitively adjudged and determined within the king's jurisdictions and authority, and not elsewhere. . . . any foreign inhibitions . . . from the see of Rome, or any other foreign courts or potentates of the world . . . to the let or impediment thereof in any wise notwithstanding. . . ." This was followed in 1534 by the Act Forbidding Papal Dispensations and the Payment of Peter's Pence, the ecclesiastical principle of the English Reformation, which deprived the Pope of all rights of nomination and dispensation and stopped payment of money to the Pope, who had impoverished the realm by taking from it "intolerable exactions of great sums of money."

The capstone came with the Supremacy Act in November of 1534, which confirmed Henry as "supreme head" of the Church of England with full power "to visit, repress, redress, reform, order, correct, restrain, and amend all such errors, heresies, abuses, offences, contempts, and enormities, whatsoever they be . . . for the conservation of the peace, unity, and tranquillity of this realm. . . ."

Parliament's Act of Succession, 1534, declared Princess Mary, daughter of Catherine of Aragon, illegitimate, and named the infant daughter of Anne Boleyn, Elizabeth, born September 7, 1533, the heir to the throne. Not to accept this decree of succession or the supremacy of the king constituted treason.

Henry's astute legal adviser in this rapid shift of worldly power from the Pope to the king was a former assistant to Wolsey, Thomas Cromwell (1485–1540), who worked ceaselessly for Henry's supremacy and became his chief adviser in ecclesiastical affairs, only to incur disfavor later and die as a traitor.

Except for the fact that Henry and not the Pope was now head of the Anglican Church, the face of religion in England had not greatly changed. Henry could hardly be called an evangelical. Basic doctrines had not been altered. One could revile the Pope, but could not speak freely against Catholic dogmas and rites. Lutheranism was still outlawed as a "pernicious poison." If Tyndale (1492–1536) had returned to England, he would undoubtedly have been tried for his heretical ideas. He had escaped the English only to be caught by Catholic authorities and martyred in Vilvorde, near Brussels. When John Frith returned to England, he was arrested and burned in London in 1533 for denying transubstantiation and purgatory. In 1535 twenty-five Anabaptists were burned in a single day. Henry had not suddenly become Protestant. He was Catholic, the only significant difference being insistence on his own supremacy.

Requiring all subjects to take the succession oath or be charged with treason immediately revealed pockets of resistance to Henry's new policies. Among others, Bishop John Fisher of Rochester refused to take the oath, and Sir Thomas More resigned his chancellorship because he could not approve. Both were beheaded on Tower Green early in the summer of 1535. Shortly before, three Carthusian priors, a Brigittine monk, and a vicar were hanged, beheaded, and quartered at Tyburn for denying royal supremacy. Prior Houghton's arm was hung over the arch of his London charterhouse. Others suffered similar fates for not abjuring the Pope. Henry's aim was royal supremacy, not reform.

An empty treasury, not religious reform, prompted Henry in 1534 to commission Thomas Cromwell to visit and examine the monasteries. When the commission reported prevalent corruption, as expected, Parliament passed a law in February 1536, allowing the crown to confiscate all monasteries with incomes of less than £200 a year. During the following three years Henry seized 376 monasteries and sold them at public auction. Temporarily Henry's financial condition was relieved, even though the takeover helped precipitate the Pilgrimage-of-Grace insurrection in 1536, which Henry ruthlessly suppressed. In 1539 a new Parliament gave Henry the remaining monasteries, making a total of 645 in all. By the end of 1540 not a single monastery remained in England. Some of the confiscated property provided pensions for dispossessed monks, some went into educational support, but most of it was sold to raise funds for the crown or given to leaders whom Henry wanted to bind more clearly to him.

Henry's overtures to the Germans in 1536 brought him as close as he ever came to the evangelical cause, and this was due more to Thomas Cranmer and Thomas Cromwell than it was to spiritual conviction on the part of Henry. Cranmer and Cromwell, who both leaned toward Luther and Zwingli, persuaded Henry that there would be advantages in his heading an evangelical alliance against Emperor Charles V. Politically, Henry felt that he needed the support of the German evangelicals, for during 1535 and 1536 he feared that Charles might unite with Francis of France and take reprisals for the way events in England had humiliated Catherine. Henry's insecurity prompted him to send a delegation headed by Edward Fox, Nicholas Heath, and Robert Barnes to the Saxon princes of the Schmalkaldic League to negotiate on religion, but Henry could not reconcile himself to the Augsburg Confession and the evangelicals could not significantly depart from it nor sanction the divorce from Catherine.

Nevertheless the negotiations did cause Henry to issue statements to establish unity and avoid contentions, known as the Ten Articles, which Cranmer pushed through Convocation June 9, 1536. These articles, although only mildly evangelical, represent the first legalized but limited acceptance of Protestant views in England during Henry's time. The first part of the articles dealt with matters necessary to salvation, the second part with ceremonies. The articles rested authority in Scripture, the early creeds, and the first four ecumenical councils. Only three sacraments were explained—baptism, penance, and the eucharist—yet the others were not denied. Auricular confession and transubstantiation were reaffirmed. Justification was defined as "remission of sins and our acceptation or reconciliation into the grace and favor of God," with the added note that "sinners attain this justification by contrition and faith joined with charity." The articles called for reverence for symbols and old ceremonies, but they warned that "none of these ceremonies have power to remit sin, but only to stir and lift up our minds to God, by whom only our sins be forgiven." The articles sanctioned prayers to the saints for the living and the dead, and inveighed against the notion that the Pope could deliver souls from pain. Throughout the articles Philip Melanchthon's deft influence is noticeable. However, negotiations with the Germans ended precipitously in 1536. In that year Catherine of Aragon and Anne Boleyn both died, relieving tension with Charles V, and Henry married Jane Seymour who died in 1537 giving birth to future King Edward VI.

Henry's advisers seized upon the situation in the mid-thirties to promote evangelical beliefs and practices. General ferment for change was already evident among many commoners and in the learned halls of Cambridge and Oxford, particularly with regard to having the Bible in the vernacular. In this area Henry was at least lenient, recognizing that certain Scriptural interpretations might even strengthen his position. William Tyndale's proscribed Bible, the first part of which appeared in 1525 and the last in 1535, circulated widely in England. Anne Boleyn persuaded Henry to read it. He was pleased, and because of Tyndale's essay on *The Obedience of a Christian Man,* which pleaded submission to civil authority, Henry was even inclined to invite Tyndale back to England. But Tyndale's criticism of Henry's divorce of Catherine abruptly ended this inclination.

Miles Coverdale's Bible of 1535, the first complete Bible in English, was based heavily on the work of Tyndale, and despite the change in the religious climate was only tacitly sanctioned. In 1528 Coverdale had fled from England to escape persecution at the hands of Bishop Tunstal of Durham and Cardinal Wolsey. He made contact with Tyndale, and by 1535 had published his Bible, probably printed in Zurich. Henry did not authorize this Bible, but it was dedicated to the king and circulated freely. Cromwell's *Injunctions of 1536* ordered every parish to provide a whole Bible in Latin and English and to encourage the reading of Scripture, though this demand was later dropped. By 1543 women, artificers, servants, farmers, and laborers were forbidden to read the Bible in their homes on penalty of a month's imprisonment. Only nobility were allowed to read the Bible, indicating Henry's fear of fanaticism among the commoners. In 1546 the Tyndale and Coverdale Bibles were both proscribed apparently to avoid biblical radicalism among the lower laity.

However, as early as 1534 Cranmer and Cromwell had initiated still another Bible translation, apparently with Henry's and Convocation's sanction. This was Matthew's Bible, 1537, the basic translation being that of Tyndale and Coverdale, the editorial combination being the work of

John Rogers using the pseudonym Thomas Matthew, later a martyr under Mary Tudor. Printed at Antwerp, it was the first English Bible to bear the king's authorization, but was not fully satisfactory.

Again Cromwell turned to Coverdale to prepare another translation. This was the Great Bible of 1539. Based on previous Bibles but largely the work of Coverdale, the printing was begun in Paris and finished in England because of inquisitorial interference. The Great Bible, so called because of its large size, enjoyed the direct patronage of Cromwell, who ordered the clergy to exhort their people to read it, "if they loke to be saved." Its title page, drawn by Hans Holbein, showed Henry VIII giving a copy of the Bible to Cranmer and Cromwell to be passed on to the people of the realm. It is also called the "Triacle" Bible, for it translated Jeremiah 8:22, "There is no more triacle [balm] in Gilead." Although these translations were superseded by better ones—particularly the Geneva Bible of 1560, the Bishop's Bible of 1568, and the King James Version in 1611—Cromwell's efforts opened the doors to further Protestant developments, for Protestant claims rested heavily on the sole authority of the Bible.

While Cromwell was promoting the Bible, Archbishop Cranmer cautiously instituted evangelical practices. He was responsible for the restrained but Protestant thrust of the *Bishop's Book,* 1537, a practical manual intended to unite religious factions. It expounded at length the Ten Commandments, the Creed, the Lord's Prayer, and the Seven Sacraments, and dealt briefly with justification, faith, good works, etc. Closing remarks emphasized the special sacramental significance of Baptism, the Lord's Supper and Penance; and Cranmer urged that "purgatory, pilgrimages, praying to saints, images, holy bread, holy water, holy days, merits, works, ceremony, and such other, be not restored to their late accustomed abuses" . . . for the "word of God hath gotten the upper hand of them all, and hath set them in their right use and estimation." However, the *Bishop's Book* never received Henry's official approval.

Protestant fortunes brightened even more with the publication in 1538 of the Thirteen Articles, the doctrinal fruit of theological negotiations with the Germans. But the brightness was soon dimmed, for Henry could not bring himself to accept Lutheran theological views. He was unwilling to forswear basic Catholic doctrine or to risk further the ire of Charles V. Accordingly, in 1539 Henry proclaimed his famous Six Articles, known as the "Whip with Six Strings." They reaffirmed six basic Roman Catholic beliefs as the law of the land: (1) transubstantiation, (2) withholding of the cup from the laity, (3) celibacy for priests, (4) inviolable vows of chastity, (5) private masses, and (6) the expediency and necessity of auricular confession. Imposition of these articles on England brought widespread harassment to many evangelicals and death to some. Denial of transubstantiation was punishable by death. A first denial of the other articles brought a forfeiture of property and imprisonment, and a second denial carried a penalty of death. Hundreds were arrested, but only a comparative few suffered death. In 1540 at Smithfield three Catholic traitors and three Protestant heretics were executed, the latter including Robert Barnes. In 1541 three men in Salisbury and two in Lincoln died for speaking against transubstantiation. In 1543 three men were burned in Windsor, one for publicly knocking the nose off an alabaster image of the Virgin. As late as 1546 several people were put to death in Smithfield. In the space of three years Henry had reversed himself, clearly indicating that the Ten Articles rested on political expediency. Henry was still Roman Catholic in his views.

Despite the Six Articles, at the insistent urging of Thomas Cromwell, Henry again tried early in 1540 to cement ties with the evangelicals of Germany through a marriage to Anne of Cleves, sister of the wife of John Frederick of Saxony, only to have the whole thing backfire. A flattering portrait by Holbein made Anne far more attractive than she was, and before the year was out Henry had Convocation nullify the marriage and had Cromwell beheaded as a traitor for having favored the Protestants. Henry then married Catherine Howard, a Roman Catholic, and entered into a military alliance with Charles V. But the alliance proved abortive. In 1542 Catherine Howard was beheaded for adultery, and in the following year Henry married Catherine Parr, who outlived him.

The final years of Henry's reign proved enigmatic for evangelicals. Besides putting to death a number of persons under the Six Articles act, Henry proscribed the use of the Bible, and published a revision of the *Bishops' Book* known as the *King's Book*. This reactionary book appeared in 1543. It declared that not all persons need read the Scriptures for themselves and it affirmed transubstantiation and communion in one kind. It required auricular confession with the sacrament of penance, and it insisted on the disputed celibacy of priests. These stringent demands may have been designed merely to cool the evangelical extremism that had been steadily growing, for Henry did not sack Cranmer, and the doors already opened to Protestantism were not irrevocably closed.

In his will Henry chose sixteen nobles, half favoring the old faith and half the new, to serve as a Council of Regency to guide nine-year-old King Edward VI (1547–53). However, two men, strongly inclined toward Protestantism, soon dominated the Council: Thomas Cranmer, the Archbishop of Canterbury, and Edward Seymour, the duke of Somerset, earl of Hertford. They encouraged the spread of Protestantism and wrote evangelical tenets into the laws and customs of the land. The Council repealed the Six Articles, legalized communion in both kinds, substituted English for Latin in rituals, permitted priests to marry, dissolved endowments for masses for the dead, sequestered holdings of religious fraternities, removed relics and images, abrogated old rules about fasting, and affirmed the Lutheran view of justification by faith. Cranmer sent Erasmus' *Paraphrase of the New Testament* and his own evangelical *Book of Homilies* and *Book of Common Prayer (First Prayer Book of Edward VI)* to all the local parishes for use in public worship. The latter was imposed on the churches in 1549 when Parliament enacted the first Act of Uniformity, which required clergymen to use the service of the *Book of Common Prayer* but left laity free to reject it. One of the most notable features of the first *Book of Common Prayer* was its attempt to avoid inflammatory statements about the Lord's Supper. Cranmer seemed to deny transubstantiation while retaining a real presence in the elements (a Lutheran influence) and to sanction a memorial view of the Supper while allowing each person to come to his own interpretation (a Zwinglian touch). This service satisfied neither the Protestants—who disliked the retention of prayers for the dead, communion at burials, and anointing of the sick—nor the conservatives, who wanted no change at all. Yet the changes continued.

An influx of Continental scholars invited by Cranmer further spread the religious innovations. Martin Bucer and Paul Fagius came from Strassburg to Cambridge; Peter Martyr of Florence and Bernard Ochino of Siena came to Oxford; and Jan Laski came from Poland to lead refugee congregations in London. Still others came from Holland and France. In their sermons, lectures, books, and disputations they further extended Protestant views and helped train the generation of divines so obstinate during the reigns of Mary and Elizabeth.

But all did not go smoothly. Seymour sought to check French influence in Scotland by contracting a marriage between Edward and the young Scottish Princess Mary. It backfired. He undertook an invasion and defeated the Scots at Pinkie in 1547, only to be defeated in his ultimate aim when the Scottish leaders suddenly betrothed Mary to the heir of France, the future Francis II. Seymour's domestic agrarian reforms met with equal frustration. In 1549 Seymour found it necessary to move with force against the restless small farmers whom his agrarian policies had been designed to help. The earl of Warwick put down the uprisings and so endeared himself to the powerful landowners that a conspiracy to displace the more lenient Seymour succeeded in October of 1549. In 1552 Warwick had Seymour beheaded, lest his popularity bring him back into favor.

Protestantism advanced under Warwick, not because Warwick had deep religious convictions, but because the Protestant program furnished guises for his own tyranny and greed. He confiscated church property for himself, and sought to win the throne for his heirs. His boldest scheme was his attempt to bypass the claims of Mary and Elizabeth to the throne and to settle the succession in the event of Edward's death on Lady Jane Grey, the granddaughter of Henry VIII's sister Mary and the wife of Warwick's fourth son, Guilford Dudley. Lady Jane Grey's royal claims were not as sound as those of Mary or Elizabeth, but Warwick persuaded Edward to enact the settlement. Cranmer consented. However, Warwick was so unpopular that even some Protestants later rallied to the support of Mary Tudor. On the accession of Mary, both Warwick and Lady Jane Grey forfeited their lives.

Meanwhile a book to replace the unpopular Prayer Book of 1549 was being readied. Unscrupulous though he was, Warwick, the duke of Northumberland did make this replacement possible. A new Act of Uniformity was passed in 1552 eliminating many of the objectionable "papal" elements in the previous Prayer Book such as prayers for the dead, exorcism, and anointing of the sick. A communion table replaced the altar and common bread the wafer, priests were referred to as ministers, and the Lord's Supper became a remembrance. Laymen as well as clergymen could be punished for using other services, and all had to attend church on Sundays.

In addition Cranmer put forth the Forty-two Articles, in which John Knox and five other theologians collaborated. These articles, authorized by Edward just a month before he died, were abrogated by Mary but later became the Thirty-nine Articles of the Church of England.

Opposition to the Protestant innovations under Edward VI came from two sources: from Roman Catholics who wanted to return to the old order, and from evangelical dissenters, later called Puritans, who wanted to purify the church along biblical lines. Bishop Gardiner of Winchester, who had helped King Henry frame the Six Articles, led the Catholic ultramontane reaction, advocating a return to papal authority. John Hooper, formerly a Cistercian monk, led in advocating just the opposite— more reform to restore "the true and pure worship of God." Under Edward VI both were imprisoned for their views. Royal supremacy demanded obedient conformity.

From early in the summer of 1547 Gardiner suspected that Cranmer's suggested reforms would be like a wedge that would force the English church farther from the old Catholic ceremonies. Once started he feared that nothing could stop the process. When Gardiner refused to support the new religious policies and disobeyed the royal authority, Cranmer promptly sent him to London's Fleet prison. Shortly after Mary Tudor became the queen, Gardiner and other Catholic bishops who had disobeyed royal authority under Edward were released from prison to take up leading roles in making England a Roman Catholic country once again.

The state sent John Hooper to prison in 1550 for refusing both to swear by "God and all the saints" and to wear vestments at his consecration as Bishop of Gloucester. Although he relented and was eventually consecrated, Hooper's expression of conscientious objection to constituted authority was prophetic of future Puritanism. In 1550 he published his famous *Godly Confession and Protestation of Faith* in defense of his position, and in his *Visitation Book,* after he became bishop, he translated his convictions into guidelines of conduct for priests under his care. Using Scripture as his standard, Hooper called for the abandonment of any "papistical doctrine which cannot be duly and justly approved by the authority of God's holy word," such as belief in transubstantiation, purgatory, veneration and invocation of saints, the mass as a propitiation for sin, enforced celibacy for priests, and liturgical uniformity. He would dispense with services in Latin, vestments, oaths in the name of saints, altars separating priests and laity, creeping to the cross, licking the chalice after communion, bowing before relics, elevating holy bread, and similar ritualisms. He also demanded an end to whoring and riotous eating and drinking. Although he opposed the "half-measures" of the Edwardian Council of Regency, he stressed the necessity of obeying magistrates even though they might be tyrannical. Popular rebellion was foreign to him; revolt would have contradicted God's word in Romans 13.

Nicholas Ridley was even more radical in his evangelical reforms. Serving as the Bishop of London, he removed the altar, installed communion tables, and abolished images, relics, and holy water.

A form of Protestantism gained ascendancy under Edward VI without any abrogation of the principle of royal supremacy. Nevertheless, it was shortlived, for when Mary became queen in 1553, she reinstituted Roman Catholicism.

Warwick's sly scheme to have Lady Jane Grey, a Protestant, succeed Edward VI failed utterly. When Edward died in 1553, the people rallied to the side of Mary, the daughter of Catherine of Aragon, who with a show of force quickly secured the throne and beheaded the unfortunate Lady Jane Grey, as well as Warwick. With Gardiner acting as the chief counselor of Mary, Catholicism was once more supreme in England. Parliament quickly declared Mary legitimate, swept aside the religious changes under Edward and returned England to the status quo at the end of Henry's reign. Protestant reformers such as Cranmer, Ridley, Hugh Latimer, and many others soon found themselves imprisoned.

The relative ease with which Mary took control suggests that the people believed that Mary's claim to the throne was at least just, not that they were clamoring for a return to Rome, even though the rootage of Catholicism in England was ancient. Mary misjudged the temper of the time in forcing a return to papal rule. A desire for fair play, nationalism, political stability, and economic security predominated. Yet Mary abolished the Prayer Book, reinstated clerical celibacy, restored the mass, and on St. Andrew's Day, 1554, solemnly knelt along with Parliament while Cardinal Legate Reginald Pole absolved the nation of heresy. Earlier, rather than accept Henry's supremacy, Pole had fled the country. His return seemed to symbolize the triumph of papalism over nationalism. But the triumph was not popular, for the English spirit of nationalism was growing. The queen's marriage in 1554 to Philip II, son of Charles V of Spain, caused many to fear that the house of Hapsburg might come to dominate the nation. Uprisings occurred in Cornwall, Devon, Suffolk, and Kent. Landholders feared that Mary might try to return to the Catholic Church the monastic lands sequestered during Henry's reign. Indeed, Mary promoted her religion with fanatic zeal. She put to death some 300 Protestant leaders, including Latimer, Ridley, Hooper, and Cranmer, and caused hundreds of others, known as Marian exiles, to flee to the Continent where they nursed their grievances and planned reprisals. Mary's barrenness and Philip's separation from her after only one year led her to believe that she was under some kind of divine judgment and that the persecution of Protestants would placate God. Her unpopularity increased when the French took Calais, the last English foothold on the Continent. England was on the verge of rebellion when Mary suddenly died of dropsy.

Elizabeth I (1558–1603) assessed the English temper more astutely. Her primary interest was statecraft, and she chose to establish a *via media* in religion that favored neither extreme papalism nor extreme Protestantism. To have politicized her reign in either direction would have weakened the broadly based interest in nationalism and political stability. She banked on the people's support of a policy of moderation. She continued to go to mass, but she forbade elevation of the eucharistic host. She reformed the Prayer Book to lessen offense to the Catholics, but reinstituted the liturgy of Edward VI. She kept the episcopal form of church government but lessened the power of the bishops. The Act of Supremacy in 1559 made her "supreme governor" rather than supreme head of the Anglican Church. Despite her attempts to be neutral, Elizabeth's *via media* tended to favor the Protestants, and in 1559 all but one of the Catholic bishops from Mary's reign resigned. Up to 2,000 beneficed Catholic priests refused to sign the Oath of Supremacy but not one was put to death. This massive resistance forced Elizabeth to lean toward the Protestants, even toward returning Marian exiles who because of their political and organizational expertise probably received more than their share of seats in Commons and church appointments. To fill the Catholic vacancies, Elizabeth called upon Matthew Parker to be Archbishop of Canterbury. He had married during the reign of Edward and had been removed from office under Mary. Four bishops who had held sees under Edward consecrated him, causing a furor over his legitimacy that has prevailed to this day. In 1896 Pope Leo XIII declared that Anglican Orders were invalid, thus denying that Anglican clergy are in the Apostolic Succession.

The Elizabethan Settlement encountered bitter Roman Catholic opposition from the very beginning, yet Elizabeth was tactful enough to avoid rebellion and excommunication for eleven years. This opposition made Elizabeth's Settlement appear all the more Protestant. Elizabeth ordered a revision of the Forty-two Articles of 1553, which were adopted in 1563 as the Thirty-nine Articles of the Church of England. The Thirty-nine Articles were definitely Calvinistic, an influence of the Marian exiles.

John Foxe's famous *Acts and Monuments of the Christian Martyrs,* widely known as Foxe's *Book of Martyrs,* also appeared in 1563. It was a documentary of legal and personal accounts of the deaths of martyrs from the earliest days of Christianity to the time of Foxe. Although it was carefully compiled, the introduction left no doubt about the author's intentions. He openly denounced the Catholics for having "slaughtered" and "murdered" thousands of people who would not bow to the dictates of the Pope, and called on Catholics to cease their striving against the Lord. It climaxed with the accounts of Protestants burned during the reign of Mary. Illustrated with woodcuts of fiery executions, the book went through many editions, sensationally arousing passions and prejudices against the Catholics. Few if any books have more profoundly influenced English thought.

Also in 1563 the Test Act became the law of the realm. It condemned anyone who in "writing ciphering printing preaching or teaching deed or act" upheld the jurisdiction of the Pope, required an oath of obedience to the queen as the supreme governor of the realm, and excluded Catholics from the House of Commons. In the same year an act dealing with maintenance in the navy established a "Protestant fast," urging the eating of fish for economic rather than religious reasons. It provided penalties for those who ate fish "for the saving of the soul of man" or "the service of God." Whether by design or not, the Elizabethan Settlement moved closer to Protestantism.

Catholic opposition to Elizabeth steadily mounted until the outbreak of the Northern revolt in 1569, a revolt involving the Duke of Norfolk and the earls of Northumberland and Westmoreland. Several thousand peasants marched and then celebrated mass in Durham Cathedral after destroying Bibles and prayer books. Although this rebellion lacked popular support and was short-lived, it signaled the use of force and intrigue to unseat Elizabeth. Rome hoped to place the embattled Mary Queen of Scots on the English throne. In 1567 Mary had lost her bid for power in Scotland and in the following year escaped from prison to take refuge in England.

Because she had claims on the throne and was an obvious threat to Elizabeth, Mary Queen of Scots was imprisoned. When Pope Pius V excommunicated Elizabeth in 1570 as a heretic and anathematized all those who supported her, Elizabeth's life was in danger. Extreme Catholics could argue that it was their religious duty to enthrone Mary. Parliament then passed a Treasons Act, 1571, requiring Mary to acknowledge Elizabeth as the rightful queen or forfeit her place in the throne succession. Parliament also passed an act in 1571 prohibiting the issuance of any Roman bulls or papal documents in England, lest a fanatic deem it his religious duty to murder the monarch. In 1570 the Regent Moray was treacherously murdered in Scotland. In 1571 the famous Ridolfi Plot to start an insurrection to unseat Elizabeth involved the Duke of Alva, Philip II, Pope Pius V, and the Duke of Norfolk. The last forfeited his life. In 1572 word reached England of the bloody Paris Massacre of Protestants on St. Bartholomew's Day to prevent a Protestant from gaining the throne of France. At the new seminary at Douai-Rheims, established by William Allen in 1568, Catholic priests were already being trained and sent to England secretly as missionaries and subversives. Cuthbert Mayne was executed for treason in 1577, and Edmund Champion, a Jesuit suspected of this activity, was apprehended and executed in 1581. Another Jesuit leader, Robert Parsons, escaped to France, where he continued to teach assassination to promote the interests of the church. An act of Parliament in 1581 set a fine of 200 marks and a year in prison for saying mass, and 100 marks and a year in prison for hearing mass, an act severely affecting all Catholics in England. In 1585 Parliament passed an Act of Association that provided for Mary's execution in the event that she conspired against the throne. Mary was widely suspected of involvement in various intrigues, but Elizabeth would not consent to Mary's execution until she was personally found guilty of treason. When Mary was found to be involved in the Babington conspiracy of 1586, Elizabeth had her executed, February 8, 1587. Suspicion of Roman Catholic priests escalated; many were expelled from England, many executed as traitors. Elizabeth's reaction to the Catholics also took the form of sending money to aid the beleaguered Huguenots in France, dispatching troops to Holland to aid the Netherlanders in their struggles against the tyranny of Spain, and encouraging English pirates like Sir Francis Drake to harass Spanish merchant ships.

Frustrated in his attempts to win England to the Catholic fold, in 1588 Philip II of Spain, who boasted he would burn his own son if he were found guilty of heresy, launched a fleet of 132 ships, "The Invincible Armada," against Elizabeth. Pope Sixtus V, who dreamed like Philip of a united Europe under one emperor and church, helped plan, finance, and launch the grand appeal to force. When the ships carrying their crack Spanish soldiers reached England, they were to be further strengthened by seasoned Spanish troops of Alexander of Parma in Holland who would cross the channel. Elizabeth appealed to the patriotism of her subjects, who outfitted some 200 smaller, faster ships with heavier cannon. In the engagements that followed, England's pirating seamen out-maneuvered, out-fought, and out-gunned the Spanish. Aided by stormy seas off Plymouth and Gravelines, the English sank all but a small number of the great Armada. In a few short weeks England had become the most powerful nation in Europe. Special printings of psalms and thanksgiving collects aided in celebrations of the triumph. The Act against Recusants in 1593 further curbed England's Catholics. Such suspicion of Catholics had been generated that restrictive anti-papal legislation grew worse in the following century and was not lifted until 1829!

During this stormy period the Puritans had by contrast remained relatively quiet, but they had by no means abandoned their drive to purify the Anglican Church of popish remnants. Nor had Elizabeth abandoned her desire to establish a *via media* of religion in England, even though the Catholic situation made her give ground temporarily. These reformers, generally called Puritans after 1563, soon became differentiated according to the form of church government they advocated. Those who desired a congregational form were called Congregationalists; a presbyterial form, Presbyterians; those who wanted to separate, Separatists; those who for various reasons would not conform, Non-conformists. All of them desired ceremonies and rituals in keeping with biblical injunctions, more preaching of the Gospel, less liturgy, and a more visible manifestation of religion in the lives of laity and ministers.

When Elizabeth insisted on royal supremacy and uniformity in worship, the Puritans became adamant. They would not wear vestments, copes and surplices that suggested a Roman Catholic separation of the laity and clergy. And Elizabeth's attempt to force uniformity by depriving them of their benefices only heightened the tension and resentment of the episcopacy that sided with the queen. Many Puritan pulpits became vacant, and new appointees were frequently stoned by a laity inclined toward Puritanism. In 1570 Thomas Cartwright (1535?–1603) lost his professorship at Cambridge and was temporarily exiled for his inflammatory advocacy of the priesthood of all believers, abolition of the episcopacy, and presbyterianism. When John Field and Thomas Wilcox in 1572 presented *An Admonition to Parliament* protesting the determined royal efforts to make clerics subscribe to *all* of the Thirty-nine Articles, both landed in jail. Cartwright's defense of the *Admonition* caused him to flee again. John Whitgift, later to become Archbishop of Canterbury, vigorously combatted the Puritans. At Oxford, a decree of 1573 required every degree candidate to subscribe to the Thirty-nine Articles, and this was extended to entering students in 1576. At Cambridge, a hotbed of religious agitation and reform from the time of Henry VIII, no such decree was issued. But Elizabeth gave ground during the turmoil with the Catholics. In 1575 on the death of Matthew Parker she appointed Edmund Grindal, a Puritan, to be the Archbishop of Canterbury, a move that temporarily placated the militants. Grindal's convictions, however, prevented him from curbing Puritan "prophesyings," which were illegal gatherings of non-conformists to study and discuss religion, and in 1577 he was suspended for a period of five years. When Grindal died in 1583, his opposite, Whitgift, became Archbishop and rigorously implemented Elizabeth's *via media*. This time was known as the years of "woeful subscription."

Resentment rapidly escalated, and some Puritans despite their acceptance of ruling authorities defiantly met in secret "conventicles," often in the woods, and called for the formation of independent congregations in which Puritan ideals could be practiced. Among these was Robert Browne (1550–1633). Drawn to Separatist views, with Robert Harrison he established an independent congregation in Norwich in 1581, only to suffer repeated harassing and imprisonment. Eventually Browne and his congregation sought refuge in Holland, where in 1582 he brought forth his *Reformation without Tarrying for Anie*, the first clear enunciation for the principle of congregationalism or independency. Browne asserted that so long as people conduct themselves properly and show respect for authority, the magistrate should have nothing to do with their religion. Neither Pope nor popeling is to control the church of God; it is therefore vain to wait any longer for the magistrate to reform the church; he is to take care of worldly matters; Christians are to reform the church in keeping with the word of God. Christians are believers who have made a covenant with God to live according to his laws. Reminiscent of the Anabaptists, he maintained that ministers are simply brethren especially designated for a particular task; ministers are not a separate clerical order. He called upon the church to initiate reformation without waiting for magistrates to act, thus defying Elizabeth's supremacy.

Browne's views aroused controversy. The sheets for his book were sent to England for binding and circulating, and two men were hanged for distributing them. Elizabeth issued a solemn proclamation against Browne's ideas.

Opposition to Whitgift's stern drive for full subscription to the *via media* radicalized many of the dissenters. The Presbyterians clamored for dissipation of control by bishops and the magistrate. They worked largely from within the system. Separatists sought to form their own independent congregations without allegiance to any outside power. The *Marprelate* tracts, 1588–89, which mercilessly criticized and ridiculed the bishops and vestiges of papalism, brought renewed attempts to suppress fanatical Puritanism. Cartwright, who had again returned to England, was arrested and tried for treason in 1590 and then freed. Others were not so lucky. In 1593, Nicolas Udal, one of the suspected authors of the *Marprelate* tracts, died in prison. And in the same year John Greenwood and Henry Barrow, both relatively young men, suffered martyrdom for organizing Separatist groups in London. John Penry, having attacked the Church of England in his *Humble Supplication in Behalf of the Country of Wales,* 1587, and suspected of complicity in the *Marprelate* tracts, fled to Scotland, returned, and was arrested, tried, and hanged in 1593 on a flimsy charge of treason. For a brief time he had associated himself with Robert Browne's church. In the same year Peter Wentworth, who agitated in Parliament for free speech, was confined a second time to London Tower, where he remained until his death in 1597.

Elizabeth's stance was at least clear. To deny the authority of the bishops, which the Puritans almost universally did, was to deny her authority for having appointed them. Not to subscribe to the Thirty-nine Articles, not to wear surplices, not to conform in ritual was to rebel against the Crown. She would not tolerate disrupting subversion, whether Puritan or Catholic. It is not surprising therefore that separate Acts against the Puritans and Recusants (Catholics who wanted the papacy to dominate) climaxed in 1593. Puritans were branded as "wicked," "dangerous," and "seditious," and Catholics as "traitorous," "dangerous," and "detestable."

Support for Elizabeth's *via media* came not only from patriots more concerned about country than religion but also from anti-Calvinistic writers like Thomas Bilson, who defended the episcopacy in his *Perpetual Government of Christ's Church,* 1593, and Richard Hooker, who drew upon Scripture and reason to justify episcopacy in his voluminous *Laws of Ecclesiastical Polity,* 1594–97. Despite protests, Elizabeth's Anglicanism prevailed. Except for the political revolt and beheading of Lord Essex, the last decade of her reign was quiet, as if the nation was waiting for her replacement.

17

State Sovereignty: Puritan Revolt, Thirty Years' War, and Absolutism

Economic and social conditions strongly affected the course of events in the seventeenth century. This can hardly be denied. Neither can the significant, if not overarching, role of religion in the same period be denied, for religion stood at the heart of the Puritan Revolt in England and the Thirty Years' War in Germany, and as a backdrop to absolute kingship in France. In these three momentous happenings, Catholicism and Protestantism clashed, and in the overall analysis both lost. Machiavellianism won, for national sovereignty rather than religious loyalty finally predominated. In Western culture the seventeenth century saw the last of the wars fought mainly over religion. After twelve hundred years, ecclesiastical sovereignty had ceased to be the organizing motif in human affairs. Whether national sovereignty, severely questioned in the twentieth century, has served humanity in a fragmented way any better than the universal sovereignty claimed by the church depends on the standard by which one judges. Vague though the content of their statement might appear, the early Christians would reply, as echoed in Augustine, that human political arrangements are proximate, that sovereignty belongs ultimately to God. In the immediate crucible of historical complexities, however, neither the questions nor the answers are clear, perhaps because people do not usually live long enough to see either the full consequences of their acts or the interpretations that others put upon them. In relating ourselves to things in space and time, as Athanasius observed, we fail to find anything that gives meaning to space and time, and the succeeding generations are not satisfied with the solutions wrought in the turmoil of their predecessors. Such was the case in the transitional events of the Puritan Revolt, the Thirty Years' War, and the rise of divine right absolutism.

PURITAN REVOLT

When James I became king of England (1603–25), both the Puritans and the Catholics expected to fare better than they had under Elizabeth. James' background was both Protestant and Catholic. His mother was Mary, Queen of the Scots. She was the daughter of James V of Scotland and Mary of Guise, France. James V died when his daughter was only a week old. She was whisked away to France, where she grew up and was educated as a Catholic. Her mother, Mary of Guise, ruled Scotland in her stead. To further strengthen the ties of Scotland with France, Mary Queen of the Scots married the future Francis II of France (1559–60), who died the same year as Mary of Guise. Mary Queen of the Scots did not return to Scotland until August 19, 1561, and by that time, despite her charm and intelligence, she was not able to turn back the Calvinism that John Knox and his predecessors had already established. Her love affairs served further to alienate her from her people. In 1565 she married her cousin, Henry Stuart, Lord Darnley, next in line as heir to the English throne. Their son became the future James I, King of England, but their marriage was brief. When Mary began dallying with David Rizzio, a court musician, Darnley and a group of conspirators in 1566 hacked Rizzio to death in the presence of Mary. Shortly afterward, Darnley contracted smallpox and was isolated in a small house outside the walls of Edinburgh. One night he was strangled and the house blown up, probably by the Earl of Bothwell, who became Mary's third husband just three months later, in 1567. Whether directly involved in the murder or not, Mary lost her waning support among the nobility of Scotland, was imprisoned, escaped, and fled to England, where she was jailed by Elizabeth in 1568. She was the center of Catholic intrigue until Elizabeth consented to her execution in 1587.

John Knox (ca. 1513–72) was not the first to bring Protestant principles to Scotland. In 1528 Catholic authorities burned Patrick Hamilton for heresy, and in 1546 Cardinal Beaton burned George Wishart. In the same year that Wishart died, John Knox joined forces with other conspirators who put Cardinal Beaton to death. For a brief time Knox preached evangelical ideas at the fortified castle of St. Andrews, but in 1547 it was captured by the French, and Knox served nineteen months as a galley slave. On his release, Knox advocated evangelical doctrines in England until the accession of Mary; he then fled to the Continent, where he met Calvin. In 1558 he published his *First Blast of the Trumpet against the Monstrous Regiment of Women,* a violent diatribe against Mary of Guise, in which he asserted that feminine rule was contrary to natural law and divine ordinance. Elizabeth would not let him pass through England on his return to Scotland in 1559. Back once again in Scotland Knox headed a reform party to establish evangelical religion. In the Treaty of Berwick, 1560, the reformers boldly arranged with the British for military aid to counteract the French army stationed in Scotland, but on her deathbed in 1560 Mary of Guise requested both the French and British to withdraw.

Knox and his followers had more than a year before the arrival of Mary Queen of the Scots in which to consolidate their Calvinistic gains. In 1560 the Scottish Parliament adopted the thoroughly Calvinistic *Scottish Confession,* or *National Covenant,* drawn up by Knox and five other ministers, and abolished papal authority and the mass. With bishops still sitting in Parliament, the *First Book of Discipline,* 1560, was not officially sanctioned, but evangelical tenets were well entrenched in the country. When Mary was forced to abdicate in 1567, Knox preached the coronation sermon for the infant James. *The Scottish Confession* was accepted by the king, council, and court in 1580, by the nation in 1581, and again in 1590 and 1638.

Although Presbyterianism eventually prevailed in Scotland, James VI of Scotland (James I of England) developed ideas of his own. An erudite scholar, in 1598 he published *The Trew Law of Free Monarchies,* in which he advocated the divine right of kings over all laws and assemblies, accountable only to God. It was a stance that gave rise to his famous motto, "No bishop, no king." James was determined on royal supremacy.

Despite his Calvinistic ties, James was in no mood to tolerate the erosion of his supremacy inherent in the Puritan stance. The Millenary Petition of 1603, presented to him as he journeyed from Scotland to London, did not receive his favor. Over a thousand Puritans asked that he "amend" certain offensive human rites and ceremonies: that use of the cross in baptism, cap and surplice in services, and the ring in marriage, be eliminated; that preaching and residency of ministers be required and clerical marriage allowed; that multiple benefices and dignities be abolished; that ecclesiastical fees be regulated; and that excommunication for trifles be abolished. James granted nothing. But he did promise and held his Hampton Court Conference with the Puritans in 1604. At that conference he authorized a new translation of the Bible, the King James Version of 1611, a translation vastly superior both to the preceding Protestant translations and to the Roman Catholic Rheims-Douai Bible of 1582–1610. Fifty scholars from Oxford, Cambridge, and Westminster cooperated to produce a work that affected broad areas of culture in England and America during the next four hundred years. The King James Bible included the Apocrypha, but by 1629 the Puritans had succeeded in eliminating it from the non-Anglican editions. James did not revise the Prayer Book, which the Puritans hated for its popish remnants, nor the Thirty-nine Articles, nor the authorized catechism. Above all, he did not yield on the episcopacy, believing that bishops bulwarked his own supremacy. A series of acts enforced his views, and some three hundred Puritans who objected lost their pulpits. James' *Book of Sports* in 1618 was intended to legalize certain sports and activities on Sundays that the Puritans had succeeded in banning. When James ordered the book read from Puritan pulpits, the furor was so great that it was withdrawn.

Puritans in England grew restive. Although they were not yet ready to revolt, many were ready to emigrate. Two influential Separatist congregations, one at Gainsborough, led by John Smyth, an Anglican clergyman, and the other at Scrooby, led by William Brewster, who was joined by William Bradford and John Robinson, resolved to leave England. They settled respectively at Amsterdam and Leyden in the Netherlands. Others joined them. Greatly concerned about their religious future, a vanguard of these questers eventually arranged for passage to America. On September 6, 1620, 101 Pilgrim venturers sailed on the *Mayflower* for America. During the next twenty years, harassment by James and his successor Charles caused more than 40,000 to seek refuge in New England.

Other groups chose to remain in Holland or return to the British Isles. John Smyth (ca. 1554–1612), feeling that if he rejected Anglican church rule he must also reject Anglican infant baptism, carried his separatism to the point of baptizing himself (Se-Baptism), and in 1609 established in Amsterdam the first modern Baptist Church—The Brethren of the Separation of the Second English Church at Amsterdam. Membership required voluntary, adult believers' baptism. Smyth himself drifted increasingly closer to the Mennonites in Holland, but others in his congregation, particularly Thomas Helwys (ca. 1550–ca. 1616), disliked this trend and felt a strong duty to return to England. With a small group of others, Helwys returned to England in 1612, and at London, in Spitalfields outside the walls, organized the first General Baptist Church in England. His successful preaching soon ended, however, for in 1612 his *Declaration of the Mystery of Iniquity,* probably printed in Holland, began to circulate, and Helwys was imprisoned and later executed. His book is noted for its outright call for complete toleration of religion, separation of church and state, inasmuch as religion is of a spiritual nature and cannot be forced. "Our lord the King is but an earthly King," he wrote, "and he has no authority as a King but in earthly causes, and if the King's people be obedient and true subjects, obeying all humane laws made by the King, our lord the King can require no more: for men's religion to God is between God and themselves; the King shall not answer for it, neither may the King be judge between God and man. Let them be heretics, Turks, Jews or whatsoever, it appertains not to the earthly power to punish them in the least measure." Helwys scored the abuse of temporal power in the hands of anyone—Catholics, Anglicans, or Puritans. *The Mystery of Iniquity* is also noted for its rejection of infant baptism and Calvinistic "particular election and reprobation," and for its acceptance of "general redemption of all by Christ." From this came the terms "General" (Arminian) and "Particular" (Calvinistic) Baptists. Baptist churches modeled after the Helwys community were connectional in polity and "General." "Particular" Baptists developed a little later in England when groups of Calvinistic Separatists adopted adult believers' baptism. Among the first to do so were members of Henry Jacob's church in London in 1633. They were congregational in polity, and soon adopted immersing instead of pouring or sprinkling as the mode of baptism.

Roger Williams' withdrawal from the Massachusetts Puritan commonwealth and settlement at Providence, Rhode Island, where a church along Baptist principles was formed in 1639, is generally regarded as the beginning of Baptists in America. In 1644 in England, Williams published his *Bloody Tenent of Persecution* in which he vigorously argued for separation of church and state and for universal toleration on the basis of reason, experience, and the Scriptures. The Baptists and other so-called "sectaries" formed the revolutionary backbone in Oliver Cromwell's army during the English Civil War.

The Catholics, who might have capitalized on James' background and his Anglo-Catholic tendencies, fared worse than the Puritans. Catholic recusants engineered a series of plots to assassinate James, the most famous being the Gunpowder Plot of 1605, in which a group of Roman Catholic conspirators led by Guy Fawkes sought to blow up the king and Parliament. Discovery of this and other intrigues caused James to order all seminarists and Jesuits to leave England. The Jesuits were arguing that any means, even assassination, might be employed to advance Roman Catholicism. James could not allow such open attacks on his royal supremacy. Many Catholics were arrested, some executed; and an oath of allegiance required Catholics to reject any papal act or excommunication that might expose rulers to violence. A far-reaching act in 1606 closed to Catholics such vocations as trustees, lawyers, doctors, and guardianships.

James saw Anglicanism as the best religious support for royal supremacy and tenaciously supported it. He reintroduced episcopacy in Scotland, and by 1612 Scotland was officially committed not only to royal supremacy but also to episcopacy on a presbyterian basis. In London he often lectured Parliament on his own divine attributes and prerogatives, but Parliament grew more and more reluctant to vote James money for his domestic and foreign policies, thus compromising his royal supremacy.

When Charles I, more truculent and absolutist than his father, became ruler (1625–49), a rebellious Parliament was in no mood to rubber stamp his adherence to divine-right monarchy. They quarreled from the beginning. But Charles was adamant. When Parliament denied his peremptory and unexplained demands for money, he levied a forced loan and imprisoned seventy-six prominent social leaders, including some members of Parliament, for refusing to contribute. In 1628 Parliament forced Charles to accept the Petition of Right, which in time safeguarded certain English liberties, but in 1629 Charles dismissed Parliament and for eleven years ruled without it.

Constantly vexed by his inability to collect taxes without the authorization of Parliament, Charles resorted to devious schemes, among which was the resurrection of an old law saying that anyone worth £40 should present himself at the time of coronation for knighting. From those gentry who had not been knighted at his crowning in 1626 Charles collected £165,000 in fines! He also turned the impost on ships, intended to raise money for defense in time of emergency, into an unpopular national tax, though with only partial success.

However, Charles' most explosive problem was religion. He appointed William Laud (1573–1645) to manage religious affairs, naming him Bishop of London in 1628 and Archbishop of Canterbury in 1633. Convinced that Anglican conformity was the way for England, Laud sternly enforced uniformity. For the Puritans he symbolized all that was hateful in state prelacy. This was the period when John Winthrop in 1630 led 1,500 Puritans to Massachusetts, and 20,000 more followed during the next ten years. Even many of the bishops objected to Laud's program. In 1637 when Laud tried to make an example of three Puritan pamphleteers by cropping their ears, they became national heroes. Open revolt erupted when Laud tried to force the Anglican Prayer Book on the Presbyterian populace of Scotland. In 1638 the Scots adopted a national covenant to die if necessary to keep their religious and political liberties. Charles' attempt to suppress the rebellion was woefully ineffective, and in 1640 the Scots invaded northern England. With an inadequate army, no money, and no popular support, Charles was forced to summon Parliament.

The Long Parliament, which sat from 1640 to 1653, soon became an even larger center of revolt than the Scots. Parliament wrested control of government from Charles through a series of constitutional acts. The king's devious tax schemes were declared illegal, the royal law courts used by Laud abolished, and the king's right to dismiss Parliament without its consent set aside. A small majority of Puritans resolved to reconstruct both the church and state. Charles did not lack parliamentary support, but his military coup in January, 1642, backfired. With four hundred soldiers he invaded the House of Commons, intent on arresting the Puritan radical leaders, only to discover they had already escaped. Mob action forced Charles to leave London, and within months the troops of the king and those raised by Parliament were locked in civil war.

Events quickly turned in favor of the Puritans, who in 1643 secured a military alliance with the Scots. In exchange for military aid, Parliament adopted the *Solemn League and Covenant* of 1643, based heavily on the Scottish national covenant of 1638, for the "reformation and defence of religion, . . . and the peace and safety of the three kingdoms of England, Scotland, and Ireland." In 1644–45 it was imposed on all Englishmen over eighteen years of age, and Anglicanism was outlawed for fifteen years. At this time a military genius in the person of Oliver Cromwell (1599–1658) surfaced. An obscure member of the Long Parliament, he enlisted in the parliamentary army and in 1643 recruited a regiment of "godly men" that won every engagement it fought. He and his men were chiefly responsible for the victory over the royalists at Marston Moor in 1644, the biggest pitched battle of the war. And he was responsible for the reorganizing of the "New Model" army (with Cromwell second in command) that defeated Charles at Naseby in 1645 and captured Charles himself in 1646. Cromwell regarded himself as one chosen by God, neither a radical Puritan, nor a Scottish Presbyterian, but an Independent, his army being his church.

The Westminster Assembly, constituted in 1643 to guide Parliament in religious decisions, produced the *Directory of Worship* 1643, which displaced the Anglican Prayer Book, wrote the famous *Short Catechism* of 1647, one of the best expressions of Calvinism, and compiled the *Westminster Confession* of 1648—all three landmarks in Presbyterianism. But tensions mounted. The Puritans were by no means united, and enforced Presbyterianism came increasingly to be resented, especially by the radical Puritan sects such as the apocalyptic Fifth Monarchy Men; the Levellers, who wanted popular male suffrage and sovereignty; the Diggers, who believed no one should own property; the early Quakers, who followed the inner light; and Baptists, who insisted on religious liberty and believers' baptism. These sects gained support in Cromwell's army, and in 1648 Cromwell issued a remonstrance against forcing religion into one mold. In the same year Cromwell crushed a combination of royalist-Presbyterian forces at Preston, and with a military coup took complete control of Parliament. His army allowed only those who agreed with his policies to participate in Parliament. Archbishop Laud had been imprisoned and executed in 1645, and Cromwell became convinced that Charles would have to be eliminated before any real peace could be effected. On January 30, 1649, Charles I was publicly decapitated as a traitor.

Cromwell was in full control, using the army to quell insurrection and repulse outside foes. In 1649 he ruthlessly crushed insurgency in Ireland, and in 1650–51 he defeated the resurgent Scots at Dunbar and Worcester. At sea he successfully fought the Dutch and the Spanish. In 1653 he dismissed Parliament, which he considered corrupt and inefficient, and made himself Lord Protector with a standing army of 50,000 men. The Cromwellian agreement with the people in 1649 granted liberty in religion to all but devotees of "popery and prelacy," but Calvinistic Puritanism later dominated (1657) in the desecration of ornate church altars, the prohibition of Christmas and other festivals, the relegation of marriage to a civil rite, and the interdiction of dancing and licentiousness.

Cromwell's significance is almost impossible to assess. He ruled like an absolute dictator but would not be titled king. When he died in 1658, his son Richard was too inept to hold the forces of power together, and in 1660 a newly elected Parliament and a coalition of those who feared political anarchy invited Charles I's son to return to England as king. The Restoration had Cromwell's body disinterred from Westminster Abbey and hung at Tyburn.

Charles II (1660–85) had spent the previous eleven years in exile and had developed a liking for Roman Catholicism and French absolutism in the person of Louis XIV. Both propensities eventually set him at odds with Parliament. The first Restoration Parliament was so thoroughly royalist that Charles kept it in session for eighteen years, from 1661 to 1679. Legal, anti-Puritan repercussions were virtually inevitable. Parliament was ardently Anglican and not only restored Anglican worship and practices, but also persecuted the Puritans and other non-conformists with a series of acts called the Clarendon Code. Over two thousand Puritans lost their pulpits, and many went to jail. Although Charles had promised religious freedom in the Breda Declaration in 1660, in 1661 Parliament passed the Corporation Act requiring all mayors, aldermen, bailiffs, and other government officials to declare armed resistance to the king traitorous, forswear the *Solemn League and Covenant,* and agree to keep Holy Communion according to the Anglican rite. The Act of Uniformity in 1662 required all ministers to have episcopal ordination, use the Anglican Prayer Book, and swear an oath not to advocate resistance to the king. The First Conventicle Act, 1664, provided fines and imprisonment for those attending non-conformist services, or for more than five extra people assembling with any household, causing the jails to bulge. The Five Mile Act, 1665, forbade ministers who refused conformity to live within five miles of an incorporated town or their former parishes, and barred them from teaching. The Second Conventicle Act, 1670, increased fines for attending non-conformist services and stipulated that fines could be collected for all from anyone connected with the group.

But sentiment in Parliament was Anglican, not Roman Catholic; royalist, not absolutist. Parliament was unwilling to sanction Charles' inclination toward Catholicism or to yield its power of taxation to the king. In 1670 in return for an immediate subsidy Charles promised Louis XIV of France in the secret Treaty of Dover to restore England to Catholicism as soon as conditions permitted. He moved to do so in 1672 when he repealed the Clarendon Code and penal laws against Catholics in a Declaration of Indulgences, which would have permitted worship in private homes. Parliament reacted sharply against this overture to Catholics, caused the indulgences to be withdrawn, and in 1673 enacted the Test Act requiring all within thirty miles of London to take communion in the Anglican way. Charles decided to move with Anglicanism and shelved his promise to Louis XIV, although on his deathbed he did confess his Catholicism.

The Titus Oates affair demonstrated that anti-Catholic feeling ran deep in England. Charles II had no legitimate male heirs. Next in line was his brother James, an avowed Roman Catholic. In 1678 Oates announced the discovery of a popish plot to assassinate Charles, massacre the English Protestants, and enthrone James. Hysteria resulted, Oates' false testimony led to many executions, and three Puritan (Whig) Parliaments were elected, in 1679–81. But Charles regained control, and persecuted non-conformists during the last years of his reign more severely than before.

James II (1685–88) tried openly to reinstitute Catholicism. He brought in Jesuits and monks, appointed Catholics to army commands, and to religious and teaching posts. But Englishmen could not forget the Spanish Armada, the Ridolfi Plot, the Babington Conspiracy, the Gunpowder Plot, St. Bartholomew's Day, and the massacre of Waldenses in Italy in 1655. In 1688 when seven Anglican bishops were charged with treason for not reading James' decree of toleration from their pulpits, the jury found them not guilty. Many Englishmen considered the birth of James' son in 1688 a hoax to secure a Catholic heir to the throne. Anglicans (Tories) and Puritans (Whigs) united in June of 1688 in issuing an invitation to William of Orange and Mary, the daughter of James, to invade England and restore liberty and religion. The Dutch army landed and moved on London without opposition. James fled to France. Parliament offered the throne to William and Mary (1689–94), and secured religious toleration, even for dissenters, in the Act of Toleration in 1689 which, however, excluded Roman Catholics and Unitarians.

Thus was the Glorious Revolution brought about. Anglicanism continued as the official religion, but royal supremacy gave way to the constitutional sovereignty of the state. With Rome still claiming papal sovereignty over all states, Catholics in England continued to suffer persecution. In 1700 they were prohibited from purchasing or inheriting land, and children were denied Catholic schooling except in their own homes. By the end of the eighteenth century, Catholics were faring better in England, but complete toleration did not come for them until 1829.

The seventeenth century began in England with strong secular interests being expressed in literature. Edmund Spenser's *Faerie Queene* appeared in 1591, Ben Jonson's *Every Man in His Humor* in 1598. Francis Bacon published his *Novum Organum* in 1620, and *Advancement of Learning* in 1622, both heralding an age of scientific experimentation. William Shakespeare (d. 1616) was at the height of his dramatic power, his numerous tragedies, comedies, histories, and sonnets dealing only slightly with religion. John Donne (d. 1631) represented a mixture of religious and secular allegory. Secular interests continued to be expressed in Thomas Hobbes' *Leviathan*, 1651; Izaac Walton's *Compleat Angler*, 1653; and in John Dryden's (1631–1700) religious poetry, which changed with the times. His *Heroic Stanzas* of 1659 eulogized Oliver Cromwell; his *Religio Laici*, 1682, celebrated Anglicanism; and *The Hind and the Panther*, 1687, extolled Catholicism.

The century ended with some of the greatest religious writing in English literature. Jeremy Taylor (1613–67) produced *Liberty of Prophesying*, 1646, religious prose at its best in his sermons, and his devotional classics, *Holy Living* and *Holy Dying*, 1650–51. But over and above these in their profound religious influence stand John Bunyan (1628–88) and John Milton (1608–74).

Arrested in 1660 for his Puritan views, Bunyan spent twelve years in prison, during which time he wrote *The Holy City*, 1665, and the autobiographical *Grace Abounding*, 1666. In a second imprisonment he wrote parts of *Pilgrim's Progress*, 1678, which made him one of the most popular and influential religious writers in all of English history. With vivid imagination and artless directness *Pilgrim's Progress* allegorizes Puritan mores and biblical insights in its depiction of the journey of Christian from the City of Destruction to the Heavenly City, and the trials and triumphs that Christian has along the way in his encounters with Mr. Worldly-Wiseman, Mr. Legality, Mr. Talkative, Mr. Facing-both-ways, Greatheart, and such places as the Slough of Despond and the Hill of Difficulty. *The Life and Death of Mr. Badman*, 1680, and *The Holy War*, 1682, are less well known, but in all his works Bunyan pictured life as a spiritual warfare and salvation as humanity's chief concern.

The literary giant among the Puritans was John Milton, whose two masterpieces *Paradise Lost*, 1667, and *Paradise Regained*, 1671, probe the mysteries of two of the Bible's most profound themes—the Fall and the Redemption of humanity. The former, on a scale exceeded only by Dante's *Divine Comedy*, treats the consequences of the rebellion of Satan and mankind against God, and the latter deals with Christ's temptations and triumph over the devil. His controversial book on divorce, 1643, advocating incompatibility of character as ground for dissolving marriage, led to the difficulties that prompted him to write *Areopagitica*, 1644, his renowned defense of freedom of the press. He defended the execution of Charles I, but because he desired complete disestablishment of church, he ran afoul of Cromwell in his later years, and his opposition to the divine-right rule of Charles II landed him in jail. In 1671 appeared *Samson*

Agonistes, an allegory based on the story of Samson in the Old Testament. It reflects Milton's bitterness toward women and the unsuccessful bid of the Puritans for power. Controversialist to the end, in a posthumous book on Christian doctrine, Milton criticized the idea of creation *ex nihilo* and the coeternality of persons in the Trinity. After 1651 he wrote in darkness, for in that year Milton became totally blind.

THE THIRTY YEARS' WAR

The British struggle over sovereignty, which saw the end of religious supremacy in England and the elevation of the constitutional state as the arbiter of human affairs, had its parallels on the Continent in the Thirty Years' War (1618–48) and the rise of absolute monarchy in France. Few wars have been so destructive and seemingly so futile as the Thirty Years' War. Some scholars estimate that up to three-fifths of Germany's sixteen million people were killed. Whole towns were decimated, some more than once. At the approach of marauding soldiers, bent more on plunder than conquest, peasants and outlying landowners fled their homes. Pillage and burning were rife. Abandoned children roamed wild like animals, foraging for food. Invading armies from Spain, Denmark, Sweden, and France left almost no part of Germany unravaged.

The Peace of Augsburg, 1555, had stabilized the religious situation in Germany for over half a century. But ardent Catholics, the Jesuits in particular, were not satisfied. They considered the arrangement a temporary truce until the conclusion of the Council of Trent, when they expected something more advantageous to be established. In 1608 militant Jesuits and nobility who stood to profit pressed demands for a restitution to Catholicism of ecclesiastical property that had fallen to the Protestants. The emperor, they said, had no right to make peace settlements without the full consent of the Pope. Tempers flared, alliances formed, and conflict followed. In 1617 Ferdinand of Styria was crowned king of Bohemia. He was the Hapsburg heir apparent to the imperial throne, a zealous Catholic, schooled and counseled by the Jesuits. He created a furor among Bohemian Protestants when he rescinded the religious liberties previously guaranteed, and in May of 1618 when a band of armed Bohemian noblemen in Prague tossed two of Ferdinand's spokesmen through a high window, the war began. The two negotiators landed in a pile of dung and survived.

The Bohemian insurgents held an advantage, temporarily. They offered the Bohemian crown to Frederick of the Palatinate, and he accepted. In 1619, however, the conflict escalated to imperial proportions, for in that year the elderly Emperor Matthias died, and Ferdinand was elected Emperor Ferdinand II (1619–37). He appealed for help and arranged deals with Catholic Maximilian of Bavaria and Philip III of Spain. Maximilian was promised the electoral seat of Frederick and some of his lands, and Philip the remainder of the Palatinate. The Lutheran elector of Saxony also sent an army, having been promised the Hapsburg province of Lusatia. The Imperial armies under General Tilly subdued the

Bohemian rebels near Prague in the fall of 1620 at the battle of White Hill, and Ferdinand exacted vengeance by confiscating Protestant property, executing leading rebels, and imposing strict Catholicism under Jesuit supervision. Imperial forces easily overran the remaining Bohemian resistance and the Palatinate, and by 1622 the war seemed to be finished. But the mercenary soldiers of fortune under Ernst von Mansfeld fled into northwestern Germany, looting and pillaging, pursued by the forces of Albrecht von Wallenstein, also a plundering soldier of fortune who had earned a great deal of wealth supplying grain to the Catholic armies. By 1626 Wallenstein had driven Mansfeld's army out of the empire and Mansfeld himself was dead, both armies leaving in their wake vast areas of desolation. In 1625 Christian IV of Denmark entered the war to prevent total conquest by the Catholics but within a year was thoroughly defeated by Tilly and Wallenstein. By 1629 when Ferdinand issued his Edict of Restitution, imperial forces controlled the Palatinate, Hanover, Brunswick, Silesia, Holstein, Schleswig, Pomerania, Mecklenburg, Bohemia, Moravia, and Austria. The Restitution demanded the restoration of all Roman Catholic property confiscated after 1552 and the expulsion of all Protestants from Catholic territories. Wallenstein was given the task of enforcement and proved so ruthless with his burning and looting that by 1630 the Catholic princes demanded that Ferdinand dismiss him.

Another phase of the conflict began when Gustavus Adolphus of Sweden landed an army on German soil in 1630. Aided by money from Cardinal Richelieu of France, who feared Hapsburg power, Adolphus, the Lutheran Lion of the North, announced that he was invading to protect Protestantism, although he also had thoughts of protecting and even enlarging his own territories. Joined by the electors of Brandenburg and Saxony, Gustavus Adolphus smashed Tilly's forces at Breitenfeld in 1631, and Tilly himself was killed the following year. The emperor recalled Wallenstein, who was defeated in 1632 at Lützen, the battle in which Adolphus was slain. Two years later Wallenstein's own soldiers murdered him.

The final and most violent phase of the war, from 1635 to 1648, began when the French openly joined the Swedes. Neither side could subdue the other, and the war dragged on until the opponents grew weary enough to settle for the Treaty of Westphalia. Basically Westphalia reasserted the Peace of Augsburg, 1555, granting each prince the right to establish Calvinism in addition to the former alternatives of Lutheranism and Catholicism, with safeguards for the minorities remaining. The son of Ferdinand, Ferdinand III (1637–57), controlled little more than his own family lands. The dream of the empire as a unified, absolute Hapsburg state had ended. Germany was fragmented into over 300 relatively small "sovereign" principalities, with the northern part principally Protestant and the southern part Catholic. Excluded from the Treaty of Westphalia were the Anabaptists and other sects who suffered renewed persecution, but generally Protestantism and Catholicism had achieved a balanced stalemate and the populace seemed to care little about which religion they were told to accept. The war brought to an end the European conflicts in which religion played a significant role.

Symbolically, Pope Innocent X's *Zelo Domini Deus*, which censured the treaty as "invalid and iniquitous," proved ineffective.

DIVINE-RIGHT ABSOLUTISM IN FRANCE

From the beginning of Henry IV's rule in France in 1589 to the end of Louis XIV's reign in 1715, national sovereignty rather than religion predominated in the policies of France. Even the revocation of the Edict of Nantes, the persecution of the Huguenots, and Louis XIV's desire to have Catholicism as the only religious faith in France point to national sovereignty rather than overriding religious concerns. These policies were quite different from those of Charles V and Philip II of Spain, who in the sixteenth century dreamed of making Catholicism once again supreme throughout Europe. Partnership of church and state continued, but in the new nationalistic states no doubt remained about the superior sovereignty of the state. Few nations exemplify this new status better than France in the seventeenth century.

Henry IV (1589–1610), the former Huguenot leader, initiated the long trend in France. He turned Catholic to secure the support of his Catholic subjects, but he also pacified his Huguenot subjects by issuing the Edict of Nantes, which guaranteed to them civil and religious autonomy. He paid thirty-two million livres to the leaders of the ultra-Catholic League to disband their troops, and he played the papacy off against the Gallican (nationalistically minded) clergy of France to undercut papal power. He retired much of the debt of France and stabilized national finances. He was on his way to fight the Hapsburg leaders to gain more territory for France when a demented Catholic monk leaped onto his carriage and stabbed him to death.

The nation drifted somewhat aimlessly under Henry's widow, Marie de Medici, during the minority of Henry's son, Louis XIII (1610–43). The Estates-General of 1614 was the last national representative body in France until the French Revolution in 1789. Marie de Medici felt that it was no longer useful. Shortly after Louis XIII assumed his rule, Cardinal Richelieu became his chief minister, in 1624. Operating on a philosophy of *raison d'etat*, he put the state above everything—above his own ambition, above church, above treaties. He ran France, but did not wish to become king. On account of intrigue, he forced the queen mother and Louis XIII's younger brother into exile, and executed nine noblemen who questioned his authority. He outraged the papacy by supporting the Lutherans in the Thirty Years' War. Because the Huguenots had become rebellious, he greatly curtailed their political and military privileges. He promoted whatever benefited the monarchy of France.

Cardinal Mazarin acted similarly as the chief minister during the minority of Louis XIV (1643–1715). In 1661 Louis XIV himself assumed direction of France boasting "I am the state," ruling with lavish pomp, at Versailles flaunting a sumptuous palace with no less than 1,400 fountains in the surrounding grounds, dining like a gourmet while others starved, arresting any who dared to criticize, demolishing the Huguenot schools and churches and revoking their religious privileges, forcing possibly as many as 250,000 to emigrate. He insisted on *un roi, une loi, une foi*—all of which meant national sovereignty through him.

By the end of the seventeenth century, national sovereignty had superseded religious sovereignty in European culture. Secularism had displaced ecclesiasticism.

The change was symbolized in Baroque architecture. It began largely as a revitalization of the militant, triumphant spirit of Catholicism, but as it ran its course in the seventeenth and eighteenth centuries, it became increasingly secular, employed for palaces, courts, castles, halls, and theaters. Certainly not all the architecture of the period expressed secularism, but there was an overall tendency to greater freedom, a movement away from religious restraints. This tendency found expression also in sculpture, painting, music, and literature. Even the mirrors that so frequently lined long sequences of rooms suggested new vistas to be experienced.

No single descriptive term encompasses the Baroque style, although certain terms recur when one tries to convey its characteristics—dramatic eloquence, flowing lines, theatrical ornateness, sensuous emotionalism, intricate designs, synthetic harmony, profuse detail, lavish surroundings, fleshly involvement in this world. Many consider it to have been rooted in the restless questing of earlier artists like Michelangelo and Leonardo da Vinci.

Two of the earliest and greatest exponents of Baroque architecture were Francesco Borromini (1599–1667) and Giovanni Bernini (1598–1680), whose works made Rome the early center of Baroque. Borromini is noted for the synthetic harmony of the Church of San Carlo of the Four Fountains in Rome and for his defiance of convention and imposing effects in the churches of St. Agnese in Piazza Narona and La Sapienza. Bernini used Baroque to enhance the total splendor of his sensuous creations and became the most famous architect in all of Europe. Patronized by five Popes, especially Maffeo Barberini (later Pope Urban VIII), Bernini's architecture, painting, and sculpture were to be seen almost everywhere in Rome. He added the two semicircular colonnades in front of St. Peter's, carved David in the act of killing Goliath, constructed an altar canopy beneath Michelangelo's immense dome of St. Peter's, and sculptured St. Teresa in the ecstasy of being pierced by divine love. For Barberini he designed a palace, built the *Scala Regina* (the royal staircase leading to the papal apartments), and dotted Rome with dramatic fountains and façades. Louis XIV invited Bernini to Paris, but rejected his plans for the Louvre, saying that his own architects could design equally lavish, imposing creations. The Louvre and the palace at Versailles epitomize on a grand scale the secular splendor of the era.

In Spain, Jose Churriguera (1650–1725) added luxuriant extremes of fantastic ornamentation to the Baroque style, an influence that extended to Mexico. The architects of Germany and Austria replaced the ruins of the Thirty Years' War with Baroque-styled palaces, altars, marble halls, residences, abbeys, churches, frescoes, and even organ cases. Among these Baroque artists were Fischer von Erlach, with his elaborate palaces and churches, and Balthasar Neumann. The spectacular splendor of the Zwinger of Dresden, the Neumann staircase in Bruchsal, and the Belvedere of Vienna point to the displacement of religion as the center of culture and suggest worldly gaiety, imagination, and freedom from religious restraints. In England, Christopher Wren (1632–1723) rebuilt more than fifty churches after London's great fire in 1666. Limitations of space, available budget, and the spirit of Protestantism introduced restraints on statuary and extravagance, but his spires and towers exhibited creative ingenuity. St. Paul's Cathedral, begun in 1675 and completed in 1710, financed with a special tax on coal, stands as his masterpiece. His more obviously secular designs included the Sheldonian Theater, Buckingham House, and Ashmolean Museum. Nicholas Hawksmoor, James Gibbs, and John Vanbrugh also championed Baroque styles, as did Grinling Gibbons, a master of wood carving and decorating with marble and metal.

Rembrandt van Rijn (1606–69), with his masterful use of light and shadow and magnificently unified canvases, and Peter Paul Rubens (1577–1640), with his dramatic sensuous creations, brought Baroque painting to new heights. With the aid of technicians who executed his designs, Rubens produced more than two thousand canvases. He traveled throughout Europe doing murals, tapestries, and paintings for royal palaces. Even though half his pictures deal with religious themes and he himself was fervently Catholic, he imparts to the viewer a sense of present joy and dramatic physical involvement.

Opera embodied the Baroque spirit in music and strongly affected church music as seen in George F. Handel (1685–1759), whose masterpieces, *Israel in Egypt*, 1738, and *The Messiah*, 1741, resound with Baroque embellishments and secular tones. By the time of Franz Joseph Haydn (1732–1809) and Wolfgang Amadeus Mozart (1756–1791) Baroque secular expressions in orchestral and operatic forms noticeably predominate over religious themes, despite Haydn's *Creation* and Mozart's *Requiem Mass*. Johann Sebastian Bach (1685–1750) may have been unpopular in his day precisely because the religious aspects in his Baroque style predominated over the secular. He distrusted the ornateness of Italian music, and unlike so many of the other Baroque artists, composed and performed his masterpieces as acts of worship. He drew upon Lutheran chorales and the evangelical tradition, and invested his works with dramatic intensity and harmonic beauty without losing the inward commitment and introspection of religious devotion. His *Mass in B Minor* intensifies the Lutheran liturgy and his Passions on St. John and St. Matthew vivify the biblical narratives.

Perhaps no two writers illustrate the Baroque style in literature and at the same time represent a trend toward secular predominance better than do William Shakespeare (1564–1616), who almost completely disregarded religion in his dramas, and John Milton (1608–74), a strong advocate of freedom of conscience. Milton's Satan is a Baroque figure, and *Paradise Lost* and *Paradise Regained* are cosmic in their grandeur, while *L'Allegro* and *Il Penseroso* are comparable to Baroque ornamentation. Despite his deep attachment to Puritanism, Milton had no wish for religious sovereignty. He wanted the state to guarantee liberty of conscience.

The Baroque style marked a broad turning away from religious ascendancy, as did developments in Puritan England, the Thirty Years' War, and the rise of absolute monarchy in France. By the end of the seventeenth century state sovereignty prevailed in the old Constantinian partnership—and has continued to prevail into the twentieth century—but already erosive forces were at work and other loyalties were bidding for attention.

18

The Age of Reason
and Piety

The displacement of absolute religious sovereignty plus an aftermath of acrimonious struggles generated two movements in the post-Reformation period that uplifted universal loyalties, transcending ecclesiastical and political particularism. These were rationalism and pietism. That their universalism succeeded only partially does not lessen their symbolic transcendence of old sovereignties so much as it points to the intransigence of cultural forms and the seemingly endless human capacity to make altruistic endeavors serve selfish, narrow ends. Rationalism and pietism were not panaceas or even alternatives to state sovereignty; rather, they were early indicators that absolute sovereignty in any form would not be viable for post-medieval, post-Reformation individuals. It is also evident that not all things in the age of reason and piety point in one direction. The realities of history are seldom encompassed in human reflective categories, any more than memory encompasses past events. But neither are they for that reason any less important in shaping culture. Realities have a way of accumulating, and the perspective of history enables one to perceive them even when imperfectly preserved.

THE AGE OF REASON

In the turmoil of the seventeenth century, rationalism began to find new devotees. It was as if people were satiated with the intolerance, persecution, and strife that accompanied religion—weary of fanatical dogmas, witchburning, heretic hunting, inquisitorial racks, and wholesale slaughter. The authoritative claims of Catholics and Protestants seemed equally unsubstantiated. Advocates on both sides put their opposites to death, each side claiming finality for its point of view. But society had grown weary. Even before the end of the Thirty Years' War, Hugo Grotius (1583–1645) in 1625 had implied that since natural law is the basis of government, the church has no reason to meddle in state affairs. The Treaty of Westphalia represented stalemate rather than victory. People disdained the fulminations of Pope Innocent X against the settlement of the Thirty Years' War. Rather than emigrate, masses accepted whatever religion the prince professed, as if it did not matter. In England the religious strife of the 1600s terminated in the Act of Toleration, and in France, where repression prevailed, events led to the French Revolution. These developments symbolize what was occurring in Western culture. The old was no longer credible; its authority had been eroded.

Gradually the new outlook of the Age of Reason developed. Philosophy combined with studies of nature to open larger vistas and opportunities. New inventions made possible better tools of discovery, and people slowly became confident that the world was not a mysterious realm directed by the inscrutable will of God, but a realm of complex relationships subject to intelligible laws. To control the environment one had but to discover those laws. A future of progress and happiness beckoned; humanity had been liberated. It was the period of Enlightenment, *Aufklärung*. Human reason in league with science made dependence on God seemingly unnecessary. Human reason stood poised to unlock the mysteries of the universe. Former distrust of human reason and culture, as seen in the traditional emphases on depravity, original sin, predestination, and self-denial, gave way to confidence in reason, free will, and the ability to build a glorious future. Ecclesiastical claims seemed to recede into remote irrelevance.

René Descartes (1596–1650), a French Catholic who spent most of his life in the Netherlands, heralded the new age. In his *Discourse on Method* he caught the spirit of the time: "There is nothing so far removed from us as to be beyond our reach, or so hidden that we cannot discover it, provided only we abstain from accepting the false for the true, and always preserve in our thoughts the order necessary for the deduction of one truth from another." Trained by the Jesuits at La Flèche and introduced to higher studies at Paris, Descartes traveled widely and in 1629 settled in Holland, where his prowess in mathematics soon gained him a wide reputation. By elaborating algebraic formulas so that they could be applied to geometric figures and solids, he founded analytic geometry, and he conceived a desire to find in all fields of knowledge a certainty comparable to that of mathematics. In 1637 Descartes published his *Philosophical Essays* including his paradigmatic *Discourse on Method*, itself a preface to three treatises in which he first stated the law of light refraction and laid out the principles of analytic geometry. *Meditations on First Philosophy* and the *Principles of Philosophy*, in which he stated the law of inertia, followed in 1641 and 1644 respectively.

Descartes' standard was lofty: All conceptions must be doubted until adequately demonstrated, and adequate proof must have the certainty of mathematics. Everything was to be doubted—revelations, concepts about God, values, physical things, opinions. Such a stance threatened church and state, but Descartes believed that strenuous doubt was necessary to discover a clear and certain foundation on which to rest knowledge. From that he built step by step to truth. In the *Discourse* he says he was willing to doubt everything as we perceive it, since our senses so often deceive us. But he could not doubt that he was doubting: *Cogito, ergo sum*—I think, therefore I am. With this premise, Descartes proceeded to deduce the existence of God and the physical universe. To do so, he assumed other working presuppositions, the main one being that in experience as in mathematics whatever can be clearly and certainly conceived as part of a logically coherent whole is true. Thus Descartes "proved" the existence of God. The thinking ego finds outside itself the idea of God, which, argued Descartes, can be accounted for only on the assumption that an existing God causes our idea. Descartes added variations of the ontological argument of Anselm and the cosmological argument of Aquinas for the existence of God. The relationship between the thinking ego and the material world proved more difficult. However, Descartes concluded that mind and matter have their source and are united in God, and that matter was given extension and set in motion by God. Our world is a mechanistic universe, initially impelled by God, and human minds, akin to God's, can discover the laws that govern all substances in their mathematical order and regularity. Starting with "I think, therefore, I am," reason can unravel the mysteries of this ordered, intelligible universe. What proved significant was not so much the details of his philosophy as the assertion that we must doubt and that we have only to proceed carefully and logically to unlock the deepest mysteries of the universe. Utopia seemed not beyond human grasp.

Standing on the shoulders of many men before him—Copernicus, Kepler, Bacon, Galileo, and Descartes—was Sir Isaac Newton (1642–1727), who rose from yeoman rural heritage to knighthood and bequeathed to science some of its most basic concepts and methods. Despite becoming renowned and honored, he led a relatively quiet life, devoting his time to mathematics, physics, alchemy, and biblical chronology. With Leibniz he is credited with developing infinitesimal calculus and contributing basically to the knowledge of laws of motion and gravitation. In 1687 Newton published his *Mathematical Principles of Natural Philosophy*, commonly referred to in Latin as Newton's *Principia*. In it he explained how the motions of the heavens could be accounted for and postulated that gravitation was the attraction of particles of matter for each other with a force proportional to their masses and inversely proportional to the square of the distance between them; he also set forth his famous Four Rules of Reasoning, which became the model for future scientific investigations. The presupposition that we live in an orderly cause-and-effect universe underlay Newton's four rules: "Rule 1, Admit no more causes of natural things than such as are both true and sufficient to explain their appearances. Rule 2, To the same natural effects we must, as far as possible, assign the same causes. Rule 3, The qualities of bodies . . . which are found to belong to all bodies within the reach of our experiments, are to be esteemed the universal qualities of all bodies whatsoever. Rule 4, In experimental philosophy we are to look upon propositions collected by general induction from phenomena as accurate or very nearly true, not-withstanding any contrary hypotheses that may be imagined, till such time as other phenomena occur, by which they may be made more accurate, or liable to exceptions." Newton's rules and theories became immensely popular. A special translation of his Latin treatise appeared under the title, "Newtonianism for Ladies." Rendered credible by his own scientific discoveries, Newton helped open the way for a scientific understanding of phenomena and fostered a deistic, mechanical view of the universe that God supposedly created and set in motion to run by fixed laws. Reason was hailed as the glorified guide of humanity; the old authorities were denigrated. Wrote Alexander Pope, "Nature and nature's laws lay hid in night: God said, 'Let Newton be!' and all was Light." The keepers of religious revelation seemed to have less claim on truth than did the verifi-able, distinct, and clear reason possessed by all rational persons. Natural reason tended toward tolerance, toward a generalized ethical theism, to-ward skepticism of supernatural claims and miracles. Religious strife over unsubstantiated, diametrically opposite dogmas seemed anachronistic. Alexander Pope caught this mood when he wrote, "For modes of faith let graceless zealots fight"; and Voltaire when he said that the atheist laughs at dogmas "but he succors the indigent and defends the oppressed."

The systematic investigation of nature fired imagination. Discoveries bore out the contention that this is an intelligible world, and that one has only to apply reason to know and control the universe. Reason was idol-ized, even worshiped, as if it were the panacea for which all had been searching. The telescope enabled astronomers to observe the regularity of the moon, planets, and stars, causing Newton to exclaim, "This most beautiful system of the sun, planets and comets could proceed only from the counsel and dominion of an intelligent and powerful Being." The microscope revealed the cellular structure and sexuality of plants, and confirmed circulation of the blood. The barometer, new scales, and the thermometer refined scientific measurements; one could weigh air, and with a new air pump make a vacuum. Logarithms and slide rules simpli-fied complex mathematical problems. Fossils in layers of earth dated geo-logical time. Twenty-five of the earth's elements became known. The bones and muscles of the body were disclosed. Carl Linnaeus' *System of Nature,* 1735, classified everything as mineral, vegetable, or animal and introduced the refinements of class, order, genus, and species. Scientific academies were founded in Italy, England, France, Ireland, Austria, Prus-sia, Russia, Sweden, and Denmark. It was as if man had finally found the key that would unlock the doors to the mysteries of the universe, and the triumphs of reason were celebrated in Abbé St. Pierre's *Observations on the Continual Progress of Universal Reason,* 1737; the French encyclopedists' *Dictionnaire universel,* 1751–65; and Marquis de Condorcet's *Progress of the Human Mind,* 1795.

Inevitably, this burst of new knowledge and the rationalistic phi-losophy that accompanied it affected religion. Dependence on God, the

Bible, and revelation seemed anachronistic. Lord Herbert of Cherbury's studies of other religions led him to deny revelation and to conclude that all religions have basic similarities, that through comparison the essential parts of all religions can be discovered. In *De Veritate*, 1624, he enumerated five such essentials: God exists, he should be worshiped, virtue is a part of worship, repentance for wrongdoing is a duty, and rewards and punishments await us in the next life. Archbishop Usher refused Lord Herbert communion when he lay dying, but later the Deists accepted him as one of the great forerunners of reasonable, universal, natural religion.

John Locke (1632–1704) profoundly affected politics, philosophy, and religion. His ideas on human liberty were embodied in the Glorious Revolution and the Act of Toleration in 1689, and his thoughts on religion provided a bridge to the natural religion of Deism. As a politician, Locke vigorously defended toleration. He believed in a state church and remained in full communion with the Church of England until he died, but he thought that the creed of a national church should be broad enough to accommodate different views, and that Christianity should not be promoted by force. His *Letters Concerning Toleration* (1689–92) show that he would allow latitudinarian practices, so long as people believed in God, sought to obey him, and looked for punishment and reward beyond this life. Such beliefs, he felt, undergirded social organization. He would not tolerate atheists for this reason, and thought that Roman Catholicism could not be tolerated because of its intolerance and subservience to a foreign overlord.

Educated for the ministry, Locke turned to science and then to politics, and filled his last years writing about religion. In 1667 he became secretary to the earl of Shaftesbury, and was deeply involved in anti-Charles, anti-James politics. In 1683 he fled to Holland, and in 1689 returned a celebrity. In *Two Treatises on Civil Government*, 1690, Locke argued for limited parliamentary government. He rejected inherited divine right rule, maintained that men have inalienable rights to life, liberty, and property, and insisted that the primary responsibility of government is to safeguard these rights. Men have the duty to resist or even to overthrow tyrants who destroy these rights. Such thoughts coalesced with rationalism and Calvinistic theories of resistance.

Locke's *Essay Concerning Human Understanding*, 1690, depicted the human mind as having the ability to intuit logically evident truths without being able to prove them. The mind at birth is a *tabula rasa*, a blank slate, upon which sensations leave impressions that the mind organizes into knowledge. Such knowledge through the senses is never absolute or final, but it is probable and reasonable. It is not logically demonstrable, but since it is not logically contradictory either, one can assent to it with probable reasons. In this way Locke could argue for the existence of God from cause and effect, demonstrate morality, and speak of the reasonableness of Christianity. In 1695 he published his *Reasonableness of Christianity*, maintaining that nothing in Christianity is inherently incredible or improbable. He explored the New Testament and concluded that Christianity is beautifully simple, harmonious, and reasonable in what it demands that we believe and do. The ethical injunctions of Christianity, the revelation of Christ as Messiah, and the miracles are not necessarily in disharmony with reason. He admitted, however, that dogmas cannot be proved. Locke did not want to dispense with revelation, but others carried his religious views much further.

John Toland (1670–1722) issued his highly controversial *Christianity Not Mysterious* in 1696. His purpose was to show "that there is nothing in the Gospel contrary to reason, nor above it, and that no Christian doctrine can be properly called a mystery." Nothing is above the comprehension of reason, not even God, and contrary contentions can be shown to be absurdities. We can have no idea of anything contrary to and above reason. Self-interested professionals introduced mysteries into Christianity, he wrote, to secure privileges and powers for themselves. Such mysteries surround Baptism and the Lord's Supper, Toland maintained. Let them be discarded for what is reasonable. He believed in Christ not because of any authority inherent in Christ, but because he could form a "clear conception" of what Christ said. Reason superseded Christ. Toland, an Irishman, had converted to Protestantism at the age of sixteen. His book aroused so much anger in Ireland that he was forced to flee to avoid imprisonment. On order of the Irish House of Commons, his book was burned by the public hangman, and one representative wanted its ashes deposited where he could trample them every day. As many as 115 replies to the book appeared. Toland's crime was the elevation of reason to a place of supremacy. His stance threatened ecclesiasticism and even the state, for Toland had dared to assert not that Christianity is reasonable in Locke's sense, but that reason is the infallible judge of what shall be regarded as revelation and truth.

Locke and Toland represent the beginning of Deism, which subordinated Scripture and tradition to reason and emphasized a reasonable ethic as the end product of religion. This reduction of everything to the primacy of reason instigated controversies throughout the eighteenth century.

In 1730 Matthew Tindal (1657–1733) asserted in *Christianity as Old as the Creation* that we need only natural religion, that God has given to all the ability to apprehend it. A perfect, universal, and immutable God is the source of both natural and revealed religion, and what God has given cannot be increased or decreased. Natural religion is God's original gift to us; it is complete. The Bible is a "republication" of natural religion, and Jesus is to be honored only as an example of how all can conform to God's will. True Christianity is not new; it is as old as creation, for God revealed himself fully in his creation. The law of nature preceded revealed law, which can add nothing to natural law. We can discover in nature all that is required of us and do it. God's gift to us for discerning law is reason, wrote Tindal, and if a thing is contrary to reason, that thing is the product of obsolescent superstition. Reason is the judge of what is reasonable. On this basis Tindal would discard the biblical miracles as superstitions, insulting to the perfectly ordered, mechanical laws that the divine Creator has set going. Reason, not the superstition added by spurious revelation, and certainly not some supposed impotency because of sin, is to guide us. This was Deism—God established an orderly universe, he gave us reason to discern and live by what he had done, and he made no further revelation.

Advocates of Deism blossomed in Germany. Christian Wolff (1679–1754), whom the pietists forced to leave Halle in 1723 or be hanged, attempted to demonstrate some deistic contentions mathematically. Herman S. Reimarus (1694–1768) openly defended natural religion, and in the *Wolfenbüttel Fragments* flatly rejected miracles, saying that the biblical writers were guilty of conscious fraud and fanaticism. The great miracle and revelation is our world; in natural religion one can find the existence of God, basic morality, and immortality. No more is needed, said Reimarus. Like Tindal, both Wolff and Reimarus made the Bible unnecessary.

Gotthold E. Lessing (1729–81) embodied rationalistic ideals in two influential works, *Nathan the Wise*, 1779, and *The Education of the Human Race*, 1780. The former is a play about an incredibly tolerant, enlightened Jew who regards various religions as but different ways to moral perfection, with no religion having absolute superiority. *The Education of the Human Race* places mankind in the third of three stages of education. The childhood stage was that of the Old Testament with its guidelines buttressed by promises of rewards and punishments. The youth stage was that of the New Testament with its ideals of self-surrender and sacrifice. The present manhood stage is geared to the demands and responsibilities of reason. Lessing thus denigrated the Bible and elevated reason; the guidelines of the Bible are childish, those of reason, mature.

In France, François-Marie Arouet de Voltaire (1694–1778) championed Deism. Educated by the Jesuits, whom he thoroughly hated, and hoping to see the last king strangled in the bowels of the last priest, he turned against all oppressive authority. Twice he was put in the Bastille. In exile in London, from 1726 to 1729, he appropriated the deistic rationalism that informed practically all his later works. With acrid wit and caustic satire, in his numerous essays, plays, philosophical works, novels, and poems Voltaire attacked the clergy, church, Bible, creeds, hypocrisy, greed, injustice, and even Joan of Arc. He was not an atheist, however, for he believed acceptance of God's existence and personal immortality were necessary bulwarks of government. He abhorred Roman Catholicism as a massive deceit, bitterly scoring it for exploitation, superstition, intolerance, and persecution. He and his fellow *philosophes* drew on Locke and Newton to frame theories of nature and society that they believed would eventually rejuvenate all of life, destroy hypocrisies, and unify all knowledge. So said the preface to the thirty-five volumes of the French encyclopaedia to which Voltaire contributed. Most important among his books were *Candide*, 1759, *Tancrede*, 1760, and *Philosophical Dictionary*, 1764.

Deism was still popular in the late eighteenth century, voiced in America by Thomas Jefferson and Thomas Paine, but it had already been dealt heavy blows by Law, Butler, Hume and Kant. Even though the French Revolution officially enshrined the Worship of Reason, the most vigorous phase of Deism had passed. Few arguments of the *philosophes* were new; they were critics rather than creators. In the nineteenth century Deism continued in other forms, particularly in liberalism. If reason was not the whole truth, neither was it untruth.

From the beginning rationalism had its opponents. Even within rationalistic circles, some drew conclusions that others would not. The world may be a machine whose parts we can classify and control, but not all were willing to draw the conclusions of Gottfried Wilhelm Leibniz (1646–1716) in his *Monadology*, published in 1720. Leibniz theorized that the world is made up of monads, each independent, but working in "preestablished harmony" with the others like so many clocks wound up by God and keeping time together. "This is the best of all possible worlds," he declared, and evil is a necessary part of the ordered whole that we do not yet understand. Alexander Pope in his *Essay on Man*, 1733, drew a similar conclusion when he wrote:

> All are but parts of one stupendous Whole,
> Whose body Nature is, and God the soul;
> . . . .
> All Nature is but Art unknown to thee;
> All Chance, Direction, which thou canst not see;
> All Discord, Harmony not understood;
> All partial Evil, universal Good:
> And spite of Pride, in erring Reason's spite,
> One truth is clear, *Whatever is, is right.*

Voltaire subjected this conclusion to merciless ridicule in *Candide*. The reasoning of the rationalists did not always coincide.

Blaise Pascal (1623–62), himself a brilliant mathematician and critic of Jesuit casuistry (see Chapter 15), felt that there was a dimension in religion far beyond the comprehension of human reason. In 1654 he had an ecstatic conversion experience, and in a burst of rapture wrote: "Fire! God of Abraham, God of Isaac, God of Jacob, not of the philosophers and savants." He regarded reason as a glorious gift: "Man is but a reed, the weakest in nature, but he is a thinking reed. . . . Were the universe to crush him, man would still be more noble than that which kills him, because he knows that he dies; and the universe knows nothing of the advantage it has over him." But finite reason can grasp only a small part of the vast universe in which we dwell. Pascal could not deify the powers of reason. Epistemologically speaking, the intuited presuppositions of reason have no more to commend them than the presuppositions of faith, and reason should not arrogantly demand proof of faith's first principles without proof of its own first principles. Reason is not the only instructor, for "the heart has its reasons that reason does not understand." Pascal was keenly aware of human greatness and smallness and could not optimistically write off sin as if it were some small error or ignorance. Eight years after he died, Pascal's fragmented *Pensées* (*Thoughts*) were collected and published. They called attention to human finitude, and greatly influenced existentialists later, but in the Age of Reason, Pascal's *Pensées* did not curb the optimistic progress of rationalism.

Still another enemy of the "general religion of nature" was Jonathan Swift (1667–1745), widely known as the author of *Gulliver's Travels*. In 1708 he published his *Argument Against Abolishing Christianity*, a biting satire in which he called attention to primordial human selfishness, which the rationalists tended to gloss over. William Law in 1731 penned a heated reply to Tindal under the title of *The Case of Reason, or Natural Religion,* in which he laid bare the incongruities and shortcomings of the rationalists.

Deism lost much of its punch when Joseph Butler blunted its arguments, and when David Hume's philosophy exposed its inherent skepticism and motivated Immanuel Kant to write his monumental critiques of reason. Butler's *Analogy of Religion,* 1736, shows the influence of Deism and at the same time a powerful reaction. He freely admitted the Deist argument that God exists and that the course of nature is uniform, but sought to curtail the growing ridicule of traditional Christianity by showing that reason is limited finally to probability and that there is just as much probability for saying the tenets of Christianity are true as for saying the tenets for natural religion are true. The same objections can be raised against both, but for this reason they need not be discarded for "probability is the very guide of life." Since the same objections can be raised against both, it is probable that they both have the same author. On the basis of probability Butler drew his analogies. Conduct now influences happiness, so it is probable that conduct will also influence the future and that the one orderer of the universe will punish and reward in proportion to vice and virtue. Since continuance is a mark of this world, it is probable that there is continuance beyond death. Revelation is not impossible for an infinite Being, and the prophecies, miracles, and deaths of the early martyrs attest its probability, even though one cannot demonstrate it. The book was immensely popular and was made required reading in many universities and seminaries in England and America.

Deism and orthodoxy both suffered under the withering attack of David Hume (1711–76), for Hume argued convincingly that cause-and-effect relationships are the products of custom and that miracles that go against the massive, observed regularity of nature are more apt to be products of faulty reporting than an actual alteration of universal uniformity in nature. Hume's *Treatise of Human Nature,* 1739; *Philosophical Essays,* 1748; *Natural History of Religion,* 1757; and *Dialogues Concerning Natural Religion,* published posthumously, 1779, made him the foremost British philosopher of his century. All our knowledge comes from experience, Hume maintained. We receive it in isolated bits via impressions on the human mind. Ideas are but faded copies of impressions. We can know the relation between ideas with logical certainty, but we cannot know actual reality with anything more than probability. Concepts of cause and effect do not come from logic, but from custom. Our minds are simply by habit accustomed to inferring causal connections in the natural world because certain things are observed in association. The existence of God cannot be proved by the causal argument of reason. Nor can the existence of the physical world be proved, though practical necessity forces us to accept it. But Hume went still further. He denied that there is any permanent "I" behind experience. Thus Hume shook the world of science and metaphysics and left no philosophical basis for immortality. In his "Essay on Miracles," which was part of the *Philosophical Essays,* Hume argued that miracles are so unlikely as to be impossible. All knowledge comes from experience, and experience informs us of the uniformity of nature, the tides, the movements of the sun, the seasons, birth and death, and so forth. The report of a miracle must offset this experienced regularity in nature, and in every case, e.g., resurrection from the dead, it is much more likely that the report is false or that the reporters are deceived or deceivers than it is that the uniform course of nature has been interrupted. In his *Dialogues* Hume showed that the arguments of natural theology for the existence of God by analogies or by *a priori* propositions are invalid, for the infinite cannot be inferred from the finite, and existence cannot be demonstrated as necessary. Hume does not say God does not exist; he simply argues that God's existence cannot be established by rational arguments or by inferences drawn from sense experience. Hume left all knowledge in the shambles of skepticism; neither science nor religion has indubitable foundations.

This was the legacy that confronted Immanuel Kant (1724–1804), the most profound of all the thinkers of the Age of Reason. His ideas set in motion concepts and trends with which thinkers still struggle. He was born and died in Königsberg in East Prussia, and was so regular in his habits that housewives set their clocks by his walks. Yet from this obscure scholar came treatises that have affected culture as profoundly as did Plato and Aristotle. He was not content to let science and morality flounder in the skepticism that Hume had promulgated. So he set forth his theory of knowledge. At age 57, in 1781, Kant startled the scholarly world with his *Critique of Pure Reason*. We have knowledge of the external world of nature via sensations imparted to the mind by our five senses. We experience these sensations in terms of the mind's forms of time and space and the twelve categories. These forms and categories are mechanisms whereby the mind organizes sense data. We have knowledge of phenomena and of sensations that the mind has organized, but no knowledge of noumena or of anything-in-itself. Consequently, our knowledge of nature is limited. It is no more absolute than our intimations of divine things, although the verifiability of sensations makes the knowledge with which science deals seem firmer than the intimations of morality, which because they are of a different nature seem vague and ungrounded by comparison. Kant effectively confined all knowledge to the realm of space and time; man cannot have knowledge of anything beyond space and time, beyond pure reason. This theory of knowledge placed traditional religious concepts and values beyond pure reason.

However, people have practical as well as pure reason. In the *Critique of Practical Reason,* 1788, and *Critique of Judgment,* 1790, Kant explored moral decisions. Practical reason convinces us that we have moral personality, freedom, and immortality. Such postulated convictions are not absolute, as the knowledge of pure reason is not absolute, and we may not in this life fully realize these moral convictions, but we must live by these convictions if life is to make sense. Kant expressed humanity's sense of moral necessity in his categorical imperative, which is present intuitively in everyone's practical reason: "So act in all things as if the maxim of your action by your will were to become a universal law of nature." The categorical imperative tells us to act in all things as if what we willed were to become universal law for all. Thus, we are not to murder for a sense of duty to murder would destroy us. On the basis of the categorical impera- tive Kant developed his ethics. Kant believed the moral law was necessary for life to make any sense at all. Practical reason demands it, and de- mands even more to escape ultimate senselessness, namely his famous postulates of freedom, immortality, and God. Without such postulates, Kant maintained, living ultimately becomes meaningless. Vice ought to be punished and virtue rewarded, yet in this life the opposite is often the case. Unless life is to be left for each individual in an utterly meaningless condition, argued Kant, there must be freedom for ethical choices, im- mortality so that vice and virtue may finally receive their just deserts, and a God to guarantee all this.

In *Religion Within the Limits of Reason Alone,* 1793, Kant applied his philosophy to religion and constructed an ethic in which the moral law is primary. Evil comes into the world through an unexplained subjective human propensity to deviate from the moral law. This propensity is seen in the frailty of our nature, impurity of heart, and downright wickedness. It chooses self-love over moral law, yet despite this choice, the evil person is still drawn by the moral law and can actualize it. Evil and the categorical imperative vie for human obedience. Jesus was for Kant an example of one in whom the categorical imperative prevailed. In this treatise, Kant reduced religion to the categorical imperative and those necessary laws and laudable practices that could be deduced from it. All else is "mere religious illusion and pseudo-service of God." Consequently, Kant de- prived the church and Scripture of any distinctive place in religion and rejected many rites and actions (including prayer and the Lord's Supper, except for fellowship) for which people claimed supernatural benefits beyond the world of reason. Natural religion was Kant's religion within the limits of reason.

Kant's impact confined religion largely to subjectively derived ethics and deprecated the historical continuity of the experience of the Christian community of faith. His overall impact was to open the floodgates to relativism. This was never intended by Kant, for he specifically set out to combat the skepticism of Hume. But in doing so, he not only demon- strated the confinement of all knowledge to the world of space and time, but he also made the knowledge of pure reason and the intimations of practical reason subjective. We never know reality; our knowledge of nature is always relative. And unless we accept reason as some kind of absolute, the postulates of freedom, immortality, and God become so much wishful hypothesizing. In science, where one might reasonably ex- pect to find agreement on reality and truth, one finds increasingly more fluidity and uncertainty. Even the forms of space and time and the twelve categories in each mind are conditioned and sensitized by all the psycho- logical, environmental, sociological, and metaphysical factors in the hu- man situation. In the realm of values this is even more pronounced. Reason may demand the postulates of freedom, immortality, and God, but the postulates are unverifiable, and the demands of reason and ulti- mate reality are not necessarily the same. Kant thus introduced subjective relativism not only on the level of knowledge but also on the level of ultimate reference.

Two eminent disciples of Kant drew opposite conclusions about reality or what is behind everything. G. W. F. Hegel (1770–1831) discarded the idea that things-in-themselves are not knowable and declared that behind reality is the Absolute Spirit or Reason, which is in a cosmic process of coming to be. Using a scheme of thesis, antithesis, and synthesis, he traced this process of coming to be through history and phenomena. No expression of the Absolute Spirit is complete, so every thesis gives rise to an antithesis, and the synthesis of the two becomes a new thesis in an on-going process. Finally all differentiations will be reconciled, and the Absolute Spirit will be embodied. One gets the impression that the final embodiment will be in the German nation and more particularly in Hegel himself. Hegel thought the Absolute Spirit found its highest expression in philosophy and that it achieved only a figurative expression in religion, symbolized by abstract ideas of the Father (thesis), the incarnate Son (antithesis), and the return of the Absolute to itself in the Holy Spirit (synthesis). Hegel believed he had found the key to all truth, and his method has had great influence.

Arthur Schopenhauer (1788–1860) in *The World as Will and Idea*, 1818, maintained that the thing-in-itself, the reality behind everything, is a great irrational Will, that this phenomenal world is a mammoth illusion, a mirage. Chairs, tomatoes, birds, and people do not really exist. All are blind objectifications of the Will. The best thing for us is simply to cease to be, to stop all desire and thus to end our sufferings and our being and become one again with the indiscriminate Will. We are like bubbles on some giant glob and the best thing for us is to burst and settle back into the glob. The bubble of existence is illusion.

Karl Marx (1818–83) dispensed with the transcendent reference in Hegel and posited the triumph of dialectical materialism in the classless society. In accepting revolution and totalitarianism until conditions are right for the perfect classless society, he along with Friedrich Nietzsche (1844–1900) built bridges to modern times, plagued with both relativism and nihilism. Nietzsche proclaimed the death of God, "exposing" the old values of love, humility, and kindness as inverted substitutes for might, and "enthroning" might as the governing factor in all human relationships. Nietzsche thus articulated the meaninglessness that has spread its mantle over modern life. This was one side of the influence of the Age of Reason; liberalism in its many forms was another. The Age of Reason can be dated, but its legacy has not terminated. Perhaps more than anything else it has led to questions about sovereignty. Who can finally determine what is right and wrong?

PIETISM

The historical challenge to the Age of Reason was pietism. Pietism was, like the Enlightenment, a reaction to the persecution, fanaticism, and destruction that accompanied so much of orthodox Catholicism and Protestantism, and, like the Enlightenment, it knew no national or denominational boundaries, but there the similarity to natural religion ended. Pietism represented a feeling that the very heart of religion had been all but lost in a maze of intellectualizing, dogmatizing, and conventionalizing. It was characterized by a Bible-centered moralism, a keen sense of human guilt and the forgiveness possible through Christ, personal conversion, a practical holiness of prayer and devotion, warm concern for the common needs of people, and an emotional outpouring of feelings and aspirations in hymns. Biblical exegesis, in-depth scholarship, and intellectual prowess were not among its strong points. For the pietists religion was not something reserved for the experts and the authorities; it had to be felt inwardly in a kind of ecstasy and expressed outwardly in good works and pious devotions. Pietism called Christians to manifest in their everyday lives the living presence of Christ within. It was a reaction to abstract formalism and creeds. It sought to make religion intensely personal and individualistic.

Among its earliest leaders was George Fox (1624–91), who in his *Journal* tells us that in 1643 "at the command of God" he left his relatives and friends and began his protest against formal religiosity and open licentiousness. He wandered about England seeking an "opening from the Lord," realizing by what he saw and heard that neither priests, nor dissenters, nor separatists had what his heart longed for—a sincere, simple manifestation of genuine Christianity. In 1647 he felt called by the Lord to preach and to trust in the inner light. Stormy years began for Fox. With rude boldness he interrupted religious services to witness to what he had experienced, only repeatedly to be thrown in jail, stoned, shipped, and haled out of town. At Launceston, he and some of his followers were thrust into the lower Doomsdale level of a jail where the excrement of former inmates came to the tops of their shoes. When they lighted straw to dispel the stench, the jailor took pots of excrement of thieves confined above and poured it through the grating. Fox's earnestness, magnetic personality, and moral integrity impressed many, and gradually his followers developed into the Society of Friends, organized in 1668, often called Quakers because the Spirit sometimes caused them to quake. Fox's missionary journeys carried him into Ireland, the West Indies, North America, and Holland. Everywhere he was persecuted. His message was inimical to privileged ecclesiasticism and state sovereignty.

Fox's vivid *Journal* was not published until 1694, but in 1675 Robert Barclay, an educated disciple of Fox, published his *Apology for the True Christian Divinity* to explain and vindicate Quaker principles and doctrines. According to Barclay the Quakers trusted in the revelation of the Spirit. "The testimony of the Spirit is that alone by which the true knowledge of God hath been, is, and can be only revealed. . . . Moreover, these divine inward revelations, which we make absolutely necessary for the building up of true faith, neither do nor can ever contradict the outward testimony of the Scriptures, or right and sound reason," yet revelations of the Spirit, said Barclay, are not to be tested by either Scripture or the natural reason of man as if the latter two were in some way superior. From the Spirit have come the Scriptures, prophecies, and the revelation of Christ as the foundation of all knowledge. From the Spirit comes rescue from the degeneracy of the Fall. The Spirit is bestowed on everyone and, if not resisted, will bring forth holiness, righteousness, and purity. Those who are led by the Spirit may and should preach without human commission, "without hire or bargaining," but may receive gifts for necessities. The Spirit, not human convenience, is to direct worship. Baptism is "a pure and spiritual thing," and communion is "inward and spiritual." Consequently the Quakers rejected ministry, external baptism, communion, and set forms of worship. No one is to force the conscience of others; rather, one is to reject all killing, banishing, fining, and imprisoning. And no one is to use conscience as an excuse to destroy his neighbor's life or estate. "Seeing the chief end of all religion is to redeem man from the spirit and vain conversation of this world, and to lead into inward communion with God," the Quakers rejected vain customs and habits "such as taking off the hat to a man, bowing and cringing of the body, . . . unprofitable plays, frivolous recreations, sportings and gamings which . . . divert the mind from the witness of God in the heart." Fox railed against ribbons and lace, costly apparel, junketing and feasting, wakes, shows, lying, and oaths, saying, however, that his religion lay not in these but in the Spirit, which led him to shun all frivolity, including art and music.

The Quakers stressed the brotherhood and equality of all. They were among the first to protest slavery, barbarous prison conditions, and inequality for women, and have become noted for their anti-militarism, educational work, philanthropy, democracy, honesty in trade, and toleration. However, the subjective nature of the inner light has also engendered schism and opened the way to the uncertainties of relativism.

In the same year as Barclay's *Apology*, in 1675, Philip Jacob Spener (1635–1705), a Lutheran, published his *Pia Desideria* (*Devout Wishes*). In it he pleaded with Christians to take their religion seriously, and to reinstate an all-believers' priesthood of service. Spener was born thirteen years before the end of the Thirty Years' War. He knew the demoralizing effects of that struggle and longed for a renaissance of moral earnestness in Germany. The Lutheran ministry had grown lax, subservient to the government, status-conscious, almost exclusively concerned with dogmatic orthodoxy. Unchecked drunkenness and licentiousness pervaded both clergy and laity. Concentration on right belief with no accompanying piety did not satisfy Spener.

One influence on Spener came from the followers of Jean de Labadie (1610–74), the Labadists, a communistically organized pietistic group that sought to appropriate the teachings of the Bible through the immediate inspiration of the Holy Spirit. Labadie, a French ex-Jesuit, joined the Reformed Church in 1650 and later withdrew to organize the followers attracted by his preaching along the Rhine River. They rejected infant baptism, seldom celebrated the Lord's Supper, held property in common, worked as manual laborers, and said marriage with an unregenerate person was not binding.

But Spener's chief influence came from reading Luther's 1520 essays and his preface to the German mass. He believed a serious commitment to Luther's idea of the spiritual priesthood of all believers would supersede a self-serving clergy and revivify the church. While a pastor at Frankfort, Spener organized small groups that met in his home for Bible reading, prayer, and discussion of sermons. He felt that a few dedicated Christians would influence others and eventually alter the outlook of the entire state church. The uplift experienced in these groups, known as *collegia pietatis*, prompted the writing of the *Pia Desideria*. In it Spener emphasized six proposals: intense Bible study to promote personal devotion; the lay fulfillment of priesthood in "fraternal admonition and correction" not only of other laity but of the clergy; an emphasis on love as well as intellectualism in religion; a seeking of truth rather than victory in theological arguments; a reorganization of the universities with higher standards of morality for professors and students; and a revival of evangelical preaching. Two years later a separate tract on spiritual priesthood stressed that all Christians are ministers although "to exercise the office publicly in the congregation before all and over all requires a special call," that all Christians have a duty to study the Bible and test the preached word against it, and that all are to avoid even the semblance of doing evil. Under attack for views that some believed would lead to schism, Spener left Frankfurt in 1686 to become court preacher at Dresden, where he encountered further opposition from the established clergy and the universities of Leipsic and Wittenberg. In 1691 he went to Berlin, where he preached with obvious success, only to be charged in 1695 by the theological faculty at Wittenberg with 284 errors. His urging the laity to study the Bible and fraternally admonish the clergy, and his insistence that right feeling was as important in religion as right doctrine, threatened the orthodox clergy and their assumed authority.

Although widely excoriated, Spener won the support of many pastors, notably of Paul Gerhardt (1607–76), who incorporated pietistic ideals in his hymns, and August Hermann Francke (1663–1727), whose educational and social ideals permanently affected pietism. Francke, Spener's most famous disciple, began his *Collegia Philobiblica* in 1689 at Leipsic. Opposition to his devotional exposition of the Bible cost him his post, both at Leipsic and at Erfurt, but in 1692 won for him a position at the newly founded University of Halle and a pastorate nearby. For more than three decades Francke dominated Halle, imbuing the university curriculum with pietism, training and placing up to two hundred ministerial graduates each year in the German church. He also established widely imitated social models—an Orphan House, a school for the poor, a Bible institute, a Latin school, publishing house, dispensary, and subsidiary enterprises. Contributions came from all over Europe to sustain his projects, especially after he published *The Marvellous Footsteps of Divine Providence*, 1707, in which he told of "miraculous" answers to prayers. Under his supervision literally thousands of children received instruction in pietism. Many entered the clergy and many became missionaries. When Frederick IV (1699–1730) of Denmark sought Protestant missionaries for India, he chose two of Francke's students—Bartholomäus Ziegenbalg and Heinrich Plutchau. Christian Friedrich Schwartz (1726–98), the most noted of the sixty missionaries who went out from Halle in the eighteenth century, labored for forty-eight years in India.

Pietism stirred the church in Germany to new seriousness, devotional zeal, biblical study, and an awareness of Christianity's social obligations. But pietism tended to reduce religion to a narrow ethical mold, it neglected intellectual pursuits despite its university ties, and it did not stem the tide of rationalism. By 1750 Halle pietism in Germany had reached its zenith.

But pietism was by no means confined to Halle and the Quakers. It had devotees in Roman Catholicism, and was virtually identified with Moravianism and Methodism. Its appeal was broad, suggesting a universal need that neither orthodoxy nor rationalism satisfied. Miguel de Molinos (1627–96), a Spanish priest and noted confessor and spiritual director in Rome, published his controversial *Spiritual Guide* in 1675. In it he posed guidelines that would eventually lead to transformation and union with God. Although more quietistic and mystical than evangelical, Molinos denigrated the externals of religion to bring the individual into an intimate fellowship with God, into a state of bliss in which the soul "desires nothing, not even its own salvation, and fears nothing, not even hell." Some nuns discarded their rosaries and images, and even abandoned vocalized prayer. Suspected by the Jesuits and Dominicans of unorthodoxy and immorality, Molinos was finally condemned and sentenced in 1687 to life imprisonment for having written sixty-eight "heretical, suspicious, erroneous, scandalous, blasphemous, and offensive" propositions. Madame de Guyon (1648–1717), a follower of Molinos, was very popular in France, for a while, and published her *Short and Easy Method of Prayer* in 1685, claiming that a divine Penman directed her hand as she wrote. Repeatedly arrested, she was finally condemned by the Pope and imprisoned for seven years.

More direct exponents of pietism were the Moravians and the Methodists. When German-speaking Bohemian Brethren from Moravia sought refuge in 1722 at Herrnhut on the Saxon estates of Count Zinzendorf (1700–60), Spener's godson, Zinzendorf, soon became their spiritual leader and dreamed of making the Moravians a *collegia pietatis* within the Lutheran Church. The Herrnhut settlement resembled a monastery in the centrality of its religious focus, good works, strict morals, and industry. The children, like those at the Halle Orphan House, were reared and trained apart from parental supervision. In opposition to Lutheran orthodoxy and rationalism, Zinzendorf stressed a "religion of the heart," excessive intimate fellowship with Jesus, the felt emotional experience of conversion, and Sermon-on-the-Mount ethics. In 1727 the community was stirred with missionary impulses and subsequently dispatched missionaries to the West Indies, Greenland, North America, Guiana, Egypt, South Africa, Labrador, Holland, England, and the Baltic States, thus inaugurating the modern missionary movement. Exiled from Saxony in 1736, Zinzendorf came to America and gave the name Bethlehem to the Moravian settlement in Pennsylvania. The Moravians expressed their evangelical piety not only in good works but also in Christ-mysticism, hymns, and liturgy. The emphasis on feeling found expression later in Schleiermacher and strongly influenced Lutheranism, but opposition forced Zinzendorf to organize a separate religious communion.

Although "pietistic" does not adequately characterize John Wesley (1703–91), pietism was significant in Wesley's inheritance and outlook, and Methodism is aptly described as the greatest expression of pietism in the eighteenth century.

The Moravians at Herrnhut directly affected the Wesleyan movement in England. It was the Moravian missionary Spangenberg who confronted John Wesley in Savannah, Georgia, with "Do you know Christ?"—to which Wesley gave an evasive answer. And it was the Moravian missionary Peter Böhler who taught Wesley that true faith meant "dominion over sin, constant peace, and a sense of forgiveness," and at Aldersgate, May 24, 1738, Wesley found the assurance of salvation that he had been seeking. His "heart was strangely warmed." It was to Herrnhut that Wesley went for reassurance and inspiration.

But Wesley drew his pietism from other sources as well. Long before he encountered the Moravians, Wesley was a student of the early Fathers, particularly Macarius, a Syrian monk, who posed devotion as the way and perfection as the goal of Christian life. Puritanism loomed large in Wesley's family background and a strict morality akin to Calvin's was evident in the Wesley societies and Wesley's own conduct. His mother, Susanna Wesley, instilled strict rules of conduct in the hearts of her eighteen children. Equally strong pietistic influences came from Thomas à Kempis' *Christian Patterns* and from Jeremy Taylor's *Rule and Exercise for Holy Living and Holy Dying*, which urged people to prepare themselves for heaven by living sober, just, and godly lives. A little later came William Law's *Serious Call to a Devout and Holy Life* and his *Treatise on Perfection* challenging Christians to order every aspect of their lives according to God's will. These pietistic strands figured heavily in Wesley's 1725 vow to give his "whole life and heart to God" and in the Holy Club at Oxford, where methodical devotions and scheduling caused Wesley and his friends to be called Methodists. His disastrous trip to America in 1735 to missionize the Indians was actually an attempt to save his own soul.

Wesley took many of his precepts from these pietistic sources. But Wesley was independent; he excluded those elements that did not suit his purposes. In particular, he rejected the mystical element in William Law and Zinzendorf. In their mysticism he sensed a nascent antinomianism. When the Moravian Philip Molther brought the "stillness" phase of theology to the Fetter Lane Society in 1739, Wesley parted company with the Moravians in the following year and organized his own group of committed believers at the Foundry in Moorfields. To avoid any semblance of trust in human works, the "still" men argued that a person should wait for the full assurance of faith from God, that any lesser faith was no faith, and that absolutely nothing should be done in preparation for full faith such as reading the Bible, praying, or taking communion. Any such activity, they said, was of the devil, a seeking of salvation by works. The Aldersgate experience was denigrated as nothing. Wesley believed the "stillness" theology to be "flatly contrary to the Word of God." He ridiculed Dionysius the Areopagite, a favorite among the Moravians at the time, as super-essential, mystic darkness. Spangenberg assumed leadership of the Fetter Lane Society, and in 1745 the Moravians advertised that they had no connection with

Wesley and his brother Charles. No amount of persuasion from Spangenberg, Böhler, and Zinzendorf could alter Wesley's conviction. He strongly believed that faith has degrees, that it grows as it is expressed in love and that the fullness of faith, perfection in love, develops gradually. Justification by faith meant forgiveness of sins and newness of life displayed in acts of love toward others. For Wesley the two went together. The freedom of faith was from sin, not from works of God. Justification by faith alone was not an invitation to antinomianism, which Wesley perceived to be inherent in the "stillness" theology.

As the Moravians during their "sifting time" drifted more and more into antinomianism (later rejected), Wesley penned tract after tract against them. He accused the antinomians of asserting that no repentance need precede saving faith, that naked faith alone is necessary to eternal salvation, and that good works need not be preached before or after faith. Their six pillars, he said, were that Christ abolished the law, Christians have no obligation to keep the law, liberty is freedom from keeping the commandments of God, assent to a biblical commandment or prohibition is bondage, the ordinances of God and good works are not necessary for believers, and believers should not be exhorted to good works. According to Wesley, some antinomians claimed they had a right to all goods and all women. Two of Wesley's earliest and ablest workers, Thomas Maxfield and George Bell, appropriated antinomianism on the basis that if Christ's righteousness is imputed to us, we need none of our own. Wesley's *A Blow at the Root*, 1762, insisted that Christians must live to God and walk as Christ walked.

In 1740 John Wesley also parted company with the Calvinists, who stressed election, as if the possibility of salvation for any but a select few had been closed by a decision of God before the world was created. Wesley was close to Calvinist George Whitefield (1714–70), who was a member of the Holy Club at Oxford and who persuaded Wesley to take up field preaching, but the publication of Wesley's sermon on "Free Grace" in 1740 brought dissension and separation of the two except for occasional contacts. Wesley believed in the sovereignty of God, but he did not accept extreme election and predestination. He believed not only that antinomianism lurked in such a stance but also that it attenuated if indeed it did not obliterate the work of Christ. Christ died for all, said Wesley; his grace is free for all, not just for those predestined, not just for a certain few. If God has already damned some and saved others, then all preaching is in vain and what one does makes no difference. Wesley quoted biblical passages to show that Christ offered salvation to all and that man has the power to respond to or resist the Spirit. In 1770 Wesley denounced Calvinism as a "poison to faith," and in 1778 deliberately published *The Arminian Magazine* to symbolize his antipredestination. The death of Christ for all is a theme repeatedly incorporated in the 539 hymns collected for the use of Methodists in 1780.

Wesley was an ordained Anglican, trained at Oxford, and during his lifetime did not separate from the Church of England. He took the whole world as his parish and, like Zinzendorf, groomed his societies as disciplined, dedicated small groups that would eventually uplift and leaven the entire church. His opponents charged him with dissension, disobedience, and disruption. In 1743 Wesley drew up rules for his Methodist societies, for all those who had a "desire to flee from the wrath to come, to be saved from their sins." As a manifestation of their continued desire for salvation, members of the societies were to avoid evil in any form—cursing, drunkenness, fighting, railing, unprofitable conversation, costly apparel, ribald songs, racy reading, theft, and so forth. They were to do as much good as possible by feeding the hungry, clothing the naked, helping the sick, instructing, reproving, being patient, living frugally. And they were to keep the ordinance of God, hear the Word, take communion, search the Scriptures, fast, and pray. The rules were guidelines for reaching perfection or full salvation, by which Wesley meant loving God above all else and neighbor as self. Unfortunately the rules tended to become ends, making pietistic moralism a continuing mark of Methodism.

Like Zinzendorf, Wesley moved gradually toward separation from the Church of England. His Societies acquired property. In 1744 the Methodists held their first conference, and although Wesley's traveling preachers were not licensed to administer the sacraments, by 1759 the movement was referred to as The Methodist Church. In 1763 Wesley's Model Deed provided doctrinal standards for his preachers, and in 1784 the Deed of Declaration legalized a continuation of the societies. Also in 1784 Wesley, though he was not a bishop, ordained Thomas Coke, and at the Baltimore Conference in 1784, Coke and Francis Asbury became America's first ordained "bishops." Afterward Wesley ordained men for Scotland, Newfoundland, Antigua, Nova Scotia, the West Indies, and even for England. But the break with Anglicanism did not come until 1795 in England and in 1870 in Ireland.

During the last fifty years of his life Wesley traveled over 250,000 miles, mostly on horseback, and delivered over 40,000 sermons. His journeys carried him throughout England, to Ireland, Scotland, Wales, Germany, and Holland. Denied the pulpit in London, he preached wherever he could find people. When he died, his followers in England numbered about 80,000 with 1,300 local and itinerant preachers. Methodists in America numbered 60,000 with almost two hundred preachers. Good organization, a system of lay preachers, warm fellowship, personal conversion, fervent preaching, and hymn-singing made the Wesleyan movement in England a potent force, credited by some historians with saving England from the disruptions of a violent French Revolution. William Wilberforce (1758–1833) illustrates the effects that evangelical pietism had on some of England's leaders. Wilberforce "converted" to the evangelical movement in 1784 and exercised his convictions in Parliament. In 1787, he began fighting slavery and won abolition of slave trading in the British dominions in 1807 and of slavery itself in 1833. His popular 400-page book, *Practical View of the Prevailing Religious System of Professed Christians,* 1797, called for serious holiness in all of life. He himself ceased card-playing, shunned luxuries, studied the Bible, and distributed a fourth of his wealth to the destitute.

The Methodists expressed their convictions in fervent hymns. They drew freely on the compositions of Isaac Watts (1674–1748), a Congregational pastor in London, who enlarged the common Psalm-singing of the time. John Wesley himself wrote and translated many hymns, but Charles Wesley (1707–88) is the acknowledged genius of English hymnody. Associated with John from the beginning, Charles left a legacy of hundreds of hymns, heavily imbued with evangelical pietism and emotional fervor.

Evangelical pietism was a powerful reaction to formal orthodoxy and rationalism. It revived personal Bible reading and individual dedication, modified intellectualism with emotional warmth, generated social concern, and rejuvenated preaching, missions, and hymnody. Romanticism became its secular ally. Although pietism did not check the tide of rationalism, its success and theology continued to challenge many of reason's precepts. But rationalism emerged strong in the nineteenth century, and ultramontane orthodoxy reasserted itself in Roman Catholicism. The Age of Reason and pietism had inherent universal appeal, but neither seriously challenged the colossus of state sovereignty. Pietism became intellectually narrow and acculturated, and rationalism lighted the path to nihilism.

19

Reaction to the French Revolution

The French and American Revolutions ushered in the nineteenth century. Both were violent rejections of old forms of exploitation. Both elevated the civil and religious rights of individuals, and both invested national sovereignty with religious fervor. This evolved in France in the nationalism of Napoleon and his successors, and in America in the nationalism of a righteous nation destined to establish the Kingdom of God on earth. In America even Roman Catholicism tended to become acculturated. The American Revolution unleashed volatile new energy directed toward turning a wilderness into a paradise. As a righteous nation chosen by God for a task at which the old world had failed, the Americans would not shackle themselves with church sovereignty, but would tolerate all churches, so long as all contributed to the nation's manifest destiny. The myth proved strong enough to withstand a civil war and was not visibly shaken until the twentieth century.

The French Revolution (see Chapter 20 for American developments) not only toppled an old regime but also served notice that rationalism would use violence to realize its ends. Many people hailed the revolution as a political victory in the extension of the universal rights of man, for it was a revolt against institutional corruption, inefficiency, oppression, and privilege. It rested on a rationalistic understanding of human worth, and was dedicated to the ideal that everyone is entitled to liberty, equality, and fraternity. Behind it was the Age of Reason. But others viewed the French Revolution as the end of law and order. Conservative

Roman Catholicism and Protestantism both recoiled from the French Revolution with a sense of horror and a feeling that something drastic had occurred. Both felt its challenge. Roman Catholicism reacted to the French Revolution by reasserting its own sovereignty. Conservative Protestantism clung to old forms while cautiously exploring new religious insights, and Liberal Protestantism tended to compromise traditional beliefs by accommodating them to psychological tenets and higher rationalistic criticism.

Wars in the interest of ultimate national sovereignty characterized the period from the French Revolution to World War II, wars that increasingly looked like glorified crusades, wars that continually claimed larger shares of the nation states' budgets. The nineteenth century was the century of warring state sovereignties, bracketed on one end by the Napoleonic debacle, on the other by World War I, and pockmarked in between with numerous clashes, imperial drives, and colonial struggles. It was the century when nation states exploited people and land, when blacks were freed and re-enslaved economically, when the American Indian was all but obliterated, when the nation state sovereignties equaled the church in shedding blood. It was the century when bullets, booze, and the Bible symbolized much of the missionary enterprise. It was also the century of great technological progress, communication and transportation strides, educational advances, social unrest, muckraking, and humanitarian concerns, when nothing seemed to shake man's boundless confidence in progress toward utopia. Karl Barth's *Epistle to the Romans,* 1919, in which he proclaimed a God "totally other" than man's cultural deity, Oswald Spengler's *Decline of the West,* 1922, and the specter of nihilism on the heels of World War I came as cultural shocks. As it took the French Revolution to shatter the old and forge a new consciousness, so it took two World Wars to awaken the West to a new consciousness that national sovereignty no longer satisfies, leaving many in the twentieth century with a great surge of nihilism and frantic groping for something more viable than nationalistic chauvinism. Nihilism marks the extent to which people have rejected both church and state sovereignty. Whether Christianity in some old or new form will transcend nihilism remains to be seen.

Religiously speaking, the French Revolution created a variety of consequences, one of which was romanticism. In Schleiermacher (discussed below) this merged with rationalism, forming an idea of religion based on feeling rather than on intellectualism or dogmatic orthodoxy. And still another was the continuance of rationalism only slightly modified as seen in Baur, Strauss, and Renan. But the most far-reaching consequence was the reassertion of ultramontane Roman Catholicism that continued to Vatican II in the twentieth century. This chapter will deal with these developments, the next with American events, and Chapter 21 with further liberal trends, fundamentalism, the social gospel, missions, and ecumenicity.

Like all major happenings, the French Revolution was complex in its origins, course, and effects. The *philosophes* had inflamed the people with expectations that the old regimes could not realize. Voltaire symbolized the period; he was denied Christian burial in 1778 but thirteen years later was disinterred and given a hero's funeral by the French National Assembly. Jean Jacques Rousseau (1712–78) in his *Social Contract,* 1762, popularized the idea that individuals are united in society for self-preservation, that society is to protect each individual and allow each as much freedom as possible. The gap between Rousseau and the authoritarian tyranny of the French monarchy did not go unnoticed. Opposition to the high-handedness of the Jesuits had forced the Pope to dissolve the Society of Jesus in 1773. The friendliness of the laity toward the local priests and lay enmity toward Rome were aspects of nationalism rooted in Gallicanism, earlier prompting Cardinal Richelieu to give priority to the affairs of France over the papacy. But the immediate cause of the French Revolution was economics. The French national debt in 1789 was comparable to that of the United States after World War II. Much of the population lived in dire poverty. This crisis motivated King Louis XVI to convoke the Estates-General in 1789, for the first time in almost two hundred years. The king wanted a fiscal way out. The Third Estate—bankers, industrialists, businessmen, and professionals—wanted to replace an entrenched aristocracy of parasitic royalty and clergy with a representative government. Confrontation came quickly.

On June 29, 1789, many members of the Estates-General took their famous Tennis Court Oath, pledging not to disband until France had a new constitution. They proclaimed themselves the National Assembly and forced the king, clergy, and nobility to acquiesce. But this political action was not enough to quell the spirit of revolt that openly erupted on July 14, when a Paris mob stormed the Bastille, the symbol of authoritarian oppression. Riotous pillaging ensued in Paris and throughout the country. The National Assembly sought to restore order by abolishing feudal dues and publishing a *Declaration of the Rights of Man and Citizen,* August 27, 1789. The *Declaration* fingered "ignorance, neglect, or contempt of the rights of man" as "the sole cause of public calamities and of the corruption of governments." It insisted on equal rights for all, freedom of press and speech, representative taxation, accountability of public servants, and the right to property. On November 2, the National Assembly seized the property of the church in France (about twenty percent of the total property), and assumed the paying of clerical salaries. The lower clergy liked this; it made incomes more equitable. Early in February, 1790, the Assembly suspended all monastic vows and made the clergy functionaries of the state. On March 29, 1790, Pope Pius VI condemned the liberal direction of the revolution, rejected the concept that law is derived from people, that all people should have representation, that Protestants should have rights in a state, and that non-Catholics should hold public office. But the protest went largely unnoticed. On July 12, 1790, the Assembly proclaimed the *Civil Constitution of the Clergy,* which completely subordinated the church to the state. Gallican sympathies were indicated by the fact that the civil constitution committee was chaired by a bishop! When the French higher clergy, one cardinal and twenty-nine bishops, finally objected, on October 30, the Assembly decreed that all clergy had to take an oath to obey the law and the constitution. At this about half the clergy balked, and in April of 1791 the Pope declared that all signers were schismatical and heretical and gave them forty days to retract. These actions divided the clergy and many of the laity in their support of the revolution, which seemed to be getting completely out of control. The king and queen attempted to flee the country but were apprehended and imprisoned. Royalists and papalists were now identified as counterrevolutionaries.

In 1792 the king was formally deposed and the newly organized National Convention decreed France a Republic. Priests who did not sign an oath to maintain liberty and equality were given fifteen days to emigrate. Many were abused, robbed, and lynched, but some 40,000 managed to leave France. The September massacres of 2,000 Frenchmen who were not enthusiastic about the Convention left the most extreme revolutionaries in control of France. In January, 1793, the Convention voted to behead the king, inaugurating the infamous Reign of Terror, 1793–94, when mob rhetoric and frenzy dominated. No one was safe. The guillotine, invented by a German who made one for each of the 83 territorial districts of France, claimed over 2,500 victims in Paris, and 10,000 in the provinces.

Charged with being anti-religious and lawless, the Convention sought to stave off foreign invasion by officially sanctioning the Worship of a Supreme Being, May 7, 1794. Libations were poured out to statues of nature, political heroes replaced saints, and churches were designated "temples of reason." Goddesses of Reason appeared in Notre Dame and in more than 2,000 village churches. Catholic clerical salaries were stopped and priests were forbidden to teach in public schools. A ten-day week was inaugurated to obliterate Sundays and saints' days. Robespierre officially celebrated Reason's Festival of the Supreme Being on June 8, 1794, by burning representations of Vice, Folly, and Atheism and raising a Statue of Wisdom. But the Worship of Reason did not have the desired effect on foreign governments, and on July 28 Robespierre was guillotined. Two days later, his supporting political commune, about sixty persons, were guillotined in less than an hour and a half. Under the Directory (1795–99), less chaos and more liberty to worship prevailed. But France was hardpressed by outside foes, and in 1799 Napoleon Bonaparte (1769–1821) worked his *coup d'état.*

Napoleon took charge of France's tottering citizen armies, stabilized the fronts along the Rhine, and then invaded Italy to wring indemnity from the Pope and a retraction of all anti-revolutionary bulls and encyclicals. When the Pope appealed to Austria, Napoleon marched on Rome, forcing the abdication of Pope Pius VI, who died in exile that same year. Radicals in Rome rioted and joined Napoleon. Some cardinals celebrated a *Te Deum* in St. Peter's to note the deposition of Pius, and the French registry tersely recorded his obituary: "Citizen John Braschi. Trade: pontiff."

To secure the new Pope Pius VII's sanction, Napoleon negotiated the Concordat of 1801, acknowledging that only the one true church could truly establish a government. He stabilized the French church, resumed paying clerical salaries, and guaranteed freedom of worship. But he retained the loyalty oath and the right to nominate new bishops. Pope Pius VII (1800–23) subscribed to these terms, believing that the future of Europe lay with Napoleon. But the Organic Articles that accompanied the proclamation of the Concordat declared that Napoleon could act as he saw fit for the advancement of France. The Pope protested ineffectively and in 1804 assisted in crowning Napoleon. But Napoleon, recalling Charlemagne, placed the crown on his own head. Subsequently Pius VII refused to play Napoleon's lackey, and in 1809 Napoleon seized the papal states and imprisoned Pius in France. Pius excommunicated Napoleon but for five years languished in prison. When Napoleon's empire began crumbling, the papacy emerged with greater moral prestige than at any time since the sixteenth century.

The French Revolution shocked Europe, and awakened people to the power of ideas and forces that had become a part of Western culture. For many, those ideas and forces connoted the disruptions and destruction that could be expected from unrestrained rationalism. They longed for the beauty and tranquillity of the past, for a renewed interest in man's universal feeling for the supernatural, for the simplicity of idealized nature. They trusted emotions more than reason for insight into human reality. They were the romanticists, and an upsurge in romanticism constituted an early reaction to the French Revolution. Indeed, romanticism had been a competing as well as initiating force in the revolution, for Rousseau was one of its earliest representatives. Rousseau's first serious essay in 1749 argued that human achievements in the sciences have not advanced human development. In *Emile*, 1762, Rousseau pitted the immediate testimony of the heart against revelation and authority in a discussion of education and religion, and made evil the doing of mankind. In *The Social Contract*, 1762, he maintained that people in their original state of nature were equal and good, and that so-called civilization had rendered them unequal and bad. He advocated adherence to the general will of the people, maximum freedom, and a return to the unspoiled original state of nature. Rousseau's political theories and civil religion appealed to the revolutionists; his emphasis on nature and the emotional side of man endeared him to the romanticists.

William Wordsworth (1770–1850), directly influenced by Rousseau's view of nature and by the French Revolution's exposure of the oppressed plight of mankind, poured his feelings into poetry. He lamented the artificiality of human "achievements" in contrast to the harmony of nature: "And much it grieved my heart to think / What Man has made of Man." In nature Wordsworth beheld God; in human society, chaos and sham. As he contemplated the destructiveness of man, he wrote: "Our meddling intellect / Mis-shapes the beauteous forms of things: / —We murder to dissect." As he contemplated the simple beauty and harmony of nature, he felt "A motion and a spirit, that impels / All thinking things, all objects of all thought, / And rolls through all things. . . ." During the same period Sir Walter Scott (1771–1832) provided imaginative escape from rationalism by using the romantic pageantry of medievalism in his popular novels, and facets of romantic reaction found expression in John Keats, Lord Byron, William Cullen Bryant, Herman Melville, and others.

In Germany romanticism blossomed in the literary creations of Johann Wolfgang von Goethe (1749–1832) and Johann Christof Friedrich von Schiller (1759–1805), but it made its most significant inroad into religion through the theology of Friedrich Schleiermacher (1768–1834). A hospital chaplain in Berlin and later professor at the university, Schleiermacher wrote *On Religion: Speeches to Its Cultured Despisers*, 1799, to counteract the arrogance of those who had relegated religion to an inferior status, as if it were something outmoded and unfit for sophisticated, intellectual consideration. In urbane circles religion was denigrated and despised. Schleiermacher's *Speeches* electrified his readers, for they saw in his essays a vigorous proponent of religion who could stand up to its deprecators. Schleiermacher boldly proclaimed religion as one of humanity's noblest pursuits, worthy of the keenest thinkers. He proposed feeling, rather than intellection or dogma, as the base of religion: "The sum total of religion is to feel that, in the highest unity, all that moves us in feeling is one; . . . that is to say, that our being and living is a being and living in and through God."

But *Speeches* was largely defensive, aimed at showing the superficiality of the detractors of religion. In his principal work, *The Christian Faith* (1821–22), Schleiermacher developed his system of dogmatics. He began not with the dogmas of the past but with an inward analysis of himself. Probing his finiteness, his creaturely existence in time, he became aware of a sense of dependence on something beyond himself, something that is the very ground of all creation. He felt that the consciousness of this dependence was an immediate consciousness of God. It was for Schleiermacher the source of all religion. Schleiermacher averred the superiority of Christianity because Christ was fully God-conscious, uniting within himself the eternal and temporal. From this God-consciousness, a feeling of Absolute Dependence, Schleiermacher then constructed his religious tenets. When the inward consciousness of God manifests itself in action, the ceremonies of religion develop; when it manifests itself in convictions, doctrines result. But always the God-consciousness precedes. Christ's perfect God-consciousness constituted his divinity. He redeems by inspiring God-consciousness in others, and in this sense we are dependent on Jesus, but the Resurrection and second coming of Christ are not essential. The sum total of the religious life is to live both individually and corporately in accordance with a consciousness of the Absolute. Sin is allowing something like self-concern to break the harmony of one's relationship to God. Goodness is promoting that relationship in the family, state, and world. The church is a social fellowship of people cooperating to preserve the feeling of God-consciousness. Schleiermacher believed the world is good insofar as it contributes to God-consciousness, evil insofar as it hinders. He believed in ultimate, foreordained blessedness for everyone, accepted the New Testament as the norm for all succeeding generations, and equated love with God. He had enough of the old not to satisfy the rationalists, and enough of the new not to satisfy the orthodox, yet his introduction of psychology into systematic theology has influenced all of modern religion.

Schleiermacher's counterpart in England was Samuel Taylor Coleridge (1772–1834), who, though not as well known, greatly influenced the transcendentalist movement in New England. His poetry, especially the *Rhyme of the Ancient Mariner*, echoed romanticism in the God who "made and loveth all." His *Aids to Reflection*, 1825, a series of aphorisms designed to promote in-depth reading, insisted that reason intuits truth and reality beyond, not necessarily contrary to, the scientific world of cause and effect, and that the conscience of man presupposes the existence of God. For Coleridge, the proofs of Christianity were not primarily intellectual, but rather internal and moral.

Hegel (1770–1831) was writing at the same time as Schleiermacher and Coleridge (see Chapter 18), saying that an Absolute Spirit is manifesting itself in the historical process. His methodology of thesis, antithesis, and synthesis, was a pattern of thought that he believed would yield truth when applied to any field of human endeavor—science, literature, art, religion. All things in history, even the French Revolution and Napoleon, were but phases in the on-going, ever-fuller manifestation of the Spirit. Thus Hegel forwarded optimistic belief in progress toward perfection. The rationalistic optimism of natural religion continued in the disciples of Hegel with little abatement.

Using Hegel's methodology, F. C. Baur (1792–1860) inaugurated a new era of biblical criticism. He depicted Peter's and Paul's understanding of Jesus as the thesis and antithesis of the New Testament, and analyzed the early creeds as their synthesis. He dated Matthew with its Judaizing tones as the oldest Gospel and declared that only Galatians, Corinthians, and Romans were genuinely Pauline letters because only they contained anti-Judaizing elements.

Appropriating aspects of Baur, Hegel, Schleiermacher, and the earlier rationalists, D. F. Strauss (1808–74) applied Hegelianism to the New Testament and concluded in his *Life of Jesus* (1835–36) that Jesus was simply a man, around whom Messianic expectations crystallized to produce the myth of Christ. Strauss not only dismissed the historicity of all supernatural elements but tended to regard the entire biblical account as a fictitious representation of religious ideas. He was summarily dismissed from his post at Tübingen. In his final work in 1872, *The Old Faith and the New*, Strauss opted for scientific materialism over Christianity.

More startling in some respects was Ernest Renan's popular *Life of Jesus*, 1863. It was beautifully written and went through ten editions in the first year. It climaxed the rationalists' presentation of Jesus as the enlightened modern man, the teacher of ethics, in contrast to seventeen centuries of Jesus as the Christ of orthodoxy. Renan regarded the Gospels as having a core of facts embellished into legend, and considered the accounts of miracles wholly unscientific and untenable. He presented Jesus as a man with ordinary emotions, preaching a message of love and dying for his perfect idealism, and the Resurrection as a product of Mary Magdalene's idealized love. He pictured the essence of religion as purity of heart in communion with a loving God who is everywhere present. Baur, Strauss, and Renan ushered in a whole new era of biblical studies.

Because natural religion, the *philosophes,* and rationalism in general informed the French Revolution, and because the revolutionaries officially exalted Reason, many Europeans regarded the horrors of the period as the awful culmination of what could be expected of rampant human reasoning. Experience had taught them a lesson; they recoiled from rationalism, and reasserted the orthodoxies of the past. This was the stance of the papacy, dramatically symbolized in one of the very first acts taken by Pope Pius VII when he was freed from prison. In 1814 he reconstituted the Society of Jesus. Throughout the nineteenth and first half of the twentieth centuries, Roman Catholicism fought rationalistic liberalism. The papacy looked disapprovingly on Febronianism in Germany and Josephism in Austria as spin-offs of the "enlightenment" that had come to such disastrous results in France. Disavowal of ecclesiastical authority could result only in uncertainty, confusion, and destruction. Rome set a course diametrically opposed to the secularizing, democratic, rationalistic forces in Western Europe. Its ultramontanism consisted in asserting that it and it alone had the divine right to control and to guide all aspects of culture. It clung to this basic attitude even though the church was no longer sovereign in Western culture.

After reviving the Jesuits, Pope Pius VII (1800–23) repossessed the papal states through the Congress of Vienna, 1815, and concluded favorable concordats with Bavaria, Sardinia, Naples, Russia, and Prussia. He wanted to prevent another French catastrophe, and in 1821 severely condemned the Carbonari revolutionaries of Naples. The Carbonari subscribed to natural religion as a sufficient basis for morality, spurned divine revelation, promoted liberalism in religion and politics, and vowed to destroy all forms of absolutism. They spread their ideas in Italy and a decade later formed part of Mazzini's Young Italy Movement, which combined with other forces to bring about the unification of Italy, bitterly fought by the papacy.

The pontificate of Pope Leo XII (1823–29) was relatively insignificant, but Pope Pius VIII (1829–30) vigorously promoted ultramontanism, as did his successors down to Vatican II. This was by design, for they understood the power inherent in legalized dogma. Pius VIII's encyclical *Traditi humilitanti*, 1829, sought to curb unauthorized, heretical, biblical translations. He condemned latitudinarianism, indifferentism, and liberalism, and reiterated that not just anyone who felt he had the Spirit but only the clergy could interpret Scripture. In the following year, the encyclical *Litteris alto* asserted the church's control of marriage by sharply condemning mixed marriages of Catholics to non-Catholics as "grave crimes," fraught with "many deformities and spiritual dangers." To show that Catholicism did not accept the principle of national sovereignty and that the church could not tolerate interference with its program, Pius declared that the spouse of Christ, the church, is by divine institution not subject to any human power.

The Catholic Emancipation Act of Great Britain and Ireland, 1829, which removed restraints imposed on Roman Catholics as far back as the reign of Elizabeth I, was the product of Catholic-Protestant liberals working together. So was the Belgian Constitution of 1831, which provided for freedom of religion in Belgium. For a while it appeared that the ultramontane stance of the papacy might be softening and that the liberals had a chance of naming a Pope, but the *Zelanti*, conservative papal zealots, secured the election of Pope Gregory XVI (1831–46), and the ultramontane march continued. Gregory sought military aid from Austria, in addition to his own troops, to maintain order in the papal states, and persistently opposed bringing in railroads and other modern improvements. He particularly countered attempts to reconcile Catholicism with modern political ideas or with the social liberalism advocated by the popular Abbé Felicite de Lamennais (1782–1854) of France. Charles X, king of France from 1824 to 1830, was a fanatical Catholic, but Gallican liberalism was still strong in France, and Lamennais felt that if the church was to prevail in the future it would have to separate itself from the monarchy and ally itself with the liberal trends among the people. Although concerned for the regeneration of society, Lamennais was actually ultramontane in loyalties. In 1823 he advocated a theocracy of man with the Pope as its supreme leader and won the approval of Pope Leo XII, who considered making him a cardinal. But the liberal ideas that Lamennais propounded in his newspaper *l'Avenir* struck Gregory as inimical to papal primacy. Lamennais and his cohorts, Montalembert and Lacordaire, used *l'Avenir* (which lasted only thirteen months) to advocate universal suffrage, self-determination for the Belgians and Poles, and freedom of the press, worship, assembly, education, and speech. When he appealed to the papacy for support, he met rebuff. Gregory had no intention of supporting a program that would acknowledge Catholicism as merely a party within the state, nor did Gregory want to administer only a spiritual lordship of the church. In 1832 his encyclical *Mirari vos* censured the idea that popular consensus is "the only criterion of certainty" and that a religion of humanity ought to prevail over the Word of God. The encyclical lashed out at "science without modesty," "unbridled license," and the loss of religious authority as a prelude to a "revolution-abyss of bottomless miseries" into which "heresy and sects have so to speak vomited as into a sewer all that their bosom holds of license, sacrilege, and blasphemy."

Stunned by this severe proscription, Lamennais and his aides submitted externally while resolving to strike back. His anonymous, but soon discovered, *Paroles d'un Croyant,* 1834, fiercely denounced papal political tyranny and praised democratic socialism. He painted the Pope as a hypocritical old man prating justice and morality while holding poison in one hand and caressing a harlot with the other. Gregory replied to this scandalous, sensational book, which soon appeared in several translations, in another encyclical called *Singulari vos,* 1834. It condemned Lamennais himself, attacked freedom of opinions and speech and "absolute liberty of conscience" as "the horrid conspiracy of the upholders of every erroneous doctrine against church and state." In the following two decades, Lamennais separated from the church, denied the whole supernatural order, was imprisoned for a year, became disillusioned with the violence of the revolutions of 1848, and ended his life as a Deist. He inspired many of the sociopolitical ideas of the later nineteenth century.

Pope Pius IX (1846–78) cemented the ultramontane position of the papacy. He engineered the dogma of infallibility in 1870, he refused to accept the nationalism that wrested temporal sovereignty from his hands, even over the papal states in Italy, and he attempted to fortify the papacy against all forms of modernism. When he first assumed the papal office, he was amenable to liberalism, fostered reforms, and even granted a more liberal constitution to the papal states. But the violent revolutions that convulsed Europe in 1848, the publication of Marx and Engels' *Communist Manifesto,* the *coup d'état* of Louis Napoleon and the Second Empire in France, and continued efforts to unify Italy under one secular government turned Pius completely about. In 1848 revolutionaries expelled Pius from the Vatican, and in 1849 Giuseppe Mazzini established a Republic of Rome, causing the Pope to renounce all forms of political liberalism and to declare that Roman Catholic liberals were traitors to their church. When French troops restored Pius to his Roman chair in 1850, he vowed to make war on modernism. Through papal pronouncements and the fanatically authoritarian journal of Louis Veuillot, *l'Univers,* Pius pursued his goal.

However, the times were not running with Pope Pius; the political conservatism following the defeat of Napoleon was waning. The 1848 revolution in France spilled over into Germany, and temporarily put the liberal leaders of the masses in control. Although the Frankfurt Parliament failed to change the political alignment in Germany and sent thousands of liberals into exile or jail, the drive toward nationalism continued in Germany. In the 1860s Otto von Bismarck recognized the inevitability of a unified Germany and resolved to make his Prussia the benefactor. He provoked a brief, successful war with Austria in 1866 and four years later engineered the victorious Prussian conflict with France. These triumphs made Bismarck a hero and enabled William I on January 18, 1871, to assume leadership of a united Germany.

The withdrawal of French troops to fight in the Franco-Prussian war enabled liberals in Italy to complete their drive toward national unification. Stopped momentarily by the reinstitution of Pius IX in 1850, the liberals regrouped behind Count Camillo di Cavour, the prime minister of Sardinia. With the military assistance of Napoleon III, in 1860 they wrested from Austria the provinces of Lombardy, Tuscany, Modena, and Parma. The papal states then revolted and by plebiscite voted to join Sardinia, giving the liberals control of northern Italy. The adventurer Giuseppi Garibaldi, with but a thousand swashbuckling followers, invaded Sicily in 1860 and with little difficulty also took the southern mainland from the corrupt Neapolitan Bourbons. Garibaldi then retired to his farm, and the northern and southern sections of Italy formed the Kingdom of Italy. The first meeting of the Italian Parliament, February 18, 1861, proclaimed Victor Emmanuel the King of Italy. Pope Pius protested saying a Catholic had broken the law, betrayed his church, and usurped a position to cover iniquity. He vowed never to recognize the title. When Austria lost to Bismarck in 1866, Venice joined the new Italian Kingdom; and when French troops left in 1870, Rome entered the new state and was chosen as its capital. Pope Pius retained only the Vatican.

"The Roman Question" concerned what to do about the Pope's territorial claims. When Pius refused to negotiate, the new state unilaterally passed the Law of Guarantees, 1871, granting the Pope privileges and immunities equal to those of the king and endowing the Pope financially for the loss of papal revenues. The papacy was also guaranteed freedom of communication and publication—"a free church in a free state." The Pope lived by the Law of Guarantees for fifty-nine years, but was not reconciled to it. He considered himself "a prisoner in the Vatican," and promulgated a *non expedit* forbidding the participation of all faithful Catholics in Italian politics. World sympathy revived Peter's Pence to compensate for financial losses. The situation was not resolved until Benito Mussolini's Fascist government abrogated the Law of Guarantees and negotiated the 1929 Lateran Treaty with the Pope. In return for recognizing the political regime of Mussolini, the Pope received sovereignty over Vatican City and a financial settlement for the loss of ancient territories.

Ultramontanism also received a further setback in Germany. The newly united Germany had a Protestant ruler, and Bismarck instituted a policy of *Kulturkampf,* "the struggle for civilization," with the intention of making the state supreme in all cultural affairs. Despite opposition from the powerful Catholic Center Party, which was organized on a confessional basis, Bismarck pushed ahead. In 1872 the state took control of schools of religion and the training of priests, and required state examinations in history, philosophy, and literature in an effort to liberalize the clergy. The militant Society of Jesus was outlawed and many monastic orders placed under police supervision. Additional enactments gave the state more control over education and marriages, the episcopacy, church property, and the press. When the Pope objected, Bismarck vowed he would not go to Canossa in spirit or flesh, but by 1886 anti-Catholic *Kulturkampf* had relaxed, and Bismarck was battling the red international of Marxism. To win the masses, he granted social insurance against illness (1883), accident (1884), and old age (1889), but at the same time repressed socialist newspapers and leaders. In 1890 William II (1888–1918) dismissed Bismarck and launched Germany on a course of heavy-handed imperialism.

Unsuccessful in Italy, partially successful in Germany, Pius IX succeeded in Ecuador, where anti-liberal forces put a devout Catholic in office and granted the papacy a concordat in 1862. It recognized Roman Catholicism as the only legal religion, with full control of education.

Against this political background Pius pursued his ultramontanism. He did not retreat. On his own authority, in 1854, Pius proclaimed the Immaculate Conception of the Blessed Virgin, a dogma long desired by Mariologists, but hardly favored by liberals. He followed this in 1864, one year after Renan's *Life of Jesus,* five years after Darwin's *Origin of Species,* with his sweeping, anti-modern, anti-liberal *Syllabus of Errors.* Pope Pius flatly censored as errors eighty rationalistic trends and ideas that countered papal supremacy. Included were pantheism, naturalism, absolute rationalism, moderate rationalism, indifferentism, latitudinarianism, socialism, communism, secret societies, biblical societies, clerico-liberal societies, and modern liberalism. Branded as unacceptable to Roman Catholicism were civil marriage or divorce, civil recognition of other forms of religion, civil control of education, national churches withdrawn from papal authority, rationalism running contrary to papal pronouncements, reason as the arbiter of truth, and the idea that the papacy should reconcile itself to democratic trends. It implied papal infallibility, the power of the Pope to coerce, and supreme control of the papacy over culture. Many shocked Roman Catholics, such as French Bishop Dupanloup, sought to soften the intransigence of the *Syllabus* by devious explanations. But Pius meant what he said. He was at war with those forces that had broken the sovereignty of the papacy.

The ultramontane drive of Pius IX climaxed in the dogma of infallibility, pronounced July 18, 1870, at Vatican Council I. Not since the Council of Trent (1545–63) had there been an ecumenical council. Pius announced his intention to call a council as early as 1867, but an air of mystery surrounded its purpose and agenda. What would be considered—infallibility, the *Syllabus,* the assumption of Mary, the Index, freedom? Speculation, debates, and even riots occurred in anticipation of what might be enacted. Pius opened the council on December 8, 1869, with some 660 delegates and 50,000 viewers participating in the pomp and ritual at St. Peter's. For three months political maneuvering and artifice ensued. Most of the delegates tended toward ultramontanism, and procedural rules insured papal control. The committees of the council were overwhelmingly ultramontane and none who opposed infallibility were included on them. The Pope by personal act fixed the rules and appointed officials. He reserved to himself the exclusive right to propose matters to be discussed, although bishops could submit proposals to a special Congregation, set up by the Pope, which screened them for decision by the pontiff. All motions of the council had to be approved by the Pope before taking effect, and silence was enjoined concerning all proceedings. Speeches could not be printed in Rome, and the Roman post office refused to distribute such literature when printed elsewhere. A simple majority might apply closure to any debate. A number of council dignitaries hotly protested these regulations, but the Pope conceded nothing. Pope Pius IX was complete master of the council.

Despite these regulations, infallibility, *the* topic considered, was vigorously debated. Many delegates grew so weary that they simply left, whereas others abstained from voting. A crucial trial vote taken on July 13 showed 451 favored infallibility, 88 did not, and 62 favored with reservations. The day of the final voting, July 18, broke with heavy rain and lightning—an ill omen for many. Only 535 of a possible 1,000 voted: 533 yea, 2 nay. The dogma declared that the Roman Church has supremacy over all other churches, and that all must submit to the Roman pontiff, who when he speaks *ex cathedra,* "that is, when exercising the office of pastor and teacher of all Christians," when defining "a doctrine regarding faith or morals to be held by the universal Church, by the divine assistance promised to him in blessed Peter, is possessed of that infallibility with which the divine Redeemer willed that his Church should be endowed for defining doctrine regarding faith or morals." Such definitions are irreformable of themselves, not from the consent of the church.

In the aftermath of the council—the Franco-Prussian War, the loss of the papal states to the Kingdom of Italy, and Bismarck's *Kulturkampf*— dissident Catholics, led by Professors Döllinger of Munich, Johann von Schulte of Prague, Reinkens of Breslau, and others who opposed the Vatican decrees, organized the "Old Catholic Church" in 1873. They forged episcopal ties with the Jansenist Church in Amsterdam. Approximately 150,000 from Germany, Austria, and Switzerland joined. Pius IX's ultramontanism had succeeded but not without cost. When the corpse of Pius was being carried to the cemetery, revolutionaries attempted to throw it into the Tiber.

Leo XIII (1878–1903), successor to Pius IX, became Pope at the age of sixty-eight and guided the church through the difficult implementation of ultramontanism during the next twenty-five years. Trained as a Jesuit, with a doctorate in canon law and practical experience as a police chief, governor, nuncio, bishop, and cardinal, Leo tackled his task with vigor and insight. He left a legacy of eighty-six encyclicals, considered by many to be the most important papal corpus since the Middle Ages. Leo's problem was how to live by ultramontane principles in a world dominated by liberalism, democratic trends, and science. Evolutionary theories derived from Darwin had come into vogue, national states were vigorously pursuing their own sovereignties, and communism was challenging capitalistic industrialism. In *Divinum Illud*, 1897, Leo said that during his pontificate he had pursued two principal goals: "the restoration, both in rulers and peoples, of the principles of the Christian life in civil and domestic society," and "the reunion of those who have fallen away from the Catholic Church either by heresy or by schism." In the same encyclical Leo depicted the Holy Ghost as "the soul" of the church and declared, "that which now takes place in the Church is the most perfect possible," and will endure forever. Many would not agree.

Leo's first significant encyclical, *Aeterni Patris*, August 4, 1879, was issued on the centennial of the day that the French Revolution abolished the feudal system in France. Leo exalted Thomas Aquinas and insisted that Thomas' philosophy be taught in all Catholic schools as the pinnacle of philosophical-theological perception. In 1880, just fifty years after Pius VIII proclaimed mixed Protestant-Catholic marriages "grave crimes," Leo issued his encyclical *On Marriage* (*Arcanum Divinae Sapientiae*). Leo warned again of the perils of marriage with those who are not Catholics, set the church with its sacrament above the power of the state to regulate marriage, made Protestantism responsible in large measure for divorce, defined the goal of marriage as the "propagation of the human race, and the bringing forth of children for the Church."

The encyclical *On Civil Government* (*Diuturnum*), 1881, proclaimed that political power must be guided by Christian doctrine, whose truths and duties alone can save society from chaos. Leo firmly rejected the notion that authority comes from the people and condemned the free spirit in Protestantism.

His encyclical of 1884 *On Freemasonry and Naturalism* attacked naturalism as a philosophy that placed nature and human reason above the supernatural order, and the Freemasons as a secret society guided by naturalism that was set on gaining control of the school system and destroying the church.

Leo's most important statement on politics came in his *Christian Constitution of States* (*Immortale Dei*), 1885, wherein he sought to answer whether a Catholic can be a good citizen in a secular state. Severe anticlericalism in France and America occasioned the statement. Leo did not retreat from ultramontanism. He insisted that the state can have different forms but should publicly profess Roman Catholicism as the only true religion; he condemned the separation of church and state but announced that Catholics could tolerate religious error in a state "for the sake of securing some great good or of hindering some great evil." He labeled liberty of thinking and publishing as "the fountain-head and origin of many evils."

An encyclical *On Human Liberty* (*Libertas Preestantissimum*) followed in 1888. By natural and divine law man, a rational creature, is not free to do evil; he is free to do good. Since the church is the guardian of natural and divine law, liberty consists in doing what the church dictates, especially since the end of all liberty is to aspire to God. Our highest duty is to respect authority and submit to law—the authority and law of the church. There can be no freedom of worship; rulers of states must preserve and protect Roman Catholicism. There can be no liberty of speech, press, teaching, conscience, or tolerance—except within the bounds laid down by the Pope. Truth and error should not have the same privileges. "The Church usually acquiesces in certain modern liberties, not because she prefers them in themselves, but because she judges it expedient to permit them, she would in happier times exercise her own liberty."

Leo's most famous encyclical, *Rights and Duties of Capital and Labor* (*Rerum Novarum*), 1891, came at a time when labor troubles were rocking the industrial establishment. The churches generally ignored or proclaimed against riots and strikes, rejected Communism, and considered riches a blessing from God and poverty a curse. So preached Henry Ward Beecher and Horace Bushnell to their fashionable congregations. Part of the power of *Rerum Novarum* came from its being one of the very first major statements from a Christian body that recognized the injustice of the plight of laborers. Leo did not mitigate any of the traditional claims of the church to superiority in society, nor did he say that society should be classless. But the rich and poor, capital and labor are bound together in a natural solidarity. They should work together for the common good of society. Where working conditions and inadequate income make workers suffer, production inevitably suffers also. So a balance dictated by brotherly concern and need should be struck. The state should promote the interests of all, both high and low. Leo strongly asserted that private property is a natural right, like marriage, and that this must be maintained by the state for the good of society. Classes naturally exist in this world; that must be accepted. But classes need not be hostile to one another, nor are they to exploit one another. Since the rich have ways of shielding themselves, the state should be especially concerned about needy workers. If a class unduly suffers, the state should step in for the sake of peace and good order. "To exercise pressure upon the indigent and the destitute for the sake of gain, and to gather one's profit out of the need of another, is condemned by all laws, human and divine," said Leo. Ultimately, however, poverty does not affect one's destiny in heaven. And one's destiny beyond this life is finally more important than having or not having goods on earth. Nevertheless, workers are not to be exploited at the expense of their own well-being. Leo sanctioned and encouraged associations among workers to improve their lot.

Leo also took note of another liberal development in scholarship—historical and literary criticism. Based largely on scientific evolution and rationalistic concepts, historical and literary criticism had caused many scholars in the Roman Catholic fold to question the stance of their church. Such prominent men as Alfred Loisy, Louis Duchesne, and Maurice D'Hulst in France; George Tyrrell in England; Hermann Schell and Baron von Hügel in Germany, and Senator Fogazzaro in Italy questioned accepted conclusions about certain events and legends in church history, the inspiration and inerrancy of the Bible, the eternity of hell-fire, the Mosaic authorship of the Pentateuch, and the reliability of scientific data drawn from Genesis. Such inquiry threatened the biblical bases of many official dogmas. Leo reacted to the direction of this modernism in his *Providentissimus Deus,* 1893, in which he upheld biblical inerrancy, saying the Bible was written "at the dictation of the Holy Ghost." He reiterated the church as the teacher, guide, and interpreter of Scripture. And in 1899 Leo paternally reprimanded "Americanism" in a letter to Cardinal O. Gibbons, Archbishop of Baltimore. "Americanism" was an attempt on the part of such men as I. T. Hecker, founder of the Paulists, to accommodate ultramontanism to other religions, eugenic reforms, social liberalism, and new historical data. Leo established a Biblical Commission in his encyclical *Vigilantiae,* 1902, to deal with dissident biblical scholars and scholarship. In 1903 the Commission put Loisy's books on the Index, and later issued rulings, binding on Catholic scholars, saying that Moses did write the Pentateuch and that the Fourth Gospel was authentic and historical. Tyrrell was dismissed from the Jesuit Order, Duchesne and Loisy lost their professorships in Paris, and other modernist scholars were forced to reconcile their views with church dogma.

Pope Pius X (1903–14) continued to wrestle with the problem of modernism. In France modernism combined with nationalism to produce the Law of Associations, 1901, which stringently curtailed ultramontanism. The French Law of Associations brought all local congregations under the direct control of the state. The state assumed authority over their continuance or discontinuance, and could require membership lists, financial statements, accounting for property, etc. In 1902 it forbade all congregations to do any educational work whatsoever. It disavowed any established religion and reduced Roman Catholicism to a status of one religion among many. This situation led to confiscation of some church property and the Law of Separation, 1905. Pope Pius bitterly objected, "We reject and condemn the law passed in France for the separation of the Church and State, as profoundly insulting to God whom it officially denies by making it a principle that the Republic recognizes no religion."

Pius X aimed his three most important encyclicals at the further inroads of modernism. *Lamentabili Sane,* 1907, condemned sixty-five modernist propositions pertaining to biblical scholarship (fifty of which were drawn from Loisy's writings). *Pascendi gregis,* a few weeks later, further condemned the "misguided" reformers of the church who were instigating schismatic movements by making religion a product of human consciousness and desires, thus abrogating the role of revelation and the church. In 1910 Pius promulgated his famous oath against modernism, which he required once a year to be taken by all professors of philosophy and theology in Catholic seminaries. In 1931 it was extended to laity and clerics at universities. The penalty for refusal was deposition.

The ultramontane stance against modern biblical scholarship was not significantly altered until Pius XII's *Divino afflante Spiritu*, 1943, which encouraged Roman Catholic scholars to incorporate the results of archeological discoveries in their biblical studies.

Pope Benedict XV (1914–22) sought to be neutral during World War I, confining his efforts to humanitarianism and the offer of a basis for peace in 1917, which was rejected by both sides. At the request of Italy, he was excluded from the peace settlement.

Popes Pius XI (1922–39) and Pius XII (1939–58) both pressed ultramontane principles. Both refused to cooperate with the ecumenical movement, except to invite all Christians to return to the Roman fold (see Chapter 21). Both sought accommodations and privileges with totalitarianism. Pius XI arranged concordats with Mussolini and Hitler, was betrayed by both, and then lashed out with major encyclicals against Fascism, Nazism, and Communism. But Pius XII during World War II left a feeling in the minds of many that the papacy irreparably compromised itself in not taking a firm stand against the wholesale slaughter of Jews.

Pope Pius XI signed the Lateran Treaty with Benito Mussolini in 1929. He recognized the political position of the Fascists, gained sovereignty over Vatican City, and received a financial settlement for loss of lands. But like Napoleon, Mussolini honored only those portions of the treaty that he wished. In June of 1931 Pius XI denounced Mussolini for breaking his agreement and for limiting Catholic action in Italy. *Non abbiamo bisogno* declared that a true Catholic could not possibly be a Fascist.

A similar concordat was arranged between Pius XI and Adolf Hitler on July 29, 1933, shortly after the National Socialist Workers' Party seized power. Pius agreed to a dissolution of the Catholic Center Party in return for a number of concessions, but Hitler did not honor the pact, except insofar as it promoted his interests. He seized Catholic schools, canceled out various concessions, and did not hesitate to pursue a policy of racism and sterilization. Catholic Reich Chancellor von Papen was removed from office less than a year after the agreement. Disappointment and disillusion prompted *Mit brennender Sorge*, March 14, 1937, in which Pius denounced "the whole Nazi conception of life as utterly, and, necessarily, anti-Christian." (See also Chapter 21.)

A few days later Pius XI condemned totalitarian Communism in *Divini Redemptoris*. The papacy disliked Communist promotion of the war in Spain, disturbances in Mexico, and efforts to promote anti-religion in Russia. Communism's anti-religion is not only "intrinsically wrong," but also "conceals in itself a false messianic idea" and uses "delusive promises," "seductive trappings," "pseudo-scientific arguments," and "deceptive tactics" to entrap its victims, who are then terrorized. Pius outlined Roman Catholicism as the only sound alternative.

Pius XII is remembered principally for his controversial stand regarding Hitler's attempted genocide of the Jews, for his encyclical *Mystici Corporis*, and for the dogma of the Assumption of the Virgin Mary. *Mystici*

Corporis, 1943, pictured the church as the mystical body of Christ, and the Assumption of the Virgin Mary, 1950, dogmatized the bodily ascension of Mary to enthronement "at the right hand of the Divine Redeemer." Pius' apparent lack of moral forthrightness in condemning Hitler's known killing of millions of Jews has become the subject of heated controversy. Rolf Hochhuth's *The Deputy,* 1964, emotionalized two continents on the issue. Pro and con documentation has been brought forth to show that although Pius did not forthrightly condemn the Nazi pogrom, he exerted great efforts to save thousands of refugees. Ironically, his first encyclical declared that he would "testify to the truth with Apostolic firmness." Archival material not yet open to historians will have to be studied before the full story is known.

The Roman Catholic Church did not significantly alter its ultramontanism before Pope John XXIII (1958–63), who called Vatican Council II. Although Vatican II (1962–65) fostered a new spirit of openness and cooperation within Catholicism, it did not change basic doctrine. Whether the new spirit can prevail without, or whether it will engender, doctrinal support remains yet to be disclosed.

20

The American Experiment

Religiously America reflected the main trends of what was happening in Europe. Discovered at a time when nationalism was coming into its own, the vast land stretches of the New World were the pawns of national empires for over 250 years. With the arrival of religious colonists in the 1600s, a new ethos gradually developed: The Old World was worn out with religious strife and prejudices; in the New World God was granting a fresh chance to found a holy Kingdom. This ethos combined with frontier individualism, necessity, and a distrust of European political forms to produce a strong American government that placed national sovereignty above specific forms of religion while at the same time allowing voluntary denominations to function. Officially, the nation established a wall of separation between church and state; unofficially, it made all churches subservient to the state. All churches might participate in the new democracy if they did not subvert national sovereignty—a condition that cast suspicion on Roman Catholicism for 185 years, subjected the Mormons to persecution and conflict with the federal government, and created tensions for Jehovah's Witnesses and religious conscientious objectors to military service. A sense of "chosenness," a sense of being God's people to do his will in the world, gave the new nation purpose and direction. Wrote Edward Johnson in his *Wonder-Working Providence of Sions Saviour in New England* (London, 1654, p. 25): "God's concern for the settlement [was] manifested by striking the Indians with a plague before the migration, thus making the waste places safe for his children." After the Revolution and the adoption of the Constitution, the Protestant churches consciously and subconsciously fused their aims with those of the body politic to produce a "righteous" kingdom, confidently believed to be God's fulfillment of the ancient promise to Israel. Youthful, confident, blessed with an abundance of natural resources, largely uncritical of itself, America rushed forward toward its manifest destiny. "In God We Trust" symbolized the guiding hand of providence. Success and growth attested divine approval. Temporary difficulties could be explained as God's tempering and chastening of occasional waywardness. United under one God and one flag, "with liberty and justice for all," the United States conquered a continent, and then felt called to export and protect democracy in the world. But in the process, democracy became tarnished, liberty and justice for all were not realized, and the sense of God's existence—much less of their own chosenness—began to fade. The push West wiped out seventy-five percent of the Indians, regarded by whites as foreigners; and the blacks, with only a three-fifths status in the Constitution, could hardly reconcile slavery and second-class citizenship with the ideals of the Declaration of Independence. In the twentieth century science, positivism, two frustrating world wars, and a burst of nihilism brought denigration and profound uncertainty about God in their wake, leaving many Christians questioning the myth of chosenness and wondering about the subservience of Christianity in the religious-political amalgamation.

This panoramic development was especially the story of the United States. Other New World countries, dominated for the most part by European nations and Catholicism, took different routes but also arrived at national sovereignty, resentful of the economic influence of the United States, which they could not avoid and on which they became increasingly dependent, especially after the Monroe Doctrine in 1823.

Following Columbus' discoveries, the Spanish explored along the coast of the Southern United States, Mexico, Central America, and the northern part of South America. Hearing of the wealth of Mexico, in 1519 Hernando Cortez led a band of conquistadors from Cuba to Mexico. Landing at a time when the ancient great white god Quetzalcoatl was expected to return, Cortez's small band overawed his Aztec opposition and with a minimum of effort took Mexico City and made Montezuma a captive. Missionaries, particularly Franciscans, followed five years later. They used both persuasion and violence to convert the Indians, and Mexico, not without difficulties, became the great outpost of Roman Catholicism in the New World. For 300 years, the Spanish dominated and exploited the land, enslaving, introducing their mores, intermarrying with the natives. In time, more than half the land belonged to the church. The Spanish governed, planted culture, and aroused hatred. In 1821, after many unsuccessful revolts, Mexico won its independence from Spain, and by 1872 under the leadership of President Juárez it separated church and state, forbade the church to participate in political affairs, and nationalized church property. Mexico's constitution of 1917 ruled the church incapable of owning property, put churches under state supervision, and said only Mexican-born priests could serve churches and that they could not participate in politics. Enforcement of the constitution after 1926 brought the closing of many churches, widespread executions, and deportation of bishops. Roman Catholicism has dominated Mexico and Central and South America, and in most of the nations the bloody path to nationalism has not been entirely dissimilar to that in Mexico.

Throughout the Southwest, Spanish expeditions, with missionaries accompanying, searched for gold and left vestiges of Spanish culture. Exploration and missionizing went hand in hand: gold for the state, souls for the church. Ponce de Leon explored Florida in 1521; De Soto discovered the Mississippi in 1541. Francisco de Coronado combed Texas, Colorado, and New Mexico in 1541–42 looking for cities of gold. Wanderers scouted the coast lands of California as early as 1542, and Jesuit and Franciscan missionaries began establishing outposts. Expeditions from Mexico planted 25 Franciscan missions in New Mexico by 1630, and 35,000 Indians were claimed as converts. More enduring settlements came in the eighteenth century when Father Junipero Serra, a Franciscan, and Father Fermin Francisco de Lasuen each founded nine missions in California and the Southwest, many of which are still standing. These spectacular explorations and early missions left a Spanish imprint on the American Southwest, but the area was not thoroughly colonized. Ineffective administration, and manipulation and exploitation of Indian labor occasioned bloody Indian uprisings in the Southwest in 1680 and 1696. Spanish explorations reached from Cape Hatteras to San Juan Capistrano, but they yielded little gold. The main thrusts of Spain centered in Mexico and South America, where in 1528 Francisco Pizarro conquered and plundered the Incan sun worshipers of Peru.

Similarly, the early French explorations lacked permanency. The French were more interested in immediate wealth from furs and fish. Jacques Cartier's trip up the St. Lawrence River to "Mont Real" gave France an early claim to Canada. Jesuit and Récollet missionaries, along with fur traders, worked with varying success among the Algonquin, Huron, and Iroquois Indians. Jesuit Father Jacques Marquette arrived in Canada in 1666, and before his death in 1675, he and adventurer Louis Joliet had explored the Great Lakes, Wisconsin, and the Mississippi down to the Arkansas River. In 1682 a soldier of fortune, La Salle, reached the mouth of the Mississippi, while Father Louis Hennepin, a Récollet priest, explored the river northward as far as Minneapolis. The French ranged across vast areas but slighted settlements, and would allow only Roman Catholics to emigrate and join the search for more pelts and converts. Yet, from Quebec to New Orleans the French eventually established a line of scattered forts and missions, only to lose the entire area by the treaty of 1763 at the close of the French and Indian War. Great Britain received Canada and everything east of the Mississippi, except Louisiana, which France ceded to Spain. In the war for independence, many of the French in these areas because of their traditional hatred of the English aided the American colonies.

The phase of colonization that predominantly shaped American life began with the English settlements along the Atlantic seaboard. The motives were commercial and religious. Some sought new economic beginnings; some sought a new haven in which to practice their convictions. In most these motives intermingled, but from the beginning the English colonists intended to settle permanently. They came primarily to build a new civilization, to carve a new Israel out of the wilderness. William Bradford's *History of Plymouth Plantation* (1620–47) recorded this ethos: "A great hope and inward zeal they had of laying some good foundation, or at least to make some way thereunto, for the propagating and advancing the gospel of the kingdom of Christ in those remote parts of the world."

Although the English attempted a few ill-fated settlements earlier, the colony of Jamestown, Virginia, established in 1607, was the first permanent English colony in the New World. King James I granted the London Company a charter to found a colony in 1606, and an Anglican priest accompanied the first group of 100 settlers. Wilderness hazards exacted a heavy toll in death and suffering, but the colony gradually grew and by 1619 had a popularly elected assembly that legally established Anglicanism and bound the colonists to conformity with the Church of England. In 1624 Virginia became a crown colony. After 1636 citizens had to pay tithes, and non-Anglicans could not vote. Special laws restricted the activities of Quakers and Puritans. Out of a population of 15,000 in 1645, only about 200 were non-conformists. However, as the population spread along Virginia's rivers, the Anglican parish system became difficult to maintain. Ever in search of more land for their plantations, especially when the demand for tobacco began to increase after 1611, the settlers pushed the Indians farther west, and the Anglican priests found regular services impossible to provide. Compounding the problem, in 1619 a Dutch military vessel landed in Jamestown with twenty indentured blacks, the beginning of a system of slave labor that made larger plantations even more desirable. The number of slaves increased from 300 in 1650 to 6,000 in 1700. Anglican ties weakened; non-conformists increased. When England's Act of Toleration, 1689, was adopted by the Virginia Assembly ten years later, Protestant dissenters who had come into the colony received liberties that further reduced Anglican control. In the following century, Enlightenment philosophy, deism, and latitudinarian tendencies combined to make Virginia even more liberal in religion. It was in Virginia that Americans first made their most radical departure from the Christian tradition; in 1776 religion was disestablished. Leaders like Thomas Jefferson and James Madison led the move. By 1787, the efforts of the faithful in Virginia could show no more than one-tenth of the people with religious ties. Yet the dream of America as a chosen people did not disappear.

A similar Puritan experiment was taking shape farther north. Dissatisfied with their lot in Holland, a group of Pilgrim Separatists negotiated for a grant of land in Virginia, and in 1620 completed arrangements with the London Company to take them to America. Financed by London merchants, the Pilgrims bound themselves to pool half their produce in America to repay the loan within seven years. When the *Mayflower* finally sailed, more than half the 101 passengers were commercial adventurers. Driven north by Atlantic storms, they landed not in Virginia but off Cape Cod. Tensions arose, and before disembarking 41 men signed the famous

Mayflower Compact for living together, the first American constitution. They chose Deacon John Carver as their governor, and on December 11 selected Plymouth, Massachusetts, as the site of their new colony. The next year they were given a patent by the New England Company, but half the colonists died during that first winter, and more might have succumbed except for the aid of friendly Indians. With the arrival of new provisions on the ship *Fortune* the following November, the Pilgrims celebrated their first Thanksgiving. Other settlers arrived, and by 1626 the Pilgrims felt secure enough to negotiate payment of their obligations to the London merchants. In 1628 the fifty-three men who contributed to the payment (though not fully completed until 1641) each received twenty acres of cleared land and the status of "freemen." The Pilgrim Separatists made landholding and orthodoxy requirements for voting. Elder William Brewster served as minister until the first Separatist pastor Ralph Smith arrived in 1629. Despite recurrent difficulties with non-Separatist settlers, Plymouth persisted until 1691 when it was absorbed by the Massachusetts Bay Colony, under whose auspices thousands of Puritans came to New England. William Bradford's *History of Plymouth Plantation* portrayed the Pilgrims as saints commissioned by God to battle Satan to establish a colony based on the teachings of Jesus.

With Charles I's dissolution of Parliament in 1629 and Laud's determined drive for Anglican conformity, waves of Puritans sought refuge and a better way of life in America. Having received a grant from the Council of New England, John Endicott led a band of followers to Salem in 1628, the vanguard of 20,000 during the next few years. In 1629 Charles I not only granted the Puritans a charter for their Massachusetts Bay Company but also conferred on them the powers of self-government. They organized a church with congregational polity, and in 1630 acquired control of the company and brought their Charter to Massachusetts, a charter that in effect allowed them to govern as they saw fit, free of parliament and king. Their religious insights did not include freedom of conscience; like Laud on the other side, they banned all diversity and unorthodoxy and gave "honest and good" laymen in the church power over religious matters, so that church and state virtually became one. The Act Against Heresy in 1646 subjected to banishment any who denied redemption through Christ, justification by faith, infant baptism, the Resurrection, or immortality of the soul. As Nathaniel Ward wrote, "All Familists, Antinomians, Anabaptists, and other Enthusiasts, shall have free Liberty to keep away from us, and such as will come to be gone as fast as they can, the sooner the better." He might also have included Roman Catholics, and especially Jesuits, who were liable to execution if they returned after banishment. Irreverence for the clergy or the Scriptures, failure to attend services, and blasphemy and atheism could bring severe punishment, including boring of the tongue with a hot iron. The people could select their own minister, but if they did not choose a minister, the court could appoint one and tax the town for his support. Suffrage was limited to church members in good standing, a rule that soon caused serious tension, for the more numerous non-church members were required to pay tithes. The Puritan saints had established a "godly" commonwealth.

For religious as well as economic reasons, Massachusetts Puritanism spawned other colonies. Both New Hampshire and Maine were outposts of the Massachusetts Bay Colony, until 1679 for New Hampshire, when it became a royal province, and until the nineteenth century for Maine. There were other offshoots as well. Thomas Hooker, a prominent Puritan divine, feeling severely harassed in England, took refuge in Holland and then came to Massachusetts, whence he led a group of settlers to the Connecticut River Valley, where a few Dutch Reformed and Puritans had already settled. In 1639 they adopted their "Fundamental Orders of Connecticut," which established a seemingly more democratic government, but which was actually very much like the Puritan model. Property, character, and religion were required for voting—provisions that disenfranchised two-thirds of the adult males. Also in the 1630s, John Davenport, who had fled from the persecutions of Archbishop Laud, helped found the colony of New Haven, which in 1639 drew up the "Plantation Covenant" form of government making church membership necessary for voting and the Bible the supreme rule in civil and religious matters. In 1662 Charles II united these two Connecticut colonies, omitting to make religion a test for voting.

Massachusetts Bay did not look kindly on "mutinous contentions of discontented persons," as Governor John Winthrop said, and in 1635 the General Court acted to expel Roger Williams and ship him back to England. From his arrival in 1631 he had objected to the authorities' punishing people for opinions and beliefs. He refused to serve a church in Boston because of the jurisdiction of magistrates in matters of conscience, and he publicly questioned the right of the English king to grant charters for lands that belonged to the Indians. To him the Indians were not ungodly, nor could he see the rightness of the "chosen" Puritans dispossessing them. Before the Massachusetts authorities could act, Williams fled south, in the midst of winter, found shelter among the Narraganset Indians, and the following year established the town of Providence on a site purchased from the Indians. Religious toleration was its hallmark; the government had to do only with civil affairs; his church was Baptist, voluntary in character. Williams' famous *Bloudy Tenent of Persecution* published in London in 1644, vigorously defended the right of conscience, even for Roman Catholics. He saw only unacceptable consequences flowing from coercion in religion. While he could not condone a national, coercive church, this did not mean that God was any the less active in what Williams was doing. Anne Hutchinson and her associates, hounded out of Boston for their unorthodox opinions and pronouncements, settled Portsmouth and Newport in 1638 to 39. Rhode Island was a haven for early dissenters, and evangelizing Baptists exported its ideas to the other settlements, often encountering resistance from civil and religious authorities.

Other colonies followed, religion and trade intermingling in their founding. Henry Hudson, under the Dutch flag, had explored the Hudson River in 1609, and in 1623 thirty families of Protestant Walloon refugees arrived in New York; some pushed up the Hudson to Albany, and others into the Connecticut Valley. Peter Minuit purchased Manhattan from the Indians in 1626 to begin the city of New Amsterdam, renamed New York when the British navy took it over with a show of force in 1664. Prophetic of the future, the liberal government instituted by the British did not interfere with either language or religion.

Concerned about the disabilities of Roman Catholics in England, George Calvert (Lord Baltimore), a recent convert to Catholicism, secured a grant from Charles I in 1632 to establish a colony for refugee Roman Catholics along the Potomac River northeast of Virginia. His son, Cecilius, succeeded to the grant, and in 1634, the first shipload of settlers with two Jesuit priests arrived. However, Protestants outnumbered the Catholics among the newcomers, and religious as well as economic tensions arose. The Jesuits challenged Lord Baltimore's proprietary rights by acquiring land directly from the Indians and by claiming military and tax exemptions for themselves, thus undercutting Lord Baltimore's policy of religious toleration, and the Protestants staged a revolt when the English Civil War began in 1642. But Lord Baltimore met both challenges and in 1649 persuaded the Assembly to pass an act of religious toleration for Christians. While liberal in many respects, it provided the death penalty for persons who denied either the divinity of Christ or the Trinity. Puritan influences in 1654 forced a repeal of the act of toleration and subverted the authority of the proprietor, only to have Lord Baltimore and toleration restored by appeal to Cromwell himself. This status was not seriously altered until the accession of William and Mary, whom a group of dissidents petitioned to make Maryland a crown colony. The petition was granted in 1691 and in the following year the assembly abolished toleration for non-Trinitarians and Roman Catholics and acted to establish the Anglican Church. By 1704 Catholic priests could not legally say mass or baptize children of non-Catholic parents, and in 1718 Catholics lost the right to vote, prompting many of them to seek refuge in the newly founded Quaker colony of Pennsylvania.

William Penn, a convert to the Society of Quakers in 1667, desired a colony where everyone could find political and religious freedom, and in 1681 his dream materialized. In payment of a crown debt to his father, Penn received a charter enabling him to begin his "holy experiment." Two thousand settlers, mostly from England but also from Germany, Holland, and France, responded in the first year to Penn's promise of religious freedom, self-government, 50 acres of free land and 5,000 acres for £100. In 1682 Penn visited his forest, Pennsylvania, issued his very liberal *Frame of Government*, helped establish Quaker meetings, and founded Philadelphia, the city of brotherly love. In 1683 he concluded a treaty with the Indians for purchase of land and future trade relations. He was intent on reducing "the savage nations, by gentle and just means, to the love of civil society and the Christian religion" and his acknowledgment and treatment of the Indians as equals probably saved the colony from bitter frontier wars. Unfortunately, however, Penn's policies did not exclude slavery, which became a rending issue of conscience in the 1700s. Penn's colony thrived, but Penn's fortunes declined rapidly. Back in England, in 1701 he lost control of his colony, and spent some of the time before his death in 1718 in debtor's prison. Delaware, which was part of Penn's experiment, acquired an independent assembly in 1702.

To attract settlers to New Jersey, proprietors Lord John Berkeley and Sir George Carteret published agreements for complete freedom of conscience and a popular assembly. In 1674 Berkeley sold the southwestern half of the colony to two Quakers, six years later Carteret's widow sold the other half to a group of proprietors, and in 1702 the whole of New Jersey became a royal colony.

The Carolinas, first settled by dissidents from Virginia, were given by Charles II to eight aristocratic entrepreneurs in 1663. The Fundamental Constitutions of 1669 provided public support only for Anglicanism, with toleration for other churches, but Anglicanism was never popular and the vast territory made effective administration almost impossible, though evangelistic work among black slaves and Indians was carried on with some success. Large numbers of Quakers and Presbyterians delayed establishment of Anglicanism until 1704 in Charleston and 1715 in North Carolina. Although the Carolinas attracted a variety of settlers, the venture was not as profitable as anticipated, and in 1729 the proprietors sold the Carolinas back to the crown, which divided them into North and South.

Georgia was created for a double purpose: to establish a buffer zone against the Spanish in Florida, and to give debtors a new start in life. James Oglethorpe with 100 settlers founded Savannah in 1733. Roman Catholics did not enjoy full religious freedom, but liberty was granted to all others including the Moravians, who arrived with Augustus Spangenberg and John Wesley in 1735. Slavery, at first prohibited, was later accepted along with the removal of the 50-acre limit on farms. Although favored, Anglicanism was not established until 1755, three years after Georgia became a royal province.

During the 170 years between the founding of Jamestown in 1607 and the Declaration of Independence in 1776, despite a large variety of religious experiences, a common ethos pervaded the American scene: God had opened up a wilderness in which to establish a paradise; the dream of the kingdom of God would be realized in the New World; Roman Catholicism had succumbed to Satan, but in America the outcome would be different. Out of England had come Wycliffe "who begat Huss, who begat Luther, who begat truth." Christ was thus pleased to be born again, as it were, of England among the English, an idea extended in Foxe's *Book of Martyrs*. But many English came to believe that the Reformation would be completed not in England, but in the New World. In America God had given Christians a fresh start. Jonathan Edwards (1703–58) saw America as a wilderness wasteland that God had chosen to "be replenished from emptiness," by God. Edwards ardently portrayed God's sovereignty in his sermons and his *Freedom of the Will*, 1754.

Throughout the colonies the mystique took hold, that God was using them to work divine mysterious purposes in history, to turn a wilderness unspoiled by the evils of the Old World into a righteous paradise. Prosperity and success in pushing back the frontiers added to the conviction. Hardships and failures, of which there were many, did not erase it. The idea of voluntaryism, so strong among the sects, grew, along with freedom of thought and a sense of the democratic equality of all men under God.

The vast distances of the frontier fostered self-reliance as well as a spirit of disobedience and insubordination toward the unrealistic regulations coming from England. Roman Catholicism, regarded as the source of many of the Old World ills, operated under disabilities, and Jews were barred from office in some areas. A pluralism of white, Anglo-Saxon Protestants held the center of the stage. Establishment of churches was still prevalent but was encountering more and more resistance from those non-church members who were required to pay tithes. This was the "new man" that J. Hector St. John de Crévecoeur described in his *Letters from an American Farmer*, 1782. This was the ethos embodied in the Declaration of Independence and the Constitution with its first amendment touching religion.

Meanwhile, four European wars spilled over into America. The first of these was King William's War (1689–97), which in Europe was the struggle between William of Orange and Louis XIV of France. On both sides the war proved indecisive, breaking out again in Europe as the War of the Spanish Succession and in America as Queen Anne's War (1701–14), with gains of Acadia, Newfoundland, and some territory around Hudson Bay for the British. Again the same basic struggle between the French and English erupted in Europe in the War of the Austrian Succession, in America as King George's War (1740–48). Neither side gained significantly in America. The fourth and decisive struggle extended from 1754 to 1763, known as the Seven Years' War in Europe, as the French and Indian War in the colonies. The English colonies had outstripped the French in population by fifteen to one, in 1754, having approximately 1.5 million population. The French had forts scattered from Quebec to New Orleans; the English had a superior navy. The military outcome might have been predicted. Both Quebec and Montreal fell to the English, and the Treaty of Paris gave England all of France's possessions in the New World except New Orleans, which the French ceded to Spain.

These wars not only schooled the colonists in the arts of defense but also forced them to cooperate. More significantly, the French and Indian War added a vast domain to the British possessions. More serious trouble developed when England attempted to exact taxes to pay for the wars and increased administrative costs. This brought the Sugar Act duty, 1764, which hurt American trade with the West Indies and the Azores, and the Stamp Act, 1765, which required stamps on all legal documents. Severe fines were imposed for breaking either. Having no elected representation in England's Parliament, the colonists resented these as well as a series of other acts, and the resentment escalated into open revolt. Anger surged through Massachusetts and Virginia, active resistance was encouraged, the Sons of Liberty were organized, tax collectors were forced to resign, and pillaging was widespread. The Stamp Act Congress, 1765, which met in New York with nine of the colonies represented, sent a list of grievances to the governmental authorities in England and declared that taxation without consent was a violation of every Englishman's right. One thousand merchants in Boston, New York, and Philadelphia boycotted British products, and Benjamin Franklin pleaded the colonists' cause before Commons. The outcry brought repeal in 1770, but not before there were clashes of troops in Manhattan and Boston. When British merchants, with the aid of Parliamentary acts, attempted to monopolize the tea trade, Samuel Adams led a group of patriots in the famous Boston tea party of 1773. In other ports tea cargoes were allowed to mold or were burned. Parliament responded in 1774 with a rash of enactments designed to force the colonies to meet their obligations. Boston harbor was closed except for food and fuel, many governmental tasks were taken over by English authorities, and lawbreakers were cited to England for trial. This crisis prompted the Continental Congress to meet at Philadelphia in September 1774, to prepare for armed resistance. Hostilities began in April, 1775, when the colonials and the British clashed at Lexington-Concord, Massachusetts. Bunker Hill soon followed, and the Second Continental Congress appointed George Washington general of the army. On July 4, 1776, the colonies declared their independence. "We hold these truths to be self-evident—that all men are created equal; that they are endowed by their Creator with certain inalienable rights; that among these are life, liberty, and the pursuit of happiness. That, to secure these rights, governments are instituted among men, deriving their just powers from the consent of the governed; that, whenever any form of government becomes destructive of these ends, it is the right of the people to alter or to abolish it, and to institute a new government. . . ." The declaration cited acts of "repeated injuries and usurpations" and closed with an appeal to the "Supreme Judge of the world" for rectitude and protection.

Surmounting incredible difficulties, the colonies forced the British to negotiate favorable peace terms in 1783. For a while the colonies with their inadequate Articles of Confederation operated virtually without a central government. In 1787 the convention to frame a constitution convened in Philadelphia, with all but Rhode Island represented. A series of compromises led to the balance of powers among the legislative, executive, and judicial branches of government, with each state having equal representation in the Senate, and representation in the House based on population. Each slave was to be counted as three-fifths of a person, and slavery was not to be prohibited for twenty years. Specific powers were granted to the central government; the states retained all others. The United States began with the adoption of the Constitution in 1789, although Rhode Island held out to the end of that year and North Carolina until 1790. In 1791 the first ten amendments guaranteeing basic individual rights received approval.

Religious tests for suffrage disappeared after 1789, and a long political struggle ensued over states' vs. federal powers. Significantly, the federal government won, but not without a bitter fight over slavery and the outbreak of a Civil War. The outcome paralleled the movement toward national sovereignty throughout the world. Nationalism triumphed, and as in so many countries in the world, this presented little or no problem, for in the process the aims of the religious bodies and the aims of the national government had coalesced in a vast cultural amalgam. The separation of church-state intended by the first amendment—"Congress shall make no law respecting an establishment of religion, or prohibiting the free exercise thereof . . ."—had great practical value for individual sects but in a larger sense had little effect on the "righteous empire" ethos.

"From the beginning," writes Robert T. Handy, "American Protestants entertained a lively hope that some day the civilization of the country would be fully Christian" (*A Christian America,* New York: Oxford University Press, 1971, p. viii), but in the process, he continues, advancement of civilization in the form of nationalism became a greater good than evangelical truth. Evangelical religion fused with political aspirations, and the nation with the blessing of the sects rushed forward to fulfill America's "manifest destiny."

The Age of Reason and Deism, both of which challenged establishment of religion, had powerful advocates in Tom Paine, Benjamin Franklin, Jonathan Mayhew, James Madison, and Thomas Jefferson. Their contentions combined with Protestant arguments for toleration, a general hatred for medieval ecclesiastical control, and frontier individualism to produce strong tendencies in America toward pluralism. No one should be compelled in matters of conscience. The conviction grew that the state should be Christian but on a voluntary basis. This process undercut the religious establishments. The Half-way Covenant in 1662 in Massachusetts, which allowed church privileges to children of the saints even though they were devoid of a personal conversion, pointed in this direction. So did the revivals in the eighteenth century, which administered a shock to the old pattern of established churches with tolerated sects. The Great Awakening spread across denominational lines from New England to Georgia, demonstrating that biblical truth and faith could not be confined, and brought a general undermining of establishment. The revivals, along with pietism, tended to make personal, emotional conversion more significant than adherence to formulated beliefs. The success of revivalists like George Whitefield (1714–70) who journeyed from England and ranged up and down the Atlantic coast, Jonathan Edwards (1703–58) in Massachusetts, Theodorus Frelinghuysen (1691–1747) and Gilbert Tennent (1703–64) in New Jersey, Samuel Davies (1723–61) in Virginia, and James Davenport (1716–57) in Connecticut seemed to indicate that God's spirit was indeed present in a great outpouring of religious fervor. Thousands gathered to hear these preachers—in churches and out in the open. On a single Sunday Whitefield is said to have preached to 15,000. Benjamin Franklin reported on Whitefield speaking to a street crowd of 6,000 in Philadelphia. In their zeal to win converts, the revivalists largely ignored denominational lines. Whitefield was an Anglican priest but he paid little heed to his church's polity; if a man confessed a love for Jesus Christ, that was enough. Wild excesses of groaning, screaming, singing, fainting, writhing, weeping, and rejoicing marked many of the meetings, described in some detail by Jonathan Edwards in his *Narrative of Surprising Conversions,* 1737. These excesses also brought sharp reactions from more orthodox quarters, for many ministers regarded the revivals as an ephemeral fad and sought to curb them. In 1742 the General Assembly of Connecticut prohibited non-residents from preaching in any church without permission of the local pastor.

The revivals began in the 1720s and reached a climax in the 1740s. In later years they were continued by itinerant ministers like the Baptist Isaac Backus (1724–1806), the Methodist Francis Asbury (1745–1816), and scores of preachers who crisscrossed the frontier on horseback. The immediate effect of the Great Awakening was thousands of converts, as if the revivalists had tapped a reservoir of emotion completely ignored by the traditional churches. In the long run Presbyterians, Congregationalists, Baptists, and Methodists profited most. A secondary effect was the diminishing of the importance of established communions. By the time of the framing of the Constitution, no church was powerful enough to demand establishment even though the nation felt committed to the reasonableness of Christian morality as a basis for government. One nation, under God, took precedence. National sovereignty prevailed, the aims of Protestantism and the aims of the nation being so intertwined as to be indistinguishable. This ethos necessitated no established churches; all were working harmoniously toward the same end. Without fanfare the remaining establishments disappeared, in Connecticut in 1818, New Hampshire, 1819, and Massachusetts, 1833.

The American settlers had learned to live with religious freedom under the civil law. One religion was not essential to peace and order, as Thomas Jefferson observed, but national sovereignty and morality were. The dismal experience under the Articles of Confederation showed the necessity of national sovereignty, and an undergirding of morality was commonly assumed to be necessary for government. Timothy Dwight (1752–1817) was only one among many who insisted that government, Christian morality, liberty, and safety were inextricably linked. Benjamin Franklin objected to ministers who preached for conversion to a particular church, but he had no objection to their preaching for good citizenship. Deists, rationalists, and traditionalists might quarrel over the nature of God, and the appropriate manner of divine worship, but they could agree in general on sociopolitical morality as a necessary foundation for government. The Bible through revelation and nature through reason disclosed similar laws. Although some men like Thomas Paine and Elihu Parker objected to all religious institutions as inventions to hamper the human spirit, most of the rationalists, traditionalists, and pietists could exult over the simple teachings and morals of Jesus. Sound government demanded as much, and it was on this level that the Protestant denominations coalesced. No single church, but rather the nation was hailed as the umbrella of God's chosen people. Although there were rivalries among the white, Anglo-Saxon, Protestant churches, under the civil law all could unite. By the beginning of the nineteenth century, Christianity in America had become acculturated as the Protestant state. Protestantism and Americanism were amalgamated. Wrote Sydney Mead in *The Lively Experiment* (New York: Harper & Row, Publishers, 1963, p. 157), "Under the system of official separation of church and state the denominations eventually found themselves as completely identified with nationalism and their country's political and economic systems as had ever been known in Christendom."

One example of this acculturation was the establishment of the public school system early in the nineteenth century. The Presbyterians, fearing a generation of "irreligious youth," at first objected to public schools and actually established over 250 parochial schools of their own. But within thirty years they had become defunct. Protestants on the whole supported the public schools because they considered their own ends and those of the nation to be so closely interwoven. This was especially the case after 1825. When Horace Mann (1796–1859), the outstanding mentor in founding public schools, developed a system of public education for Massachusetts in 1837, he did so with the intention of promoting Christianity, not in a sectarian sense but as part of the moral fiber of the nation. Mann wanted all dogmatic sectarian theology excluded, but he wanted the Gospel included in all courses of study, for he regarded the Bible not as something polemical but as a base for peace and unity. Protestants accepted the public school system because they identified their own aims with those of the nation. The Bible rather than contentious creedal statements seemed to be a neutral basis for all. The distinction between religion and chauvinism faded. Efforts were made to legalize Sunday as a national day of rest, to outlaw drinking, to legislate Protestant morality. Ezra Stiles Ely, a Presbyterian pastor, published *The Duty of Freemen to Elect Christian Rulers,* 1828.

This identification of nationalism and Protestantism accounted in large measure for the anti-Catholic feeling that manifested itself during the same period. The Pope was regarded as a foreigner, and Catholics as little short of subversive subjects. In the first half of the nineteenth century, immigrants poured into the country. By 1860 foreign immigrants numbered about one-eighth of the population. Following the Napoleonic War and the failure of potato crops in Ireland, Bavaria, and the Rhineland, emigration on a large scale took place. During the period 1841 to 1855 a fifth of the Irish population emigrated, settling largely in the cities on the Atlantic seaboard as common laborers. Lutherans, Reformed, and Jews also came, but the large majority were Roman Catholics.

Bishop John Hughes (1797–1864) of New York actively opposed public education, and sought to gain public funds for Roman Catholic parochial schools. This activity prompted state after state to ban aid to sectarian schools and set up the public system, which was Protestant in ethos. It also contributed to the developing nativism. Protestant clergy and laity began to fear the enlarging Catholic population, which by 1860 numbered over 3,000,000, the largest single church body in the United States. The divine right of the Pope to dictate to secular governments, advocated by the papacy even more firmly after the French Revolution, caused Protestants to fear internal subversion. Lyman Beecher (1775–1863), Horace Bushnell (1802–76) and other clergymen preached anti-Catholicism. Samuel F. B. Morse (1791–1872), inventor of the telegraph, believed that Catholic missions in this country were spearheads of a subversive infiltration to overthrow American democracy. His book, *Foreign Conspiracy Against the Liberties of the United States,* 1835, charged that the Roman Catholic Church was the extension of a foreign government whose stated principles were inimical to American democracy, and that emigration was deliberately encouraged by European Catholic despots to undermine American democratic processes. Such feelings about the Catholics erupted in mob action in Boston in 1834 when stories about convent immoralities began to circulate; a mob burned the Ursuline Convent at

Charlestown. Maria Monk's *Awful Disclosures,* 1836, about her forced life as a priest's mistress, heralded an avalanche of similar writings. This attitude emotionalized the formation of the Native American party in 1837. It sought to limit immigration, exclude Catholics and foreign-born citizens from public office, and require aliens to live in the United States twenty-one years before being eligible for citizenship. In 1849 the Order of the Star-Spangled Banner formed in New York "to place in all offices of honor, trust, or profit, in the gift of the people, or by appointment, none but native-born Protestant citizens." This movement became prominent in the 1850s as the Know-Nothings, because members professed to know nothing. As the American party they controlled several state legislatures in 1854 to 55, and in 1856 ran Millard Fillmore for President.

Protestant nationalism also dictated treatment of the Mormons. Their doctrines of polygamy and celestial marriage affronted Protestant morality, and their insistence on political independence defied the nation's concept of chosenness. The golden tablets, which Joseph Smith (1805–44) found at Palmyra, New York, and translated with the aid of the angel Moroni, implicitly questioned biblical adequacy. The *Book of Mormon* was published in 1830, and the next year Smith and his followers moved to Kirtland, Ohio, and then to Caldwell County, Missouri, only to be forced by popular antagonism to retreat to Nauvoo, Illinois. Under Mormon leadership, Nauvoo became Illinois' largest city, and Smith ran for president in 1844, promising to free slaves and prisoners. In 1843 he received his revelation to practice polygamy. When word of this circulated, outraged citizens and state militia attacked. Smith and his brother Hyrum were arrested and wantonly shot in jail by members of a mob in 1844. The Mormons then split, the Reorganized Church of Jesus Christ of Latter-Day Saints disavowing polygamy and settling in Iowa, and the main group under Brigham Young (1801–77) trekking west to establish their State of Deseret in Utah, then part of Mexico. When Utah was acquired by the United States in 1848, the Mormons requested statehood but were denied. Repeated misunderstandings and clashes between Mormons and federal troops culminated in 1887 in confiscation of Mormon property and jailing of hundreds of polygamists. Three years later the Mormons discontinued polygamy, and when Utah became a state in 1896, its constitution specifically forbade polygamy.

The Civil War interrupted but did not allay this country's feeling of divine mission. Both North and South claimed providential guidance; both felt called to lead the nation to its manifest destiny. In the final outcome, those who championed states' rights vs. national sovereignty lost. And after the war, Protestant churches North and South continued the march to manifest destiny.

Economics and states' rights lay at the heart of the Civil War, but slavery proved to be the moral issue over which the abolitionists were willing to risk destruction of the national union. It became the overriding issue that God would have to arbitrate by giving victory to one side or the other. The nation could not endure half slave and half free; both sides had somehow sinned; only God's purging would decide which should prevail.

Both North and South were convinced of the righteousness of their views. In the colonists' early years, slavery was not seriously questioned. Slaves in the North as well as in the South were common, but economic developments rendered slavery unprofitable in the North, lucrative in the South. As the plantations of rice, indigo, tobacco, and cotton grew in the South, the need for slave labor increased. The population in 1790 was roughly 4,000,000, with slaves comprising about one-eighth of the total. Already slave-holding was profitable. The invention of the cotton gin by Eli Whitney in 1793 made it even more so. Within ten years cotton exports multiplied by 200, the number of slaves doubled, and by 1860 the number of slaves rose to 4,000,000. Cotton had become king from the Atlantic Coast to Texas and as far north as Missouri. Slaves sold for as much as $2,000 each on the auction block. The Constitution had promised no prohibition of slavery for twenty years, and King Cotton bade well to imbed it permanently. Although the Northwest Ordinance of 1787 had prohibited slavery north of the Ohio River, men like Jefferson had voiced strong opposition to human bondage, and the Quakers had sent a petition to Congress in 1790 objecting to the institution, it was not until the abolitionist movement in the 1820s that the divisions on slavery began to harden.

Earlier in the nineteenth century, some of the leading churches were ambiguous in their stances. The Methodists at their Christmas Conference in Baltimore, 1784, directed Methodist ministers to emancipate their slaves, and a general plan was drawn for laity, but within six months the whole matter was suspended. Bishop Francis Asbury skirted the issue, and Methodists generally compromised on the issue to satisfy brethren from the South and to avoid conflict with several state laws prohibiting manumission. Antislavery agitation fared little better among the Baptists, each resolution against slavery being greeted with such controversy in local associations that the matter was generally tabled. The Presbyterians by 1818 forced strong resolutions through their General Assembly, but these were almost totally ineffective in the South. Roman Catholics, Protestant Episcopal churches, and Lutherans avoided taking a stand in these early agitations. Congregationalists, Unitarians, and Quakers, rooted mainly in the North, took bold, aggressive antislavery stances. Many Christians from both North and South united in the effort to ship free blacks back to Africa, and Baptists, Methodists, and Episcopalians endorsed the American Colonization Society, formed in 1817. Backed by the national government and private donations, the Society sent its first shipload of eighty-nine blacks to Sierra Leone in 1821, but by 1830 the infeasibility of the scheme brought its demise.

Meanwhile the abolition forces began attacking on a broad religious-humanitarian-political front. William Lloyd Garrison, Benjamin Lundy, Theodore Dwight Weld, Lewis Tappan, James G. Birney, Elijah P. Lovejoy, Frederick Douglass, Wendell Phillips, Salmon P. Chase, and a host of others flooded the country with antislavery literature and speeches. Tempers flared, tensions rose. Mobs in the North and Midwest often broke up abolitionist meetings. Weld, Garrison, Tappan, and other abolitionists suffered physical violence. Many considered the abolitionists irresponsible. Yet they were powerful enough to run James G. Birney for President on the Liberty Party ticket in 1840 and 1844, and thwarted much of the Fugitive Slave Act in 1850. Harriet Beecher Stowe's *Uncle Tom's Cabin*, 1852, raised antislavery sentiments to a new pitch. Within five years it sold 500,000 copies.

The South reacted with powerful biblical, humanitarian, and political arguments of its own. Clergymen argued that slavery was not contrary to the Bible, that it was an institution divinely sanctioned in Scripture, that it provided obvious benefits for inferior blacks while at the same time enabling the superior white civilization to exist and prosper.

The Methodists, after several splinter groups had formed, split over the issue in 1844; the Baptists, after severe in-fighting, split in 1845; and the Presbyterians experienced a series of Old and New School splits from the mid-1840s to the outbreak of the war. Congregationalists and Unitarians, most of whom were in the North, and Quakers, who were almost totally against slavery, did not split. For various reasons other major church bodies chose not to take a stance. The divisions in the churches heralded the division in the nation which from 1861 to 1865 resorted to armed conflict.

Churches North and South enthusiastically supported their respective governments, appealed to God for military victory, and ministered to the combatants. Perhaps more than any other single person, Abraham Lincoln, often called the greatest theologian of the century, sensed the awful tragedy of the destruction wrought and the blood spilled, yet felt divinely called at all costs to preserve the Union. After the war, despite the overriding problems of Reconstruction, churches North and South once more joined in the effort to realize the righteous kingdom conceived in the beginning.

Anti-Roman Catholicism flared again. Protestants viewed the papacy as subversive both of religion and government, inasmuch as the Pope officially claimed superiority in all temporal and spiritual matters. The Ku Klux Klan, formed in the South to keep blacks from achieving social and political power, was violently anti-Catholic and persisted into the twentieth century. The American Protective Association, founded in Iowa in 1887, had as its avowed purpose the curbing of Roman Catholic political power, denying public office to Catholics, limiting immigration of Catholics, and protecting public funds from parochial schools. In 1884 Reverend Samuel Burchard labeled the Democratic party, which had gained strength from Irish immigration, as the party of "rum, Romanism and rebellion." Although Catholic leaders like Isaac Thomas Hecker (1819–88), founder of the Paulists in 1858, Cardinal James Gibbons (1834–1921), and John Ireland (1838–1918) believed in the separation of church and state and sought to Americanize the church, they were rebuffed by Pope Leo XIII's papal letter to Gibbons in 1899. Leo condemned efforts to modernize the church as bringing into question the church's right to decide on all moral and doctrinal matters. This papal rebuff served to heighten and substantiate the fears of the nativists. Some of the labor problem at the end of the nineteenth century rooted in anti-Catholic nativism, for immigrant Catholics comprised much of the labor force, and strikes appeared to impede the nation's manifest destiny. Newspapers carried stories and editorials blaming Catholics. The railroad strike of 1877 was bloody with battles between the workers and the police and militia. The strike of the McCormick Harvester Plant in 1886 brought death to 6 pickets and a retaliation bomb in Haymarket Square killed 8 policemen and injured 27 persons. Of the 7 "anarchists" who were tried, 4 were hanged, 1 committed suicide, and 2 were sentenced to life imprisonment. The Carnegie Steel Plant strike in Homestead, Pennsylvania, 1892, took 8,000 militia to quell, after battles between 300 Pinkerton detectives and laborers left 10 killed, and 60 wounded. The Great Pullman Palace Car Company strike in 1894 necessitated 2,000 federal troops to keep order. Between 1881 and 1900 the Bureau of Labor reported 23,798 strikes.

The bearers of the national Protestant mission could be deterred neither by Roman Catholic subversives nor by anarchists nor by demands of poor people whose dire poverty was regarded as God's judgment on them (cf. Deuteronomy 28). Andrew Carnegie, John D. Rockefeller, G. F. Baer, and other entrepreneurs of business believed that their wealth was God's providential blessing; preachers like Henry Ward Beecher, Horace Bushnell, Josiah Strong, and Russell Conwell were expounding poverty as the result of vice. Those who were blessed would complete the manifest destiny, would carry the principles of the righteous kingdom throughout the world. America's civilization, blessed by God, would be the springboard for the moral conquest of the world. As early as 1830 Alexander Campbell renamed the journal of the Disciples of Christ the *Millennial Harbinger*, for he felt that American civilization was the harbinger of the millennium—the perfect society of the Scriptures. In the nineteenth century the belief in America as a redeemer nation, elected to live out a new and sacred history, was still firmly fixed in the nation's collective memory. Speaking at the turn of the century, Indiana's Albert J. Beveridge (1862–1927) gave this public faith vivid expression before the United States Senate: "God has not been preparing the English-speaking and Teutonic peoples for a thousand years for nothing but vain and idle self-contemplation and self-admiration. No. He has made us master organizers of the world to establish system where chaos reigned. He has given us the spirit of progress to overwhelm the forces of reaction throughout the earth. He has made us adept in government that we may administer government among the savage and senile peoples. Were it not for such a force as this the world would relapse into barbarism and night. And of all our race He has marked out the American people as His chosen nation to finally lead in the redemption of the world" (cited in Ernest L. Tuveson, *Redeemer Nation*, Chicago: University of Chicago Press, 1968, p. vii).

But already forces had begun to build in America and in the world that would call such righteous identification of nation and church into question (see Chapter 21). These forces were complex and multiple in their influences, but two of them especially affected the American religious ethos, one directly and the other indirectly. One was the development of independent religious expression among blacks, causing many to question and eventually to reject the American synthesis of Christianity and culture. The other was the struggle of women for civil rights and more substantial recognition in religious leadership, a drive for equality in culture and religion that raised basic questions about the structures of both.

THE NEGRO CHURCH

The Negro church in America until the twentieth century was not essentially different from its white counterpart, despite the fact that the black church incorporated into itself the "invisible institution"—elements from its African heritage. Even after 1900 the vast majority of black religious groups could be so categorized. Nevertheless, nascent within the blacks' search for identity and integrity were differentiating forces that would draw many blacks closer to an African Muslim heritage, cause some to look for non-white rootage in ancient Ethiopian Christianity, and prompt others to find religious outlets in cult developments.

Symbolic of the earlier period of the black church was Booker T. Washington (ca. 1858–1915), son of a mulatto slave woman, author of the popular *Up from Slavery*, 1901. Although born a slave, he won for himself an education, graduated in 1875 from Hampton Institute, Virginia, and was for a time a part of its faculty. Hampton Institute started in 1868, largely as a result of the Freedmen's Bureau and the efforts of the American Missionary Association, which had heavy Congregationalist backing. As the director of Tuskegee Institute, which opened July 4, 1881, Booker T. Washington became a renowned educator of blacks, the most widely known and revered black leader in his time. At the Atlanta Exposition in 1895 he delivered his famous "Put down your buckets where you are" speech. He asked whites of the South to invest in the future of their faithful, cooperating Negroes, and Negroes to further the place of their birth. In effect he accepted the segregation and social inequality that prevailed at the end of the nineteenth century. This was the "Atlanta Compromise" soon scorned by many blacks.

Symbolic of the later period and a transitional figure into the twentieth century was W. E. B. DuBois (1868–1963), a prolific American black author, born in Massachusetts, and educated at Fisk University, Harvard University where he received a Ph.D. degree, and the University of Berlin. Professor of Latin and Greek at Wilberforce University (1894–6), of history and economics at Atlanta University (1897–1910), co-founder of the National Association for the Advancement of Colored People (NAACP), 1910, and director of its publications (1910–32), and professor of sociology at Atlanta University (1932–44), DuBois won worldwide recognition as a black leader. He sought to make blacks aware and proud of their African background, of which he found many vestiges in the blacks' speech, mores, and the invisible institution. He vehemently repudiated Booker T. Washington's Atlanta Compromise and openly condemned black segregation and social inequality in *Souls of Black Folk*, 1903. DuBois called a meeting of Negro leaders at Niagara Falls, 1905, to organize for rights of Negroes. The resulting Niagara Movement's first conference, 1906, resolved to claim for Negroes "every right that belongs to a free-born American, civil and social, and until we get these rights we shall never cease to protest and assail the ears of America with the stories of its shameful deeds toward us." Not satisfied to have whites and their Christian God set goals for blacks, he broke with the NAACP in 1934. DuBois typifies a push for equality on a broad front among blacks in the twentieth century.

Before the Civil War, ninety percent of the black population in the United States was in the South, and by 1900 seventy-two percent was still in the South. The institution of slavery in the South did not look favorably on separate, organized churches among Negroes. Whites feared that separate black churches might prompt conspiracy or rebellion among the slaves. Escape plots and insurrection were not uncommon, the most famous being those connected with Gabriel Prosser in 1800, Denmark Vesey in 1822, and Nat Turner in 1831. David Walker's *Appeal*, 1829, urging slaves to revolt against their masters aroused widespread fear among owners. In the late 1700s Quakers who opposed slavery initiated the famous Underground Railroad, which enabled thousands of slaves to escape into Canada through Illinois, Indiana, Michigan, Ohio, Pennsylvania, and Massachusetts (by ship). Levi Coffin, Frederick Douglas, Sojourner Truth, and Harriet Tubman were only a few of the active leaders in this movement. Southern states offered high rewards for the capture of those engaged in this extensive enterprise. Separate Negro congregations might abet these activities. Those blacks who experienced conversions in the lively frontier revivals conducted mostly by the Baptists, Methodists, and Disciples of Christ, usually became segregated parts of white congregations. As early as 1787 the Methodists actively evangelized slaves for church membership. These successful missions increased in the first half of the nineteenth century. Conversion and the frontier revivals gave Negroes a semblance of equality, but only a few scattered separate black congregations formed. Those few that did form patterned themselves after the Baptists and Methodists. The autonomous congregational polity of the Baptists especially helped in the formation of early groups in Virginia, Maryland, and the Carolinas. One such Negro Baptist church in Silver Bluff, South Carolina, dates back to 1773.

Still scattered and few in the South, in the North a number of Negro churches started. Growing racial consciousness increased the desires of blacks to manage their religious affairs, so that after 1800 several independent churches developed in Illinois, Louisiana, Massachusetts, New York, Ohio, and Pennsylvania. Many Negroes as well as whites got involved in the Underground Railroad. Richard Allen (1790–1831) and Absalom Jones, both free Negro Methodists, founded the Free African Society in Philadelphia, 1787. In 1791 this group adopted a polity similar to that of the Protestant Episcopal Church. Jones became their pastor and eventually received ordination. Allen stayed within Methodism, in 1792 founding the Bethel African Methodist Episcopal Church, consecrated by Bishop Francis Asbury, from whom Allen received ordination in 1799. However, denigrating segregation practices in white religious assemblies prompted delegates from several black congregations to meet in Philadelphia in 1816 and formally establish the African Methodist Episcopal

Church, with Richard Allen as its first bishop. This AME church spawned other churches and circuits and by 1863 was strong enough to purchase Wilberforce University in Ohio. The African Methodist Episcopal Church Zion originated within segregated John Street Methodist Church in New York City. Bishop Asbury in 1796 gave permission for Negro members to withdraw and form their own congregation. They constituted themselves a separate church from Allen's AME church in 1821. James Varick became their first bishop in 1822. By 1900 these two Methodist-related churches had nearly a million members.

The Negro churches rendered an immense religious and social service, both in the South and North. Freedom in the North did not mean non-discrimination or civil rights; many former slaves were subject to unscrupulous schemes of kidnapping and extradition under Fugitive Slave laws. Under slavery, Negroes by law were viewed as property, less than human beings; like any other property they could be bought and sold at will. They had few effective means of redress against cruelty and were generally kept in ignorance. Revolts were fiercely quelled. In their churches, however, Negroes found solace and a sense of integrity, decision-making, freedom, and responsibility. They had opportunity to develop organizational and leadership skills. Some black businesses had their genesis in the efforts of churches to meet the economic needs of their people. Negro churches were poorer than those of the whites, their black leaders generally had more limited education, and they developed different styles of worship, but theologically little difference existed. Both white and black churches stressed revival conversion, personal right living, and rewards in heaven. However, racial consciousness harbored future changes.

During the Civil War period blacks grew increasingly aware of the issues involved. In the North some blacks became outspoken abolition leaders, and in the South many slaves made their way to the Union army and volunteered. January 1, 1863, President Abraham Lincoln issued the Emancipation Proclamation declaring freedom for slaves within states in rebellion. Although the Emancipation did not apply in all states, it marked a political policy shift from simply confining slavery to its existing boundaries to outright conferral of liberty on more than three million slaves. Anti-slavery feelings were running so high in England and France that the Emancipation helped stave off foreign military intervention to aid the South. The thirteenth constitutional amendment, which took effect in 1865, abolished slavery completely.

Although the war ended master-slave relationships, the miserably poor economic resources of most blacks after the Civil War made them relatively easy prey to legal and illegal exploitation. Following the war, freed slaves wandered the South like dispossessed refugees. As the former masters had little capital for hiring labor, a system of tenant farming soon emerged. Black tenants and others mortgaged their future harvests in exchange for the means to live and raise crops. This was basic to the economy of the South. The Black Codes passed by provisional southern states in 1865–66 severely restricted mobility of blacks and locked the vast majority of southern Negroes into sharecropping dependency. Organized white vigilantes of the Ku-Klux-Klan type harrassed, abused, threatened, flogged, and murdered resisters. Race riots broke out in New Orleans and Memphis, prompting the return of military rule. The fourteenth and fifteenth amendments to the Constitution, 1868 and 1869, gave equal rights to Negroes as citizens, prohibiting any abridgement on account of color or previous servitude. Some Negroes were elected to state legislatures and other offices. Two won seats in the U.S. Senate and thirteen became members of the House of Representatives. The Freedmen's Bureau, 1865, was active for four years and carried educational projects until 1872. It provided food, medicine, school facilities, and legal aid for freed blacks; regulated wages; and helped distribute 800,000 acres of confiscated land in 40-acre plots, although much of the land was actually returned to its former owners. Along with such church agencies as the American Missionary Association (heavily Congregational) the Freedmen's Bureau established lower and higher schools. Among the most successful and enduring were Atlanta University in Georgia, 1865, Fisk University in Tennessee, 1866, Howard University in Washington, D.C., 1866, Talladega College in Alabama, 1867, and Hampton Institute in Virginia, 1868. Literally hundreds of missionaries and teachers worked among the Negroes. The blacks organized their churches in enlarging conventions and conferences—the Colored Primitive Baptists, 1866, and the Colored Methodist Episcopal Church, 1870, being typical. However, interest in succoring Negroes gradually waned. Federal military control relaxed. The Freedmen's Bureau collapsed, 1862, the Supreme Court invalidated the Civil Rights Act in 1883, poorer segregated schools resulted from the far-reaching "separate but equal" decision in the Plessy v. Ferguson case, 1896, and in the last quarter of the nineteenth century general segregation in the South and to a considerable extent in the North made a mockery of the thirteenth, fourteenth, and fifteenth amendments. Reconstruction had failed.

Negroes soon had virtually no political voice in the South. Grandfather clauses (no one could vote unless his grandfather had voted), literacy tests, poll taxes, and other rules, applied unevenly to whites and blacks, effectively disfranchised Negroes, especially in the primaries of the Democratic Party. Jim Crow laws after 1883 restricted or excluded Negroes from many public facilities, restaurants, hotels, trains, and buses. They could not serve on juries; their testimony was deemed unequal to that of whites, and miscegenation was made illegal, although sex between white men and Negro women was tolerated and rape often overlooked. President Woodrow Wilson curtailed jobs for blacks in the Federal Civil Service in 1913. Thus, White Supremacy, which regarded Negroes as biologically and morally inferior, became embedded in social mores and law, and set a prevailing ethos for blacks in the first half of the twentieth century.

Despite this situation or perhaps because of it, one out of every four blacks in the United States was in a church. There they found refuge, a sense of belonging, leadership training, and some economic and educational help. With rapid industrialization and the labor needs of World Wars I and II large numbers of Negroes migrated to the metropolitan northern centers, creating changes. The church's place as a social center lessened, and a restive revolutionary spirit increased.

Liberals in politics and religion in the 1900s began various drives to gain civil rights for blacks. They were plagued by guilt and stung by foreign totalitarian tyrants justifying their own actions or nullifying American protests of maltreatment of minorities by pointing to the American black situation. The main thrust to gain civil rights, however, came from the Negro community. W. E. B. DuBois deliberately rejected the 1895 Atlanta Compromise of Booker T. Washington and proved to be the prophet of a more militant mood among blacks.

To be sure, not all black groups were militant. Large numbers continued to be parts of or modeled themselves after the established churches, though with some differences. Around 1906, William J. Seymour inaugurated a Pentecostal revival in Los Angeles that spawned over 4,000 churches and spread across the country and into Latin America. Already strong among white churches, Pentecostalism appealed especially to the economically deprived. Father Divine's Peace Mission in New York flourished with its chicken dinners for the poor during the Depression. Started by George Baker (d. 1965) in Georgia, it moved north to Brooklyn, Harlem, and Philadelphia, with "farm" branches in other cities. It stressed prohibition of drinking, smoking, gambling, cursing, stealing, and dancing; declared sex would but increase the world's misery; and barred use of the words "Negroes" and "Whites." Many of his followers regarded him as divine, as God. Sweet Daddy Grace's United House of Prayer for All People, begun in 1925 by Charles Emmanuel (d. 1960) became noted for public baptisms with fire hoses, wild dancing, spiritual ecstasies, and the luxurious living and autonomous power of its leader. Militant black groups raised questions about such religious organizations, even though they obviously brightened the lives of thousands of ghetto inhabitants.

Black nationalism had already begun to rise. Marcus Garvey (1887–1940), a Jamaican, dreamed of leading blacks in a redemption of Africa for Africans. He founded the Universal Negro Improvement Association in 1914 to awaken Negro self-consciousness. His followers spoke of a Black Madonna and Child and a nonwhite God. The seeds he sowed bore fruit in the Black Muslim movement initiated by Timothy Drew (1866–1929), a North Carolinian. Building on his interest in Islamic religion, Drew founded the Moorish Science Temple of America in 1913, urging his followers to call themselves Moorish Americans rather than Negroes. He called himself Noble Prophet Ali Drew and circulated *The Koran* and the writings of Garvey among his followers. Internal strife resulted in the murder of one of Drew's leading assistants and of Drew himself in 1929. However, Wali Farad Muhammad claimed he was a reincarnation of Drew and established strong Temples of Islam in Detroit and Chicago. He mysteriously disappeared in 1934. Robert Poole who took the name of Elijah Muhammad rose to dominance in Chicago. He exalted Farad and claimed for himself direct messages from Allah, which he published in *Muhammad Speaks.* He prophesied the end of Christianity and the rise of a Black Nation led by him that would rule the earth by the year 2,000. During World War II he and some of his followers went to jail for refusing to kill. Nevertheless, the movement continued to expand, especially among youth, zooming in membership to over 100,000 in the 1960s, its exact strength not known.

Malcolm Little (1925–65), known as Malcolm X, son of a Baptist minister in Nebraska, converted to the Black Muslims while serving a six-year prison term (1946–52) and became an inspired national apostle with a huge following. He left the Black Muslims in 1964 and founded a Black Nationalist Muslim Mosque and an Organization of Afro-American Unity to coalesce black liberation efforts. Unfortunately, he was assassinated in Harlem, February 21, 1965. His influential autobiography appeared posthumously. While these and other black movements evidence alienation and even despair, other groups, especially the NAACP, sought and won concrete gains for blacks.

The National Association for the Advancement of Colored People, founded in 1910, and directed from 1916 to 1930 by James Weldon Johnson, attempted to protect basic rights for blacks by recourse to courts of law. Its success was gradual but substantial. Prodded by various court decisions, in 1949 President Harry S. Truman issued two executive orders that ended segregation in the armed forces and in the federal civil service. But the signal victory of the NAACP came in 1954 when the Supreme Court ruled unanimously against racial segregation in public schools. The ramifications of the decision shook the social ethos of the nation. Yet implementation of the decision was painfully slow. In 1957 President Eisenhower moved federal troops into Little Rock, Arkansas, to support a court order to integrate the city's Central High School. In the following years, aroused college students, civil rights advocates, and the liberal churches mounted a sustained drive to equalize rights for blacks in all areas of society. Dr. Martin Luther King, Jr., who in 1955 successfully directed a boycott against Jim Crow buses in Montgomery, Alabama, became the first president of the newly organized Southern Christian Leadership Conference. He stood for peaceful, non-violent resistance. Sit-ins, already a tactic of the Congress of Racial Equality organized in 1943, multiplied throughout the South in an effort to integrate lunch counters, theaters, playgrounds, and other facilities. The Student Nonviolent Coordinating Committee launched "freedom rides" on interstate buses and trains. Voter registration drives made blacks aware of their political power. In 1962, despite legal machinations, rioting, and threats from the governor, the first black, James H. Meredith, registered at the University of Mississippi. Dr. King, Jr., won significant victories in Birmingham, Alabama, in 1963. His speeches, books, and deeds made him the living symbol of the blacks' struggle for equality.

The struggle was not without cost. Thousands of civil rights activists were jailed, untold numbers beaten, scores killed. Buses were bombed and burned. The year 1963 climaxed with 250,000 freedom marchers converging on Washington, D.C., where they heard King's moving "I Have a Dream" speech from the steps of the Lincoln Memorial. The dream did not immediately materialize. In 1964 King received the Nobel Prize for peace but that year there were more riots, in the North as well as the South, and in the summer of 1965, 25,000 civil righters gathered at

Selma, Alabama, to conduct the last of the great interracial demonstrations. Blacks had come to feel that they had to do it alone, and whites were turning increasingly toward Vietnam. Despite the meeting of the black churchmen in 1966 in Harlem who decried past otherworldly religious concerns and resolved to work for the reign of God in this world, a feeling had developed that traditional white Christian standards of right and wrong had become irrelevant, and that only might counted. Pent-up frustrations of blacks erupted into riots, notably in the Watts District of Los Angeles in the summer of 1965, in Detroit and Newark in 1967. The assassination of Dr. King on April 4, 1968, occasioned a nationwide upheaval of rioting and burning, as if his murder were proof that the time for Christian non-violent resistance had passed.

Many blacks have joined in the promotion of black revolution, even demanding "reparation" payments from other churches. In 1968 the Rev. Albert B. Cleage, Jr., pastor of the UCC Shrine of the Black Madonna in Detroit, published *The Black Messiah*, picturing Jesus as a revolutionary black leader. *Black Theology and Black Power*, 1969, by Professor James H. Cone, a leading black theologian, at Union Theological Seminary, New York, expressed a revolutionary theme that Cone actively promoted in developing nations.

At the beginning of the 1980s one can say that nationwide segregation and discrimination have significantly altered and decreased in schools, churches, housing, politics, the military, and the job market. Old bastions have cracked. In 1978 the Mormon Church in Salt Lake City declared its priesthood open to worthy Negro males and Joseph Freeman, a black, was ordained an elder. However, one could hardly say segregation and discrimination have ceased. Unemployment among blacks in the 1970s ran significantly higher than among whites, and racial disturbances continued to erupt in various cities. Blacks have increasingly developed political acumen and power. In the 1980s a black nominee for the presidency appears possible. As more than fifty percent of the blacks have entered the mythical middle class status, revolutionary tendencies have subsided, but the search for integrity and identity continues. The problems of uncertainty in religion plague Christianity and cut across racial lines regardless of discrimination.

WOMEN AND THE CHURCH

Women in America, both black and white, represent another group struggling for civil rights and a sense of equality in religious affairs, a struggle that extends worldwide, especially in predominantly Christian countries. They have had to struggle in the secular world for legal identity, the right to vote, equality of opportunity in professions, equal pay for equal work, and in the churches for ordination and high clerical positions. Like other denied groups they have had to be belligerent just to be heard. During the last century and a half their voices have been heard, and many barriers have fallen, but not all the goals have been achieved.

Women have been a mainstay in Christianity since its beginning, but have found access to ordained leadership roles and historical recognition very difficult, except in some "off-shoot" groups. Entrenched male domination of society, traditional mores and customs favoring men, Eve's creation from Adam's rib and her role as temptress, Paul's admonition that women are to keep quiet in church, and an ideal of asceticism that equated sin with sex and denigrated women as minions of temptation have all been part of a complex of factors that have denied women equal status in society and the church. Such a condition prevailed generally in Christendom until the nineteenth century. The second half of the twentieth century witnessed dramatic changes, some of which have shaken established customs and raised basic questions about Christianity's structures, creating turmoil in some churches and renewal of strength in others. In the 1980s abortion, contraception, and ordination are still controversial subjects, particularly in Roman Catholicism, the largest segment of Christianity; Pope Paul VI's *Humanae vitae,* 1968, rejected all methods of artificial birth control. In Protestantism contraception in various forms and ordinations of women have become commonplace, but the moral implications of abortion have prompted contradictory stances. Symbolic of the changes, by 1980, after centuries of disfranchisement, women have the right to vote in most countries, and in 1982 the United Church of Christ reported that fifty-two percent of its students preparing for ministry were female.

Early in the nineteenth century women perceived freedom to vote as the basic right on which all the other equalities rested, but woman suffrage did not come easy. In the 1830s and 40s many dedicated American women, despite scorn and ridicule, pushed for enfranchisement. Lucretia Mott, Lucy Stone, Ernestine Rose, Abigail Foster, Angelina and Sarah Grimke, Elizabeth Cady Stanton, Susan B. Anthony, and Margaret Fuller became nationally known as progenitors of voting rights for women. Their efforts met with limited success, but prepared the way for the future. In 1848 at a convention in Seneca Falls, New York, sixty-eight women and thirty-two men adopted a Declaration of Principles demanding equality in education, preaching, teaching, and work. "We hold these truths to be self-evident: that all men and women are created equal. . . ." The declaration depicted human history as "a history of repeated injuries and usurpations on the part of man toward woman, having in direct object the establishment of an absolute tyranny over her." It urged women to assume the sacred duty of securing for themselves the franchise. Other conventions followed, including a national convention in Worcester, Massachusetts, in 1850. In 1852 Susan B. Anthony and Elizabeth Cady Stanton joined forces to work for equality, and in 1869 they established the National Woman Suffrage Association to secure an amendment to the Constitution. Lucy Stone and Julia Ward Howe led another group, the American Woman Suffrage Association, to work on state levels. In 1890 these two groups coalesced as the National American Woman Suffrage Association, headed successively by Elizabeth Cady Stanton and Susan B. Anthony. Beginning with Wyoming, between 1890 and 1918, fifteen states included woman suffrage in their constitutions, although the "Anthony Amendment" to the U.S. Constitution did not get past the U.S. Senate in 1887 or 1914. However, in response to continued pressure, the House in 1918 and the Senate in 1919 passed a constitutional amendment. August 18, 1920, Tennessee became the thirty-sixth state to ratify the nineteenth amendment establishing woman suffrage as part of the U.S. Constitution. A similar victory for women came in Great Britain in 1918.

An Equal Rights Amendment (ERA) has not fared as well. Although U.S. laws have prohibited discrimination of women on account of sex since 1964, and although the Supreme Court in 1971 declared discrimination based on sex was in violation of the fourteenth amendment, a constitutional change insuring equal rights for women has not been accepted. The House of Representatives in 1971 and the Senate in 1972 passed such an amendment, but the necessary states failed to ratify, even though in 1978 the period for ratification was extended for thirty-nine months beyond March 1979. The new deadline passed without the necessary number of states ratifying. Many women still feel unequal legally to men. In Canada a Bill of Rights insuring no denial of rights because of sex passed in 1960.

In the churches ordination of women has proved most troublesome. Early revivals conducted by Charles G. Finney (1792–1875) may well have initiated changes that later led to ordination. He and other frontier revivalists encouraged women who experienced dramatic conversions to testify in public. Invited to repeat their testimonies in other settings, some women in effect became evangelists, witnessing not only to their conversions but also voicing other concerns. Various churches tried utilizing deaconnesses before 1900 in visitation and missionary enterprises. The Methodists were modestly successful, but their deaconnesses were not officially recognized until 1889. Methodist women received limited ordination as supply pastors in 1924 and full ordination rights in 1956. With women's suffrage constitutionalized in 1920, barriers to women in secular and religious offices weakened. Restrictions on women in the armed services ended officially in 1948, and most other professions have opened up, but the turbulent 1960s, when so many people lost confidence in religion, revealed a broad split among the churches on female ordination. Friends, Baptists, United Church of Christ members, and Methodists, having long utilized the talents of women, accommodated with little fanfare to the increased ordinations of women. United Presbyterians and the Lutheran Church in America followed suit, but more traditional churches and conservative pockets in liberal groups soon became embroiled in controversy. The Anglican Church, the Roman Catholic Church, the Mormon Church in Salt Lake City, Conservative Jews, and other "traditionalists" by 1980 had taken no definitive actions. Nevertheless, agitation goes on, particularly in Roman Catholicism. The papacy has reiterated its opposition to ordination of women, despite open demonstrations by nuns, priests, and laity favoring ordinations of women. Thousands have expressed their indignation by defection. In 1980 Roman Catholic seminarians numbered only 13,000 in contrast to 1970 when there were twice that many. Thousands of nuns since the 1960s have left their orders; many have defied the papacy by getting married. Whether traditional rigidity regarding female ordination is fading has not become clear. What is clear, however, is that the struggles of blacks and women for equality, identity, and integrity as persons have radically affected society and Christianity. The larger issue of worldwide religious uncertainty has not been allayed. Whether troubled Christianity can move beyond uncertainty in the last quarter of the twentieth century remains to be seen.

21

Retrenchment, Outreach, Reappraisal, and Uncertainty

To the scientific secularism and burgeoning nationalism of the nineteenth century, Christendom reacted with a variety of attitudes. Catholicism symbolized retrenchment; it stood like a fortress against all the forces commonly associated with modernism and defended revealed religion as seen by the papacy with surprising vigor. Roman Catholicism reluctantly accepted religious pluralism and national sovereignty, without abandoning its assertion that it is the one true church and that it should by right dictate in all temporal and spiritual matters. Not until Vatican II did it show any openness to new trends, and since the upheaval that surrounded Vatican II, many signs have pointed again to retrenchment, as if Roman Catholicism looked briefly for a new place to stand, found only uncertainty, and turned again to historically proven ways.

The Oxford Movement was a reaction within Protestantism similar to Roman Catholicism's reaction to modernism; it was a return to tradition, and many of its adherents converted to Roman Catholicism. The Ecumenical Movement was fed by deep desires for Christian unity and was led almost entirely by Protestants, but it too floundered in the twentieth century, buffeted by internal disagreements and external events. Within Protestantism serious theological cleavages emerged, roughly identified as Liberalism and Fundamentalism. Liberalism in general adjusted to the trends of modernism, adapted its own beliefs to those of science, and entered the twentieth century confidently expecting human progress to bring social panacea, only to find those expectations shattered by two destructive world wars. Fundamentalism in general balked at adjusting to a modernism that continued to erode its biblical basis of authority. It fought Darwinism, secular rationalism, and liberalism by asserting its famous Fundamentals—biblical inerrancy, the virgin birth, substitutionary atonement, physical resurrection, and miracles—only to be overwhelmed by ridicule in the "monkey trial" of 1925. Liberalism and fundamentalism have struggled to piece together their broken cisterns in the face of the twentieth century's relativistic uncertainty about God, morals, reality, and meaning. Signs of hope and despair have surfaced but are by no means clear. Thus Protestantism without a centralized authority reacted to the powerful forces of modernism in varied ways, compromising and running with some, resisting and retreating from others. The turmoil produced many new sects, people searching for a firm place to stand. Old standards slipped, new positions met with skepticism, and uncertainty with its many attendants became pervasive.

THE OXFORD MOVEMENT AND ECUMENISM

A Protestant return to tradition and a burst of evangelical strength manifested themselves early in the nineteenth century. The Oxford Movement in England, which was in part a reaction to the French Revolution, epitomized the return to tradition. Many devout Christians distrusted critical rationalism and political reform and longed for the certainties of orthodoxy. John Keble (1792–1866) was among them. *The Extraordinary Black Book* of 1831 showed that scandalous immorality was rife in ecclesiastical circles. Liberal Unitarians had grown stronger and were demanding that the blot left on them by the Act of Toleration be removed. In 1772, 250 clergymen, led by Theophilus Lindsey, petitioned Parliament for relief from subscribing to belief in the Trinity. When denied, Lindsey withdrew from the Anglican system and established the first Unitarian church in London. By 1813 Unitarians were no longer required to accept the Trinity. The Congregational Union of England and Wales in 1833 objected to "the imposition of any human standard, whether of faith or discipline" and "reserved to everyone the most perfect liberty of conscience." Lord Byron (1788–1824) as an English poet of revolt expressed the weariness of man in bondage to institutions. Industrial classes and liberals were demanding a voice in government. The newly founded London University required no religious tests, and the Reform Bill of 1832 diluted Anglican landowners' privileges by extending the franchise. In 1829 the Roman Catholic Emancipation removed many restrictions from Catholics and allowed them to hold seats in Commons, as well as other public offices.

Leaders in the Oxford Movement resisted this erosion; either the Church of England was established or it was not. If established, then it should be honored as such. On July 14, 1833, John Keble preached his famous sermon on National Apostasy, in which he accused the nation of infringing on apostolic rights and disavowing the sovereignty of God. He insisted on sacramentalism, saying that salvation was possible only through the sacraments and that bishops in the apostolic succession were essential in administering them. He called for a return to Prayer Book orthodoxy, and implied that sectarian evangelicals and enthusiasts with their emphasis on preaching and reform had strayed from true Christianity. Keble was soon joined by John Henry Newman (1801–90), author of "Lead, kindly Light, amid the encircling gloom," and Edward B. Pusey (1800–82). In *Tracts for the Times* and other publications they cogently defended orthodox views, insisted that the state had not created the church and had no right to destroy it, and gradually drifted closer to Roman Catholicism. In *Tract XC*, 1841, Newman argued that the Thirty-nine Articles were really in harmony with Catholicism, that the articles condemned Roman corruptions but did not outrightly reject purgatory, pardons, images, relics, invocation of saints, the five extra sacraments, and masses, and that those who are Catholic in heart and doctrine should subscribe to them. In *Via Media of the Anglican Church* Newman hit hard at the inadequacy of the Protestant appeal to the Bible and the multiplicity of subjective views that must follow for lack of a guiding principle. The Oxford reformers were charged with Jesuitism, subversion, and betrayal of Anglicanism. For preaching a doctrine of Real Presence in the sacrament, Pusey was suspended from preaching at Oxford University for two years. W. G. Ward lost his university degrees for publishing *Ideal of a Christian Church*, 1844, in which he declared his right to hold Roman Catholic views and still be an Anglican. The Oxford reformers leaned so close to Roman Catholicism that on October 9, 1845, Newman and several hundred other Englishmen joined the Roman Catholic Church. Defections to Rome became numerous, and in 1864 Newman issued his *Apologia Pro Vita Sua* in defense of his succession. Henry E. Manning (1808–92), Archbishop of Chichester and a prominent tract writer, joined the Roman Catholic Church in 1851, became Archbishop of Westminster, and in 1875 was made a cardinal. He staunchly supported the papal infallibility of Vatican I. Newman was not ultramontane and did not become a cardinal until 1879. Pusey, the recognized leader of the Oxford Movement after 1845, pressed hard during the next seventeen years for reunion with Rome. No other movement did more to revitalize religion in England in the mid-nineteenth century.

The Oxford Movement was more than retrenchment. It embodied the ecumenical stance of Rome (let all return to Roman Catholicism). Its influence was widespread, but Protestantism in general did not choose this pathway to unity. A significant surge toward oneness in Christ was already developing among Protestants in the nineteenth century, almost as if the churches sensed the weakness of their divided loyalties. Beginning with missions, it gave rise to ecumenicity in the next century—only to be rebuffed by Rome and sidetracked by onslaughts of secularism, theological differences, organizational problems, and directional uncertainty.

Protestant missionary efforts lagged far behind those of Roman Catholicism, which through its monastic orders, particularly the Jesuits and Franciscans, had penetrated most areas of the world by 1800. Neither early Lutheranism nor Calvinism fostered missions; whether this was for lack of opportunity and means, indifference, wars, eschatology, or doctrine is not known. In 1651 Wittenberg's theological faculty showed little

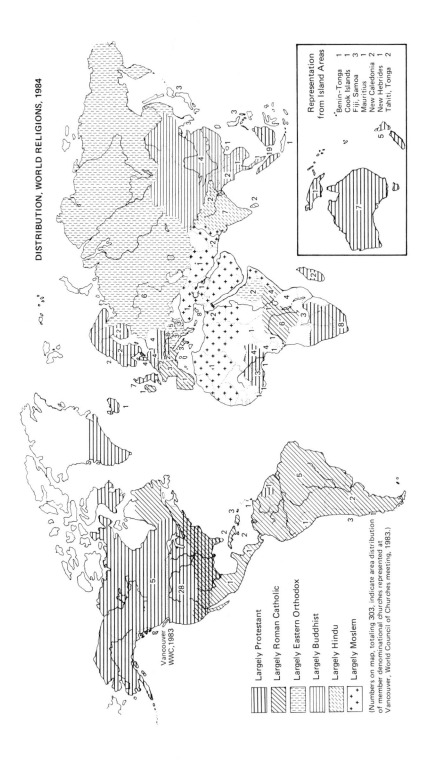

DISTRIBUTION, WORLD RELIGIONS, 1984

Representation
from Island Areas

Benin–Tonga   1
Cook Islands   1
Fiji, Samoa   3
Mauritius   1
New Caledonia   2
New Hebrides   1
Tahiti, Tonga   2

Vancouver
WWC, 1983

Largely Protestant

Largely Roman Catholic

Largely Eastern Orthodox

Largely Buddhist

Largely Hindu

Largely Moslem

(Numbers on map, totaling 303, indicate area distribution
of member denominational churches represented at
Vancouver, World Council of Churches meeting, 1983.)

interest in missions on the grounds that countries still languishing in heathenism were obviously under the judgment of God. Baron von Weltz, who died as a missionary in Dutch Guiana, proposed a Lutheran missionary society in 1664 but met with little encouragement. Lutheran missions were sparse until the rise of Spener-Francke pietism and the formation of the Danish-Halle Mission in 1705, which in the following year sent missionaries to India. Zinzendorf's Moravians at Herrnhut continued this interest in missions, sending Leonard Dober and David Nitschmann to the West Indies in 1732, and Christian David in the next year to Greenland. These self-supporting Moravians penetrated into North America, Labrador, Southern Asia, Africa, the Caribbean Islands, and remote parts of Europe. Other Protestant missions were similarly sporadic. John Eliot (1604–90), a Puritan pastor, undertook to evangelize the Indians of New England and to organize them according to Exodus 18, efforts that led to translating the Bible into Mohican in 1663. Several English groups were organized to evangelize the colonies—the Society for Propagation of the Gospel in New England, 1649, the Society for Promoting Christian Knowledge, 1699, and the Society for the Propagation of the Gospel in Foreign Parts, 1701. Those who believed in election felt that the elect everywhere should be called forth to glorify God, and those who believed in voluntary acceptance of Jesus thought that Christ should be presented to all. Rationalism hindered both groups by fostering the belief that in nature and reason people everywhere had access to the essential truth in revelation. The big push in Protestant missions did not come until Jonathan Edwards published a biography of David Brainerd (1718–47), whose brief work among the American Indians directly inspired William Carey, who in turn inspired scores of others.

William Carey (1761–1834), a British cobbler who had taught himself Latin, Greek, Hebrew, Dutch, and French, had a conversion experience in 1779 that turned him from Anglicans to the Baptists, among whom he began preaching. In 1792 he published *An Enquiry into the Obligation of Christians to Use Means for the Conversion of the Heathen,* a small, subsidized book that virtually electrified a lethargic England to the need to obey Christ's command to go into all the world. In the same year a sermon at Nottingham in which Carey exhorted his hearers to "expect great things from God" and "attempt great things for God" resulted in the formation of the Particular Baptist Society for the Propagation of the Gospel amongst the Heathen. The following year Carey with his large family set sail for India. By the end of the year, the ship reached the Bay of Bengal. Lack of funds and illness brought him to the verge of despair, but Carey became self-supporting through his work at an indigo factory at Malda, and later through teaching. A genius in language, Carey within five years had translated the New Testament into Bengali and was preaching in the natives' own tongue. By 1809 he printed the entire Bible in Bengali and parts of it in twenty-six other languages and dialects. For thirty years he was professor of Oriental languages at Fort William College at Calcutta. His widely publicized letters caused scores of others to aspire to missions.

Directly inspired by Carey, 200 ministers in 1795 formed the London Missionary Society to promote interdenominational missionary work among the heathen. Following this came the Religious Tract Society, 1799, and the Bible Society, 1804. Probably no other agency has promoted missions as widely and as successfully as the London Missionary Society.

In America the missionary fervor of students at Williams College and Andover Theological Seminary stirred New England to revival pitch, and in 1812 Adoniram Judson and Samuel Newell sailed with their brides from Salem on the *Caravan*, and Luther Rice, Samuel Nott, and Gordon Hall sailed from Philadelphia on the *Harmony*. Five months later they reached Calcutta. Judson (1788–1850), after studying baptism in the New Testament, became convinced that immersion was the only way and was baptized by Carey in Calcutta. To support Judson in the field the American Baptists organized their own foreign missionary society in 1814. Though Judson learned Burmese, not until 1819 did he hold his first worship service, and not until 1834 did he complete the Bible in Burmese. Like Carey, he overcame obstacles, and was a living inspiration for the hundreds who followed his pioneering. In Europe and America, a score of missionary societies sprang into being, and by 1825 the Protestant missionary effort had expanded into the Pacific islands and was penetrating deeper into the Orient and Africa. Everywhere the missionaries evangelized, started schools, translated Scriptures, and established stations.

Missionaries quickly perceived the evils of competing in the field and vindicating their theological differences. If the body of Christ is one, should not they be one? Their field discussions led to the calling of world conferences in New York and London in 1854. A series of meetings followed, the eighth being the World Missionary Conference at Edinburgh in 1910, followed by the *Lambeth Appeal* in 1920, which engendered the three major thrusts of the ecumenical endeavor—the International Missionary Council, 1921, the Universal Christian Conference on Life and Work at Stockholm in 1925, and the World Conference on Faith and Order at Lausanne in 1927. The latter two merged to form the World Council of Churches in 1948, which the IMC joined in 1961.

Other developments fed into these missionary moves toward ecumenicity. One of these was the appeal for a federation based on individuals rather than churches. As early as 1835 Samuel S. Schmucker (1799–1873), a Lutheran professor of Theology at Gettysburg, published his *Fraternal Appeal to the American Churches*, 1838, followed by an *Overture for Christian Union* in 1845. In 1846 representatives from around the world met in London and organized the Evangelical Alliance. It opposed Roman Catholicism and promoted biblical authority, eschatology, an annual week of prayer, and generally conservative doctrines. It championed liberty, and its journal, *Evangelical Christendom*, served as an ecumenical press service in its day.

On still another level, formations of national church federations began to take shape. Led by Josiah Strong (1847–1916) and Elias B. Sanford (1843–1932), the Federal Council of Churches of Christ in America became a reality in 1908, with 31 of the major American denominations subscribing. Forty-two years later it represented 144,000 local congregations that embraced 32,000,000 members. In 1950 the Federal Council of

Churches merged with other interdenominational groups to establish the National Council of Churches of Christ in the United States. Between 1905 and 1946, similar federations developed in France, Switzerland, Germany, New Zealand, Great Britain, Canada, and Australia. The need for a united voice to combat secular forces along with theological guilt for not being one in Christ motivated these moves toward union.

In addition many churches recognized their similarities, buried their differences, and merged—the United Free Church of Scotland, 1900; the South India United Church, 1908; United Lutheran Church, 1918; United Church of Canada, 1925; the Methodist Church, 1939; and the Church of South India, 1947.

Youth played a major role in missions and ecumenicity through George William's (1821–1905) organization of the Young Men's Christian Association in London in 1844, and through John R. Mott's (1865–1955) Student Volunteer Movement. In the same year that the World's Alliance of the YMCA was formed, 1855, the YWCA was organized and expanded into the World's YWCA in 1894. The interdenominational Y encouraged youth everywhere to live by Christian ideals. Mott, a Methodist layman, worked in the Y as a collegiate organizer in the United States and Canada until he took over the Student Volunteer Movement for Foreign Missions, an organization inspired by Dwight L. Moody. From 1888 to 1920 Mott promoted the SVM, which caught the imagination of college youth in America and Europe. By the thousands they volunteered and vowed to become missionaries—their watchword, "the evangelization of the world in our generation." Three-fourths of the missionaries from North America have come from the Volunteers, a total of more than 20,000 recruits! With Karl Fries of Sweden, Mott founded the World's Student Christian Federation, 1895, "to deepen the spiritual life of students, and to enlist students in extending the Kingdom of Christ . . . that they all may be one." Countries from around the world invited Mott to organize their youth. The Anglican Church made him a canon, the Russian Orthodox Church granted him a doctor's degree, and in 1946 he received the Nobel Peace Prize. When the World Missionary Conference convened at Edinburgh in 1910 he was chosen as chairman. Most of the ecumenical leaders were connected with that seminal conference. Among its ushers were William Temple, John McLeod Campbell, John Baillie, Kenneth Kirk, and Sir Walter Moberly. How to carry the Gospel to all the non-Christian world and cooperation and unity among churches received major attention. Mott served as chairman of the continuation committee, which became the International Missionary Council in 1921, directed by Mott until 1942. It sought to coordinate missionary activities and to develop indigenous national leaders. Significantly, racism and secularism were the subjects for discussion at the IMC world conference in Jerusalem, 1928.

Following the key Edinburgh Conference of 1910, Anglicans issued the *Lambeth Appeal,* 1920, which instigated intercommunion discussions of the doctrinal and practical aspects of ecumenism. Despite profound disagreement on ordination, the Lord's Supper, and episcopal versus congregational polity, the feeling that unity ought to prevail prompted the major Protestant churches to shelve their differences to convene the Universal

Christian Conference on Life and Work at Stockholm in 1925. Under the leadership of Nathan Söderblom (1866–1931), a Swedish Lutheran pastor, the Life and Work conference studied ways to alleviate the world's social ills.

Realizing that social action without agreement on doctrine was truncated, Charles H. Brent (1862–1929), an American Episcopal missionary bishop, organized the Faith and Order World Conference, which was held at Lausanne in 1927. The conference frankly faced the churches' differences on ministry, sacraments, and polity. Ten years later, while meeting separately at Oxford and Edinburgh, the conferences on Life and Work and Faith and Order voted to form a World Council of Churches, "a fellowship of churches which accept our Lord Jesus Christ as God and Savior." World War II prevented actual union until 1948 at Amsterdam, when the World Council of Churches became a reality. John R. Mott was chosen as its honorary chairman. The WCC conceived of itself not as a superchurch but as an organization for counsel, exchange of opinion, study, and promotion of common projects. It assumed no authority over individual churches.

At the World Council meeting in New Delhi, 1961, a massive study and discussion of "Jesus Christ the Light of the World" resulted in an appeal to all governments to "renounce the threat of force" and actively seek peace. Considerable publicity accompanied the admission of Eastern Orthodox churches; many observers interpreted this as admitting Communism.

The World Council embraces 303 member churches, but by no means all existing denominations. Fundamentalists tend to regard the WCC as a suspect fellowship that has fostered social action and compromised doctrine. Carl McIntire, after being deposed from the Presbyterian Church of the U.S.A., formed two splinter Presbyterian churches of his own and organized the International Council of Christian Churches and the American Council of Churches. He has vigorously opposed and disrupted WCC meetings. The more moderate evangelicals, who accept the Bible as an infallible authority, formed the World Evangelical Fellowship in Holland in 1951. Since the mid-1950s Protestant ecumenical fervor has noticeably diminished, almost as if the churches have lost so much status in the world that it does not matter.

Although the Roman Catholic Church sent official observers to the WCC meeting in New Delhi, it has held aloof from Protestant ecumenical developments, claiming that it is the one true church and that ecumenical unity must mean return to an acceptance of papal "authority and supremacy." The encyclical *Mortalium Animos*, 1928, invited all "separated children . . . to humbly beg light from heaven . . . to recognize the one true Church of Jesus Christ." In 1950, *Humani Generis* warned against compromise with modernism, and the bodily ascension of the Virgin Mary was dogmatized, both of which dampened ecumenical overtures.

In 1962 Pope John XXIII convened Vatican Council II. Protestant observers and consultants were invited to Rome. The unusually open, self-critical stance displayed at Vatican II led many to forecast radical changes in Roman Catholicism's traditionally ultramontane position, but major church dogmas were not altered. The liberal hopes born at Vatican II have not been realized under succeeding Popes Paul VI (1963–78), John Paul I (1978, 34 days), or John Paul II of Poland (1978–). The papacy has reproved dissidents, refused ordination of women, rejected clerical marriages, balked at freer birth control rules, and censored liberal theologians. Karl Rahner (b. 1904), a distinguished Jesuit theologian, has stirred controversy and new understandings by forthrightly exposing religious problems and interpreting Thomistic thought in modern existential terms in *Spirit in the World* (1968), but fundamental changes have not occurred. Hans Küng (b. 1928), professor at the University of Tübingen, West Germany, was appointed official theologian at Vatican Council II. For many years he has sought to show an affinity between Roman Catholicism and Karl Barth on the doctrine of justification. In December 1979 he was severely censored by the papacy. Since Vatican II thousands of disappointed priests, nuns, and monks have disavowed their religious vocations. Nevertheless, the attitude of Rome has altered. Dialogue and cooperation with other churches have become commonplace. Collegiality has restored a measure of authority to bishops around the world, but without a displacement of papal primacy. The lay apostolate and diaconate encouraged in Vatican II have given a semi-clerical status to some lay leaders. Catholics have increasingly regarded Luther not simply as a "wild boar" but as a true reformer who must be reassessed; at Vatican II many delegates wore buttons praising Luther. Vernacular languages have replaced Latin in the mass. The Vatican decree on Ecumenism, November 21, 1964, committed Rome to recovery of the union of Christendom. Wide-ranging formal and informal dialogues have resulted in an effort to bridge ancient differences about the church, ordination, authority, the eucharist, and related topics, even papal primacy by divine versus human right. Twelve years of conferences and consultations between Anglican and Roman Catholic churches ended in 1982 with "substantial agreement" on central subjects but without official implementation. In the same year, five-year conversation between Methodist and Catholic churches and four-year talks between Disciples of Christ and Catholic churches ended with "encouraging" reports but no implementation. The Greek Orthodox and Catholic churches have found much in common but not enough to patch their ancient schismatic rift. Dramatic breakthroughs have not occurred; however, serious conversations on various levels continue.

LIBERALISM AND FUNDAMENTALISM

The larger struggle in the nineteenth century, however, was to make Christianity relevant to a changing world in which ecclesiastical authority was no longer sacrosanct. In Catholicism this prompted a war on "modernism" (see Chapter 19), and in Protestantism, agonizing reappraisals that resulted in compromise, adjustment, turmoil, and uncertainty. The French Revolution had dramatically broken old lines of authority. Science had opened up new fields of knowledge, and technology had burgeoned. By 1800 the Industrial Revolution was in full swing, with its accompanying problems of human exploitation, urban congestion, and slum subsistence. Men in power may have been satisfied with Adam Smith's *Wealth of Nations,* 1776, which argued for laissez faire in trade; and with Thomas Malthus' *Essay on the Principles of Population,* 1798, which argued that pestilence, famine, and war were nature's way of balancing the food supply and population; and with David Ricardo's *Principles of Political Economy,* 1817, which laid down the "iron law" that wages will not fall below subsistence, for then men could not work, nor rise so high as to engender a larger population and a shortage of jobs. But the masses of men were not satisfied, and the violent revolutions that rocked Europe in the 1830s and '40s gauged the unrest as deep.

Increasing numbers of people believed that governments should take the profit motive out of economics in order to promote the general welfare. Traditional evangelical beliefs inspired some of these efforts, and humanistic idealism quite apart from religious convictions inspired others. Count Henri de Saint-Simon, Charles Fourier, and Louis Blanc theorized and planned communities that operated not for individual profit but for the common good. Robert Owen translated these ideas into actuality by establishing experimental communal colonies at New Harmony, Indiana, in 1825, and later at Ralahine and Tytherley in Great Britain. These communal societies failed, but they charted a new outreach. More than any other man Karl Marx (1818–83) put these notions into a disciplined system of thought. He saw history as inevitably leading to socialism because he believed history to be determined by dialectical materialism, the conflict of economic forces in which the masses would emerge victorious. He advocated a classless society of economic and social justice and preached a revolution to inaugurate its establishment. In 1848 he and Friedrich Engles published their *Communist Manifesto:* "Let the ruling classes tremble at a Communistic revolution. The proletarians have nothing to lose but their chains. They have a world to win. Workers of the world, unite!" Auguste Comte (1798–1857) espoused a love of humanity that he said should replace love of God if mankind is to have sound social doctrine. His lectures on positivism defended a religion of humanity as the culmination of man's expanding stages of knowledge—the theological, concerned with God; the metaphysical, concerned with nature; and the positive, concerned with universal law. The third stage should yield government by universal social laws as revealed in science, religion, and experience, not by obligations to a supernatural deity. John Stuart Mill (1806–73), who learned Greek at three and wrote history at twelve, translated Comte's ideas into a utilitarian religion of humanity. An economist of note, Mill wrote *On Liberty* (1859), *Utilitarianism* (1863), and *Three Essays on Religion* (1873), all advocating utilitarian programs as means of realizing a truly democratic society. Otherwordly striving and worship of a supernatural God did not interest him, only what was useful for relieving human need now. In America Henry George (1839–97) published *Progress and Poverty,* 1879, recommending public ownership of lands in order to protect the rights of laborers who improve the land; and in 1888 Edward Bellamy (1850–98) pictured a utopian society in *Looking Backward, 2000–1887.*

Many Christians believed that Christianity could and should respond to the conditions of oppression wrought by technology and human greed.

William Wilberforce fought slavery, winning abolition of it in British dominions in 1833. Lord Ashley campaigned for a ten-hour working day, adequate care for the mentally ill, and public health programs. J. F. D. Maurice (1805–72), perhaps the period's most influential theologian, founded the Christian Socialist Movement, 1848–54, and the Working Men's College, 1854. He won assistance from J. M. Ludlow (1821–1911), a layman, who had seen the revolutionary upheavals in France, and from Charles Kingsley (1819–75), rector of Eversley. A prolific author, Kingsley wrote a series of novels dealing with social conditions—*Alton Locke, Tailor and Poet; Yeast, a Problem; Hypatia;* and *Westward Ho!* Maurice, Kingsley, Ludlow, and others agitated for better working conditions; they rejected poverty as a judgment from God, as well as Calvinistic predestination and the kinds of theology that devalued social responsibility now. Their *Politics for the People* initiated cooperatives for tailors and other tradesmen and sought to make industry and government more responsive to the people.

Though the Christian Socialist Movement soon faded out, others continued to struggle to make Christianity relevant to the social conditions. Steward Duckworth Headlam and other English high churchmen formed the Guild of St. Matthew in 1877 for social reform, and in 1889 founded the Christian Social Union, which carried on a program of study and investigation of working conditions in factories and blacklisted workshops with poor standards. In Switzerland Leonhard Ragaz and Herman Kutter promoted cooperatives, folk schools, settlements, and pacifism. In Germany there was Johann Heinrich Wichern (1808–81) with his schools, agencies, and missions for seamen, prisoners, the underprivileged, and the unemployed. But perhaps none had more impact on their times than did William Booth (1829–1912) and Walter Rauschenbusch (1861–1918).

William Booth represents evangelical, pietistic Christianity's concern for the social plight of the individual. He had been associated with the Methodist New Connection, formed in 1797, but withdrew to work more fully in his efforts to rescue London's "submerged tenth." His street preaching and missions in East End London in 1864 met with phenomenal success. Within eleven years he had thirty-two stations promoting evangelism and social services among London's destitute. His workers, because of the strict discipline and chain of command, became known as the Salvation Army. By 1888 Booth had established 1,000 British corps and had dispatched patrols to other nations. Marked success accompanied the Army's work in most of Continental Europe (including Russia), the United States, Scotland, Ireland, Wales, Canada, Australia, New Zealand, South Africa, India, Ceylon, Japan, and China. Booth's *In Darkest England and the Way Out*, 1890, graphically compared the social darkness in England to Africa's darkness as pictured by David Livingstone and H. M. Stanley. In London, in one year, he noted 2,157 people had been found dead; 2,297 had committed suicide; 30,000 were living in prostitution; 160,000 had been convicted of drunkenness; and more than 900,000 were classed as paupers. He then told about the Army's rescue efforts—missions, shelter stations, food depots, job training centers, city and farm colonies, and preaching. A huge chart pictured a sea of unbelief, insanity, deceit, theft, drunkenness, adultery, and murder from which the Army was netting the drowning. In one year, 1889, the Army dispensed 192 tons of bread, 140 tons of potatoes, 25 tons of sugar, 46 tons of flour, 12 tons of rice, 15 tons of meat, 15 tons of jam, and similar large amounts of other foods. Booth's experience of late-nineteenth-century life was hardly one of genteel Victorian morality, and his work brought dramatic awareness of dire social need.

The more traditional response of evangelical, pietistic Christianity to social conditions came in revivalists' efforts to change the hearts of men and thereby affect the total social sphere. Peter Cartwright (1785–1882), Charles G. Finney (1792–1875), Dwight L. Moody (1837–99), and Henry Drummond (1851–97) led the field. Cartwright, a Methodist, one of many frontier revivalists, won thousands of converts on the frontiers of Kentucky and Illinois. He published his *Autobiography* in 1856. Finney, a Presbyterian, sometimes termed the first professional revivalist, became a professor and later the president at Oberlin College. While many of the revivalists opposed an educated ministry, Finney had trained for law and knew Latin, Hebrew, and Greek. After being "invaded" by the Holy Spirit, he held revivals in America and England; his *Lectures* at Oberlin provided revivalism with a methodology and a theology. This early revivalism, which was greatly concerned with slavery, drink, debt, debauchery, repentance, and surrender, reached its height in the 1850s.

After the Civil War, the evangelism of Dwight L. Moody, a layman, created another great awakening. He toured England and America preaching against the sins of sexual immorality and drunkenness, and in the face of rationalistic and scientific trends upheld biblical inerrancy and authority. He crossed denominational lines in organizing massive prayer meetings, Bible conferences, and revivals, and pleaded for cooperation in world missions. His Northfield School for Girls, Mount Hermon School for Boys, and Moody Bible Institute for laymen trained thousands of evangelical workers.

Henry Drummond, an English scientist concerned with bridging the gap between science and religion, wrote his popular *Natural Laws in the Spiritual World*, 1883, while a professor of science at the Free Church College in Glasgow. It went through thirty-five editions and was translated into French, Dutch, German, and Norwegian. In 1889 at Dwight L. Moody's college at Oxford, he delivered one of the most famous sermons ever preached, *The Greatest Thing in the World*, in which he interpreted love (I Corinthians 13) as patience, kindness, generosity, humility, courtesy, unselfishness, good temper, guilelessness, and sincerity—"these make up the supreme gift, the stature of the perfect man."

Throughout most of the nineteenth century, fundamentalism and liberalism operated out of a common evangelical tradition, namely Calvinistic Puritanism. Scottish Common Sense Philosophy, with roots in Francis Bacon's inductive scientific method, was widely adopted and used as a tool to reconcile scientific discoveries and biblical convictions. Thomas Reid (1710–96), a Scottish philosopher, formulated common sense philosophy in response to John Locke and David Hume. Reid published his *Inquiry into the Human Mind on the Principles of Common Sense* in 1764, and by mid–nineteenth century it predominated as a philosophical basis for religion in America and England. He boldly asserted that human beings intuitively know and believe in the existence of a real world, cause and effect, the moral character of actions, and an existing real self or soul. Common sense, he said, is a reliable guide to truth, open to all with eyes to see. This common sense view of reality had a strong appeal in revolutionary America. Democratic and anti-elitist, common sense philosophy could be adapted readily to traditional Christian views. Careful observation and classification of data from nature and Scripture, it was affirmed, would yield compatible truths. Calvin's radical understanding of sinful human nature was pushed aside. The universe is governed by a rational system of laws, unified laws that science discovers in nature and religion in Scripture. Both are guaranteed by God. A careful study of the Bible reveals moral laws for society just as science reveals natural laws through the facts of science. Since the same benevolent God is the source of both and since the universe is rational and unified, the discoveries of science cannot but confirm and be compatible with biblical truth. Joseph Butler's *Analogy of Religion*, 1736, and William Paley's *Natural Theology*, 1802, were commonly used to prove Christian truths. The insights of Immanuel Kant, F. C. Baur, D. F. Strauss, and Ernest Renan went unappropriated, if not ignored. Higher criticism seemed far removed from practical religion in America. The Civil War demonstrated God's judgment in history. Revivalism in the Cartwright and Finney style continued to bring converts into the fold. A great revival in 1857–58 came largely from noonday prayer meetings led by lay businessmen, and Dwight L. Moody's triumphant tours of England and America came in the 1870s. By 1870 Protestants commonly thought of America as a Christian nation.

Unsettling forces were about to take their toll, however. These forces were already loose in Europe: their legacy was to reduce concern with religion and even to question its validity and value. Charles Darwin (1809–82) published the *Origin of Species* in 1859, followed by the *Descent of Man* in 1871. The theory of evolution challenged the Bible's validity as a source of truth as well as the claim of human beings to moral uniqueness. How could either be so if all life forms evolved over thousands of years from a common, low form? How could the Genesis story of creation be made to conform to evolution? Some Christians adamantly rejected Darwin in favor of an inerrant, inspired Bible; these were Protestant evangelicals as well as Roman Catholics who frowned on "modernism." In the United States eleven states passed laws against evolution. When *Essays and Reviews*, 1860, appeared in England sanctioning free inquiry into religion, a storm of protest followed. Two of its seven writers, H. B. Wilson and Rowland Williams, were officially deprived for denying biblical inspiration and the reality of hell. Eleven thousand clergymen and 137,000 laity signed statements reaffirming their belief in inerrancy and eternal punishment. For publishing *The Pentateuch*, challenging the Old Testament's historical accuracy, John W. Colenso, Bishop of Natal, was deposed in 1863 and excommunicated three years later.

A split characterized later as Fundamentalism versus Liberalism was beginning to take shape, because others in Protestantism chose to regard evolution as part of God's providence and sought increasingly to accommodate religion to science. Herbert Spencer (1820–1903) presented evolution as a manifestation of the Absolute on which all knowledge depends. John Fiske's *Cosmic Philosophy*, 1874, accepted evolution "as God's way of doing things" while at the same time vindicating a religious epistemology comformable to both science and philosophy. Henry Ward Beecher (1813–87) referred to himself as a "cordial Christian evolutionist," and Lyman Abbott's *Theology of an Evolutionist*, 1897, presented evolution as God's providence and progress in history, thus contributing to the notion at the turn of the century that humanity was rapidly advancing toward the kingdom of God on earth. In humanity's progress, sin, like the lower forms of evolution, was being left behind.

Henry Ward Beecher, eminent, eloquent, and respected, was among the first of the evangelicals to adjust to evolution. As such, he was a transitional figure into full-fledged liberalism. The son of Lyman Beecher and the brother of Harriet Beecher Stowe, who wrote *Uncle Tom's Cabin*, he opposed slavery and after the Civil War became more and more liberal and progressive in spirit. He upheld "virtuous" wealth as a model for the poor, stated many views ambiguously so as not to offend, and waffled on traditional doctrines such as future punishment in hell. Revered nationally, he weathered a split jury's decision in 1874 exonerating him of the charge of adultery with a parishioner. Although a member of the Congregational Association, he was virtually independent as the minister of a large, comfortable Victorian church. When charges of heresy surfaced among the Congregationalists, he simply threatened to withdraw from the Association. In 1885 he published *Evolution and Religion* in which he subscribed to evolution and pictured God not only as evolving new forms in nature but also evolving a new civilization in the great advances of science, philosophy, and morality. He identified this broad evolutionary progress with the Kingdom of God. For Beecher, the supernatural was manifesting itself in our natural world; the Bible was no longer the primary source for authoritative Christian views. Human experience had displaced it. Sin, equated with animality, was an obstacle to be overcome by cultivating the higher qualities of life.

Evolution and historical progress received increasing consideration in the biblical works of Brook F. Westcott, Joseph B. Lightfoot, Fenton John A. Hart, and Julius Wellhausen. They realigned traditional interpretation of the Bible with the truths of historical research. Wellhausen's *History of Israel* showed that the Old Testament writings were products of their times. But perhaps the book that most symbolized the reconciliation of science and religion was *Lux Mundi*, 1889, by a group of English scholars led by Charles Gore (1853–1932). They confessed in the preface that they were committed Christians trying to explain their faith in a time of "profound transformation, intellectual and social." They accepted the Bible as reasonable, explained incongruities in terms of progressive evolution, and by saying that the Holy Spirit works in nature as well as in man and the church they reconciled Christian doctrines to historical and scientific research. This immensely popular book influenced theology for four decades. By 1909 many Christians could quote with approval William Herbert Carruth's poem *Each in His Own Tongue:*

A firemist and a planet,
    A crystal and a cell,
A jellyfish and a saurian,
    And caves where the cave men dwell;
Then a sense of law and beauty,
    And a face turned from the clod—
Some call it Evolution
    And others call it God.

Influenced by science, the Scriptures, and Hindu concepts of reality, Mary Baker Eddy (1821–1910) institutionalized a variety of traditional and non-traditional elements in Christian Science. Following her experience of healing, in 1875 she produced *Science and Health with a Key to the Scriptures* in which she expounded on matter, evil, sin, sickness, and death as illusions. "God is all-in-all; God is Spirit. Matter is an illusion. Since man is Spirit and body is illusion, there can be no illness." Christian Science has been doubted and ridiculed, but many believers have witnessed to its truth and it persists as an important part of the American scene.

The optimism that greeted the twentieth century was rooted in rationalism's projection of man's capabilities for good, scientific evolution, and the idea of progress. Charles M. Sheldon's *In His Steps* envisaged the dawn of the regeneration of Christendom. The question in Earl Marlatt's hymn, *Are Ye Able?* was answered with a lusty, "Lord, we are able. . . . Remold and make us like Thee divine." Through economic betterment, social improvement, and more education, primitivism and sin would be evolutionized away. This theological outlook with its disparagement of Calvin's sinfully depraved man and doctrines of election, its comfortable fellowship with science, its this-worldly orientation, and its belief in human perfectibility, came to be characterized as liberalism. Henry P. Van Dusen listed its presuppositions as devotion to truth, deference to science and the scientific method, tentativeness about any metaphysical certainty, continuity between revelation and natural religion and between Christ and other men, and dispassionate tolerance and confidence in human reason. In 1917 the United States entered World War I (1914–18) jubilantly confident that it would make the world safe for democracy and usher in a political brotherhood of all humanity by removing a corrupt social structure from the path of human progress. Harry Emerson Fosdick (1878–1969), a Baptist and one of America's most popular preachers, rejected easy, automatic betterment in *Christianity and Progress,* 1922, but called for continued progress through the conquest of ignorance, sin, inefficiency, apathy, and carelessness. In *Adventurous Religion*, 1926, Fosdick subordinated creeds to contemporary tasks, authoritarianism to free inquiry, and ecclesiasticism to principles that create personal character and social progress. The Bible as a source for authoritative Christian truth became but one of many sources.

For those who regarded the Bible as essential to authoritative Christian truth, such developments, though complex, ambiguous, and gradual as they were in their unfolding, seemed like heresy. Far from believing that human efforts and progress were in continuity with the Kingdom of God, conservative evangelicals with strong ties to revivalism and pietism began insisting on a divinely inspired, inerrant Bible. They viewed the progress hailed by liberals as a march toward a catastrophic divine judgment of God on the sinful pretentions of human beings. Morality and civilization were at stake; modernism was not basically Christian, according to their standards. Conservatives were keenly aware of the problem early in the 1870s. In the 1873 meeting of the Evangelical Alliance, heated arguments erupted about how to respond to Darwinism. Some thought Scripture and science were still in conformity, others that they were incompatible and irreconcilable. Some saw a way out in Kant's limitation of knowledge to the realm of science; values and morals were beyond and higher than science. But still the devastating blows of Darwinism had to be combatted; the Bible interpreted by "right" reason had to be defended. Traditional Christianity and civilization were threatened!

From these developments, identifiable, visible Fundamentalism gradually emerged with its emphasis on Scriptural inerrancy, literalism, antimodernism, prophecy, dispensational millenarianism, revivalism, divine control of history, and distrust of evolutionary progress. However, fundamentalism was not a unified front, and for the most part it operated within the churches and did not spawn large schisms. Key, symbolic figures in the unfolding of fundamentalism were John Nelson Darby, Jonathan and Charles Blanchard, Dwight L. Moody and his associates, and conservative theologians comprising a group expressing Princeton Theology.

John Nelson Darby (1800–82), founder of the Plymouth Brethren in England, was the apostle of dispensational millenarianism in America as early as the 1840s. The Plymouth Brethren, although never large in numbers, became widespread in England, on the Continent, and in the United States. From 1862 to 1877 Darby spent much time in America touring and working, especially in the larger cities. Calvinist in background, distrustful of the ability of human beings, Darby preached a dispensationalism that depicted large biblical "periods" as no longer specifically relevant. The revelations in those periods were suitable for those times. Under Moses people were to keep the law; under the present period of Grace, they are to turn to Christ. The present period of Grace, the sixth, will end in divine judgment; the seventh period of the Kingdom will be the millennial reign of Christ. Present civilization will end in doom; only a righteous remnant of true believers will survive. By 1900 dispensational millenarianism was fast becoming a distinctive mark among fundamentalists.

The trend away from humanistic liberalism became more visible. Acrid arguments broke forth in many religious gatherings. Henry Ward Beecher was openly attacked as a hypocrite who had sold out to modernism. The transitional figure into specific fundamentalism was Dwight L. Moody (1837–99). He himself tried to remain non-controversial and was consumed with winning souls for Christ, but most of his chief co-workers were committed dispensational millenarians. He and Ira Sankey, his song leader, won thousands of converts in their international revivals. Moody began as a YMCA worker in Boston, moved to Chicago, sold shoes, and in 1860 quit the shoe business to give full time to ministry. In 1864 he organized his non-denominational Chicago church. Rising to worldwide fame as a revivalist, he moved to Northfield, Massachusetts, closer to his schools for boys and girls and the site of his influential international summer conferences. The 1886 conference generated the Student Volunteer Movement the following summer. Their enthusiastic motto was "evangelization of the world in this generation." Moody made emotional Prodigal-Son appeals to sinners to accept redemption through Christ and regeneration through the Holy Spirit. He avoided controversial topics in the interest of presenting the Gospel message of God's love.

Although Moody was more interested in conversion and holiness of life than in millenarianism, it was present in his message, for he was consciously trying to save all he could before the coming catastrophe. In his leading associates dispensational millenarianism became a distinguishing mark. Among these lieutenants were Charles Blanchard, founder of the Moody Bible Training Institute and drafter of the doctrines affirmed by the World's Christian Fundamentals Association, 1919; Reuben Torrey, world evangelist and author of *What the Bible Teaches*, 1898; William J. Erdman and A. J. Gordon, initiators of the annual Niagara Bible Conferences where "dispensational" prophecy was diligently propagated; and C. I. Scofield, author of *Rightly Dividing the Word of God* and the famous *Scofield Reference Bible*, 1909, which became indispensable for millions of Bible teachers and preachers as they attempted to interpret the inerrant words of Scripture and maintain a unitary view of the Bible. Scofield's typology, based heavily on numerology and apocalyptic texts in Daniel and Revelation, partitioned history into seven periods, and in the process reduced history since Christ to a kind of parenthesis that would soon end in the inauguration of the millennial reign of Christ. In this scheme the coming of the Kingdom of God as the unfolding of a human, historical process was regarded as a Satanic ruse to blind people to their real situation. Dispensational devotees often denounced liberal church leaders as apostates.

The opposing forces of liberalism and fundamentalism rapidly gathered for a showdown—each camp convinced of its own rightness. Under the leadership of President W. Rainey Harper, the Divinity School at the University of Chicago became a stronghold for liberalism after the 1890s. In 1913 fundamentalist Baptists founded the Northern Baptist Seminary in Chicago intentionally to counter the liberal influence of the University of Chicago. Professors Shailer Mathews and Shirley Jackson Case militantly enjoined fundamentalism. When J. Gresham Machen called for the overthrow of liberalism in *Christianity and Liberalism*, 1923, attacking liberalism as alien, unchristian, and unscientific, Shailer Mathews replied heatedly in his *Faith of Modernism*, 1924. Presbyterians, Baptists, Disciples of Christ, and Methodists were visibly shaken by the fundamentalism-liberalism controversy. Fosdick eventually lost his Presbyterian pulpit, Machen was suspended from the ministry, and many lesser figures suffered similar fates.

Particularly irritating to the fundamentalists was the social gospel of Walter Rauschenbusch (1861–1918). Despite laudable aspects of his works, the fundamentalists believed the social gospel was in effect an effort to usher in the Kingdom of God through acts of human beings. Born in Rochester, New York, just seven years after his father emigrated from revolution-torn Germany, and educated in both America and Germany, Rauschenbusch brought together in himself liberalism and evangelism, social concern and individualistic pietism. As minister of the Second German Baptist Church in Hell's Kitchen, New York City, he saw the castoff wrecks of depersonalized economic aggrandizement and the suffering caused by the exploitation of the destitute, the immigrants, the poor, and the old. Like an Old Testament prophet he fought back, tirelessly denouncing, writing, and organizing. As editor of the newspaper *For the Right* he advocated public ownership of railroads and utilities, more equitable taxation, safer and better working conditions, social security insurance, parks and playgrounds, libraries, abolition of child labor, and curbs on capitalism. In 1907 he published his first book, *Christianity and the Social Crisis*, in which he analyzed the biblical development of social religion, and in 1917 brought out his most famous book, *A Theology for the Social Gospel*, in which he set forth a theological basis for social reform, calling for an assault on the Kingdom of Evil particularly in the public sphere if the Kingdom of God is ever to be realized. Yet he emphasized that social reform must also look to personal, spiritual regeneration. As Professor of Church History at Rochester Theological Seminary, Rauschenbusch led a host of dedicated Christians concerned with meaningful application of Christian principles to society—Washington Gladden, who preceded him in calling for unions, cooperatives, profit sharing, and socialization of railroads and utilities; Josiah Strong, who contended that greed for money was corrupting the nation; Graham Taylor, who taught Christian Sociology at Chicago Theological Seminary; Harry F. Ward, who got a social creed stated in the purposes of the Federal Council of Churches; Ernest Troeltsch with his monumental *Social Teaching of the Christian Churches;* and many more. In the 1920s and '30s governments in Europe and America enacted into law many of the proposals of the social gospel. Fundamentalists attacked Rauschenbusch saying he and his kind had substituted the social gospel for the Gospel.

The fundamentalists belligerently voiced their views through summer conferences, Bible institutes, and their widely disseminated work, *The Fundamentals: A Testimony to the Truth,* published in Chicago in twelve paperback volumes from 1910 to 1915. It was distributed free to virtually everyone involved in ministry in the English-speaking world. Financed by California oil millionaires Lyman Stewart and his quiet brother Milton, *The Fundamentals* mounted a broad attack on modernism, stressing biblical inerrancy, soul-saving, prayer, and so forth, but avoiding politically controversial subjects and minimizing dispensational millenarianism in order to build alliances with other groups against liberalism. Many respectable authors contributed. An already important alliance was with Princeton Seminary, especially in the personages of A. A. Hodge, B. B. Warfield, and J. G. Machen. As early as the First International Prophetic Conference in 1878, conservative Princeton Calvinists concerned with millenarianism were drawn into the orbit of the fundamentalists. They found common ground in opposition to modernism, the social gospel, and the

Kingdom through human progress. Machen's scholarly *Virgin Birth of Christ*, not published until 1932, was a classic defense of one of the fundamentalists' five essential beliefs.

The publicized climax in the clash between the liberals and fundamentalists came in the sensational J. T. Scopes' trial, 1925. Scopes, a teacher of high-school biology at Dayton, Tennessee, had defied a Tennessee state law that forbade teaching evolutionary theory in public schools. The prosecution featured William Jennings Bryan (1860–1925); the defense, Clarence Darrow (1857–1938). Bryan defended biblical inerrancy; Darrow ridiculed biblical literalism. The state Supreme Court eventually reversed Scopes' conviction.

Although many leaders in the 1920s were beginning to recoil from liberalism, two of its most forceful expressions came later. One was the *Humanist Manifesto,* 1933, formulated by a group of liberal thinkers who believed Christianity was outmoded. It asserted that the universe is self-existing and not created, that humanity and culture are products of natural evolution, that supernaturalism must be rejected in favor of human values, and that our proper goal is fulfillment of life now. The second was John Dewey's *A Common Faith,* 1934, which asserted that religion should give way to the projection of humanity's ever-enlarging experiences into a harmonized whole that embraces everything. Dewey's humanistic ideals and democratic principles embodied in a philosophy of learning-by-doing directly affected educational practices and theories around the world.

World War I, the Depression, and World War II dealt heavy blows to liberalism's optimistic progress. Rauschenbusch felt that World War I was a step backward, and wore a black armband to symbolize his disillusionment. In 1919, a Swiss pastor, Karl Barth, startled the theological world with his epochal *Epistle to the Romans.* With the strength of a massively scholarly mind committed to biblical revelation, he proclaimed God to be "totally other" than man's cultural deity. Barth attacked the "reasonableness" of Christianity, the subjectivism of Protestant theology, and the analogies of Aquinas as devious exaltations of man. The Bible is not a literary collection, a program for social reform, nor a fortress of proof-texts for status culture. It is the Word of the transcendent God, and its revelation must not be compromised by human speculations. He wrote a mighty "no" to the submersion and loss of God in culture. He presented the classical reformers' biblical doctrines of sinful man and exhibited the existential intensity of Pascal and Kierkegaard. Although his basic contentions did not change, his *Church Dogmatics,* begun in 1932, showed a deepened awareness of cultural complexities. Oswald Spengler countered progressive betterment with his *Decline of the West* (1918–22), in which he expounded a thesis of imminent disintegration. Sigmund Freud, Carl G. Jung, and Alfred Adler uncovered subconscious, irrational recesses in the human mind that fundamentally altered man's trust in human reason as the gateway to utopia. American churchmen were basically unaware of these new theological insights, for they were still attached to the liberal orientations of Albrecht Ritschl's value judgments as seen in *The Christian Doctrine of Justification and Reconciliation* (1870–74), Adolf Harnack's *History of Dogma* (1886–89), and his *What Is Christianity?* (1901), William

James' *Will to Believe* (1905), the social idealism in Leo Tolstoy's religious essays, and the optimistic "new" thrusts of John Dewey in philosophy and education. As the counter-progress theology filtrated into the American scene, Harry Emerson Fosdick, Reinhold Niebuhr, Walter Lowrie, Edwin Lewis, Walter M. Horton, and others made critical assessments of liberalism and prepared the way for the impact of Europe's theology of crisis, or neo-orthodoxy, as it became known. On the fringes of the theology of crisis, more traditionally orthodox, were England's William Temple, Sweden's Anders Nygren and Gustaf Aulen, France's Jacques Maritain, Russia's Nicholas Berdyaev and Sergius Bulgakov, and Switzerland's Emil Brunner.

More than any other person, Reinhold Niebuhr (1892–1971) broke the myopia of liberalism with his shattering analysis in *Moral Man and Immoral Society* (1932), *Reflections on the End of an Era* (1934), *An Interpretation of Christian Ethics* (1935), and his monumental Gifford lectures in England, *The Nature and Destiny of Man* (1941–43). He spearheaded neo-orthodoxy in this country, recalling the depths of human sinfulness and its direct and devious effects in political and social structures. He lacked the optimism of Rauschenbusch, believing that the best human intentions and achievements would still be permeated with sinful pride, and would therefore always be less than the kingdom of God. He vigorously advocated political and social reform, but realized that escape from all error and human contamination was impossible. People, therefore, should not put final trust in some program, environmental improvement, education, or political panacea. To do so would be to live with illusions. We are to express love for others, but not expect those expressions to be final. Niebuhr put his trust in the God who is beyond, yet in, history, whose love and forgiveness ennoble human life, and whose promises rescue human life from despair. His optimism came from trust in the ultimate triumph of God rather than from trust in the penultimate schemes of man. Whenever people do not trust in God, said Niebuhr, they fall into despair because their schemes do not and cannot ultimately succeed, or they surround themselves with pretentious, illusory idols of success that eventually prove even more disastrous. Whenever trust in God prevails, people achieve what they can in love, and the whole of history takes on meaning as it moves toward the end of history when God's forgiving love will triumph over all evil. Niebuhr was deeply conscious of human sin, which infects all human achievements and ideals; this made him cautious and critical; it did not make him pessimistic about life's final course.

With Paul Tillich (1886–1965) liberalism and neo-orthodoxy reached a new synthesis. A native of Germany, active in Christian social movements, Tillich immigrated to the United States when Hitler came into power in 1933. From 1933 to 1956 he taught theology at Union Theological Seminary. He drew heavily on Karl Barth but insisted that no single biblical norm is necessarily final. His Americanizing experience impressed on him the need to unite religion and culture in theological reflection. Aware that secularism had become a dominant factor, Tillich risked presenting Christianity in philosophical terms in order to communicate more fully with secular culture. He predicted the closing of the gap between the sacred and secular realms. In some sense Tillich achieved his goal, but in doing so he left his "Ground of Being" surrounded by vagueness and became the acknowledged godfather of the Death-of-God theologians. Man's religious questions arise out of his situation, Tillich maintained, and doctrines are presented as resolutions, but the answers are never final. In *Courage to Be*, 1952, he analyzed man's anxieties about death, meaninglessness, and guilt, which result from man's encounter with nonbeing, and proposed participation in God as the source for courage to exist fully. He characterized life as a "continuous attempt to avoid despair." But in asserting that God is above God, that the traditional God of theism will disappear, and that God is not a self or a person, Tillich offered a God with whom specific relatedness seemed virtually impossible. By describing God as the inaccessible creative ground of being Tillich wrapped God in mystery beyond knowledge. He defined faith as an unconditional surrender to ultimate concern, to that which gives reality and meaning to our existence, being-itself. He posited objects of faith (e.g., doctrines of God) as symbols pointing beyond themselves to being-itself, which is beyond existence. We can speak of God only symbolically; to elevate anything in this world to an unconditional status is to engage in the demonic, to which man is always prone. In this human struggle, love, power, and justice are always ambiguous; they find their unity only in God. By faith we know forgiveness and acceptance, and by faith we gain the courage to be while still involved in the ambiguities of this finite situation. With wide interests in art, history, and culture, Tillich considered religion an aspect of the human spirit, and so gave his religious speculations an existential-secular rather than traditional turn. His major works were all written in America: *The Shaking of the Foundations* and *The Protestant Era* (1948), *Love, Power, and Justice* (1954), *Theology of Culture* (1959), and *Systematic Theology* (1951–1963, three volumes). He risked expressing traditional doctrines in modern dress.

UNCERTAINTY

The turmoil within Christianity in the last two centuries was heightened by assaults on Christianity from without, leaving uncertainty a dominant mark of the twentieth century. Epistemological relativism, which for centuries lurked beneath the surface of Western culture, emerged in the past 450 years to question previously accepted truths and standards. Martin Luther opened the door to modern relativism when at Worms he stood alone and defied the papacy on the basis of Scripture and individual conscience, thus theoretically introducing as many authorities into Protestantism as there are individuals. David Hume furthered relativism when he effectively questioned miracles, revealed religion, cause-and-effect thinking, and the existence of a permanent experiencing "I." Immanuel Kant limited all knowledge to the phenomenal world of the five senses, the world of science, thus closing off the realm of noumena, which Kant nevertheless asserted to avoid practical and ultimate irrationality. But Kant's postulated assertions, and even the forms of space and time and the twelve categories through which all phenomenal impressions pass, harbored an element of subjectivism that has become the hallmark of modern relativism. Through such giants and lesser figures, relativism came steadily into view. A host of thinkers contributed to and extended the trend, dramatizing and emotionalizing the current human plight in literature, philosophy, art, music, government, language, and war. Truth is subjectivity, cried Sören Kierkegaard, the mentor of a host of existential thinkers who have pictured truth as passionately individual. Martin Buber's classic *I and Thou*, 1923, deepened the impact of existentialism in religion. Even science felt the force of relativism as shown in Einstein's theory of relativity. Other thinkers explored the consequences of these trends and called into question the sources, values, and relevance of all standards. If our grasp of truth is both relative and subjective, who can finally say what is truth—what is right and what is wrong? This has resulted in a pervasive feeling among Westerners that final truth and value are beyond human grasp, leaving everyone and every nation an end in itself. Feodor Dostoyevsky (1821–81) poignantly posed the problem for moderners when he wrote in *The Brothers Karamazov*, 1879, "If God does not exist, then everything is permitted." In *The Possessed*, 1871, Dostoyevsky argued that if there is no final standard (God), then individual freedom is the most meaningful reality and suicide its supreme expression.

Friedrich Nietzsche (1844–1900) fragmented many of the cultural religious notions of the nineteenth century. Interpreted by some as a protofascist, he called for the abandonment of all the stifling elements in society, so that the basic human motive, will to power, could be realized in the exceptional superman whom he pictured as surpassingly intelligent, mentally and physically disciplined, yet above moral scruples in his ruthless pursuit of creative victory. Nietzsche proclaimed a this-worldly antithesis to God, for he believed life has no meaning except what humanity gives to it. In *Thus Spoke Zarathustra* (1883–84), *Beyond Good and Evil* (1886), *Toward a Genealogy of Morals* (1887), and *The Antichrist* (1888), Nietzsche announced the death of God. He depicted the Christian values of pity, humility, kindness, and gentleness as herd morality that must be abolished, since such slave values hinder the creative manifestations of the superman. He extolled might—with no standard for the application of might—as the governing factor in all human relationships. Nietzsche, who had studied for the ministry and whose father was a Lutheran pastor, thus posited a dilemma that has spread its mantle over modern life. With values in doubt, on what basis would people organize their lives? Jacob Burckhardt (1818–97), a historian and philosopher of culture whom Nietzsche praised, foresaw voluntary acceptance of individual leaders, saviors, and usurpers.

Waves of uncertainty swirled through society giving rise to twentieth-century nihilism and meaninglessness. Nihilism (derived from the Latin *nihil* meaning "nothing") came from nineteenth-century Russia in reaction to injustices in political and social life during the time of Czar Alexander II. Philosophically it rests on our human inability to lay hold of absolutes, so that valuations rest on subjective relativism, and no one can finally identify right and wrong. Profoundly dissatisfied with things as they were, Dmitri Pisarev and his followers in the 1850s advocated the smashing of everything that could be smashed; denied any distinction between good and evil; rejected standards imposed by state, religion, and family; claimed there is no right—only might; made personal happiness the only law; and used terrorism and violence to destroy all forms of social organization and control. Erratic, unrestrained immediacy reigned as individual freedom. Ivan Turgenev popularized the term nihilism in his novel *Fathers and Sons* (1862). Pisarev carried to an extreme what Ecclesiastes characterized as "Eat, drink, and be merry for tomorrow you die."

In the twentieth century, nihilism connotes not so much anarchistic revolution as a mood of despair, a sense of emptiness and meaninglessness, a feeling that all of life finally ends in the nothingness of death, that moral norms cannot be justified by rational argument, and that one view is as good as another. This in turn has engendered various reactions: suicide, indifference, detachment, conformity, frustration, despair, violence.

Nihilism in the later connotation appeared strongly in the aftermath of World War I. The isms for which many had sacrificed proved to be tawdry slogans and masks for greed. People felt disillusionment and frustration. T. S. Eliot voiced these feelings in "The Love Song of J. Alfred Prufrock" (1917), "Gerotion" (1920), *The Waste Land* (1922), and *The Hollow Men* (1925). In Prufrock he pictured the emptiness and triviality of measuring out one's life in coffee spoons; in *The Waste Land,* a human desert of rootless, sterile, aimless characters, a land from which faith in God has departed, a land of weariness, spiritual despair, and chaos, a land of corpses, crawling rats, and bones; in *The Hollow Men,* the barrenness and insignificance of life. Although Eliot adopted a religious stance a few years later, he made a generation conscious of nihilism. Franz Kafka's *The Trial* (1925), probed a sense of absurdity, bafflement, frustration, and loss of values in relating to the institutions of culture. Edna St. Vincent Millay invested many of her poems with a view of life as fruitless and absurd and of death as the final no. She wrote of people sitting in a "circle of toys," gathering "baubles" while all the time death is "beating the door in." "Life is nothing," she lamented, the end being "the brains of men eaten by maggots."

Albert Camus, Nobel Prize winner in 1957, made nihilism a dominant theme mingled with a sense of despairing hope in *The Stranger* (1942), *Myth of Sisyphus* (1943), and *The Plague* (1947). After World War II he wrote, "We live in a world where one must choose between being a victim and an executioner—there's nothing else."

In Germany, Martin Heidegger in his *Being and Time,* 1927, philosophized on life as care and dread brought to nothingness in death, and the Christian God as no longer living, leaving all with the necessity of grasping and shaping life in face of ever approaching death. France's Jean-Paul Sartre popularized his disgust with the emptiness of routine living in *Nausea* (1938), *No Exit* and *The Flies* (1943). Every person is his own final norm and must choose freedom. In *Being and Nothingness* (1943), Sartre philosophized on ultimate nothingness, rendering all of life meaningless except for what one invests it with, until death. Death conquers all; it reduces us to Being-in-itself, sheer thingness.

Other literary thinkers played the same dirge in different keys—Tennessee Williams, Ernest Hemingway, W. H. Auden, Wallace Stevens, William Butler Yeats, Edward Albee, Richard Rubenstein, Jack Kerouak, John Berryman, and Samuel Beckett. In a series of novels and plays, Samuel Beckett (1906–), known as the prince of nihilists, writes about the absurdity of all living that ends in the nothingness of death. When he won the Nobel Prize for literature in 1969, he characterized it as one more absurdity of an absurd world. *Waiting for Godot* (1952) vaulted Beckett to worldwide fame. *Molloy, Malone Dies, The Unnamable, Krapp's Last Tape, Watt,* and other works dwell on a world without God and the emptiness of human lives that end in the void of death. None articulates the ethos of nihilism better than Beckett—all of life "from naught come to naught gone."

Nihilism found conscious expression in the Dada art of the 1920s in the work of Hugo Ball, Hans Arp, Tristan Tzara, and André Breton; their message—only chaos is real. In 1922 Tzara spoke of Dada as an embodiment of nothingness, uselessness, and disgust: "What dominates is *indifference.* . . . For everything is relative. What are the Beautiful, the Good, Art, Freedom? Words have a different meaning for every individual. . . . There is no common basis in men's minds. . . . Everything seems absurd to me. . . . What interests a Dadaist is his own mode of life."

These views had their effects on the churches. They eroded a sense of transcendence and traditional bases for Christian morality.

Paralleling and forming a part of this ethos were the virulent national sovereignties of the twentieth century. Nietzsche may not have been protofascist, but the value vacuum that he helped create proved fertile for such political systems. If there is no right, only might, totalitarianism has an open invitation. Two centuries earlier Hobbes had outlined the matter in his *Leviathan.* When self-preservation pits man against man in a continual state of war in which life is "solitary, poor, nasty, brutish, and short," then totalitarianism for the sake of a protective order seems acceptable. The value vacuum of nihilism and relativism is not the only cause of the complex rise of twentieth-century Leviathans of Communism, Fascism, Nazism, and extreme chauvinism, but neither is it coincidental that these arose in such powerful anti-Christian forms at a time when traditional Christian values had been eroded. The rise of Hitlerism in Germany, says Helmut Thielicke in *Nihilism: Its Origin and Nature,* 1950, was a tragic consequence of the meaninglessness that pervaded society. Knowing that blood and nation are not final absolutes, Hitler nevertheless absolutized them. He unleashed a holocaust against the Jews and the most destructive war in human history. In the absence of God, Hitler assumed divine prerogatives. Perhaps better than others, Hitler sensed the inherent power of the transcendent sovereignty of Christianity and Judaism; the former he tried to manipulate, the latter he tried to destroy.

From the time that the Weimar Constitution was adopted, July 31, 1919, until Hitler established the Third Reich, Germans cringed under the national humiliation of the imposed peace treaty that ended World War I. The National Socialist German Workers' Party capitalized on this feeling. February 25, 1920, at Munich, the Nazi party set forth its program for recovery of national dignity: the union of all Germans, colonies to nourish the nation, nationalization of business, profit-sharing, free education, religious liberty for those who do not endanger the state or disturb the moral sensibilities of the German race, citizenship for all with German blood, and exclusion of Jews. Hitler's colleague, Gottfried Feder, authored the statement. Few people thought the Nazis could succeed. They did not assess as cogently as did Hitler the intense drive toward nationalism that enveloped Germany in the latter part of the nineteenth century. Nor did they judge accurately the power of anti-Semitism, both ancient and modern, that had infused Western culture. Except for a brief period in the Middle Ages, from 700 to 1095, when Jews enjoyed an apartheid status, one can search in vain from the days of the early church to the twentieth century for a period when the Jews were not severely persecuted by so-called Christian regimes in Europe. During the Reformation, Luther had turned on the Jews in savage fury. His tirade against the Jews, 1543, was republished by Hitler without change. Lutheran states restricted Jews to ghettos and the wearing of yellow badges. Hitler's apologists were able to justify their own actions against the Jews by pointing to Catholic and Lutheran legislation in the past. H. S. Chamberlain (1855–1927), an Englishman enamored with German culture, who spent his life in Germany and Austria, and who eventually became a citizen of Germany and a friend of Hitler, captured this anti-Jewish ethos in his massive two-volume *Foundations of the Nineteenth Century* (1889–1901). He denigrated the Jews as barriers to the free development of the German spirit. Other tomes and pamphlets swelled this attitude. Alfred Rosenberg's *Myth of the Twentieth Century*, 1930, attacked the Jews, Christians, Masons, Marxists, pacifists, and feminists as sources of poisonous dark blood that must be eradicated from German veins. He could accept Christ as an Aryan, but not the Jewish ideal of deliverance and not the Christian concept of love, which conflicted with German ideals of honor. He exalted military heroes, celebrated Germanic unity, and envisioned a German folk church without Christian and Jewish symbols. Rosenberg was the official philosopher of National Socialism and a member of Hitler's inner circle. In *The German National Church*, 1932, Ernest Bergmann, professor of philosophy at Leipsic, depicted the divine creative impulse of the Germans as the modern God to displace degenerate Christianity and Judaism.

As the Nazis gained strength, a veritable worship of Hitler developed. Youth joined in growing numbers; they had their mountaintop torchlight and bonfire services, their rites of passage, their Brown Batallions, Storm Troopers, and Swastika. Hitler promised them victory over slavery, the Red Front, and Reactionaries. In 1932, Christian leaders, in support of Hitler, issued the "Platform of the German Christians," which called for a national folk church free of Christian and Jewish "deterioration and bastardization" to achieve the divine commission to the Germans.

The year 1933 was critical for Hitler's Nazism. The burning of the Reichstag, February 27, 1933, caused such social turmoil that Hitler was voted dictatorial powers for the next four years by a margin of 441 to 94. The program of the Nazis as set forth in their earlier platform and in Hitler's 800-page *Mein Kampf* quickly went into effect. Non-Aryans were dismissed from the civil service, the Nazi party was declared to be the only legal political organization, and sterilization of undesirables was instituted. Catholics and Protestants cooperated. July 20, 1933, the Catholic Center Party in Germany was formally dissolved and a concordat between Pope Pius XI and the German Nazis announced. In October of 1933 German bishops celebrated the 450th anniversary of Luther's birth by pledging fealty to "our Leader Adolf Hitler as a gift from God's hand." When President Paul von Hindenburg died in 1934, Hitler became both president and chancellor, the full dictator of Germany. On May 31 of that same year, a group of Confessing Church Christians led by Karl Barth issued a statement at Barmen that rejected any identification of the Christian message with national-racial politics. Also in that same year the Nazis dismissed Roman Catholic Vice-Chancellor von Papen from the Reich government, virtually disavowing the concordat with the papacy, but it was not until 1937 that Pius XI issued *Mit brennender Sorge* condemning Hitler's broken promises and interferences with the church. Because the papacy did not specifically condemn the Nazi pogrom against the Jews, even though Roman Catholics helped thousands of Jewish victims, the papacy was severely criticized in such well-documented, controversial works as Rolf Hochhuth's *The Deputy* and Gunther Lewy's *The Catholic Church and Nazi Germany,* both in 1964.

Following the end of the war in 1945, the full extent of the Nazi horror became known. Six million Jews died in Hitler's Final Solution at such infamous concentration death camps as Dahlem, Dachau, Buchenwald, Auschwitz, and Treblinka. Hundreds of protesters like Martin Niemoeller were thrown into prison; others like Dietrich Bonhoeffer were put to death. On October 19, 1945, surviving leaders of the Confessing Church, despite their resistance to Hitler, acknowledged corporate guilt for Nazism in their Stuttgart Declaration before the World Council of Churches.

This surge toward totalitarianism was not confined to Germany. Similar military regimes developed in Russia, Italy, Spain, Japan, China, and other countries.

World War II left many unsolved problems. The dropping of the atomic bomb on Hiroshima and Nagasaki in 1945 sent psychic shock waves around the world. It left a feeling that such force could not be employed in all-out war without the destruction of mankind. Backgrounded by the war's destructive aftermath, with Russia in possession of the bomb and obviously advancing technologically, a jittery America waged the inconclusive Korean War to contain Communism and advanced into the cold war of the 1950s. Dwight D. Eisenhower, who had commanded the Allied Forces in the victorious push against the Nazi Axis, vowed to go to Korea if elected President. With his election in 1952 a war-weary America began the strange era of the 1950s. Billy Graham's worldwide evangelistic campaigns attracted millions of hopeful seekers, and the individualistic pietism that developed, inspired perhaps by the father figure of Eisenhower, showed a deep desire to return to the stable security of older values; at the same time a "beat generation" became noticeably visible. Veterans returning from Korea were intent on establishing themselves, getting an education. College campuses were quiet, and the postwar religious revival lulled the churches into sociopolitical complacency.

Yet the 1950s were not calm. Problems of church and state had once more come to the forefront, with Protestants charging that Catholics were using questionable political means to get public money for their religious enterprises. In 1949, Paul Blanshard, a Quaker journalist, published his sensational *American Freedom and Catholic Power,* and A. P. Stokes published his three-volume *Church and State in the United States* in 1950, showing that Catholic-Protestant problems were by no means dead. In 1949 the press featured sensational stories about denial of religious freedom and human rights in Spain. When Franco gained power in 1939 at the end of Spain's bloody Civil War, Protestant schools were closed and an accord with the papacy made Roman Catholicism the sole religion of the country. When restrictions were relaxed in 1945, the Protestants established chapels and schools and became vigorously active, only to suffer ecclesiastical curtailment and harassment in the succeeding years. The Federal Council of Churches of Christ in America published accounts of the situation in 1949 and secular journalists confirmed the stories. This was regarded as an example of what Catholicism would do in any country in which it had sufficient political power.

However, Communism had come to be the demon to be curbed. As in foreign affairs Communists had to be stopped at all costs, so in domestic affairs they had to be uprooted. Protestant rightists and Catholic extremists joined men like Senator Joseph R. McCarthy, Senator W. S. Jenner, and Representative H. H. Velde in a witch-hunt for Communists and un-American activists. Those in the highest positions were not safe from accusations. J. B. Matthews, chief of McCarthy's investigating staff, published an article in *American Mercury* in which he asserted that 7,000 liberal Protestant clergymen provided the bulwark of Communist strength in America. Three senators resigned from the investigating committee in protest. Methodist Bishop G. Bromley Oxnam, an opponent of Cardinal Spellman, was among the accused. His *I Protest,* 1954, along with statements from leading church bodies and televised committee hearings finally exposed the false allegations, demagoguery, and inquisitorial tactics for which McCarthyism now stands.

At the beginning of the turbulent sixties, Gabriel Vahanian published *The Death of God: The Culture of Our Post-Christian Era,* 1961. The book not only revived Nietzsche's famous phrase but also marked a decade of "post-Christian" uncertainty in which values, churches, the establishment, government, and the military seemed to lose their credibility. Two years later, Bishop J. A. T. Robinson's *Honest to God* appeared in Great Britain, and in 1965 Harvey Cox's *The Secular City* was marketed. These and other publications reflected massive uncertainty about the relevance of religion in secular society. Credibility gaps yawned, not only about the validity of the church in a secular world but also about the reality of the existence of God. Rabbi Richard Rubenstein's *After Auschwitz,* 1966, argued that God is a Nothingness from which all things come and into which all things finally collapse. Reflecting on the extermination of 6,000,000 Jews, Rubenstein concluded that we are alone in the world, with only ourselves to depend on, that the Nazi horrors made God as pictured in the Bible no longer believable, that final human destiny is simply death. We must now live without ultimate hope, said Rubenstein, creating for ourselves whatever meaning we can. Thomas J. J. Altizer and William Hamilton popularized the Death of God in articles, speeches, and books. Even Vatican II, with its strident criticisms and insistence on change, added to the shaking of foundations. A trickle, then hundreds and thousands of monks, nuns, and priests in defiance of the papacy began getting married and leaving the clergy. Emotive standards of morality eroded and displaced traditional norms. Thousands of young men, supported by millions who saw no viable reason for fighting in Vietnam, refused service in the military and fled to Canada and Sweden. Profound distrust of government developed. Countercultures mushroomed. Drugs became a way of life to fight off frustration, loneliness, and despair. Timothy Leary became the high priest of seeking for new divine dimensions in LSD. Cults, mostly outside the established churches, multiplied, promising varieties of salvation by peaceful and violent means. Oriental modes of thought—Zen Buddhism and Transcendental Meditation (made popular by the Beatles)—gained wide acceptance. These cults grew out of disillusion, despair, loss of faith in established churches, relativized values, and desperate searching for meaning. We mention two such cults, the People's Temple and the Unification Church, to illustrate the disarray in religion.

In November of 1978 in a remote jungle spot in Guyana called Jonestown, over 900 members of the People's Temple and their leader Jim Jones committed mass murder-suicide by drinking juice laced with cyanide. Born in 1931 in Lynn, Indiana, to a mother who believed she had borne a messiah, Jones launched himself early on a preaching career among Methodist churches in Indiana, Kentucky, and Ohio. He reportedly performed miracles. In 1955 he raised $55,000 to start his own People's Temple in Indianapolis. After a few years, fearing nuclear destruction, Jones moved with his family and followers to Belo Horizonte, Brazil, then back to Indianapolis in 1963, at which time he was ordained by the Disciples of Christ. Again to escape nuclear destruction, he moved in 1965 with about 100 followers to Ukiah, California. The People's Temple thrived, and Jones and his members became known for social and political work in San Francisco, especially among poor blacks and whites. Upon the death of Father Divine, Jones claimed to be his reincarnation. In 1973 Jones purchased an 800-acre tract in Guyana, and in 1973 started his congregational suicide drills. Success brought more temples in Los Angeles and San Francisco; he appeared on platforms with Rosalyn Carter and Walter Mondale; he won recognition for his drug programs, free clinics, and food distributions. Apostates were hated. The press began investigating defectors' grim stories of beatings, misuse of funds, sex, etc. Precipitously in 1977 Jones moved with 800 followers to Guyana. When Congressman Leo Ryan tried to investigate the mysterious death of one cult member, Ryan and his party were slain. Shortly thereafter the world learned of the mass suicide—of misplaced sovereignty in one man.

Rev. Sun Myung Moon (1918–) founded his Unification Church in 1954 in Korea. His anti-Communism brought favors from the Korean government, and he amassed a private fortune. His work spread to Japan, and in 1973 he shifted his main base to the United States, stressing that he needed America's help to fight the evils of Communism. He spoke of rescuing America from drugs, immorality, and crime, and restoring its righteous mission in the world. From his followers, mostly middle-class youth converted in intense conferences, he demanded surrender of all worldly goods and ties, full obedience and loyalty, and unquestioning acceptance of his *Divine Principle*, which updated the Bible. They number about 2,000,000. He claimed to have had a mountaintop experience in which he was told by Jesus to finish Jesus' mission. In the Garden, Eve had sex with Satan; she then seduced Adam, thus corrupting the human race. Jesus was sent to start a new human race by having children of a virgin. He was not divine, and the crucifixion aborted his mission. Jesus won spiritual but not physical salvation. God eventually found Moon to complete the mission and start a pure race through the offspring of virginal marriages of Unification Church members—arranged by Moon. When humanity is finally saved, Moon will be the absolute spiritual ruler and savior of mankind.

The American dream of a righteous empire faded before the incongruities of Vietnam, unrealized liberty and justice for all, and the demonic depths in rational humanity. More historical perspective is needed to assess the twentieth century religiously, but in its legacy few would leave out relativism, nihilism, totalitarianism, and uncertainty. The sovereignty of the church has been abolished, that of the state is under grave question, and individual sovereignty has lost social credibility. The late 1970s and early 80s have witnessed the revival of some of the traditional moral authorities that previously suffered destructive erosion, but the story is not yet complete. Dostoyevsky's tale of the Grand Inquisitor poses an enigma for our time. The old Cardinal jails Christ and upbraids him for returning and disturbing things. Without speaking, Christ then kisses the Inquisitor on his bloodless lips. Is it a kiss of gratitude for having arranged life better without Christ? Or is it a kiss of forgiveness? The questions symbolize the uncertainty that has come to Christendom.

General Bibliography

EARLY CHURCH TO 500 A.D.

AYER, J. C. *A Source Book for Ancient Church History.* New York: Charles Scribner's Sons, 1913.

BAINTON, R. H. *Christian Attitudes Toward War and Peace.* New York: Abingdon Press, 1960.

BARRETT, C. K. *Signs of an Apostle.* London: Epworth Press & Methodist Publishing House, 1970.

BATTENHOUSE, R. W. *Companion to the Study of St. Augustine.* New York: Oxford University Press, 1955.

BAUR, WALTER *Orthodoxy and Heresy in Earliest Christianity.* Philadelphia: Fortress Press, 1971.

BETTENSON, H. *Documents of the Christian Church.* New York: Oxford University Press, 1963.

BRANDON, S. G. F. *Fall of Jerusalem and the Christian Church.* London: S. P. C. K., 1951.

BROCK, P. *Pacifism in Europe to 1914.* Princeton: Princeton University Press, 1972.

BROWN, PETER *Augustine of Hippo.* Berkeley: University of California Press, 1967.

CADOUX, C. J. *The Early Church and the World.* Edinburgh: T. & T. Clark, 1955.

CARRINGTON, P. *The Early Christian Church.* Cambridge, Eng.: Cambridge University Press, 1957.

CHADWICK, HENRY *Early Christian Thought and the Classical Tradition.* New York: Oxford University Press, 1966.

COCHRANE, C. N. *Christianity and Classical Culture.* Oxford: The Clarendon Press, 1940.

CONZELMANN, HANS   *History of Primitive Christianity.* Nashville: Abingdon Press, 1973.

COUNTRYMAN, L. WILLIAM   *The Rich Christian in the Church of the Early Empire: Contradictions and Accommodations.* New York: Edwin Mellen Press, 1980.

CULLMANN, O.   *Christ and Time.* Philadelphia: The Westminster Press, 1964.

———   *The Early Church.* Philadelphia: The Westminster Press, 1956.

———   *Jesus and the Revolutionaries.* New York: Harper & Row, Publishers, 1970.

DANIELOU, J., and H. MARROU   *The First Six Hundred Years.* New York: McGraw-Hill Book Company, 1964.

DAVIES, J. G.   *The Early Christian Church.* New York: Holt, Rinehart and Winston, Inc., 1965.

DAVIES, W. D.   *Christian Origins and Judaism.* Philadelphia: The Westminster Press, 1962.

DÖRRIES, HERMANN   *Constantine the Great.* New York: Harper & Row, Publishers, 1972.

FIGGIS, J. N.   *Political Aspects of St. Augustine's City of God.* Gloucester, Mass.: Peter Smith, 1963.

FREND, W. H. C.   *The Donatist Church.* Oxford: The Clarendon Press, 1952.

———   *The Early Church.* Philadelphia: Fortress Press, 1982.

———   *Martyrdom and Persecution in the Early Church.* Garden City, N.Y.: Anchor Books, 1967.

GILES, E.   *Documents Illustrating Papal Authority, 96–454.* London: S. P. C. K., 1952.

GOPPELT, LEONARD   *Apostolic and Post-Apostolic Times.* New York: Harper & Row, Publishers, 1970.

GRANT, F. C.   *Hellenistic Religions.* New York: Liberal Arts Press, 1953.

GRANT, R. M.   *After the New Testament.* Philadelphia: Fortress Press, 1967.

———   *Augustus to Constantine.* New York: Harper & Row, Publishers, 1970.

———   *Gnosticism and Early Christianity.* New York: Columbia University Press, 1959.

HARNACK, ADOLF VON   *The Mission and Expansion of Christianity in the First Three Centuries.* New York: Harper & Row, Publishers, 1962.

HINSON, E. GLENN   *The Evangelization of the Roman Empire: Identity and Adaptability.* Macon, Ga.: Mercer University Press, 1981.

JONAS, HANS   *The Gnostic Religion.* Boston: Beacon Press, 1958.

KING, N. Q.   *Emperor Theodosius and the Establishment of Christianity.* Philadelphia: The Westminster Press, 1960.

LASSUS, J.   *The Early Christian and Byzantine World.* New York: McGraw-Hill Book Company, 1967.

LIETZMANN, H.   *A History of the Early Church.* Cleveland: The World Publishing Company, 1961. 4v.

MARKUS, R. A.   *Saeculum: History and Society in the Theology of St. Augustine.* Cambridge, Eng.: Cambridge University Press, 1970.

MARXSEN, W.   *The Resurrection of Jesus of Nazareth.* Philadelphia: Fortress Press, 1970.

MEER, F. VAN DER   *Atlas of the Early Church.* London: Nelson, 1958.

MOMIGLIANO, A.   *The Conflict Between Paganism and Christianity in the Fourth Century.* Oxford: Clarendon Press, 1963.

MOWRY, LUCETTA   *The Dead Sea Scrolls and the Early Church.* Chicago: University of Chicago Press, 1962.

NYGREN, ANDERS   *Agape and Eros.* Philadelphia: The Westminster Press, 1952.

O'CONNELL, R. J.   *St. Augustine's Confessions, Odyssey of Soul.* Cambridge, Mass.: Harvard University Press, 1969.

PARKES, JAMES *A History of the Jewish People.* Baltimore: Penguin Books Inc., 1964.

SCHMITHALS, WALTER *Gnosticism in Corinth.* Nashville: Abingdon Press, 1971.

SCHWEITZER, F. M. *A History of the Jews.* New York: The Macmillan Company, 1971.

STEVENSON, J. *Creeds, Councils and Controversies: Documents.* London: S. P. C. K., 1966.

――― *A New Eusebius.* London: S. P. C. K., 1957.

TESELLE, EUGENE *Augustine, the Theologian.* New York: Herder and Herder, Inc., 1970.

WADDAMS, H. M. *The Struggle for Christian Unity.* New York: Walker & Company, 1968.

WADDELL, HELEN *The Desert Fathers.* New York: Henry Holt, 1936.

WILKEN, R. L. *The Myth of Christian Beginnings.* Garden City, N.Y.: Doubleday & Company, Inc., 1971.

WORKMAN, H. B. *The Evolution of the Monastic Ideal.* London: Epworth Press and Methodist Publishing House, 1927.

――― *Persecution in the Early Church.* London: Kelly, 1906.

MEDIEVAL CHRISTIANITY, 500–1450

ANDERSON, C. S. *Augsburg Historical Atlas of Christianity in the Middle Ages and Reformation.* Minneapolis: Augsburg Publishing House, 1967.

CANNON, W. R. *History of Christianity in the Middle Ages.* Grand Rapids, Mich.: Baker Book House, 1983.

COHN, N. R. C. *The Pursuit of the Millennium.* New York: Oxford University Press, 1970.

COULTON, G. G. *Life in the Middle Ages.* Cambridge, Eng.: Cambridge University Press, 1928–30.

DANIEL-ROPS, HENRY *Cathedral and Crusade, 1050–1350.* New York: E. P. Dutton & Co., Inc., 1957.

――― *The Church in the Dark Ages.* New York: E. P. Dutton & Co., Inc., 1959.

DAVIS, C. T. *Sources of Medieval History.* New York: Appleton-Century-Crofts, 1967.

DEANESLY, MARGARET *A History of the Medieval Church.* Scranton, Pa,: Barnes & Noble, Inc., 1960.

FAIRWEATHER, A. M. *Aquinas on Nature and Grace.* Philadelphia: The Westminster Press, 1954.

GILCHRIST, J. T. *The Church and Economic Activity in the Middle Ages.* New York: The Macmillan Company, 1969.

GILL, J. *The Council of Florence.* Cambridge, Eng.: Cambridge University Press, 1959.

GILSON, ETIENNE *The Spirit of Medieval Philosophy.* New York: Charles Scribner's Sons, 1936.

HABID, MARION A. *St. Francis of Assisi, Writings and Early Biographies.* Chicago: Franciscan Herald Press, 1973.

JACOBS, E. F. *Essays in the Conciliar Epoch.* Notre Dame: University of Notre Dame Press, 1963.

JARRETT, BEDE *Social Theories of the Middle Ages, 1200–1500.* New York: Frederick Ungar Publishing Inc., Co., 1966.

KAMINSKY, HOWARD *A History of the Hussite Revolution.* Berkeley: University of California Press, 1967.

KNOWLES, DAVID *The Middle Ages.* New York: McGraw-Hill Book Company, 1968.

LEA, H. C. *A History of the Inquisition in the Middle Ages.* New York: Russell & Russell Publishers, 1955.

LOOMIS, LOUISE R. *The Council of Constance.* New York: Columbia University Press, 1961.

McFARLANE, K. B. *John Wycliffe and the Beginnings of English Non-conformity.* Mystic, Conn.: Lawrence Verry, 1952.

MARGULL, HANS J. *The Councils of the Church.* Philadelphia: Fortress Press, 1966.

MOORMAN, JOHN *A History of the Franciscan Order.* Oxford: Clarendon Press, 1968.

PETRY, R. C. *Late Medieval Mysticism.* Philadelphia: The Westminster Press, 1957.

PETRY, R. C., and C. L. MANSCHRECK *A History of Christianity.* Grand Rapids, Mich.: Baker Book House, 1981. 2v.

POWELL, J. M. *Innocent III.* Lexington, Mass.: D. C. Heath, 1963.

RUNCIMAN, S. *A History of the Crusades.* Cambridge, Eng.: Cambridge University Press, 1951. 3v.

RUSSELL, J. B. *A History of Medieval Christianity.* New York: Thomas Y. Crowell Company, 1968.

——— *A History of Witchcraft, Sorcerers, Heretics, and Pagans.* London: Thames and Hudson Ltd., 1980.

SPINKA, MATTHEW *Advocates of Reform from Wyclif to Erasmus.* Philadelphia: The Westminster Press, 1963.

——— *John Hus: A Biography.* Princeton: Princeton University Press, 1968.

TAYLOR, H. O. *The Medieval Mind.* Cambridge: Harvard University Press, 1959. 2v.

TIERNEY, BRIAN *The Crisis of Church and State, 1050–1300.* Englewood Cliffs, N.J.: Prentice-Hall, Inc., 1964.

——— *Foundations of Conciliar Theory.* Cambridge, Eng.: University Press, 1955.

VOLZ, C. A. *The Church of the Middle Ages.* St. Louis: Concordia Publishing House, 1970.

RENAISSANCE AND REFORMATION, 1450–1700

ABBOTT, W. C. *The Writings and Speeches of Oliver Cromwell.* Cambridge: Harvard University Press, 1937–47. 4v.

BAINTON, R. H. *Erasmus of Christendom.* New York: Charles Scribner's Sons, 1969.

——— *Here I Stand.* New York: Abingdon Press, 1950.

——— *Hunted Heretic: Servetus.* Boston: Beacon Press, 1953.

——— *The Travail of Religious Liberty.* Philadelphia: The Westminster Press, 1951.

——— *Women of the Reformation, in Germany and Italy; in France and England.* Minneapolis: Ausburg Publishing House, 1971, 1973.

BANGS, CARL *Arminius.* New York: Abingdon Press, 1971.

BARBOUR, H. *The Quakers in Puritan England.* New Haven: Yale University Press, 1964.

BENNETT, JOHN W. *Hutterian Brethren.* Palo Alto, Calif.: Stanford University Press, 1967.

BOULENGER, JACQUES *The Seventeenth Century in France.* New York: G. P. Putnam's Sons, 1963.

BRAILSFORD, H. N.   *The Levellers and the English Revolution.* Palo Alto, Calif.: Stanford University Press, 1961.

BRAITHWAITE, W. C.   *The Beginnings of Quakerism.* Cambridge, Eng.: Cambridge University Press, 1961.

BRIDENBAUGH, CARL   *Vexed and Troubled Englishmen, 1590–1642.* New York: Oxford University Press, 1968.

BROMILY, G. W.   *Zwingli and Bullinger.* Philadelphia: The Westminster Press, 1953.

BURNS, E. M.   *The Counter-Reformation.* Princeton: Princeton University Press, 1964.

CALVIN, JOHN   *Institutes of the Christian Religion,* tr. J. T. McNeill. Philadelphia: The Westminster Press, 1960.

CARLSON, L. H.   *Writings of Henry Barrow, 1587–1590.* London: George Allen & Unwin Ltd., 1962.

CLARK, SIR GEORGE   *The Later Stuarts.* Oxford: Oxford University Press, 1961.

CLARK, HENRY W.   *History of English Nonconformity.* N. Y.: Russell & Russell Publishers, 1965.

CLEBSCH, WILLIAM A.   *England's Earliest Protestants.* New Haven: Yale University Press, 1964.

DAVIES, GODFREY   *The Early Stuarts.* Oxford: Oxford University Press, 1959.

DICKENS, A. G.   *The English Reformation.* New York: Schocken Books Inc., 1964.

DOLAN, J. P.   *History of the Reformation.* New York: Desclee Co., 1965.

DURNBAUGH, DONALD   *The Believers' Church.* New York: The Macmillan Company, 1968.

EMERY, R. W.   *The Friars in Medieval France.* New York: Columbia University Press, 1962.

FIGGIS, J. N.   *The Divine Right of Kings.* New York: Harper & Row Publishers, 1965.

FLETCHER, C. R. L.   *Gustavus Adolphus and the Thirty Years' War.* New York: Capricorn Books, 1963.

FOX, GEORGE   *Journal of George Fox.* Cambridge, Eng.: Cambridge University Press, 1952.

FOXE, JOHN   *Book of Martyrs.* Boston: Little, Brown and Company, 1966.

GARDNER, JAMES   *Lollardy and the Reformation in England.* New York: B. Franklin, 1964. 4v.

GEYL, PETER   *The Netherlands in the Seventeenth Century, 1609–1648.* New York: Barnes & Noble, Inc., 1961–64. 2v.

GRITSCH, E. W.   *Reformer Without a Church: Thomas Muentzer.* Philadelphia: Fortress Press, 1967.

HALLER, W.   *Liberty and Reformation in the Puritan Revolution.* New York: Columbia University Press, 1955.

———   *The Rise of Puritanism.* New York: Columbia University Press, 1938.

HARBISON, E.   *The Christian Scholar in the Age of the Reformation.* New York: Charles Scribner's Sons, 1956.

HENDRIX, SCOTT H.   *Luther and the Papacy: Stages in a Reformation Conflict.* Philadelphia: Fortress Press, 1981.

HILL, CHRISTOPHER   *God's Englishman.* New York: The Dial Press, Inc., 1970.

———   *Puritanism and Revolution.* New York: Schocken Books Inc., 1968.

HILLERBRAND, HANS   *The Reformation.* New York: Harper & Row, Publishers, 1964.

HORSCH, JOHN   *The Hutterian Brethren, 1528–1931.* Goshen, Ind.: Mennonite Historical Society, 1931.

———   *Mennonites in Europe.* Scottdale, Pa.: Herald Press, 1950.

IGNATIUS OF LOYOLA *The Spiritual Exercises,* tr. Anthony Mottola. New York: Doubleday & Company, Inc. 1964.

JEDIN, H. *A History of the Council of Trent.* St. Louis: Herder and Herder, Inc., 1957. 2v.

JONES, R. T. *Congregationalism in England.* London: Independent Press, 1962.

KNOWLES, DAVID *Christian Monasticism.* New York: McGraw-Hill Book Company, 1969.

KNOX, JOHN *History of the Reformation in Scotland.* London: T. Nelson, 1949. 2v.

LITTELL, FRANKLIN *The Origins of Sectarian Protestantism.* New York: The Macmillan Company, 1968.

LOCHER, G. W. *Zwingli's Thought: New Perspectives.* Leiden: E. J. Brill, 1981.

LUTHER, MARTIN *Luther's Works,* ed. by J. Pelikan and H. Lehman. St. Louis: Concordia Publishing House, 1955– . 55v.

MCFARLANE, K. B. *Origins of Religious Dissent in England.* New York: The Macmillan Company, 1966.

MCNEILL, J. T. *The History and Character of Calvinism.* New York: Oxford University Press, 1954.

MANSCHRECK, CLYDE L. *Melanchthon: The Quiet Reformer.* New York: Abingdon Press, 1958.

NEALE, J. E. *Queen Elizabeth.* New York: Doubleday, Anchor Books, 1957.

OLSEN, V. NORSKOV *John Foxe and the Elizabethan Church.* Berkeley: University of California Press, 1973.

PATER, CALVIN A. *Karlstadt as the Father of the Baptist Movements.* Toronto: University of Toronto Press, 1983.

POWICKE, F. M. *The Reformation in England.* New York: Oxford University Press, 1958.

REARDON, BERNARD M. G. *Religious Thought in the Reformation.* London: Longman, 1981.

RENWICK, A. M. *The Story of the Scottish Reformation.* Grand Rapids, Mich.: Wm. B. Eerdmans Publishing Company, 1960.

RIDLEY, JASPER *John Knox.* New York: Oxford University Press, 1968.

RIEDEMANN, PETER *Confession of Faith.* Rifton, N. Y.: The Plough Publishing House, 1970.

RILLIET, JEAN *Zwingli: Third Man of the Reformation.* London: Lutterworth Press, 1964.

SPENER, PHILLIP JACOB *Pia Desideria,* tr. T. G. Tappert. Philadelphia: Fortress Press, 1964.

STRYPE, JOHN *Annals of the Reformation.* New York: Burt Franklin, 1964. 4v.

TAPPERT, T. *Book of Concord.* Philadelphia: Muhlenberg Press, 1959.

TORBET, R. G. *A History of the Baptists.* Valley Forge, Pa.: Judson Press, 1963.

WALTON, R. C. *Zwingli's Theocracy.* Toronto: University of Toronto Press, 1967.

WEDGEWOOD, C. V. *The Thirty Years' War.* N. Y.: Doubleday, Anchor Books, 1962.

WENGER, J. C. *The Complete Writings of Menno Simons.* Scottdale, Pa.: Herald Press, 1956.

———— *Even Unto Death.* Richmond, Va.: John Knox Press, 1961.

WILLIAMS, GEORGE H. *The Radical Reformation.* Philadelphia: The Westminster Press, 1962.

WILLIAMS, GEORGE H., and A. M. MERGAL *Spiritual and Anabaptist Writers.* Philadelphia: The Westminster Press, 1957.

WOLFE, D. M. *Leveller Manifestoes of the Puritan Revolution.* New York: Humanities Press, Inc., 1967.

MODERN CHRISTIANITY, 1700 TO PRESENT

AHLSTROM, SYDNEY E.   *A Religious History of the American People.* New Haven: Yale University Press, 1972.

BATOR, VICTOR   *Vietnam, A Diplomatic Tragedy.* New York: Oceana Publications, 1965.

BILLINGTON, R. A.   *The Protestant Crusade, 1800–1860: Origins of American Nativism.* New York: The Macmillan Company, 1938.

BIOT, FRANÇOIS   *The Rise of Protestant Monasticism.* Baltimore: Helicon Press, 1964.

BONNOT, BERNARD F.   *Pope John XXIII. An Astute, Pastoral Leader.* New York: Alba House, 1980.

BORDIN, RUTH   *Women and Temperance: The Quest for Power and Liberty, 1873–1900.* Philadelphia: Temple University Press, 1981.

BOURDEAUX, MICHAEL   *Religious Ferment in Russia.* London: Macmillan & Co. Ltd. 1968.

BROCK, PETER   *Pacifism in the United States.* Princeton: Princeton University Press, 1968.

CARTER, P. A.   *The Spiritual Crisis of the Gilded Age.* DeKalb, Ill.: Northern Illinois University Press, 1972.

CAVERT, SAMUEL   *The American Churches in the Ecumenical Movement, 1900–1968.* New York: Association Press, 1968.

CHADWICK, OWEN   *The Victorian Church.* New York: Oxford University Press, 1966. 2v.

CLARK, ELMER T.   *The Small Sects in America.* New York: Abingdon Press, 1949.

COCHRANE, A. C.   *The Church's Confession Under Hitler.* Philadelphia: The Westminster Press, 1962.

CRAIG, G. R.   *From Puritanism to the Age of Reason, 1660–1700.* Cambridge, Eng.: Cambridge University Press, 1950.

ELLIS, J. T.   *American Catholicism.* Chicago: University of Chicago Press, 1969.

FRAZIER, E. FRANKLIN   *The Negro Church in America.* New York: Schocken Books, Inc., 1964.

GAUSTAD, E. S.   *Historical Atlas of Religion in America.* New York: Harper & Row Publishers, 1962.

GAY, PETER   *The Enlightenment.* New York: Random House, Inc., 1966.

GISH, A. G.   *The New Left and Christian Radicalism.* Grand Rapids, Mich.: Wm. B. Eerdmans Publishing Company, 1970.

GOODWIN, R. N.   *Triumph or Tragedy: Reflections on Vietnam.* New York: Random House, Inc., 1966.

GRUNBERGER, RICHARD   *The 12-Year Reich.* New York: Holt, Rinehart and Winston, 1971.

HALES, E. E. Y.   *Revolution and Papacy, 1764–1846.* Garden City, N.Y.: Hanover House, 1960.

HALL, DAVID   *The Antinomian Controversy: A Documentary History.* Middletown, Conn.: Wesleyan University Press, 1968.

HANDY, ROBERT T.   *A Christian America.* New York: Oxford University Press, 1971.

——— *A History of the Churches in the United States and Canada.* New York: Oxford University Press, 1977.

——— *The Social Gospel in America, 1870–1920.* New York: Oxford University Press, 1966.

HANSEN, KLAUS J.   *Mormonism and the American Experience.* Chicago: University of Chicago Press, 1981.

HASLER, AUGUST B. *How the Pope Became Infallible: Pius IX and the Politics of Persuasion.* New York: Doubleday and Co., 1981.

HENNESEY, JAMES *American Catholics: A History of the Roman Catholic Community in the United States.* New York: Oxford University Press, 1981.

HENRY, STUART C. *George Whitefield: Wayfaring Witness.* New York: Abingdon Press, 1957.

HOLLOWAY, MARK *Heavens on Earth: Utopian Communities in America, 1680–1880.* New York: Dover Publications, Inc., 1966.

HOPKINS, C. H. *The Rise of the Social Gospel in American Protestantism.* New Haven: Yale University Press, 1940.

HUDSON, WINTHROP S. *Religion in America.* New York: Charles Scribner's Sons, 1965.

KRADITOR, A. S. *The Ideas of the Woman Suffrage Movement, 1890–1920.* New York: Columbia University Press, 1965.

LATOURETTE, K. S. *Christianity in a Revolutionary Age.* New York: Harper & Row, Publishers, 1959–62. 5v.

LEWY, GUENTHER *The Catholic Church and Nazi Germany.* New York: McGraw-Hill Book Company, 1964.

McAVOY, T. T. *A History of the Catholic Church in the United States.* Notre Dame: University of Notre Dame Press, 1970.

MARSDEN, GEORGE M. *Fundamentalism and American Culture, the Shaping of Twentieth-century Evangelicalism, 1870–1925.* New York: Oxford University Press, 1980.

MARTY, MARTIN E. *Righteous Empire: Protestant Experience in America.* New York: The Dial Press, Inc., 1970.

MEAD, SIDNEY E. *The Lively Experiment.* New York: Harper & Row, Publishers, 1963.

MELVILLE, KEITH *Communes in the Counter Culture: Origins, Theories, Styles of Life.* New York: William Morrow & Co., Inc., 1972.

MILLER, PERRY *Errand into the Wilderness.* Cambridge, Mass.: Harvard University Press, 1956.

MORGAN, E. S. *Visible Saints: History of the Puritan Idea.* New York: N.Y.U. Press, 1963.

NEILL, STEPHEN *A History of Christian Missions.* Baltimore: Penguin Books, 1964.

NELSEN, H. M., et al. *The Black Church in America.* New York: Basic Books, Inc., Publishers, 1971.

OUTLER, A. C. *John Wesley.* New York: Oxford University Press, 1964.

RECKITT, M. B. *Maurice to Temple: A Century of the Social Movement in the Church of England.* London: Faber & Faber Ltd., 1947.

ROUSE, RUTH, and STEPHEN NEILL *A History of the Ecumenical Movement, 1517–1948.* Philadelphia: The Westminster Press, 1952.

SANDEEN, ERNEST R. *The Roots of Fundamentalism: British and American Millenarianism 1800–1930.* Chicago: University of Chicago Press, 1970.

SCHMIDT, MARTIN *John Wesley: Theological Biography.* New York: Abingdon Press, 1963.

SCHNEIDER, ISIDOR *The Enlightenment.* New York: George Braziller, Inc., 1965.

SIMPSON, ALAN *Puritanism in Old and New England.* Chicago: University of Chicago Press, 1955.

SMITH, SHELTON, et al. *American Christianity: An Historical Interpretation, Documents.* New York: Charles Scribner's Sons, 1960–63. 2v.

SONTAG, FREDERICK, and J. K. ROTH *The American Religious Experience.* New York: Harper and Row, Publishers, 1972.

STOKES, ANSON P. *Church and State in the United States.* New York: Harper & Row, Publishers, 1950.

TRACY, PATRICIA *Jonathan Edwards, Pastor: Religion and Society in Eighteenth Century Northampton.* Hill, 1980.

TUVESON, ERNEST L. *Redeemer Nation.* Chicago: University of Chicago Press, 1968.

WALSH, H. H. *The Christian Church in Canada.* Toronto: Ryerson Press, 1956.

WALZER, MICHAEL *The Revolution of the Saints: Origins of Radical Politics.* Cambridge, Mass.: Harvard University Press, 1965.

WILLIAMS, GEORGE H. *The Mind of John Paul II. Origins of His Thought and Action.* New York: Seabury Press, 1981.

(For additional original writings, consult library listings under historical figures, e.g., Ambrose, Aquinas, Augustine, Bernard of Clairvaux, Hildebrand, etc.)

Index

Abbott, Lyman, 320
Abelard, Peter, 120–21, 133
Act of Toleration, 210, 235–36, 283
Acts of Peter, 33
Acts of the Apostles, 9–10, 30, 37
Adamites, 150
Adler, Alfred, 325
Adolphus, Gustavus, 238
Agape, 3, 4, 8
Agricola, Rudolf, 163
Aidan, 105
Alaric, 79, 88
Albertus Magnus, 129, 135
Albigenses. *See* Cathari
Alcuin, 108
Alexander of Hales, 129, 169
Alexis, Metropolitan, 102
Allegory, 40, 41, 50, 51, 80, 121
Allegro, John Marco, 2
Allen, Richard, 298–99
Allen, William, 224
Alva, Duke of, 207–8, 224
Ambrose of Milan, 64–66, 69, 72–73, 91
American Revolution, 263, 288–89
Anabaptists, 177, 181–88, 238

Anagni, 140
Angelico, Fra, 153, 159
Anselm of Canterbury, 133–34
Anthony, St., 56
Anthony, Susan B., 304
Anti-Catholicism, in America, 280, 284, 286, 288, 292–93, 295
Antinomianism, 29, 30, 32, 38, 260
Apocalypticism. *See* Eschatology
Apocrypha, 33, 203
Apollinarianism, 64
Apostles' Creed, 32, 34, 43
Apostolic Succession, 34, 35, 36, 37, 42, 43, 45, 55, 78, 85, 112
Apotheosis, 21
Appeal to the German Nobility, The, 171
Aquinas, Thomas, 67, 128, 129, 132–39, 140, 275
Arianism, 56, 60–66
Aristides, 21
Aristotle, 133, 136
Armada, Great, 207
Arminianism, 192–93, 231
Arminius, J., 192
Arnauld, Antoine, 201
Arnobius, 27

Arnold of Brescia, 120–21
Asbury, Francis, 261, 290–91, 294, 298
Asceticism, 25, 26, 27, 29, 31, 32, 37, 44–46, 48, 49, 51, 53–54, 55, 58, 63, 66, 68, 115–16, 117, 121, 154, 156, 195, 197, 208
Athanasius, 34, 51, 57, 60–63, 66, 228
Atheism, 246, 291, 328
Athenagoras, 21, 38, 41, 42
Atom bomb, 332
Atonement, 48, 51, 133
Attila, 80, 88, 89
Augsburg Confession, 176–77
Augustine of Canterbury, 86, 106
Augustine of Hippo, 11, 59, 67–78, 90, 91, 104, 111, 144
   City of God, 67–68, 75–78, 80
   Confessions, 67–70
Aurelius, Marcus (emperor), 21, 22
Authority, 1–2, 28–37, 33, 34, 35, 37, 43, 44, 45–46, 60, 77–78, 98, 104, 138–39, 147, 172, 178, 188, 211, 217, 327
Averroists, 136
Avignon, 143
Avvakum (priest), 99

Babington conspiracy, 224
Babylas of Antioch, 23
Babylonian Captivity, 142, 152, 155, 211
Babylonian Captivity, The, 172
Bach, Johann Sebastian, 241
Backus, Isaac, 290
Bacon, Francis, 129, 236, 245
Baer, G. F., 296
Baptism, 28, 51, 70–71, 85, 91, 187–88
Baptists, 231–32, 234, 285, 290, 291, 294, 298, 311–12
Bar Kochba, 17
Barbarians, 58, 75, 78, 79–80, 81, 85–86, 88, 89
Barbarossa, Frederick (emperor), 119, 121, 126
Barclay, Robert, 255–56
Barmen confession, 332
Barnabas, Letter of, 26, 33, 38, 41
Barnabites, 197
Barnes, Robert, 213, 216, 218
Baroque architecture, 240–42
Barrow, Henry, 226

Barth, Karl, 264, 325, 332
Barton, Bruce, 2
Basil of Caesarea, 57, 63
Basilides, 30, 31
Baur, F. C., 264, 269, 319
Beatles, 334
Beckett, Samuel, 330
Bede, Venerable, 106, 108, 115
Beecher, Henry Ward, 276, 296, 320
Beecher, Lyman, 292
Beghards, 124
Bellamy, Henry, 316
Bellarmine, Robert, 200, 209
Benedict of Nursia, 80, 86–88, 92
Benedictines, 86–88, 106–7, 112
Berengar of Tours, 111
Berkeley, John, 287
Bernard of Clairvaux, 116–17, 120
Bernini, Giovanni, 240
Beveridge, Albert J., 296
Bible, English, 217–19, 230
Biblical criticism, 319–20
Bilney, Thomas, 214
Bilson, Thomas, 227
Bismarck, Otto von, 272, 273
Blanchard, Charles and Jonathan, 322, 323
Blanchard, Paul, 333
Blandina, 22
Blaurock, George, 181, 184
Boccaccio, Giovanni, 153, 154
Bockelson, Jan, 186–87
Boethius, 86
Bogomiles, 124
Böhler, Peter, 260
Bonaparte, Napoleon, 100, 263, 266–67
Bonaventura, 129
Bonhoeffer, Dietrich, 332
Boniface (missionary), 88, 90, 106–7
Booth, William, 317–18
Borgia, Caesar, 156, 159
Borgia, Lucrezia, 156
Borromeo, Charles, 209
Borromini, Francesco, 240
Botticelli, Sandro, 153, 159
Bradford, William, 231, 282–83, 284
Brainerd, David, 311
Bramante, 159
Brent, Charles H., 314
Brenz, Johann, 203
Brethren of the Common Life, 152, 164

Brewster, William, 231, 284
Browne, Robert, 226
Bruni, Leonardo, 154, 163
Brunner, Emil, 326
Bruno, Giordano, 205
Bryan, W. J., 325
Buber, Martin, 328
Bucer, Martin, 178, 180, 185
Bullinger, Heinrich, 191
Bunyan, John, 236
Bushnell, Horace, 276, 292, 296
Butler, Joseph, 251, 319
Byzantine Empire, 94–101

Caesaropapism, 81, 85, 94–103, 107
Cajetan, Cardinal, 170, 196
Calvert, Cecilius, 286
Calvert, George, 286
Calvin, John, 67, 178, 185, 188–93
Campbell, Alexander, 296
Camus, Albert, 329
Canisius, Peter, 200, 209
Canon, Biblical, 28, 32, 33–34, 37
Canossa, 114
Capuchins, 196–97
Caraffa. *See* Pope Paul IV
Carey, William, 311–12
Carnegie, Andrew, 296
Carruth, William Herbert, 320–21
Carteret, George, 287
Carthusians, 115–16, 152
Cartier, Jacques, 282
Cartwright, Peter, 318
Cartwright, Thomas, 226–27
Case, S. J., 323
Cassian, John, 74
Castellio, Sebastian, 191
Castiglione, Baldassare, 159, 160
Cathari, 121–23, 125, 129, 162
Catholic Emancipation Act, 270
Cavour, Camillio di, 272
Celestius, 73–4
Celibacy, 19, 26, 37, 49, 55, 73, 112
Celsus, 21, 37, 38–39, 51
Celtes, Conrad, 163
Cerularius, Michael, 96
Cervantes, Miguel de, 160
Champion, Edmund, 224
Charlemagne, 90, 107–9
Charles I (England), 232–34
Charles II (England), 234–35
Charles V (emperor), 159, 172, 196, 203

Charles IX (France), 206
Chaucer, Geoffrey, 154
Chekhov, Anton, 100
Chelčický, Peter, 150
Chilperic, 88
Christology, 30, 41, 43, 46, 48, 50, 51, 53, 59–66, 80–82, 95, 96, 108, 121. *See also* Jesus
Chrysoloras, Manuel, 154
Chrysostom, John, 64–66
Church, concept of, 59, 70–72, 91, 148–49
Church and state, 16–27, 53, 58–66, 71–72, 75–78, 80, 89, 93–103, 125–27, 181, 210–27, 280, 287, 333
Churriguera, Jose, 240–41
Cicero, 66
Cistercians, 116
Civil religion, 45–46, 93–103, 207, 263, 281, 289–91, 292–94, 296
Civil rights, 302–3
Civil War, American, 293–95
Clarendon Code, 234–35
Clement of Alexandria, 23, 33, 38, 46–49
Clement of Rome, 20, 26, 33, 35, 36, 38, 85
Clergy, development of, 28, 32, 33, 37
Clericis laicos, 141
Clovis (France), 89
Cluny, 112, 115–16
Coke, Thomas, 261
Colenso, J. W., 319
Coleridge, Samuel T., 268–69
Colet, John, 163, 165, 212
College of Cardinals, 113, 117
Columba, 105
Columbanus, 105
Columbus, 160
Comnenus, Alexius, 117, 118
Comte, Auguste, 316
Concerning Heretics and Those Who Burn Them, 185
Conciliarism, 140, 148, 152, 155, 161
Confutation, 176
Conrad of Gelnhausen, 146
Constans, 59, 62
Constantine (emperor), 24, 25, 27, 53, 58–59, 60, 62, 107
Constantine II, 62
Constantinople (Byzantium), 49, 52, 57, 64, 98, 117, 150, 153

Constantius, 24, 62–63
Constitution, U.S., 289
Contarini, Gasparo, 196
Conwell, Russell, 296
Cop, Nicolas, 188
Copernicus, Nikolaus, 245
Cortez, Hernando, 281
Councils
    Basel, 147–48, 155, 202
    Chalcedon, 57, 64, 81, 85, 95
    Clermont, 117
    Constance, 146–47, 148, 155
    Constantinople, 49, 52, 57, 63–64,
        80, 81
    Ephesus, 74, 80
    Florence, 98, 148
    Fourth Lateran, 111, 122, 124, 127,
        148
    Nicaea, 24, 53, 55, 59–66, 81, 85
    Sardica, 62
    Trent, 194, 202–5
    Vatican I, 204, 209, 274
    Vatican II, 202, 204, 209, 264, 279,
        307, 314–15
Coverdale, William, 217–18
Cox, Harvey, 333
Cranmer, Thomas, 214, 215, 216,
    217–18, 219–20
Crévecoeur, St. John de, 288
Cromwell, Oliver, 232–34
Cromwell, Thomas, 214, 216, 217–19,
    286
Crusades, 117–19, 125
Cyprian of Carthage, 23, 59, 70

Dada art, 330
Dante, Alighieri, 153
Darby, John N., 322
Darrow, Clarence, 325
Darwin, Charles, 273, 308, 319, 322
De Soto, Hernando, 282
Dead Sea Scrolls, 19, 54
Death of God, theologians, 326,
    333–34
Decius (emperor), 23, 49
Declaration of Independence, 289
Deism, 246, 248–51, 290
Descartes, René, 244–45
Determinism, 51, 61, 91, 137. See also
    Predestination
Dewey, John, 325, 326
Diatessaron, 33
Didache, 26, 33, 38, 39–40

Diggers, 234
Diocletian, 23, 24, 58
Diognetus, 27
Dispensations, 1, 322, 323
Divine Right, 239–42
Dobneck, Johann, 167
Docetism, 30, 31, 36, 43, 48. See also
    Gnosticism
Dominicans, 122, 125–26, 128–30,
    132–39, 144, 150
Domitian, 20, 22
Donatello, 153, 159
Donation of Constantine, 107, 154–55,
    156
Donatists, 24, 59, 67, 70–72
Donne, John, 236
Dort, Synod, 193
Dostoyevsky, Feodor, 100, 201, 328,
    335
Douglas, Frederick, 294
Drummond, Henry, 318
Dryden, John, 236
DuBois, W. E. B., 297–98, 301
Duchesne, Louis, 277
Dürer, Albrecht, 157, 175
Dwight, Timothy, 291

Eastern Orthodox Church, 93–103,
    314
Ebionites, 11, 30, 55
Eck, Johann, 171
Eckhart, Meister, 129, 150–52
Ecumenism, 93, 103, 155, 307, 311–15
Eddy, Mary Baker, 321
Edict of Milan, 23, 53
Edict of Nantes, 206
Edward I (England), 141
Edward III, 142
Edward VI, 217, 219–22
Edwards, Jonathan, 287, 290, 311
Einstein, Albert, 328
Eisenhower, D. W., 332
Election, 78, 168, 192. See also
    Predestination
Eliot, John, 311
Eliot, T. S., 329
Elizabeth I, 158, 186, 222–27
Emmanuel, Victor, 272
Endicott, John, 284
Engels, F. See Marx, Karl
Enlightenment. See Rationalism
Epiphanius, 52
ERA, 305

Erasmus, Desiderius, 163, 164–66, 179
Erdman, William, 323
Eschatology, 14, 15, 25, 27, 32, 41, 55, 76, 78, 92, 186, 268, 322, 324–25
Essenes, 18, 19, 54
Eusebius of Caesarea, 18, 21, 24, 60–61
Eusebius of Nicomedia, 60–62
Eutychianism, 64, 80, 81
Evolution, 319–21
Eymericus, Nicolaus, 162

Fall, the, 43, 61, 70, 73, 75–76, 138, 144, 173, 256
False Decretals, 109, 110, 155
Farel, William, 188
Father Divine, 301
Fawkes, Guy, 232
Febronianism, 270
Federal Council of Churches, 312
Ficino, Marsilio, 163, 212
Fifth Monarchy Men, 233
Finney, Charles G., 305, 318
Fisher, John, 198, 213, 216
Fiske, John, 320
Fosdick, Harry Emerson, 321, 326
Four Prague Articles, 150
Fox, George, 255–56
Foxe, John, 212, 223
France, New World, 282
Francis of Assisi, 119, 130–32
Francis I (France), 188
Franciscans, 128, 130–32, 144, 162, 281–82, 309
Francke, August Hermann, 257–58
Franklin, Benjamin, 288, 290, 291
Frederick of Saxony, 169–70, 171
Free will, 50, 51, 67, 72–75, 154, 173, 187, 260, 276
Freedom of the Christian Man, 172
French and Indian War, 282, 288–89
French Revolution, 244, 263–67
Freud, Sigmund, 325
Friends of God, 151
Frith, John, 216
Fundamentalism, 307–8, 315–27

Gaiseric, 80, 88
Galba, 20
Galerius, 24
Galileo, 245
Gallican Confession, 192
Gallicanism, 88, 265

Gardiner, Stephen, 221–22
Garibaldi, Giuseppi, 272
Garrison, William Lloyd, 294
Garvey, Marcus, 301
George, Duke of Saxony, 173
George, Henry, 316
George of Poděbrady, 150
Gerhardt, Paul, 257
German Theology, 151
Gerson, John, 146
Ghiberti, Gian, 196, 198
Gibbons, James, 241, 277, 295
Giotto, 153
Gladden, W., 324
Gnosticism, 21, 26, 29, 30, 31–32, 33, 34, 35, 36, 37, 38, 43, 44–45, 48, 49, 60, 68, 133
God, proofs of existence of, 134, 136
Goethe, Johann, 167, 267
Golden Bull, 152
Gordon, A. J., 323
Gore, Charles, 320
Gorki, Maxim, 100
Gormarus, F., 192
Gospel of Thomas, 33
Gospels, 33. *See also* Matthew; Mark; Luke; John
Gottschalk, 111
Grace, 69, 71, 72–75, 77, 138, 189, 192–93, 201, 260. *See also* Justification
Graham, Billy, 332
Great Schism, 142, 146, 152, 155, 211, 224–25
Grebel, Conrad, 181
Greenwood, John, 226
Gregory of Nazianzus, 52, 57, 63
Gregory of Nyssa, 63
Gregory of Tours, 89
Grey, Lady Jane, 220–22
Grindal, Edmund, 225
Groot, Gerhard, 152
Grotius, Hugo, 244
Gui, Bernard, 122–23
Gunpowder Plot, 232
Gutenberg, Johann of, 160
Guyon, Madame de, 258

Hadrian, 21
Hagia Sophia, 81, 95
Half-way Covenant, 290
Hamilton, Patrick, 229
Handel, George F., 241

Handy, Robert T., 290
Harnack, Adolf, 325
Harper, W. Rainey, 323
Haydn, Franz Joseph, 241
Headlam, S. D., 317
Hecker, Isaac, 277, 295
Hegel, G. W. F., 67, 254, 269
Heidegger, Martin, 329
Heinrich of Langenstein, 146
Helwys, Thomas, 231
Hennepin, Louis, 282
Henotikon, 81
Henry II (France), 192
Henry II (Germany), 110
Henry III (Germany), 110, 112–13
Henry IV (France), 206, 239
Henry IV (Germany), 113, 114, 117
Henry V (England), 143, 212
Henry V (Germany), 114
Henry VI (Germany), 126
Henry VII (England), 158, 212, 214
Henry VIII (England), 142, 157, 185,
    210–19
Herbert of Cherbury, Lord, 247
Hilary of Gaul, 74
Hildebrand. See Pope Gregory VII
Hincmar, 109
Hippolytus, 27, 30, 31
Hitler, Adolf, 3, 278–79, 330
Hobbes, Thomas, 236, 330
Hochhuth, Rolf, 279, 332
Hodge, A. A., 324
Hofmann, Melchior, 186
Holbein, Hans, 218
Holy Spirit, 34, 50. See Trinity
Honorius (emperor), 74, 79
Hooker, Richard, 227
Hooker, Thomas, 285
Hooper, John, 221–22
Horton, W. M., 326
Howe, Julia Ward, 304
Hubmaier, Balthasar, 181, 185, 186, 187
Hudson, Henry, 285
Hughes, John, 292
Hugo of St. Cher, 169
Huguenots, 192, 205–6, 239
Humanism, 140, 154, 163, 165, 196,
    213
Humanist Manifesto, 325
Humbert, Cardinal, 111, 113
Hume, David, 251–52, 318
Humiliati, 123, 124
Hundred Years' War, 152, 158

Hus, John, 148–49, 171
Hussites, 149–50
Hutchinson, Anne, 285
Huter, Jacob, 187
Hutten, Ulrich von, 164

Iconoclasm, 96
Ignatius, Patriarch, 109
Ignatius, St., 21, 25, 30, 33, 35–36, 38,
    55, 85
Imitation of Christ, 116, 152
Incarnation, 1–15, 43, 51, 61, 144,
    168. See also Christology; Jesus
Indians, 280, 281, 285–86, 287, 311
Individualism, 152, 177, 263
Indulgences, 169–70, 204
Inerrancy, of the Bible, 1, 277, 325
Infallibility, 104, 109, 139, 170, 204,
    271, 274
Inquisition, 122–23, 125, 130, 153,
    161, 162–63, 195–96, 205
Institutes of the Christian Religion, 178,
    188–90
International Missionary Council,
    312–13
Interims, Augsburg, Leipsic, 176–77
Investiture, lay, 112–14
Ireland, John, 295
Irenaeus, 30, 31, 33, 36, 38, 40, 42–
    44, 85
Ivan the Great, 97–98
Ivan the Terrible, 98–99

Jacobs, Henry, 231
James, St., 6, 7, 19, 29
James I (England), 229–32, 283
James II, 235
James, William, 326
Jamnia, 33
Jansen, Cornelius, 201–2
Jefferson, Thomas, 283, 290, 291, 294
Jehovah's Witnesses, 280
Jerome, 52, 57–58, 73, 91
Jerome of Prague, 149
Jerusalem, destruction of, 6, 17
Jesuits, 194, 198–202, 235, 265, 270,
    284, 309
Jesus, 1–15, 18, 26, 29, 30, 31, 32, 33,
    37, 54, 60, 269. See also Christol-
    ogy; Incarnation
Jews, 2, 13, 16–20, 29, 53–54, 133, 162,
    164, 196, 278–79, 288, 333–34
Joachim of Fiore, 124

John, Gospel of, 7, 10, 11, 13, 26, 29, 33
John, King (England), 126–27, 211
John the Baptist, 5
Johnson, Edward, 280
Johnson, James Weldon, 302
Jones, Jim, 334–35
Jonson, Ben, 236
Josephism, 270
Josephus, 17, 19
Juárez, Benito, 281
Judaizers, 13, 21, 29, 32, 36, 38
Judson, Adoniram, 312
Julian (emperor), 25, 63
Julian of Eclanum, 74
Jung, Carl, 325
Justification, 91, 168, 189, 204. *See also* Grace
Justin, 81, 86
Justin Martyr, 21, 27, 38, 41–42
Justinian (emperor), 81, 86, 95

Kafka, Franz, 329
Kant, Immanuel, 67, 251–54, 319
Keble, John, 308–9
Kepler, Johannes, 245
Kierkegaard, Sören, 328
Kilwardby, Robert, 140
King, Martin Luther, Jr., 302–3
King George's War, 288
King William's War, 288
Kingsley, Charles, 317
Know-Nothings, 293
Knox, John, 178, 221, 229–30
Ku Klux Klan, 295, 300
Küng, Hans, 315

La Salle, René de, 282
Labadie, Jean de, 256
Labor strife, 295–96
Lactantius, 24, 27
Lambeth Appeal, 312
Lamennais, Abbé, 271–72
Langton, Stephen, 126
Lapsi, 23
Latimer, Hugh, 213, 222
Laud, William, 232–33
Law, in Aquinas, 137–38
Law, Old and New, 7–8, 11, 29–30, 40
Law, William, 251–52
Lazarus, 11
Le Fevre, Jacques, 163, 188
Leary, Timothy, 334

Leibniz, G. W., 250
Lenin, Nikolai, 101
Leo III (emperor), 96
Leonardo da Vinci, 153, 159, 240
Lessing, Gotthold E., 249
Letters of Obscure Men, 164
Levellers, 233–34
Lewy, Gunther, 332
Liberalism, 270, 272, 307–8, 315–27
Licinius, 24
Lightfoot, J. B., 320
Linacre, Thomas, 163, 165, 212
Lincoln, Abraham, 295, 299
Lindsey, Theophilus, 308
Linnaeus, Carl, 246
Lippi, Filippo, 153, 159
Loci Communes, 173
Locke, John, 247–48, 318
Logos, 10–11, 41, 42, 46, 48, 51, 60, 61
Loisy, Alfred, 277
Lollards, 143, 211–12
London Missionary Society, 311–12
Lord's Supper, 51, 110–11, 180, 219. *See also* Sacraments
Lothair, 109
Louis VII (France), 119
Louis XI, 158, 161
Louis XIII, 239
Louis XIV, 235, 239–40
Love, agape, 4, 8–10, 12–15
Loyola, Ignatius, 198–200
Lucian, 21, 37, 38–39
Ludlow, J. M., 317
Luke, Gospel of, 5, 8–10, 13, 32
Luther, Martin, 8–11, 67, 158, 162, 165–77, 185, 213, 315
Lux Mundi, 320

Maccabeans, 17, 19
McCarthy, Joseph R., 333
Machen, J. Gresham, 323, 324–25
Machiavelli, Niccolo, 159–60
McIntire, Carl, 93, 314
Madison, James, 283, 290
Magna Carta, 127, 211
Maimonides, Moses, 133
Malcolm X, 302
Malthus, Thomas, 316
Manicheism, 32, 67–70, 76, 85
Mann, Horace, 292
Manning, Henry E., 309
Mansfeld, Ernst von, 238

Manz, Felix, 181, 184
Marburg Colloquy, 180–81
Marcellus, 62
Marcion, 30, 31, 32, 33, 34, 42, 43, 51
Marian exiles, 222–23
Maritan, Jacques, 326
Mark, Gospel of, 5, 6, 13, 26
Marprelate tracts, 226
Marquette, Jacques, 282
Marriage, 26, 27, 45, 48, 55, 58, 73, 113, 125, 175, 204, 270, 275. *See also* Asceticism; Celibacy; Virginity
Marsiglio (Marsilius), of Padua, 146–47
Martel, Charles, 83, 90, 106
Martin of Tours, 89
Martyr, Peter, 220
Martyrs, early, 25–34, 36
Mary, Queen (England), 223–24
Mary, Queen of Scots, 224, 229–30
Mary, Virgin, 5, 58, 80, 95, 111, 139, 144, 278–79
Marx, Karl, 67, 254, 272, 273, 316
Masada, 17
Mathews, Shailer, 323
Matthew, Gospel of, 5, 7, 8, 13, 26
Matthis, Jan, 186
Maurice, Duke, 205
Maurice, J. F. D., 317
Maurus, Rabanus, 107, 111
Maximus, 24, 51, 80
Mayhew, Jonathan, 290
Mazarin, Cardinal, 239
Mazzini, Giuseppe, 270, 272
Mead, Sydney, 291
Melanchthon, Philip, 164, 167, 169, 173, 176, 180, 191, 196, 203, 217
Melchiorites, 186
Melito, 21, 22
Melville, Herman, 267
Mennonites, 231
Messiah, 7, 12–13, 17, 18, 29
Methodism, 258–62, 291, 294–95, 299
Michelangelo, Buonarroti, 153, 159, 240
Militades, 21
Mill, John Stuart, 316
Millay, Edna St. Vincent, 329
Miltitz, Karl von, 171
Milton, John, 236–37, 241
Minuit, Peter, 285
Missions, 90, 104–7, 257, 258, 264, 281–82, 309–12

Modernism, 271–77, 307. *See also* Liberalism
Molinos, Miguel de, 258
Molther, Philip, 259
Monasticism, 53–58, 63, 86–88, 90, 105, 112, 115–17, 128–39
Monophysitism, 80, 95
Montaigne, Michel de, 160
Montanists, 27, 37, 45, 53
Moody, Dwight L., 313, 318, 322–23
Moon, Sun Myung, 335
Moravians, 258–61, 311
More, Thomas, 163, 213, 216
Mormons, 282, 293
Morse, Samuel, 292
Mortalium Animos, 314
Mott, John R., 313–14
Mott, Lucretia, 304
Mozart, Wolfgang, 241
Muhammad, Elijah, 301
Muhammad, Wali Farad, 301
Münster, 186–87
Müntzer, Thomas, 173
Muratori, 33
Murner, Thomas, 167
Muslims, 59, 82–85, 117, 301
Mussolini, Benito, 273
Mysticism, 140, 150–52, 208

NAACP, 297–98, 302
National Council of Churches, 313
Nationalism. *See* Sovereignty, state
Nazarenes, 7, 11
Nazism, 278, 330–32
Negro Church, American, 297–303
Neo-orthodoxy, 325–27
Neoplatonism, 69, 76–77
Neri, Philip, 197
Nero (emperor) 6, 17, 19
Nerva, 20
Nestorianism, 64, 80, 81
New Testament, 4–13
Newman, John Henry, 309
Newton, Isaac, 245–46
Nicene controversy, 57, 58, 59–66. *See also* Council, Nicaea
Nicholas of Cusa, 107, 154–55
Nicoliatans, 30
Niebuhr, Reinhold, 326–27
Nietzsche, Friedrich, 167, 254, 328, 330
Nihilism, 3, 60, 262, 264, 281, 328–35
Nikon, Patriarch, 99

Ninety-five Theses, 158, 169–70
Nominalism vs. realism, 133–35, 140
Nygren, Anders, 326

Oates, Titus, 235
Occam (Ockham), William, 129, 145–46, 164
Ochino, Bernardino, 196, 197
Oda of Canterbury, 112
Odilo, Abbot, 115
Odovakar, 80, 81, 86
Oecolampadius, Johann, 180
Oglethorpe, James, 287
Old Believers, Russian, 99
Old Catholic Church, 274
Oldcastle, John, 211–12
Olivetan, Pierre, 163
Ophites, 30
Oratory of Divine Love, 295–97
Origen, 23, 27, 33, 38, 49–52, 57, 90
Original sin. *See* Sin
Ostromsky, 100
Otho, 20
Otto I (Germany), 110
Otto III, 110
Owen, Robert, 316
Oxford movement, 308–9
Oxnam, G. Bromley, 333

Pachomius, 56
Pacifism, 88, 165, 187
Paganism, 67, 75–78, 105
Paine, Thomas, 290, 291
Palestrina, Giovanni, 209
Paley, William, 319
Pantaenus, 48
Papacy, 36, 62, 80, 81, 85–86, 90, 91, 107–14, 125, 128–29, 140, 142, 161
Papias, 26
Parker, Elihu, 291
Parker, Matthew, 223
Parsons, Robert, 224
Pascal, Blaise, 67, 201–2, 250
Patrick, St., 105
Paul, St., 4–5, 6, 7, 10, 11, 12, 17, 22, 26, 29–30, 32, 33, 35, 37, 38
Paul of Thebes, 56
Paula, 58
Peace of Augsburg, 176, 205, 237
Peace of Passau, 176
Peasants' Revolt, 143, 173–75, 211

Peckham, John, 140
Pelagianism, 67, 72–75, 85
Penn, William, 286
Penry, John, 226
Pepin, 80, 107
Perpetua and Felicitas, 23
Persecutions, early, 19–27, 32
Peter, St., 6, 7, 10, 13, 18, 29, 35, 36, 37, 55, 85
Peter of Ailli, 146
Peter the Great (Russia), 100–1
Peter the Hermit, 118
Petition of Right, 232
Petrarch, Francesco, 153, 154
Philips, Dirk and Obee, 187
Philip II (France), 122, 126
Philip II (Spain), 159, 161, 206–7
Philip IV (France), 141
Philo, 19, 50
Philotheos, 98
Photius, Patriarch, 109
Pia Desideria, 256
Picards, 150
Pico della Mirandola, 163, 212
Pietism, 243, 254–62, 311
Pilgrims, 231, 283–84
Pisarev, Dmitri, 328–29
Pius, Antonius, 21
Pizarro, Francisco, 282
Plato, 41, 48, 133, 154
Pliny of Bithynia, 19, 20, 21
Plotinus, 69
Pole, Reginald, 203, 222
Polycarp, St., 21, 25, 33, 36, 38, 42
Poor Catholics, 123–24
Poor Clares, 132
Pope, Alexander, 250
Popes
 Adrian IV, 121
 Alexander II, 113
 Alexander IV, 162
 Alexander V, 146
 Alexander VI, 159, 161
 Benedict IX, 110
 Benedict X, 113
 Benedict XI, 142
 Benedict XIII, 147
 Benedict XV, 278
 Boniface VIII, 140–42, 171
 Callistus, 45
 Calixtus III, 155
 Clement II, 110
 Clement VI, 142, 146, 169

Popes (*cont.*)
Clement VII, 143, 197
Clement XI, 202
Clement XIV, 202
Damasus I, 57, 58, 63, 85
Eugenius III, 117, 121
Eugenius IV, 147–48, 202
Gelasius I, 86
Gregory I, 90–91, 92
Gregory VII, 110, 112, 113, 115, 203
Gregory XIII, 147, 208
Gregory XVI, 270
Honorius III, 82, 111, 129, 131, 169
Innocent I, 85
Innocent III, 119, 124–27, 128–29,
131, 162, 211
Innocent VIII, 162
Innocent X, 239
John VIII, 109, 118
John X, 109
John XI, 109
John XII, 109–10
John XIII, 110
John XXII, 132, 145, 151
John XXIII, 147, 149, 278, 314
John Paul I, 315
John Paul II, 315
Julius II, 166, 171
Leo I, 80, 81, 85, 88
Leo IX, 96, 110, 113
Leo X, 164, 166, 169, 172, 213
Leo XIII, 132, 223, 275–77, 295
Lucius III, 122
Martin V, 147, 149, 202
Nicholas I, 109
Nicholas II, 113
Paul III, 196, 203
Paul IV, 196, 202, 204, 205
Paul V, 208
Paul VI, 315
Pius II, 155, 159, 161, 202
Pius V, 132, 203, 207–8
Pius VI, 265–66, 304
Pius VII, 266–68, 270
Pius VIII, 270, 275
Pius IX, 271–75
Pius XI, 133, 278, 332
Pius XII, 278
Sixtus II, 23
Sixtus IV, 156
Sixtus V, 203, 224
Urban II, 117–18, 169
Victor, 36

Popes, Anti-
Felix V, 148, 155
Guibert, 117
Nicholas V, 146
Wibert, 111
Porphyry, 69
Praemunire, 211, 214
Predestination, 31, 73, 74–75, 78, 173.
See also Election
Presbyterians, 178, 225, 226, 233, 287,
291, 295
Presuppositions, 1–4, 30, 50
Prierias, Sylvester, 170
Prisca, 23
Probabilism, 201
Protestant principle, 3
Puritans, 210, 225–27, 229–37,
283–85
Pusey, Edward B., 309

Q source, 5
Quakers, 234, 255–56, 286–87, 294,
295
Queen Anne's War, 288
Quesnel, Pasquier, 202
Qumran community, 18, 19, 54

Radbertus, Paschasius, 111
Rahner, Karl, 315
Raphael Sanzio, 159
Rasputin, Gregory, 101
Rationalism, 2, 243–54, 263–67
Ratramus of Corbie, 111
Rauschenbusch, Walter, 317, 323–24,
325
Reconstruction, 299–300
Reid, Thomas, 318–19
Reimarus, Herman S., 249
Relativism, 156, 157, 166, 251–54,
256, 308, 327
Relics, 58, 91, 106, 112, 127, 162, 169,
198
Rembrandt van Rijn, 241
Renaissance, 152–57, 159, 161
Renan, Ernest, 2, 264, 269, 273, 319
Renewal, Catholic, 194–209
Rerum Novarum, 276
Resurrection, 6, 7, 8, 9, 10, 11, 12, 14,
34, 41, 42, 54, 61–62, 73, 76, 268
Reuchlin, Johann, 163–64
Revelation to John, Book of, 5, 19, 22,
26, 33
Revivalism, 290, 291, 298, 305, 318

Rheims-Douai Bible, 230
Ricardo, David, 316
Ricci, Matteo, 201
Richelieu, Cardinal, 238, 239, 265
Ridley, Nicholas, 221–22
Ridolfi Plot, 224
Rimsky-Korsakov, 100
Ritschl, Albrecht, 325
Robespierre, 266
Robinson, John, 231
Rockefeller, John D., 296
Rome, fall of, 75, 79
Roscellinus, 133–34
Rosenberg, Alfred, 2, 331
Rousseau, Jean Jacques, 265, 267
Rubens, Peter Paul, 241
Rubenstein, Richard, 330, 333–34
Rubianus, Crotius, 164
Runcarii, 124
Russian Christianity, 94–103, 153
Ruysbroeck, John, 151–52

Sacraments, 21, 55, 59, 66, 67, 70, 77,
    113, 138, 143, 149, 180, 217
Sacrosancta, 147, 202
St. Bartholomew's Day, 206
St. John of the Cross, 208
Sales, Francis de, 208–9
Sanford, Elias, 312
Sartre, Jean-Paul, 329
Sattler, Michael, 184–85
Savonarola, Girolamo (Jerome), 161–
    62, 195
Schell, Hermann, 277
Schleiermacher, Friedrich, 258, 264,
    267–68, 269
Schleitheim Confession, 184–5, 187
Schiller, Johann, 267
Schmalkald (Smalcald) League, 205,
    216
Schmucker, Samuel S., 312
Scholasticism, 128, 132–39, 180
Schools, public, 107–8, 291–92
Schopenhauer, Arthur, 254
Schweitzer, Albert, 25
Scofield, C. I., 323
Scopes' trial, 325
Scott, Sir Walter, 267
Scotus, Duns, 129, 144–45
Scripture and Tradition, 28, 77–78,
    203
Separatists, 225, 226, 231, 283–84
Septuagint, 33, 50

Sergei, Metropolitan, 102
Serra, Junipero, 282
Servetus, Michael, 190–91
Severus, Septimus, 22, 48
Seymour, Edward, 219
Shakespeare, William, 160, 241
Sheldon, Charles M., 321
Shepherd of Hermas, 27, 33, 38, 40, 50
Sigismund (emperor), 149, 150
Simons, Menno, 187
Sin, 46, 48, 49, 50, 55, 67, 68, 69, 70,
    72–75, 91, 104, 137, 144, 189,
    320, 321, 326
Six Articles, 218
Sixty-seven Articles, 180
Slavery, 256, 264, 281, 286, 287, 289,
    293–94, 295, 317
Smith, Adam, 316
Smith, Joseph, 293
Smyth, John, 231
Social gospel, 316–18, 323–24
Söderblom, Nathan, 314
Sovereignty, church, 59, 66, 88, 90,
    104–14, 139, 140, 150, 156, 181,
    209, 210–27, 228, 264, 271–77,
    308. *See also* Church and state
Sovereignty, divine, 16, 54, 65, 189,
    190
Sovereignty, individual, 152, 157, 263
Sovereignty, state, 16–27, 59, 65, 88,
    119, 140, 142, 146, 152, 153, 158–
    59, 160, 172, 175, 207, 228, 243,
    263, 264, 265, 277, 280, 289, 291,
    293–95, 296, 298, 308, 330
Spain, New World, 281
Spangenburg, Augustus, 259–60, 287
Spencer, Herbert, 320
Spener, Philip, 256–57
Spengler, Oswald, 264, 325
Spiritual Exercises, 199–200
Stalin, Joseph, 102
Stanton, Elizabeth Cady, 304
Stokes, A. P., 333
Stone, Lucy, 304
Stowe, Harriet Beecher, 295
Strauss, D. F., 264, 269, 319
Strong, Josiah, 296, 312, 324
Stuart, Henry, 229
Stuttgart Declaration, 332
Stylites, Simeon, 56
Suetonius, 20
Supererogation, 40, 55
Suso, Henry, 151

Sutri, Synod of, 110
Sweet Daddy Grace, 301
Swift, Jonathan, 250–51
Symphonia, 94–103
Synergism, 73, 91, 204

Tacitus, 19, 90
Tatian, 27, 33
Tauler, John, 150
Taylor, Graham, 324
Taylor, Jeremy, 236, 259
Tchaikovsky, 100
Tempier, Stephen, 140
Ten Articles, 216–17
Tennent, Gilbert, 290
Teresa, St., 208
Tertullian, 19, 23, 27, 30, 31, 33, 37,
    38, 40, 44–46, 85
Tetzel, Johann, 169–71
Theatines, 197
Theodosius I, 25, 63, 64, 66, 72
Theodosius II, 74
Theophilus of Alexandria, 52, 65
Therapeutae, 54
Thielicke, Helmut, 330
Third Rome, 98–103
Thirty-nine Articles, 223, 225, 227
Thirty Years' War, 161, 205, 207,
    237–39, 244
Thomas a Kempis, 150, 198
Tikhon, Patriarch, 101–2
Tillich, Paul, 326–27
Tilly, Count von, 237
Tindal, Matthew, 248–49
Titian, 159
Toland, 248
Toleration, 44, 185, 188, 191, 210,
    231–32, 234, 235, 247, 283, 285,
    287, 291, 333
Tolstoy, Leo, 100–1, 326
Torrey, Reuben, 323
Torquemada, Domingo de, 123, 162
Trajan (emperor), 19, 20
Transubstantiation, 110–11, 125, 204,
    218–19
Treasury of Merits, 40, 169
Trinity, 18, 42, 44, 46, 50, 60, 61–64,
    71, 77, 96, 122, 135, 190–91
Troeltsch, Ernst, 28, 54, 324
Truce of God, 117
Truth, Sojourner, 298
Tubman, Harriet, 298
Turgenev, Ivan, 329

Tyndale, William, 215, 217
Tyrrell, George, 277
Tzara, Tristan, 330

Udal, Nicolas, 226
Ulfilas, 88
Ultramontanism, 88, 209, 264, 271,
    274, 275–77
Unam sanctam, 141
Uncertainty, 3, 281, 327–35
Unitarianism, 2, 235, 294, 295, 308
Universities, 112–21, 128–29, 133,
    169, 200, 203, 212
Ursulines, 197
Utraquists, 149–50

Vahanian, Gabriel, 133
Valentinian I, 63
Valentinian II, 66
Valentinus, 30, 31, 34, 42–43
Valerian, 23
Valla, Lorenzo, 107, 154
Van Dusen, Henry P., 321
Vandals, 75–78. *See also* Barbarians
Vesey, Denmark, 298
Vespasian, 17, 20
Victor, 36, 85
Victorinus, 27, 69
Vincent of Lerins, 74–75
Virginity, 26, 55, 58, 66. *See also* As-
    ceticism; Celibacy; Marriage
Visitation Articles, 175
Vives, Juan, 163
Vladimir of Kiev, 97, 101
Voltaire, 110, 264
Voluntaryism, 178, 188, 280, 287, 290
Vulgate Bible of Jerome, 57–58, 85,
    154, 165, 203

Waldenses, 123–24, 126, 162, 190
Wallenstein, Albrecht von, 238
War, just, 72, 89
War of Roses, 152, 158
Ward, Harry F., 324
Ward, Nathaniel, 285
Ward, W. G., 309
Warfield, B. B., 324
Warwick, Earl of, 221–22
Washington, Booker T., 297, 301
Washington, George, 289
Watts, Isaac, 261
Weld, Theodore D., 294
Wellhausen, Julius, 320

Wescott, B. F., 320
Wesley, Charles, 261–62
Wesley, John, 259–62
Westminster Assembly, 233
Whitby, Synod of, 90
Whitefield, George, 260, 290
Whitgift, John, 225–26
Whitney, Eli, 294
Wichern, J. H., 317
Wilberforce, William, 261, 317
Wilfred, 106
William of Aquitaine, 112
William of Champeaux, 133–34
William and Mary, 235, 286
Williams, George, 313
Williams, Roger, 231–32, 285
Willibrord, 106
Winthrop, John, 233, 285
Wishart, George, 229
Wolsey, Thomas, 212–13, 214, 217
Women, 37, 54, 57, 83, 90, 146, 163, 208, 256, 297, 303–6
Wordsworth, William, 267–68
Works, good, 91, 117–18, 168, 204. *See also* Justification; Synergism

World Council of Churches, 93, 314
World Missionary Conference, 312
Worms, Diet of, 166, 172
Worship, 28–29, 32, 33, 40, 87, 92, 99, 100, 180, 219, 241, 266
Wren, Christopher, 241
Writing, 108
Wycliffe, John, 142–43, 147, 148, 211

Xavier, Francis, 201
Ximenes, Cardinal, 163, 195–96

Yaroslav, 97
Yeats, William Butler, 330
Young, Brigham, 293

Zealots, 17, 19
Zeno (emperor), 81
Zinzendorf, Count, 258–60
Zizka, John, 150
Zosimus, 74
Zwingli, Ulrich, 176, 178–85